Deep Complexity and the Social Sciences

NEW HORIZONS IN INSTITUTIONAL AND EVOLUTIONARY ECONOMICS

Series Editor: Geoffrey M. Hodgson
Research Professor, University of Hertfordshire Business School, UK

Economics today is at a crossroads. New ideas and approaches are challenging the largely static and equilibrium-oriented models that used to dominate mainstream economics. The study of economic institutions – long neglected in the economics textbooks – has returned to the forefront of theoretical and empirical investigation.

This challenging and interdisciplinary series publishes leading works at the forefront of institutional and evolutionary theory and focuses on cutting-edge analyses of modern socio-economic systems. The aim is to understand both the institutional structures of modern economies and the processes of economic evolution and development. Contributions will be from all forms of evolutionary and institutional economics, as well as from Post-Keynesian, Austrian and other schools. The overriding aim is to understand the processes of institutional transformation and economic change.

Titles in the series include:

An Economic Analysis of Innovation
Extending the Concept of National Innovation Systems
Markus Balzat

Evolutionary Economics and Environmental Policy
Survival of the Greenest
Jeroen C.J.M. van den Bergh, Albert Faber, Annemarth M. Idenburg and Frans H. Oosterhuis

Property Rights, Consumption and the Market Process
David Emanuel Andersson

The Evolution of Path Dependence
Edited by Lars Magnusson and Jan Ottosson

Economics, Culture and Social Theory
William A. Jackson

Deep Complexity and the Social Sciences
Experience, Modelling and Operationality
Robert Delorme

Deep Complexity and the Social Sciences

Experience, Modelling and Operationality

Robert DELORME

Emeritus Professor, Université de Versailles, France

NEW HORIZONS IN INSTITUTIONAL AND EVOLUTIONARY ECONOMICS

Edward Elgar

Cheltenham, UK • Northampton, MA, USA

Published by
Edward Elgar Publishing Limited
The Lypiatts
15 Lansdown Road
Cheltenham
Glos GL50 2JA
UK

Edward Elgar Publishing, Inc.
William Pratt House
9 Dewey Court
Northampton
Massachusetts 01060
USA

A catalogue record for this book
is available from the British Library

Library of Congress Control Number: 2009938428

ISBN 978 1 84980 026 6

Printed and bound by MPG Books Group, UK

To
Mauricette
Sandrine
Jérémie

Contents

Part II *Modelling*

Main abbreviations and symbols

ADCX: anchored deep complexity
CEPREMAP: Centre d'études prospectives d'économie mathématique appliquées à la planification (until 2005), Centre pour la recherche économique et ses applications (since 2005), Paris.
CTSP: critically transactional systemic process
CX: complexity
CX1, CX2, CX3, CX4, CX5, CX6: the successive formulations of DCX, ending in CX6 = EDCX
DCX: deep complexity
EBB: effective building block
EDCX: Effective Deep Complexity
FBB: formal building block
FODCX: first-order deep complexity
GDP: gross domestic product
GP: generative process or generative principle
INRETS: Institut national de recherche sur les transports et leur sécurité, France
m : meta-level
NDCX: non-deep complexity
o : object level
OP1, OP2, OP3, OP4, OP5: the organising principles of CX5 and CX6
OP1: behaviouralist self-reflexivity
OP2: composite self-similarity
OP3: conjunction
OP4: abduction
OP5: construction
OP6, OP7, OP8: the operational principles of CX6
OP6: autonomy of CX5
OP7: situation recognition
OP8: action in a deeply complex situation
P: product of *GP*
PEW: the generic process of enquiry into the world *W*
PR: procedural rationality
RISE: regime of interaction between the state and the economy
R4: road risk regulation regime

SODCX: second-order deep complexity
SR: substantive rationality
SSM: Soft Systems Methodology
W: the world external to *PEW*; *W* includes *W1* and *W2*
W1: the world external to *W2*
W2: the process of enquiry into *W1*
* : elementary recursive duality
** : nested double recursive duality

Figures

Tables

Preface

> The hard sciences are successful because they deal with the soft problems; the soft sciences are struggling because they deal with the hard problems.
>
> Heinz von Foerster (2003)[1]

This book is about deep complexity in social sciences. Deep complexity, abbreviated as DCX, is a term introduced here to denote the particular kind of complexity experienced in problem-situations which no method available in the current scientific literature can seemingly deal with satisfactorily. These situations I call deeply ill-structured problem-situations.

The book is a long argument about how some deeply ill-structured problem-situations in social sciences can nevertheless be dealt with in a scientific manner. In order to analyse deeply ill-structured problem-situations, I argue that one needs to step outside the limits of the prevailing scientific paradigm and its disjunctive reasoning. This paradigm, which enjoys monopoly status in the hard sciences, excludes from its scope everything that cannot be grasped through the range of its concepts and tools. Deeply ill-structured problem-situations fall outside the boundaries of this paradigm. Yet it has succeeded in appearing as the sole, exclusive way to do science. But is it necessarily the unique way to put to work what is commonly understood as defining science?

Science is a particular activity in the production of knowledge. It combines five properties: it is about some object or subject matter pertaining to some reality; it aims at some truth value or validity; it relies on an explicit conceptual and methodological framework; it is systematically exposed to public criticism and test; and it is subject to error and revision. The disjunctive, 'either–or' reasoning is obviously compatible with this definition. But I claim in this book that this definition is also compatible with a conjunctive framework based on 'and', and that this framework makes it possible to accommodate deeply ill-structured issues. Furthermore, I argue that this can be done while encompassing the classical framework.

Social science is not the only area in which deeply ill-structured problem-situations can be experienced. However, the argument developed here is grounded in experience gained in economics and in research on safety management in socio-technical systems in transport and industry, which are limited to the domain of the social sciences.

This book is the outcome of a long enquiry that began with a reflection on how to deal with an obstacle I encountered in research on the long-run evolution of public expenditure in France as compared with that in Germany. This obstacle arose when I discovered that the empirical identification of very robust, multidimensional configurations of interactions between the state and the economy was irreducible to a theoretical modelling with the available, classical concepts and tools of analysis. These configurations were called 'regimes of interaction between the state and the economy', or RISEs. The question to which there was no answer was: What is the theory underpinning the RISE? Without such a theory, the RISE could be no more than an empirical conjecture, remaining broadly unintelligible within the realm of economics. It is this question which triggered the research presented in this book.

The effort to pursue this analysis evolved into the design of a theory of deep complexity. My initial intention was not to design a theory of complexity but simply to explore to what extent the problem that I perceived as complex might be addressed with material provided in the fast-growing literature on complex systems. I soon discovered a new dilemma which I discuss at length in this book. In short, complex systems are mostly addressed in the modelling literature via computer simulations without a satisfactory theory of complexity conceived in its own right. When complexity is addressed in its own right, it is done so outside this literature, most often at a philosophical level without any noticeable disciplinary modelling. The challenge is to build a bridge between the rich philosophical thinking about complexity and the work being done in empirical research. This is not a matter of adding up separate, disjunct notions but of constructing the '*and*', that is, of creating and organising knowledge.

While I was engaged in this work, I took on responsibility for a graduate programme on safety management in transport and industry. In the course of my work in this area, I discovered that the irreducible potentiality and actualisation of very rare but very large accidents in these activities created deeply ill-structured problem-situations which had the same structure as the one I experienced in economic theory. They are described in Chapter 3. This work in economic theory and in transport and industrial safety research forms the basis on which the arguments of this book are developed.

It is only with the hindsight provided by the work in Chapter 6, on 'Generality', that it became clear that there was an essential difference between the kind of complexity on which I had been working and the complexity found in the complex systems literature. This difference needed to be identified in its own right. Hence, the term 'deep complexity'. It designates the irreducibility to a satisfactory, or more precisely, to use Simon's term, a satisficing level of reduction in a given problem-situation, using classical disjunctive tools.

The purpose of this book is to present in full transparency a theory of deep complexity. Deep complexity is thus distinguished from 'plain' or non-deep complexity in the sense that the latter is dealt with without the perceived need to step outside the classical, mostly unnoticed, specific disjunctive framework within which it is developed.

This book is, therefore, the unplanned outcome of an initial phase of muddling through in an attempt to find a way out of a blockage confronted in economic theory. This led to the heuristic construction of a tentative local solution which appeared original when it was compared to similar situations of blockage, notably in the economics literature. It became necessary to model it and to explore it progressively, step by step, in an effort to reveal its general character.

The result is what I call Effective Deep Complexity, or EDCX. It is effective in the sense that it constitutes a complete alternative to the classical framework. It ranges from epistemological foundations to empirical applications; it is encompassing and includes the classical framework.

EDCX has a threefold character. The logical order would command to present it from the more general to the more specific, as an alternative framework first, then as a theory of deeply complex situations, and finally as a decision-and-action support process. However, this is not the sequence in which the argumentation was constructed. Construction is one of the principles of EDCX. Hence the priority given to it. The construction of EDCX originated with a blockage in a problem-situation for which a hypothetical way out was designed. It was modelled and generalised in a second step. It is put to work in several instances in a final step. Therefore, EDCX is primarily a *theory of deeply complex situations*. In the specific case which triggered this work, the situation of an irreducible blockage arose from the identification of robust, many-sided configurations of state economy interactions through time series analysis and a cross-country comparison. Their robustness made them appear as regimes of interaction between the state and the economy (RISEs). EDCX is a theory of the problem-situation created by the RISE. It informs the RISE and makes it a product of a theoretical framework rather than being a theory of the RISE directly. It does so by the way in which it brings an answer to the question of what theory underpins the RISE. It is therefore not a direct theory of particular empirical objects, but a theory of the situations created, at least in part, by some empirical objects when no satisficing solution can be found within the classical disjunctive framework. Two instances of it are developed in Chapter 8, the road risk regulation regime (or R4) in road safety, and the complex duality of competition and organisation in the market economy.

Second, since DCX situations cannot be grasped within the classical framework, the EDCX framework that had to be designed, and which informs DCX situations, is an *alternative analytical framework*. EDCX differs in an essential way from the complexity one finds in the complex systems literature. It is an alternative to both the classical analytical framework and to the classical systems approach to which most of the complex systems literature belongs. Nevertheless, it does not exclude or negate, but subsumes them, and reckons their relevance to non-deeply complex (NDCX) problem-situations.

Third, EDCX relies on an intrinsic, essential connection between knowing and action which makes it a *decision-and-action support process*. In deeply complex situations, the main obstacles to thinking and action are intellectual and behavioural. EDCX provides a way to unblock these obstacles. Instances of it in road safety governance and in structural economic policy are presented in the final chapter.

The argumentation of this book is constructed through a chain of several loops. It begins with an empirical deeply complex problem described in Part I, on experience. Its modelling is developed in Part II. It leads to a model of Effective Deep Complexity. Its operationality is defined and illustrated with applications to road safety management and economic theory in Part III.

This work found its inspiration in the ideas of three outstanding scientists: Herbert Simon's behaviouralist approach, Heinz von Foerster's recursive thinking, and John von Neumann's intuitive sense of complexity. It is thanks to a critical and hopefully constructive assessment of their contributions that I was also able to assess critically and constructively the path-breaking contributions of John Maynard Keynes on uncertainty, John Dewey on transactional thinking, and Edgar Morin on complexity thinking.

I hope that it will be manifest that there is no hubris in this book, rather the opposite. It follows from a fallibilist stance and a general hypothesis through a transparent argumentation which is exposed to public criticism. It is not the case that I have a theory and then want to make it operational. I start from something that makes sense in practice but not in theory. I need the reader's goodwill about the way the argumentation is developed for it does not fit into any known pigeonhole. It unfolds as a concatenation of recursive patterns and processes. It is my hope that its end will justify its beginning. As René Descartes put it: 'I will be very pleased if those who want to object to me do not hasten to do so, and that they try to understand everything I have written before judging one part; for all holds together and the end serves to prove the beginning.' [2]

NOTES

1. H. von Foerster (2003), *Understanding Understanding*, New York: Springer, 191.
2. R. Descartes (1638 [1969]), 'Lettre à Mersenne', in C. Adam et P. Tanney (eds), *Oeuvres de Descartes. Correspondance* I, Paris: J. Vrin, 484.

Acknowledgements

During the long enquiry of which this book is the outcome, I benefited from my interactions with a number of individuals. Although it was difficult to explain publicly what was going on in my research as long as the manuscript was not completed, which compelled me to a continual, yet cheerful stoicism, I found interest for what I was doing and support in a variety of seminars and conferences. Among those who invited me repeatedly to present my ideas in development and created the occasions to sharpen and enrich them, several names come immediately to my mind. They are Jerzy Hausner, from the Cracow University of Economics, Poland; Atle Midttun, from the Norwegian School of Management, Oslo; Paul Bush, from California State University, Fresno; and John Foster, from the University of Queensland, Brisbane.

I express also my deep appreciation to the 28 scholars and experts who agreed to join with me in research teams studying the transforming Central and Eastern European countries, in the 1990s, and road safety governance, in the 2000s, without knowing what would come out of exploring a still to be defined deeply complex perspective in these endeavours. Their names are mentioned in Chapter 8, pp. 385 and 410.

I learned a lot from my discussions with Stefano Solari about the state in the Italian economy, and with Jean-Daniel Weisz about German institutionalism and the state in the German economy. I also found support in one way or another from Robert Boyer and Pascal Petit in the *régulation* group at CEPREMAP (Centre pour la recherche économique et ses applications), and from Charlie Dannreuther, Richard Morris and John White.

However, four persons deserve special mention. Christine André, from CEPREMAP, was my first accomplice in the construction of the observations on public spending. She continues her research on international comparisons of social public spending and has remained faithful to the priority given to empirical observation. Jean-Louis Le Moigne, from the University of Aix-en-Provence-Marseille, helped me discover second systemics and another aspect of Herbert Simon's work, and has remained an enthusiastic and unflagging correspondent with whom I could test my ideas. Sylvain Lassarre, from INRETS (Institut national de recherche sur les transports et leur sécurité), helped me discover the subtlelties of transport safety, notably of road safety. And Yong-Joon Jeon, from EasyM Energy Holdings Ltd, Seoul and Paris, devoted considerable effort to getting the manuscript in shape for publication.

Last but not least, CEPREMAP, EAEPE (the European Association for Evolutionary Political Economy, that I chaired from 1993 to 2003), MCX (the European Programme for Modelling Complexity), and the University of Versailles-Saint-Quentin-en-Yvelines provided unparalleled institutional and scientific environments for this work.

Needless to say, any remaining errors are my sole responsibility.

Part I

Experience

A twofold experience is depicted in the two chapters of this part. Chapter 1, 'Heuristics', reports the experience of bumping into an apparently insolvable obstacle. This led to the heuristic construction of a path without abandoning the subject matter, given its empirically established robustness. This subject matter is about the relationship between the state and the economy as it arose from long-run time series for France, and from an international comparison between France and Germany. It led to a notion of characteristic multidimensional configuration of this relationship or regime of interaction between the state and the economy (RISE) which appeared irreducible to a known satisfactory toolkit. A heuristic way out is constructed through extending Simon's behaviouralist pattern to a self-reflexive setting. A notion of anchored deep complexity (ADCX) emerges from it.

In Chapter 2, ADCX is presented as a hypothesis. Whether ADCX is already addressed in the literature is then examined. Hence the title 'Originality'. A review is made of the uses of complexity or analogous notions in economic theory, in the complex economic systems literature, in management science, and in transdisciplinary sources and forms of complexity. A wealth of contributions is found in economic theory, notably Keynes's theory of uncertainty which comes closest to deep complexity. But we will find that its anchoring is not satisfactory. No other available notion seems to accommodate ADCX, which leaves the issue of its theoretical status entirely open and will necessitate to theorise it in Part II.

1. Heuristics

> One has to be constantly on guard against treating the material as constant and homogeneous. It is as though the fall of the apple to the ground depended on the apple's motives, on whether it is worth while falling to the ground, and whether the ground wanted the apple to fall, and on mistaken calculations on the part of the apple as to how far it was from the centre of the earth.
> But do not be reluctant to soil your hands...
>
> John Maynard Keynes (1938)[1]

1.1 INTRODUCTION

The purpose of this chapter is to describe the circumstances of the emergence of a particular obstacle I encountered while doing empirical research in economics. This obstacle triggered my interest in exploring a heuristic way to come to grips with it. The obstacle appeared impossible to deal with using the usual analytical tools. I found that I could not rely on the classical cannons of economics. None of the shortcuts, simplifications and algorithms of that literature was of any help. Realising this, I was forced to search an alternative intellectual strategy. This effort led to my work on what I call 'deep complexity'. Deep complexity could never have been devised through some sort of hypothetico-deductive inference. It arose, instead, from my realisation that the robust empirical outcome of my research could not be tackled by the methodology of standard economic theory. It was the effort to deal with this methodological blockage that led to my formulation of deep complexity. This encounter with deep complexity (or DCX for short) is presented in the next section. The construction of a pathway and of a tentatively fruitful conjecture of 'anchored' deep complexity (ADCX) is developed in the final section.

1.2 EXPERIENCING DEEP COMPLEXITY

1.2.1 A First Encounter with Deep Complexity in Economic Analysis

A. *Step one*: Public expenditure in France in a time series perspective

The problem which triggered my interest in deep complexity arose while I was involved in research conducted several years ago on the long-run growth of public expenditure in France during the twentieth century. This research was aimed at filling a gap which consisted in the absence of France from the main comparative international studies. This omission was due to an apparent lack of confidence in the French data covering the period prior to 1950. My interest in this subject came from my previous, rather abstract, theoretical research on national indicative planning in France, and the need this created for prolonging it by an empirical inquiry about the role of the state in economic activity and its comparison with other countries. In order to move forward in this direction it was therefore necessary to build or rebuild the time series which were needed. Christine André, a mathematician at CEPREMAP joined this project. It took us almost two years of work on original public accounts at the Ministry of Finance in Paris before we could test the time series obtained for France and compare them with international data (Delorme and André, 1983; Delorme, 1984, 1992). For this purpose, we followed the framework available in the international literature.[2]

Public spending includes the outlays funded mainly by taxation, social security contributions and borrowing, and which emanate from public entities defined by their capacity to act in the name of legitimate power or sovereignty over a population of a territory. They cover central and local government, and social security, and constitute the 'state'. Beyond the disaggregation of spending and funding by levels of government, public spending needs to be structured according to economic categories of resource use and to its functions or areas. The former are salaries, consumption, investment, transfers and subsidies, and debt interest. The latter bear mainly on general administration, justice, police, defence, transport and infrastructure, industry, agriculture, education, urbanism and housing, social security, and debt interest.

Without entering into the details, it is worth mentioning that the long-run path of evolution in France is on the whole crudely similar to other countries. The ratio of public spending to gross domestic product (GDP) was about 10 per cent before World War I. It fluctuated a lot, between 15 and 20 per cent, during the interwar period. It rose progressively from a little more than 30 per cent after World War II to 50 per cent since the 1990s. The bulk goes to social security (health, pensions, unemployment) and education. On the whole, these areas represent more than 50 per cent of public spending and about 25 per cent of GDP by the beginning of the twenty-first century. It is higher in Sweden. Germany's ratio evolved since the

1980s roughly like France's, but with three to four percentage points below with a widening of this gap at the beginning of the 2000s.

Economic analysis suggests a variety of perspectives on public expenditures. We examined, among other hypotheses, the available theoretical explanations about the determinants of public spending. Several hypotheses were tested and it was found that most of them had limited relevance for particular, local matters, under precise and sometimes very constraining conditions. An example is the theme of the productivity lag in the public sector. It is viewed by some as a cause of the growth of public expenditure relative to overall economic activity. It was demonstrated that the empirical evidence for this thesis is difficult to establish, even in the cases most suited to it, such as the provision of services in health, hospitals and education. It leaves wide open the issue of the rationale for projecting this kind of assumption to other domains of public expenditure.

It was found difficult to detect 'laws' in the evolution of public spending in France. A displacement effect, the threshold phenomenon favouring the growth of public spending during and after big shocks like the two world wars, was shown to be present. We were driven to emphasise historical events and tensions of political, social and economic origins (notably in education throughout the twentieth century, and in the painstaking implementation of a social security system achieved in 1945 after several decades of debate). However this does not mean that the evolution was totally hectic and unpatterned. Although the long-run growth of public expenditure has followed an irregular path like that in other European industrialised countries, this path is composed of stabilised periods separated by unstable phases of transition or crisis. It led to a periodisation in which institutions play a central role. This makes it possible to identify successive configurations or patterns.

It was also found that limiting our investigation to public spending was too restrictive. It meant not paying attention to the reasons why, in a given domain, public action would be performed through spending rather than some other more qualitative form such as the obligation for individuals to buy the service, in part or totally. Social insurance, housing, education are among the domains which illustrate moving arrangements over time between direct public spending and qualitative forms. Another domain pertains to the nationalisation and privatisation of corporations in banking, finance, insurance, transport, energy and other industries.

Other questions arise: Why public spending rather than some other form of state action? What is the rationale for state action rather than some form of non-public (that is, private) collective action? Consider social insurance funding. Its funding varies over time and across countries. It combines on the one hand compulsory and non-compulsory funding, and on the other hand public forms (taxation, social contributions) and private forms (mutual benefit, non-profit health insurance financed by employers and employees). The latter do not enter public spending. This is not a minor matter since social security as a whole represents roughly two-thirds of public spending and 30 per cent of GDP in France at the beginning of the twenty-first century. These considerations point to the need to take into account the evolving nationwide arrangements which surround public spending. The way they are institutionalised, and therefore rendered more enduring, must be carefully examined.

Therefore, in order to understand the evolution of public spending, it appeared necessary to explain why action in a given domain was in the form of spending rather than in some other form like qualitative action through regulation, law or incentives of state origin. This question points to the issue of the various forms of state action. It triggers in turn the question of the public rather than the private origin of action. Economic theory offers a whole spectrum of theories concerning this issue. They range from preconceptions of a benevolent state, for example, public goods theory, to the opposite, a bureaucratic state, for example, public choice theories.

To summarise, the insight was that it was not possible to take public spending independently of the other forms of public action, and to take public action autonomously from other forms of collective action. Another way to present it is that it is not possible to take the public expenditure form as given separately from other forms, except in trivial instances where it is specific to an area such as defence or general administration. Therefore expenditure evolution comes 'after' explaining the expenditure form which itself comes 'after' explaining the public form. This enlarged setting makes it possible to understand better the role of some institutions in the evolution of public expenditure.

We employ D.C. North's definition of institutions as formal and informal rules of the game and their enforcement characteristics (North, 1994). Two institutions which must be given special attention are education and social security. Education and its distribution between public and private institutions has been a long-standing political issue since the end of the nineteenth century in France. It was settled at the beginning of the twentieth century but this issue still arises from time to time. Social security as a system was created by law in 1945 and has remained until now the framework of the French welfare state. These institutions were not the outcomes of rational choices. They emerged as compromises settling deep tensions between political, social and economic forces. Along with property rights, the rule of law and universal suffrage, these two *institutionalised compromises* on education and social security appear at the top level of a hierarchy of formal institutions in France.

These qualitative and quantitative features were the ingredients which, when combined, enabled us to detect rather stabilised or slowly evolving configurations of what may be called interactions between the state and the economy. The current configuration has been in place since the end of the 1940s and the 1950s. Although it is currently under heavy pressure from persistent unemployment, globalisation, deregulation and liberalisation fostered by European integration, and from numerous incremental changes toward more flexibility, it is still the initial framework with its institutionalised compromises which serves as a point of reference.

This periodisation appeared consonant with the socio-economic periodisation developed in *régulation* theory (Boyer and Saillard, 2002).[3] *Régulation* theory aims at depicting the trajectories of capitalist economies. The two programmes were initially developed autonomously. However the convergence of their results, notably their periodisations and the role of institutions, led to a connection being established between our findings and the five institutional 'forms' or domains of *régulation* theory (that is, forms of competition, the monetary regime, the wage-labour nexus, the state regime and the international regime). We formulated the hypothesis that these enduring configurations needed to be characterised as specific regimes of interaction between the state and the economy or RISEs.[4] What remained to be determined was whether what had been devised for one country might be relevant for other countries.

These results were obtained for one country, France. The question of their more general representativeness called for an international comparison. However, this comparison had to be an in-depth inquiry. It could not rely on the available public finance data because they ignored the qualitative and institutional aspects. The price that must be paid for inquiring in depth is the necessary limitation of the size of the sample of the countries involved in the study. The obvious limitations of resources imposed this constraint. We chose to focus on the comparison with Germany because of its close economic ties with France. Further researches have included Central and Eastern European countries in transition (Delorme, 1996), Italy (Solari, 2000) and Germany after its unification (Weisz, 2005). In the following sections we will concentrate on the comparison of France with Germany.

B. *Step two*: A comparison with Germany

The overall evolution of public expenditure in the Federal Republic of Germany is not very different from its French counterpart. The long-run periodisation is quasi-similar, and social expenditures as a percentage of total public spending and as a percentage of GDP have also followed approximately similar paths. However, the French ratio of public spending to GDP remained higher than the German ratio by three to four percentage points crudely averaged, since the 1980s, with a recent widening after year 2000. The German state–economy interactions could hardly be understood if three outstanding features which form their background were not explained from the outset.

First, *a heavy imprint of economic structures and historical origins*. A peculiarity of Germany is the widespread reference to the 'German economic model' or the German variety of capitalism, although its demise has periodically been evoked since the 1970s. Does there exist a German model of state–economy interactions? How does one articulate the German model of capitalism? Such questions first appeared in the wake of what came to be called the 'German miracle' of the 1950s and 1960s.

Second, a dominant feature of the German model is its long-standing *strength in industry*, notably in chemistry, mechanical engineering, machine tools and automobile manufacturing. It dates back to the beginning of the twentieth century and has been associated with high-quality products and recurrent trade surpluses throughout the post-World War II period.

Third, and foremost, is a multisecular, *deeply rooted style of decentralised political and economic life.* It might be better depicted as a polycentric federalism. The 'state' in Germany today means 17 states: the *Bund* (federal government) and the 16 *Länder* or regional states. Germany was a mosaic of state and state-like territorial entities until its unification under Prussia and Bismarck's action in the nineteenth century. There were more than 300 states by the end of the eighteenth century.

The most noticeable institutions and other enduring features can be listed as follows, according to the institutional forms of *régulation* theory:

- The competition regime – Market-led prices. World market orientation. High-quality products. Important role of large corporations and dense and strong sector of medium-sized enterprises. Close connections between banks and industry, which have eroded since the 1990s. Today's influence of globalisation (moving towards larger place of shareholder value) and predominance of European Union competition policy.
- The monetary regime – Independence of the Bundesbank. Price stability as a powerful imperative (induced by the societal trauma of the hyperinflation of the 1920s). Tight monetary policy. Transfer of these strong features to the European Central Bank since its creation in 1999.
- The wage–labour nexus – This notion includes three subgroups: the direct wage and labour relations; the 'indirect wage' or social security; and skills and the training and educational system. The main elements of the first subgroup are, first, the *Tarifautonomie*. It is the right of trade unions and employers' associations to regulate wage policy and working conditions without state interference. It implies that there is no minimum wage and no compulsory arbitration by the state (Fichter, 2005, 95). A recent attempt to introduce a minimum wage is under debate. Other components of this subgroup are sectoral contract agreements between trade unions and employer's associations. Branch-wide industrial unionism. Dual system of interest representation between works councils, codetermination and enterprise management, and trade unions and employers' associations. The

former are legally institutionalized organs of employee representation at the enterprise level for workplace issues (works councils) and at the company board level (codetermination). Trade unions intervene in collective bargaining.

The second subgroup is the social welfare state. It was initiated at the end of the nineteenth century on the basis of contributions by employers and employees. It has kept this imprint and is organised in arrangements at national level, and regional and sectoral levels (Fichter, 2005, 96).

Furthermore, this system of labour relations includes an extensive legal and judicial framework for dealing with labour disputes that are not directly resolved by the affected parties. This framework contains measures that range from mediation and arbitration to a network of labour courts (ibid., 96).

Finally, the German educational system is characterised by its dual structure between vocational training and classical schooling. Vocational training is based on classroom attendance and practical training courses inside the enterprise, and institutions of more specialised qualification at a higher level. It reflects a long-standing, society-wide concern with institutionalised skill identities and it ensures the availability of a highly skilled workforce.

- The state – A deeply entrenched federalism is the cornerstone of the role and meaning of the state in Germany as has been outlined above. An instance of it is the principle of subsidiarity.

  It entails a highly intricate political decision-making structure that has been called a 'negotiation state' by Esser (Beck et al, 2005, 3). It has been a 'political integrating force' since World War II. It is based on the 'adoption and transformation of corporatist political structures from National Socialist Germany' and on the introduction of a liberal capitalism 'under political competition between Christian Democrats and Social Democrats, who eventually found common ground in the politically mediated compromise between capital and labour' (ibid., 3). This foundational institutionalised compromise has been described by Wolfgang Streeck as a 'compromise … negotiated and institutionalised at a time when the communist wing of the workers movement and the authoritarian voices of German capital … were excluded from political participation' (quoted in Beck et al, 2005, 3). This fundamentally centrist political culture still prevails (Uterwedde, 2003, 37).

  Other features of the German state are the extensive judicial framework, already mentioned, and the highly intricate economic public sector. The latter combines mixed economic entities and cooperative structures at the local and regional levels (Weisz, 2005). These activities range from transport and energy to finance (savings institutions and agricultural credit cooperatives).
- The linkage with the international economy – From its inception, the Federal Republic of Germany espoused a liberal economic orientation toward the world market. It was consonant with its already acquired specialisation in

> industrial, technologically intensive, high-quality products. After the 1950s, the German economy almost constantly generated trade surpluses. The preservation of these surpluses has been considered 'a primacy of German economic policy'. It has been accompanied by a stability-oriented monetary policy, fiscal discipline and relations between capital and labour which on the whole constituted 'an unwritten productivity coalition and consensus to ensure international competitiveness, high quality, and high employment standards'. Despite current changes, 'this kind of mercantilism' still prevails today according to Beck et al., 2005, 233.

On the whole the German state–economy relations seem to express today more than ever the two opposing forces of rather fast market-led change, on the one hand, and of relatively inert, slowly evolving institutional and ideational resilience on the other (Allen, 2005). Globalisation, deregulation and European integration put growing pressure on the welfare state and on corporate governance, with its tendency toward extending shareholder value. Yet, however intense these forces may be, they affect a society characterised by a broad, politically centrist consensus on competition, the stability of money, and a world market orientation. These aspects differentiate Germany from France. Things are also changing in France, but from a departure point in which none of the characteristics mentioned above for Germany was prevailing. The 'adaptation' to a market-led world economy will undoubtedly take longer for France than Germany.

Other lasting features of Germany's political economic system must be emphasised. There is a 'participatory, regulatory, and negotiated settlement culture' of German welfare state institutions and organised interests (Fichter, 2005, 97); there is a climate of conflict partnership (ibid., 101) between strong collective bargaining partners embedded in a framework of 'pragmatic strength of conflict and cooperation, which enables incremental change and adaptation' (ibid., 105); there is the presence of 'institutional and habitual factors' that permit voice rather than exit options 'for the main societal actors in their relations to one another and thus force them into constant dialogue and negotiations' (Beck et al., 2005, 227). An aspect of this interplay pertains to the so-called corporatist policy structures of Germany, with its central association of employers as well as more regionally oriented chambers of industry and commerce and of handicrafts that make possible an 'interest-oriented self-organisation' (ibid., 4).

These factors may be affected by the tide of globalisation. However they have proved to be most enduring thus far. They rely on institutional and organisational as well as deeply rooted ideational features. They point to an overall coherence of which the state–economy interactions are one dimension which cannot be severed from the other dimensions before it is investigated and duly characterised.

The contrast with the French policy structures and economic policy-making is clear. Although both economies are capitalist, are now under the European monetary and competition policies, are part of the globalisation trend and can be represented with the same institutional domains, the description above shows differences in their institutions, in their organisation, in their societal actors' strengths, and ideas. To take an example, the decision by the central government in France, at the end of the 1990s, to reduce the legal labour week to 35 hours would have been unimaginable in Germany given the strength of *Tarifautonomie*. If the state is a part of an organically coordinated capitalism in Germany, France might be characterised by its central state imprint resulting from the relatively weak influence of societal actors.

C. *Step three*: The RISE hypothesis

The comparison of France with Germany reveals two different, robust national configurations of state–economy interactions. A number of lasting differences may be clustered as follows: institutions (industrial relations, vocational training, decentralised and cooperative federalism, judicial apparatus); organisational arrangements (corporatist, negotiation-based, importance of intermediary-level organisations, connections between financial institutions and industry); actors and strategies (trade unions, importance of the *Mittelstand*, the sector of medium-sized business); and the discourse coalitions (social market economy, consensus on monetary stability and world competition). These features that we detailed for Germany signal lasting differences with France. They make up enduring national frameworks although these countries are otherwise clustered in the same variety of a 'continental European capitalism' (Amable, 2005) and abide by the European integration and European Monetary Union.

These differences are often recognised but do not seem to have been specifically structured into more encompassing frames which articulate both differences and similarities. I suggest that these national configurations of the relations between the state and the economy can be represented as regimes of state–economy interaction (RISEs) built on the basis of their structural, institutional, functional and organisational forms, and their actors.

They can be mapped in a double entry form (Figure 1.1), with structural and institutional aspects in lines and functional dimensions in columns. Each one needs to be disaggregated further.

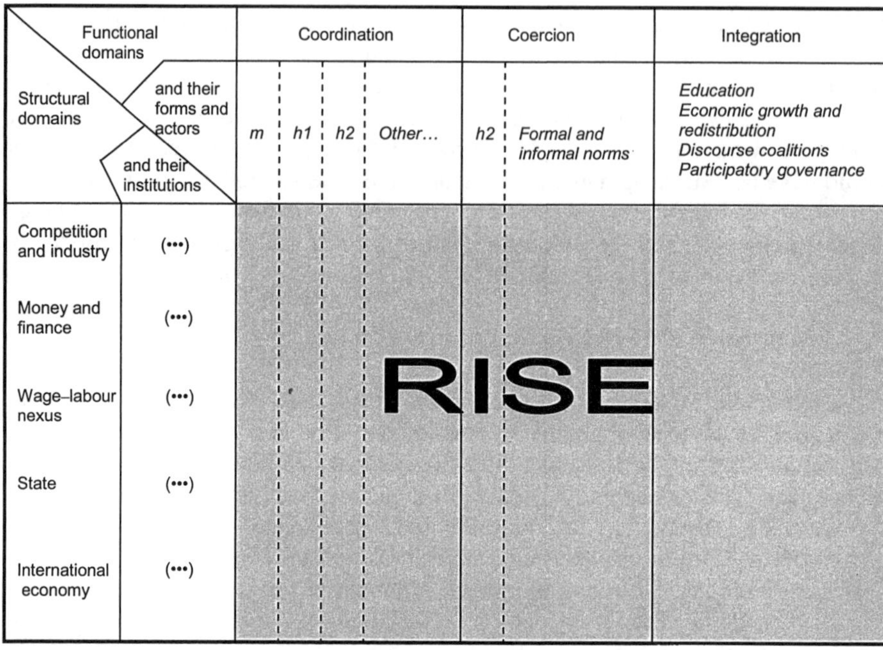

Figure 1.1 The structure of a regime of interaction between the state and the economy (RISE)

The RISE rests on several assumptions:

1. The state–economy interactions are not the whole of an economy. They pertain to both less and more than the economy. To 'less', in the sense that a market-led capitalist economy includes private activities that are not under the direct influence of state structures or agents. And to 'more' in the sense that the state extends to political and societal domains that are beyond the economic domain proper.
2. Some basic ingredients of what an economy is can be viewed through the metaphor of a game such as football. They consist in a hierarchy ranging top-down from the nature of the game, to the rules of the game, then to the organisation of the play of the game, and the players. The first level does not discriminate between French and German economies since they are both capitalist economies with property rights and the rule of laws. The rules of the game are the institutions. The third category pertains to the regularities observed in the unfolding of the game, that is, its organisation. As in soccer, although there is one unique rule, the organisation of the players on the field,

and the tactics followed, vary across teams and may also vary during a game. And the players are the economic agents and other relevant societal actors such as organised interests and associations.

3. The institutions are structured according to the institutional 'forms' or domains of *régulation* theory. Several institutions may operate in a domain. The typical instance are the institutions of the wage–labour nexus.
4. Institutions have three main functions: coordination; coercion; and integration or legitimacy building and preservation. Each one of these functions can be performed through various organisational forms. *Coordination* is the proper economic task pursued at the macro, meso and micro levels. It is the function for which its main organisational forms are disaggregated in Figure 1.1. They include a variety of intricate forms. The most elementary are 'pure': the market (*m*), private hierarchies, that is, private corporations (*h1*), public hierarchies (*h2*) including the state and the public and semi-public sectors. Finally there are networks, associations, clans, and so on (*n*). They coexist with their hybrid forms of concrete activity like *mh1* for markets between private corporations and organisations which represent a very large part of market transactions. One may have alliances between *h2* and *h1*, and with other forms in *n*. We have no space here to be more explicit, but it is clear from the two countries on which our investigation bears that it would be heroic to reduce the state–economy interactions to market transactions. *Coercion* is intrinsic to the sovereignty of the state. It includes the regalian functions (general administration, police, courts, defense, foreign relations). Coercion is attached to the public hierarchies *h2* but is also reflected in several norms, formal and informal. Among the former is the more or less centralised or decentralised style of governance. Among the latter are strong traditions such as the *Tarifautonomie* in Germany. *Integration and legitimacy building* covers the areas that appear necessary to the formation of what can be broadly understood as a societal consensus, instances of which are education, economic growth and distribution, discourse coalitions (Lehmbruch, 2001), and participatory governance.

The structure of the RISE is represented in Figure 1.1. The state–economy interactions proper bear primarily on all the cells of column *h2* and of the line 'State', plus some cells in the coercion and the integration columns. Crossing the lines and columns are the institutional and organisational arrangements that were detected in the investigations of the French and German cases summarised above. They can readily be positioned in the figure. It suffices to say here that the density of these arrangements appears higher in Germany, notably for the wage–labour nexus and the organisation of the state. State–economy interactions reflect a quasi omnipresence of the central government in France whereas a more complicated sharing among public levels prevails in Germany. Moreover, actors and ideas do play a role although it is difficult to represent it in a schematised setting. The structural character of Figure 1.1 would need to be complemented with functional and processual aspects in order to reflect more fully the RISE.

1.2.2 A Wicked Problem

A. In search of a theory

A.1 The Challenge

The RISE is the robust outcome of an empirical investigation. Yet, however robust it may be, it appears as a strange object for economic analysis. It is a configuration of interdependent components that is not produced with the usual inductive or hypothetico-deductive analytical tools of economic theorising. It rests on the observation of two cases and is therefore primarily abductive, a notion that will be explained in the next section. Moreover, it was constructed on the basis of the carefully checked observation of quantitative and qualitative phenomena independently of any reference to a pre-existing 'theory of the state', given the high degree of ideological controversy attached to it.

It would therefore be exposed to the limitations of any purely empirical inquiry, notably its possible arbitrariness in the choices made in the course of research, and its limited, monographical bearing, if it were not informed by a theory. Reflecting on what kind of theory can accommodate the RISE is the object of this section.

At this point we need to distinguish between the construction of the observations and their results, and the organisation of the results. Whereas the former is autonomous of theory, the latter is influenced in part by *régulation* theory since the structure of the institutional domains of the RISE entails the institutional forms of *régulation* theory. This connection followed from the observation that our periodisation on the French case and the qualitative insights about the role of institutions were consonant with those of *régulation* theory. In this sense, the RISE might be called *régulationist*, notwithstanding the terminological ambiguity about the fact that the state in a *régulation* perspective is in no way limited to regulatory functions. However, the connection of the RISE with *régulation* theory requires more than mere convergence on the aspects mentioned above. This needs to be further elaborated. We are therefore driven back to what can be expected from a theoretical appraisal of the state–economy interactions under the form of enduring configurations: the RISEs.

If we assume that the RISE is worth being taken as an object of theorising, several questions must be considered: How does it emerge and develop as an enduring configuration? How do differences in the RISEs across countries occur? How many of these differences are enduring and evolving? Finally, what will be the impact on economic analysis and policy-making of the RISEs and their differences across countries?

Central to the RISE is the role of the state in the economy. To sum up, it is several dimensions at once. As an institutional domain, it contains many institutions within it. It is a combination of institutional functions, all of which have the unique attribute of sovereignty derived from the coercion function. It is also an economic actor. The coordination function *h2* is exerted through procedures and organisational forms.

In the RISE, the state appears as an intricate relational entity rather than having an absolute nature. It is grasped through what 'it does' rather than through a perception of its presumed a priori nature. Its characteristics are not deduced from a priori considerations. It can be observed quantitatively and qualitatively.

The state is institutional and organisational, and it is an actor among other actors, institutions and organisations, even if it holds a specific position on each of these items. Therefore it combines several logics of interactions and is yet a unified, integrated entity rather than the piecemeal addition of independent parts. Finally, it cannot be reduced a priori to one of these dimensions through some sort of ad hoc hypothesis holding other dimensions constant. The view which emerges from the RISE is a relational, interactive, integrated and complex state. This view does not oppose reducing aspects of it to analytical treatment. It obviously would be irrelevant to require that the RISE be fully depicted by a theory. Thus, reduction is necessary, but it needs to be constructed. There is a difference between reduction done *ex post*, after having constructed the whole from which the reduction is performed, and a reduction done through an immediate assumption without reference to a previously constructed whole. In sum, the reduction from a constructed whole is a priori different from the spontaneous reduction from an unconstructed whole in economics. The former is a priori more informed and less arbitrary than the latter and is retained here.

We turn now to the theoretical status of the RISE. How can we move from its hypothetical and conjectural character to a theoretical formulation? What can be expected from a theory of the RISE? If we reason with respect to a final purpose, the focus would be to improve policy-making and the knowledge upon which it is based. The RISE is a pattern which renders explicit a number of interdependent features that are the substance of past and present policy-making. It reveals how the interaction of the state and the economy differs across countries. It shows how to make sense of international comparisons and how any sort of crude benchmarking is doomed to fail. It demonstrates how change is about a specific configuration to start with, and how some change, when it is not minor, can put into motion a number of interdependent factors. Finally, it suggests that what can be expected at most from policymaking is to evolve the configuration that has been inherited rather than changing rapidly and profoundly the configuration itself.

Since institutions play an important role in the RISE, we turn now to economic institutional theory in order to assess whether there are analytical views that might underlie the RISE hypothesis.

A.2 Candidate Answers

The first perspective we will consider is the game-theoretic approach to comparative institutional analysis that has been developed by several authors recently, notably by Masahiko Aoki (2001, 2007). In Aoki's conceptualisation, an institution is 'self-sustaining, salient patterns of social interactions, as represented by meaningful rules that every agent knows and are incorporated as agents' shared beliefs about how the game is played and to be played' (Aoki, 2007, 6). In this view, institutions are endogenised as game equilibria implying agents' summary representations '(rules cum beliefs) regarding how the game is being played' (ibid., 9). Institutional dynamics appear to involve interactions of economic, political, social and organisational factors, in which organisations are players of the game. These factors thus define four 'exchange domains' including linkages among them from which arises 'a complex structure of overall institutional arrangements' (ibid., 14). Two types of linkages follow from the game-theoretic perspective: linked games and institutional complementarities when institutions are interdependent and mutually reinforcing. It 'explains why there can be a variety of overall institutional arrangements across economies'' (ibid., 17), and it suggests how institutional change can result from mechanisms based on counterparts of equilibrium linkages. Three such mechanisms are: 'Shumpeterian bundling innovation' (institutional innovation of the Silicon Valley); 'overlapping social embeddedness' (Italian industrial districts); and dynamic complementarities as formulated in the Momentum Theorem by Milgrom et al. (1991), an example of which is the role played by the institutions of contract implementation in Hong Kong in the transition of the Chinese economy to a market economy (ibid., 25).

The relationships between the state and other institutions in the economic domain are derived by Aoki from his conceptualisation of the state as an equilibrium phenomenon of a game in the polity domain (Aoki, 2001, 151). It is based on the distinction of the government as an organisation and player of a game in the polity domain and the state as 'a stable order of relationships between the government and private agents' to which the government is itself submitted (ibid., 152). Three prototypes of the state are identified: democratic, predatory and collusive, with various ramifications. The democratic and collusive states ramify notably into liberal democratic ('rule of law, labour subjected to market discipline') and social-compact corporatist ('rule making delegated to associations, labour represented by an organization') types. The former is illustrated by the USA, the latter by Germany (ibid., 163 – 164).

Aoki's conceptual and analytical thinking is intuitively appealing. It would even seem hard to think of stable states resulting from social interactions between competing or adversary interests that might not be interpreted as game equilibria in Aoki's fashion. Nevertheless this analysis raises some problems with respect to the RISE.

The first problem is the issue of the strategy followed for empirical validation. Aoki relies on examples based on resemblances between conceptualisations and particular empirical situations in specific sectors. Even Aoki's core instance of the complementarity of lifetime employment, imperfect labour market and the main bank system in Japan has been challenged (Streeck, 2005). It seems to be more an *ex post* discovery in the 1960s and 1970s than the outcome of designs since there is no point in historical time 'when the three elements were jointly designed' (ibid.). According to what criteria of empirical validation can this analysis be extended to situations having no equivalent in the empirical situations taken as examples? This seems to remain an open issue. The two world wars played an important role in shaping the French and the German RISEs. Can they be included in a game-theoretic perspective? The types of state mentioned above are bird's - eye views which lead to cluster commonalities at a highly general level of abstraction without any knowledge of what is lost in terms of possibly relevant distinctions between national patterns belonging to a common cluster.

A second problem arises from the multidimensional character of the RISE. The RISE contains features about institutions, forms of organisation, players as organisations, hegemonic discourse coalitions, and their combinations. It is more than institutions and players. It relies on coordination, coercion and integration, not merely on coordination. To take coordination alone, the interaction between the state and the economy involves modes of coordination such as markets, hierarchies, networks and associations that go beyond the dualism of state and market. These features and their combinations cannot be posited a priori. They require to be addressed as an empirical question first, on the basis of which a further theorising can be developed.

The third and perhaps the most important problem is the overall challenge the RISE presents to theorising. It lies in the issue of how to articulate the overall global combination level with the diversity of the component sectoral parts. The identification of the former under the state-type patterns provides little information on the latter. And the reliance on sectoral aspects of the whole does not illuminate the unity of the whole. Moreover, the search for state types is oriented toward clustering based on the search of commonalities. But this search should not be at the expense of neglecting differences when they are enduring and relevant to understanding the specificities of each nation. How to articulate global and sectoral levels within one RISE, and the similarities and differences across RISEs, is the central difficulty in theorising about the RISE. The game-theoretic approach does not solve these problems.

Another theoretical perspective on economic institutions is found in the comparative institutional analysis of the 'varieties of capitalism' literature (Hall and Soskice, 2001). In contrast with the game-theoretic perspective, it is based on an empirical, inductive analysis of modern capitalist economies. It emphasises the coexistence of different types of capitalist economies which are characterised by substantially different institutional structures (Amable, 2000, 645). These institutional structures are composed of coherent, complementary institutional arrangements which make up overall configurations defining the actual varieties of capitalism. In a recent study of 'five capitalisms', Amable defines institutions as political economic rules and equilibria, that is, as the outcomes of strategic game interactions between actors within a power structure (Amable, 2005, 50–53). The analysis is based on 21 countries of the Organisation for Economic Co-operation and Development (OECD). It is a principal component analysis aimed at identifying groups of countries with common characteristics, in the 1990s. Five institutional domains are considered: competition in the product markets; labour market regulation; financing; social security and education (ibid., 27). Five groups of economic systems are identified: market led, social-democrat, continental European, Mediterranean and Asian.

Of interest here is the continental European capitalism which includes notably Germany and France. They are clustered on the basis of the five institutional areas mentioned above which compose 'specific architectures of complementary institutions' defining an overall coherence (ibid., 32). It offers a welcome refutation of the idea that current globalisation and its strengthening of market-led tendencies would imply a 'one best way' to high levels of economic performance. It is however disconcerting to find Germany and France in the same model after having detected such a strong difference in their RISEs in the present study. The absence of the state in the institutional domains that were selected may explain this discrepancy.

We are left with a political economy of institutional complementarities which indicates that France and Germany belong to the same pattern, whereas the state–economy interactions model indicates that they are two different political economies.

The political economy of institutional complementarities presented in Amable's study is oriented toward finding similarities and gathering them into clusters rather than toward identifying the in-depth institutional factors that differentiate political economies within a given type of capitalism, that is, here, Germany and France within the continental European variety.

Taken at face value, it is a political economy that ignores state–economy interactions. Then there is no choice but to accept that either it overlooks the latter and should include them, or that the political economy of institutional complementarities does not normally account for the state–economy interactions, in which case a political economy of state–economy interactions in its own right is needed.

The French and German cases demonstrate how the neglect of state–economy interactions may be problematic when economic policy-making is envisaged. The two countries have profoundly different modes of governance. These differences are not totally ignored but they remain casually evoked. The conceptualisation of the RISE provides an explicit, though partial, specification. It is not accommodated by the theoretical perspectives reviewed above.

Amable stresses that considering single institutions in the economy may be misleading and that it is 'necessary to have the whole institutional picture in mind before attempting some reform with an improvement of economic performance in mind' (Amable, 2000, 659). It is all the more perplexing to notice that the characterisation of the state and its interactions with the economy are absent. If it may be agreed that models of capitalism 'are not variants of one unique, pattern, each has an internal logic and synergetic effects that are entirely specific' (ibid., 676), our research suggests strongly that within the continental European model which includes France and Germany, there are also two different modes of state–economy interactions. This feature sets the theoretical challenge: it is to articulate into a unified setting both the similarities and differences which compose empirical, historically generated, intricate and robust combinations, the RISEs.

Considering the limitations of the analysis evoked above, it may be tempting to return to the initial step, *régulation* theory, and take it as the theory that, after all, informs the RISE.

Régulation theory is indeed wide-ranging and can accommodate a priori most of the features of the RISE. It is a research program that initially emphasised the long-term transformations of national forms of capitalism, addressed the alternation of periods of rapid and slow growth, and specified the diversity of national trajectories. The historical and geographical variability in the modes of adjustment of economic variables, in other words the mode of *régulation*, is at its heart. The state appears as one of the five institutional forms mentioned above. *Régulation* theory deals with the dynamics of an economy with a wealth of institutions and organisations that interact through markets and other modes of interactions. It is conceived from the start as an alternative to mainstream theory and its axioms of rationality and equilibrium deemed to operate through the sole mechanism of interdependent markets.

Régulation theory relies on four 'pillars' or founding methodological hypotheses (Boyer, 2002, 5–6): multidisciplinarity, empirically based theorising, historicity, and a constant concern for maintaining a limited recourse to ad hoc hypotheses. They are complemented by a central theoretical hypothesis: that economic actors interact primarily on the basis of a set of institutions that imply a variety of situated rationales (ibid., 14). None of these hypotheses contradicts what is done in the construction of the RISE. Therefore *régulation* theory can be viewed as a background framework for the RISE.

It is primarily a set of organising principles and an approach to analysis. Its substantive accounts bear mainly on macroeconomic notions. Thanks to its openness and flexibility, *régulation* theory can accommodate the RISE. But the RISE and its variety across periods and countries could hardly be inferred and specified from modes of *régulation*. Calling the RISE '*régulationist*' would denote a broad reference to the methodology of *régulation* theory rather than to a *régulationist*, well-specified substantive theory of the state–economy interactions. *Régulation* theory directs attention primarily toward a methodological issue. This is not surprising in view of its emphasis of the variability of *régulation* through time and across nations within the framework of evolving modes of *régulation*. It goes against the tendency of looking for a substantive model that would be valid for all times and in all places. In this way the substance of the RISE is connected to capitalist market-led economies specifically. Consequently, the issue of what kind of theory one may build for a subject matter characterised by its singularity remains wide open.

B. In search of a methodology

Even if we accept *régulation* theory as a broad theoretical background for the RISE, a finer-grained perspective may be needed in order to assess better the degree of generality of the RISE and its implications for state action and structural governance.

Can a finer-grained, more highly specified theory of the RISE be conceived? Can the theoretical status of the RISE hypothesis be fully established? The theoretical contributions we have reviewed do not offer satisfactory answers. This situation suggests that in the absence of a fully satisfactory available theoretical frame, it becomes necessary to construct theoretical arguments solidly based on an appropriate methodology. This is the pathway to which *régulation* theory invites us. We assess it below.

B.1 The Challenge

The French and German RISEs are historically, empirically and nationally constructed. They reveal enduring and evolving intricate combinations of institutional, organisational and discursive features which frame and inform the state–economy interactions as subsets of larger societal regimes of reproduction. Let us recall that 'institutional' connotes stuctural and functional aspects of institutions. The epithet 'organisational' denotes both non-random, persistent regularities in the operational unfolding of the functions and the actors as organisations operating in the name of organised interests. The reference to the societal level is simply meant to signal that the RISE bears only on a specific aspect of the social realm. Although the hypothesis of the RISE might be extended to other countries, we continue to restrict our analysis to France and Germany.

Any satisfactory method or methodology should account for the two main characteristics of the RISE: the articulation of wholes and parts, and the diversity of RISEs across countries. The former relates to the unity and internal diversity, to the many-sidedness and the mutual interdependencies which constitute a RISE. The latter suggests strongly that the RISEs are singularities and that there is no one best way for structural economic policy making.

How to reduce and simplify while preserving these intrinsic properties? The RISE appears irreducible to any one-sided view that would be either global or based on the analysis of isolated parts.

B.2 Candidate Answers

An immediate candidate method for many-sidedness is the systems approach. However it remains little more than a language and suffers from a lack of unified and firm methodological foundations. We will consider this problem later in this book. Simon's near decomposability of so-called complex systems (Simon, 1969 [1996]) requires that the whole to be nearly decomposed be known from the start, and a priori helps little in the very construction of the articulation of whole and parts.

Another perspective would be the acceptance of a combination of various methods as a kind of methodological pluralism. It is however an interim, defensive posture, the rationale of which is to defend the legitimacy of heterodox approaches. Its main weakness is its potential lack of coherence.

A still different path to an open, many-sided view is *régulation* theory. Within the limits of its foundational hypotheses, it is explicitly presented by Boyer as originating in the 'juxtaposition and transformation of a collection of tools and different approaches' (Boyer and Saillard, 2002, 17). The strength of its methodology seems to reside, it is claimed, in the realism of its hypotheses and the relevance of its conclusions (ibid., 15). It fits with the 'specific scientificity' advocated by the same author and his co-authors which departs from the economics mainstream epistemology 'built on the pattern of the physical sciences and for their needs' and whose fruitfulness 'material [in economics] that seems different from what it usually deals with' is questionable. This 'new form' of scientificity is 'modest or intermediate'. It is not derived from the unity of a 'canonical model'. It does not contain, for example, a set of methodological (microeconomic foundation, rationality of behaviours) and technical axioms (convexity, differentiability) controlling the construction of models of economic theory. It accepts a 'well tempered' recourse to ad hoc hypotheses when they are 'relevant' and relies in the end on an idea of greater realism and fruitfulness (Amable et al., 1997).

A notion of eclecticism arises from these views. It may be the sole reasonable attitude toward a very intricate, many-sided subject matter in the socio-economic domain. Its *raison d'être* as an alternative to mainstream methodology is to propose a way of knowing which is at least as good as the mainstream one. Thus it claims to be more realistic and to achieve more relevant conclusions. This is where a serious problem arises. The realism of hypotheses is undoubtedly a welcomed requirement. But it does not adequately address the instrumentalist methodology which underpins most of mainstream economic theory. In mainstream theory it is the realism of results that counts, whatever the realism – or lack thereof – of assumptions (Delorme, 1999). Therefore the issue becomes one of comparison of different degrees of realism of the outcomes of theories. The protocols of validation which operate in the hard sciences through controlled experimentation simply cannot be applied to material as intricate as the RISE. Whether there exist other ways to assess the realism of theories appears to remain an open question for further methodological thinking.

The 'relevance of conclusions' is an equally problematic notion. How can one evaluate it otherwise than through the process leading to the conclusions? This process cannot rely only on the realism of hypotheses for the reason given above.

An eclecticism without unambiguous answers to these two issues is a floating eclecticism. Although it relies on a set of shared basic hypotheses, its claims to realism and relevance do not rely on unambiguous criteria. It leaves wide open the issue of constructing a methodology underlying the RISE.

B.3 Why Stick to the RISE?

In consideration of these difficulties, why stick to the RISE? Why not give up on such a problematic notion and address analytically its tractable parts in a piecemeal way? There are several reasons for not doing this. First, there is no criterion or general rule for sorting out the parts of the RISE that could be taken autonomously from their context in the RISE. Second, the RISE is a very robust empirical outcome. It provides a structured, though hypothetical conceptualisation of the broadly shared belief that the conditions, constraints and possibilities of structural economic policy-making vary across countries. This alone makes it worth exploring why there is no one best way in this domain. Not only have the method and the results been exposed to public criticism and proved to be very robust thus far, but it is even possible to say that this present discussion on an appropriate theory would have never come to the fore if it had not first been so deeply rooted in empirical research. Finally, one must make a choice prompted by the profound divide within the economics profession. This is illustrated by the exchange between Simon and Rubinstein included in the final chapter of Rubinstein's book (Rubinstein, 1998).

Simon writes in his criticism of Rubinstein's modelling that: 'At the moment we don't need more models; we need evidence that will tell us what models are worth building and testing'. He adds that economic theory should describe 'real-world phenomena … those that actually occur' (ibid., 190). Rubinstein claims that 'Models of economic theory are meant to establish "Linkages" between the concepts and statements that appear in our daily thinking on economic situations ... [and] are viewed as being analogous to models in mathematical logic' (ibid.). He adds that in this approach a model 'does not have to be verifiable in the way models in the sciences must be … The test lies in the ability to derive insights about the concepts dealt with' (ibid., 192). He thus seems to espouse the view of 'economic theory as an abstract discussion of models' (ibid., 191). There is no room for the RISE in this view. Needless to say, Simon's view is the one preferred here.

B.4 The Implications of Sticking to the RISE

The decision to stick to the RISE creates a messy situation, for we have no available satisfactory methodology to transform the RISE from an empirical conjecture into a notion informed by theory. From the discussion about floating eclecticism, there follows another direction to be explored, the search of an unfloating or anchored eclecticism. Eclecticism can be anchored methodologically if it is subject to declared-in-advance, unambiguously discriminating criteria rather than the mere realism of hypotheses or the relevance of conclusions. This will necessarily entail an exploration of, and a decision about, meta-criteria to determine the methodological criteria. These meta-criteria are of an epistemological character and involve a discussion of the scientific nature of the operation that is envisaged. Some may believe that this is likely to discourage analysis by its very broadness (Amable et al., 1997, 272–273). Then there seems to be no way to face this challenge other than pursuing it with an analysis based on a flawed methodology, or simply giving up with this subject matter.

Yet, the choice made here is different. It is to start with the phenomenal situation creating this wicked problem. It is wicked because it is irreducible to a known methodology and creates a situation of ignorance for the scientist. It invites us to explore whether the scientist's behaviour in this context is much different from the behaviour pioneered by Herbert Simon under the name of bounded (or procedural) rationality.

1.3 CONSTRUCTING A PATHWAY

1.3.1 A Simonian Situation: Procedural Rationality

Simon studied situations in which the observed behaviour of agents denotes a sort of reasonableness or rationality that he coined 'procedural'. These 'complex' or ill-structured problem-situations differ from simple, stable and transparent problem-situations in which what Simon calls 'rationality' can be a reasonable way of behaving.

Procedural rationality is synonymous with bounded rationality in Simon's thinking. Their difference from substantive rationality is a major theme. Literature on modelling 'bounded rationality' has been flourishing since the 1980s in economics but the uses of the term in that literature often differ from the meaning of the concept coined by Simon. This divergence in meaning will be examined later.

Part of the difficulty with the use of Simon's notions of rationality appears to arise from the fact that he did not systematise these notions in a general unified theory but presented them in a plurality of models and contributions pertaining to several disciplines ranging from psychology to management, organisation theory, economics and artificial intelligence.

Although a 'comprehensive coherent theory of bounded rationality is not available' (Selten, 2001, 14), one cannot but be impressed by the unchanged orientation of Simon's works since his 1943 dissertation published in 1947 (Simon, 1947 [1976]. In the first edition of *Administrative Behavior*, objective rationality (in the sense of substantive rationality later on) and subjective rationality (procedural rationality later on) were introduced. Bounded rationality appeared in the second edition (1957). It was distinguished from global rationality. Procedural rationality and substantive rationality appeared in a paper presented in 1973 and published in 1976 (Simon, 1976). The notion was presented by Simon under the term 'bounded' solely in the entry in the *New Palgrave* (Simon, 1987b) and in *Models of my Life* (Simon, 1991). Simon's indifferent use of the two words may create some ambiguity. He seems to have used the term 'procedural rationality' when discussing psychology, and 'bounded rationality' when discussing economics. It is tempting to consider bounded rationality as a kind of rationality simply intended to supplement a complete or substantive rationality, understood as 'the rationality assumption' as does J. Elster (1989, 31). Then bounded rationality would be secondary to a core notion of rationality. But it appears that this view runs opposite to both the substance and the logic of these notions.

Bounded rationality is not bounded or limited relative to a main or complete rationality. It is not secondary to a primary notion. The converse is true as will be shown below. In order to avoid this possible ambiguity, I choose to use the term 'procedural'.

A. What procedural rationality is

According to Simon rationality is substantive when it is defined by the result of a procedure, it is procedural when it relies on the procedure itself: 'Behaviour is substantively rational when it is appropriate to the achievement of given goals within the limits imposed by given conditions and constraints … Behaviour is procedurally rational when it is the outcome of appropriate deliberation. Its procedural rationality depends on the process that generated it'. (Simon, 1976, 130–131). Procedural rationality may be expected in situations that are not 'sufficiently simple as to be transparent to [the] mind'. Then 'we must expect that the mind will use such imperfect information as it has, will simplify and represent the situation as it can, and will make such calculations as are within its powers' (ibid., 144). Using the correct available algorithm is the usual way to operate in substantive rationality. There is no interference between the decision-maker and the way to solve a problem. No such thing is, by definition, available when uncertainty, ignorance or complexity prevail. In this case, decision embodies search and deliberation. A solution is then constructed through a heuristic search in which it is reasonable to retain 'an alternative that meets or exceeds specified criteria, but that is not guaranteed to be either unique or in any sense the best'. This defines *satisficing*, a term introduced by Simon in 1956 (Simon, 1987b). A situation is satisficing when it is adequate to some aspiration level.

It is the degree of complexity of the situation that determines which behaviour is rational. In procedural rationality, decision alternatives are not given but found, one after the other, in a search process that is guided by aspiration levels. An aspiration level is a value of a goal variable that must be reached or surpassed by a decision alternative. The search process goes on until an alternative meets the aspiration level and is thus satisficing. A 'situation' is the combination of cognitive resources, of a purpose or a problem, and of an environment.

In situations that are complex, procedural rationality calls for 'a very high ratio of empirical investigation to theory building'. It requires 'painstaking factual study of the decision-making process itself' (Simon, 1987a, 39). Simon goes on to say that economics without psychological and sociological research to determine the givens of the decision-making situation, the focus of attention, the problem representation, and the processes used to identify alternatives, estimate consequences, and choose among possibilities, such economics is a 'one-bladed scissors' (ibid., 40). Thus Simon uses the metaphor of a pair of scissors where one blade is the cognitive limitation of the human mind and the other is the structure of the environment. Minds with limited cognitive resources can nevertheless be successful by exploiting structures of their environments: studying only one blade is not enough, 'it takes both for the scissors to cut' (Gigerenzer and Selten, 2001, 4).

Accordingly, procedural rationality can be defined as a behaviour or process of matching a heuristic search of alternatives with the structure of an environment. This process is itself defined by an aspiration level and a stopping criterion consisting in satisficing. Rationality is procedural when it obeys this process.

The heuristic search as opposed to an algorithmic use of tools is fundamental to it. It has been described as an 'ecological rationality' of the heuristic exploitation of regularities in the environment by 'Homo heuristicus'. It is distinguished from the *Homo economicus* of standard economic theory: 'a heuristic is not good or bad, rational or irrational, in itself, but only relative to an environment, just as adaptations are context bound' (Gigerenzer, 2004, 403).

Behaviour and the epithets and substantives derived from it are another source of confusion about behavioural rationality that Simon constantly denounced in a combative tone. Simon's 'behaviouralism' is still often confused with 'behaviourism'. Behaviourism sticks to the observable facts of stimuli and responses. Behaviouralism is a framework that speaks about what goes on inside the head, it prefers humans to rats (Simon, 1985, 297). Elsewhere, Simon states that: 'behavioural economics is best characterized not as a single specific theory but as a commitment to empirical testing of the neoclassical assumptions of human behaviour and to modifying economic theory on the basis of what is found in the testing process' (Simon, 1987b, 221). And he adds that: 'whereas neoclassical economists think in a behavioristic manner, through assuming that people are solving constrained maximization problems, behavioral economics aims at addressing what lays between the ears' (Simon, 1991, 232). This commitment of behavioralism to empirical enquiry and testing is well illustrated by the advocacy by Gigerenzer and Selten of 'bounded rationality as the key to understanding how actual people make decisions without utilities and probabilities', and 'dispense with optimization' (Gigerenzer and Selten, 2001, 3,6).

B. What procedural rationality is not

A way to clarify the meaning of procedural rationality is also to expose what it is not in order to avoid possible distortions. It is neither optimisation nor irrationality or fallacies in judgement and decision-making.

B.1 Optimisation under Constraints

There is a class of models known as optimisation under constraints that is referred to in the literature as 'bounded rationality' (for example, Sargent, 1993) and which started with taking searching costs into account without abandoning the goal of optimisation in the modelling of searches (Stigler, 1961). A predecessor of these models was Friedman's methodology of the 'as if' conjecture (Friedman, 1953) in which the question is not whether agents actually optimise but whether they act as if they were doing so. Then, as long as optimisation predicts behaviour, one need not be concerned with the actual reasoning of agents. In this case, as Gigerenzer states it, 'the bounds in rationality are just another name for constraints, and bounded rationality is merely a case of optimisation under constraints' (Gigerenzer, 2004, 391). Simon constantly rejected these models as psychologically unrealistic and as misusing his concept of bounded or procedural rationality. A substantial criticism of this distortion is offered by Gigerenzer and Selten (2001) and Gigerenzer (2004).

B.2 Cognitive Illusion and Errors

Gigerenzer also denounces convincingly a second distortion, the notion that bounded rationality is the study of cognitive illusions (Gigerenzer, 2004, 396). Against Kahneman et al. (1982), Gigerenzer argues that systematic deviations from the 'economists' rationality model' cannot be properly called errors in judgement resulting from the limitations of human cognition. It would be incorrect to presume that since bounded rationality follows from human cognitive limitations, the study of such errors alone would be the object of the study of bounded rationality. To do so would be to rely on only one blade of the pair of scissors of bounded rationality, ignoring completely the environment blade. The view of cognitive illusions and errors relies only on the cognitive blade, 'and compares it with laws of probability rather than with the structure of the environment. One blade alone does not cut well' (Gigerenzer, 2004, 397).

B.3 Substantive Rationality

In the following discussion, Simon's original concepts are exploited and extended to draw a comparison between procedural rationality (PR) and substantive rationality (SR). PR starts with a heuristic search of alternatives. SR starts with the application of an algorithm, optimisation in most cases, to the substance of the problem. They are compared in Figure 1.2. Each contains both procedure and substance, and heuristic and algorithmic aspects, but they differ in the ways these features are combined.

The first difference between the two types of rationality is that PR relies on a heuristic procedure whereas SR relies on an algorithmic procedure. The heuristic procedure aims at setting a problem first, before attempting to solve it. The algorithmic procedure aims at problem-solving with the assumption that the problem is well formulated.

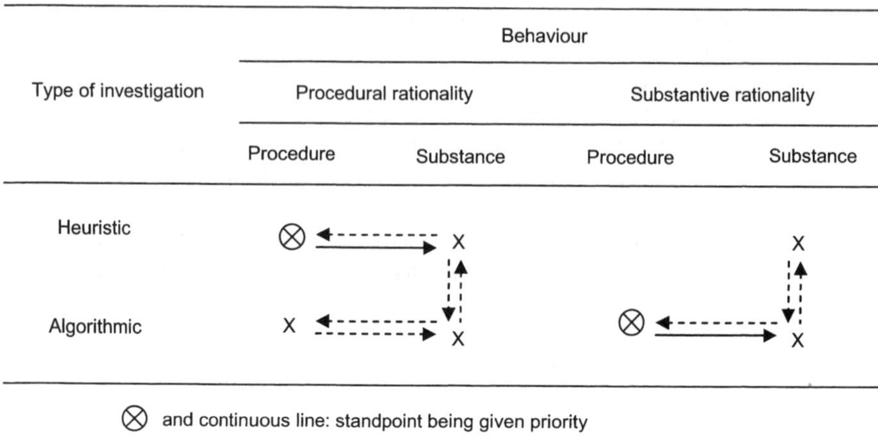

Figure 1.2 Comparison of procedural and substantive rationality

The second difference follows from their asymmetry. Although they both contain iterative steps symbolised by the dotted arrows, they are not symmetrical. PR subsumes SR in the way the heuristic search may uncover stable and transparent regularities between procedure and substance. These would appear as algorithm-like regularities in the sense that they can be dealt with algorithmically. On the other hand, SR rules out the plurality of a priori admissible conducts, learning and variable preferences, which constitute the heuristic search procedure.

In this way, substantive rationality excludes genuine procedural rationality whereas procedural rationality subsumes substantive rationality. However, an issue that requires clarification is the degree of separation between what is procedural and what is substantive in these two types of behaviour. It seems reasonable to consider that they *both* contain procedure *and* substance but that they differ in the weight and the priority given to them. A behaviour of procedural rationality is primarily concerned with heuristics and the definition of some level of aspiration that is, with procedure. But since it is purposeful behaviour it is aimed at obtaining some final result, that is, some substance. Substantive rationality is primarily concerned with the result, that is, optimisation or equilibrium, and under given conditions and hypotheses, the result sought can be obtained. It excludes from its domain of relevance the irreducibility to a known method, that is, deep complexity, as well as uncertainty not amenable to probability, that is, radical uncertainty. When the term 'heuristic' is evoked in a SR setting, it refers to iterations about substance and whether or not it can be grasped with the tools of available algorithms.

A consequence of this comparison is the fluidity established between the two notions. It is an asymmetric fluidity that is informed by procedural rationality.

1.3.2 A 'Post-Simonian' Construction of a Way Out

In the Simonian decision-making situation, rationality pertains to the behaviour of an agent observed by an observer, here, a scientist. A reflexive, procedurally rational behaviour prevails when the situation is ill-structured. A similar messy situation is experienced in our quest of a satisfactory theoretical and methodological frame for the RISE. There is, however, a big difference with the Simonian situation: in the present case, the agent is the observer-scientist. Here, complexity arises from the cognitive irreducibility to a known scientific procedure or algorithm. This is a case of deep complexity. It differs from the complexity studied by Simon and dealt with through the near-decomposability technique (Simon, 1969[1996]). Simon's complexity is not irreducible, whereas deep complexity denotes the irreducibility to a known technique of reduction, including near-decomposability. In summary, near-decomposability relies on the knowledge of the mechanisms through which the parts interact both in forming sub-blocks and in forming a whole, and there are no internal relations between the parts; they are things that are assembled and can be disassembled up to the point of near-decomposability. It might be claimed that the RISE is an instance of reduction and of decomposability into institutional and organisational forms. Yet, while the RISE would lead to a satisficing, and therefore reducible, outcome in Simon's setting, in our case, it is the problem.

The RISE is a conjecture whose validity cannot be based on a straightforward argument of realism as is done by Simon. Realism can be more readily assessed in issues of micro decisions than in broader and macroeconomic issues.

We are left with the problem of how to proceed as a decision-maker. We have no other option but to engage in a heuristic search for an alternative. But this means entering a self-reflexive process in which the observer is assumed to be a Simonian decision-maker. This is a step that Simon never made. He took a posture similar to a positivist empirical scientist to denounce the unrealism of the decision behaviour postulated by neoclassical economics. He advocated a more realistic view of decision-making based on empirical inquiry (Simon, 1992).

The search for a solution to the problem presented here will be based on a self-reflexive practice of procedural rationality. Though procedural rationality includes reflection and deliberation, the shift to a self-reflexive setting exposes it to the logical difficulties of self-reference. Simon kept away from these complications. The construction of a way out sought here is therefore truly post-Simonian, though it relies on Simonian tools and concepts. The design of a procedurally rational way out requires that we clarify the issue of self-reflexivity before we address the consequences of self-reflexivity on procedural rationality.

A. Self-reflexivity

Self-reflexivity entails recursion and self-reference. The latter entails the threat of infinite regress. These two questions are addressed below.

A.1 Recursion and Self-reference

Self-reflexivity pertains both to reasoning and behaviour. It can be represented as recursion. Recursion designates the application of a repeated procedure such that the result at each step is given in terms of the result at the next step. It can be symbolised by a closed loop between a generating principle and its product (Figure 1.3).

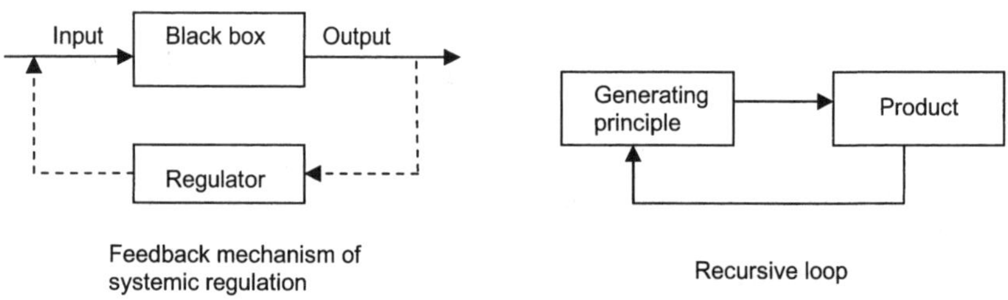

Figure 1.3 Feedback and recursion schematised

The recursive loop differs from feedback. In feedback, a part of the output of a system is picked up as information. It is used as the input of a command or controlling system whose orders are directed to the input of the controlled phenomenon whose variations are maintained within given limits (negative feedback). In the recursive loop the product is producing what produces it. The process is not directed from the outside, although it is not separated from it and can be influenced by it. But the recursive loop is to itself its own program (Dupuy, 1982).

A simple example will help figure out how recursion and procedural rationality are connected when self-reflexivity operates. Let us make a detour and consider a thought experiment derived from an easily conceived game.

It is a game with several players gathered together in a room, in which the aim is to discover a story. One of the players goes out while the others choose a story. Then the first player comes back. The game for him/her is to reconstitute the story by means of questions asked to the other players. Yes or no are the only admitted answers. The unfolding of the game is a process of interaction between the player's imagination and an existing story known only by the other players.

Usually the game converges, through trial and error, toward the discovery of the story (Dupuy, 1982).

Now let us consider the following variant. The rules remain unchanged, but only for the player who goes out and will ask questions. In his/her absence, the others decide not to choose any story. They simply agree on an arbitrary convention for answering. It may be to answer yes if the question asked ends with a vowel, no in the opposite case. They also agree on a rule of non-contradiction of answers. Then the game progresses as a random interacting process produced by the player's imagination and the outcome of the answers. This outcome is only constrained by the consistency of meaning attributed by the player to the story he/she believes he/she is reconstituting. A well-constituted story may emerge. In such a case it is pure invention. It is perceived as such by the outside observers formed by the group of other, answering, players. But for the player who asks the questions and who is ignorant of the true rule of the game, the situation appears similar to the previous game. The player believes that he/she comes nearer to a given story until there emerges a story that appears to be a well-constituted story.

In the initial game the process is guided by an end state. Something given, already existing in the real world independently of the player, must be discovered. The trial and error process is driven by its end:

In the second variant, the player believes that the story has a meaning and an end that are exterior to him/her. But simultaneously it is he/she who generates and invents this meaning and this end. The recursive loop relates to the fact that the invention of a result is both a cause and a consequence of the unfolding. At each step, the outcome of reasoning produces what will produce it in the next step, like a self-referential spiral.

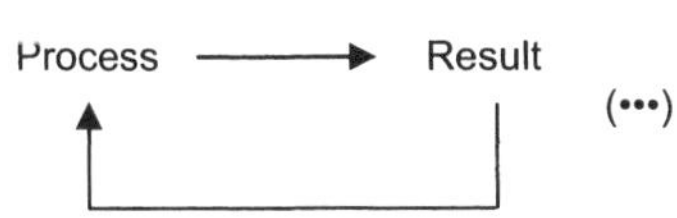

It must be noted that ending with a 'well-constituted' or satisfactory result, thus stopping the process, is not warranted. Moreover, the result is unpredictable both to the outside observer and, naturally, to the player. Here process and result are respectively equivalent to generating principle and product. The game develops as the search for a matching between the heuristics of the questions asked by the player and the answers given by the environment consisting in the group of players. If the outcome looks reasonable and satisficing to the player, it constitutes procedurally rational behaviour.

However, two problems arise immediately from this self-reflexive recursion: the threat of an infinite regress, and the matter of subjectivity. In scientific practice, subjectivity needs to be 'eliminated' or controlled by the submission to external criteria and testing. The possibility of infinite regress raises the issue of a stopping rule. We turn first to a discussion of the infinite regress.

An important implication of recursion is the fluidity between its terms, in which they may become transformed into each other at each step. Equivalent representations of recursion are the loops between generative principle and product, between procedure and substance, and between procedural rationality and substantive rationality.

For behavioural rationality, it means that PR and SR are not separate absolutes. They can alternatively be transformed into the other term, depending upon changes in the purpose, in the level of aspiration, in the cognitive resources, and in the environment. This will be the case provided that the standpoint is first one of procedural rationality, since it subsumes SR and allows this fluidity. In other words, the level of difficulty of a task is not fixed once and for all. It is susceptible to variation over time through changes in some of the factors which determine it. If the level of difficulty is low, SR may be relevant. If it is high, deliberation and reflection on an adequate procedure, focusing on process rather than substance or outcome, again becomes relevant. The notion of relevance is tied to the search for a satisficing situation. Satisficing is the central notion and the key difficulty.

First, satisficing has no determinate content. Nothing prevents someone from deciding procedurally to be 'substantively rational', whereas the opposite seems to be ruled out a priori. Second, it is exposed to infinite regress. This is implied by the very recursion loop linking, say, deliberation and its outcome. Entering a deliberation process at time t_o is itself the result of a previous deliberation and so on. An infinite regress threatens the search for a justification of a decision about behaving procedurally or substantively in the absence of a cutting-off criterion not provided by satisficing. Moreover, this infinite regress is associated with another problem known as the self-referential paradox.

A.2 Self-referential Problems

To study the implication of the procedurally rational choice between procedural and substantive rationality (which we continue to symbolise as PR and SR), we rely on their fluidity mentioned above. Indeed, it is possible to be more accurate and to distinguish a strong and a weak meaning for both notions, in the following way:

- Strong SR: global optimising rationality.
- Weak SR: recourse to routines, to algorithms that can be changed, and to second-best optimisation.

- Weak PR: recourse to heuristics, to pre-established reasoning permitting deliberation, the convergence of which is not established, but that are satisficing.
- Strong PR: no available satisficing heuristic; a complete deliberation is needed in order to conceive a heuristic.

As we have already stated, it is reasonable to consider that several of these notions are not congealed, especially between weak PR and weak SR. The very presence of learning must logically bring some fluidity. The goal of PR reasoning is to reduce uncertainty and to identify a local situation in which SR reasoning is relevant, thus allowing some gain in accuracy. Conversely, a practice of weak SR in a local situation subject to sudden important change is likely to be less and less relevant since the conditions of stability, simplicity and transparency would be likely to regress. This would logically create an incentive to rely less on SR algorithms and more on heuristic investigation of the weak PR type.

In the following presentation, we consider weak SR only, whereas admissible PR can be either weak or strong. Strong SR is not considered because it excludes logically any fluidity with PR.

A kind of cycle or spiral arising between these behaviors cannot be ruled out with successive steps indicated by t_0, t_1, and so on:

$$\text{PR } t_0 \rightarrow \text{weak SR } t_1 \rightarrow \text{PR } t_2 \rightarrow \text{weak SR } t_3 \cdots$$

A cycle can be generated. Indeed its formal structure is analogous to that of the self-referential paradox. It can be shown in the following way.

Let us consider its well-known liar's paradox form: 'This statement is false'. This assertion is false when it is true and true when it is false. The paradox originates in the confusion or lack of distinction between an object level and a meta-level.

One may write, in the logic of propositions:

[1] B = non A
with B: false, A: true

Proposition [1] is itself true. Then 'B = non A' (object level proposition) is true, it is therefore A (meta-level proposition), thus:

[2] A = non A

Confusing the levels produces the paradox. In order to avoid it, it is necessary to distinguish a meta-level, that is, here, the observer level, and an object level, that is, the 'observed'.

Now, referring to procedural rationality PR and to substantive rationality SR, we may write:

[3] A: {PR = SR is false}
[4] B: {PR = SR is true}
with B = non A as in [1] above,
A: true ; B: false.

Is this proposition self-referential? In order to answer this question, we follow the reasoning inspired by H. von Foerster (1977) and J.P. Dupuy (1982).

Let us define an operator symbolised by 'op' ('op' stands for operator) that connects an output y with an input x:

[5] $y = op(x)$

There is self-reference for object x (x can be a number) whenever the operation produces the object itself:

[6] $op(x) = x$

More generally, if op is an application of a set S on itself, x is a fixed point of op: if the object or the number x exists, it remains invariant in the operation op. This fixed point is also called an eigenvalue or an eigenbehaviour (von Foerster, 1977).

Replacing x by its expression in [6], one obtains:

[7] $x = op(op(x))$

and, developing [7]:

[8] $x = op(op(op(\ldots)))$

which suggests a way to define the eigenvalue: the iteration stops when one can find a number or an object such that equation [6] is obtained.

An illustration in which this is not obtained follows from [2]:

A = non A
= non (non (A))
= non (non (non (...)))

It suggests that the operator of negation 'non' has no fixed point in this logic: it is the principle of non-contradiction.

In the present case we have:

A = non B [4]
B = non A [3]
A = non (non (A))
B = non (non (B))

The operator non (non( )) has two eigenbehaviours, A and B. This can be generalised: if there is a path leading to A or B, then one moves indefinitely in a cycle from A to B to A: A, B, A, B, … true, false, true, false … It defines the self-referential paradox.

The expected paradoxical self-referential nature of the cycle presented above is confirmed. The application of self-reflexivity to procedural rationality leads to a paradox in the absence of a stopping rule. In spite of it, a way to go on is to cut off in the self-referential spiral, using the meta-level standpoint of the observer-scientist. There seems to be no better way to cut off than by means of satisficing originating from a judgement that is itself satisficing, but at the meta-level. The main lesson of the argument developed above is that the deep kind of complexity experienced here cannot be solved in the sense of reducing it to a simple model or expression.

This self-reflexive complexity arises when we are forced to admit that *how to decide about a complex problem is itself a complex problem*. It reflects a deep complexity (DCX). It appears as a genuinely second-order deep complexity (SODCX) distinguished from the initial, object-level, or first-order deep complexity (FODCX). SODCX cannot be solved but it can be dealt with. It calls for a SODCX meta-level procedurally rational reasoning and behaviour.

We need to shift from solving a well-formulated problem to the task of setting the problem first. In a deeply complex situation, it appears that the issue of what a good explanation is cannot be solved without relying on procedure. And a satisficing procedure is the outcome of deliberation and design rather than of a deductively predefined choice.

In Figure 1.4 we offer a schematic view of the differences between the standard approach of substantive rationality, Simon's procedural rationality, and the 'post-Simonian', self-reflexive, procedural rationality. This last term is called 'second order complexity', or SODCX.

A first distinctive character of SODCX is the absence of separation between the observer and the observed. It arises from self-reflexivity, that is, the observer's reflexivity. Substantive rationality is symbolised by a one-way influence of procedure on substance (P → S) for the observed. In Simonian procedural rationality, the observed is deliberating, and the pattern is recursive. In second-order deep complexity, this recursion extends to the observer.

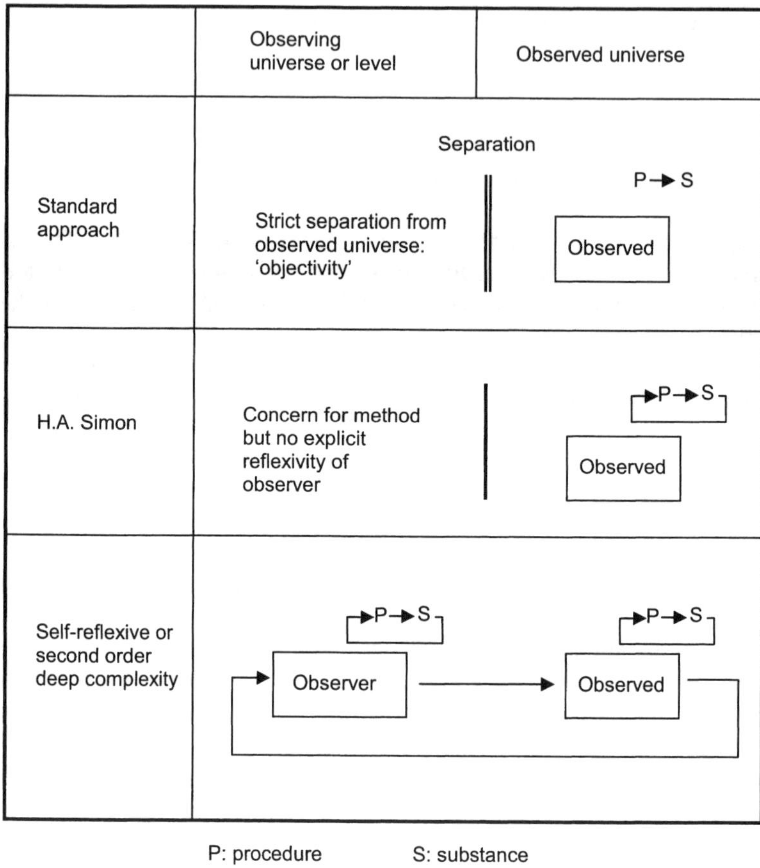

Figure 1.4 Three perspectives compared

B. Designing a way out

B.1 The Task before us: Two Layers of Heuristics

Let us recall where we stand at this point. It was found that the situation about the RISE was similar to the cognitive situation in which decision-makers behave procedurally in the terms described by Simon. For Simon, observation shows that agents facing a complex problem do not optimise under constraints but develop heuristics. Acknowledging this feature is a matter of commitment to a behavioural approach and to realism. An implicit assumption of this standpoint is that the observer has no complex problem of description and that it is a matter of plain, indisputable obviousness. It is at this point that our analysis differs from Simon's.

We extend the behavioural assumption to the observer. This introduces a self-reflexive procedural rationality, a thing in which Simon seemingly never engaged. This is why we use the epithet 'post-Simonian' for the reasoning developed here. No reliance on realism can render 'obvious' the process, the subject matter and the outcome of self-reflexive behaviour. What is called for is a self-reflexive procedural deliberation which involves the matching of a heuristic search with an environment.

What can the substance of this heuristic search be? Our purpose is to design a heuristic that can accommodate the RISE, which means that it satisfies the conditions that were defined above for non-floating eclecticism; that it grasps; that it grasps the properties of unity and diversity; and that it incorporates the singularity of the RISE. These properties were the sources of the irreducibility which defined the deeply complex problem-situation. It was, however, only an initial complex situation; it was followed by a second situation of irreducibility when we uncovered the consequences of self-reflexive procedurally rational behaviour. In this situation the challenge is to control subjectivity and to deal with infinite regress and the paradoxical character of the choice of procedural or substantive rationality. Self-reflexive behaviour entails that to decide about a deeply complex problem is itself a deeply complex problem rather than simply a matter of realism. Therefore, it requires a specific heuristic search.

The outcome is that two layers of heuristics are involved. At the first layer, the aspiration level was to devise heuristically a procedure of which the RISE can be a product, and that must be matched with the conditions that generate deep complexity (non-floating eclecticism, controlled subjectivity, dealing with infinite regress, and self-reflexive indeterminacy). It is a first-order procedural rationality following from a first-order deep complexity (FODCX). At the second layer, the aspiration level is to design heuristically a procedure that can produce the first-order procedure subject to the condition that it can be matched with an environment of scientific practice, that is, that it be scientific and operational. It is a second-order procedural rationality which includes deep complexity, scientific practice and effectiveness, constituting what may be called a second-order deep complexity (SODCX). The chronological sequence in our presentation is from first order to second order, whereas the logical sequence is from the more encompassing, that is, second order, to the particular, that is, first order. Thus, SODCX subsumes FODCX.

The task ahead is to devise a satisficing procedure that accommodates the RISE. But since satisficing has no determinate substantive content and may lead to subjectivism, it needs to be controlled by submitting it to an external constraint. This constraint cannot but be related to the environment of the research process. Here, the relevant environment is scientific practice. The constraint consists of making compatible the three dimensions around which our argumentation has revolved until now. They are: inclusion of deep complexity, scientific practice and operationality. They define an aspiration level for which it is reasonable to consider that a wide agreement on the following global injunction may be obtained: *embody deep complexity, do science and be operational.* A theory will be appropriate or satisficing if it meets these three conditions. Let us now explore how it can be done.

B.2 Deep Complexity

The necessity of including deep complexity in the procedure is self-evident. It means maintaining the properties of the RISE that generated the deadlock: its multidimensionality, its irreducibility to induction or deduction, its inclusion of satisficing, of unity and diversity, of singularity and of self-reflexive procedural rationality.

There is however one implication of deep complexity that is less obvious and must be made clear. It follows from self-reflexive recursion and bears on the conjunction introduced between the observer and the observed. This conjunction of the observer and the observed is inherent to this procedure and determines the orientation of its reasoning. In this way it goes against the foundational separation between observer and observed that is classically considered the *sine qua non* condition for the objectivity of scientific method. It is his credit that Jean-Louis Le Moigne insisted, after others, on the limits of this view. He is highly critical of the way a specific logic derived from Aristotelian axioms has won a universal status in science, whereas other logics remain almost unknown or disdained. As an alternative to the three axioms of disjunctive or Aristotelian logic, Le Moigne presents three 'axioms' of conjunctive or 'systemic modelling' in his work on the modelling of complex systems (Le Moigne, 1990, 32–36).

Every logical system has its own, inevitably arbitrary basis. The nature of the propositions which may be considered as axiomatic is a matter of discussion. Our purpose here is not to develop a pure logic but a heuristic. To this end we introduce the three 'axioms' of complexity modelling, inspired to a large extent by Le Moigne, as working assumptions in our development of a heuristic for deep complexity.

- *The axioms of disjunctive modelling*

The reality to be modelled is perceived through three axioms. A and B stand for propositions:

1. Identity: A is A.
2. Non contradiction: A cannot be simultaneously B and $\overline{B}$ (not-B).
3. Excluded middle: A is either B or $\overline{B}$.

- *The assumptions of deep complexity*

The phenomena to be modelled are perceived through three axiomatic assumptions:

1. *Operationality and intentionality.* Modelling is the conjunction of the modeller's purpose with his/her environment. It eliminates the analytical disjunction between causes and effects. Action and interaction, as opposed to 'things', and process, not its result, are the basic categories.

2. *Irreversibility.* Action and process take place over time. Time is perceived as irreversible.

3. *Included middle.* Operation or action is perceived as generating a product. The generating principle and its product are not separable.

The propositions presented as 'axiomatic' assumptions of deep complexity are much less codified, propagated and familiar than those of disjunctive modelling. It may thus make them appear rather abstract and strange. Yet, if we reflect on the rationale of the axioms of classical logic which form the basis of analytical theorising, we will see that they are not more obvious than the complex ones. It is habituation which makes them look familiar and self-evident to the point where we never refer to them explicitly, as if they were the unsaid basic consensus to be preserved from questioning.

B.3 Scientific Practice

When it is viewed from a basic, practical level, what distinguishes doing science from other cognitive activities may be learnt both from the dictionary definition and from the observation of the day-to-day activity of scientists. Regarding the former, there seems to be a wide consensus on the combination of three elements. Doing science involves the search for some explanation of some reality and systematically testing it (Granger, 1990). According to this view, scientific practice consists pragmatically in an activity of production of knowledge that combines five properties: it is about some object or subject matter; it aims at some 'truth' value or validity; it relies on an explicit methodological and conceptual framework; it is systematically exposed to public criticism and test; and it is subject to revision. It seems reasonable to consider that these views converge and form a common reference to all scientific activity. While this is a widely shared vision, disagreements over different conceptions of science do arise. These disagreements arise mainly from the various ways of conceiving explanation, reality and testing.

Explanation is taken here in a broad sense. It refers to the operation of producing knowledge. It can be causal explanation in a strict sense, but it can also be prediction, representation, design or understanding. For the purpose at hand, the main disagreement exists between the goals of causal explanation and prediction of mainstream economics, on the one hand, and the emphasis on representation common to most heterodox views on the other. The important notion of abduction is especially relevant to the context of deep complexity and its singularity features. It is Charles S. Peirce who revived abduction and pioneered its modern usage. In his terms, 'abduction… amounts … to observing a fact and then professing to say what… it is that gave rise to that fact ' (Hanson, 1965, 89). In the abductive inference some surprising, unexplained fact or phenomenon *P* is observed; *P* would be explicable 'as a matter of course' if a hypothesis *H* were 'true' or valid; hence there is reason to think that *H* is 'true'. In induction, *H* is expected to emerge from repetitions of *P*. In deduction, *P* emerges from some 'unaccounted-for creation of *H* as a higher-level hypothesis' (Hanson, 1965, 86).

The second disagreement occurs over what is to be considered *reality*. The subject matter of science bears on the real world. But here there is a profound separation between two positions. One is ontological realism. It attempts to know the nature of reality by discovering its laws, thus viewing reality as 'objective' in the sense of being independent of the mind. Presumably the statements produced will be scientific because they depict a reality independent from the observer's eye.

Another view of reality contends that true reality is beyond reach and that we know it only through our experience of phenomena. This is known as phenomenological realism. Instead of being discovered, laws and other statements are invented. Scientific practice aims more at diminishing our ignorance than at establishing truths. This is a fallibilistic standpoint. Deep complexity fits well with it. It is based on a rich intellectual tradition which has been maintained for a long time although it has often gone untaught because of the overwhelming influence of the disjunctive, positivist scientific doctrine in science. This tradition is known nowadays as constructivism. Its modern revival finds roots in Dewey's 'participatory knowing', in Piaget's genetic epistemology, in Simon's 'design', and in the 'construction of reality' perspective offered by Bateson, Morin, von Foerster, von Glasersfeld, among others, who will be discussed in Chapter 6. Although positivism has been slowly eroded for decades in natural sciences, it is still pervasive in economics. It finds its strength in the ignorance of constructivism as an alternative point of view. Positivism thrives on the unspoken consensus that promotes immunising stratagems, which destroys the possibility of identifying when a theory is false or irrelevant, and which deprives economic theory of a possibility to learn from its errors. The practical invulnerability of most analytical positivist economics is its main weakness.

This brings us to the third feature, *testing*. This is the most difficult question in economic science, for it lacks a final arbiter. The situation is incomparably better in natural science, where experimentation and controlled observation provide criteria for empirical validation. Insofar as we are interested in empirico-theoretic scientific practice, not in formal science, a final arbiter rests on controlled protocols of empirical validation. It is not an overstatement to say that standard economics is in a disastrous state in this regard. Exceptions can be found in simple, transparent enough problems such as those for which substantive rationality is relevant at a micro level. They can also be found at the macroeconomic level where some problems are simple enough to enable reasonably reliable predictions. This difficult state of affairs is widely admitted in the literature on economic methodology. But, until recently, one must say that its influence has been almost nil on the way most economists work. The greatest part of economic theory consists mainly in conversation at a formal and abstract level. As a consequence, a final arbiter is avoided.

B.4 Putting Scientific Knowledge to the Test

There are two other features that are closely linked to scientific practice. They pertain to the manner in which reasoning is conducted and is communicated. It needs a language. As any other language, it is made with signs, symbols and rules. The first feature has to do with the requirement contained in the triplet of communicability, systematicity and cumulativeness of science. Communication is the basis for diminishing confusion and establishing systematicity thanks to which some progress and cumulative knowledge may be envisaged. These notions point to the importance of the way scientific knowledge is represented and communicated. It is the second feature.

At this stage it is necessary to emphasise that every science embodies its statements and results in signs. Semiotics, the science of signs, comprises three fields called investigating languages by Carnap, also termed portions of semiotics by Morris or levels of communication by Weaver. *Syntax*, also called syntactics by Morris, or the technical level by Weaver, pertains to the relations of signs to one another independently of the relations of signs to objects or to interpreters. *Semantics* deals with the signification of signs understood as the relation of signs to the objects. *Pragmatics* designates the relation of signs to their interpreters, thus dealing with the origin, the uses and the effects of signs (Morris, 1971). From our action-oriented standpoint scientific practice may be expressed as covering necessarily these three fields (Figure 1.5).

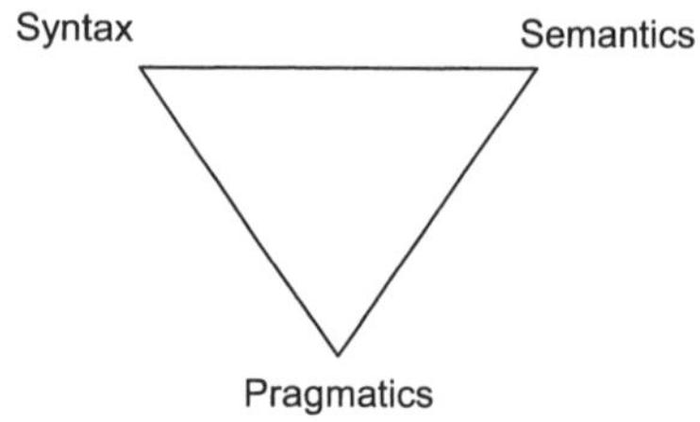

Figure 1.5 Three levels of communication

Within the economic discipline, perspectives can be differentiated according to the relative weights they give to each of these levels of communication. The mainstream formal orientation focuses on syntax while most heterodox dissident perspectives emphasise the two other vertices of the triangle. The ideal is a balance. Since the standard perspective in economics gives priority to syntax, in the case of radical uncertainty, it is no surprise that primacy will be given to the method over the object of inquiry, that is, to syntax over semantics. Exclusion of radical uncertainty, because it cannot be captured with the standard analytical toolkit, illustrates this point. In consequence, the tools are taken for granted and applied to situations which are made to adapt to them through the use of ad hoc assumptions.

A different approach is to start from problematic situations and empirical facts and try to adjust the method and syntax applied to them, thus putting the bulk of adjustment on the pragmatic and syntactic levels of discourse. Yet this procedure does not mean that facts can be taken a priori for granted. They are inevitably arbitrary. However we would find it difficult to express our experience of reality without relying on facts. Thus, it seems reasonable to admit that some adaptation of the facts is inevitable. Of course it does not mean that observation will be modified in order to fit the observer's own preferences. Adjusting facts means making them relevant to the question addressed. In the research done on the RISEs, we found that it was impossible to address public spending in the long run independently of public finance. We also discovered that it would be quite difficult to investigate public finance over time and in international comparisons independently of the other forms, both quantitative and qualitative, of interaction between the state and the economy. Thus, the facts investigated were initially public spending, then public finance, then quantitative and qualitative dimensions of the public sector.

One would expect that in any empirical science consistency prevails not only in the manner the signs are used, in the way they are relevant and in the way they combine in syntax, but also in the overall consistency of the triangle. It is difficult here not to think of the discrepancy which exists in economics between professed and actual method. It is the price paid to preserve formalism. It illustrates how excessive formalism may constrain scientific practice by preventing the study of empirical situations that do not fit with its syntax. Mainstream economists ask the public at large, first, to accept that economics relies mainly on syntax and must be programmatic for the time being; and, second, to believe that it will have empirically relevant results in an ever- postponed future. The alternative approach also has its own price: it is the weakness of its syntax, the evasiveness or the absence of a body of founding logical principles. Here we face once again the ongoing debate over the trade-offs of 'well-derived' versus 'empirically relevant' theories.

B.5 Operationality

Until now our discussion has remained at the logical and the methodological levels. The next task is to combine in an operational way what has been stated about scientific practice and about deep complexity. This will enable us to apply these results to actual cases and to compare them with alternative theoretical perspectives. We still need to submit deep complexity to the test of its adequacy to the problem. This operational test, it is claimed, relies on three rules: consistency, communicability and relevance.

Consistency

Consistency is concerned with avoiding the discrepancy between professed and actual method and an imbalance between the three elements of the semiotic triangle. Although it is difficult to define substantively a balance between these elements, it can be defined procedurally as mutually adjusting semantics and syntax up to the point where the actually practised pragmatics meets the declared pragmatics, that is, the professed method. This may be summarised as: preach what you can do, do what you preach. In the study of a phenomenon perceived as deeply complex, for which there exists no available satisficing substantive theory or model, empirical investigation comes together with abduction in the attempt at theorising. Hence, the priority given to the object of study and to the semantics over the syntax.

Communicability

It may look trivial to insist on communicability as a rule. Yet it conditions both potential systematicity and cumulativeness. Above all, it is a precondition for mutual criticism and the real exercise of control within and outside the scientific community. It implies transparency and voluntary exposure to criticism. It runs opposite to the immunisation so often denounced by methodologists in economics (Caldwell, 1991). Even if it may look too idealistic to believe in the elimination of immunisation, the least that can be done is to eliminate hidden immunisation. A way to foster transparency is the comparison between theories for a given problem in a meliorative strategy. This requires that statements be designed in a way that makes comparison possible. This means that when immunisation is introduced, it is made explicit. One finds here that in a deeply complex situation, contrary to the usual saying, the proof of the pudding is less in the eating than in the making.

Relevance

In line with the fallibilistic stance of the complex perspective, relevance amounts to reducing ignorance and arbitrariness in theorising. Emphasising the reduction of arbitrariness seems fruitful because of its generality and because of its capacity to be used as a criterion for comparison and for assessment. We express it in the following propositions:

1. There is no non-arbitrary way of reasoning. There is no non-arbitrary ultimate foundation.
2. There are relative degrees of arbitrariness. They can be identified through comparison.
3. The aim is to reduce the relative degree of arbitrariness for a given problem.

C. Anchored Deep Complexity (ADCX)

The conditions established about deep complexity, scientific practice, and operationality constitute what we have named 'anchored deep complexity', abbreviated as ADCX. It provides a way out of the two successive deadlocks that we encountered. It is a framework that structures and constrains the initially floating eclecticism and the methodological and theoretical pluralism involved in the RISE. It also constrains the potential subjectivity of self-reflexive procedural rationality. It structures a way to cut off the indeterminacy of satisficing through the reliance on its exposure to public test, criticism and judgement. Therefore ADCX consists in the combined outcome of the first- and second-order heuristics. It is abductively connected with the RISE. In its present state, it does not produce a theory of the RISE, but it does produce the conditions that make it possible to address the theoretical foundations of the RISE.

Our insistance on two layers of heuristics underscores the point that the procedure meeting the conditions set out for self-reflexive procedural rationality is rather demanding. It does not suffice to identify the sources of a cognitive block at the object level of a problem-situation and design a representation of the phenomenon which creates the block such as the RISE in the present case. The RISE creates an irreducible difficulty because of its empirical robustness, because of its many-dimensional character, because of its apparent initial indecomposabilty as long as its articulation between whole and parts is not informed in a way that organises its unity and diversity, and because of its singularity as a unified, integrated setting. The possible systemic character that seems to follow from these traits is not a solution; it is the problem. This is first-order deep complexity (FODCX).

At a second-order level, the question of how to behave about a deeply complex problem is itself a deeply complex problem. It is self-reflexivity. There seems to be no other way to deal with it than to have it match with its environment of scientific practice and operationality.

A satisficing heuristic will have to accommodate these two levels, that is, depth and submission to scientific practice and operationality, or depth and anchoring. Starting from the RISE, we had to develop a first-order heuristic (FODCX and H1), and then a second-order one (SODCX and H2) in a recursive pattern (Figure 1.6).

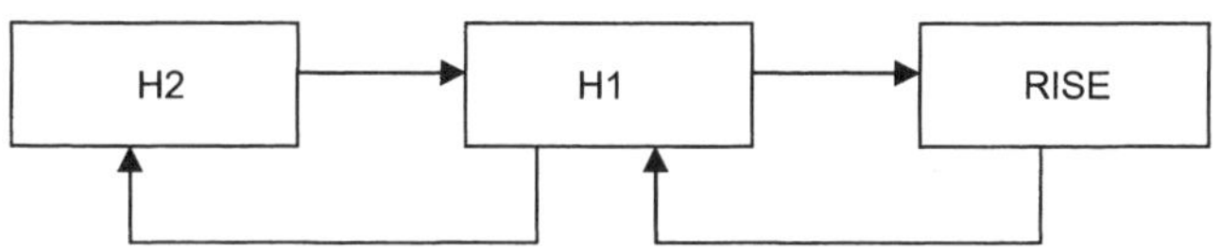

Figure 1.6 Two layers of heuristics for the RISE

Finally, ADCX may be considered as a generating principle whose product stimulated its own production. This sentence simply describes the overall recursive loop between an initial empirical observation transformed into an empirical conjecture and next into a conjecture produced by a structured procedure (ADCX combining H1 and H2), schematised on Figure 1.7.

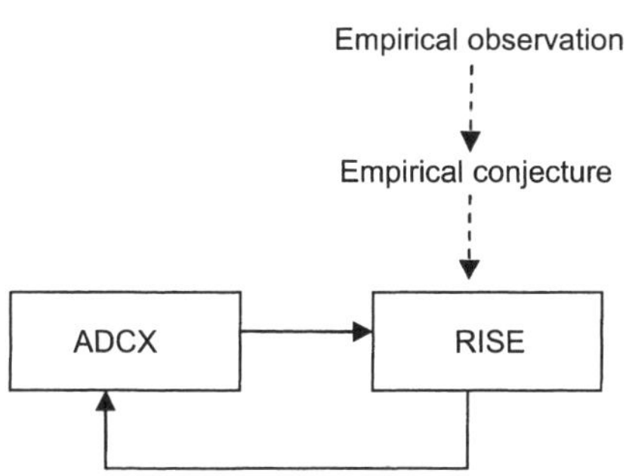

Figure 1.7 Anchored deep complexity and the RISE

1.4 CONCLUSION

We have developed a procedurally rational, self-reflexive heuristic which entails stepping outside the classical logical framework based on the axiom of the excluded middle. Its development was triggered by the irreducibility of the problem-situation to the cognitive framework of decomposability into separate parts that prevails in science, and by our simultaneous rejection of replacing it with an altogether non-decomposable substitute that would derive from a purely holistic view.

Both aspects of parts and of the whole seem to be present in the material under scrutiny and need to be taken on board although they classically negate each other. It was suggested to move beyond this block through the introduction of an 'included middle' hypothesis. Doing this is more than changing a hypothesis within a cognitive framework. It is a change of framework. It defines deep complexity as an irreducibility to a satisficing situation in the existing decomposability framework, and which necessitates stepping outside it. It is subject to the common constraint of abiding by scientific practice and is therefore explicitly anchored to declared-in-advance criteria of scientific practice. It reflects a structured heuristic but the question of where it brings the argument remains wide open. Is it merely heuristic and tinkering, or is it a move toward an alternative framework? Is it new, or are there antecedents or equivalents in the literature? These are the questions that need to be addressed in the next chapter.

NOTES

1. Letter to Roy F. Harrod (1938, 1973) in *The Collected Writings of J.M. Keynes*, D. Moggridge (ed.), Vol XIV, Macmillan.
2. Notably the studies by A.T. Peacock and J. Wiseman (1967), S.P. Gupta (1967), F.L. Pryor (1968), and R.M. Bird (1970). They were followed in the next decades by a long list of studies on the growth of public spending in capitalist countries which were surveyed by V. Tanzi and L. Schuknecht (2000).
3. I follow the use introduced in the book edited by R. Boyer and Y. Saillard (2002). The French term *régulation* avoids the confusion with 'regulation'.
4. The term 'regime' is preferred to 'mode' used in past publications (Delorme, 2002). A regime connotes dynamic interactions in a processual perspective, a feature that the static character of a mode does not convey.

2. Originality

> The difficulty lies, not in the new ideas, but in escaping from the old ones, which ramify, for those brought up as most of us have been, into every corner of our minds.
>
> John Maynard Keynes (1936 [1965])[1]

> Never will man penetrate deeper into error than when he is continuing on a road which has led him to great success.
>
> Friedrich August von Hayek (1955)[2]

> In economics (along with the other moral sciences) … it is often impossible to bring one's ideas to a conclusive test either formal or experimental.
>
> J.M. Keynes (1936 [1965])[3]

> It is high time … that we take our ignorance more seriously.
>
> F.A. Hayek (1967)[4]

2.1 INTRODUCTION

The imaginary dialogue between J.M. Keynes and F.A. Hayek placed in the epigraph reflects the philosophy of this chapter. Its purpose is twofold. It is to determine where anchored deep complexity, hereafter ADCX, stands in the growing literature on complexity and complex systems in both economic theory and other social sciences, and it is to investigate whether there exists a theoretical framework that may accommodate ADCX. The depth of the notion of complexity arrived at in Chapter 1 is its first distinctive trait, before its being anchored to specific criteria. Since it was introduced in a heuristic way there is a need to assess its apparent originality by comparing it with existing views on complexity that may already convey a similar meaning or at least stand close to deep complexity. I will restrict this comparison to the views that appear equivalent or potentially equivalent to deep complexity. It will be rather unexpected to discover the wealth of economic theory in this respect. Why, then, none of the existing perspectives appear to accommodate ADCX is the issue that will be addressed. The ADCX hypothesis will be clarified first in the next section. An outcome of it will be to address depth prior to anchoring in two successive steps. It will pave the way for taking cognisance of deep complexity in economic theory (section 2.3), in management and organisation science (section 2.4) and in several transdisciplinary forms of irreducibility (section 2.5). It will be shown in conclusion that anchoring is the central pending issue.

2.2 THE ADCX HYPOTHESIS

At this stage, ADCX stands as a hypothesis for answering the search of a theoretical frame underpinning the RISE. However it is not a theoretical frame in the usual way of bearing directly upon the specific substance of the RISE. It is rather about how the RISE, as an entity, is informed by a frame, that is, ADCX itself, abiding by scientific criteria. The insight is that the problem-situation becomes underpinned by a framework based on ADCX and such that the RISE can be its product, whereas the RISE could not be a product of the 'classical' methodological and theoretical framework in the initial insolvable problem-situation.

2.2.1 Depth

The initial element of originality of ADCX is its very depth. No other reference to this kind of deep complexity seems to exist in the present-day literature although Hayek casually evoked an 'essential' complexity (Hayek, 1978). Keynes introduced a closely related notion under the labels of organic interdependence and uncertainty. This will be addressed in section 2.3. The idea of essential complexity was also evoked by Gaston Bachelard in 1937, in the context of quantum physics (Bachelard, 1937, 143). Deep complexity will call for differentiating it from non-deeply complex problem-situations ranging from plain complexity to simplicity.

The first appearance of depth was with the initial recognition that there was no existing way of dealing satisfactorily with the RISE. The important term is 'satisfactorily'. It has the meaning of 'scientifically satisfactory' here. It appeared progressively that several robust traits of the RISE were strictly not compatible with notions that seem fundamental to what we may call the 'classical' or 'normal' scientific discourse in economics. First there is the organic interdependence of the RISE which makes it problematic to tackle it as if it were composed of separate parts from the outset. It goes also against a merely holistic view. It calls for putting to work the Pascalian circular, oscillatory knowing process between the parts and the whole expressed in a famous statement of Blaise Pascal's *Pensées*:

> Since everything, then, is both caused and causing, dependent and supporting, mediate and immediate, and all hold together by a natural and unnoticed bond which ties things most distant and most different, I hold it equally impossible to know the parts

> without knowing the whole, and to know the whole without knowing the parts in detail. (Pascal, 1662, [1963], 527)

In such a process there is no basis for hypothesising its outcome before the process of knowing has unfolded enough and developed an improved knowledge of how the parts and the whole combine into a more or less robust and evolving arrangement.

A direct implication of this organic interdependence of the RISE is its *singularity* or uniqueness. It does not mean that we are compelled to a mere monographic description and that there are no elements of similarity between different RISEs. Rather it orientates the enquiry towards working out how difference and sameness combine into singular configurations. Induction and deduction are no longer appropriate as basic methods of inference in this case. It calls for an *abductive* reasoning. Finally the excluded middle tied to classical logic needs to give way to the possibility of carrying out a 'third', *included* term or 'middle' thanks to which it is no longer unreasonable to work with notions whose truth *or* falsity can be replaced by appropriate truth *and* falsity. These traits compose a consistent setting. They are definitional properties at the epistemological, methodological and theoretical levels of what appears as an initial classical cognitive framework and, through the step-by-step introduction of alternative traits, as an alternative cognitive framework.

Facing the kind of difficulty provoked by the recognition of the robustness of the RISE leads to a choice between two options. One is to satisfy with either a merely empirical description or its connection to an eclectic, methodologically pluralist argumentation under an umbrella perspective like *régulation* theory or a so-called systems theory. In this case, it leaves unanswered the conditions of its scientific coherence contrasted to those of the classical approach. Therefore it appears underspecified comparatively to the classical framework. The other option is to take this irreducibility 'more seriously', to paraphrase Hayek, and not to satisfy with a floating eclecticism. It will consist in exploring whether it is possible to design an alternative. Its substance can be envisaged in the following way. If the initial, irreducible problem-situation is to be theorised and underpinned by a theoretical frame in an abductive way, it will have to be the product of a setting informing it theoretically in the sense of integrating the three basic traits of the RISE that are incompatible with the corresponding definitional traits of the classical framework. These traits included in deep complexity can be summarised in the following way: beyond atomism or holism, singularity and similarity, and the 'third' beyond the excluded middle.

Therefore the initial recognition of the absence of a way to deal satisfactorily with a problem-situation in a given cognitive framework is complemented by the recognition of the need to step outside this framework. It is the recognition that dealing with the problem is not a matter of another theory within this framework but calls for another framework. The impossibility of reducing the initial problem to either a cause effect analysis or to a covering law explanation signals the impossibility of reaching a satisfactory solution within the initial, classical disjunctive framework.

At this stage the depth of complexity consists in two things. It is the intractability or unsolvable character of a problem-situation within a given cognitive framework, and the thrust towards the search or construction of an alternative framework.

The insight brought here suggests that a way out is an abductive reasoning informed by a conjunctive setting. If a satisfactory situation is attained using this procedure, it necessarily means that the initial irreducibility has been transformed into some reducibility. But if it is reduced, is it still deeply complex? This twofold substance of deep complexity may understandably look strange at this stage since it includes both an irreducibility and a reduction to be actualised within an alternative cognitive framework for a seemingly unchanged problem-situation. The answer is that the word 'solution' does not mean the same thing and depends upon the cognitive framework which informs it.

Let us go back to the RISE. The point is that the RISE is intractable when viewed within the initial, classical cognitive framework that I symbolise by F1. The RISE cannot be a product of F1 in the sense that it cannot be grasped abductively with a pattern based on disjunction (excluded middle), on atomism or holism, and on induction and deduction solely. In the alternative cognitive framework F2 combining conjunction, the Pascalian circularity, and abduction, the problem-situation created by the RISE becomes informed by F2 in such a way that it can be a product of F2 (Table 2.1).

Table 2.1 Two cognitive frameworks

F1 Disjunctive	F2 Conjunctive
Disjunction (logic of '*either…or*')	Conjunction (logic of '*and*')
Atomist *or* holist	Pascalian circularity (parts *and* whole)
Induction, deduction	Abduction first (*and* induction, *and* deduction)

The irreducible 'RISE-in-F1' becomes an informed 'RISE-in-F2'. F2 is recursively constructed after the initial blockage in F1; it is such that the insolvable problem-situation in F1 becomes a possible product of F2. The RISE remains intractable in F1 but becomes informed and theoretically structured by F2 through abduction, in a second step (Figure 2.1).

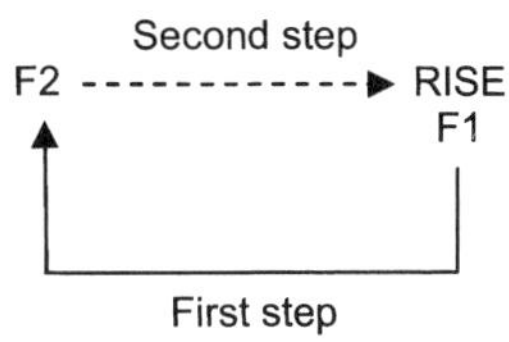

Figure 2.1 Depth schematised

There follows from this abductive argumentation that deep complexity consists in a specific articulation of F1 and F2 in which F2 encompasses F1 in the sense that it does not exclude F1 and makes it appear possibly relevant locally, as a special case, when the conditions defining it are met. It does not eliminate the irreducibility in the disjunctive setting of F1. If some satisfactory reducibility were achieved within F1 there would be no rationale for investigating an alternative framework. The reducibility obtained in F2 is therefore of a different qualitative order than the one envisaged in F1. This qualitative difference can be characterised in terms of closure and openness: F2 is closed with respect to the criteria defining it as a specific cognitive framework, and open with respect to its possible outcome by definition of its irreducibility. Therefore deep complexity appears as a process comprising a definitional closure and an openness of its possible outcomes. This feature adds a fundamental component to the above characterisation. It is a dynamic, processual framework of knowing which combines reducibility and irreducibility, that is, its definitional or operational closure, and the openness of its possible outcomes. The former is procedural, the latter is substantive.

Additional remarks on substantive open-endedness appear as follows:

1. At this stage, the openness of outcome or substantive open-endedness is what follows from the operation of ADCX about the RISE. ADCX does not determine the particular substance of the RISE, it only makes the RISE appear as the product of a procedure abiding by criteria of scientific practice, however indeterminate the RISE may prove to be.
2. The goal is to reduce indeterminacy as much as possible rather than to eliminate it at any price.
3. The remarks above imply that the investigation is not restricted to a constraint of necessary determinacy or reduction to a satisfactory outcome to be attained. This is the basic meaning of openness: it is the irreducibility to 'reducibility-in-all-cases'.

2.2.2 Anchoring

The metaphor of anchoring denotes the procedural closure, that is, the tying of deep complexity to declared-in-advance criteria whose fulfilment ensures its acceptability in its cognitive framework. Here this framework is scientific practice. The very reasons that led to deep complexity suggest that there is a need to draw a distinction between the problems which can be addressed scientifically within the traditional framework and those which necessitate another framework. The recognition of this distinction is the first big step. It follows from a fundamental distinction about scientific practice between a common substance (the production of knowledge about some subject matter, systematically put to the public test of its validity) and at least two ways to fulfil it, the two sets of principles F1 and F2 introduced above.

At first sight F1 and F2 match roughly the possibilities and constraints that are specific to natural science on the one hand and to human and social sciences, or anthropo-social sciences, on the other hand.

In physics, the observation of the world does not change it to an extent that would invalidate its basic properties, which makes it possible to view it atomistically, disjunctively, inductively and deductively with strict protocols of validation. In economics the same protocols of validation are intrinsically much less exact and operative since the production of knowledge aims both at describing and bringing change in a world that is not inert but likely to react to new knowledge, and in which internal relations cannot be eliminated wholly to make it compatible with the atomist and disjunctive view. Individual consumption is a function of prices, income, tastes and expectations. Production is a function of expectations, price, income, and technology. The economic material is a blend of lawlike relations and of internal and changing relations whose disentangling should be a subject of research rather than being eschewed through ad hoc assumptions which neutralise what might trouble the working of the disjunctive atomist overall pattern.

The day-to-day practice in natural science is intrinsically enslaved to strict, mostly empirical protocols of validation. This type of control cannot be transposed to social science in general. It cannot but rely on a control of the procedure through which statements on the social universe are made. This is the main reason for the utmost importance of anchoring social science practice to pre-declared criteria about its scientific content and coherence.

Anchoring is therefore a necessary condition for theorising. Its content must be such that it enables a theoretical reasoning rather than being merely philosophical or methodological, or even pure practical know-how, though all these aspects are necessary dimensions that an effective alternative framework should comprise. If the ultimate justice of peace in human social science resides in action, the ADCX hypothesis suggests that we may need to temperate the popular wisdom that the proof of the pudding is in the eating by adding that it is primarily in the making when deep complexity prevails. At any rate, anchoring should help avoid the kind of situation evoked by W.W. Bartley III, about Lewis Carroll, in which the 'proof of the spoof' would be in the 'putting'(Bartley, 1977; Falletta, 1985).

To conclude, a test of the originality of ADCX will be to assess whether there is a theoretical body in economic theory or elsewhere which accommodates fully the four defining components of ADCX: the intractability of the problem-situation; the shift to an alternative framework; its substantive open-endedness; and its procedural closure or anchoring.

2.3 DEEP COMPLEXITY IN ECONOMIC THEORY

Our purpose in this section is to scrutinise the theoretical economic perspectives which come close to ADCX as defined above and are most susceptible to accommodate all or parts of it. It must be said at the outset that there are two aspects to this question in economic theory, one at a very general level, the other at the level of specific theoretical contributions.

At a general level, one cannot bypass the divide which has characterised the developments of economic theory since the beginning of the nineteenth century. It is the divide between what has progressively dominated the discipline and has imposed itself as a mainstream, standard theory since the middle of the twentieth century, and the variety of non-standard, heterodox perspectives. In this way, one might interpret heterodox economic theory in terms of a perceived irreducible lack of knowledge stemming from the established predominating framework and the search or the construction of alternative frameworks. It would fit the definition of ADCX provided the openness of the theoretical outcomes is preserved. A notable exception would be Marxian theory and its reduction of capitalist economic evolution to a classless end-state of rest, which runs counter to the openness of outcome that is intrinsic to ADCX. One would hardly disagree with J.M. Keynes that the seeds of this broad divide find an illustration in the debate between Malthus and Ricardo in 1817. In a letter to Malthus, Ricardo accused him of having 'always in ... mind the immediate and temporary effects of particular changes' whereas he himself 'puts these immediate and temporary effects quite aside and fixes his whole attention on the permanent state of things which will result from them' (Keynes, CW X, 97).[5] Ricardo was investigating the theory of the distribution of the product in conditions of equilibrium in a money-neutral economy, whereas Malthus was concerned with 'what determines the volume of output day by day in the real world' of a monetary economy. As it is reported by Keynes, Malthus replied that by supposing 'what is not at all true practically', one 'precludes himself from drawing any practical inferences from his hypotheses'. Keynes comments that 'the almost total obliteration of Malthus's line of approach and the complete domination of Ricardo's for a period of a hundred years has been a disaster to the progress of economics'(ibid., 98). Keynes wrote these lines in 1922.

The focus on the implications of equilibrium in an abstract economy reduced to market exchange conditions enabled a so far apparently irresistible tendency to import into economics the tools and methods which proved successful in physics in a thrust pulled by the ambition of making of economics a 'modern science' (Mirowski, 1989; Clower, 1994; Clower and Howitt, 1997; Israel, 1996; Louçã, 1997) and through relying on the tacit premises of disjunctive logic, deductive – inductive reasoning and an atomistic view of the material of the economy. As I have already written, most of the counter-reactions to it may be viewed at first sight as instances of a concern for deep complexity. They would range notably from Veblen and the institutionalist tradition, and the German Historical School, to Austrian and Keynesian traditions, and most present-day heterodox movements.

Such a level of generality is however helpless in terms of our theoretical concern as opposed to purely philosophical, methodological or even practical perspectives. Although it may be difficult to separate these aspects, we are interested at this stage in the perspectives that comprise criteria making up an anchoring and thus providing reference points for harnessing deep complexity about a substantial subject matter, that is, offering tools for dealing theoretically with deep complexity. It naturally does not mean that the non-theoretical views are uninteresting. They will be fully relevant when we will have to investigate the foundations for theorising deep complexity later on in this book. At the moment we merely inquire about the existing contributions in economic theory having a clearly discernable theoretical content and that are susceptible to accommodate the depth and the anchoring of ADCX. Therefore this excludes any loosely or floating eclectic perspective.

Given these qualifications, DCX seems to be approached in three broad strands in economic theory, which are irreducibility to hard science, radical uncertainty, and the more recent upsurge about complex systems.

2.3.1 The Irreducibility to Hard Science

Although the irreducibility to hard science is a general argument that appears in most non-mainstream perspectives and thus overlaps with radical uncertainty, I single it out here to depict perspectives in which it is found independently from any specific reference to uncertainty. Under this heading, one finds notably contributions by Alfred Marshall, Walter Eucken and Nicholas Georgescu-Roegen, and also *régulation* theory, already discussed in Chapter 1.

A. Alfred Marshall and the intricacy of the material of economics

Several authors reacted to the pronounced shift towards abstraction and deduction that had originated with Ricardo and continued notably with Senior, Jevons, Walras, Pareto and culminated in the present period in the wake of Hicks, Arrow and Debreu's works. Without engaging in a full review, and apart from Marx and the German Historical School, several authors need to be mentioned if we follow T. Hutchison (1984): Sismondi stressed in 1819 the importance of ignorance as a source of economic instability; Jones insisted in 1833 on the place of experience and observation as against the pretence to deduce principles of wide applicability from a small set of general assumptions and invited to 'look and see' instead of reasoning from a priori principles; Leslie emphasised the place of the unknown in the economic world, in 1879. The open-ended character of economic evolution seems to have followed a line of influences from Darwin to Veblen's famous article on *Why is economics not an evolutionary science?* (Veblen, 1898) and his plea for a conception of evolutionary economics as a 'theory of a process of cultural growth as determined by the economic interest, a theory of a cumulative sequence of institutions stated in terms of the process itself'.

It is however Alfred Marshall who appears as the main precursor of the recognition of the notion of complexity in economic theory in a way comprising both a criticism of classical economists as founders of economics on a scientific basis, and ideas for an alternative perspective.

Marshall's 'gradual change of attitude towards mathematico-economics' is manifest in his inaugural lecture at Cambridge on '*The Present Position of Economics*', in 1885, as reported by Keynes (Keynes, CW X, 262). Although he maintains in it his continuity with Ricardo and the classical economists, and his critique of the historical school's rejection of formalism, Marshall points out what he believes to be the oversight of Ricardo and his followers: 'that man himself is in a great measure a creature of circumstances and changes with them ... They regarded man as so to speak a constant quantity, and gave themselves little trouble to study his variations ... Their most vital fault was that they did not see how liable to change are the habits and institutions of industry' (Keynes, CW, X, 196).

He claims in his *Principles of Economics*, through the successive editions from 1890 to 1920, that economics is a science but that it differs from the 'harder' sciences, particularly mathematical physics (Marshall, 1961, 31). It aspires to be a science of social complexity (Marchionatti, 2002a, 6) in which the 'forces of which economics has to take into account are more numerous, less definite, less well known, and more diverse in character than those of mechanics; while the material on which they act is more uncertain and less homogeneous' (Marshall, 1961, 772).

Marshall defines economics as 'a study of men as they live and move and think in the ordinary business of life' (ibid., 14). He sees biology as 'the Mecca of the economist' (Comim, 2000, 25–26) and he maintains that economic reasoning cannot be merely abstract and thus unable to 'disentangle the interwoven effect of complex causes', and must start with facts. Facts by themselves teach nothing, 'reason alone can interpret and draw lessons' with the help of 'trained common sense … as the ultimate arbiter in every practical problem' (ibid., 36), a trained common sense itself 'aided by appliances of organised analysis and general reasoning, which facilitate the task of collecting, arranging, and drawing inferences from particular facts' (Marchionatti, 2002b, 14).

These insights illustrate an irreducibility to the working of natural science which originates in the recognition of the complex material of the economy. It is not yet identified with specific consequences like the tension between history and theory, and radical uncertainty, but it is nonetheless fully precursory in the way Marshall appears to view complexity 'not only in the object of study – the natural and social processes – but in the knowledge used to analyse these processes' (Comim, 2000, 33). Ideas close to Marshall's will be found in Keynes's thinking on uncertainty.

B. Walter Eucken's 'Great Antinomy' and *Régulation* theory

The 'Great Antinomy', an expression coined by German economist Walter Eucken, is the cornerstone of Eucken's book *The Foundations of Economics* published in German in 1939 and in English in 1950. Eucken is one of the founders of Ordnungstheorie or the theory of economic order which provided the intellectual framework of both the Ordo liberal tradition in Germany after World War II, and the so-called social market economy model of economic policy that has been habitually used to depict the German economic model since the 1950s (Labrousse and Weisz, 2001). Like *régulation* theory, Ordnungstheorie is concerned with the connection between the historical character of the economy and the necessarily theoretical dimension of economics. How to transcend their dichotomous, dualistic treatment and grasp them into a unified setting is the issue that both perspectives seek to resolve.

The Great Antinomy denotes the tension between the 'individual historical' and the 'general-theoretical' inherent features of economic life and economics: 'The economist has to see economic events as part of a particular individual-historical situation if he is to do justice to the real world. He must see them also as presenting general-theoretical problems if the relationships of the real world are not to escape him'(Eucken, 1939 [1950], 41). Because of this intrinsic duality, economic life presents the economist with a 'complex phenomenon' that cannot be reduced to either one or the other duals: 'Because established doctrines fail before the Great Antinomy, we must make a completely new approach to the subject-matter itself. Simply to continue on existing lines, either "historical" or "theoretical", is impossible' (ibid., 101). This does not mean rejecting theorising.

Eucken suggests solving the Great Antinomy by way of a morphological analysis conceived of as preparing for the next step of theoretical analysis. He develops a method of 'isolating abstraction' which starts with the observation of a historical fact or phenomenon whose 'significant salient characteristics' are extracted and abstracted in ideal-types. It contrasts with the 'generalizing' abstraction which involves a 'withdrawal from actual economic phenomena' since it leads to the identification of common traits of different phenomena whereas the phenomenological unity of a fact is preserved in the reduction to the salient features of an individual phenomenon which defines isolating abstraction (ibid., 107, 219).

Different economic orders (or systems, or socio-economic arrangements) can be identified through the use of this morphological apparatus in which form and process appear as central notions. 'Thinking in orders' is the motto of this view of economic life as an organic whole considered in connection with other social sciences, notably history, business administration and law.

The parallel between *régulation* theory and Ordnungstheorie is striking although the former was developed independently – and even in ignorance – of the latter. Both theories attempt to answer the question of integrating into a unified setting the two traditionally irreducible features of history and theory in economics. Ordnungstheorie relies on a microeconomic standpoint and provides a morphological perspective highlighting form and process. *Régulation* theory starts from a macroeconomic standpoint and develops a morphological theory articulating form and process at the macroeconomic and intermediary, meso levels. In both instances, the morphological schemes combining form and process, whether they are orders or modes or regimes of *régulation*, appear as the common answer to the problem of irreducibility with which they are confronted. It is an irreducibility of such an importance that it leads their authors to reject unambiguously the conventional doctrines and their methods. Most of the ingredients of deep complexity are present in these perspectives except for a firm anchoring either on the methodological or the theoretical side. The former calls for improvement in *régulation* theory, with its floating eclecticism. The latter is the main weakness of Ordnungstheorie. This approach had practically no theoretical descendance and almost vanished. Both instances point indirectly to the challenge of anchoring firmly deep complexity.

C. Nicholas Georgescu-Roegen and dialectical penumbra

The irreducibility to hard science takes a still different form in Nicholas Georgescu-Roegen's work. An important part of it is the distinction between arithmomorphic and dialectical reasonings.

Arithmomorphic concepts are '*discretely distinct*' in the same way as numbers are. They are the basic material of analysis. On the other hand, dialectical reasoning employs concepts 'that are distinct but not *discretely* distinct... they may overlap with their opposites ... Whereas an arithmomorphic concept is separated from its opposite by a vacuous boundary (a null set ...) a dialectical concept is separated from its opposite by a *substantial* penumbra' within which 'both A and non-A are true' (Georgescu-Roegen, 1979, 322–23). Dialectical concepts are not perfectly or exactly circumscribed: 'Instead, they are bounded by a *dialectical* penumbra, that is by a penumbra surrounded by a penumbra surrounded by a penumbra ... in an infinite progress – which is the specific peculiarity of dialectics' (Georgescu-Roegen, 1988, 300). According to Georgescu-Roegen, analysis and dialectics are the 'two and only two irreducible modes' through which 'we get in mental contact with the inner and the outer reality' (ibid., 300), that is, the phenomena 'around and even within us' (1979, 322). He emphasises that the domain of dialectics is everything that is subject to qualitative change, 'that is, that does not consist of mere accretion, or its opposite, or of just locomotion' which means that dialectical concepts 'cover the greatest area of what we think and communicate' (1988, 301).

Georgescu-Roegen's distinction hits at an issue similar to the one we had to face with the RISE. It is about how to account for features that appear to negate each other and yet are 'true' in the sense that 'within any penumbra both A and non-A are true' (1988, 304). We relied on an included middle principle as a way out. Here the consequence is that both methods are needed, in a view of the economy being subject to both quantitative and qualitative change. The irreducibility to an analytical framework alone is however only one component of deep complexity. Dialectical reasoning cannot be as precise as an arithmomorphic statement but it can be entirely 'correct' (1979, 323) although it is sometimes denounced as 'muddled-thinking' (1988, 301). It is nevertheless not an acceptable reason to reject dialectical reasoning, just as in the art of painting 'we should not blame colours for the horrible works some "painters" may produce with them' (ibid.). Still, this view leaves wide open the issue of how one establishes the correctness of this type of reasoning, that is, its anchoring to criteria of validity.

2.3.2 Radical Uncertainty

With radical uncertainty we focus on a specific source of irreducibility. It is the irreducibility to a numerically determinate probability. This property is designated in a variety of ways among which are genuine uncertainty (O'Driscoll and Rizzo, 1985), true uncertainty (Davidson, 1991), fundamental uncertainty (Hamouda and Smithin, 1988; Winslow, 1989), structural uncertainty (Langlois, 1994), partial ignorance (Loasby, 1976), procedural uncertainty (Dosi and Egidi, 1991) and uncertainty plainly stated (Keynes, CW, XIV, 113–114; Shackle, 1972 [1992]) or radical uncertainty here.

Brian Loasby characterised radical uncertainty in the following terms: 'When someone says he is uncertain, what he usually means is not just that he doesn't know the chances of various outcomes, but that he doesn't know what outcomes are possible. He may well be far from sure even of the structure of the problem that he faces' (Loasby, 1976, 9). This structure denotes a state of 'partial ignorance' a term in which the adjective is meant to infer that there is not a total absence of any relevant knowledge.

Radical uncertainty differs unambiguously from several concepts often termed uncertainty. In rational expectations theory, uncertainty corresponds to a situation of numerically determinate probabilistic knowledge. Bayesian decision-making reduces uncertainty to mere risk through the requirement of a prior probability distribution. Procedural uncertainty originates from incomplete knowledge in problem-solving (Dosi and Egidi, 1991) which differs from the axiomatic theory of rational choice in which uncertainty originates from incomplete information about the occurrence of a known list of events. In a similar vein, in Arrow's definition, uncertainty consists in not knowing which state of the world is the true one. But 'each state of the world is a description which is complete for all relevant purposes' given that the world is considered 'to be in one or another of a range of states' (Arrow, 1974, 33–34). This presupposes a complete knowledge of the structure of the world. If however we take uncertainty to mean that we do not know with certainty a listing of all possible states of the world, then uncertainty is about the structure of the world. This is the basis of Langlois's distinction between parametric uncertainty, in which states of the world are known, and structural uncertainty, in which not all states of the world are known (Langlois, 1994, 119–121). The latter does not lend itself to numerical measurement.

Radical uncertainty is a source of irreducibility that takes on various forms in economic theory. These are tied to specific authors or traditions of thought. Three major forms appear to stand out. They derive respectively from event uniqueness (F. Knight), from historical time and ignorance (the Austrian tradition), and from organic interdependence (J.M. Keynes). G.L.S. Shackle developed a subjectivist conception of uncertainty which combined Austrian and Keynesian aspects and will not be addressed here in its own right (Shackle, 1972 [1992]).

A. Event uniqueness: Frank Knight

Frank H. Knight's distinction of risk and uncertainty is a classic (Knight, 1921 [1964]). Knight's analysis relies on the distinction between two situations. In the first situation of 'a prior probability', it is possible to establish an 'Absolutely homogeneous classification of instances completely identical except for really indeterminate factors' (ibid., 224). It is illustrated by throwing a die. The second situation is 'statistical probability' (ibid., 225). It rests on an empirical classification of events which occurred in the past, which can be attached to the same class of risk over which a statistical frequency can be computed: 'The principal subject for investigation is thus the *degree* of assimilability, or the amount of homogeneity of classes securable, or stated inversely, the *degree of uniqueness* of various kinds of business contingencies' (ibid., 247).

An event is uncertain when the probability situation is that of 'estimates': there is *no valid basis of any kind* for classifying instances (ibid., 225). Homogeneity, equivalence or assimilability are thus attached to risk whereas uniqueness characterises uncertain situations.

For Knight, uncertainty or radical uncertainty denotes clearly a situation of irreducibility to statistical probability. This irreducibility is a property of the external world of events.

B. Historical time and ignorance in the Austrian tradition

Another conception of radical uncertainty follows from the subjectivist tradition in economics as represented by the Austrian tradition. Radical uncertainty faced by market participants is one of the constitutive aspects of the modern Austrian school, according to Israel Kirzner (1987). Here we touch upon a tradition which appears as a whole original cognitive framework. It will therefore be of the utmost interest to assess whether it provides an alternative framework for deep complexity and to what extent it can accommodate the four traits of intractability of problem-situation, alternative framework, substantive open-endedness, and anchoring or procedural closure which compose the ADCX hypothesis.

The use and limitations of knowledge in society have been a constant concern of the leading Austrian figure of Friedrich Hayek (1945). The way he connected it to 'complex phenomena' appeals more, however, to 'complex structures of human interaction' than to explicit radical uncertainty, and will be evoked in section 2.5.

The connection of radical uncertainty with 'real' or historical time and ignorance is most clearly developed in O'Driscoll and Rizzo's book *The Economics of Time and Ignorance* (1985).

B.1 Intractability

In Austrian economics, radical or genuine uncertainty is the outcome of a chain of influences which develop from a fundamental focus from which follow successively a subjectivist view, historical time, and an ignorance which entails radical uncertainty (O'Driscoll and Rizzo, 1985).

The prime focus of Austrian economics is the articulation of economic order with action. Action depends on the objectives, perceptions and expectations of the actor which are subject to change (Loasby, 1988, 155). From it follows the general presupposition of subjectivism according to which, on the one hand, individual choice is autonomous, 'not rigidly determined by external events', and on the other hand, economics is primarily about 'the thoughts leading up to choice, and not about things or the interaction of objective magnitudes' (O'Driscoll and Rizzo, 1985, 2). All action takes place in 'real', historical time, a 'dynamic continuous flow of novel experiences'. The flow is not *in* time 'as it would be in space, it *is* or constitutes time' (ibid., 60). Real time is irreversible; its passage involves creative evolution in the sense that processes produce unpredictable change, that is, novelty.

Choices made in real time 'are never made with complete knowledge (either deterministic or stochastic) of their consequences' (ibid., 3). Ignorance, for the Austrian subjectivists, is specific. Its meaning can be grasped by means of comparison with the standard 'subjectivist' theory of probability which portrays the uncertainty of the future as a probability distribution defined over an exhaustive set of events. Here, ignorance is different. It denotes the unlistability of all possible outcomes: 'It is not merely that we do not know which possibility out of a given set will occur, but the set itself is unbounded as a reflection of the essential dynamic nature of time' (ibid., 4). Therefore, according to these authors 'ignorance is not something that... can be avoided or overcome', it is 'ineradicable' in a world of 'real time' and leads to 'genuine uncertainty' (ibid., 4).

Genuine ignorance in this context designates a 'total ignorance' about the future while the conditions of the present are of partial ignorance (Vaughn, 1994, 163), a term in which the adjective is meant to infer that there is not a total absence of relevant knowledge.

B.2 An Alternative Framework

Although radical uncertainty is a common central theme of Austrian economics, it does not necessarily translate into an alternative to an initial, problematic framework. Austrian economists are divided as to whether their approach supplements the mainstream or is an alternative to it (Vaughn, 1994). It is worth noting here that in Karen Vaughn's presentation the option of an encompassing alternative seems to be ignored. Indeed Austrian economics displays an internal diversity which renders necessary to clarify it before we can go further.

What is Austrian economics? All 'modern-day Austrians', to use Vaughn's phrase, claim their founding ancestor and reference in Carl Menger and his *Principles of Economics* published in 1871 (ibid., 3). Vaughn claims that the concern for the notions of time and ignorance permeates Menger's original works, 'primarily in his descriptions of market processes and in his linking of economic growth to the generation and dissemination of knowledge in society' and extends to Ludwig von Mises' and Friedrich Hayek's works in the 1920s and 1930s. Menger is linked with Jevons and Walras as an originator of subjective value theory, and as a marginalist. But he believed that subjective theory leads not towards, but away from the formalism permitted by equilibrium, and he leaned towards the notion of order and evolutionary biology rather than towards physics (ibid., 6).

After the debates over central planning led by von Mises and Hayek in the 1920s and the 1930s, and again Hayek's denunciation of constructivism that reopened the issue of limited knowledge and ignorance, a revival of Austrian economics started in the 1970s and explains the terms modern Austrian economists use to define it (ibid., 8–9).

Austrians agree with neoclassical economics that human beings attempt to act rationally to achieve their goals, but they differ sharply with the equilibrium consequences inferred by the neoclassical approach. This has been the Austrians' central target since the beginning. This criticism maintains that the neoclassical concept of equilibrium already assumes the solution of the economic problem, 'which is the problem of discovering – or inventing – possibilities and making good use of them' (Loasby, 1988, 156). All Austrians agree that human action always takes place in time and under conditions of ignorance. This defines a 'dynamic' subjectivism which characterises not only preferences, but also knowledge and expectations.

Besides their criticism of equilibrium, Austrians denounce the neoclassical neglect of process, its high level of formalism at the expense of practical relevance, its high level of aggregation and neglect of heterogeneity and, not least, its perception of uncertainty as rational, probabilisable ignorance.

Instead of focusing on what sets of actions by individuals would be mutually consistent by assuming that the processes of adjustment are sufficiently rapid, effective and neutral to dispense from studying them and divert attention to their end-states, Austrians assume that knowledge, perceptions and expectations are subject to change 'as each of us tries to act sensibly in a world which is beyond our comprehension' (Loasby, 1988, 155).

Finally, all Austrians seem to agree that this overall critical view 'requires some adjustment in the way economists understand human action in the real world'. But their unity ends at this point. They disagree about 'whether the adjustment should take the form of arguing for changes in the use of the equilibrium-maximization framework of neoclassical economic theory to better reflect Austrian insights, or whether it should strive to overturn that theory and replace it whole cloth with another' (Vaughn, 1994, 163). Thus, two sharply different views bearing on the relationship with neoclassical economics divide modern Austrian economics.

One side of the divide is led by Israel Kirzner. It emphasises equilibrating processes as opposed to equilibrium states but otherwise accepts much of the corpus of neoclassical economics, notably the idea of equilibrium as an end state in a market process. According to Vaughn, these economists see their role as one of providing a theoretical supplement to show how equilibrium can in principle be achieved.

The other side is inspired by Ludwig Lachmann, following J.M. Keynes – who was not an Austrian – and G.L.S. Shackle, and inspires O'Driscoll and Rizzo, and Vaughn. They claim that taking time and ignorance seriously requires one to abandon conventional concepts of equilibrium and to develop a whole alternative paradigm. As mentioned by Roger Garrison, Lachmann used to ask: 'How can we be sure that the forces of equilibrium will prevail over the forces of disequilibrium?' Garrison adds that Kirzner and others 'pursued substantive issues as if they were sure enough' whereas Lachmann 'allowed his doubts to dominate his thinking' (Garrison, 1995). I have attempted through the developments above to make clear why it is only this latter, Lachmannian perspective, that defines an Austrian thrust towards an alternative framework in modern Austrian economics.

This is however not the end of the story for one finds in another, not 'modern' Austrian contribution, by Friedrich Hayek, a plea for complexity based on limitations of knowledge faced with 'complex phenomena' and requiring a radical shift away from the scientism illustrated by neoclassical economics. The paradox, given the sources of the divide within modern Austrian economics, is that Hayek emphasised equilibrating forces and spontaneous order operating within the economy as long as government policy does not attempt to disturb them through constructivist strategies, and appears thus rather Kirznerian in his premises and Lachmannian in his epistemological conclusion. The prevailing source of Hayekian complexity is not radical uncertainty. Hayek explicitly refers it to Weaver's contribution, which will be evoked later on in this chapter.

B.3 Substantive Open-endedness

Open-endedness is a consequence of the processual, evolutionary perspective of the Lachmannian perspective illustrated by O'Driscoll and Rizzo. There is no endpoint toward which the process must lead, it has no absolute beginning, there is no single path that it must follow.

Loasby praises Austrian economics in that it is an 'open system' with its emphasis on 'subjective assessments and incompletable knowledge' (Loasby, 1988, 166). Vaughn evokes the intellectual proximity with evolution: 'Evolution is the language of process and change ... It is also ... about the development of an open-ended system ... in which the focus of attention is on explaining the emergence of the present from the past rather than predicting the future' (Vaughn, 1994, 175).

Open-endedness seems to be even intrinsic to the 'catallaxy' rather than the 'economy' emphasised by Hayek. An economy, it is argued, 'presumes some single intelligence that wishes to "economize" on resources to achieve some articulable set of objectives' (Vaughn, 1994, 5). A catallaxy is a system of overlapping sets of rules and institutions within which heterogeneous individuals cooperate and compete, with often conflicting goals. These actions, interactions, their unintended consequences, and the new knowledge that they produce as a by-product constitute a never-ending process. This substantive open-endedness masks however a substantive closure with the primacy of markets which seems to be accepted as self-evident. The market is the unique way of channelling the pursuit of individual advantage in Austrian economics. Other forms of organisation seem absent. This closure is substantive, it is not about procedural criteria. It is not compatible with the open-endedness of ADCX.

B.4 Procedural Closure

The procedural anchoring of Austrian economics is its Achilles heel. Vaughn, after O'Driscoll and Rizzo, aptly mentions that an urgent task for this approach is to formalise a method for explaining indeterminate, open-ended processes (Vaughn, 1994, 87). As long as such a formalised pattern is missing, Austrian economics has no chance of escaping from being accused of concentrating too much on mere methodology, and of lacking actual economic analysis. This issue is also relevant for any investigation of deeply complex problem-situations. It explains why anchoring is so important and why, in the end, the way radical uncertainty is tackled in the Austrian approach does not accommodate ADCX.

C. Organic interdependence: J.M. Keynes on uncertainty

Keynes's macroeconomic approach through aggregates, his disbelief in the self-adjusting capacity of an economic world reduced to market exchange, and his reliance on discretionary government policy for influencing the level of economic activity are features that explain the Austrian economists' criticism of 'Keynesianism', although the radical uncertainty they envisage leads some of them to the same conclusion as Keynesian uncertainty, that is, the need of a radical departure from mainstream economics.

However, the source of Keynesian uncertainty is different. It lies in organic interdependence. Keynesian uncertainty is a by-product of Keynes's logical theory of probability. The publication of Keynes's *Collected Writings* in the 1970s triggered a rediscovery of an author whose contributions display a continuity between the early work on probability and the later works on economics. A rich debate took place in the 1980s and the 1990s over this issue and seems to have ended in favour of the continuity thesis. I have found elements in Keynes's writings and in the scientific debates which, with the hindsight of the ADCX hypothesis, convinced me of the major importance of Keynesian uncertainty for complexity thinking in economics, although it does not dispense, in hindsight again, from the task undertaken in the next chapters of this book.

Keynes's conception of radical uncertainty deserves to be made clear because it will be a reference point in our argumentation. Its source is organic interdependence. It operates through the limitations of the use of probability-based induction in the 'moral sciences' as distinguished from natural science. Moral sciences denote sciences of human society and of the mind or, in present-day terminology, the human and social sciences. Probability itself is specific and depends on a probability relation or argument whose meaning will necessitate to be clarified.

Keynes's theory of probability is exposed in *A Treatise on Probability* published in 1921 whereas his explicit considerations on uncertainty stretch over a variety of publications after 1931. Keynes was not an explicit systematiser. He seemingly never set down his views systematically. His works contain no essay on his method. His ideas are scattered among his works. It explains the divergence of interpretations of his works between those who claim that he repudiated his earlier theory in the 1930s and those who maintain that there is a consistent unity. A wealth of contributions to this debate appeared in the 1980s and the 1990s, notably about Keynes's vision (O'Donnell, 1989), Keynes's method (Carabelli, 1988) and his theory of uncertainty (Lawson, 1985), and other contributions to which it is not possible to do justice here. This reconstruction of a consistency led to a view which appears in hindsight broadly compatible with the ADCX hypothesis developed here and which explains why it may be fruitful to be explicit about it in order to identify better what difference remains with ADCX and what problems it presents.

C.1 Intractability: From Probability to Uncertainty

Keynes's theory of probability in *A Treatise on Probability* is a theory of logic embracing deductive logic as a special case. It is concerned with the logical foundations of rational but non-conclusive argument: 'the typical form of all arguments in daily life, science, policy-making and so on' (O'Donnell, 1991, 5). The rational element was identified with logic, the non-conclusive element was identified with probability. Keynes sought to 'emphasise the existence of a logical relation between two sets of propositions in cases where it is not possible to argue demonstratively from one to the other' (Keynes, CW VIII, 9). Thus Keynes's theory of probability does not deal with events or material processes as such but with propositions. Probability, in the probability relation, relates to the relation between premises and implications. On this view, every argument proceeds from a given premise h to a conclusion a via a probability relation written a/h by Keynes:

$$p = a / h$$

where p represents the probability of some proposition *a* on the basis of the available evidence *h*. The discovery of new evidence *h1* does not entail that the previous argument is wrong, it only gives rise to a new argument *a/hh1*.

It forms an inductive framework in which: ‘An inductive argument affirms, not that a certain matter of fact *is* so, but that *relative to certain evidence* there is a probability in its favour’ (ibid., 245).

The probability is viewed by Keynes as the degree of belief in a proposition that it is rational to hold, given the available evidence (Gerrard, 1992, 84). It is therefore epistemic: it is a property of knowledge or of belief, not a property of external reality.

In the *Treatise on Probability*, Keynes set out that the main types of argument used in establishing probability relations are analogy (an initial probability rises from likeness and unlikeness) and induction (the multiplication of instances strengthening or weakening the initial probability) (Brown-Collier, 1985, 14). He stresses that an implicit assumption that is central to these modes of reasoning in natural sciences is what he calls the assumption of atomic uniformity:

> The system of the material universe must consist, if this kind of assumption [the atomic character of universal law] is warranted, of bodies which we may term … *legal atoms*, such that each of them exercises its own, separate, independent, and invariable effect, a change of the total state being compounded of a number of separate changes each of which is solely due to a separate portion of the preceding state … Each atom can, according to this theory, be treated as a separate cause and does not enter into different organic combinations in each of which it is regulated by different laws. (Keynes, CW, VIII, 276 – 277)

Five years later, in his essay on Edgeworth, Keynes assessed the validity of the atomic hypothesis for the study of human behaviour:

> The atomic hypothesis which has worked so splendidly in physics breaks down in psychics. We are faced at every turn with problems of organic unity, of discreteness, of discontinuity – the whole is not equal to the sum of the parts, comparisons of quantity fail us, small changes produce large effects, the assumptions of a uniform and homogeneous continuum are not satisfied. (Keynes, CW, X, 262)

Thirteen years later, in 1939, Keynes used the same theme in his critical review of Tinbergen’s work in econometrics (CW, XIV, 285–286, 316). Systems which do not exhibit an atomic uniformity are called *organic*: ‘A system is organic if we do not have knowledge allowing us to assume atomic uniformity such that each of the basic constituents of the system exercises its own *separate*, *independent* and *invariable* effects’ (Brown-Collier, 1985, 16). Keynes believed the economic world or the world of social relations to be organic. The atomist view assumes that the relations between the basic components of a reality are *external*, meaning by this that the essential qualities of an 'ultimate' component – an 'atom' – exist independently of its relations. The organist view, in contrast, assumes that relations are *internal*, meaning by this that the essential qualities of a basic or 'ultimate' component are the outcome of its relations (Carabelli, 1988, 1994; Winslow, 1989, 1995).

The view of the social world as organic implies that the assumption of atomic uniformity cannot be applied generally to it as is the case for the natural world. Therefore one can no longer rely on the probability relation as the sole means of inductive inference. The situations in which the atomic hypothesis may be relevant need to be justified explicitly in each case; they no longer benefit from a 'legal' status. Organic interdependence does not preclude atomist analysis but it highlights its limitations to local situations in which the environment may be viewed as given and relations external. Therefore organic interdependence encompasses atomicity. It underpins the claim that the main distinguishing characteristic of economics is the lack of homogeneity, uniformity and continuity in its material. The motives behind economic behaviour will change with changes in the relations within which agents live (Winslow, 1986, 423). Contextualisation and the need to characterise the configurations of regularities, institutional and organisational, follow from this perspective and appear fully compatible with the view taken about the RISE in Chapter 1 above.

Internal relations generate however a problem of circularity in placing us under the necessity of knowing everything at once and therefore ruling out the possibility of rational induction. Whitehead coined this problem in the following terms, as quoted by Winslow (1989, 1175): 'In so far as there are internal relations, everything must depend upon everything else. But if this be the case, we cannot know about anything till we equally well know everything else'. Whitehead's way of avoiding this problem consisted in introducing two notions. The first was to assume that internal relations form a nested hierarchy containing different layers of different degrees of generality and stability, thus enabling identification of the possibility of regularities. The second was the limitation of the factors taken into account to the relations relevant to a particular occasion of experience, what Whitehead calls the 'extensive continuum' and Keynes a 'finite system' (Winslow, 1989). But then knowledge requires judgement and some rational basis for believing.

It calls for a move from the formal logic of probability, of a logical relationship between premises and implications, to the field of human logic and the empirical relationship between premises and the actual world. Probability relates to the consistency between degrees of belief but it cannot explain the basis of these degrees of belief. These premises of the probability relation are assumed as true knowledge. The move to the world of economic and social relations necessitates a shift to a theory of practical rationality which encompasses speculative rationality and relies on reasonable behaviour in circumstances of 'vague knowledge'

(Keynes, letter to Urban, Marchionatti, 2002a) when premises are not true but uncertain.

In his review of Ramsey's *Foundations of Mathematics*, Keynes took from Ramsey the distinction between formal logic and human logic. Keynes writes that: 'Formal logic is concerned with nothing but the rules of consistent thought'. Human logic is concerned with something in addition to these rules, the 'useful mental habits for handling the material with which we are supplied by our perceptions and by our memory and perhaps in other ways, and so arriving at or towards truth; and the analysis of such habits is also a sort of logic' (CW, X, 338 –339).

These successive moves reflect the change of emphasis by Keynes, from a formal theory of probability to the problem of uncertainty. Keynes writes explicitly in the *General Theory* (Keynes, 1936 [1965], 148) that by 'very uncertain' he does not mean 'very improbable' and in his 1937 *Quarterly Journal of Economics* article he states that:

> By 'uncertain knowledge'... I do not mean merely to distinguish what is known for certain from what is only probable. The game of roulette is not subject, in this sense, to uncertainty ... The sense in which I am using the term is that in which the prospect of a European war is uncertain, or the price of copper and the rate of interest twenty years hence ... About these matters there is no scientific basis on which to form any calculable probability whatever. We simply do not know. (CW, XIV, 113–114)

In Keynes's view, uncertainty arises when the probability relation is numerically indeterminate and not comparable to other probability relations. Following Lawson, the lack of knowledge and uncertainty coincide:

> Given the available evidence, the probability in a particular proposition may or may not be known. When it *is* known but is calculated at less than unity then the situation is not one of uncertainty. The latter arises when the probability relation itself is unknown, or more importantly, is numerically indeterminate in the literal sense that there is no basis upon which it could be determined. (Lawson, 1985, 915)

Therefore improbability and uncertainty are distinct concepts. The former implies measurability, the latter implies an 'inherent unknowableness' (Perlman and McCann, 1996, 13). Both immeasurability and unknowableness point to the irreducibility to some degree of reduction because of a lack of knowledge, or ignorance. In the self reflexive behaviouralist setting of DCX, it is an irreducibility to a satisficing level of reduction.

Tony Lawson (1988, 1994) has brought a clarification of the main conceptions of probability and uncertainty in economic analysis. Table 2.2 is adapted from his presentation, with a complement.

Table 2.2 Accounts of probability and uncertainty in economic analysis (adapted from Lawson, 1994, 353)

Uncertainty	Probability: **Epistemic** Probability is a form of knowledge or belief	Probability: **Aleatory** Probability is also an object of knowledge
Situation of numerically measurable probability	Subjectivists (Savage, Friedman, etc.)	Rational expectations proponents (Muth, Lucas, etc.)
Situation of numerically immeasurable probability	Keynes Austrians	Knight

Probability is either merely epistemic (it is a form of knowledge or belief) or it is essentially aleatory (it is an object of knowledge as a property of the external world). Uncertainty is often associated with probabilistic knowledge which implies a situation of numerically measurable probability. The radical or fundamental uncertainty upheld by Keynes implies an absence of probabilistic knowledge in a situation of immeasurable probability.

Austrian uncertainty comes close to Keynes's uncertainty according to the two criteria used in Table 2.2. Yet it denotes also ignorance – partial about the present, total about the future. Keynes's uncertainty is not merely about the future. It is logical, between any two propositions for which probability is immeasurable. It does not imply a total ignorance about the future.

C.2 An Alternative Cognitive Framework

It should be clear by now that Keynesian uncertainty is assimilable with the kind of irreducibility that is present in deep complexity. It is a different notion from the commonsense understanding of complexity as an attribute of the material under investigation, which is the way Keynes uses the term when he evokes the complexity derived from the material being 'capable of variations of degree in more than one mutually incommensurable direction at the same time' (CW, V, 88). An illustration is what Anna Carabelli writes about Keynes's view of the 'complexity' of a monetary macroeconomy, that is, 'a system … possessing attributes such as organic interdependence among variables, non-homogeneity through time and space, non-numerical measurability, physical heterogeneity, openness, incompleteness, indivisibility, secondary qualities, contingency and change' (Carabelli, 1992, 3–4).

Keynes's views on uncertainty in social and human science, and especially in economics, denote a radical departure from the perspectives of natural science and 'classical' economic theory. They also form an alternative framework which would be hardly understandable without having in mind the subject of Keynes's criticism and the evolution of his scientific interests. It is a particular alternative which does not reject what it criticises but encompasses it in a setting whose characterisation is not self-evident, but which ends unequivocally in an encompassing, alternative framework, as I shall attempt to summarise below:

1. Keynes was a student of the theory of probability before he became an economist. His scientific works denote a move from an emphasis on the former to a concern with practical decision-making processes in the economic world. He conceived the former as a general theory of logic whose subject matter was, as O'Donnell puts it: 'the *philosophical foundations of rational but non-conclusive argument*, the typical form of all arguments in daily life, science, policy making and so on. The rational element ... was identified with logic, the non-conclusive element was identified with probability, and the two elements were welded together by the conception of probability as a generalised logic' following from 'Keynes's distinctive notion of probability as a *logical relation* between virtually any pair of propositions' (O'Donnell, 1991, 5). This move from the *Treatise on Probability* to the *General Theory* is therefore a move from a theory of logical or speculative rationality to a theory of practical rationality.
2. This move was not a rejection of the initial concern. It retained an element of continuity with Keynes's constant preoccupation about how to deal adequately with human decision-making in the face of an absence of certainty, be it probability or uncertainty. Rather, it was a move to consider rational behaviour in circumstances of 'vague knowledge', when the premises are not 'true' but uncertain. Furthermore it entailed a constant concern about how knowledge, as a basis for action, is established.
3. The theory of knowledge was fundamental in Keynes's edifice. It was a theory of knowledge for action aimed at modifying reality, not a speculative theory (Carabelli, 1988, 240). Although it might be problematic to claim that explanatory and descriptive purposes were absent from it, the notion about knowledge that arises from Keynes's works is its 'projective, ... essentially operative' character (ibid., 234).
4. A major part of theoretical knowledge is based on the assessment and the criticism of established theories. Criticism reveals the points that appear important to its author. In this respect, Keynes had a profound concern for the status of premises, tacit or explicit. His criticism of the premises of classical theory was not primarily concerned with their empirical relevance. Rather, it was directed at their lack of generality. They were adequate to

situations in which the atomic hypothesis was relevant, which ought to be extremely rare in a world of organic interdependence. The tacit premises of 'logical independence' were the crucial point for the introduction of the atomic hypothesis (Carabelli, 1994, 141). Keynes writes in the fourth sentence of the preface of his *General Theory*: 'For if orthodox economics is at fault, the error is to be found not in the superstructure, which has been erected with great care for logical consistency, but in a lack of clearness and of generality in the premises' (Keynes, 1936 [1965], v).

A consequence of Keynes's overall position is that it was foreign to the debate between realism and instrumentalism. Carabelli writes that: 'Keynes was not interested in material ontology – that is, how things are in reality – but in how things are actually *known* (or, rather, probably known) by us'. The distinction he made in the *Treatise on Probability* was between '*causa essendi*' ('cause of why a thing is what it is') and the '*causa cognoscendi*' ('cause of our knowledge of the event') (Carabelli, 1994, 149).

For Keynes, only reasoning rather than the mere observation of matters of fact could raise doubts about a theory. He saw the strength of classical theory to lie in the consistency between its conclusions and its tacit premises. He was therefore critical of the attempts at refutation of the 'self-adjusting school' by those among the 'brave army of heretics' (Keynes, 1936 [1965], 371) who believed either that the straightforward observation of facts and history would suffice, as did the German historical school, or who rejected the classical conclusions but did not notice the tacit classical premises, and were therefore inconsistent and doomed to failure in front of the 'citadel' of classical theory (Keynes, CW, XIII, 488–489).

One may infer from this that Keynes's method for criticising the classical theory is indeed an approach for the search of an alternative which comprises three steps: firstly, the clarification and the identification of the tacit premises, secondly, the assessment of the extent to which these premises may be unduly restrictive and thirdly, the building of an alternative theory based on a less restrictive set of premises.

The benefit for knowledge was aptly coined by Brian Loasby who wrote that equilibrium theory 'excludes consideration of the consequences of ignorance, and leaves one in ignorance of the effects of what is excluded' (Loasby, 1976, 218). In the same vein, Austrian theory excludes consideration of the consequences of other relevant forms of organisation besides the market – through its tacit premise of the universal supremacy of the market – and introduces in this way an ignorance about the effects of what it excludes.

5. Organic interdependence is the alternative advocated by Keynes throughout his works. It is itself premised upon a non-demonstrative, non-conclusive or

> ordinary logic which makes the classical assumptions appear as a special case.
>
> Then the question arises of the nature of this alternative. Is it holist? Is it eclectic? At least it seems that it can hardly be assimilated to rationalism or to empiricism, the 'two traditional horns of epistemology... and the two leading trends in which one can sketchily divide economic methods in our century' (Carabelli, 1988, 245, 247). Keynes's own methodological position seems to stand apart, making it difficult, if not impossible to classify his position in economics in a clear-cut way, along conventional lines. He seems to have stood in a 'middle position', and to represent a 'third stream' in economics (ibid., 247). For O'Donnell, 'whether in philosophy, economics or politics, Keynes is typically an exponent of a middle way' (O'Donnell, 1989, 325).
>
> And although Keynes denounced atomism as a general premise not adequate to social science, he did not propose to replace it by a holist perspective. Keynes's method perceives the individual as organic in the sense of being internally related to other individuals: 'the nature of the individual as well as her perception of herself are functions of and change with her interaction with other individuals' in the whole (Rotheim, 1989–90, 322). Rotheim aptly states that 'the individual is neither autonomous nor *a priori*' in Keynes's view. A Keynesian organic system 'is not one that replaces parts with wholes. Instead, it is one that causes parts to be continually redefined as they collectively interact' (ibid.).

Keynes's perspective on knowledge and theory transcends the conventionally understood dualisms: he was neither individualist nor holist, 'neither deductionist nor empiricist, neither objectivist nor subjectivist, neither materialist nor idealist, neither rationalist nor irrationalist' (Dow, 1991, 149). In the absence of the 'third way' terminology that would characterise Keynes's theory of knowledge, Sheila Dow suggests following Victoria Chick's depiction of Keynes's theory as an 'exercise in containment' which transcends the opposition between dual terms by allowing each a place in theorising, 'each dealing with a different aspect of complex subject matters' (ibid., 150).

However something more, still, seems to be conveyed by Keynes's concern with premises being general enough to account for features that otherwise would remain excluded and ignored. Keynes's alternative is an encompassing one in which the sufficient generality of the premises is the prime concern. It introduces a priority to generality, and thus differs from a plainly eclectic practice. This is what seems implied when the recourse to atomist assumptions may be relevant, but as a special case of an otherwise more general, organically based method.

C.3 Substantive Open-endedness

Open-endedness was a pervasive aspect of Keynes's theory. It was the unsurprising outcome of the substitution of an assumption of organic interdependence to the tacit introduction of the atomic – or simplicity – hypothesis. The notion of an organically interdependent and 'complex' world could no longer be approached with the atomistic logic and called for a logic in line with it. This logic was evoked by Keynes in the first paragraph of his *Treatise on Probability*:

> The course which the history of thought has led Logic to follow has encouraged the view that doubtful arguments are not within its scope. But in the actual exercise of reason we do not wait on certainty, or deem it irrational to depend on a doubtful argument. If logic investigates the general principles of valid thought, the study of arguments, to which it is rational to attach *some* weight, is as much a part of it as the study of those which are demonstrative. (CW, VIII, 3)

This logic relies therefore on non-demonstrative arguments. In his review of Ramsey's *Foundations of Mathematics*, in 1931, Keynes took from Ramsey the distinction between formal logic and human logic:

> Formal logic is concerned with nothing but the rules of *consistent* thought. But in addition to this we have certain 'useful mental habits' for handling the material with which we are supplied by our perceptions and by our memory and perhaps in other ways, and so arriving at or towards truth; and the analysis of such habits is also a logic ... in attempting to distinguish a 'human' logic from formal logic ... Ramsey may have been pointing the way to the next field of study when formal logic has been put into good order and its highly limited scope properly defined.' (CW, X, 388–89)

In his discussion with Roy Harrod in 1938, Keynes reiterates this conception of logic when he declares that: 'economics is a branch of logic, a way of thinking' rather than a 'pseudo-natural-science' (CW, XIV, 296). Keynes maintained this view about logic throughout his career. In several places in the *Treatise on Probability*, he referred to 'ordinary language' – and equivalent expressions – in terms of its priority over mathematical language and in praise of its semantical character in contrast to the synctactical character of mathematical language (Carabelli, 1988, 142–143).

Therefore there is no doubt about the substantively open character of Keynes's alternative as it is expressed by an 'open' ordinary language rather than by a 'closed' artificial language. This leads to the question of how one can establish 'general principles of valid thought' with an ordinary language logic.

C.4 Anchoring

Anchoring, the fourth component of ADCX, designates the means by which substantive openness is submitted to a procedural closure. Keynes did not state it in these terms but he was fully concerned with the question of the validity of arguments that are not underpinned by formal logic.

Indeed it seems to me that three ways in which a notion of 'anchoring' is present in Keynes's theory can be detected. First are the writings in which validity or correctness of conclusions appear. The former is evoked as 'valid thought' and 'valid argument' in the first pages of the *Treatise on Probability* (CW, VIII, 3–4). The latter is part of Keynes's characterisation of economics: 'The Theory of Economics does not furnish a body of settled conclusions immediately applicable to a policy. It is a method rather than a doctrine, an apparatus of the mind, a technique of thinking, which helps its possessor to draw correct conclusions' (CW, XIII, 856).

The significance of these remarks and notions derives from Keynes's conception of logic embracing both deductive logic and 'the rational kernel in all non-deductive forms of human reasoning' (O'Donnell, 1989, 161), and in which economics appears as a branch of logic, a subordinate to domains 'concerned with the general principles of rational choice and conduct namely, philosophy and logic' (ibid.). However distinct from natural science economics is, it is a branch of science, and as such 'the application of logic and rational analysis to the material presented as sense-data' (CW, X, 438). Logic and rationality require to be explicated. The branch of logic that Keynes evokes is 'human logic' as distinct from 'formal logic'. As logic, they both pertain to sets of principles for valid thought. But they differ in the way mentioned above in the paragraph on open-endedness. Economics belongs to 'human' or ordinary, non-conclusive or non-demonstrative logic. In economics, it is often impossible to bring one's idea to a conclusive test either formal or experimental (Keynes, 1936 [1965], vii – viii). Rationality is related to having some reason to believe: the reasonableness of a belief depends on whether or not we have some reason to hold it. A belief is reasonable if it is adequate in a given situation (Carabelli, 1988, 161).

A second type of anchoring follows from uncertainty: 'As living and moving beings, we are forced to act … Yet we must be guided by some hypothesis. We tend, therefore, to substitute for the knowledge which is not attainable certain conventions' (CW, XIV, 124). This anchoring consists in conventions which appear as substitutes to the knowledge which is unattainable. Conventions are essentially agreed, shared rules of behaviour which enable individuals to take action in situation of uncertainty: 'In practice, we have tacitly agreed, as a rule, to fall back on what is, in truth, a *convention*' (Keynes, 1936 [1965], 152).

A third kind of anchoring follows from the need to protect the 'system against infinite regresses of reason' (O'Donnell, 1989, 90). It is obtained by 'direct knowledge', that is, 'the result of contemplating the objects of direct acquaintance' which is distinct from the knowledge obtained 'indirectly, by argument, through … the probability-relation (CW, VIII, 12). Direct knowledge (or intuition) eliminates infinite regresses 'through providing putatively true knowledge incapable of further proof' (O'Donnell, 1989, 93). O'Donnell lists several cognate terms used interchangeably, among which are intuition and judgement as the commonest synonyms.

To recap, what we may call Keynes's notion of anchoring appears to rely on human logic, reasons to believe, conventions, direct knowledge and judgement. Judgement covers several components and we can summarise the list by conventions and judgement.

From this presentation one may feel that the criterion of choice between statements or models is rather elusive. It is however consistent with Keynes's insistence on the non-conclusive character of logic in moral or social science, especially in economics. To repeat, the lack of homogeneity, of uniformity and continuity following from internal relations (or organic interdependence) of the material of economics explained the inapplicability of the atomic hypothesis. On the hypothesis of internal relations, motives behind economic behaviour will change with changes in the relations within which individuals live. Therefore the regularities observable in behaviour which depend on these motives will also change (Winslow, 1986, 423). The outcome of this is that economic theories are seldom true or false in any absolute sense except that of logical consistency. As Chick states it 'A theory one describes as "true" captures important features of reality as one perceives it. A theory which is "true" in that sense can become "false" through the mere passage of time, not because it is, or ever was, "wrong", but because the world has changed' (Chick, 1992, 2). Organic interdependence, time and change impose limitations on knowledge which are reflected in the acceptance of a reasonable practice of economics as a science based on a mixture of logic, persuasion rhetoric and practical judgement (Carabelli, 1988, 167; O'Donnell, 1989, 92–93).

Conventions and judgement, as well informed as is possible, may therefore be the ultimate stage about the issue of anchoring. There seems to be little ground for disagreement on this. However the substance of conventions and the quality of the information on which judgement is based are still matters to be discussed.

Keynes's edifice is built on the notion of a human logic adequate to moral science and distinguished from abstract rules of consistent thought or formal logic. There is nothing in between this formal logic, which is equated indeed with the classical disjunctive logic, and ordinary, human logic. Yet the strength of scientific discourse depends on its exposure to public test and criticism, which implies that it relies on means of checking and criticising. These in turn require criteria of judgement and choice. The more the criteria are specified, the better the check, the easier the assessment and the clearer discussion and criticism may be.

In reducing de facto formal logic to disjunctive logic, Keynes overlooks the possibility of a formal but non-disjunctive logic, a logic accounting for the irreducibility which is intrinsic to deep complexity or uncertainty. The price to be paid for this flaw is the lack of reference marks against which the validity or not of a reasoning can be assessed and compared with an alternative argumentation, at a theoretical level. One must admit that Keynes's logic is underspecified in this respect.

Conventions in science present two impediments. Once established, a convention can be self-enforcing and lead to an entrenchment that the citadel status of the mainstream seems to illustrate well. Beyond that, a convention can be self-defeating. Although a valid argument might be an argument like Darwin's, elaborated from the standpoint of 'a plain man with an obvious argument for all to see' (Cannon, 1968, 162), and although a degree of belief could be rational and thus not merely a matter of the believer's psychological state of mind 'but one which all rational men under similar circumstances would share' (Braithwaite, 1973, xxi) one cannot forget Marshall's warning that man is in a great measure a creature of circumstances and changes with them. In judgement as such, left unspecified, nothing prevents in ordinary logic a convention arising according to which economics is to abide by disjunctive logic because, as is often heard, it is the way 'modern' science is practised in the prevailing 'circumstances' like natural or 'exact' science. Only Keynes's judgement avoids this. It relies in the confidence in the superior rationality and judgement of the investigator or the scientist. It ends in intellectual elitism.

It is the immense merit of Keynes to have pointed out relentlessly the irreducibility of human and social sciences to natural science. But in leaving a void between 'formal logic', reduced to disjunctive logic, and human logic, Keynes's construction abandoned formal criteria to the former and left conventions and judgement underspecified in the latter.

The ADCX hypothesis suggests an alternative formal set of principles of conjunctive logic accounting for the irreducibility of deep complexity and aims at organising a reasoning adequate to it, ensuring its coherence and helping to assess its value for action. The ADCX hypothesis as such does not specify how to operationalise these principles. But it provides the impulse to inquire further in this direction.

As it stands at this stage, the ADCX hypothesis relies on a convention of scientific practice and on a scientific judgement subject to explicit, declared-in-advance criteria. The convention bears on scientific practice itself, on a conjunctive, encompassing logic, and on criteria following from it, providing hopefully an effective alternative for theorising, and which are to be elaborated.

The judgement bears first on obedience to the criteria above by the process of investigation and theorising. And it is also a judgement of the relevance of the features of the subject matter which need to be included or excluded, that is, whether there is matter for deep complexity or not. This judgement does not preclude any extra scientific judgement and its own value, distinct from scientific value. The judgement envisaged here is simply a judgement of deep complexity and scientific relevance. It is limited to it and has nothing to say about any other criterion.

At this stage, could it be envisaged simply to use the Keynesian framework and improve its specification as indicated above? The answer is rather negative since this suggestion would bring in a tacit assumption about equating deep complexity with radical uncertainty. Keynes's uncertainty, and radical uncertainty in general, do actually consist in deep complexity. Keynes's view on uncertainty is the one that comes closest to ADCX. The main apparent difference is the underspecification of its anchoring. Therefore, that Keynes's uncertainty is deeply complex is beyond discussion. But can Keynes's theory of uncertainty, even if it is more specified, be a theory of DCX? Nothing tells us a priori that uncertainty can be taken as the unique or as the most relevant representation of deep complexity before we have investigated other forms of deep complexity. The outcome expected from this inquiry will be either that all forms of DCX reduce to radical uncertainty, or that a theory of DCX proper is required, which will account for the variety of its forms and for the anchoring that has been so deficient thus far.

2.3.3 Complex Economic Systems

Complex economic systems refer to the growing domain which has been based for about three decades now on the import, in economics, of the developments of complex, non-linear dynamics which gained pace in the early 1970s in mathematics and natural science and which have been bolstered by the continual advances in computers and software.

This new field is interdisciplinary. It is mainly concerned with studying the general attributes of evolutionary natural and social systems, and notably structural change driven by non-linear dynamics and exposed possibly to follow unstable and chaotic trajectories (Garnsey and McGlade, 2006, 1). Under such names as complexity theory, complexity science, complex adaptive systems or non-linear science, complexity-driven research has spread over a variety of disciplines and given rise to an already important, and still rapidly growing literature.[6]

Although it is trivial to say that there must be complexity in any complex system, there is little consensus on the sense of the term, which seems to mean 'all things to all people' (ibid.). Yet there is a spontaneous consensus on taking complexity as a property of the imagined, computed or observed world external to the imagining, computing or observing actor. There seems thus far to be little difference from Keynes's concern with the complex organic interdependence of the economic material. However there is a profound divide about the consequences of this complexity of the subject matter. For Keynes, it justified both agents' and observers' uncertainty, which was akin to deep complexity. Here the concern about the epistemic implications of the complexity of complex economic systems is very uneven. It ranges from a quasi deep complexity in some works, to an absence of any explicit concern in other works, with an intermediate position denoting a concern but without deep complexity. I will present instances of each of these three cases, with the hope that discussing how deep complexity is partly taken into account or simply absent will help gain some insight into the nature of the challenge that it presents.

A. Quasi deep complexity in multi-agent dynamic systems

A representative contribution is in the work done by Brian Arthur and the so-called Santa Fe approach to complexity. Complexity is taken as the common property of systems composed of multiple, heterogeneous elements which are reacting to the pattern or the aggregate behaviour these elements co-create. In the economy, elements are agents who react to the aggregate world that their actions, strategies and expectations create. Time enters through processes of adjustment and change. Complex systems are systems in process that continually evolve and unfold over time: 'As the elements react, the aggregate changes, and as the aggregate changes, elements react anew' (Arthur, 1999, 107). The immediate consequence is a differentiation from the standard, neoclassical conception of the economy. How it relates to ADCX is discussed next.

A.1 Intractability

Although no precise definition of complexity seems to be proposed, Arthur, Durlauf and Lane suggest that complex systems exhibit six properties that they borrow from John Holland (Arthur et al., 1997):

- dispersed interaction among locally interacting heterogeneous agents, which prevents from relying on a representative agent hypothesis;
- no global controller for exploiting opportunities arising from these interactions;
- cross-cutting hierarchical organisation with tangled interactions and a plurality of levels of organisation;
- continual learning and adaptation by agents;
- perpetual novelty as ecological niches are continually created by new markets, new technologies, new behaviours, new institutions; filling a niche provides new niches;

- out-of-equilibrium dynamics, the economy operates far from an optimum (or global attractor), improvements are always possible and, indeed, occur regularly.

These features of the global economy in the aggregate make it a difficult subject for the traditional mathematics used in economics, according to Holland. Indeed they compose a kind of proxy for an irreducibility to standard economics and an insolvability within its cognitive framework. Technically the features listed above are related to what Holland refers as adaptive non-linear networks. A little later, Arthur mentioned that he avoids explicitly 'exact definitions of complexity and complex systems which vary widely' (Arthur, 1999, 109).

A.2 An Alternative Framework

In studying the unfolding of the patterns that are created by economic agents, the type of process described above departs unequivocally from conventional economic theory. It does not simplify its questions in order to seek analytical solutions (what behavioural elements – actions, strategies, expectations – are consistent with the aggregate patterns these elements co-create), but turns to the question of how actions, and so on, might react in general (might endogenously change with) the aggregate patterns they create. 'The result – complexity economics – is not an adjunct to standard economic theory but theory at a more general, out-of-equilibrium level' (Arthur, ibid., 108).

If the process contains non-linearities in the form of positive feedbacks arising from increasing returns, it will exhibit a multiplicity of potential solutions, an unpredictability of the outcome actually reached, a tendency to be locked in, a dependence on the historical path taken, and will not necessarily be the most efficient economically.

Computation and simulation tend to substitute to deductive and inductive analysis. At the 2002 Conference of the EAEPE (European Association for Evolutionary Political Economy) in Aix-en-Provence, Arthur presented a comparison of 'old' and 'new' economics (Table 2.3).

Table 2.3 Arthur's comparison of 'old' and 'new' economics

Old economics	New economics
Equilibrium economics (elements consistent with ...)	Out-of-equilibrium economics (elements react to ...)
Simplified assumptions (e.g. homogeneous agents)	More realistic assumptions (e.g. heterogeneous agents)
Rational, deductive behaviour	Adaptive, evolutionary behaviour
Analytical, equation-based	Algorithmic, agent-based
Outcome: static equilibrium simple stationary	Outcome: evolving pattern complex perpetually novel

A.3 Substantive Open-endedness

The complex outlook thus conceived emphasises the formation of structures rather than the consistency conditions attached to given structures as in the equilibrium perspective. This approach to complex systems entails a 'process-and-emergence' economics in which the properties appearing at the macroscopic level are not deducible from an understanding of the components. The outcomes are typically multiple, history-dependent, phase-locked, non-predictable and asymmetric (Arthur, 1999). Novelty prevails. In their introduction to the volume, Arthur, Durlauf and Lane argue that the approach has implications for economic theory at the cognitive, structural and methodological levels.

First, the cognitive and behavioural foundations. In the complex perspective, agents have to make sense of their problems, they do not optimise in the standard rational sense because an optimal course of action cannot be defined. They experience first.

Second, the structure of interactions. Whereas in general equilibrium agents interact through impersonal markets, structure matters in complex economies in a variety of ways: through networks; through socially supported procedures, that is, institutions; and through recursive structures in which economic entities are themselves comprised of entities and exhibit reciprocal causation between different levels of organisation.

A.4 Anchoring

The same authors address the issue of the validity of the approach via a discussion about 'what counts as a problem and as a solution' (Arthur et al, 12–13). They write:

> While papers here have much to say on cognition and structure, they contain much less discussion on what constitutes a problem and a solution from this new viewpoint.

> Perhaps this is because it is premature to talk about methods for generating and assessing understanding when what is to be understood is still under discussion. (Arthur et al., 12–13)

It is an intellectually honest way to ask the question about the kind of knowledge that is obtained through simulating the highly intricate societal processes. There is a gulf between the simulation of the functioning of an engine or of an aircraft, and the simulation of the dynamics of a human society. To say the least, there still seems to be no systematic corpus of knowledge on the kind of research strategy following from simulation that would be adequate to understand the empirically derived highly intricate problems of which the RISE is an instance. The process-and-emergence view is highly suggestive of the degree of ignorance that accompanies the equilibrium view.

However the question of what insight it brings to an empirically based problem as the RISE also seems to be 'under negotiation'. Theorising on the basis of experience first may still be a safe method, while running simulations first may be suggestive but still leaves uncertainty about how to transform the outcome of simulation into solid knowledge for action in the actual world.

This suggests that experience and simulation are not opposed to each other. It is a matter of priority. In this way it would seem problematic to make simulation outcomes direct the meaning given to experience, rather than operating the other way round: starting with experienced problem-situations and using simulation as a tool, among others, to help understand experience.

B. A complex system perspective without deep complexity

The complex system perspective in economics is dominated by the notion of complex adaptive systems. It does not oppose multi-agent models and their intrinsic interactional and adaptive characteristics. But whereas the latter emphasise processes, it is the system's characteristics that are emphasised in the complex adaptive system perspective.

I will discuss a telling instance of addressing the economy as a complex system. It is provided by John Foster in two recent articles whose titles are explicit: '*From simplistic to complex systems in economics*' (2005) and '*Why is economics not a complex systems science?*' (2006). I present below my understanding of Foster's position in a summarised and simplified way. Notwithstanding this condensed reporting, I believe it is sufficient to capture the central challenge that it has to face in the end.

Foster's general approach develops as a reaction against what he conceives as major defects exhibited by the mainstream and some heterodoxies in economics. Standard economic theory centres on constrained optimisation in the allocation of resources. It cannot account for historical time since it deals more with outcomes than with processes. Temporal trajectories capture only manifestations of historical processes rather than the processes themselves. And some heterodox perspectives (post-Keynesian and, I should add, neo-Schumpeterian) seem more concerned with developing dynamical models than to employ complex systems theory (Foster, 2005). For Foster, the gulf between economic theory and historical research is widening. It presents the threat of economics bifurcating into either 'a branch of applied mathematics' or 'a business school specialism that deals with aspects of market behaviour and business strategy' (ibid., 24).

Foster's goal is to replace prevailing 'simplistic' theories based in constrained optimisation with 'simple' theories derived from a complex systems perspective upon the economy. Intractability is therefore not the triggering factor. Foster's standpoint is ontological, it is based on a vision of what the economy is, from which all theoretical inquiry should derive. In a nutshell, the economy is a complex adaptive system. Each of these terms needs to be explained.

As a system, the economy is a network structure whose integrity derives from a set of rules. These rules constitute a connective structure. Connection and elements are central. As a complex system, it is a dissipative structure, that is, a system that imports free energy and exports entropy in a way that enables it to self-organise its structural content, subject to boundary limits. This analogy borrowed from Prigogine's work on physico-chemical settings is enriched for the economic domain with the 'much greater role that knowledge has in the processes of acquiring and deploying free energy' and with dealing with the behaviour of systems in history (Foster, 2006, 1076).

As a complex adaptive system, the economy combines the four properties of being a dissipative structure, of being a whole in itself, of exhibiting some degree of structural irreversibility, and of experiencing an evolutionary process expressed in historical time (Foster, 2005). Dissipative structures are so-called because they dissipate unless energy is fed in from outside to maintain them (Prigogine and Stengers, 1984).

The term 'complexity' refers to 'the connective structure (or lack of thereof) of a system' (Foster, 2005, 4) and relates to a state of "ordered complicatedness" (Foster, 2006, 1076). No single definition of complexity is adequate according to Foster. However he proposes to discern different orders of complexity within which different types of complex systems can be classified, from first-order complex systems (physico-chemical settings, when energy is imposed on elements), to second-order complex systems (in the biological domain, where a system can receive information 'and translate it into a knowledge structure of some kind'), to third-order complex systems (human beings, with imagination, anticipation, design and creativity), to finally a fourth order of complex system (the interactive knowledge case in which 'mental models interact with each other') (Foster, 2005, 5–6).

Foster applies this setting to Keynes's macroeconomic theory and claims that Keynes had in mind a system that contained features 'we can now identify as belonging to a complex adaptive economic system'. In contrast to the neoclassical synthesis version of the Keynesian system, Foster argues convincingly that there is no supply – demand dichotomy at the aggregate level in Keynes's system, 'only a network of connections through which income and expenditure flow in exchange for goods and services' (Foster, 2006, 1082). He contends that a limitation of Keynes's analysis is that the macroeconomic level of inquiry is inappropriate to capture the complexity of processes in an economic system. Keynes focused merely on stock and flow-of-funds consequences of interactions whereas the meso-level, intermediate between the micro- and macro-levels, is the most appropriate approach to identify the generic rules and their connections that govern the behaviour of complex systems (ibid., 1084). Foster concludes that the economy is a complex adaptive system and its theorising can produce a unified analytical framework for heterodox economics, following Potts (2000), (ibid., 1087).

Thus, the alternative and open-ended properties of ADCX are manifestly present in this intuitively insightful and involved construct. The properties of intractability and anchoring are however totally ignored.

There is even an irony in praising Keynes for his concern with features of a complex adaptive system, indeed for the organic interdependence of the material of the economy, and in ignoring the fundamental epistemic consequence drawn from it by Keynes, and which underlies his economic analysis, that is, uncertainty or deep complexity.

Keynes unearthed a central tacit premise of classical economics consisting in an atomic world and the usage of an analytical toolkit consistent with it, making classical economics a 'citadel'. He was sarcastic about the inconsistency, or the myopia, of the 'brave army of heretics' who rejected the conclusions of standard theory but remained silent on its premises.

One has to admit that Keynes's criticism applies dramatically well to the purely ontological perspective developed by Foster. It is an ontology of connections which remains silent on the – possibly ontological – connection between ontology and epistemology. It posits that the – necessarily cognising – subject or scientist who affirms ontological statements about the world, reduced to the world external to him/her, knows what the world *is* and that there is no need to explain how he/she knows what the nature of the world is.

If it is taken at face value, and however suggestive it may be, Foster's argument, as any purely ontological argument, relies on asking the reader to believe what some scientist knows as the true world, like a high priest, rather than advancing it as a hypothesis to be assessed through an explicitly stated methodological frame and research strategy, and explaining what might disconfirm or disprove it.

The purely ontological standpoint leads to a war of ontological beliefs since it offers no other way for answering the question of how it is known that some ontology is the true ontology.

Beyond this particular case, it reveals the Achilles heel of classical systems theory since its inception in the 1940s, that is, its rejection of standard analytical conclusions and its silence on the tacit premises which ensure the consistency of the standard analytical approach. Classical and most complex systems alike, are faced with the challenge of their consistency, all the more as beyond their ignorance of Keynes's revolution with uncertainty, they also ignore Heinz von Foerster's conceptual revolution with second-order cybernetics and the inclusion of the observing system into the systemic problem-situation when complexity is deemed to be present (Andreewsky and Delorme, 2006).

C. Conceptual pluralism

In the book they edited on *Complexity and Co-evolution: Continuity and Change in Socio-economic Systems* (2006), Elizabeth Garnsey and James McGlade set out to demonstrate that the complexity perspective provides a new context in which to understand the behaviour of socio-economic systems and to provide an analytical framework 'that forces us to reconsider the nature of causality and the process of evolution' (McGlade and Garnsey, 4). They write: 'What is really radical about the world as defined by the new paradigm of complexity is that it alters our notions of time and reversibility, of space (action can occur at a distance) and of causality which may be non-proportional' (ibid., 12). They stress the potentially profound consequences of this complexity perspective for conventional epistemological premises, quoting Katherine Hayles: 'When a dichotomy as central to western thought as order/disorder is destabilized it is no exaggeration to say that a major fault line has developed in the episteme' (ibid., 2; Hayles, 1991, 16). They also converge with the ADCX hypothesis when they seem to endorse the rejection of the tradition of a two-valued logic and its replacement by a conception in which the terms (in this case order and disorder) are not antagonistic and fixed states but rather are 'stages in a process of dynamic and transformational becoming', following Stephen Wolfram (Garnsey and McGlade, 2; Wolfram, 2002, 1068). However they do not attempt to define complexity in its own right for 'by its very nature... complexity resists easy reduction to a set of law-like statements or general principles' (Garnsey and McGlade, 2–3). They therefore fall back on defining complexity as a set of characteristic properties of complex systems that have been summarised by Bernard Pavard and Julie Dugdale as a set of the four related properties of non-determinism and non-tractability, limited functional decomposability, distributed nature of information and representation, and emergence and self-organization (ibid., 3; Pavard and Dugdale, 2000).

They advocate an approach in which complexity is no new 'master narrative' or totalizing explanation that can provide formulaic solutions', but which 'enlarges our capacity to understand human-environment co-evolution as recursive', and that 'expresses new dimensions defined by partial connections, fragmented temporalities and multiple mappings' and which leads to 'a model of conceptual pluralism as opposed to strategies based on scientific reductionism' (Garnsey and McGlade, 12). They address frontally the epistemological problem that this perspective raises. They argue that 'explanations are arbitrary descriptions of a continuous learning process, in contradistinction to explanation as a nomothetic goal' and that the idea of any single and optimising solution is spurious and should be replaced by a paradigm of learning, following Peter Checkland, in which any model representation is no more than a 'carrier of insight through a variety of related arguments and meanings', in which models of 'socio-cultural' phenomena are necessarily incomplete and contingent, which creates the need of a variety of model scenarios at different temporal and spatial scales.

These considerations end in the advocacy of a position expressed earlier by McGlade (2003) in which: (1) no single map or model is sufficient to describe a complex entity; (2) models can be viewed as discrete knowledge systems reflecting distinct points of view or problem-sets; (3) 'each model potentially serves a different purpose, just as a geological map, a street map, or an aerial survey, all generate different but complementary information on the landscape' (ibid., 12–13). This position defines indeed a programme whose implementation, as underlined by the two authors, runs counter to the current discourse 'within which Complexity Theory or Complex Adaptive Systems ... is situated, and indeed to modelling in the social and natural science generally' (ibid., 13).

To summarise, Garnsey and McGlade advocate an evolutionary perspective for political economy in which a better understanding is not to be found in the adoption of any single set of rules, of epistemology or of ontology such as is claimed by those wishing to create a new orthodoxy in complexity studies. Their insistence on diversity, on accounting for co-evolution and complexity issues in the absence of any overarching – and explicit – ideological perspective echoes Delorme and Dopfer (1994), Finch and Orillard (2005) and even *régulation* theory.

However a problem comes again from the floating eclecticism that this posture entails. The challenge is now to move beyond these provisional, interim positions and explore how to anchor deep complexity and make of it an open-and-closed alternative. The argumentation about a 'complex' conceptual pluralism that was reviewed here reveals indirectly the need to have a strict characterisation of deep complexity in order to avoid a floating eclecticism.

2.4 DEEP COMPLEXITY IN MANAGEMENT THEORY

Organisation and business management is a discipline in which a growing awareness of the limitation of traditional methods has given rise for nearly three decades now to a rich reflection about taking decisions in organisations when the situations create intractable problems.

The interest for evoking this field is that it deals directly with problems of reasonable behaviour in contexts of ill-structured problem-situations that present the same difficulty of intractability or of irreducibility to a known established method as the one that was encountered about understanding the RISE. It differs from economics in the sense that here, the decision or behavioural pattern is the immediate crucial subject matter. It is a ubiquitous issue in all human and social science. We have already got acquainted with a central contributor to its study, Herbert Simon. Another insightful perspective pertains typically to management and was initiated by Peter Checkland under the name of Soft Systems Methodology. It will be assessed in detail in Chapter 6. Its main originality is explicitly to include the decision maker into systems management. Whereas in complex economic systems, the most that we detected was a quasi deep complexity, with B. Arthur, management theory provides several instances of deep complexity. However, their weakness is about anchoring. Although they exhibit the other three dimensions of ADCX (intractability, search of an alternative, open-endedness of outcomes), they fail on anchoring and the boundary conditions it sets about open-endedness. Complexity is also commonly taken as a feature of the subject matter, an instance of which is the 'densely interconnected networks' in which organisations operate and in which 'the wider ramifications of decisions cannot be ignored' (Rosenhead and Mingers, 2004, 1).

It signals a common reluctance to attempt to characterise complexity in its own right, a feature that we have already noticed with the complex economic systems perspective.

Rosenhead and Mingers review several formulations generated independently, in which their authors rely on a dichotomy of problem situations, with one of the two categories unsuited to the application of traditional optimising methods. They list Russell Ackoff contrasting 'messes' with 'problems' in operations research and systems management (Ackoff, 1979); Hans Rittel and his 'wicked' versus 'tame' problems in design (Rittel and Webber, 1981; Rittel, 1982); Donald Schön's 'swamp' versus 'high ground' in systems management (1987); Peter Checkland's 'soft' versus 'hard' systems thinking in management systems (1998) (Rosenhead and Mingers, 2004, 4–6).

Perspectives akin to deep complexity can also be found notably in works by Chris Argyris (1993), D. Schön and M. Rein (1994), Michael Jackson (2003), R.D. Stacey, D. Griffin and P. Shaw (2000), and the more philosophical work by H. Tsoukas and Mary Jo Hatch (2001) as well as in non-English language literature, some instances of which are, in French, J.-L. Le Moigne (1990), D. Génelot (1998) and M.-J. Avenier (2000).

This wealth masks however a common weakness on the anchoring issue. ADCX is not accommodated as such. It remains to assess whether there can be a connection of deep complexity with other forms of irreducibility or intractability of problem-situations, in the next section.

2.5 ALTERNATIVE TRANSDISCIPLINARY SOURCES AND FORMS

Beyond radical uncertainty, any form of irreducibility creating a problem-situation likely to lead to actualise the four components of ADCX is a potential source of deep complexity. The list may be long. In the following, I characterise four main potential sources and forms of deep complexity. They are indecomposability, uncontrollability, deterministic unpredictability and incompressibility. Other aspects of radical irreducibility such as incommensurable stakeholders' values, and even the limit case of radical disagreement on how to disagree, would carry us rather far away from our initial concern at this stage.

2.5.1 Indecomposability: W. Weaver

In a classical article on 'Science and complexity', Warren Weaver, a mathematician with the Rockefeller foundation, identified three classes of scientific problems: simplicity, disorganised complexity and organised complexity (Weaver, 1948).

Problems of *simplicity* occur when there are a small number of significant factors and a large number of insignificant factors. Typically, 'physical science before 1900 was largely concerned with two-variable problems of simplicity' (ibid., 537).

Problems of *disorganised complexity* are those in which the number of variables is very large, and in which 'each of the many variables has a behaviour which is individually erratic, or perhaps totally unknown' (ibid., 538). Yet the system as a whole possesses 'certain orderly and analyzable average properties'. It is typically the domain of statistical mechanics. Simplicity and disorganised complexity are therefore both eminently quantifiable, the former by concentrating on specific elements, the latter by statistical techniques. These two ranges occupy positions at opposite extremes of Weaver's three classes. Organised complexity sits in a middle region between these two end points.

Organised complexity refers to problems which exhibit 'the essential feature of organisation .... which involve dealing simultaneously with a *sizable number of factors which are interrelated into an organic whole*' (ibid., 539). These problems are typical of 'biological, medical, psychological, economic, and political sciences' and cannot be handled with the techniques that work effectively on a large degree of randomness.

Weaver's concern echoes the concern Keynes expressed earlier about the implications of organic interdependence. The new thing is that Weaver addresses natural science as well as social science. He points to the consequences of acknowledging the features of organisation as opposed to analytical decomposability, a feature which underpins the development of the systems perspective (von Bertalanffy, 1968).

Indecomposability is different from Simon's notion of near decomposability. Near decomposability is a method to reduce indecomposability to a satisfactory level and thus solve the initial irreducibility up to this level. Irreducibility as a source of deep complexity is therefore solved. The remaining component of indecomposability is judged insignificant. No such degree of solution can be achieved in the indecomposability envisaged here.

This kind of irreducibility due to organisation inspired Hayek's characterisation of what he called essential complexity in his Nobel Memorial Lecture (Hayek, 1975[1989]): 'the social sciences, like much of biology but unlike most fields of the physical sciences, have to deal with structures of *essential* complexity, i.e. with structures whose characteristic properties can be exhibited only by models made up of relatively large numbers of variables' (ibid., 4). Organised complexity means that theory cannot do more than pattern predictions 'predictions of some of the general attributes of the structures that will form themselves' (ibid.).

In organised complexity, the character of the structure depends only in part on the properties of their elements and the frequency with which they occur and to a large extent on the manner in which the individual elements are connected with each other (ibid.).

A criterion to measure the degree of complexity of different kinds of abstract patterns is the 'minimum number of elements of which an instance of the pattern must consist in order to exhibit all the characteristic attributes of the class of patterns' (Hayek, 1967, 25). This minimum number of elements is usually large in social sciences, which defines essential complexity. It is akin to the definition of complexity found in computational or algorithmic information theory, notably Gell-Mann's 'effective' complexity (see below).

A final remark is about the apparent similarity of indecomposability with the immediate epistemic implication of organic interdependence in Keynes's uncertainty. They both point to a central feature of organised phenomena. Indecomposability can be partial, total or nil. If it is total, the phenomenon can be perceived holistically as a unity. If it is nil, it can be perceived atomistically. It is in the intermediate situation that the difficulty lies. Simon's near decomposability reflects a situation in which the problem-solver knows how to obtain a satisfactory solution, a satisfactory mixture of what part is decomposable and what part is not decomposable, in which case irreducibility is solved. Deep complexity denotes the situation in which no satisfactory solution is obtained.

Since Keynes reckons that atomicity can be relevant in special cases, his argument is akin to partial indecomposability. The atomicity or decomposability tacit premise cannot be taken as a general, founding preconception or principle.

At this stage organisation means two things. First, it entails internal relationality between its elements. Partial unsolved indecomposability is positively linked to the degree of internality of the elements composing the phenomenon that is studied. It also influences its dynamics since what is joined or connected in this context gets necessarily transformed.

Second, it denotes the presence of regularities or structured relations, in contradistinction to random elements, which are not amenable to statistical techniques and whose role cannot be assumed away on a general basis. Similarly, these regularities are not the product of mechanistic interactions, they rather originate from an historical evolution.

This twofold irreducibility suggests forcefully that organisation also concerns the organisation of the knowing process in the problem situation which generates irreducibility to a well-structured problem situation. It gives rise to the hypothesis of a complex organisation, in which irreducibility is neither a mere property of an extraneous object, nor of a subjective mind, but of their relationship.

2.5.2 Uncontrollability: W.R. Ashby

A way to conceive of complexity as linked to the relationship between a knowing subject and an extraneous object can be derived from the formulation of control or regulation of systems initiated by W. Ross Ashby under the terminology of the 'law of requisite variety' (Ashby, 1956, 1958a).

Ashby argues that when the scientist 'faces a complex system', the classical methods become inappropriate. He introduces the scientist's limitations on the basis of her/his capacity to obtain an acceptable outcome defined in terms of the '*power of appropriate selection* (of the right answers from the wrong)' which defines intelligence according to Ashby (1958a, 94). The variety of a set of elements is the number of elements that can be distinguished. Regulation or control is aimed at achieving a goal against a set of disturbances. A set D of disturbances is met by a set R of responses. The actual outcomes are themselves a subset P of the set of possible outcomes. The controller or regulator acts in order to limit the variety of the outcomes. This variety of outcome depends itself on the varieties of disturbances and of responses. The law of requisite variety states that, with the varieties of D, R and P denoted respectively by V_D, V_R and V_P, the minimum value of V_P is V_D-V_R when they are measured logarithmically:

$$V_P \geq V_D\text{-}V_R$$

Let us symbolise V_P minimum by V_P^*. If V_D is given, V_P^* can be further reduced only by a corresponding increase in V_R. Restricting the outcomes to the subset that is valued as satisfactory demands a sufficient level of variety in R. Given V_D, to improve the control requires to increase V_R.

If V_R is increased up to V_D, then $V_P^* = 0$. In the "normal", problematic situation, V_R is inferior or at most equal to V_D which implies that $V_P^* \geq 0$. A situation in which V_R would be strictly larger then V_D would be trivial. It defines simplicity. In this case it is easy to obtain the minimum variety of the outcome: the outcome is unique, its variety is zero, and the law of requisite variety is also trivial in this case. Of interest for our purpose is the way Ashby extends his analysis to scientific work by considering the scientist as a regulator in the sense of control. Then scientific research may be viewed as a process of regulation through the selection of appropriate answers where D is the set of possible questions and R is the set of possible answers. The goal of scientific practice is to select answers enabling one to obtain adequate outcomes. It is precisely here that the scientist's ability can be limited. It is limited in the case of complex situations. Ashby defines the complexity of a system by the heterogeneity of its parts and by their strong interaction. Asking what kinds of scientific strategies should then be used, Ashby advises to beware of accepting the classical scientific strategies without scrutiny. They have come mainly from physics and chemistry. These disciplines are not typical because of two peculiarities:

> The first is that their systems are composed of parts that show an extreme degree of homogeneity: contrast the similarity between atoms of carbon with the dissimilarity between persons. The second is that the systems studied by the physicist and chemist have nothing like the richness of internal interaction that have the systems studied by the sociologist and psychologist. Or take the case of the scientist who would study the brain. Here again is a system of high complexity, with much heterogeneity in the parts, and great richness of connexion and internal interaction. (Ashby, 1958a, 95)

The consequence is that:

> Both of these qualities of the complex system – heterogeneity in the parts, and richness of interaction between them – have the same implication: the quantities of information that flow, either from system to observer or from part to part, are much larger than those that flow when the scientist is physicist or chemist. And it is because the quantities are large that the limitation is likely to become dominant in the selection of the appropriate scientific strategy ... We must beware of taking our strategies slavishly from physics and chemistry. They gained their triumphs chiefly against systems whose parts are homogeneous and interacting only slightly. Because

> their systems were so specialised, they have developed specialised strategies. We who face the complex system must beware of accepting their strategies as universally valid. (ibid., 96)

Thus the main issue becomes how to define an appropriate scientific strategy. Instead of doing away with complexity, Ashby advocates the search of new methods taking into account the limitation whenever the degree of complexity of the object of enquiry is above this limitation. Among these methods is what he calls 'operational research'. Instead of aiming at analysing the behaviour of the system and tracing a whole chain of causes and effects, it attempts to answer more the 'how' than the 'why': the 'ultimate aim is not understanding but the purely practical one of control' (ibid., 97).

Extension

This presentation can be extended. Let V_D measure the complexity of the object of enquiry as defined by Ashby, and V_R indicate the richness of the scientist's repertoire of answers measured by its variety. Then the difference V_D - V_R provides another definition of complexity. It takes explicitly into account the investigator's ability or competence. It is close to the competence–difficulty gap introduced by R. Heiner in 1983.[7]

Although Ashby's argumentation remains naturally related to the control of input–output systems, that is, to the first cybernetics, and although he refers here to complexity as being objectal, as a property intrinsic to a subject matter[8], one should not underestimate the fruitfulness of his reflection. Ashby's reasoning about intelligence provides a way for introducing complexity not as an absolute property but as a relationship between an observer and the observed world, which obviously pulls us beyond Ashby's own analysis. We pursue this extension below.

Let us consider that the aim of scientific practice is to reduce V_P to some target level. This level is zero if the goal is to obtain one single determinate value of the result. It is positive if obtaining two or more values is considered acceptable. We thus have to consider two notions of the variety of the outcome, namely V_P^* and the acceptable level of V_P, which we denote as V_P^a. The aim of this control game is now to make V_P^* coincide with V_P^a.

Three situations can be distinguished. The first is *simplicity*. It was evoked above. In this case one may consider that V_R is permanently greater than or equal to V_D. Then V_P is maintained at zero in all cases.

The second situation may be termed *complication*: $V_R \leq V_D$. The problem of control is to lessen V_P since $V_P \geq V_D - V_R$. According to the law of requisite variety we have: $V_P^* = V_D - V_R$. This value of V_P is itself such that $V_P^* \geq V_P^a$.

Whenever V_P^* can be lessened so as to equate V_P^a, the scientist's goal is achieved. Then complication denotes any situation in which, given some aspiration level, it is possible to solve the problem at hand.

Complexity occurs when $V_P^* > V_P^a$. It is then impossible to obtain a satisfactory control or to reduce V_P to a given target required for scientific practice. In this case V_R remains strictly inferior to V_P.

These values of variety refer to quantifiable measures. In a more general view, a qualitative dimension such as meaning might be included. Then the scientist is confronted with a still more complex situation, one in which V_D is replaced by a combination (V_D, m), m standing for meaning. The gap between V_P^* and V_P^a might be wider in this case of generalised complexity based on quantitative and qualitative factors. The list below summarises our presentation.

$$\begin{array}{lll} \text{Simplicity} & V_R \geq V_D & : \quad V_P = V_P^* \\ \text{Complication} & V_R \leq V_D & \left\{ \begin{array}{l} V_P \geq V_D - V_R \\ V_P^* = V_D - V_R \\ V_P^* \geq V_P^a \end{array} \right. \\ \text{Complexity} & V_R < V_D & : \quad V_P^* > V_P^a \end{array}$$

Ashby's 'new method' for controlling complex systems may be assessed against the component properties of ADCX. Intractability within the classical methods, those practised 'in physics and in chemistry' is clearly acknowledged. Two features, heterogeneity in the parts and richness of internal interaction seem to define complexity. They are close to Keynes's organic interdependence, to Arthur's multi-agent interactions, and to Weaver's organised complexity.

An alternative method is defined. It is called 'operational research' whose ultimate aim is control rather than tracing a whole chain of causes and effects. It opposes control, the search of the 'how', and instead focuses on understanding, the search of the 'why'.

A substantive open-endedness is undeniably present. However, an explicit account of anchoring is absent. The issue of how to assess the validity of control in comparison with the validity of classical methods is not addressed apart from a putative greater realism. It is therefore manifest that anchoring is not an issue for Ashby. Then the criticism addressed by Keynes towards the 'brave army' of heterodox economists seems to apply here as well but for a different reason. For Keynes, organic interdependence calls for an ordinary logic. Ashby's diagnosis ignores this implication and relies on a suggestive tool whose effective validity in science is not addressed. Yet the relationship between observer and observed world as an intrinsic feature of the situation is a forceful insight, as well as the threshold represented by the scientist's 'limitation' in the face of complexity. The notion of complexity thus introduced serves to discriminate between 'classical' and 'operational research' methods. Ashby is explicit on this when he states that:

> measurement of the quantity of information, even if it can be done only approximately, will tell the investigator where a complex system falls in relation to his limitation. If it is well below the limit, the classic methods may be appropriate; but should it be above the limit, then if his work is to be realistic and successful, he must alter his strategy to one more like that of operational research. (Ashby, 1958a, 98)

Here Ashby is overoptimistic and seems to believe in the operational bearing of information measurement in non-physical matters. He was writing in a time of high confidence in the newly introduced thinking about general systems, first cybernetics and operational research. He portrays an activity of control in which the controller sits in exteriority to what is supposed to be controlled, with the mere aim of practical control rather than of understanding. It is foreign to the ADCX hypothesis, in which communication and understanding through the interaction between the observer and the observed, rather than mere control, are the key words.

To conclude, the emphasis on the gap between the levels of variety of an object of control and of its controller, and its limitation with respect to ADCX, invite further investigation into the sources of these two kinds of varieties. On the side of the matter to be controlled, von Neumann's intuition about complex automata provides a powerful insight beyond Ashby's reference to heterogeneity and richness of internal interaction. On the controller's side, the capacity to control depends on knowledge which itself relies on a level of information defined qualitatively and quantitatively. The former, von Neumannian perspective pertains to deterministic unpredictability. The latter is tied to information theory and its limit of uncompressibilty. These themes are addressed in the next paragraphs.

2.5.3 Deterministic Unpredictability: J. von Neumann

John von Neumann addressed the problem of complexity in his work on self-reproducing automata. It provided a setting of deterministic unpredictability before this property became a trademark of the theories of chaos which developed in the 1980s and the 1990s, though in a quite different setting.

There was no systematic development of a 'theory of complexity' by von Neumann. But he formulated an insightful intuition which inspires the present book to a large extent.

Von Neumann used the terms 'complication' and 'complexity' interchangeably. He introduced what he called 'the concept of complication' in the following way:

> The discussions so far have shown that high complexity plays an important role in any theoretical effort relating to automata, and that this concept, in spite of its prima facie quantitative character, may in fact stand for something qualitative – for a matter of principle … We are all inclined to suspect in a vague way the existence of a concept of 'complication'. This concept and its putative properties have never been clearly formulated'. (von Neumann, 1961, 312)

> There is a concept which will be quite useful here, of which we have a certain intuitive idea, but which is vague, unscientific, and imperfect … I know no adequate name for it, but it is best described by calling it 'complication'. (von Neumann, 1966, 78)

Complication does not pertain to the structure or the composition of an object in von Neumann's view, but to the potentiality to do things, to the productive potentiality in an organisation: 'I am not thinking about how involved an object is, but how involved its purposive operations are. In this sense, an object is of the highest degree of complexity if it can do very difficult and involved things' (1966, 78–79).

These remarks led von Neumann to consider two categories of automata. One is living organisms. They reproduce themselves with no decrease in complexity. Over long periods of evolution they are indirectly derived from others which had lower complexity. Therefore, complexity is even increasing: 'organisms appear to have gotten more elaborate in the course of time' (1966, 78). An opposite conclusion derives from considering artificial automata:

> An automaton A, which can make an automaton B, must contain a complete description of B and also rules on how to behave while effecting the synthesis … complication … is degenerative … an organization which synthesizes something is necessarily more complicated, of a higher order, than the organization it synthesizes. (1966, 79)

The idea of a threshold defined as a certain level of complexity enabling to differentiate between non-complexity and complexity emanates from von Neumann's conclusion to his lecture at the Hixon Symposium in 1948:

> All these are very crude steps in the direction of a systematic theory of automata. They represent, in addition, only one particular direction. This is, as I indicated before, the direction towards forming a rigorous concept of what constitutes 'complication'. They illustrate that 'complication' on its lower levels is probably degenerative, that is, that every automaton that can produce other automata will only be able to produce less complicated ones. There is, however, a certain minimum level where this degenerative characteristic ceases to be universal. At this point automata which can reproduce themselves, or even construct higher entities, become possible. This fact, that complication, as well as organization, below a certain minimum level is

degenerative, and beyond that level can become self-supporting and even increasing, will clearly play an important role in any future theory of this subject. (1961, 318)

Von Neumann presents a similar idea in his comments on formal logic:

> It is characteristic of objects of low complexity that it is easier to talk about the object than produce it and easier to predict its properties than to build it. But in the complicated parts of formal logic it is always one order of magnitude harder to tell what an object can do than to produce the object ... There is thus this completely decisive property of complexity, that there exists a critical size below which the process of synthesis is degenerative, but above which the phenomenon of synthesis, if properly arranged, can become explosive, in other words, where syntheses of automata can proceed in such a manner that each automaton will produce other automata which are more complex and of higher potentialities than itself. (1966, 51, 80)

There is no other more explicit formulation on complexity by von Neumann. This may explain why his views are often referred to as a conjecture, following Gödel's comment[9]. We propose to define complexity using von Neumann's insights in the following way.

Let us first locate the origin of complexity with reference to one's ability to describe an object or to predict its behaviour. Although complexity remains a qualitative notion we simply admit that it is possible to refer to the notion of a level of complexity and that a proxy for it is the level of difficulty of depiction.

Let us also perceive an object through what it can do. It follows that complexity can be defined as the situation in which there exists a certain level of difficulty of depiction such that for objects below this level, it is simpler to describe what they do or how they behave than how they are made or structured. The opposite occurs for objects above the threshold level.

It leads one to consider that a basic notion enabling one to conceive some complexity lies in the relationship between what we may call a generating principle and what is generated. Then this renders it possible to state the above definition in the following way.

Two situations can be distinguished, non-complexity and complexity. In non-complexity, it is easier to describe what is generated (*P* or product) than the generating principle (*GP*). The opposite occurs in complexity. This definition is summarised below with symbols D for the difficulty of depiction, NCX for non-complexity, and CX for complexity:

$$\begin{cases} \text{NCX}: & \text{D}_{GP} \geq \text{D}_{P} \\ \text{CX}: & \text{D}_{GP} < \text{D}_{P} \end{cases}$$

Complexity thus defined can be conceived in an absolute and in a relative sense. The absolute conception means that a full depiction of P is out of reach. The relative definition is more operational for theorising purposes. It means that the depiction of P that can be achieved remains unsatisfactory compared to some given goal or, equivalently, remains below some aspiration level. Two basic insights follow from this characterisation. First, what a thing can do is more important than what it is. Second, the notion of a threshold separates what behaves in a complex way from what behaves in a non-complex way.

2.5.4 Incompressibility

Let us recall that the indecomposability and uncontrollability forms of irreducibility suggested to envisage a complexity relation. This relationship is between two terms, the observer and the observed world, for short. With von Neumann's complexity, we introduced the observed world side. We address now the observer's side via the theory of information and the notion of incompressibility. Information is however in no way limited to an observer. Yet, although it may be considered in an object-based way, it contains features which are directly relevant to knowledge and ignorance and the capacity to solve problem-situations. Both aspects will be evoked below although it is the latter that will matter most for our purpose.

The concept of information is most elusive. It means that something is added to a stock of knowledge. Knowledge is the outcome of organising information by the mind. Gregory Bateson defined information as a difference which makes a difference (Bateson, 1972). And the higher the degree of improbability of an event, the higher is the information that the actual occurrence of the event will produce. These ideas pertain to a message conception of information. Another conception is about structure. Then information means the creation of regularities, of shapes or forms that can be recognised by an outside observer in contradistinction with randomness in which no structuration, no regularity characterises the behaviour of what is observed. In this second meaning, information means 'in-formation'. It is related to organisation, the appearance and operation of durable, though evolving, regularities in a phenomenon of interest. In a broad sense these two notions vary in opposite ways: the higher the degree of organisation (that is, of structured information), the lower the degree of message-information, and conversely. The occurrence of an event in a situation of radical uncertainty about this event, that is, of non-probability, is also a case in which the information produced should be at a maximum.

It is therefore worth noticing that there currently exists no universal or general theory of information, even in mathematics and physics (Delahaye, 1994, 13–14). This seems due to the fact that information is related to some value, utility or content considered in connection with some purpose in some given situation.

Then the more the measure of information is disconnected from semantic and pragmatic content, the more it is supposed to gain in objectiveness or objectivity. But it may become quite problematic in matters or disciplines in which the semantic and pragmatic features are constitutive of the subject matter and can hardly be neutralised.

These few remarks were aimed at introducing the necessity to be careful and this subject-matter. I shall rely on two main mathematical theories of information with the aim of clarifying their connection with complexity and deep complexity in domains in which syntactic, semantic and pragmatic features do count, that is, in social science, and especially in economics.

These two theories of information are the statistical or probabilist formulation of information introduced by Claude Shannon in the 1940s, and the algorithmic theory of information introduced independently by several scientists in the 1960s, notably Andrei Kolmogorov, Ray Solomonoff, Per Martin-Löf and Gregory Chaitin.

A. Statistical information: Shannon's formulation

Shannon's formulation is sometimes called 'complexity'. It is concerned with message and communication, and is based on a priori probability. Probability can be conceived as reflecting the lack of a priori information about the result of an experiment or of an event. If no information exists on whether an alternative is more likely than another one, the alternatives are attributed equal probabilities. Shannon has elaborated a mathematical expression for this lack of information which is identical (except for a constant) to the entropy measure used in physics as a measure of disorder:

$$H = -\sum_i p_i \log p_i \qquad i = 1, \ldots, n.$$

H is maximum for total disorder or randomness, that is, a total absence of organisation or of regularities. Let us symbolize it by H_m. The degree of organisation can be characterised by its redundancy R defined below:

$$R = \frac{H_m - H}{H_m} \quad \text{or} \quad H = H_m(1 - R) \quad \text{with} \quad 0 < R < 1$$

Redundancy can in principle vary from nil to 'total' or 1. H is maximum when R is nil or close to nil because the knowledge one has of a phenomenon is never totally nil. Conversely, this knowledge is never total, hence $R < 1$: H is minimum when R is maximum, close to 1.

This measure of information is sometimes used in biology and in social science. About its use in biology, Delahaye writes: 'I believe that it is absurd to reduce biological information in order to make it fit with a mathematical theory of information or even with a physical theory of information' (Delahaye, 1994, 26). The same can be said about its use in economics, all the more as H is purely syntactic. It has no semantic or pragmatic content.

A last point is a problem of abused terminology. Given the strict limitation mentioned above, H is to a theory of information the same as the measurement of temperature with a thermometer is to a theory of heat: it is simply a measure along a strictly specific dimension, nothing more. Equating H with a 'theory of information', as is too often done in economics, designates either a tiny bit of theory whose usefulness should be argued in every case, or its author's disputable level of information.

B. Complexity and algorithmic information

When complexity is conceived via algorithmic information it may mean at least two different things. In one sense it means 'orderless, without any regularity, random, chaotic and in another sense, it means 'organised, highly structured, rich in information' (Delahaye, 1994, 97–98). Delahaye suggests to call the former 'random complexity' and the latter 'organised complexity'. Random complexity itself covers different notions among which are algorithmic complexity proper and computational complexity. We address these notions below.

B.1 Algorithmic Complexity

A general way of defining complexity related to algorithmic information is what Murray Gell-Mann calls 'crude complexity'. It is: 'the length of the shortest message that will describe a system, at a given level of coarse graining, to someone at a distance, employing language, knowledge, and understanding that both parties share (and know they share) beforehand' (Gell-Mann, 1995, 34).

Let us recall that the information value V of an object or a string s is related to some goal G:

$$V_s = V(s, G)$$

If G is to compress s as much as possible with a computer M, then V_s is the length of the shortest program which, when introduced in M reconstitutes s. The information value is this incompressible content of s, expressed in bits, for M. A bit is the smallest piece of information which permits distinguishing two possibilities or objects having equal probability. It is expressed in binary notation by either 0 or 1. Turing's conceptualisation in 1936 of a universal mechanism of computation makes it possible to express the length of the shortest program capable of generating *s* in terms of a universal computer. This reasoning is the basis of algorithmic randomness from which the notions of algorithmic information content (AIC) and algorithmic complexity are derived.

Let us start with the definition of a random string. The basic idea is that the information contained in such a string cannot be compressed or expressed in a more reduced form. A random string contains no regularity that will permit it to be compressed. Incompressibility is common to all random strings. A string of bits is random if the shortest algorithm enabling its introduction in a computer contains the same number of bits than the string. The length of the shortest program that will cause a standard universal computer to print out a string of bits and then stop defines the algorithmic information content (AIC), also called the algorithmic randomness or the algorithmic complexity of the string. AIC is maximal for random strings.

Strictly speaking, the complexity of a string is the number of bits that must be introduced in a computer in order to generate that string. It is thus equal to the length of the minimal program generating the string. If this length is equal to the length of the string then the string is random. A string is not random if it can be demonstrated that there exists a shorter program generating the string. Conversely, in order to prove that a given string is random one must establish that there does not exist a shorter algorithm capable of generating it.

AIC was introduced in the 1960s by several scientists, most of them working independently from each other. AIC is commonly denominated Kolmogorov complexity (K complexity) after the name of the Russian mathematician Andrei N. Kolmogorov although it seems that Ray J. Solomonoff introduced first this notion, in the USA, previous to the contributions by A.N. Kolmogorov, P. Martin-Löf and Gregory J. Chaitin (Delahaye, 1994, 45; Chaitin, 1996, 69). The Kolmogorov complexity of a finite string *s* is expressed by:

$$\mathrm{K}(s) \equiv \text{length of the shortest program that generates } s.$$

K(*s*) or K complexity corresponds to the general definition above with G = [compress for the universal machine M]. It is a descriptional definition of information. It increases with disorder and the lack of structure or of regularity of a system to be described or a message string to be generated.

AIC is uncomputable. The reason is that there is no procedure for finding all the procedures that would permit further compression. There is no way of knowing exactly which strings are random. We cannot in general be sure that the AIC of a given message string is not lower than we think it is (Gell-Mann, 1995, 38–39). For this reason, we can only place an upper boundary on AIC. Since its value may be below that boundary, AIC cannot be computed.

Since the algorithmic information content of an object is the length of the smallest computer program whose execution generates this object, it seems more general than Shannon's definition because it does not rely on a probability distribution given a priori. Yet it has two flaws.

First, consider the chain of the first billion digits of number π. Its K complexity is rather small because it can be generated by a short algorithm. Yet this string has a high information value because it embodies an important and long computation. Hence the interest for a computational definition of information.

But, above all, AIC has one property that makes it unfit for our purpose. It is a measure of randomness. But randomness is not what is usually meant by complexity in scientific practice and even in ordinary discourse (ibid., 41). This is illustrated by the proverbial monkeys sitting at typewriters. The question is: What are the chances that a group of monkeys will, in a given period of time, type the works of some author, say Victor Hugo? This is a random process. The chance that the material typed would resemble a passage of Hugo's work is extremely small although it is not nil. Then comparing the work of Hugo and the material typed by the monkeys would inevitably lead one to conclude that the work of the monkeys has larger AIC. It would be more complex than Hugo's since the latter is less random and much more structured.

B.2 Computational Complexity

B.2.1 Logical depth

That complexity is a relative notion, even in physics, is well illustrated by Charles Bennett's presentation of logical depth (Bennett, 1990). Bennett states that: 'at an intermediate level of humility, one can attempt to discover general principles governing the creation and destruction of complexity in the standard mathematical models of many-body systems' (ibid., 138). The 'formulation of suitable definitions of complexity' imposes that on the one hand they 'adequately capture intuitive notions of complexity, and on the other hand are sufficiently objective and mathematical to prove theorems about' (ibid.). Bennett proposes 'logical depth' as a most suitable candidate for a measure of complexity in physics.

Bennett mentions that the notion of logical depth developed by him was first described by G. Chaitin in 1977 (Bennett, 1988, 229). He introduces depth as a better measure of the value of a message than algorithmic information (AIC). In his view, the value of a message resides not in its information content (its unpredictable parts) nor in its obvious redundancy (order) but in what he calls its 'buried redundancy', that is, 'parts predictable only with difficulty, things the receiver could in principle have figured out without being told, but only at considerable cost in money, time, or computation'. He adds: 'in other words, the value of a message is the amount of mathematical or other work plausibly done by its originator which its receiver is saved from having to repeat' (Bennett, 1988, 230). A typical sequence of coin tosses has high information content but little value. An ephemeris, giving the positions of the moon and planets over a period of years, contains no more information than the equations of motion and the initial conditions from which it was calculated, but it saves its owner the work of repeating this calculation. Its value lies therefore in its depth rather than in its information. Naturally the word 'value' is understood here in terms of the contribution to achieving a goal ascribed by the operator, observer or designer. Here, value relates to the contribution to reducing the duration of computation.

The logical depth of an object is: 'the execution time required to generate the object by an incompressible universal computer program, i.e., one not itself computable as output of a significantly more concise program' (Bennett, 1990, 142). Logical depth is measured by the duration of the computation that generates a given object from a minimal program. It also measures the plausible amount of mathematical work needed to create this object (Bennett, 1989, 791). This computation represents, then, a plausible causal history of the object. It is an intrinsic property defined in terms of the possible histories an object might have had, not in terms of its actual history. An object is called deep only if there is no short computational path to construct it from a concise description (Bennett, 1989, 792–793). The demarcation between deep and not deep depends then on defining what is meant by 'a short computational path' which seems to be left unanswered.

An important issue is how organisation might be associated with logical depth. It must be noted that organisation-based complexity entails the existence of structured regularities and is thus opposed to complexity based on randomness, on the absence of order or regularities. According to Bennett, complexity cannot increase quickly except with very low probability. Logical depth is associated with long computation or elaboration and satisfies what he calls a slow-growth law by construction.

In order to understand how this property of slow growth is obtained, we cannot do better than to quote Bennett:

> Logical depth computerizes the Occam's razor paradigm, with programs representing hypotheses, outputs representing phenomena, and considers a hypothesis plausible only if it cannot be reduced to a simpler (more concise) hypothesis. Logically deep objects, in other words, contain internal evidence of having been the result of a long computation or slow-to-simulate dynamical processes and could not plausibly have originated otherwise. Logical depth satisfies the slow-growth law by construction. (Bennett, 1990, 142)

It has been proposed to link this kind of complexity, in this frame of reasoning, to an idea of organisation and to call it organised complexity (Delahaye, 1994, 108). Organised complexity can increase only slowly over time. Any attempt at formalising the notion of organised complexity must satisfy this assumed property. Logical depth conforms with this requirement since deep objects can be generated only very slowly by deterministic processes.

There can be sudden erasures but not sudden increases. Then accepting to equate organised complexity with logical depth gives a clue to 'explaining' the slowness of the appearance of organised complexity in any deterministic universe with small depth at its origin.

B.2.2 Crypticity

Logical depth designates the answer to the question: How difficult (lengthy, laborious) is it to go from a concise (short, minimal) program or a highly compressed schema to a full-blown (complete) description of the system itself?

In the reverse way one may ask: How difficult is it, starting with a system, to compress its description into a program or schema? The answer provides another notion of complexity, also introduced by Bennett, under the name of crypticity. This kind of complexity is the difficulty, given an object, of finding a plausible hypothesis to explain it. Bennett proposes to call 'cryptic' the objects having this kind of complexity: finding a plausible origin for such an object is like solving a cryptogram (Bennett, 1988, 231). The crypticity of a message string is the minimum time required for the standard, universal computer, starting from the string, to find one of the shorter programs that will cause the machine to print out the string and then stop. If we suppose that the message string results from the encoding of a data stream studied by a theorist, then the crypticity of the string is a rough measure of the difficulty of the theorist's task.

B.3 Organised Complexity

A different concern may be with the regularities of a string or a system rather than the description of all the components. This is at the basis of a notion introduced by Gell-Mann under the name of 'effective complexity'. It corresponds roughly to a notion of organisation evoked in the introduction of this section. Since we will refer to 'effective deep complexity' in a quite different sense in Chapter 6, it is preferable to avoid any ambiguity between these terms and refer to Gell-Mann's complexity as organised complexity.

Gell-Mann proposes to found complexity on the non-random aspects of a system or a string and to relate it to the description of its regularities. This kind of complexity is 'effective' or organised to the extent that it is not related to the description of a whole system or string but only to its regularities. Organised complexity is thus the length of a concise description of the regularities of an object (Gell-Mann, 56).

The description is achieved by a complex adaptive system. It separates regularities from random features in a given data stream and condenses regularities into a schema. Complexity can be defined as the length of the schema. These regularities are themselves of a certain type and inevitably partial. They depend on the goal pursued and on the level of detail up to which the object is to be described, or coarse graining. Grammar is an example of a schema for a language. The complexity of a language can thus be related to the length of a textbook describing its grammar. In other words, the organised complexity of an entity relative to a complex adaptive system that is observing it and constructing a schema is 'the length of a concise description of the entity's regularities identified in the schema' (ibid., 56).

Naturally one must assume that the observing system (it can be a human being) is efficient, otherwise the organised complexity of the entity will have more to do with the particular observer's capability than with the properties of the entity observed. However there is no general algorithm for picking out every kind of regularity (ibid., 57).

We can summarise this definition by:

$$\text{G-M}(s) \equiv \text{length of a concise description of the regularities of } s.$$

Organised complexity achieves its maximum for intermediate values of AIC. It is null for maximal AIC. In that case there is no regularity in the entity being described and the length of the schema summarising regularities is zero. Conversely, when AIC is near zero, the string is completely regular and displays total order. The length of a concise description of it must be very small.

B.4 A Comparison

B.4.1 Five notions of complexity

We have come across five notions in the previous section. We synthesise them below. We symbolise the operation through which *a* generates *b* by an arrow going from term *a* to term *b*: $a \rightarrow b$.

First is *AIC* or *Kolmogorov complexity*. It is the size in bits of the shortest program K(*s*) generating a finite string *s*. We symbolise it by the initial of its initiator's name:

$$\text{K:} \quad K(s) \rightarrow s$$

Second is organised complexity. It is the length of the shortest program G-M(*s*) generating s^* where s^* stands for the regularities in *s*:

$$\text{G-M:} \quad \text{G-M}(s) \rightarrow s^*$$

Third is *logical depth.* It is the execution time t required from a standard, universal computer to generate an object or string s from its minimal description or program K(s). Let us symbolise logical depth by B for Bennett, and use the subscript t to designate time:

$$\text{B:} \quad [\text{K}(s) \rightarrow s]_{t}$$

Fourth is *crypticity*. It is the execution time for generating a minimal K program from s. We say '*a*' minimal program because there exists no way, no algorithm for knowing the shortest program. Let us symbolise one of the shorter programs by K_{min} , and crypticity by B':

$$\text{B'}: \quad [s \rightarrow K_{min}]_{t}$$

Fifth, an additional notion of crypticity can be introduced, in a Gell-Mannian way so to speak. It is the execution time for generating a minimal G-M program from s^*. We denote such a program by G-M_{min} and this kind of crypticity by *G-M'*:

$$\textit{G-M'}: \quad [s^* \rightarrow \text{G-M}_{min}]_{t}$$

B.4.2 A graphical comparison of B, G-M and K

A crude sketch of the plausible variations of B, G-M and K is proposed in Figure 2.2. It is adapted from Gell-Mann. We combine in this graph the variations of K or AIC on the horizontal axis, of G-M on the left vertical axis and of B on the right vertical axis. The variations of G-M with respect to AIC or K have already been dealt with above. Let us consider logical depth B and AIC.

If the AIC of a message string is near zero because the message is completely regular then the execution time of the shortest program is certainly small [ex: 'PRINT 100 billion ones'] although the printing may take some time if the printer is not rapid. Now, if the string is random, with maximal AIC for a given message length, then going from the shortest program [ex: PRINT followed by the string] to printing out the string will require very little computation. Logical depth is again low.

As Gell-Mann points out, this situation resembles the way maximum organised complexity varies with AIC. Logical depth is smaller near both ends of the interval of variation but it can be sizable anywhere in the intermediate region between maximum order and maximum disorder. We follow freely Gell-Mann's reasoning for the rough sketch of depth in Figure 2.2.

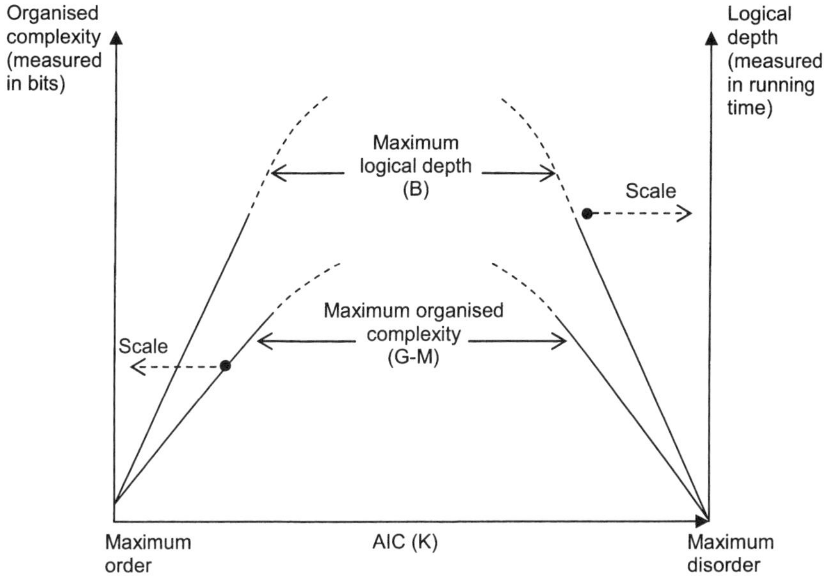

Figure 2.2 Organised complexity and largest possible logical depth crudely sketched as functions of algorithmic information content. Freely adapted from Gell-Mann (1995, 59, 104)

Depth can be large for values of AIC for which organised complexity is still small at both ends of the interval, near maximum order and maximum disorder. The curves pictured on the figure are only suggestive and result from a crude sketch.

B.4.3 A comparison of the relative sizes of K, B and G-M for some objects

We pursue the comparison of the relative sizes of K, B and G-M (organised complexity) for some objects in Table 2.4.

Table 2.4 A crude comparison of the relative sizes of K, B and G-M for some objects

	Crystal	π (10^9 digits)	Living entity	Gas (cloud, smoke)	Human society, economy
K	small	average -	average +	large	average +
B	small	average	large	small	very large
G-M	small	small	average to large	small	very large

This sketch is based on Delahaye (1995, 1997) for the first two lines and the first four columns of data input. We add to it a third line about G-M organised complexity and a fifth column, on human society and the economy. A crystal is a very redundant and ordered object. It can be described by a short and rapid program. For the first 10^9 digits of π, it is difficult to find out the shortest program, but every known short program for π implies a non-trivial computation time. It thus seems reasonable to consider that the logical depth of π is sizable, at least average. G-M for π is certainly small since there appears to be no regularity in it. For a living entity, K is certainly rather large but less than if it were totally random and disordered; B is certainly large because of the slow growth law. Saying something on the size of G-M may look debatable in the present state of knowledge. Are the regularities contained in the living known? The answer depends on the kind of regularities one considers relevant for describing the living. It may range from a rather limited size – when it is confined to the genetic program – to a very large size in case a more complete depiction of a human being would be the goal. It seems reasonable to consider than G-M ranges from average to large in this case. A gas or smoke, or a cloud, are prototypes of a random string. For them, K is at its maximum but B is certainly small since the minimal program is of the form 'Print *s*' and is as long as *s* itself. This minimal program is thus long but the computation it performs is not longer than that of a program generating a string of same length with zeros or ones only. Consequently it has low depth. G-M is also small because of the absence of regularities. Finally, for a human society or an economic system, K is not maximum since such a system is structured, whereas B and G-M are very large.

B.5 Concluding Remarks

Among the notions reviewed, it is the Gell-Mannian crypticity which appears the most suggestive for our purpose since it describes the theorist's tasks of modelling as the design of a concise representation of the regularities which are important enough to describe the behaviour of an involved phenomenon. However it has one important flaw. It assumes that how to depict *s*, that is, the initial situation, in a satisfactory or valid way, is not problematic and is taken for granted. But how to describe an object before expressing it as a string for which a short description is looked for is not a trivial task in our domain.

Moreover organisation remains a property of an objectal world, that is, external to the observer. The organisation of the relation between them is not envisaged. This brings us back to uncontrollability if we want to account for this relationship, and leaves wide open the issue of the depth of complexity.

This paragraph began with organisation and ends with information. Uncompressibility points to an irreducible barrier to simplification, that is, to modelling. Deep complexity in modelling denotes a lack of information transformed into a lack of knowledge, that is, a lack in the organisation of thought for which an anchoring is called for.

2.6 CONCLUSION

We inquired in this chapter on whether we could find a theoretical framework that would accommodate ADCX, anchored deep complexity. We discovered that several perspectives address issues roughly equivalent to deep complexity, in economics and in management science. In economics, the approach closest to deep complexity is Keynes's theory of uncertainty. However the anchoring of deep complexity remains an unanswered issue. It seems to have no equivalent or analogue in the literature. It calls for theorising ADCX in its own right. Although it is unusual to include a table in a conclusion, I can think of no clearer way for summarising the argument developed in this chapter. Table 2.5 synthesises it. The cells are either filled with a • or are empty. The • denotes the cases in which the components of ADCX defining the four columns are explicitly addressed. The cells are empty when the components are not addressed.

A second result is that to take deep complexity as an extension or a by-product of systems is a trap. The complex system perspective seems invariably to pull the analysis towards making complexity dependent on a prior characterisation of a system as a tacitly existing entity independent from the observer's mind.

Third, deep complexity is not restricted to radical uncertainty in economics and ill-structured problem-situations in management theory. Several other transdisciplinary forms exist. A relativity of complexity is strongly suggested by this diversity. Yet, a common feature is also suggested by the extension of uncontrollability. It is the relationship between what is the object of control and the controller, in which case it is the notion of a *complexity relation* that needs to be stressed and explored, rather than a complexity intrinsic to the external world.

The exploration of the relativity of deep complexity follows logically from it. It is a first step of the modelling of deep complexity undertaken in Part II.

Table 2.5 Synthesis of Chapter 2

ADCX	Intractability	Alternative framework	Substantive open-endedness	Procedural closure, anchoring
Irreducibility to hard science				
• Marshall	•			
• Eucken	•			
• *Régulation*	•	•	•	Floating eclecticism
• Georgescu-Roegen	•	•	•	
Radical uncertainty				
• Knight	•			
• Austrians	•	•		
• Keynes	•	•	•	Ordinary language
Complex economic systems				
• Quasi DCX (Arthur, ...)	•	•	•	'Under negotiation'
• Without DCX (Foster, ...)	•	•	•	
• Conceptual pluralism (Garnsey & McGlade)	•	•	•	Floating eclecticism
DCX in management theory	•	•	•	
Alternative transdisciplinary sources and forms				
• Indecomposability (Weaver)	•			
• Uncontrollability (Ashby)	•			
• Deterministic unpredictability (Von Neumann)	•			
• Incompressibility	•			

NOTES

1. J.M. Keynes (1936 [1965]), viii.
2. F.A. Hayek (1955), *The Counter-Revolution of Science. Studies in the Abuse of Reason*, Glencoe: Free Press, 105.
3. J.M. Keynes, op.cit, vii–viii.

4. F.A. Hayek (1967), *Studies in Philosophy, Politics and Economics*, Chicago: University of Chicago Press, 39.
5. All references to Keynes are the *Collected Writings* (1971–1979) denoted CW, with the exception of the *General Theory* (1936 [1965]).
6. Rosser (1991, 2000, 2004) provides a general view of the literature about conventional, object-based, complexity.
7. It is noticeable that Heiner refers in passim to Ashby's 1956 book - and to Wiener - but appears to ignore Ashby's 1958a article which comes close to the idea of the competence-difficulty gap (Heiner, 1983, 567, fn19). Heiner mentions that posing the problem in terms of competence and difficulty was suggested to him by A. Leijonhufvud (ibid., 562, fn 7).
8. In a later contribution, Ashby expressed a different view on complexity that will be documented in Chapter 3.
9. Kurt Gödel was asked by A.W. Burks, the editor of the *Theory of Self-Reproducing Automata*, to clarify the reference made by von Neumann to a theorem of Gödel 'that you can perform within the logical type that's involved everything that's feasible, but the question of whether something is feasible in a type belongs to a higher logical type' (von Neumann, 1966, 53). Gödel replied that he thought that von Neumann was referring to 'the fact that a complete epistemological description of a language A cannot be given in the same language A, because the concept of truth of sentences of A cannot be defined in A'. Gödel added that this theorem is the true reason for the existence of undecidable propositions in the formal systems containing arithmetic and that he formulated it explicitly not in his paper of 1931 but in 1934, whereas the same theorem had been proved by Tarski in 1933 (ibid., 55–56).

Part II

Modelling

We discovered in Part I that the notion of complexity which arose in our enquiry on the RISE (regime of interaction between the state and the economy) appears to have no complete equivalent in the available scientific literature on complexity, although irreducibility is a common and essential property of the forms of complexity that we reviewed, and especially of Keynes's perspective on uncertainty.

We learned three things in Chapter 2:

- ADCX (anchored deep complexity) is not accommodated in the literature on complexity, be it scientific or on complexity thinking more generally;
- DCX (deep complexity) is not explicitly reckoned and therefore not differentiated from non-deep complexity;
- CX (complexity) takes on several forms but is not characterised and theorised in its own right as a specific irreducibility proper.

The finding that the kind of ADCX that emerged in Part I has no satisfactory equivalent in the literature on complexity renders it necessary to inquire further into its meaning. The straightforward consequence is that before studying how to *anchor* deep complexity, we need to have a firm grip on *deep* complexity, and before we know deep complexity better, we need in turn to characterise *complexity* in its own right. These tasks define our modelling agenda. It will be developed in four chapters.

Chapter 3 is on the characterisation of the relativity of complexity considered in a generic way. It will reveal the interest of introducing a threshold. It will find support in safety management in industry and transport. The outcome will be to emphasise that complexity is best understood as a property of a situation rather than of an object.

Chapter 4 is on deep complexity as a product. It will be characterised in quantitative terms as a gap in epistemic and practical resources, and qualitatively as non-separability. This non-separability will be modelled via a generic recursive relationship between a generative process and its product, thus opening the way toward appraising deep complexity as a process.

Deep complexity designed as a process in Chapter 5 will lead to identify five organising principles whose combination makes up a notion of deep complexity accommodating the conditions imposed with anchored deep complexity in Part I, and symbolised by CX5.

This leaves open the issue of the scientific status and of the generalisability of CX5. It will be addressed in Chapter 6. Chapter 6 will take the issue further, with the need to complement CX5 with three operational principles whose combination with CX5 will deliver a final, sixth notion of deep complexity: CX6 or Effective Deep Complexity (EDCX). The generality of EDCX will follow from its overall property of being an alternative to the classical analytical framework. It will constitute an encompassing, alternative cognitive framework.

3. Relativity

Draw a distinction.
G. Spencer Brown (1969)[1]

3.1 INTRODUCTION

The object of this chapter is to put to work the first step of the agenda sketched out in the preface to Part II. It is to characterise complexity proper before we can shift to deep complexity in the next chapter, and to its anchoring in Chapters 5 and 6.

Part I revealed that complexity takes on a variety of forms of irreducibility, beyond the distinction which arose de facto between deep complexity and 'ordinary', non-deep complexity. Before we assess the value of this distinction in next chapters, we need to work out the meaning of the irreducibility that is constitutive of both notions. For this purpose, we will concentrate on irreducibility proper and assume that deep complexity and non-deep complexity are subsets of a generic notion of complexity plainly understood as irreducibility. This is an assumption which will have to be assessed later on. It will allow us to deal with 'complexity' in this chapter without being concerned with its possible depth. It will drive us to construct the basis from which deep complexity can arise, an issue that will be addressed in Chapter 4.

Therefore we undertake the study of the characteristic properties of complexity rather than taking complexity as a property of complex systems. As soon as we ask what is common to the forms of complexity underneath irreducibility, we find a mixture between the views which emphasise a subject-based as opposed to an object-based irreducibility, the views which rely on the combination of these aspects, and the views which seek a remedy in the measurement of irreducibility. However, none of them appears fully convincing. This apparently irreducible diversity about the properties of irreducibility suggests strongly that any theorising of complexity cannot avoid facing it head on from the start.

The strategy that we will follow will be to investigate the factors which jointly make up irreducibility rather than trying to establish a nomenclature of the properties of irreducibility which would be doomed to failure in the absence of a firm unified grounding on which to base it. Irreducibility needs to be endogenised via an understanding of how it is generated. The basis for doing this will be all the more effective as irreducibility is an unambiguous feature of it. The area of safety science and safety management offers such an opportunity. It is concerned with preventing accidents, notably major accidents or catastrophes in fields such as industry, transport, public health and environment. Irreducibility means here the impossibility to eliminate the risk of major accident. The clear-cut fashion in which irreducibility manifests itself in this domain will offer a basis for assessing its bearing for other activities, notably economics.

It will lead us to establish a twofold relativity of complexity, a relativity based on a plurality of elementary factors and dimensions first, and on the problem-situations, thus making complexity totally independent from any particular disciplinary framework. The term 'relativity' denotes that complexity is not absolute and intrinsic to objects or subjects. Indeed we will argue in this chapter that for complexity to depend only on objects would necessitate neutralising several other relevant dimensions. Yet one can observe that most of the literature on complex systems still relies on an object-based notion of complexity. This is clear from our presentation in the last chapter. We wish to show in the present chapter that this is too limited in the sense that it presupposes that very specific conditions are met.

The idea that complexity is not intrinsic to objects does not mean that it would therefore depend entirely on the observing or designing subject. Several dimensions are at stake and need to be made explicit. Among them is the subject. But it does not boil down to mere subjectivity as will be argued below. Then it is appropriate to speak of the relativity of complexity to a plurality of dimensions.

This chapter contains six sections. In section 3.2 we explain how complexity is not intrinsic to objects. This raises the issue of subjectivity addressed in section 3.3. Measuring complexity is usually considered as an antidote to subjectivity. However, we argue in section 3.4 that measurement leads to a kind of useless universal irreducibility if it is not complemented by a threshold discriminating between complexity and non-complexity. The consequence is the need for explaining how a threshold may be built. This endogenisation of irreducibility is undertaken in section 3.5 through a detour via the field of safety management. It leads to highlighting eight dimensions of complexity (section 3.6), all of which are necessary in order to characterise a situation, which brings to an ending point this journey from the complexity of objects to the complexity of situations (section 3.7).

3.2 COMPLEXITY NOT INTRINSIC TO OBJECTS

W. Ross Ashby initiated a fruitful reflection on the roles of subject and object in the attribution of complexity, at the Sixth World Congress of Cybernetic Medicine in Naples in 1972 (Ashby, 1973). Ashby's contribution stands out in this domain and offers a basis for starting our enquiry. Although Heinz von Foerster pioneered it for systems, it is Ashby who first illustrated the issue with respect to complexity proper in a contribution which went almost unnoticed in the literature on complexity, with the notable exception of John Casti.

In an attempt to clarify the meaning of the word 'complex' applied to systems, Ashby proposed to measure the degree of complexity by the quantity of information required to describe a system (the vital system in his own domain), and to compare the complexity of some given object, say the brain of a sheep, to two different operators, say a butcher and a neurophysiologist. He wrote:

> To the neurophysiologist the brain, as a feltwork of fibers and a soup of enzymes, is certainly complex; and equally the transmission of a detailed description of it would require much time. To a butcher the brain is simple, for he/she has to distinguish it from only about thirty other 'meats', so not more than $\log_2 30$, i.e. about 5 bits, are involved. (Ashby, 1973, 1)

He went on to comment: 'This method admittedly makes a system's complexity purely *relative to a given observer*; it rejects the attempt to measure an absolute, or intrinsic, complexity; but this acceptance of complexity as something in the eye of the beholder is, in my opinion, the only workable way of measuring complexity' (ibid.).

This statement suggests in a very simple way that complexity cannot be viewed as a property intrinsic to an object. Yet this simplicity is only apparent. We will show why this is so in the next sections. Meanwhile we must notice that closely related views have been developed by other authors after Ashby.

Among them are Robert Rosen (1977, 1987, 1991) and John Casti (1979, 1994, 1997). For Rosen complexity is a function of the number of ways

> in which we are able (or desire) to interact with a system. Indeed ... *any* system can be made to appear complex in this sense. A system like a stone typically is regarded as simple, because we interact with it in only a few ways. For a geologist, who multiplies the number of ways in which he interacts with a stone, such a system can appear infinitely complex. Thus complexity is indeed a function of the number of ways available to interact with a system. (Rosen, 1977, 229)

More specifically, a stone is a simple 'system' in Rosen's view because we typically interact with it in only a few ways and, basically, a single mode of description is sufficient to describe these ways. Organisms are complex because 'we can interact with them at many levels, and describe these interactions in many different ways' (Rosen, 1991, 477). In this conception, a system is complex if two conditions are met. First it is possible to interact with it significantly in many distinct ways. Second, each of these ways 'requires a different mode of description of the system to encompass it' (ibid.). A system is complex if it is impossible to obtain one single valid description of it: there exist more than one description of the system and these descriptions cannot be reduced to one. Systems complexity is thus made to depend on the number of modes of interaction with a system and on the number of different descriptions to which these modes of interaction give rise. In Rosen's terms, complexity is a function 'not only of a system's interactive capabilities, but of our own' (Rosen,1985, 322).

Such a relativistic view of system complexity is also espoused by J. Casti. Casti starts from considering some system N and an observer who interacts with it. Here the term observer refers simply to some other system which interacts in some way with the target system N. Casti's claim is that 'the complexity of the system N as seen by the observer is directly proportional to the number of [...] *inequivalent descriptions*' that the observer can generate (Casti, 1994, 276). Two descriptions are inequivalent if they cannot be transformed one to the other by a simple relabelling of the variables used to formulate them. Like Rosen, Casti uses the stone example. A 'stone on the street' is a much more complex object to a geologist than to an unskilled observer because of the larger number of inequivalent descriptions available to the former. The unskilled observer can 'weigh the stone, throw it, break it apart, kick it – and that's about it' while the geologist can 'perform various sorts of chemical analyses on the stone, use carbon-dating techniques on it, x-ray it and so on' (Casti, 1997, 22–23). The complexity of the stone is thus clearly a relative matter, 'depending on the nature of the system with which the stone is interacting' (Casti, 1994, 277).

At this stage it seems difficult to escape from relating complexity to an actor whatever the name we use to state it. Csanyi (1989) evokes semiotic complexity, Vallée (1990) the grain of observation and the selected resolution level, Salthe (1993) an actor-related complexity, Gell-Mann (1995) the actor's choice about coarse-graining.

3.3 THE ISSUE OF SUBJECTIVITY

A lesson from the last section is that in general complexity cannot be crudely dependent on a given object. For this to be true other variables must be neutralised. One of these pertains to the actor or operator. But this should not symmetrically entail a sort of crude subjectivity, notwithstanding Ashby's statement that complexity is 'purely relative to a given observer'. It is no surprise that we find on this issue the same variety of standpoints as appeared in the previous chapter. Measurement is highlighted in some conceptions, while the emphasis is on the interaction with the observing system or on judgement in others. In the quest to avoid crude subjectivity, while not returning to crude objectivity, one finds a traditional pathway through the conception and use of a measure of complexity.

All the authors quoted above introduce it. We will make it explicit below and will comment on it in the next paragraph. However another pathway to control individual subjectivity exists. It pertains to the reference to the field of activity. We will show that it is necessarily present in Ashby's definition of complexity if we want to make sense of it, but it seems never to be explicitly dealt with, to our knowledge. We will examine this dimension below, after having addressed the issue of measurement.

3.3.1 Measurement

The definition of complexity, its measurement and the question of how to deal with non-reducibility are often intertwined. Let us recall that for Ashby complexity is the length of a description of an object. But he does not use it in the absolute. His reasoning is comparative, which is another form of relativity. Thus the brain of a sheep is more complex to a neurophysiologist than to a butcher. In Rosen and Casti's conceptions, a stone is more complex to a geologist than to an unskilled observer. We may go on in this vein: any given object is more complex to a skilled, expert operator than to an unskilled, non-expert one.

It thus seems to follow that if skill is positively linked to the number of distinctions one is able to draw about a given phenomenon of interest, then the more you are skilled, the more complex the phenomenon is likely to be to you. However, we will show later on in this chapter that even this apparently sound inference has no general validity. It must be qualified because it rests on a partial view of the relativity of complexity. One must complement it with the level of aspiration.

Relating the complexity attached to a phenomenon to an observing or designing actor immediately entails the question of subjectivity and of the remedies in order to avoid it or to control it in scientific activity. Indeed this question is often intertwined with the issues of measurement of complexity, of its definition and of how to deal with non-reducibility. Rosen and Casti provide again neat illustrations of this.

Rosen states that two questions arise from complexity thus understood: '(1) Is there one class of interactions, and consequently one mode of system description, from which all the others can be derived (the problem of reductionism), (2) Is there any kind of measure of interactive capacity which will allow us to define complexity in other than subjective terms?' (Rosen, 1991, 477). Addressing reduction, Rosen relates complexity to 'the idea of many non-equivalent subsystems; i.e. modes of description or encoding which cannot be transformed or reduced to one another' (ibid., 322–323). It is this multiplicity of descriptions which 'precludes any one class of subsystems, or any one mode of system analysis, from being universally valid over all system properties. Indeed, the lack of such a universally valid strategy for system analysis is but an alternate definition of complexity' (ibid., 322).

A tentative answer to Rosen's questions is proposed by Casti. It is inspired by Rosen's theory of modelling. Casti relates the complexity level to the number of equivalence classes that an observer creates in the process of coding informal observations into a formal language, using symbols and syntax. In Casti's words this is a 'necessary – but far from sufficient' condition for 'complexity to become a science' (Casti, 1994, 277–278). An additional constraint comes from the necessity 'for any such formalization to respect the fact that complexity is a subjective concept'. And, given the fact that no system is isolated, it is actually 'other systems like observers or controllers that are responsible for deciding upon the particular formalization to be used' and it is these systems 'that ultimately render the verdict as to what is and isn't complex' (ibid., 278). This is about the end of Casti's book on complexification. Although we would hardly disagree with the importance attributed to the observer, the issue of making subjectivity and science compatible seems to remain broadly unanswered. Can the judgement on complexity or non-complexity be the outcome of mere subjectivity? Can such a question be answered satisfactorily without a theory – or an encoding, in Rosen's terms – of the behaviour of the observing system? Although these authors acknowledge the epistemic character of complexity, they appear to avoid any explicit reference to the behaviour of the cognising system and thus leave the issue unanswered. These considerations clearly call for an investigation about what is meant by the relativity to a given observer – is it mere subjectivity? – about what a satisfactory knowledge consists of, and about what insight can be gained from measurement.

3.3.2 The Field of Activity

The need to refer to the field of activity as a way to control individual subjectivity arises from the incomplete remedy to subjectivity that measurement provides. Measurement does not preclude authors who propose it from refering to the role of observers in complexity. This is clear from last paragraph for Ashby, Rosen and Casti. Gell-Mann and others relate complexity to the level of coarse-graining chosen by the observer. Given these limitations of measure as a remedy to subjectivity, how does the reference to the field of activity come in? It occurs quite naturally in the wake of Ashby's definition.

Ashby compares two observers (a butcher and a neurophysiologist) of the same object (the brain of a sheep) who have the same purpose of depicting it. Both Rosen and Casti portray similar pairs of observers comprising a non-expert and an expert, for example, an unskilled observer and a geologist, who are supposed to describe a stone. Notice that although the definitions of complexity differ between Ashby, for whom complexity is the length of a description, and Rosen and Casti, for whom complexity is a number of different (Rosen) or inequivalent (Casti) descriptions, these differences have no consequence on the common claim that complexity is not a property of the objects to be described but of the observers. Then what are the differences between the observers? Rosen and Casti oppose an unskilled observer to a skilled, scientific observer. Ashby's example looks more interesting because no such obvious opposition is introduced.

In the absence of any explicit qualification made by Ashby, the implication follows that the butcher and the neurophysiologist are 'normal', representative operators in their respective fields of activity. They are portrayed in the postures of what common sense expects a butcher and a neurophysiologist to do in their ordinary activities. Both observers are skilled in their respective fields of activity. Ashby's butcher is an average, trained butcher in the field of butchery, and his neurophysiologist is an average, competent scientist in the field of neurophysiology.

It is what is commonly expected, in terms of required quantity of information, from standard observation in butchery and in neurophysiology, rather than the individual observers themselves, which differentiates between complexity to the representative butcher and complexity to the representative neurophysiologist. Thus, we started in this example with a common object, a unique purpose and observers who are similar from the standpoint of competency. We do not need to rely on their personal choices or states of mind to differentiate between complexities. We can avoid pure subjectivity through adding an explicit consideration of the field of activity and its associated standard of performance to the above three dimensions. Beyond the element of subjectivity attached to deciding on a purpose, the only remaining subjectivity arises from the functioning of the community of actors in a given field at a given time. Whoever does not abide by the standards is likely to be sanctioned sooner or later by the community, or at least, to have trouble in staying within it, be they a butcher or a scientist.

3.3.3 Against Loose Complexity

At this stage, there is a rationale for introducing the level of aspiration and satisficing. It originates in severe limitations of the notions of complexity presented above.

First, what happens to Ashby's complexity when we reason within a given field instead of considering two different fields? Let us consider two observers belonging to a given field. In Ashby's conception they cannot but be equally representative and competent. Therefore the quantities of information they use to describe a given object must be similar. Then complexity cannot be compared: the object cannot be more complex to any observer. Only two different objects taken in the same field could result in one being more complex than the other, to a similar degree to both observers. It is a case in which complexity would be related to objects, which runs counter to the argument. Ashby's view is therefore incomplete on this account. Rosen and Casti's argument does not avoid this impasse. Since it is based on a difference of skilling, it can be extended to two observers in the same field, one being skilled, the other unskilled. According to their definitions, a given object always appears more complex to the skilled observer than to the unskilled. But if we consider equally competent observers describing a given object in a given field, are they bound to find it equally complex? It does not seem so, for an additional source of differentiation can come from their levels of aspiration. And different levels of aspiration for a given observer of an object account as well for variations in complexity. But it is not the end of the story. A given level of aspiration is not always fully actualised. Satisficing is not automatically achieved. Then, apart from the polar trivial cases in which the level of aspiration is 100 per cent achieved or not achieved, there arises the question of what degree of achievement is good enough for cases in-between these two extremes. Satisficing can be either purely subjective or dependent on a standard of operation in a given field. If a goal in science is to reduce the length of descriptions, then can a description be reduced to a satisfactory length? What is a satisfactory or satisficing length?

3.4 MEASUREMENT AND IRREDUCIBILITY

Irreducibility is congenital to complexity. But it presents a challenge in two ways. The first difficulty originates from the attempts to avoid subjectivity through designing a measure for complexity. It will be shown that this is disappointing since it entails ignoring practically the very idea of irreducibility. The second difficulty is almost opposite. It relies on a loosely defined notion of universal irreducibility. Then the matter looks as if we were condemned to choose between the Charybdis of complexity without irreducibility and the Scylla of irreducibility everywhere. We will conclude this section with considerations on the pitfalls which should be avoided in theorising complexity and on the need to include additional dimensions in it.

3.4.1 The Irony of Measurement

From the characterisations proposed by Rosen and Casti, it seems that whenever two or more descriptions of a system can be reduced to only one or can be made equivalent, then complexity no longer holds by definition. Complexity is non-reducibility. Yet none of the definitions mentioned above deals explicitly with irreducibility. This notion appears only in a programmatic way in the first part of the interrogation set out by Rosen. And yet none of these definitions can do without introducing some form of irreducibility.

It is either comparative irreducibility (object A is more complex than object B to an observer if its description requires more information – Ashby – or requires a larger number of different or inequivalent descriptions – Rosen and Casti) or absolute irreducibility in an abstract sense (complexity is the length of the shortest program describing the regularities of a system – Gell-Mann). In the comparative sense, what is pertaining to A cannot be reduced to B, and in the absolute sense there is supposedly no shorter program.

A synthetic view in a comparative setting is proposed by Duncan Foley in his introductory chapter to Peter Albin's book:

> The intuitive concept of complexity that lies behind most measures is that simple systems are easy to describe with a small amount of information, while the description of a complex system requires a large amount of information. This idea can be unpacked in several different contexts, which turn out to be closely related. We can, for example, measure the complexity of a system by the size of the smallest computer program capable of describing it. More complex systems require larger programs. Or we could measure the complexity of the system by the computer resources required to represent it, in time and memory. A more complex system requires more time and memory to describe than a simple one. Or we could measure the complexity of a system by the richness of the language required to describe it. A simple system can be described by a minimally structured language, while a complex one requires a language rich in possibilities. (Foley in Albin, 1998, 41)

Behind the apparent simplicity of defining the intuitive concept of complexity above is the question of what 'required' stands for. We are told that something is more complex because it requires more information, and so on, to be described. But how do we know that 'more' is required? How is the level, amount or size of what is required determined? Is there an accepted criterion or a standard of what is required? If so, is it of such a nature that it is given and does not necessitate to be explained? If we do not know how the required level is determined, how can we make sense of such a measure of complexity for our own theoretical purposes? The only difference introduced here between simplicity and complexity is the difference between a small and a large amount of information. But in both cases the description can be given. This intuitive concept of complexity results in equating complexity with complication since it implicitly comprises a satisfactory description. This definition cannot account for situations which, instead of being such that 'the description of a complex system requires a large amount of information' (in the first sentence of the quotation above), are situations in which a *satisfactory* description of a complex system requires *such* a large amount of information *that it cannot be performed*. In this sense there exists a threshold between simplicity or complication on the one hand, and complexity on the other hand. This threshold of irreducibility is absent in the comparison made along a quantitative continuum or along the scale envisaged by Albin.

Albin's theory of the complexity of social and economic systems is based on the sophistication of the machines needed to describe or represent them. It is inspired by Noam Chomsky's theory of formal languages. The potential complexity of a language generated by a grammar in Chomsky's hierarchy depends on the restrictions imposed on the procedures for producing new words: the more they are restricted, the less complex the language is. Four levels of increasing linguistic complexity are thus distinguished: regular languages first, then context-free languages, then context-sensitive languages and finally unrestricted languages. Albin transplants this four-step taxonomy to computational complexity, to non-linear dynamical systems, and to cellular automata. In computational complexity, complexity ranges from a finite automaton (computers with no memory) to computers with fixed-size memory, then to computers with variable-size memory and finally to universal computers (Turing machines). In non-linear dynamical systems, complexity ranges from systems with a unique globally attracting equilibrium state, to systems with a periodic attractor, then to systems with a chaotic attractor, and then to social and economic systems. Finally, taking a cellular automaton as a simplified representation of general nonlinear dynamical systems, the complexity of cellular automata increases from a first level in which automata evolve to uniform states from arbitrary initial conditions, to a second level in which they evolve to periodic patterns, to a third level in which they evolve to non-repeating complicated patterns and to a fourth level in which they evolve to propagating irregular structures. These third and fourth levels represent the boundaries and barriers to rationality studied in Albin's book.

In this schema the qualitative hierarchy of a system is therefore defined as its position within a four-step hierarchy. Nevertheless, however sophisticated it is, this qualitative taxonomy of complexity degrees contains no explicit threshold and seemingly does not make it possible to answer the questions asked above without specifying the meaning of 'satisfactory'. This absence of a threshold is also detrimental to the operational usefulness of the measures of complexity proposed by Ashby, Rosen, Casti and Gell-Mann.

We represent the various measures of complexity evoked above in Figure 3.1 in a way enabling us to compare them with a quantitative threshold of complexity. Variations of complexity can be read on the vertical axis in terms of the particular selected measures. It is the length of a description for Ashby (L) and Gell-Mann (L'), the number n of inequivalent descriptions for Rosen and Casti, and a broad notion of amount of information (I) required for description for Albin and Foley. We include in the terms 'quantity of information' both information measured in bits and the number n of inequivalent descriptions since there is a positive relationship between n and the information required to describe the phenomenon to which n applies. Notice that all measures, except Gell-Mann's effective complexity, are expressed in comparative terms. The aim pursued in Figure 3.1 is heuristic. It is to compare *L*, *L'*, *n* and *I* with the threshold *T*, not to compare these measures mutually. Measures are in units of information and vary along a vertical scale. The lower limit is 1. It defines full reducibility. Irreducibility may start with 2 in the absolute. It is the inferior limit of effective complexity *L'* since it is 'not simple' but left unspecified by Gell-Mann. These magnitudes have otherwise no specified upper limit: they can be very large and even tend to infinity. The constraints we impose on these magnitudes are summarised below (with all symbols explained in the legend of Figure 3.1):

$$1 < L, n, I \leq +\infty$$
$$2 \leq L', T \leq +\infty$$
$$L_A^a < L_B^b$$
$$n_{A'} > n_{B'}$$
$$I_s < I_\ell$$
$$T_1 < T_2 < T_3$$

Every one of these measures has to be compared to some cutting-point criterion. This particular threshold discriminating effectively between non-complexity and complexity for the individual or community operator is a priori undetermined. It is attached to the particular level of reduction that the operator considers good enough. It can be set at any level larger than or equal to 2 since potential complexity starts with the impossibility to reduce to less than 2. Actual complexity depends on the level at which the threshold is set. We will devote the next section to explaining it. Here we simply need to point out that this actual level can define three configurations: it can be lower than the lowest of the measures (T_1). It can be above the highest measure (T_3). And it can be at an intermediary level (T_2).

If the relevant level is T_1, then there is complexity in all cases. If it is T_2, the comparative measures discriminate effectively between non complexity and complexity. Gell-Mann's 'effective complexity' *L'* is effectively complex in the sense advocated here whenever $L' \geq T$ (it is arbitrarily set at the level of T_1 in Figure 3.1). Finally everything is non-complex when the threshold is set at a level T_3 higher than any of the measures.

The difficulty arising with these measures is immediately apparent when they are confronted with the threshold. The measures are consistent only for the T_2 case. Everything is complex with T_1, everything is non-complex with T_3. These measures thus fail to provide a general way of discriminating between complexity and non-complexity. They leave this distinction unspecified. Gell-Mann seems to admit it when he writes that 'Simplicity refers to the absence (or near-absence) of complexity' (1995, 27), and leaves the issue of their distinction unanswered. Yet it would seem difficult to assert that a short description can be complex if the word 'complex' is to retain any meaning. How could one make sense of equating complexity with simplicity? Yet this possibility exists in these definitions, in the absence of any discriminating point or threshold between complexity and non-complexity.

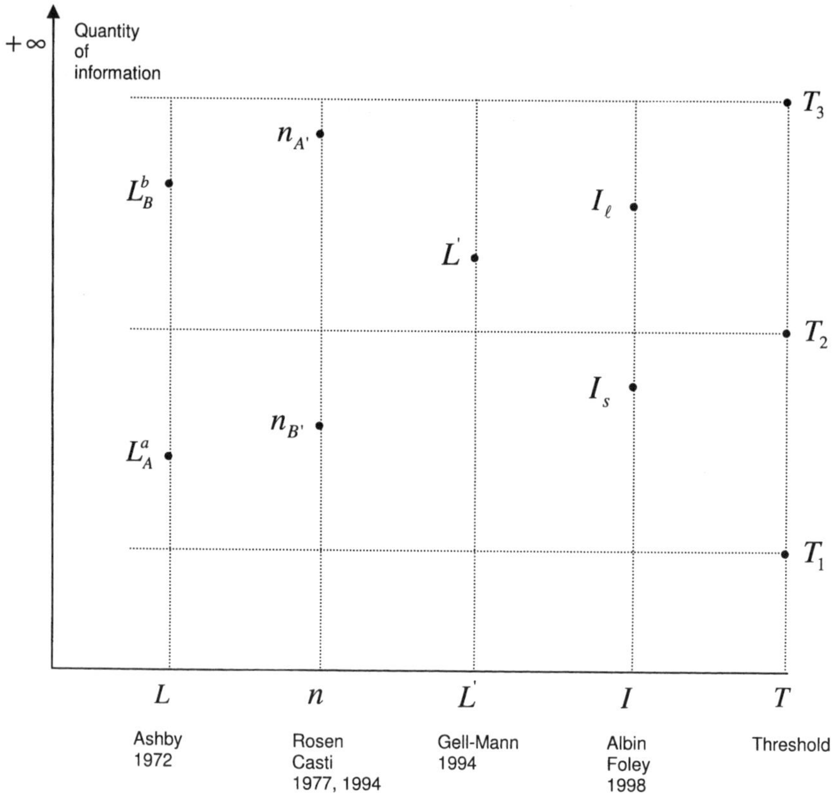

Legend: *L*, *L'*: length of description
A, *B*: competent operators in their respective fields a and b
n: number of inequivalent descriptions
A': skilled operator
B': unskilled operator
I: amount of information required for description (*s*: small; *ℓ*: large)
Ti (*i*=1, 2, 3): size of threshold between non-complexity and complexity

Figure 3.1 Measures of complexity, and thresholds of complexity compared

Complexity measured without specified irreducibility thus leads to an inconsistency. Irreducibility can hardly be measured along a kind of quantitative continuum, in the way temperature measures heat. One cannot avoid specifying a cutting point. A way to solve this plain inconsistency is to explicitly introduce a threshold. This threshold cannot but be based on an explicit recognition of the actor's role. It is rendered possible through referring to a level of aspiration and to satisficing. Then genuine complexity is an irreducibility to a satisficing level of reduction. Non-complexity signals the achievement of a satisficing situation for the observer.

The irony of the proposed measures of complexity is that they cannot prevent from falling into a sort of loose universal complexity, whereas they are aimed at bringing accuracy and rigour in all cases, and objectivity in cases in which subjectivity is deemed damaging.

3.4.2 Universal Irreducibility is Useless

Universal complexity is the expression used by physicist Jean-Marc Lévy-Leblond to denounce the uselessness of having complexity or irreducibility everywhere. It is worth summarising his argumentation because it illustrates *a contrario* the point we have already made on the need to define a threshold derived from a level of aspiration. Lévy-Leblond relates the complexity of a system to the non-linear interactions between different levels in a hierarchical and heterogeneous structure. He mentions that the term 'intricacy' might better describe these features. But then, according to him, any real system, in physics and in biology, is complex. There is therefore a danger of loose, uninformative universality, and of triviality in the use of such a notion of complexity. Yet one of the achievements of physics has been 'to treat large areas of the universe *as if they were not complex*, through linear and/or homogenous schemas which are deprived from the circularity and/or heterogeneity constituting complexity' (Lévy-Leblond, 1991, 129). He adds that although the description of the physical world naturally evokes its complexity, its theoretical analysis avoids it. Physics is based on a deliberate effort to avoid dealing with complexity as such. This avoidance is closely related to the mathematisation of theoretical physics. In other words, although complexity may be a general standpoint, it has little usefulness in the scientific practice of physics.

This argument is not new and one would hardly disagree with being doubtful about the usefulness of loose, universal complexity. We will develop a notion of restricted complexity in the next sections and yet end with a result opposite to Lévy-Leblond's claim. Our claim will be to deal with the world as if it were complex first, and then, simplify whenever it is possible.

However, rejecting universal complexity does not imply that non-complex, simple schemes are always satisfactory. An explicit assumption about the level of aspiration needs to be introduced here. It enables one to show that Lévy-Leblond stands within a particular limit. The particular level of aspiration of the physics he describes is not to depict the complexity of the world, it is to depict regularities by means of analytically tractable tools and to test these depictions. Although reality remains partially perceived, this knowledge remains good enough given the standards of the discipline. Quantum physics illustrates it: although there is much debate on what quantum reality is, its formalisms provide powerful tools of prediction (Mugur-Schächter, 1997). Thus complexity or its absence is highly dependent on the level of aspiration within a given field or discipline, beyond the factors already mentioned above.

There are indeed two aspects in Lévy-Leblond's criticism of the scientific discourse on complexity. One is against the very notion of complexity and the universality surrounding it. This would include the idea of intricacy proposed by him. The other aspect is rooted in the scientific practice of physics which consists of striving toward reductionism, and is performing well. I would argue that these two aspects complement one another and fit well with what I develop here, although at first sight the contrary may appear to be the case. Indeed there is no surprise in relation to the first aspect. However useful complexity – defined as the length of a description, the size of a computer program, the size of resources in time, the number of inequivalent descriptions of an object, or even intricacy – may be in the respective fields in which these definitions are elaborated, its operationality remains quite problematic in our case. We must find a way of distinguishing complexity and non-complexity unequivocally. We need a restricted notion of complexity. As regards the second aspect, one should not overlook the factors which make the reductionist strategy acceptable in the field on which Lévy-Leblond concentrates, that is, physics. It is a particular field of activity, a particular observer community with a particular purpose (depiction and prediction) and a particular level of aspiration (depiction of regularities tested against empirical evidence). Outcomes appear satisfactory or not through their screening with these criteria. In another field or discipline, things may go differently because of different purposes, different levels of aspiration and methods for assessing the acceptability or satisficing character of a situation. This will be illustrated abundantly in the next section. Then we are left with the question of how to define an operational notion of complexity.

It is worth noticing that from the same premise about the uselessness of unrestricted, loosely defined, universal complexity, Lévy-Leblond and the conception advocated here end with opposite conclusions. This is quite understandable once the fields of activity and the levels of aspiration and of satisfactory performance are taken into account. Levy-Leblond's claim that non-complex tools work in physics for a broad class of issues cannot but be associated to a properly adjusted level of aspiration. It might no longer be true for a different, more ambitious level of aspiration. I explained in Chapter 1 why I encountered irreducibility about the RISE given the level of aspiration imposed in the economics field. Then irreducibility is a real issue.

3.4.3 The Need for a Cutting Point

Our exploration of the relativity of complexity has driven us to introduce several dimensions thus far. The issue of how to avoid crude objectivity led us to introduce the operator's purpose and skill. But then crude subjectivity had to be avoided. We found a solution in the reference to the field of activity and its standards of operation. This, together with the limitations of measurement, rendered it necessary to take explicitly into account a level of aspiration and whether a situation good enough for the operator, in a given field of activity, was achieved or not. We showed that these notions were alluded to (level of coarse-graining by Gell-Mann, 'required' level by the other authors) but were never addressed as an issue in their own right. Yet this is a key factor since it signals the possibility of not achieving what is 'required', that is, of not having irreducibility to a satisfactory level of reduction.

In these examples, the level of aspiration is never mentioned. It does not play any limiting role. It is such that it is always possible to achieve a satisfactory description or analysis. This is implicit in Ashby and his followers' presentations for whom complexity merely entails lengthier descriptions. Lévy-Leblond neutralises complexity in physics through adjusting the level of aspiration. This renders it possible to achieve a satisfactory outcome given the operating standard, once the level of aspiration has been adjusted or reduced to what the available method and tools in a discipline make it possible to tackle. Objects which cannot be tackled are left out or removed to the 'all other things equal' category. In economics, this amounts to leaving these objects unstudied although it is common to refer to a temporary exclusion, making a possible future inclusion depend on a hypothetical improvement of the analysis.

These considerations point clearly to the need to include both a level of aspiration and satisficing in the design of a threshold between non-complexity and complexity. In conclusion, the operational relevance of a complexity measure depends on the threshold. It remains to explain how this threshold is designed or, in other terms, to endogenise it.

3.5 IRREDUCIBILITY ENDOGENISED

3.5.1 A Detour via Safety Management

Given an operator purposefully addressing an object of interest in a given field of activity with a given level of aspiration, the outcome is satisfactory or satisficing whenever the level of aspiration is actually achieved. This means that in this case it is possible to reduce the difficulty of achieving the particular level of aspiration to a satisficing level. This defines reducibility and irreducibility *a contrario*.

We showed the necessity of introducing a criterion (threshold or level of aspiration) against which the difficulty of performing a task can be qualified unambiguously as complex or not complex. We thus go beyond the definitions of complexity proposed above since this shift points to the need to explain how this criterion arises. Endogenising complexity therefore calls for a behavioural setting building on what is of value in Ashby and other authors, which can be summarised by saying that the operator's role must be made explicit and at the same time not reduced to plain subjectivity.

In Ashby's example of the brain of a sheep, the task to be performed by a butcher is non-complex given the standard level of aspiration in the field of butchery. It must be noticed that the task retained is mere description. According to Ashby, description is complex for the neurophysiologist. We showed that this outcome presupposes a level of aspiration in neurophysiology remaining above what can be achieved. But the outcome might be non-complex if the level of aspiration were lower.

At this stage, coming back to the RISE, one may wonder whether it was found complex because of an excessive requirement due to an overly ambitious level of aspiration. We propose to address this issue through examples taken in a domain combining the same factors as the ones singled out above, but in a possibly clearer way due to the very clear-cut nature of the issues. This domain is safety. Two fields stand out in this respect, industrial high-risk technologies and transport. A sub-domain pertains to the precautionary principle. These examples will suggest the necessity to introduce an additional distinction, the one between cognitive satisficing and practical satisficing.

Safety management and safety science provide possibly the best examples of domains in which irreducibility – the impossibility to eliminate major accidents totally – is a permanent key issue. The literature in this domain is recent and growing. It includes notably Perrow (1984 [1999a]), Reason (1993, 1998), Rasmussen (1997), Rasmussen and Svedung (2000), Paté-Cornell (1993), Amalberti (1996, 1997, 1999, 2001), Vaughan (1996) and Hollnagel (2004). It shows that several levels for addressing this issue are present with their corresponding models, going bottom-up from the front-line operators and human-machine interactions to the workplace level, to the organisational level, to the socio-technical system level, to the regulatory level, and ultimately to the level of society. In the following, I select three representative contributions. They are those by Charles Perrow at the system level, by James Reason on organisational accidents, and by René Amalberti on human-machine ergonomic interactions. I summarise them and will reflect on the common lesson for our purpose that can be extracted from these studies.

3.5.2 Normal Accidents

In his book, *Normal Accidents: Living with High-Risk Technologies* published in 1984 with a second edition in 1999, Charles Perrow, an organisational theorist, advanced the proposition that accidents are inevitable in complexly interacting and tightly coupled systems like nuclear power plants, chemical plants, aircraft, and so on, regardless of the skills of their operators, managers and designers. The term 'normal accident' – or its equivalent 'system accident' – is meant to signal that it is inherent to systems having certain properties arising from a particular combination of the interactions between their components and the technical coupling. The proposition follows from it that most high-risk systems have characteristics that make accidents in them inevitable and even "normal". Hence the idea that accidents cannot be eliminated totally, although the goal is to eliminate them. This constitutes a clear instance of irreducibility. However, it is necessary to go into a more detailed presentation of Perrow's argument in order to avoid possible confusions. We will mention some basic definitions first, then introduce interactions and coupling, and finally combine them and focus on the potential for normal accident of interactive complexity with tight coupling.

A. Definitions

Accidents are distinguished from incidents on the basis of levels in the system. Systems are divided into four levels of increasing aggregation: units, parts, subsystems and systems. Incidents pertain to damage to units or parts. Accidents involve damage to subsystems or the system as a whole. Both incidents and accidents affect or even stop production. There are two types of accidents, 'normal' and, one might say, 'non-normal'. The former involve the unanticipated interaction of multiple failures while the latter involve one or more component failures (units, parts or subsystem) that are linked in an anticipated sequence. Perrow calls them component failure accidents. Both accidents stem from component failures. But a normal, or system accident differs from a component failure accident in that the interaction between several failures is unexpected, even incomprehensible to the operators, the managers and the designers of the system.

B. Interactions and complexity

In the normal accident model, complexity resides in the character of interactions among the components of the system (operators at every level, parts, and procedures). A more detailed view of the system is conveyed by the notion of the DEPOSE system (design, equipment, procedures, operators, supplies and materials, and environment). These interactions are either linear or 'complex', depending both on the way they appear in the sequences of production and maintenance and on how they affect the operators. Linear interactions are 'those interactions of one component in the DEPOSE system with one or more components that precede or follow it immediately in the sequence of production' or in the maintenance sequence. They are in expected and familiar sequence and are quite perceptible even if unplanned. Complex interactions are those in which components can interact outside of the familiar production and maintenance sequences, in unplanned and unexpected ways, which renders the interactions 'either not visible or not immediately comprehensible' (Perrow, 1999a, 77–78). These notions are detailed in Table 3.1.

Table 3.1 Complex and non-complex interactions compared (adapted from C. Perrow, 1999a, 88)

Complex interactions and systems	Non-complex interactions and systems
Proximity (tight spacing of equipment, proximate production steps)	Special segregation (equipment spread out, segregated production steps)
Many common-mode connection of components not in production sequence	Common-mode connections limited to power supply and environment; majority of dedicated connections
Limited isolation of failed components (interconnected subsystems)	Easy isolation of failed components (segregated subsystems)
Personnel specialisation limiting awareness of interdependencies	Little personnel specialisation
Limited substitution of supplies and materials	Extensive substitution of supplies and materials
Unfamiliar or unintended feedback loops	Few unfamiliar or unintended feedback loops
Multiple and potentially interacting control parameters	Few, single purpose and segregated control parameters
Indirect or inferential information sources	Direct, on-line information sources
Limited understanding of some process	Extensive understanding of all processes

A few comments about Table 3.1 are needed. The comparison between interactions is borrowed from Perrow with some minor changes inspired by a desire for clarification. The main difference is in the labelling of the two columns. We substitute 'complex interactions' for 'complex systems' and 'non-complex interactions' for 'linear systems' in Perrow. The difficulty is more with the adjectives than with the systems wording. One may well consider that the combination of several or all of the interactions in each column characterises the overall property of a system. It seems preferable at this stage to stay in the direct continuation of the definitions of interactions just given above. Why oppose complex and linear as Perrow does, instead of either complex and non-complex or linear and non-linear? Perrow explains that linear means both 'simple' in the sense of 'easily comprehensible' and not simple in the sense of sophisticated processes and technologies which nevertheless consist of interactions in expected sequence. He adds that on the other hand the term 'non-linear does not readily convey the notion of possible incomprehensibility, while the term complex does' (ibid., 78). A minor problem arises from Perrow's view that the opposite of complex is 'simple' when what is not complex can be either simple or complicated. We subsume both properties under the term 'non-complex'. This difference does not affect the overall characterisation of interactions.

C. Coupling

Coupling is a term borrowed from mechanics. It can be tight or loose. Tight coupling means the absence of slack or buffer, or give between two items. What happens in one directly influences what happens in the other. When a system is tightly coupled, processes can happen very fast and cannot be interrupted. The failed parts cannot be isolated from other parts for at least a time. There is no alternative way to keep the production going safely. Recovery from the initial disturbance is not possible; the disturbance will spread. Tight coupling entails prescribed steps to the operator, and invariant sequences that cannot be changed, at least for some time.

Table 3.2 is adapted from Perrow and lists half-a-dozen criteria for comparing the tendencies found, respectively, in tightly coupled and loosely coupled systems. These are tendencies that are mentioned here as almost polar cases for the sake of simplicity. In actually functioning systems it is a matter of degree and no system is likely to have all the characteristics listed in either one or the other columns.

Table 3.2 Coupling tendencies compared (adapted from C. Perrow, 1999a, 96)

Criteria	Tight coupling	Loose coupling
Possibility of delays in processing?	No	Yes
Order of sequences	Invariant	Can be changed
Methods available to achieve a goal	Only one	Alternative method available
Availability of buffers and redundancies	Designed-in, deliberate	Fortuitously available
Slack in resources (personnel, supplies, equipment)	Little possibility	Possibility
Possibility of substitution of resources	Limited and designed-in	Fortuitously available

D. Interactions and coupling combined

The combination of interactions and coupling results in four combinations of systems. They are, in Perrow's terms: linear (non-complex) interactions with loose coupling (examples: single-goal agencies, most manufacturing); linear interactions and tight coupling (examples: rail transport, marine transport, dams, power grids); complex interactions and loose coupling (examples: universities, multi-goal agencies); and finally complex interactions with tight coupling (examples: nuclear plants; aircraft, chemical plants). This last combination is most relevant to our purpose since it describes the situation in which the potential for system or normal accidents is highest. Interactive complexity means that any part of the system may be interacting with other parts in ways that no designer anticipated and that no operator can understand. When these unanticipated interactions of comparatively small failures are combined with tight coupling, the conditions exist than can defeat the safety system, that is, the plant, the aircraft, and so on.

Normal accidents differ from catastrophes. They have a catastrophic potential but catastrophes are rare. Perrow estimated in the first edition of his book that out of the roughly 3000 reports of events every year in the USA filed by the 70 or so nuclear plants, roughly 300 were accidents, out of which 15 to 30 might have been normal accidents (Perrow, 1999a, 71).

To paraphrase Perrow, normal accidents lie in the system, not in the components (ibid., 351). By their very definition, normal accidents cannot be eliminated notwithstanding the proclaimed goal of avoiding catastrophes (Perrow, 1999b, 70). In this way, normal accidents are irreducible to a level ensuring that catastrophes or major accidents would be reduced to zero.

3.5.3 Organisational Accidents

In *Managing the Risks of Organizational Accidents* (1998) James Reason emphasises the organisational factor in accidents, in addition to the human and technical factors. Like Perrow, he claims that the conventional approach to ensuring safety – that is, building in more warnings and safeguards – fails. Perrow showed that system complexity makes failures inevitable. Typical precautions, by adding to complexity, may even help to create new categories of accidents. Hence the need for a renewed framework for analysing risk. Reason addresses safety management from the standpoint of the organisational characteristics of modern technologies. He thus extends Perrow's analysis with a special focus on a notion of opacity. I summarise Reason's analysis under the headings of organisational accidents, defences-in-depth and latent conditions. I will point out to the results in terms of complexity.

A. Organisational accidents defined

Reason distinguishes two kinds of accidents: those that happen to individuals and those that happen to organisations. Although it may sometimes not be easy to draw a dividing line between them, their comparison through different criteria shows the relevance of treating them as different kinds of events. They differ in frequency, in their context of occurrence, in their causes, in magnitude and spread, and in the defences built against them.

Organisational accidents (OA) are rare; individual accidents (IA) are comparatively more frequent although they are quite reduced in number nowadays compared to their past frequency. Following Reason, though comparatively rare, OAs occur within complex modern technologies such as nuclear power plants, commercial aviation, the petrochemical industry, chemical process plants, marine and rail transport, not to mention banks and stadiums. Recent events in blood transfusion and food contamination may render it necessary to enlarge the list. OAs are thus a product of recent times, of technological innovations that have modified the relationship between systems and their human components, whereas IAs have remained practically unchanged in nature. OAs have in general multiple causes involving many persons operating at different levels and at different times, whereas in IAs a specific person or group is often both agent and victim. OAs are often catastrophic and can affect uninvolved populations, assets and the environment, whereas IAs are usually limited to the people concerned and have a limited spread. Any accident means that the defences ensuring the safety of people and assets, and separating hazards from people and assets, were breached. An essential difference between OAs and IAs arises from the defences.

B. Defences-in-depth

Defences-in-depth are the barriers and safeguards ensuring the functions of understanding, awareness, guidance, warning, restoration, interposition, containment, escape and rescue. These functions, taken in this order, correspond to successive layers of protection, one behind the other, each guarding against the possible failure of the one in front, in a sequence ranging from creating understanding and awareness of the local hazards in a first step, to providing the means of escape and rescue should hazard containment fail, in the final step.

The multiplicity of these overlapping and mutually supporting means of safety has changed the character of industrial accidents. Modern technological systems are largely single-failure-proof. In earlier or traditional technologies, there still are relatively high numbers of individual accidents. In modern technologies, systems are largely immune to isolated failures, and individual accidents are comparatively rare. The main danger comes from organisational accidents involving causal contributions from people distributed both through the system and over time. In earlier technologies, human activities were primarily productive. Modern technologies consist of largely automated systems that are more opaque to their operators. Human operators become controllers. They are increasingly remote, both physically and intellectually, from the productive processes which they nominally control. There follows from this the 'insidious build-up of latent conditions' (Reason, 1998, 8).

C. Latent conditions

Human beings contribute to accidents in two ways. The most common is unsafe acts with immediate adverse effects, which defines active failures. However it is more and more recognised that persons working in complex systems make unsafe acts for reasons that generally go beyond individual fallibility and psychology. These reasons are *latent conditions*. In Reason's terms, latent conditions are to technological organisations what resident pathogens are to the human body:

> Like pathogens, latent conditions – such as poor design, gaps in supervision, undetected manufacturing defects or maintenance failures, unworkable procedures, clumsy automation, shortfalls in training, less than adequate tools and equipment may be present for many years before they combine with local circumstances and active failures to penetrate the system's many layers of defenses. They arise from strategic and other top-level decisions made by governments, regulators, manufacturers,

> designers and organizational managers. The impact of these decisions spreads throughout the organization, shaping a distinctive corporate culture and creating error-producing factors within the individual work places. (ibid., 10).

Latent conditions are thus always present in complex systems since they relate to 'basic organizational processes: designing, constructing, operating, maintaining, communicating, selecting, training, supervising and managing ... They are the generic essentials of any productive process' (ibid., 36). Contrary to active failures, latent conditions have no immediate impact, they can lie dormant for a time, doing no particular harm until they interact with local circumstances to defeat the system's defences. While most active failures are committed at the front line, human-system interface, latent conditions are spawned in upper echelons and within related processes. Latent conditions pathways may combine with local workplace factors to defeat the defences, independently of any unsafe act being committed. Unsafe acts are not a necessary condition for organisational accidents. This necessary condition is the rare conjunction of several holes in successive defences, and of latent conditions.

Reason suggests tellingly, through the comparison of a virtual stagecoach accident with a jumbo jet accident, that a similar person-centred investigation would have little or no chance of improving the jumbo jet system's safety. Defences-in-depth are ambivalent: they both protect and may be a dangerous concealment, notably through relocating the error opportunities through adding components and linkages rendering the system more opaque to its operators, and even through contributing to an increased feeling of safety and diminished alertness. They thus contribute to an enlarged presence of latent conditions.

D. Synthesis

- Latent conditions are inevitable. They threaten all hazardous domains involving modern technologies whereas individual factors affect these domains with much variability.
- Identifying and eliminating latent conditions is a main road towards improved safety. But it can only be a continuous, never-ending process: as one problem is addressed, others will spring up in its place.
- Often the factors that caused an accident look obvious after the fact. But it is also often overlooked that some prior indication of a disaster 'is only truly a warning if you know what kind of disaster you will suffer' (Reason, 1998, 39). Yet, from the perspective of those involved, many accidents are 'impossible accidents', they occur because 'people do not believe that the accident that is about to occur is at all possible' (Wagenaar and Groeneweg, quoted by Reason, 1998, 39). Knowing how events turned out biases our judgement of

the actions of those on the spot, following what psychologists call the bias of outcome knowledge (Fischhoff, 1975).

- There is an asymmetry of application. The organisational approach thus described complements the traditional approaches based on individuals and on the human-machine interfaces. But while the organisational approach is applicable to limiting personal injury risks, the person-based approach helps little in dealing with the kind of irreducibility entailed by organisational factors of organisational accidents. These kinds of inevitability and irreducible opacity are features which safety science and safety management applied to complex systems must live with.

3.5.4 Irreducible Risk and High Safety

The analyses of normal and organisational accidents tell us that it is not possible to eliminate major accidents in modern technologies because of system characteristics and of organisational latent conditions. This is a strong result which constitutes our background for further reflection. It emphasises a kind of irreducibility that is intrinsic to the functioning of modern systems combining high technology, high specialisation of operators and competitive pressures endlessly pushing toward improved productive and commercial performances. These analyses are developed from the standpoint of failures, errors and accidents, at a global level. They can be complemented in several directions. First, there is the reverse side of accidents, that is, safety management. Among the systems studied by Perrow and Reason there are systems that achieve a high level of safety with inevitable, but rare, major accidents, such as commercial aviation, nuclear plants and modern railways. They provide an interesting case for studying the limits of safety improvements and the conditions under which residual risk is rendered acceptable. Second, these analyses leave little room for an explicit consideration of how the tasks are performed by front-line operators. Yet they are the immediate and mediating links between systemic and organisational factors on the one hand, and events on the other hand. Ergonomics applied in contexts of high-safety systems provides another view of acceptable risk and of irreducible risk at the operators' level. We address these topics below. A third direction is to complement high safety and acceptable residual risk at the regulatory and societal level through the precautionary principle which will be addressed in the next section.

Perrow's and Reason's analyses of risk are challenging since they convey the idea of the inevitability of major accidents in systems and organisations based on modern automated technologies, whatever the efforts made by human beings, be they the designers, the managers or the operators. Yet this kind of endogeneity remains partial. It can be furthered in two directions while retaining the general idea that much can be learned through the study of limit situations, those of persisting, high residual risk in otherwise so-called high-safety systems (HSS). The first direction consists in the notion of acceptable risk. The second comes from the cognitive ergonomics of safety at the front-line operators' level.

The very irreducibility of risk and the unavoidability of major accidents, even in HSS, create an interrogation on risk acceptance and on what level of safety is safe enough or satisficing to the persons involved. In such a context of irreducibility, risk acceptability and the methods used to achieve it offer examples of putting into practice the notion of threshold introduced above, and of exploring further its implications for complexity.

We will proceed in two steps. The next step will be to enquire at the micro level of front-line operators. We will address the regulatory level in a further step, in a section on the precautionary principle. We will thus have covered four levels of irreducibility in safety management and safety science, going from the micro to the organisational, the systemic, and the regulatory and societal levels.

A. High-safety systems (HSS)

HSS (high-safety systems) are those in which the probability of a major accident involving at least one fatality is approximately of one in a million operations. Such systems include commercial aviation, nuclear power plants and modern railways. In commercial aviation, the domain on which we focus, this average of 10^{-6} risk is based on the number of take-offs and landings. In 1995 this figure varied by a factor of 42 across the world's air carriers from 1 over 260 000 in the worst cases to 1 over 11 000 000 in the best cases (Reason, 1998, 191). At the beginning of the 1990s, it varied by a factor of ten across geographical areas, from 5.10^{-6} in the worst cases (East European countries, Africa, some Asian countries) to $0.5.10^{-6}$ in the USA (Amalberti, 1996, 30). Historically, this risk decreased rapidly until the end of the 1960s and reached its present level by the middle of the 1970s. It has not diminished since this period. A kind of asymptote has thus been present for more than three decades. Without any further progress in safety and given the trend in traffic growth which existed before the 11 September, 2001 events, it was commonly expected that the number of major accidents would have doubled in 2010 compared to 2000, which would amount to about 50 major accidents per year. The figure of $0.5.10^{-6}$ risk of disastrous accident (human death or other important consequences) per safety unit (varying according to industry and transportation mode) may be regarded as the safety asymptote for today's ultra-safe macro-technical systems such as the nuclear industry, civil aviation and the European railways system (Amalberti, 2001, 110).

These figures summarise one of the paradoxes of HSS: modern technological systems perform better and are more reliable than their predecessors, yet residual risks appear more intolerable than in the past. Another paradox lies in the fact that there seems to be no limits in gains in productivity and performance due to technical progress, yet there appears to be a limit on gains in safety. This limit is illustrated by the average 10^{-6} plateau for major accidents.

What is the character of this limit? It does not seem to be technical, particularly in aviation. A jump to a 10^{-7} risk might not be out of reach intellectually in two decades or so in the future. But it would be a different system (Durand and Alliot, 1999). Its costs would be very high. It remains out of reach in practical terms.

B. The issue of acceptable risk

Acceptability of risk has several meanings. Accepting a risk can correspond to the risk of failure or of accident that the system's operators and users accept consciously, although solutions for reducing this risk exist but are not implemented because of various reasons (cost, loss of productive performance, resistance to the changes of behaviour this would entail – as it is the case in road traffic safety, and so on). In a broader way, risk acceptance may derive from the absence of solutions for diminishing the risks of major accidents in the short run and in the medium term. All HSS are instances of it. In this case risk acceptability is linked to a given technology. When this acceptability vanishes, the technology is likely to be abandoned altogether. Examples of it are the Zeppelin airship in 1937 and recently the decisions to abandon nuclear power generation in Sweden and in Germany. An additional distinction between two kinds of risks and safety is especially relevant in HSS. There are the risks due to current failures and incidents and their reduction to a very low level, which is a defining characteristic of HSS. And there are the inevitable risks of major accidents. Due to the difficulty of improving safety in HSS and considering the growth of traffic and the pressures towards gains in performance, the issue becomes more to maintain the existing level of safety and to render acceptable the risk of major accidents to both users and society in general.

Several solutions can be conceived in order to determine what society regards as safe enough. Fischhoff et al. (1981 [1999]) present a list of seven criteria desired of an approach to making acceptable-risk decisions. They require it to be comprehensive, logically sound, practical, open to evaluation, politically acceptable, compatible with institutions and conducive to learning. The ALARA (as low as reasonably acceptable) approach summarises a number of different approaches. Reason (1998) mentions four of them. Firstly, the feasibility or ALARP approach (risks to be kept as low as reasonably practicable) obeys technological and economic logics since sufficient safety is deemed to exist at the point beyond which it is neither technologically nor economically feasible to do more. Secondly, in the comparative risk approach, sufficient safety is determined on the basis of comparisons to others risks that are voluntarily accepted (road transport, smoking, railway transport, choice of air travel, and so on.). A third way is the *de minimis* approach, which corresponds to the definition of high-safety systems usually retained, commonly taken as 10^{-6} risk or better. An extreme approach is the zero-risk approach for which safety would entail no risk of major accident. It may be proposed by strong opponents to an activity such as nuclear power plants but in practice it entails abandoning the activity at stake.

Finally an additional important approach must be mentioned: it is the participatory approach. Various actors participate more or less directly and more or less formally to the decision-making process. Whether they become co-decision-makers or remain simply informed actors is naturally a big issue. In all cases the main idea seems to win acceptance of a risk. In HSS, in which it is difficult to improve safety, risk acceptance tends to be more and more crucial, whereas in non-HSS a clear priority goal is to improve safety since the scope for improvement within a given system is large.

A significant improvement in HSS often seems to entail that a change of system be carried out, which is not a short-run or even medium-term practical solution. Then, within an existing system, improvements can be sought through a number of factors, either systemic or pertaining to the front-line operators. Such an approach is developed by René Amalberti, in terms of cognitive ergonomics contrasted to pure engineering (Amalberti 1996, 1997, 1999).

C. Cognitive ergonomics of risk

Ergonomics is often presented as a way to study 'real-life tasks' (Rasmussen and Jensen, 1974) and thus allows going beyond considering merely nominal systems and cognitive aspects. Integrating human beings at work is, so to speak, intrinsic to it.

With hindsight, it is worth enquiring whether ergonomics as a discipline contains generalisations capable of operating as a test of what we reported about our experience in the first chapters of this book. Our experience was entirely driven by our encounter with a form of irreducibility and consisted in a sort of muddling through in order to carry out a given task. Safety ergonomics also deals with a form of irreducibility when it faces irreducible risk. But we ignored this proximity when we started our enquiry. Indeed, although some pioneering work in this domain was done in the 1970s and the 1980s, it is only recently, thanks to work done on systemic and organisational accidents, that it became possible to attempt to develop these insights with an ergonomic perspective. In his book published in 1996, René Amalberti starts with an explicit, albeit critical, reference to Reason's book on human error (Reason, 1993). Amalberti emphasises safety rather than error. An abundant literature exists in this field. We rely mainly on the analysis conducted by Amalberti on safety in high-safety technologies. These include nuclear power generation, commercial aviation and railways. Following Amalberti, we will concentrate on safety in aviation. He models how front-line operators manage safety, based both on empirical observation of operators at work such as aircraft pilots in the cockpits during flights, and on simulations run with the operators. This modelling derives from the study of normal conditions during work, not of accidents, in high-technology systems. The general setting is ergonomic cognitive psychology. It stresses real-life tasks in natural conditions of work, which justifies the term of *ecological safety* used to denote this approach. We summarise what this perspective tells us and then present it in a more detailed fashion.

There first arises the idea that optimisation is not possible because of limited cognitive resources. What is observed instead is a cognitive compromise between the three goals of safety, performance and minimisation of the physiological and mental impacts of performance (fatigue and stress). The case studies reported support Amalberti's claim that the first risk perceived by the operator is not the risk of accident but the risk of losing control of the situation, hence a dynamic *cognitive compromise*, in which satisfying behaviour prevails. Carrying out the tasks and stabilising the system through just sufficient or good enough behaviour, with an instantaneous situation likely to evolve and a system not fully known or understood, summarises this dynamic compromise. Overall, the notions of cognitive compromise and ecological safety are central to Amalberti's argumentation. It differs from the engineering model. The engineering model typically focuses on how the performance of front-line operators such as pilots or control-room operators is influenced by the characteristics of the workplace, notably by the informational properties of the human – machine interface. As Reason puts it, safety is viewed as something that needs to be 'engineered' into the system and that is often expressed in quantitative probabilistic terms. In this approach, reducing human failures depends heavily on effective human engineering – that is, the ability of the system's designers to tailor the system appropriately to the cognitive capacities of its operators.

It is at this point that an ergonomic perspective brings something new through considering both the cognitive and practical capacities of operators. While Reason criticises the engineering model because it downplays the role of organisational factors, the cognitive ergonomic approach to safety also contains a criticism of the engineering standpoint but for a quite different reason: it criticises its focus on optimisation as a way to improve safety. In effect, all HSS are based on a progressively built (engineered) optimisation of safety components. However, this strategy is all the more effective as important safety margins exist, when safety is still below a high safety level. A rather common idea is that a system is designed in order to operate at a maximum safety level but is prevented from achieving it because of the failures it undergoes. There follows from this the goal of eliminating all human and technical failures identified in the system. As Amalberti mentions, this view relies on two wrong postulates of modern safety: first, that a safe system is a system with no failure; second, that all failures must be eliminated. These postulates have progressively locked safety to a dead end in HSS, however effective they are, to repeat, in non-HSS.

First are the paradoxical effects of automation and the need to keep the human operator closely associated with automated systems, since their safety depends ultimately on human intervention in case of their failure (Bainbridge, 1987). Human-centred automation is gaining support, notably in aviation (Billings, 1997) and air traffic control (Villiers, 1998). Second, in HSS, safety management cannot rely on past accidents because of their scarcity. It relies on precursors, weak signals and incidents and their systematic elimination. Yet the presence of incidents is useful in that it maintains an awareness and alertness among operators. Naturally a compromise must be practised between the extremes of leaving all incidents undetected and striving towards eliminating all of them. Consequences of their systematic elimination are a growing confidence in the working of the system and an increased productive performance accompanied by a narrowing of operators' margins for action. These evolutions tend to create the conditions for increasing the risk of serious failures of the same kind as that following from the latent conditions accumulating in organisations analysed by Reason. The very serious incidents which occurred repeatedly in nuclear plants in Japan in 1995, 1996 (Triendl, 1999) and in 1999 (Science et Vie, 2000) came as an enormous surprise in a country in which the nuclear sector used to be considered as the safest in the world because it produced a minimum number of incidents.

The model of ecological safety opposes the optimising model. It is based on empirical testing with operators in concrete situations, notably aircraft pilots. It shows that the operator's goal is to keep control of the situation, that is, staying within acceptable safety margins given the level of performance aimed at. When errors are made, the operator first reduces the level of performance in order to control errors better and continue to operate. The regulating variable appears thus to be the feeling of controlling the situation rather than the number of errors. Excessively automated solutions impoverish the awareness of the situation by the operator.

Amalberti's thesis is that in order to improve safety or to maintain an already high safety level together with increasing productive performance, it is necessary to accept minor failures or errors, not to attempt systematically to eliminate them. The reason is the excessive fatigue and stress that such a strategy would impose on the operator. Then a balance has to be found. A safe system is not a system without failures, it is a system in which failures and errors are kept under control. Similarly, good operators are not those who do not make errors but those who are able to detect and restore from errors. Thus in order to improve or at least to maintain at its present low magnitude the level of major risk in HSS, it is necessary to accept minor risks.

Figure 3.2 represents a model of operators' behaviour inspired and freely adapted from Amalberti. Amalberti describes what he calls a 'cognitive compromise' between the 'cognitive cost of acquiring the know-how', the 'cognitive cost of operating in real time' and a targeted level of performance (Amalberti, 1996, 194). The higher the level of performance required from operators is, the higher both costs are. We differ slightly from this through reasoning on rising levels of difficulty instead of costs, and through distinguishing a cognitive difficulty from a practical difficulty. The latter does not mean that the two notions exist separately. Nevertheless one can learn how to operate but lack the minimum practical resources needed to operate in real conditions. Conversely one can have the practical resources but lack some minimum knowledge required. This is a limit situation in which either the operator knows the principles at work but has no practical competence, or the operator has some empirical experience but no knowledge of the theory. This situation corresponds to point M in Figure 3.2. The compromise depends then on the cognitive and practical difficulties entailed for a given level of performance. Figure 3.2 depicts two kinds of areas, inside and outside the pentagon MNOPQ. This figure has a purely heuristic purpose. Lines are drawn symmetrically with respect to the bisecting line for the sake of simplicity. The same goes for the dotted lines delimitating areas (A), (B) and (C) inside the pentagon and for starting at point M from equal minimum levels of cognitive and practical resources OK and OL.

The compromise is achieved inside the pentagon. Outside of it are areas beyond the limits of the compromise. Let us recall that the compromise depicts the conditions under which the operator is able to keep the situation under control. In area (A) there are margins for improvement. It is a 'comfort' area. These margins can be used in area (B) in order to increase the performance thanks to incentives and an improved motivation. It is the 'motivated' area. Self-limitation of performance through error detection and restoration are counteracted by increasing performance requirements. Fatigue and stress are mounting in this area.

Area (C) depicts an artificial range accessible only with artificial aids. These aids entail a diminishing overall number of failures enabling an increased performance. This is accompanied by a potential growing number of non-detected and non-restored errors. It is the 'artificial' area. Imposing the system to go beyond the limit point M' – or beyond OP – disrupts the artificial compromise and creates the conditions of a major failure; OP then represents a sort of safety barrier induced by the pressures toward increased performance given the bounded cognitive and practical resources of the operator.

Areas I to V symbolise situations of lack or loss of control. In area I, the absence of control is due to the lack of minimum knowledge. In area II, it is due to the lack of minimum practical resources. Area III corresponds to a work overload: the loss of control is due to a deficient practical adjustment. Similarly the loss of control in area IV arises from a lack of knowledge due to a cognitive overload. Finally area V symbolises the loss of control due to the multiplication of non-detected errors and to both deficient practical adjustment and deficient knowledge.

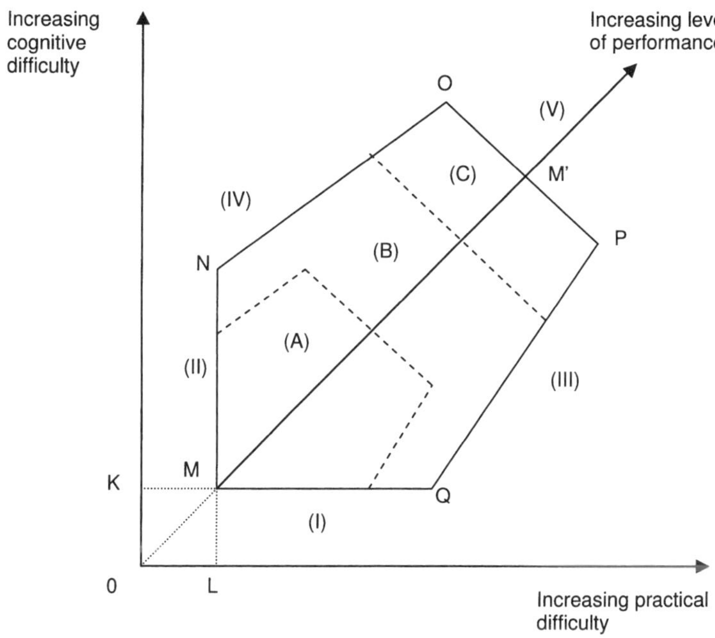

Figure 3.2 A stylised operator's compromise between performance and safety

The ecological compromise corresponds to areas (A) and (B) in which the operator adjusts the level of performance to his/her cognitive and practical capacities in real time. In the case of a perceived risk of disruption, the level of performance is reduced in order to achieve a balance again, gain an understanding of the situation and then try to achieve an improved performance. Indeed it is a compromise between performance and safety that is described here. It complements Reason's model of latent conditions: they accumulate especially in area (C) of artificial compromise and beyond M', after which the potential for major failure can develop since it is no longer checked by the operator's control of the situation. Three operational sources of irreducibility of accidents at the operator's level are thus identified with areas III, IV and V. This brings a behavioural setting endogenising irreducibility in addition to the systemic and organisational standpoints evoked above.

This model illustrates how risk reduction can resist optimising. Engineering and technical fixes do diminish the risks of current failures and improve performance, but they also contribute to growing latent conditions of major failures. This model suggests strongly that mere optimisation and elimination of errors is not an appropriate strategy, because of the irreducible risk of major failures in HSS. There is no linear connection between small accidents and major accidents. Amalberti's model tells us that a way to limit major failures is to rely more on the compromise that trained operators naturally tend to practice. This model also illustrates how the study of limit conditions (here the risk of major failure) feeds back on the current functioning of a system and is thus necessary to the understanding of its day-to-day management.

3.5.5 The Precautionary Principle

With the precautionary principle we tackle risk management at the level of public authorities. Yet it is not limited to a regulatory domain. The precautionary principle may entail the decision to act or not to act. And when it is decided to act, it can be regulatory action as well as funding research or informing the public about the potential risks.

The precautionary principle is particularly interesting for our purpose because it extends the notion of acceptable risk of the last section to situations that are not limited to HSS and to modern technological systems. It thus offers an opportunity to explore in more detail how acceptable risk can be defined at the societal level. Since the precautionary principle is triggered by a gap between knowledge and risk in a specific situation, the very idea of an acceptable risk is another term for a threshold of risk, above which it is not acceptable.

A. Definition

Precaution as it is understood in the precautionary principle arose from a concern about environmental pollution in the 1970s. The Oslo Commission on sea pollution which was created in 1972, and the London Final Act of 1987 on the protection of the North Sea, were decisive steps followed by the declaration of the environment ministers of OECD (Organisation for Economic Co-operation and Development) in 1991. The precautionary principle was explicitly recognized at the United Nations Conference on Environment and Development (UNCED) in Rio de Janeiro in 1992. It is listed as Principle 15 of the so-called Rio Declaration (June 1992) among the principles of general rights and obligations of national authorities:

> In order to protect the environment, the precautionary approach should be widely applied by States according to their capabilities. Where there are threats of serious or

> irreversible damage, lack of full scientific certainty shall not be used as a reason for postponing cost-effective measures to prevent environmental degradation. (CEC: Commission of the European Communities, 2000, 26)

This principle has been progressively consolidated in international environmental law, and it has since become a general principle of international law. The WTO (World Trade Organization) agreements confirm this observation. They establish close links between international trade and environmental protection although the term 'precautionary principle' itself is not explicitly used.

This international status has been complemented by the recognition of the principle in national law in several countries, including a French law in 1995 which states that: 'The absence of certainty, given the scientific and technical evidence existing at the moment, shall not delay taking effective and proportional decisions aimed at preventing a risk of high and irreversible damage to environment at an economically acceptable cost'. It was incorporated in the French national constitution in 2005.

The Commission of the European Communities declared that 'following the example set by other Members of the WTO, the Community is entitled to prescribe the level of protection, notably as regards the environment and human, animal and plant health, which it considers appropriate', and that to this end, 'reliance on the precautionary principle constitutes an essential plank of its policy' (CEC 2000, 12). The CEC innovated here, since the European Union Treaty does not define explicitly the precautionary principle and prescribes only the protection of the environment. The CEC emphasised that the scope of the precautionary principle is much wider in practice than the environment and covers human, animal and plant health. Moreover the Commission considered that 'the Community like other WTO members, has the right to establish the level of protection (...) that it deems appropriate' (ibid., 3).

B. Principles of application

We will rely here on the European Commission communication since it defines a scope for the precautionary principle which makes it particularly relevant to decision-makers, notably public authorities having tasks of risk management.

Recourse to the precautionary principle should start with the identification of 'potentially dangerous effects deriving from a phenomenon, product or process', first, and second, with the evidence that 'scientific evaluation does not allow the risk to be determined with sufficient certainty' (CEC, 2000, 4).

The European Commission insists that 'the absence of scientific proof of the existence of a cause – effect relationship, a quantifiable dose/response relationship or a quantitative evaluation of the probability of the emergence of adverse effects following exposure should not be used to justify inaction' (ibid., 17). The precautionary principle covers those circumstances where 'scientific evidence is insufficient, inconclusive or uncertain and there are indications through preliminary objective scientific evaluation that there are reasonable grounds for concern that the potentially dangerous effects on the environment, human, animal or plant health may be inconsistent with the chosen level of protection' (ibid., 10).

Real difficulties emerge at this point. First, 'objective' scientific evaluation may not preclude a division among scientists or expert groups. The very existence of divergent views presented by competent scientists on a particular issue may indicate, or even increase, a state of scientific uncertainty. Second, the bulk of the responsibility is shifted to the decision-makers' judgement: 'Judging what is an "acceptable" level of risk for society is an eminently political responsibility. Decision makers faced with an unacceptable risk, scientific uncertainty and public concerns have a duty to find answers' (ibid., 4).

Besides the decision to act or not to act, which is linked to the two triggering factors of identification of a danger and of scientific uncertainty about the risk evoked above, there is the question of how to act. The decision to do nothing may be a response in its own right since the decision-makers' duty to respond does not necessarily mean that measures always have to be adopted. The Commission emphasises that the appropriate response is the result of a political decision, 'a function of the risk level that is 'acceptable' to the society on which the risk is imposed' (ibid., 16). A key issue is the legitimacy of the measures that make possible to achieve what society considers an acceptable risk or, equivalently, a satisfactory level of environmental protection or health. The Commission's solution is that all interested parties should be involved 'to the fullest extent possible in the study of various risk management options that may be envisaged' (ibid., 17).

3.5.6 Pulling the Threads Together. Cognitive and Practical Irreducibility

Our aim in this section was to clarify and explain how the difficulty of performing a task appears complex or not complex. This rendered it necessary to make the operator's behaviour explicit. In the hope of finding properties that might be helpful, we chose to explore a field in which these factors are essential and have been studied for years, that is, safety science and management.

There are a variety of approaches in safety management covering several levels ranging from the front-line level of individuals, to the human – machine, workplace level (engineering, cognitive ergonomics), then to the organisational level, to the system level, to the regulatory level, and finally to the societal level. We concentrated our attention on four perspectives connected to several of these levels. We started with the kind of irreducibility attached to system or normal accidents. We continued with the inevitability of opacity and latent conditions linked to organisational accidents. Then we emphasised the irreducibility to zero of the residual risk of major accident in high-safety systems. This issue is fully addressed in the ongoing developments on the precautionary principle. Indeed the precautionary principle forces to a synthesis of all the aspects that we encountered, including its built-in emphasis on the societal level of the issue of acceptable risk.

The European Commission emphasises the procedural character of what is an acceptable risk: it is acceptable if it is legitimate and thus involves the participation of all interested parties in the study of various risk management options that may be envisaged 'once the results of the scientific evaluation and/or risk assessment are available in an as transparent as possible' procedure (CEC, 2000, 17).

The precautionary principle illustrates the search for, and the construction of, broad guidelines of action in a context of radical uncertainty with high collective stakes residing in high and irreversible risks to the environment and human, animal and plant health. It entails the same kind of difficulties as those we found with the residual risk of major accident in high-safety systems. In all these fields the goal is to avoid any major accident. Yet it is known that this cannot be achieved. There is a cognitive irreducibility. But it does not prevent these technologies from continuing to be operated. Whether or not this means a genuine social acceptance of this risk varies a lot across the particular fields: there is more divergence of opinions about nuclear plants than about commercial aviation. The very fact that they are continuously and normally operated in most countries can be taken as an indication of a broad practical acceptance of the risks attached to them.

Given the general level of aspiration of avoiding any major accident, one is forced to accept the existence of a gap between this goal and available knowledge. This cognitive gap characterises a cognitively non-satisficing situation. Yet the very idea of acceptable risk can be interpreted from a practical standpoint. Since a risk is accepted, it is in some way satisfactory or satisficing for the people who accept it. It connotes a practically satisficing situation.

The people alluded to may range from a few individuals to a whole population and society. A division is likely to occur within the population and interested parties with respect to the acceptable character of risk: some will consider it acceptable, others will not. Controversy often reigns. There may even be a majority or a predominant expression of practical non-satisficing, thus refusing a given risk. The parallel with our argument above becomes obvious when we replace some of the European Commission's terms by our own terms: 'chosen level of protection' by level of aspiration, 'insufficient scientific evidence' by absence of cognitive satisficing and 'judging what is an acceptable level of risk for society' and 'involvement of interested parties' by action in order to obtain a practical and judgmental satisficing.

Several remarks need to be added at this point. First, as in our argument, the assessment of cognitive satisficing comes first, before moving to practical satisficing, in case cognitive satisficing cannot be achieved.

Second, our reference to practical satisficing simplifies a process in which judgement is also present. Judgement receives a central role in A. Marshall and J.M. Keynes's views and in G. Vickers's concept of an appreciative system (Vickers, 1995). The former were addressed in Chapter 2, the latter will be examined in Chapter 6. Since our aim at this stage is to differentiate cognitive satisficing from other forms of satisficing, it seems justified to synthesise the latter under the label of practical satisficing whatever the degree and type of judgement involved in it. We will remove this simplification and explicitly address judgemental reducibility in the next chapter.

Furthermore, whether practical satisficing is achieved or not is most often a matter of public debate and of the evolution of public opinion about acceptable risk. It has a social origin and is not subjective in the usual sense of the term. It is evolving and linked to experience and learning. Thus the search for practical satisficing is not separate from knowing. In this sense the wording used until now to differentiate the two sorts of satisficing may be misleading, in conveying the idea that practical satisficing has no cognitive content. It might be justified to denominate it as cognitive and practical satisficing, thus differentiated from initial cognitive satisficing.

However entangled knowledge and practice may be, this discussion suggests that it is useful to maintain the distinction between the two kinds of satisficing. For the sake of simplicity it seems better to retain the terms *cognitive satisficing* and *practical satisficing* to connote, respectively, a *cognitive irreducibility* and a *practical irreducibility* when satisficing of either kind is not achieved. The threshold of non-complexity – complexity is thus conceived as part of a behavioural frame combining the components of complexity analysed above and is thus endogenised.

3.6 EIGHT ELEMENTARY DIMENSIONS OF COMPLEXITY

How do the previous developments fit with our initial concern about the regime of interaction between the state and the economy (RISE)? It will appear that it was necessary to introduce progressively eight dimensions in the notion of complexity that is relevant to our purpose.

Now, let us leave safety management and suppose that we are in a scientific field. The purpose is to depict an object, and the level of aspiration is to depict it theoretically, not in a purely empirical way. Suppose that there is no available knowledge enabling us to depict it in a satisficing way. Suppose, then, that we shift to the search for a practical way out of the issue and suppose that we do not find an available procedure, technique or basis of agreement within our specific scientific community, enabling to achieve a practically satisficing outcome – that is, an outcome acceptable to the community. This is what we described in Chapter 1 in our inquiry in the state-economy relationships. And this is what the RISE is about. In most cases, when the level of satisficing is such that it enables finding some procedure to deal satisficingly with an otherwise cognitively complex problem, the situation obtained receives a practical solution and is not complex. The central variable is the level of satisficing. It is decided individually or set at a community level in a field of activity, whatever the field is. It is generally not explicit. A consequence is that there is no predeterminate criterion telling whether a problem or a situation is complex or not. Whether a satisficing state of affairs is obtained in a field is usually a source of debate among practitioners. In our case, the tension about the RISE was obvious.

It proved not possible to find a satisficing, practical way to proceed in a first step. This drove us to reflect on an appropriate method in a next step, to which we will come back in the next chapter. The kind of irreducibility which appeared is a limit case since it is the result of both cognitive and practical complexity. It was developed through a pragmatic and principled progression. Genuine complexity appears at the end of the process in the case where practical satisficing cannot be achieved. It might be asked whether such a limit notion of complexity is not due to extreme and excessive requirements. The long detour we made via safety management and the precautionary principle proved that without using the concepts developed here, a similar problematic setting exists in these fields. With the RISE, we are in the same situation as those sections of the population who consider that some risks are not acceptable, while the others consider them acceptable, or are indifferent. This is far from being an exceptional or unrealistic situation. It is a final step in our journey to a notion of complexity grasping the complexity that we experienced with the RISE. It proved necessary to introduce eight factors or dimensions. A synthesis is proposed in Table 3.3.

Table 3.3 details the variables or dimensions on which complexity (CX) or non-complexity (NCX) are dependent. The first seven dimensions are: the object or phenomenon of interest, the purpose, the representative operator or agent, the field of operation or activity, the level of aspiration or goal sought, cognitive reducibility, and practical reducibility. The norm consistent with the field (column 4) is a necessary, but not sufficient, ingredient of the level of aspiration: it must be complemented with the particular level of difficulty addressed. This is what the entries in column 5 stand for. Indeed the level of aspiration combines a standard of behaviour in a given field with a goal ascribed to a particular operation entailing a variable level of difficulty, from low to high. Satisficing means here reducibility to a satisfactory level, that is, to a level consistent with the level of aspiration. Irreducibility or complexity occurs when this level cannot be achieved. Thus reducibility and satisficing are synonyms in this setting. Achieved satisficing is symbolised by the plus sign (+), and non-satisficing by the minus sign (-), in columns 6 and 7.

Table 3.3 From object to situation: eight elementary dimensions of complexity

1 Object	2 Purpose	3 Operator	4 Field	5 Level of aspiration	6 Cognitive/ substantive reducibility	7 Practical/ procedural reducibility	8 Character of situation
Brain of a sheep	Description	Butcher	Butchery	Given by 4	+	+	NCX
	Description	Neurophy-siologist	Neurophy-siology	Given by 4 but variable according to level of difficulty addressed	+(if 5 low)	+	NCX
					-(if 5 high)	+	NCX
						-	CX
High-risk technologies and high-safety systems	Production and safety	Manage-ment Front-line operators	Industry Transport	No major accident	-	+	NCX
						-	CX
Precautionary principle	Production and safety	Public authorities	Environment Public health Public policy	No major accident	-	+	NCX
						-	CX
Public expenditure and role of the state in the economy (RISE: Regime of interaction between the state and the economy)	Description Understand-ing Explanation Representa-tion	Economist	Political economy Economics	Meeting scientific standards given by 4:			
				1) through doing away with RISE	+	+	NCX
				2) through not doing away with RISE	-	-	CX

Cognitive satisficing means that there is no gap between the level of aspiration and the cognitive resources necessary to achieve it. It is a cognitive, substantively rational satisficing or reducibility. The definition of practical satisficing or reducibility is less straightforward since it derives from a notion of acceptable result as was shown in the previous paragraph. When a cognitive satisficing cannot be achieved substantively, a procedurally rational search is called for in our behaviouralist setting. It might be envisaged to achieve in this way a satisficing that would be purely cognitive, but it would be most unlikely that in this process, no practical resource would be mobilised. Indeed, in the case of a block on the purely cognitive resources, the examples taken in safety management tell us that what remains feasible is to rely mainly on practical resources. Hence the de facto association made here of cognitive and substantive reducibility or irreducibility in column 6, and the association of practical and procedural reducibility or irreducibility made in column 7. Complexity emerges in the absence of practical satisficing.

The information contained in column 8 defines the situation, non-complex or complex, resulting from the combination of columns 6 and 7. This character of the situation is a dimension of complexity whose relevance will be revealed fully in Chapter 4 when the present argument is developed in a next step differentiating an object level synthesised by the character of situation (column 8), and a meta-level whose starting point is this object-level situation.

We are now able to structure the developments of the last section on the basis of the eight dimensions of complexity. This is described in Table 3.3, starting with the sheep brain example, continuing with the safety management case and precautionary principle, and ending with the RISE.

3.7 FROM COMPLEX OBJECT TO COMPLEX SITUATION

Section 3.2 of this chapter is entitled 'Complexity not intrinsic to objects', meaning that complexity does not depend only on objects in general. We can say now that for complexity to depend only on object, six other factors or dimensions must be neutralised. It is these dimensions that produce the relativity of complexity. These dimensions are the product both of the willingness to avoid crude objectivity, crude subjectivity and crude irreducibility, and of the willingness to retain an operational notion through an endogenously built threshold. We end up at this stage with a notion of complexity restricted to a particular kind of situation.

There is a second, extended meaning in which we may compare an object and a situation. While, in the narrow sense, referring merely to the object (column 1 of Table 3.3) assumes that all other factors are given, in the extended meaning we wish to compare an object and a situation, for instance a 'complex system' and a 'complex situation'. Our construction enables us to do this through synthesising the properties arising from the first five dimensions (columns 1 to 5 of Table 3.3). They can be synthesised in two ways, from a cognitive standpoint (column 6) and from a practical standpoint (column 7). This simplification enables us furthermore to clarify the meanings of complexity and non-complexity (simplicity and complication), as is shown in Table 3.4. We differentiate simple, complicated and complex situations. Reducibility is obtained in the first two cases, easily or with little resources in simplicity, with more resources in complication.

Table 3.4 From simplicity to complex situation

	Character of object from the standpoint of reducibility		Character of the resulting situation	Symbols
	Cognitive reducibility	Practical reducibility		
1	+ Simplicity	+ Simplicity	+ Simplicity	NCX
2	+ Complication	+ Complication	+ Complication	NCX
3	- Complexity	+ Complication	+ Complication	NCX
4	- Complexity	- Complexity	- Complexity	CX
5	+ Simplicity or complication	- Complexity	- Complexity	CX

In this way of synthesising the factors on which complexity depends, it is possible to have a cognitively complex object and yet a non-complex situation if the object is in practice non-complex (line 3). In this case there are tools or a technique for treatment of the object which prove to be satisfactory to the extent that they render it possible to achieve a satisfactory situation. We can have a complex system and a non-complex situation. This demonstrates why dealing with complex systems differs from dealing with complexity. We are seeking a theory of complex situations, not basically a theory of complex systems.

A situation is conceived in cognitive and practical terms. Indeed these two aspects cannot be separated in the conception developed here. And action and experience implied in the practical aspect are central. This can be shown through reflecting on the configuration appearing in lines 3 and 5. Line 3 illustrates cases of 'working in practice but not in theory' (La Porte and Consolini, 1991). Line 5 reflects cases of cognitive reducibility and practical irreducibility. Speculative thinking is an example. Science fiction is another instance. Otherwise it can be the initial step of a process necessarily comprising practical experience. An example is automated systems imagined to improve air traffic control performance (Durand and Alliot, 1999, 61). Then the initial cognitive phase cannot stabilise independently of a next, practically satisfactory stage. Otherwise we would have to assume that cognitive reducibility or satisficing might exist although it would not be satisficing in practice. This would be absurd. How could we make sense of knowledge if it were not checked in practice? Only speculative thinking or pure theorising separated from empirical testing can fit with this configuration. It could be at most transitory for our purpose and would necessitate it to be empirically complemented and tested. Therefore a complex situation arises from a cognitive and practical irreducibility and is best represented by the configuration shown in line 4. Furthermore, contrary to what happens with object-based complexity, the operator is *in* the situation, he/she is not facing a situation from outside.

The notion of complexity that we obtain is more general than the traditional object-based notion, contrary to what the questioning of the relevance of relying on a limit case evoked in the previous section would suggest. It is even worth emphasising that it is thanks to exploring a limit situation that a more general and more consistent notion could be built. For this, it proved necessary to shift away from Ashby's notion of complexity to complexity defined as the irreducibility to a satisficing level of reduction.

3.8 CONCLUSION

We explored in this chapter the consequences of conceiving complexity as an irreducibility to a satisficing level or degree of reduction. This irreducibility depends on eight elementary factors and dimensions, including the capacity to characterise the problem-situation as complex or not. This structuration is based on a behaviouralist setting. Complexity emerges when no cognitive and no practical satisficing reduction can be achieved.

Relativity is intrinsic to complexity. For an object-based complexity to be relevant, the other dimensions would have to be neutralised, which would be an extreme, limiting situation. Complexity is always relative to an epistemic situation, whatever the field or discipline. It is a property of complex systems in the special case in which the object is a system and the purpose is to deal with it. This is not definitional of complexity. Complexity is a property of a problem-situation defined by the combination of the factors and dimensions which appear in Table 3.3.

Thus we ended with a notion of complexity of a situation as a limit case emerging after the pathways to reducibility had failed in a sequence of eight steps representing factors or dimensions of complexity. We compared several examples which showed that what we obtained on the state – economy relations is not exceptional. The possibility or impossibility of sufficient reduction was established in each case and it supplied the character, complex or not complex, of the resulting situation. The argument contained in Table 3.3 thus sets the stage for connecting complexity with the epistemic situation, whatever the activity is. However, this is based on four examples only. A further enquiry into more general characteristics of complexity is needed. It is undertaken in the next chapter.

NOTE

1. G. Spencer Brown (1969), *Laws of Form*, London: George Allen & Unwin Ltd, 3.

4. Deep complexity as product

> During my conferences with these gentlemen, I was convinced with no less certainty than surprise, that if men of learning have sometimes fewer prejudices than others, they more tenaciously retain those they have.
>
> Jean-Jacques Rousseau (1742)[1]

4.1 INTRODUCTION

The object of this chapter is to explore the immediate implications of the relativity of complexity that was established in Chapter 3. Complexity was shown to depend on eight elementary factors and dimensions, and to be a property of an epistemic problem-situation. These findings were condensed in Table 3.3. Then, when complexity holds in this behaviouralist setting, where can we go from Table 3.3? An immediate answer is that this intractability calls for the search of an alternative setting in which the initial block can be stuctured. This depicts the initial stages of anchored deep complexity (ADCX) introduced in Chapter 2. But this time, deep complexity will no longer be the mere outcome of a heuristic procedure. It will be the product of a theoretical reflection on irreducibility taken as an object of enquiry in its own right.

This reflection will be developed in three stages. First, drawing on the results of Chapter 3, we will characterise complex irreducibility as a quantitative gap in epistemic resources, in section 4.2. Second, the necessary differentiation of epistemic resources into purely cognitive, practical and judgemental resources will open the way for a particular kind of judgement, a judgement of self-reference, giving rise to a ninth dimension with the distinction between an object level and a meta-level of reasoning. Deep complexity follows from it. Third, this differentiation of resources also opens the way for a qualitative characterisation of deep complexity as non-separability. This will lead us to characterise deep complexity through a fundamental, generic recursive relationship between a generative process and its product, thus opening a new way toward appraising complexity as a process in Chapter 5.

4.2 QUANTITATIVE IRREDUCIBILITY

Irreducibility to a satisficing level of reduction defines a behaviouralist complexity. It denotes a specific kind of difficulty pertaining to knowledge at large. It can be expressed by the difference between the resources needed for a satisficing reduction and the resources which are available. A situation is complex whenever the former are larger than the latter and this positive difference cannot be reduced to zero. This is what appeared in Table 3.3. But it was not explained. We do it now, in two steps. A generic expression of this resource gap is elaborated first. It will require two transformations before it qualifies as the category of complexity we arrived at, that is, the second-order complexity (SOCX) of Chapter 1 reappraised as deep complexity. A primary transformation consists in differentiating resources. It will be dealt with in quantitative terms. The second transformation entails a qualitative shift combined with quantitative terms. It will be addressed in section 4.3.

4.2.1 A Resource Gap

Let us go back to the process through which complex and non-complex situations were generated in Table 3.3. Reducibility or not in columns 6 to 8 results from a level of difficulty entailed by a level of aspiration for achieving a purpose or performing a task in a field imposing a standard of performance. There is no absolute measure of the level of difficulty. It depends on the level of aspiration, on the resources available, and on the standard. All these notions can be expressed in terms of difficulty defined as the amount of resources needed to perform a given task.

The field (column 4) dictates the standard acting as a constraint upon satisfactory activity in the field. Customs, and sanitary and commercial regulations, set the standards in butchery. Explicit standards are common in manufacturing. In scientific practice, they are set mainly by peers. In economics, editorial boards, referees and reviewers of journals, recruitment and tenure committees, and other specific sources of influence such as the most renowned university departments and research units, and the committees awarding prizes, notably the Bank of Sweden Prize in Economic Sciences in the Memory of Alfred Nobel, are the groups which determine institutional incentives, and shape de facto the standards of good scientific practice (Churchman and Ulrich, 1980; McCloskey, 1989; Colander, 1994, 2003). Let us symbolise by D^* the amount of resources needed to match the standard reigning in a given field. Since we are not going to compare levels of difficulties and of resources across fields, but will attempt to formulate properties that are valid independently of the differences across fields, we do not need to identify the fields.

The goal in performing a task i is to match the level of aspiration (column 5). We denote by $\hat{D}^i$ the difficulty or amount of resources needed for it. Given the social or community feedback on the specific activity at stake, the level of aspiration is not set freely. It is constrained by D^* and cannot be inferior to it: $\hat{D}^i \geq D^*$.

Finally, the amount of available resources ($\overline{D}$) enters into play in columns 3, 6 and 7. $\overline{D}$ stands for the maximum level of difficulty that can be dealt with effectively with the available resources. This upper limit of the available resources may be considered as given in the short run. It may range from a very small, practically nil level, to some finite upper limit Z at a given point in time. $\hat{D}^i$ and D^* can range from small, but not nil levels, to arbitrary large levels. We assume that $\hat{D}^i$ and D^* have the same minimum level measured as a unit of the cognitive and practical resources in which $\hat{D}^i$, D^* and $\overline{D}$ are expressed. How to measure these magnitudes is an open question which can be left out since we are only interested in comparing them in relative terms. D^* has no determinate relationship with $\overline{D}$: it can be lower than, equal to or higher than $\overline{D}$.

Should we index the available resources $\overline{D}$ on a specific task i? The resources available to an operator are normally considered in connection with a task to perform or with a range of tasks. This seems to be especially true for cognitive and practical abilities. It seems however less true for judgemental resources. The faculty of judgement connotes more a general ability than a capacity connected to specific tasks. Available resources are thus diversified in this respect, which points to the need to differentiate them explicitly in a next step. Yet, since we are characterising a resource gap in general at this stage, we will keep the general notation $\overline{D}$ for the available resources.

$\overline{D}$ can be changed through acquiring additional resources and learning but is given in the short run. Then adjustment can take place in the short run only through $\hat{D}^i$.

The diversity i of purposes and tasks one may envisage is very large and has no conceivable limit. Therefore i may range from one to a very high, practically infinite figure.

These conditions are recapitulated below:

$$0 \leq \overline{D} \leq Z \;; \qquad 1 \leq \hat{D}^i; \qquad D^* < +\infty\;; \qquad i = 1,2,\ldots,+\infty$$

We can now express the resource gap of complexity in general terms as the irreducibility to zero of the excess of the resources needed over the resources available to perform a task satisfactorily or achieve some goal. Complexity itself follows from this positive difference between the two levels of difficulties. It can be expressed in two ways, either directly as the difference itself or as an increasing function of this difference. Let us symbolise by DD^i the difference of difficulties pertaining to task i. In the first way, complexity derives from DD^i_1 such that:

$$DD^i_1 \equiv \hat{D}^i - \overline{D}$$

In the second way, complexity derives from DD^i_2 such that:

$$DD^i_2 \equiv f(\hat{D}^i - \overline{D}) \text{ with } f(0) = 0 \text{ and } f' > 0.$$

In both cases, the behavioural constraint applies:

$$\hat{D}^i \geq D^*$$

Irreducibility or non-satisficing corresponds to the situation in which the level of aspiration remains higher than the available resources: $\hat{D}^i > \overline{D}$. These cases are represented in Figure 4.1.

Complexity as difference DD^i_1 is illustrated by Figure 4.1a. Satisficing is achieved when reducibility is obtained. It can be achieved in two ways, 'from below' and 'from above'. 'From below' means that if we start from a 'low' level of aspiration such that $\hat{D}^i < \overline{D}$, this level of aspiration can be increased while reducibility continues to be obtained up to the limit set by the available resources: $\hat{D}^i \leq \overline{D}$. 'From above' means that if we start from a 'high' level of aspiration, above the resources available, then this level of aspiration must be reduced enough in order to match $\overline{D}$: $\hat{D}^i \geq \overline{D}$.

In Figure 4.1a, the area under the bisecting line and the one ordinate is not admissible. Points A, B and C represent characteristic situations. In A, 'the level of aspiration' $\hat{D}^i$ is larger than D^* but both are inferior to $\overline{D}$, then reducibility is achieved. In B the level of aspiration cannot be met because it is larger than $\overline{D}$. Although $\overline{D}$ is itself above D^*, no satisficing can be achieved. In C both the level of aspiration and the standard cannot be achieved. The area of non-complexity is delimited by ordinate 1, by $\overline{D}$ and by the bisecting line. Complexity corresponds to the area above $\overline{D}$ and above the bisecting line. Complexity as DD^i_2 is illustrated in Figure 4.1b.

In sum, a general expression of complexity is:

$$DD^i_j > 0 \quad \text{with } \hat{D}^i \geq D^* \qquad j = 1,2$$

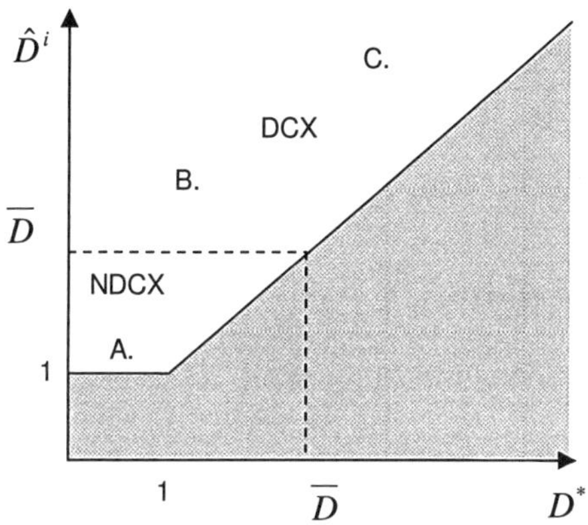

4.1a Deep complexity derived from $DD^i{}_1 \equiv \hat{D}^i - \overline{D}$, subject to $\hat{D}^i \geq D^*$

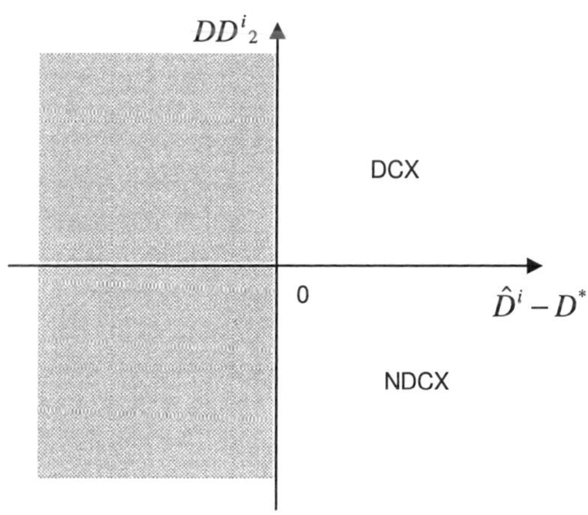

4.1b Deep complexity derived from $DD^i{}_2 \equiv f(\hat{D}^i - \overline{D})$, subject to $\hat{D}^i \geq D^*$

Figure 4.1 Elementary quantitative irreducibility

It is clear from the expression above that complexity is strictly determined by the positive sign of $\hat{D}^i - \overline{D}$ in both cases. This renders it possible to simplify through dropping the subscript j and reducing $DD^i{}_j$ to $DD^i \equiv \hat{D}^i - \overline{D}$.

Then we express a first, elementary notion of complexity (CX1) as:

$$\textbf{CX1}: \quad DD^i > 0$$
$$\text{s.t.} \quad \hat{D}^i \geq D^*$$

4.2.2 Resources Differentiated

A. Pure cognition, practice and judgement

The general expression of complexity CXl requires to be complemented in several directions. These directions will lead to progressively enriched and more specified expressions of complexity: CX2 and CX3 in this chapter, and CX4 in the next chapter. We concentrate now on the move from CXl to the complexity of situation CX2.

This notion denotes a restricted conception of complexity, for it is only when the practical resources do not suffice (column 7 of Table 3.3, Chapter 3) that the situation can be characterised as complex. The practical resources are themselves activated when the purely cognitive resources do not permit achieving a satisfactory outcome. This distinction is connoted by the reference to cognitive and practical irreducibility in columns 6 and 7 of Table 3.3. It is clear from the examples taken that cognition is not separated from practice. Referring to pure cognitive resources does not mean that cognition is absent from practical resources. It simply depicts a situation in which the acquired, already existing knowledge of a tool, of a technique or of an algorithm is sufficient to carry out a task satisfactorily. These cognitive properties of column 6 are a composition of the mainly cognitive aspects detailed in the previous five columns. They pertain to the substance of the task independently of the practical aspects of column 7. The Simonian notion of substantive rationality characterises a behaviour which relies on this kind of resource. It may be called cognitive resource, for short. Two gaps are thus explicitly distinguished in Table 3.3, a cognitive gap in column 6 and a practical gap in column 7. Yet a further reflection reveals that an additional, less explicit distinction is operating in columns 6 to 8 and requires a specific resource. This resource is needed to identify when satisficing is obtained in columns 6 and 7, and to identify the situation as complex, in column 8, when satisficing is not obtained in column 7. This third resource is *judgement*. It is present in columns 6 to 8, in combination with the purely cognitive and practical resources in columns 6 and 7, and is alone in column 8. Characterising the overall situation in this column may look strange since it denotes a sort of final dead end and insurmountable obstacle. Accepting this very possibility requires therefore more than the practical resources of column 7. In fact a divide occurs here between two conceptions, one that puts an end to the process of enquiry at this stage, and another that attempts to pursue the enquiry but in a quite specific way, relying therefore on a specific kind of resource not activated in the previous steps. It is a *judgement of situation* which complements the judgements of cognitive and practical reducibility. It will itself be complemented by a judgement of *self-reference* connected to deep complexity, in the next section.

B. Substance and procedure

Both practical and judgemental resources pertain to procedural rationality (PR). Indeed the three kinds of resources are not separated, they are facets of a whole epistemic capacity but come into focus differently, depending on the degree of difficulty encountered. And it seems reasonable to introduce them in a sequence going from the simple to the most difficult. Heuristics, procedural rationality and capacity of judgement characterise the situation in which cognitive resources do not suffice. We identified it in Table 3.3 as practical and judgemental. The judgment of situation lies in the capacity to identify the resulting situation as complex or not complex. But this leads immediately to another judgement, on what to do next when the situation perceived is complex. Moving toward a second-order, meta-level, is the answer we bring. Second-order or deep complexity will follow from it.

At this stage, it will be helpful to rely explicitly on a behavioural setting. We will gain in simplification of our argument while not altering its content. Cognitive reducibility means that the available knowledge is sufficient to achieve a satisfactory outcome – to perform the task satisfactorily – without inquiring further about an appropriate procedure. To repeat, it is similar to substantive rationality. But if cognitive irreducibility prevails, this makes necessary to enquire about an appropriate procedure, and to put it into practice. Practice, cognition and judgemental resources are naturally not insulated from each other in this search for what is identified as practical reducibility in Table 3.3, but is nothing else than a practice of procedural rationality in Simonian terms. And the activation of procedural resources naturally includes the characterisation of the situation. Thus we can simplify the differentiation into the two categories of substantive and procedural resources in connection with substantive and procedural rationality, and will symbolise them by SR and PR respectively. Reducibility or irreducibility can then be considered from substantive and procedural standpoints. What are the consequences of this differentiation of resources on $\hat{D}'$, D^* and $\overline{D}$? Let us start with $\overline{D}$. It depends clearly on the nature of resources and needs to be indexed on substantive resources ($\overline{D}^s$) and procedural resources ($\overline{D}^p$).

For what concerns D^*, it seems reasonable not to split it into substantive and procedural standards. If the very notion of a standard is to retain some signification, be it explicitly stated or empirically imposing itself through the day-to-day functioning of a community, it can hardly depend on the nature of the resources considered. Resources signal different ways for operating in a field. The three types of resources considered here, including judgement, to be addressed below, are different dimensions complementing each other, starting with pure cognition, then activating practice, and judgement ultimately, in the attempt to match a given standard at a given logical level which is here the object level.

Finally, the same goes for the level of aspiration $\hat{D}^i$ as is clear from Table 3.3. $\hat{D}^i$, which can be for instance 'aspiring to no major accident', does not vary according to the nature of the resources envisaged.

Complexity is now dependent on a differentiated resource gap:

$$DD^{is} \equiv \hat{D}^i - \overline{D}^s$$
$$DD^{ip} \equiv \hat{D}^i - \overline{D}^p$$
$$DD^{ir} \equiv \hat{D}^i - \overline{D}^r$$

with $r = s, p$ (s = substantive resources, p = procedural resources).

Four combinations of these substantive and procedural resource gaps can be envisaged. They provide a criterion for differentiating complexity from non-complexity (simplicity or complication), as is shown in Table 4.1.

Table 4.1 From simplicity to complexity

Configuration	Substantive gap	Procedural gap	Resulting situation	Symbols
1	$\hat{D}^i < \overline{D}^s$	$\hat{D}^i < \overline{D}^p$	Simplicity	NCX
2	$\hat{D}^i \leq \overline{D}^s$	$\hat{D}^i \leq \overline{D}^p$	Complication	
3	$\hat{D}^i > \overline{D}^s$	$\hat{D}^i \leq \overline{D}^p$	Complication	
4	$\hat{D}^i > \overline{D}^s$	$\hat{D}^i > \overline{D}^p$	**Complexity**	CX

A second expression of complexity emerges from Table 4.1:

$$\textbf{CX2}: \; DD^{ip} > 0$$
$$\text{s.t. } \hat{D}^i \geq D^*$$

The complexity of situation follows from procedural irreducibility since it is the ultimate point in assessing whether the reduction that is achieved can be satisficing or not. Then, what to do next can only be dealt with through judgement. Procedural rationality and informed deliberation may be considered as other names for it, although it is appropriate to use them with more restricted meanings in the present context. The kind of judgement called for at this stage differs from the judgement already evoked above in assessing cognitive and practical satisficing. It is addressed in the next section.

4.3 THE NINTH DIMENSION

4.3.1 From Object Level to Meta-level

Procedural irreducibility is a decisive factor leading to a complex situation. Yet it does not obey any clear-cut criterion. It is a matter of judgement: some people will be ready to satisfice while others will not. In the case of the RISE (regime of interaction between the state and the economy), I found myself clearly in the second category. As an object in its own right, the RISE resists conventional analysis. No procedure seems to work satisfactorily. The situation is complex. Judgement plays a central role. It has two facets. One has already been evoked. It lies in the capacity to judge whether satisficing is obtained or not. It is thus present in the identification of substantive and procedural reducibility and, finally in the recognition of the complex or non-complex character of the situation. It is a third category of resource understood in a broad, epistemic sense, but it does not add simply to the other two resources since it is intimately connected with both substantive and procedural resources and it comes as the decisive factor in the identification of the resulting situation. The second facet lies in the answer to the question about what to do when the situation is perceived as deeply complex. The answer I propose is to shift to a meta-level thanks to a self-referential reasoning. This is a big move since we are no longer in the original Simonian setting although what appears at the meta-level obeys the behavioural pattern. Simon kept away from self-referential reasoning. What I develop may therefore be termed post-Simonian. It relies on the move from the object level to the meta-level. It adds a ninth dimension to the eight initial dimensions pertaining to the object-level, which are therefore genuine elementary dimensions of quantitative irreducibility.

Although we explored a way out of the obstacle of the complexity of situation, which was developed in Chapter 1, the above characterisation of complexity tells us that other alternatives exist, however problematic implementing them might be.

One might think first of reducing the level of aspiration through lessening primarily the level of cognitive, substantive difficulty addressed, and identifying the level of aspiration thus adjusted with an s superscript: $\hat{D}^{is}$, and, in cases where it does not suffice, adjusting also the level of practical p difficulty identified as the level of aspiration thus adjusted for procedural purposes: $\hat{D}^{ip}$. However, there may exist reasons which prevent this reduction. In our case, the very robustness of the RISE was the main factor for not doing away with it. Abandoning the RISE considered in its own right and limiting the inquiry to the analytically tractable aspects would change the object of inquiry. It would boil down to adjusting the level of aspiration to analytical tractability. There is a priori nothing wrong with this provided it remains consistent with the most robust empirical properties of the object or, more broadly, with the constituting properties of the task at hand. This could hardly be done on the RISE.

Another strategy might be envisaged. It would be aimed at increasing the available resources $\overline{D}$. It is ruled out in the short run since we assume competency in a given field. But it can be effective over time through learning, and scientific and technical progress. Moreover, procedural resources may also evolve and render acceptable in the future what was irreducible in the short run. In this way interactive learning and the evolution of perceptions may be a powerful way for modifying $\overline{D}$.

A third attitude is to acknowledge the difficulty and leave the issue open for further inquiry but unsolved for the time being. Arthur et al. (1997) illustrate this. We have already evoked how they seem to admit that adaptive non-linear networks present a difficulty of a special kind for economic analysis. They wonder about the nature of the problem and the concepts to be used in the frame of what they call the Santa Fe approach. They come close to a complexity of situation but they do not question the relevance of the procedure, and thus implicitly seem to assume that the tools and the procedure available at the object level will suffice to carry out the task. The very idea of complexity of situation remains unknown.

A fourth strategy stems from the explicit recognition of the complexity of situation and is adopted here. Since the task cannot be performed satisfactorily, the ultimate obstacle must lie with the procedural step. The rationale is to explore how to improve the procedure, not through reducing $\hat{D}^{ip}$ but through changing it qualitatively. How can this be done? Since we assume that the operator is competent, it can hardly be done directly through the use of procedural resources which would be available but would have remained unused. The only path left is to inquire as to how the procedure is generated and to act at the generating level. This requires differentiation between an initial, object level, and the level at which the procedure is generated, that is, a meta-level. Instead of attempting to solve the problem at the object level, it tells that if this problem cannot be solved, then it is worth enquiring on how the problem is designed. This leads one to design a procedure at the meta-level and then connects this procedure with the object level. This strategy is developed below.

In a deeply complex situation irreducibility appears total since no solution to procedural irreducibility seems to exist. Yet it is at this very step, not at the substantive step, that practical resources, deliberation, ingenuity, and so on, that is, judgement, can be activated in order to elaborate a reasonable procedure. But it is not a procedure that can directly replace the initial, irreducible one. The problem is to design a satisficing procedure for elaborating an itself satisficing procedure for the initial problem. There is a qualitative difference between these procedures because they belong to different logical levels. The former is at the meta-level, the latter is at the initial, object level. This distinction is central although it is, so to speak, neutralised in current practice by focusing attention on substantive aspects and by assuming that proof-tested techniques or methods are available, which avoids the issue addressed here through rendering it unnecessary to reflect on a meta-level. We thus bump into a complexity including an object-level or first-order irreducibility, and a meta-level or second-order problem of reducibility. In our experience with the RISE, we designed a procedure at the second-order level that we named anchored complexity, and thanks to which it became possible to address the RISE in a way that was compatible with explicitly stated criteria meeting a standard of scientific practice. This may look strange, although it arose from a case study. It is not surprising once we perceive this step in our theoretical characterisation of complexity as intermediary between a phase of identification of quantitative irreducibility, which we initiated above, and a next phase, to come, of identification of qualitative irreducibility. Notice that second-order, deep complexity emerges from quantitative irreducibility and will necessitate refering to qualitative reducibility and irreducibility in order to be fully characterised.

4.3.2 The Emergence of Second-order, Deep Complexity

Deep complexity emerges as a second order complexity. It adds a new dimension to irreducibility that is based on the distinction between logical levels. A move beyond Table 4.1 becomes necessary. It appears in Table 4.2, which includes a complex situation at the object level – the object-level row is line 4 of Table 4.1 – and second-order complexity created by referring to a meta-level. In fact, second - order complexity denotes the new situation created by combining the two levels.

The substance (task or object) at the meta-level is to design an acceptable, satisfactory procedure for dealing with the object-level substance. This result at the meta-level abides itself by explicit criteria included in a meta-procedure which is itself the outcome of a higher, meta-meta, logical level. One advantage of this argumentation is to render explicit and to clarify a plurality of steps which might otherwise be nothing else than tacit preconceptions.

Table 4.2 From object level to meta-level: the emergence of second order complexity

Logical level	Substance	Procedure	Situation created
Object	Substantive irreducibility	Procedural irreducibility	Complex
Meta	Procedure for dealing with the object level	Abiding by explicit criteria	**Second order complexity**

The information presented in Tables 3.4, 4.1 and 4.2 helps us understand where deep, second-order complexity stands in comparison with the already known forms of complexity discussed in Chapter 2. Deep complexity follows from the recognition of a complex situation. This recognition is central to our argument. The difference with the existing literature arises from it. While in classical object-based forms of complexity it is implicitly assumed that it is possible to go ahead procedurally ($\hat{D}^{i} \leq \overline{D}^{p}$) which amounts to remain in configuration 3 of Table 4.1, deep complexity arises from case 4. It is the complexity of situation which triggered the shift to a self-referential, meta-level reasoning.

The procedure we introduce considers the outcome obtained at the object level (complex situation) as the object of inquiry at the upper, meta-level. This procedure is also called second-order complexity because it originates from complexity of complexity at the object level. It is detailed in Table 4.3 with the explicit consideration of higher logical levels. Table 4.3 is constructed on the basis of Table 3.3: its upper part on object level is transplanted from Table 3.3. Although the setting at the meta-level is similar to that at the object level with its sequence developed in eight steps, its substance is different. The object at the meta-level is the object-level problem, it consists in the complex situation. The purpose is to design a satisfactory procedure for dealing with the object-level problem. This needs to be made explicit. The operator is naturally the same as before but he/she operates differently since he/she is self-referentially contemplating from a meta-level what he/she can do at the object level. Given the obstacle arising from the object level, the task at the meta-level consists in rendering compatible a level of aspiration $\hat{D}^{i}_{m}$, the resources available $\overline{D}_{m}$ and the standard D^{*}_{m}, with the *m* subscript indicating the meta-level.

Table 4.3 The ninth dimension of deep complexity

Ninth dimension	Elementary dimensions: 1 Object	2 Purpose or task	3 Operator	4 Field	5 Level of aspiration	6 Cognitive/ substantive reducibility	7 Practical/ procedural reducibility	8 Character of situation
Object level	Public expenditure and role of the state in the economy (RISE)	Description	Economist	Political economy Economics	1) See Table 3.3 2)	+ -	+ -	NCX CX: shift to meta-level
Meta-level	Object level complex situation	Design a procedure for dealing satisficingly with object level situation	Modeller, designer as self-referential operator (here economist)	Political economy Economics	Achieve a satisficing procedure meeting standards of scientific practice	-	-	DCX : shift to meta-meta-level
Meta-meta-level	Meta-level deeply complex situation	Design a procedure for dealing satisficingly with meta-level situation	Same as at meta-level	- d° -	- d° -	Constraint of bringing an end point Construction of this end point as goal on the modelling agenda		

In a similar way, we index the object-level entities with the subscript *o*. Therefore from now on we will have to differentiate the task at the object level $({}^{\iota}_{o})$ from the task at the meta-level $({}^{\iota}_{m})$, $\hat{D}^i_o$ from $\hat{D}^i_m$, D^*_o from D^*_m, $\overline{D}^r_o$ from $\overline{D}^r_m$, with $r = s, p$ (s = substantive resources, p = procedural resources). This differentiation can in principle include higher levels than *m*, that is, a meta-meta-level *mm*, and so on. Let us symbolise this new dimension by ℓ.

The differentiation of logical levels introduces a ninth dimension. Complexity becomes expressed through a generalised resource gap:

$$DD^{ir}_{\ell} \equiv \hat{D}^i_{\ell} - \overline{D}^r_{\ell}$$

with $\ell = o, m, mm$ (o = object level, m = meta-level, mm = meta-meta-level);
$r = s, p$ (s = substantive resources, p = procedural resources).

The level of aspiration at the meta-level is to achieve a satisficing procedure meeting the standards of the field; here, scientific practice. It is to achieve a situation such that $\hat{D}^i_m$ is not larger than $\overline{D}^r_m$ and not lower than D^*_m, the explicitly stated standard of satisficing practice in the field.

Table 4.3 describes the emergence of deep complexity. The first line is about the object-level situation. It begins with the RISE as object, though any one of the other objects of Table 3.3 might have been chosen as well. The behaviouralist setting appears with the level of aspiration. If it is not higher than the available cognitive/substantive, and/or practical/procedural resources, then the situation is not complex. If it is higher, then the situation is complex and requires a shift to the meta-level. The second line is about this meta-level. Its object is the object-level problem-situation. In this case the task is to design a procedure for dealing in a satisficing way with the object-level problem-situation. At this stage of the depiction of how deep complexity arises, no satisficing procedure is available (minus signs in columns 6 and 7). There is no available way out at the meta-level. It has to be constructed. It creates a *deeply complex situation* which necessitates to be addressed from an upper, meta-meta-level. The third line is about the meta-meta-level. Its object is the meta-level deeply complex situation. The task is to design a model that will be used at the meta-level in order to be put to work on the object-level problem-situation. Once this model is designed, it will be available at the meta-level. The aim of this modelling is to be operational at the object level. The construction of this end point is the goal of the modelling agenda.

It must be stressed that the achievement of a satisficing outcome at the meta-level is not synonymous with solving the problem of the initial complex situation. Indeed, irreducibility cannot be solved in the sense of achieving a final solution to it. But it becomes dealt with in a specific structured way. This way consists in designing criteria abiding by explicit constraints informing judgement. It is different from object-level judgement in which the basis of informed judgement remains unknown: informed judgement comes as an exogenous resource filling the irreducible cognitive gap about performing a task, whereas the task at the meta-level is to design a procedure for dealing satisfactorily with the object-level situation (Table 4.3), that is, to design an informed judgement.

In conclusion we arrive at a third notion of complexity (CX3) or deep complexity. It arises through a bottom-up reasoning which began with a first-order, object-level irreducibility, and shifted to a second-order, meta-level.

It is expressed as:

$$\textbf{CX3:} \begin{cases} DD_o^{ip} > 0 & \text{s.t.} \quad \hat{D}_o^i \geq D_o^* \\ DD_m^{ip} \geq 0 & \text{s.t.} \quad \hat{D}_m^i \geq D_m^* \end{cases}$$

CX3 is an intermediary and ambivalent concept. Having it greater than or equal to zero at the meta-level reflects both its static and its processual character. Statically, it is the product of a heuristic hypothesis in Chapter 1 whereby a satisficing procedure was assumed to hold at the meta-level. Hence the reduction of the resource gap to zero. Processually, this assumption must be transformed into the product of an endogenising mechanism whose origin cannot but be at the meta-meta-level, in a top-down process. Prolonging the search for a satisficing up to this level implies that the meta-level is not satisficing, that is, that the resource gap is positive. It is only in a next stage, when a satisficing is constructed at the meta-meta-level, that the meta-level satisficing can be defined. This will entail conceiving deep complexity as a process, a task that will be undertaken in the next chapter.

The quantitative expression of deep complexity is also incomplete. The very combination of logical levels means that we are no longer dealing with mere quantitative complexity. It denotes a qualitative aspect that we must address now.

4.4 QUALITATIVE IRREDUCIBILITY

4.4.1 Duality and Non-separability

At first sight the notion of qualitative irreducibility conveys the idea that something is not amenable to something else and that the difference between these things remains essential to the extent that it designates a difference in nature. However, qualitative irreducibility can be found in the literature with different meanings. Let us illustrate this with two examples. Michael Smithson writes that: ‘fuzzy set theory made a strong case early on for being distinct from and irreducible to probability’ (Smithson, 1989, 108). In the same way, Tony Lawson evokes ‘social structures … that are irreducible to people’ and to events (Lawson, 1997, 159). However, one might object that this idea can be expressed in quantitative terms and transformed into an irreducibility to less than two distinct terms or entities, which brings us back to a quantitative threshold of two and is synonymous with ‘not amenable to less than two’. This is similar to Rosen and Casti’s definitions of complexity as irreducibility to less than several or at least two inequivalent descriptions of a phenomenon. The limit case or threshold of two may serve to define complexity since it is the most that can be achieved in relation to reduction and all other cases are compounds of it:

$$CX = (A, B)$$

In this expression A and B are two distinct notions, or entities, not amenable to one another. Inequivalent descriptions are an example. They can be viewed as two entities standing side by side, separated and autonomous from each other, composing a pair denotating a dualism or a dichotomy of its components. It is quantitative: only the number of irreducible terms counts, independently of the particular substance of these terms. Here, we know only that they are descriptions, but the very nature of these descriptions plays no role.

We claimed above that this notion of quantitative irreducibility needed to be reframed in terms of a resource gap.

A. Duality, neither dichotomy nor dualism

A closer scrutiny at the two examples above suggests that they are not equivalent. Their respective terms do not stand in similar relations in each pair. Fuzzy set theory and probability theory can be viewed as two inequivalent and irreducible theories or descriptions, although this is much debated, and thus represent two separated terms, whereas social structures and agents are definitely not separated. They reciprocally shape each other. These examples illustrate two types of relations: external and internal. 'Two objects or aspects are said to be externally related if neither is constituted by the relationship in which it stands to the other' (Lawson, 1997, 164). Water and bottle, stone and wood, table and chair, tea and milk, provide examples. In contrast, two objects or notions are said to be internally related 'if they are what they are by virtue of the relationship in which they stand to one other' (Lawson, ibid.). Predator and prey, landlord and tenant, employer and employee, are examples. It seems appropriate to associate dualism or dichotomy with the former example, and to denote by *duality* the relationship characterising the latter.

In duality the terms are necessary to each other insofar as each term depends on the other term for its definition and for the role it plays. This is different in dualism: when the description of a phenomenon cannot be reduced to less than two, these two descriptions need not have any intrinsic definitional connection and can be considered autonomously from each other. This is *a fortiori* true for more than two descriptions. In one case they are conjoined or combined; in the other, they are disjointed. There is more to qualitative irreducibility than mere dualism or dichotomy of separated and insulated entities. We have seen it in different instances. The (observer, observed) pair arose from a perceived irreducible problem at the object level. This very problem provided the rationale for also distinguishing substantive and procedural rationality. Another instance stems from conceiving complexity as an irreducible composite of order and disorder (Chapter 2). As soon as the entity resulting from the combination of order and disorder can be identified as either one or the other, it loses its complex character. Thus, not only can complexity not be assimilated to one of the terms, but it is also not amenable to a pair of terms whose contributions could be divisible and counted separately or combined quantitatively. The kind of complexity we uncover consists in an essential connection between the components: they are not separable, although they are different and none is reducible to the other. Duality denotes this kind of articulated unity or non-separability. It is essential to the extent that it is not merely a property of complexity: it is complexity.

In duality, the terms are irreducibly different and yet necessary to each other. They cannot be separated lest the very notion of duality disappear. In this sense there is a unity created by the internal relation. The character of each term which is relevant for the purpose at hand depends on the other term. Irreducibility in this case is no longer a matter of number but of nature, that is, of the quality of the relationship between the terms.

B. Three root dualities

We have encountered thus far a diversity of pairs with the character of duality: observer and observed, operator and operated, procedural rationality and substantive rationality, institutions and agents, meta-level and object level, process and product, procedure and substance, order and disorder, and even an apparently strange combination of reducibility (meta) and irreducibility (object) which opens the way to stating that complexity appears in CX3 as an obstacle (product of the object-level process) which triggered the search for a solution at the meta-level. Therefore complexity is also a pair (obstacle, solution). Duality takes on a variety of components and of meanings in the developments leading to second-order complexity. Some pairs contain terms negating each other, of the (A, not-A) type reminiscent of dialectics and of a 'unity of opposites'. But a majority of the pairs are different and contain complementary aspects, of the process and product type.

A challenge resides in the fact that in order to be operational we must structure and reduce this heterogeneity of pairs. A way to do it is to select the basic pairs that we had to introduce in our argument. Indeed three pairs stand out as a common background from which all other considerations in our argument derive. We started with the Simonian frame of procedural and substantive rationality and symbolised it by (PR, SR). Then we introduced self-reference and the object and meta-logical levels through the reference to von Foerster. And we developed an argument starting from the observation of some complex phenomenon of interest, and seeking to design a pattern of which the phenomenon is an outcome, which is congruent with von Neumann's intuition on complexity. This third pair associates a generative mechanism or process (GP) and an outcome or product of it (P); we symbolise it as (*GP, P*). These three pairs are ever present, they interact and are seemingly sufficient to account for the complex situations that can be encountered. It can be shown with the other two pairs mentioned above. Let us take the (order, disorder) pair. The complexity it represents at the object level (disorder) is complemented with second-order complexity or order at the meta-level. The (observer, observed) pair appears easily as an instance of the three pairs respectively. The observer is connected with procedure, is meta and is a generative process compared to the respective substantive, object and product qualities of what is observed. It seems that whatever the details of a complex situation are, the second-order complexity to which it leads follows from the use of these three pairs. Thus it is appropriate to call them *root pairs* or *root dualities*.

4.4.2 Asymmetry and Recursion

A. Asymmetry and the generic duality

A common aspect of the root pairs is the *imbrication* of the terms in a hierarchical order. It works in the following way. In the (PR, SR) pair, common behaviour commands starting with SR and shifting to a PR behaviour if SR is not satisficing in a first step. But the aim remains to simplify as much as possible, not to stay at PR if the possibility of simplifying to SR exists. In this sense PR is more general and enables one to envisage a set of possibilities, none of which reduce to SR, but in which some simplifications of an SR character may be achieved. This works in both ways, in the move from SR to PR (bottom-up) and in the move from PR to SR (top-down). My claim is that a permanent tension in purposeful behaviour is to achieve a satisficing simplification even if this simplification is partial in the sense that the PR step remains active.

The pair (PR, SR) can itself be considered as a specific instance of a more general process and product pair in which the asymmetry is obvious.

A similar kind of imbrication exists between the object and the meta-levels. Common behaviour commands to work at the object level. It is only when a satisficing result cannot be achieved that a shift to the meta-level becomes necessary. Imbrication means that one term emerges from the other, but in an asymmetric way in the sense of a hierarchical order between them. It is not interaction between terms of equal status since one is more general than the other.

In the kind of complex situation in which we are, a key point is the identification of the object-level situation (Table 3.3, column 8). If it is not complex, there is no need to activate the meta-level. One can proceed at the object level through (PR, SR) and (process, product). If the situation is complex, then our model activates the meta-level, that is, the (meta-level, object level) pair. The other pairs are particular, contingent pairs, whose nature depends on the specific task or issue at stake. Notice the central role of the (meta-level, object level) pair. You can need to activate PR and process at the object level and still satisfice, that is, obtain a non-complex situation. Naturally it is even more obvious when you can rely simply on SR and product, when you are confident in the effectiveness of your toolkit and of the available algorithms. A soon as you need to activate the meta-level, the three pairs enter into interplay, whereas only two pairs need to be active at the object level.

Our argumentation shows that it is not necessary to include the meta-level when the situation is non-complex. Then only the other two root pairs (PR, SR) and (process and product) are operationally present. The third pair comes into play in a complex situation and in second-order complexity. In the simplest situation of all, only the right-hand side terms of the pairs that is SR, product and object level need to be considered. PR and process are explicitly introduced when the situation becomes more complicated, but is still satisficing. The meta-level becomes explicitly necessary in the complex situation. Things appear as if the right-hand side terms of the dualities were considered first and as if the left-hand side terms were called for only in the case of a failure to satisfice with the right-hand side terms. This depicts a setting in which the terms can be alternatively activated and deactivated in an ordered way, depending on whether satisficing is achieved or not. This is what was shown in Tables 3.3, 3.4 and 4.2 at the object level only; and in Tables 4.2 (meta-level introduced) and 4.3 (meta-level detailed).

Asymmetry occurs within a given level and across levels. In the former case it is the imbrication in the pairs (PR, SR) and (process, product); in the latter, a third imbrication is added, between meta- and object levels. The former type of imbrication is present at both levels. And the latter denotes a self-referential order resembling a tangled hierarchy (Hofstadter, 1985) or a Russian doll construct, with fluidity between levels. Each level can be contemplated from a higher level in a nested self-referential spiral or hierarchy with a permanent fluidity and no absolute prior level: the meta-level is itself an object level when it is considered from a meta-meta-level.

The search for reduction and simplification is also our purpose. It seems clear from the developments above that the pair (process and product) is more general than the other two and can represent complex duality considered in a generic way. Literally, this generic duality consists of a process leading to something (or a generative process) and the thing to which the process leads (product or outcome). It would indeed be more accurate to consider that the outcome is already there, and to use the past for what led to it: a time dimension is intrinsic to the process and product duality. In order to simplify the symbols and to avoid confusion in the rest of this book, we take as synonymous process and generative mechanism, and product and outcome respectively, and will stick to the pair (generative process, product), that is (*GP*, *P*), as the generic pair for complexity without making the time dimension explicit. All other pairs or cases derive from a simplification or particular specifications of it.

B. Recursion

Recursion is a process whereby the result of an operation is run again through this operation. This general definition is given specific contents adapted to its domains of application, notably in mathematics, in programming and in logic and systems theory. On the mathematical side, let the sequence $\{y_n\}$, in which y_n can be any real number, be defined for $n = 1,2,3\ldots$ by the equation $y_{n+1} = f(y_n)$. This equation expresses y_{n+1} as a function of the previous term in the sequence which defines recursion. When the new term depends on several of the previous terms in the sequence $\{y_{n+k}\}$ defined for $n,k = 1,2,3,\ldots$, a more general form is:

$$y_{n+k} = f(y_{n+k-1}, y_{n+k-2}, \ldots, y_n)$$

In programming, recursion is a technique whereby a procedure is divided into a sequence of repetitions of itself. The recursive process can go on forever if it does not contain a stopping rule. Fractals are an example of recursive geometry in which entities break up into copies of themselves in an endless process.

Recursion is also a process of self-referential reasoning (H. von Foerster) and of formal calculus of self-reference (G. Spencer Brown, 1969; F. Varela, 1979). It is a mechanism of circular self-reproduction of components and relationships in a system. Recursion can in principle be applied on its own results without limits. It is a process that operates on the product of its own operation or, to paraphrase E. Morin, it is a process in which the result produces what produces it.

This view fits well with the pattern of duality presented here in which one term emerges from the other. However, these terms are not interchangeable, the interaction is asymmetric. To show this, let us recall the shift from a complex situation to the meta-level.

The meta-level and object-level duality is always present, but the explicit reference to the meta-level may not be needed. In our development, the key point is not the existence of, but the role played by, the meta-level.

When it is satisficing to stick to the object level, the meta-level remains neutralised and, so to speak, deactivated. In this case, the existing tools and algorithms are performing well enough; there is no need for an active and explicit self-reference. The only consciousness coming close to self-reference that is needed is about using one's competence and adequate tools and algorithms. If it is not enough, then practical and judgemental satisficing enter into play. The whole process was depicted in sections 4.2 and 4.3 above.

Shifting to the meta-level results from not satisficing at the object level or, in other words, from the emergence of a complex situation and from the willingness not to be paralysed by this obstacle but to 'move up' to the meta-level and activate it.

In this shift the very process in operation at the object level and its product become the object of operation at the meta-level. The product at the object level triggers an operation reshaping the process but at a different, higher level at which the newly reshaped process will itself lead to a new outcome, a meta-product different from the initial object product which triggered the new overall process at the meta-level.

Two aspects are present in this process: besides the hierarchically ordered imbrication of terms defining asymmetry, there is a recursion denoting the reshaping of the generative mechanism. Self-reference provides an instance of it. The product produces what produces it. There is more to recursion than a mere oscillating or iterative process because the generative process *GP* is not at the same level as product, as is illustrated by the way deep complexity emerged in Chapter 1.

Other instances are abundant. Among them is the paradigmatic conception of learning proposed by Jean Piaget in 1937: 'Intelligence (and therefore the process of knowing) does not start with the knowledge of self, nor with the knowledge of things, but with the knowledge of their interaction; it is through dealing simultaneously with both poles of this interaction that intelligence organizes the world through organizing itself' (Piaget, 1937, 311). In characterising man in evolution, Theodosius Dobzhansky also depicts a recursive process: 'By changing what he knows about the world man changes the world that he knows; and by changing the world in which he lives man changes himself' (Dobzhansky, 1962, 347), to which we might add that by changing himself man changes what he knows, and so on. Reporting on an urban renewal programme, Herbert Simon states that 'Each step of implementation created a new situation; and the new situation provided a starting point for fresh design activity' and adds that: 'The real result of our actions is to establish initial conditions for the next succeeding stage of action' (Simon, 1969 [1996], 162).

Again, the importance of asymmetry should be noticed. Like recursion, it is a specific type of asymmetry since it is given a content or value. This value is a particular process based on the three root dualities and identified in a generic way as a generative mechanism *GP* and its outcome *P*. And there is more to it than feedback because *GP* is not left unaffected by the backward influence: it is reshaped. This leaves space for learning and dynamics since a time dimension is necessarily present through the unfolding of one loop after the other, which indeed composes a spiral of successive loops over time in which process and product evolve. For the sake of simplification, we do not index over time the expressions used, unless it is explicitly needed. The cases encountered in the developments above can be expressed graphically in terms of process *GP* and product *P* (Figure 4.2).

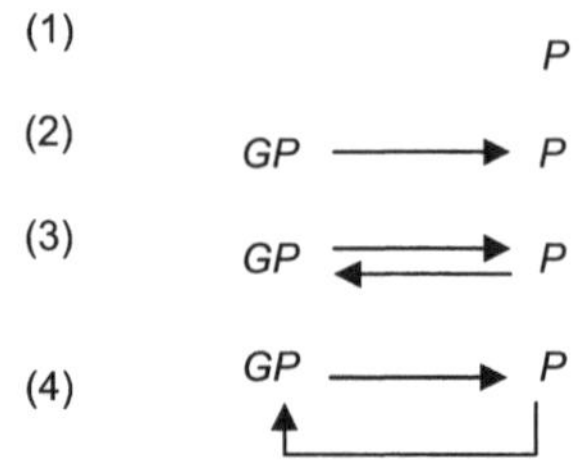

Figure 4.2 From simplicity to generic recursive duality

Case (1) represents a situation in which the product can be treated as a mere object, without paying attention to the process which generates it. Case (2) represents a one-way, cause-and-effect, means – ends relation. Case (3) represents iteration, interdependence or feedback: information is taken into account on the output side and channelled back as input without *GP* being affected. No learning occurs, or it is so small that it does not affect *GP*. Case (4) represents recursion. It is a specific iterative process. Its specificity is symbolised by the line with square angles from *P* to *GP*. Not only is *GP* affected by *P* but the square angles symbolise that explicit criteria and constraints are compelling. All in all we obtain what may be identified as a recursive loop combining re-entry or recursion *stricto sensu* from *P* to *GP* and an operation from *GP* to *P* whereby something becomes actualised. This adds to the asymmetry between the terms of duality another form of asymmetry between the operations connecting the operator and the operated. An alternative way of presentation is to introduce the star sign $*$ as a symbol of the recursive loop. Then $(GP{*}P)$ is identical to the symbol:

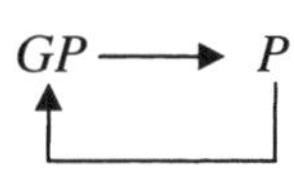

The star is here a full line sign, which should prevent any confusion with a superscript used here for symbolising a standard, and with a subscript. $(GP{*}P)$ is the elementary qualitative component of complexity. It symbolises the more general situation from which it is possible to simplify to cases (3), (2) or (1).

This echoes Gaston Bachelard's words: 'What is simple is always merely simplified' (Bachelard, 1937, 143), and directs attention to the process of simplification rather than to the belief that there exist things which are simple by their very intrinsic nature.

Cases (1) to (3) are not complex. They can be dealt with at the object level. Case (4) is complex. It necessitates an explicit shift to the meta-level.

We end with a notion of complexity consisting in a recursive asymmetric duality with a specific content of three root pairs (PR, SR), (ML, OL) and (*GP*, *P*) reduced to the (*GP*∗*P*) generic loop.

C. Complex duality

It might be tempting to equate the pairs introduced above with dialectical notions. But it would only be a superficial similarity. Formal similarities with dialectics can be found when the terms of the dualities are clearly antagonistic. This is typical of (order, disorder). However this is by far not the most representative instance. The complex loop is informed by a *GP* and *P* relationship which constitutes its landmark. Indeed, possible antagonisms at a given logical level are transformed through the move to the (meta-level, object level) pattern in which the meta-level operates as a generative process. This basic difference can be made clear through the comparison with Nicholas Georgescu-Roegen's distinction between analytical and dialectical reasoning. But let us start with a founding reference.

Drawing on Friedrich Hegel and Karl Marx, Friedrich Engels proposed to identify three basic 'laws' of dialectics, namely the transformation of quantity into quality and vice versa, the interpenetration of opposites and the negation of negation (Rosser, 2000) Indeed one may connect the pairs mentioned above to one or more of these properties of dialectics. The interpenetration or unity of opposites is central to Georgescu-Roegen's distinction between analysis and dialectical reasoning and to his claim that the distinctive characteristic of dialectical concepts is to overlap with their opposites: 'It is thus possible for a given dialectical entity to be both A and non-A. Dialectical concepts are not perfectly circumscribed. Instead, they are bounded by a *dialectical* penumbra' (Georgescu-Roegen, 1988, 300). The penumbra 'is itself bordered by dialectical penumbra, and so on in an infinite dialectical reduction' (Georgescu-Roegen, 1979, 323). This opposes arithmomorphic concepts whose characteristic is to be discretely distinct and immutable: an arithmomorphic concept is separated from its opposite by a null set whereas a dialectical concept is separated from its opposite by a substantial penumbra within which:

> 'both A and non-A are true … this penumbra is not a perfectly defined arithmomorphic entity in the sense that we always know whether a given instance is within the penumbra or outside it. The dialectical penumbra does not divide the whole spectrum of the concept into three arithmomorphic domains: the domain of A, of non-A, and of both A and non-A". (ibid)

This connects with the issue of the limitation due to the excluded middle in logic and the need to overcome it, that we mentioned in Chapter 1. However, the above argument works with opposites while most of the pairs that appeared in our own argumentation are of a different type: observer and observed, process and product, meta and object, and so on. This fact points to the need to conceive reduced notions enabling the capture of this heterogeneity between the pairs.

The approach of penumbra is a much debated issue. Some maintain that it can be dealt with using fuzzy logic, a claim firmly opposed by Georgescu-Roegen (1979, 328). And there is the debate about whether fuzzy logic can ultimately rely on a probabilistic approach (Smithson, 1989; Laviolette, 1995).

Assimilating our argumentation with classical dialectics would therefore be confusing. A majority of the pairs are not composed of opposites but of complementary aspects in the sense that they mutually specify each other in a specific way based on asymmetry. Therefore the presence or absence of antagonism or of opposites (S. Lupasco, 1951 [1987]; E. Bernard-Weil, 1988) is of minor interest. The main issue is asymmetric recursion in the (*GP**P*) frame.

D. Root dualities and recursion

Complexity expressed by (*GP**P*) is the product of three root pairs. These root pairs illustrate three already mentioned intellectual influences. They are those of H.A. Simon for the (PR, SR) behavioural setting, of H. von Foerster for the (meta-level, object level) pair and self-reference, and of J. von Neumann for the process and product pair. It is fair to add the combined influences of J.-L. Le Moigne complementing Simon, and of F. Varela and E. Morin in complement of von Foerster.

These influences complement each other. Simon and von Neumann's insights lack the Foersterian self-referential, recursive dimension; von Foerster and von Neumann's contributions lack the Simonian and post-Simonian behavioural setting; and Simon and von Foerster lack the von Neumannian notion of a product whose complexity outpasses by far the complication of the process which produces it.

The full interplay of these three root pairs is the landmark of deep complexity. If the interplay is only partial, with non-separable (PR, SR) and (process, product) being tackled at the object level only, the meta-level being not activated, recursion being not needed, then non-deep complexity prevails. The basis of the distinction resides in the shift whereby the closely connected aspects of meta-level, self-reference and recursion are deneutralised and activated.

An example of recursion coming immediately to mind is what we developed in Chapter 1. It can be read entirely through the lens of Table 4.3. In the first steps of the process I proceeded from column 1 to column 6, then I identified a phenomenon called RISE in column 7 which created a complex situation like the one depicted in column 8. I explored, in a move from column 8 'back' to column

1, and so on, at the meta-level, how to conceive a satisficing generative mechanism, what I called anchored complexity, which illustrates recursion.

A source of difficulty for the reader may arise from the fluidity of the meta- and object levels and standpoints. Since these levels are always relative to each other, there does not exist an absolute position 'above' the other, the meta-level is itself the object level of a meta-meta-level, and so on. A self-referential, recursive behaviour of some operator X acting from a meta-level on an object-evel phenomenon can itself be contemplated by another operator Y observing X. Then it becomes necessary to locate the locutor or enunciator acting as a self-referential modeller. The present statement that you read is made from the standpoint of the author-modeller modelling self-referentially his own purposeful behaviour in operating on an object. But this enunciator's behaviour is similar to the behaviour of any operator, either 'operated' (observed, designed) or operating, in the general behavioural pattern (PR, SR).

4.5 CONCLUSION

After having introduced the meta-level, it is now possible to explain that the dimensions of complexity introduced in Table 3.3 are elementary because they pertain to the object level only. Table 4.3 is then the necessary complement of Table 3.3 and completes the characterisation of complexity as the product of a process.

Irreducibility takes on two forms: a *quantitative resource gap* and a *qualitative recursive duality*. This is still partial for two main reasons. First, the shift from complexity as an irreducible obstacle at the object level (complex situation) to a solution at the meta-level may create a feeling of ambiguity, if not of misunderstanding, since saying that by virtue of duality it is possible to obtain simultaneously obstacle and solution may appear as a conjuring trick as long as it is not reappraised, whatever the care that might have been taken to explain every new step in this bottom-up process. Second, the irreducibility introduced here is not plain irreducibility. It cannot be fully characterised by remaining at the level of product. It ensues that deep complexity is itself complex. Then, tackling it as a product cannot but be more than one part of the story as long as it is not worked out also as a process. This is the task we address in the next chapter.

NOTE

1. J.-J. Rousseau (1742 [1994]), *Les Confessions* II (2), Paris: GF Flammarion, 26.

5. Deep complexity as process

> The mind and the world jointly make up the mind and the world.
>
> Hilary Putnam (1981)[1]

5.1 INTRODUCTION

The argumentation developed in Chapter 4 was about one side of the coin since it originated in a substantive, first-order problem and produced a second-order setting, with a second-order complexity. The perception of a first-order complex situation triggered the shift to the second-order level. The characterisation of complexity as both an irreducible resource gap and a recursive duality derived from conceiving it as the product of the interplay of several factors, and ended in condensating these properties in the $GP*P$ building block. Now, this building block introduces to process as a 'whole series of continuous actions' according to the dictionary definition in two ways: in containing process and in being itself part of a process. First, process is in the essence of the recursive duality since complexity vanishes as soon as the generating process GP can be neutralised. When it is operating it entails a process of actualisation from GP to P and of recursion from P to GP, and again of actualisation, and so on in a sort of spiral unfolding over time until a stopping point is reached. Defining a stopping rule will then be on the agenda of this chapter. Indeed this image of a spiral indexed over time depicts the second way in which process contains the building block. Another way to state it is that we moved from complexity as an obstacle at one level to a kind of solution at a second level. Then several questions arise. How can complexity be both an obstacle and a 'solution'? Isn't second-order complexity only a limit case? Can we derive from it a broader notion of complexity?

We address these issues below. We characterise complexity as a nested process in section 5.2. It results in a meta-complexity as a fourth characterisation of complexity. In section 5.3, we recapitulate and establish a systematic pattern of the necessary components of the process that we have built thus far. We had to work out five organising principles whose combined operation establishes the consistency of deep complexity and brings an anchoring to it.

5.2 A NESTED PROCESS

The move from deep, second-order complexity, to objects is a move from a meta-level to a first-order, object level. It is the converse of what was shown in the emergence of second-order complexity since in that case, it resulted from a shift from a complex situation, or first-order complexity, to the meta-level. After having defined complexity as an irreducible resource gap, this was the basis for characterising an asymmetric recursive duality attached to complexity as a product. These properties are naturally not susceptible to disappear when the kind of complexity arrived at in the bottom-up procedure is taken as the starting point of a top-down process. But they need to be complemented before we achieve a full characterisation of deep complexity. First, the basic duality provides an elementary building block which is never isolated. It operates as part of a nested pair. Second, these nested pairs operate themselves in a sequence of logical levels.

5.2.1 The Generic Pattern: Nested Double Duality

A process appears in the move from object level to meta-level and from meta-level to object level. This applies within a recursive loop with process being *GP* and product being *P* . But a recursive loop at the object level can be viewed from a meta-level. Then the whole loop is *P* compared to the loop at the meta-level. Indeed our own experience about the RISE reveals two successive moments illustrated respectively by Tables 3.3 and 4.3.

Complexity emerged from a sequence of steps at the object level. Then we enquired on how to produce a *GP* whereby this product at the object level might be dealt with satisfactorily. We designed a process at the meta-level whose product P_m was reshaped as GP_o for the object level. Indeed we connected two successive elementary (*GP*∗*P*) loops. Second-order deep complexity (SODCX) was designed as a product of a first-order deep complexity (FODCX). Now, given this knowledge and availability of SODCX as a meta-notion, can we use it as a resource in order to deal with object level phenomena and problems?

It is manifest that both moves rely on the combination of two successive dualities. This combination is specific: the loops are hierarchically ordered and overlapping as shown in Figure 5.1. This specific connection between consecutive loops provides a generic pattern.

In Figure 5.1, the upward arrow from *GP* at object level to *P* at the meta-level stands for the bottom-up shift described in the emergence of deep complexity in Chapter 4. The downward arrow from *P* at the meta-level to *GP* at the object level stands for the top-down move.

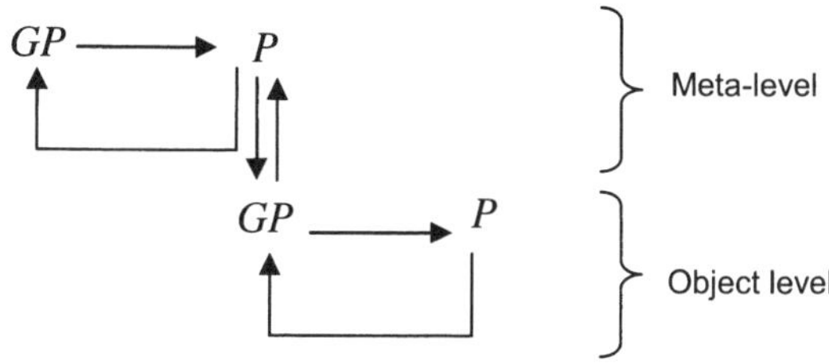

Figure 5.1 Generic nested double duality

Starting a task with having in mind deep, second-order complexity means that the task is envisaged at a meta-level first, then at the object level. At each level, the ($GP*P$) generic duality operates fully or partially. It operates partially at the meta-level if it leads to a non-complex situation at this level and fully at the object level if the situation is potentially complex, as will be shown later on in this section.

This two-level pattern is generic. More than two levels can be envisaged when it is attempted to derive the standard at the lowest level from progressively more remote foundational principles, as will be shown below or, more generally, when it is attempted to derive a property at a given level from the meta and higher (meta-meta, and so on.) levels. Fluidity characterises these hierarchically ordered levels to the extent that every level is meta for the level immediately 'below' it, or enveloped by it, and is in turn the object level for the level immediately 'above' it, or enveloping it.

Thus we find a sequence of dualities considered at successive levels and organised by pairs composed of a meta-level and an object level. This creates a fluidity of double dualities generating the process of complexity. There is no logical reason for limiting the number of levels; an infinite regress of paired levels might even be theoretically envisaged. Each level may become in turn meta or object. Any operator is at a meta-level for a task to be performed (object level). He/she is in turn at an object level when he/she is either observed by another observer or when he/she is relying on criteria and principles emanating or imposed upon him/her from a meta-level. Any level is dependent on the levels immediately connected to it, above and below it. This constitutes a guidepost for basing our argumentation on a three-level process of paired recursive dualities. Another aspect of fluidity pertains to the fact that these paired dualities are nested. The observer observing an observer observing an agent exemplifies typically this case. This was done in Chapter 1 when we designed a reflexive scheme based on procedural and substantive rationality.

The generic presence of paired dualities complements the qualitative characterisation of deep complexity: deep complexity relies qualitatively both on a recursive duality and on the pairing of this duality at two consecutive levels. The introduction of the meta-level renders obvious that what seemed natural before shifting to it, that is, operating at the object level, is but a specific kind of behaviour, however usual it is. Any level is part of a pair of levels and can be in turn meta and object with respect to the other level. Most of the developments of Chapters 2 and 3 pertained to the object level.

To recapitulate, the generic structure of deep complexity is composed of two building blocks. The first and most elementary is the generic duality *GP*P*. The second is the paired duality, that is, duality applied to itself. We symbolise it by *GP**P*. The former is internally processual since process is represented by the * connecting *GP* and *P* within a single duality. The latter adds external process to the former: the double duality is ** generated. It is more general and conveys a fuller notion of complexity conceived as process. The double duality characterising it is nested in a fluid way in which the elementary loops operate alternatively as *GP* and *P* according to their relative positions in the logical level structure. This double duality is the operational or effective building block of complexity compared with the formal building block of the elementary duality. We symbolise them by *FBB* and *EBB* respectively:

$$GP{*}P \equiv FBB \text{ (formal building block of deep complexity)}$$
$$GP{**}P \equiv EBB \text{ (effective building block of deep complexity)}$$

We explain in the next paragraphs how this process works for second-order complexity (CX3) defined in Chapter 4 and we extend it to a notion of deep, meta-complexity (CX4).

5.2.2 The Modus Operandi of Second-order Deep Complexity CX3

We recall in a first step how second-order complexity emerged as a way to address a first-order complex situation. We reframe in terms of recursive duality the process that we experienced.

We started with asking if the object-level situation we obtained was satisficing. The answer was negative. Then we considered that this situation could be viewed as the product of a generating procedure. We enquired about such a procedure and could not find a satisficing one at the object level. In other words we started with P_o (outcome at the object level) and looked for a GP_o, or, equivalently, with $\hat{D}_o^i > \overline{D}_o^s$ (that is, $DD_o^{is} > 0$) in a first step and $\hat{D}_o^i > \overline{D}_o^p$ (that is, $DD_o^{ip} > 0$) in a second step, and then shifted to the meta-level (Figure 5.2). We notice here the equivalence between using the terms of the generic duality, GP and P, and using the terms related to the resource gap DD^i pertaining to a task i. This denotes that the qualitative and quantitative views of deep complexity boil down to a unique process, which is comforting for the approach followed. It also illustrates the higher degree of integration and generality of the process conception of complexity, when compared to the product conception, since it envelops the latter.

Every move can be figured out qualitatively and quantitatively. However the pattern in which the moves occur is governed by the building blocks *GP*P* and *GP**P*. Qualitatively, the moves are from an initial P_o to GP_o at the object level and to P_m and GP_m and so on at the meta-level and downwards back to the object level. Quantitatively, the process starts with assessing the sign of DD_o^{is}. If it is positive, the move is to DD_o^{ip}, etc. DD_o^{is} is equivalent to P_o, DD_o^{ip} to GP_o, and so on. This equivalence within the generic duality is illustrated explicitly on Figure 5.2.

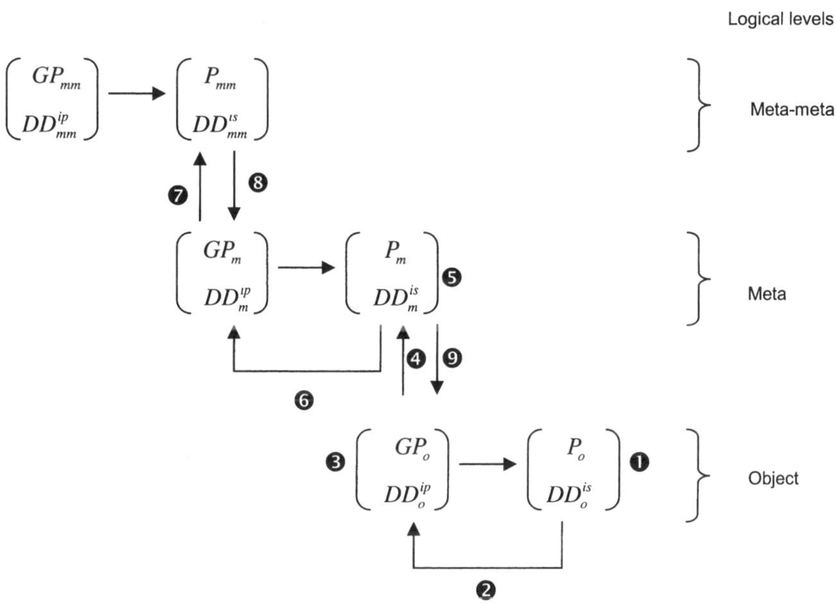

Figure 5.2 From first-order to second-order complexity

At the meta-level, we looked for a procedure GP_m (or DD_m^{ip}) producing a P_m (or DD_m^{is}) subject to $\hat{D}'_m \geq D^*_m$, and such that this P_m, which is a product at the meta-level, is transformed into a reshaped procedure at the object level (a modified GP_o or DD_o^{ip}) such that it may become satisficing at the object level. This adjusted or reframed procedure is consistent by construction with the meta-standard D^*_m. If it were not satisficing at the object level then it would be necessary to go on with the recursive process, back to the meta-level. We impose to design reducibility at the meta-level. But the possibility of irreducibility at the meta-level cannot be ruled out on a logical basis. It is a matter of judgement. Our judgement imposes to stop at D^*_{mm} for founding D^*_m. One can think of this stopping rule as an operational device imposing to combine and concentrate into D^*_{mm} the still 'higher' or 'deeper' level foundations, thus avoiding the trap of a potential quasi infinite regress.

Concrete examples of this process are our own experience with the RISE (Chapter 1) and those reported in Tables 3.3 and 4.3. The process can be described as a sequence of steps. It is represented in Figure 5.2 with nine moves denoted by the circled figures ❶ to ❾. The first step ❶ was cognitive irreducibility (the RISE as a conjecture; column 6 of Table 3), complemented in a second step ❷ by practical irreducibility (column 7, Table 3.3) leading to identify a complex situation (column 8, Table 3.3) in a third step ❸. The shift to self-referential theorising at a meta-level, that is, the shift from Table 3.3 to Table 4.3, is the fourth step❹. In the case of the RISE as well as in Table 4.3, once the reasoning is conducted at the meta-level, the first question is whether there exists a cognitive reducibility at this level: is there an available substantive way of satisficing, after having enquired through columns 1 to 5 of Table 4.3? If the answer is positive, we go back to the object level with a GP_o reframed in compliance with column 6 of the meta-level (Table 4.3): it is a $GP_o^{'}$, it is satisficing (complying with the meta-level requirements) but not necessarily a solution to the initial problem: it does not bring necessarily an end to the object level recursive process. This is a fifth step ❺. If the answer is negative a sixth step ❻ is triggered in order to design a procedure at the meta-level (GP_m or DD_m^{ip}) which is satisficing in the now usual sense of abiding by the immediately higher and 'deeper' level constraint in step ❼ (here: $GP_m = P_{mm}$ or equivalently: $DD_m^{ip} = DD_{mm}^{is}$). Thus, in an eighth step ❽, the process goes back from the meta-meta-level to the meta-level in producing P_m or DD_m^{is}, and finally shifts to the object level in a ninth step ❾. In the case of the RISE, we had no available ready-to-use procedure at the meta-level and were driven to enquire about designing a GP_m abiding by the rules of scientific practice in use in the scientific field in general, and then to go back to the RISE at the object level, through steps ❼ to ❾.

Figure 5.2 describes our own experience with the RISE and with the processes reported in Tables 3.3 and 4.3. It depicts the move from an initially identified first-order deep complexity to the process triggered by the irreducibility of this complexity, or complexity of complexity. It is the origin of the wording 'second order'. The whole process is triggered by a kind of bottom-up move followed by a move back to the initial object-level issue. The way SODCX operates combines bottom-up and top-down moves which unfold until a satisficing procedure is achieved. This obviously contains a time dimension through which learning takes place. Indeed this process may be described as a learning process. This time dimension is not made explicitly apparent through time indexes, for the sake of the simplicity of the representation. But it is ever present in the unfolding of the process.

The process goes back to the object level moving downwards from ❽ and ending with a reshaped $GP_o^{'} \neq GP_o$. The time content of the process transforms the static elementary pattern of Figure 5.2 into a spiral unfolding over a time dimension. Picturing and formalizing it would add complication and little substance to our argumentation and is not undertaken here.

A new situation follows from the process depicted thus far. It results from an asymmetry between the initial bottom-up process through which SODCX emerged, and the top-down process from meta- to object level.

The bottom-up process arose from the recognition of complexity of situation or FODCX at the object level, and the continuation of the reasoning about complexity of complexity or SODCX (expression [1] below). It led one to judge that in order to avoid a many-step regress, satisficing should be achieved at the meta-level under the constraint coming from a meta-meta-level standard (expression [2]). It is the complexity of the product P which drives us to rely on the generative process GP through the nested double duality combining P at the object level and GP at the meta-level. This is expressed by CX3 combining [1] and [2]:

$$\textbf{CX3:} \begin{cases} DD_o^{ip} > 0 \quad \text{s.t} \quad \hat{D}_o^i \geq D_o^* & [1] \\ DD_m^{ip} \geq 0 \quad \text{s.t} \quad \hat{D}_m^i \geq D_m^* & [2] \end{cases}$$

Expression [2] informs that the resource $\overline{D}_m^p$ and the level of aspiration $\hat{D}_m^i$ are adjusted to each other at the meta-level: $\hat{D}_m^i \geq \bar{D}_m^p$. This resource is procedural, it denotes a method rendered satisficing and abiding by a constraint D_m^* itself shaped by D_{mm}^*.

5.2.3 Meta-complexity CX4

Moving back downwards to the object level makes it possible to reappraise the object-level situation through a newly informed $GP_o^{'}$. This was described in Figure 5.2. Thus this process consists in achieving satisficing at the meta-level.

Here is where, with the benefit of hindsight, the question arises of using this result as a method for addressing complexity in a reverse, top-down way. SODCX was generated in a bottom-up way. In terms of the generic duality, we started with P and explored how to design a GP of which P is a product. This necessitated to move from the object level to the meta-level. Now, once this GP is constructed, it appears as a starting point, at a meta-level, for addressing object-level problems. This can in principle be done whatever the particular problem is, since this kind of complexity derives from the epistemic situation regardless of the particular task leading to it. Thus this GP appears as a resource or a method $\overline{D}_m^p$ available at the meta-level, provided by a meta-meta-level process $\overline{D}_{mm}^s$, and itself producing a $\overline{D}_m^s$ transformed into a $\overline{D}_o^p$ at the object level, through the sequence:

$$GP : \overline{D}_{mm}^s \longrightarrow \overline{D}_m^p \longrightarrow \overline{D}_m^s \longrightarrow \overline{D}_o^p$$

This GP is nested. It is aimed at providing a procedure at the object level ($\overline{D}_o^p$) whose satisficing character depends on the substance of the problem i and $\overline{D}_o^{is}$. If $\overline{D}_o^{is}$ is too low compared to $\hat{D}_o^{is}$, leading to $DD_o^{is} > 0$, then $\overline{D}_o^{ip}$ is activated. If it is not satisficing, $\overline{D}_m^s$ will itself be activated. In our own experience with the RISE, the meta-meta resource is the content of 'doing science', the meta-resource consists in defining a scientific practice, and the object-level resource is adjusted to it.

There is however a big difference with the original SODCX. Indeed in the top-down procedure for addressing object-level problems, we are a priori not certain about the character of the object-level problem: it is only potentially complex. In starting from a meta-level standpoint, we engage in a search, in a recognition of the object-level situation. It does not follow from a previously identified complex situation at the object level. Then there is no rationale for sticking to the 'SODCX' wording. The object-level situation is a priori indeterminate, it can turn out either deeply complex or non-deeply complex. This constitutes an asymmetry between the bottom-up and top-down processes. The top-down process connotes another kind of complexity, in which reducibility holds at the meta-level but is only potential at the object level, together with the irreducibility of the pair constituted by the two levels, as illustrated in Figure 5.3. It looks appropriate to call *meta-complexity* this kind of deep complexity.

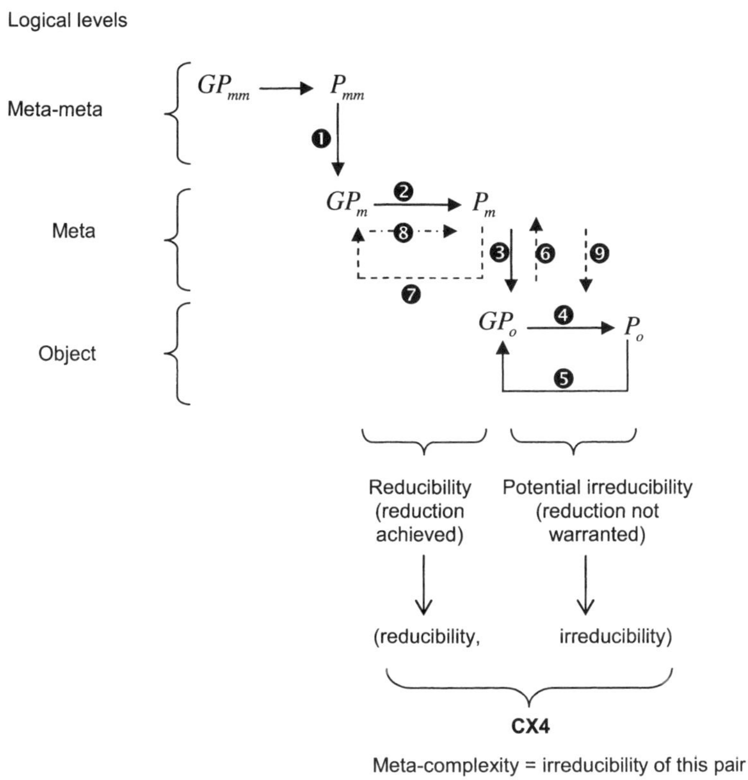

Figure 5.3 The modus operandi of CX4

Meta-complexity can be formally expressed as CX4:

$$\mathbf{CX4:}\begin{cases} DD^{ip}_{mm} = 0 & \text{s.t.} \quad \hat{D}^{i}_{mm} \geq D^{*}_{mm} \\ DD^{ip}_{m} = 0 & \text{s.t.} \quad \hat{D}^{i}_{m} \geq D^{*}_{m} \\ DD^{ir}_{o}\ \text{indeterminate} & \text{s.t.} \quad \hat{D}^{i}_{o} \geq D^{*}_{o} \end{cases}$$

Meta-complexity as CX4 thus operationalises the kind of complexity that we have been looking for since the beginning. The apparent irony one may find in the wording disappears with the irreducible presence of complexity as a resource, method or solution, and as an obstacle. Meta-complexity embodies the nested, recursive and behavioural duality of this deep complexity. It is not any sort of available method. Its content emerges throughout the developments from Chapter 1 to this chapter. It can be systematised through the notion of five organising principles, as described in the next section.

Meta-complexity is schematised in the language of nested recursive dualities in Figure 5.3. Meta-complexity follows from SODCX read in the top-down way and formally resembles ❽ and ❾ of Figure 5.2 considered in a detailed way. But it is different in content from merely taking these steps ❽ and ❾. It is a starting point informed by the nested generic duality *EBB* whatever the character of the object-level situation may turn out to be.

Meta-complexity starts with a method deemed to be satisficing at the meta-level: it is produced by a meta-meta procedure ❶ and produces itself a meta-outcome P_m through ❷. Here, step ❶ is scientific practice, ❷ is a particular style of scientific practice applied to the issue at hand (the state – economy relationship) through method ❸ and substantively through ❹. If it does not turn out to be satisficing, a new move can be triggered back to the method ❺, to the process ❻ and ❼ generating the method, then back to a new adjustment at the meta-level ❽ and back again to the object level ❾. The process stops as soon as a satisficing outcome is achieved. Such a situation may begin at step ❹. Similarly to Figure 5.2, this representation should be indexed over time and pictured as a spiral to ensure its generality.

The dotted arrows signal potential moves furthering an initial process whereby meta-complexity operates as an available process of enquiry into a problem, from ❶ to ❹, and ❺ if an adjustment or iteration is needed at the object level. If it is not satisficing, then the iteration continues through reactivating the meta-level through steps ❻ to ❾ and so on.

Finally the nestedness follows from the double duality pattern connecting meta- and object-level loops. Indeed, given one level as the starting point, all other successive steps and loops appear to belong to the other level in a sequence repeating the building block duality in both upward and downward moves.

5.3 FIVE ORGANISING PRINCIPLES FOR CX4

We built our reasoning on the basis of a difficulty we encountered with the substance of our subject matter. It was the starting point of a process turning out as second-order deep complexity expressed in CX3 and whose formal modus operandi was depicted in the last section. Meta-complexity was established in the reverse way, starting from a formal standpoint. Implicit in it is the idea that the CX3 process is already known and that its results serve as the starting point in CX4. There is no doubt that CX4 could not be conceived if CX3 had not been conceptualised before it. In our case study, the notion of the RISE results from a CX3 procedure. Once it is known, it can be used as an assumption in new research on state – economy relationships and be put to the test. Whether the task proves non-deeply complex or deeply complex will depend on the cognitive situation which will emerge out of the first seven dimensions presented in Table 3.3. Although one may think of complexity as either CX3 or CX4, it is manifest that CX3 appears mainly as an intermediary notion since its result renders it possible to concentrate on CX4 as a starting point, thus avoiding having to reinvent the CX3 process in every case as if we were in ignorance of its outcome. However this does not eliminate CX3. It keeps its operational relevance whenever an iterative bottom-up move is needed from a given logical level to a higher level. These upward and downward processes were depicted in Figures 5.2 and 5.3. Meta-complexity CX4 is an ending point in our formal characterisation of the kind of deep complexity which emerged in our research. If our argumentation is valid, CX4 cannot but be a standpoint for further analysis and new research. But then it requires to be based on strong operational pillars. This is the task we address now in this section: what are the necessary resources of the modus operandi of CX4 which arise from the argumentation developed so far? This argumentation depicts an involved process. It relies on organising principles whose working is not straightforward. It is this working that we now attempt to establish. We claim below that five organising principles are at work in the modus operandi of CX4.

5.3.1 Behaviouralist Self-reflexivity

The process of effective complexity starts reflexively in the operator's mind with the consciousness of a potentially complex situation whatever the field of activity is. It is synthesised by CX4. This reflexive process is structured by the behaviouralist setting introduced by Herbert Simon and extended by us to self-referential situations.

Our argumentation started with the hypothesis that a researcher behaves like the agent portrayed by H.A. Simon with respect to substantive and procedural rationality. The behaviouralist setting emphasised by Simon relies on the notions of level of aspiration and of satisficing together with the two concepts of rationality. This hypothesis extends Simon's pattern to a self-referential level, a thing Simon appears to have constantly avoided.

Simon argued for procedural rationality on the basis of empirical investigation resulting in evidence of a type of behaviour at odds with substantive rationality. He did not commit himself to inquire about what may happen when procedural rationality ends in procedural irreducibility, that is, non-satisficing for the observer, at a meta-level. He stayed at the object level. This excluded the very idea of complexity of situation, and, consequently, the very rationale to differentiate object and meta levels. Simon's stance is not on the notion of complexity encountered here. Indeed we take support in his basic setting of reasonable behaviour for an extension involving being explicit about the content of this behaviour, viewed from its inside. It differs from observing agents' behaviours from the standpoint of an external observer. It deserves to be emphasised that this sort of post-Simonian move is triggered by the shift to the meta-level. It is endogenous to second-order complexity, and therefore, to effective complexity CX4. It is one of the peculiarities of complexity that although Simon envisaged it mostly as near decomposability – which we depict as complication, not effective complexity – he provided the tools and the impetus against the often unwarranted reliance on substantive rationality in standard economics and advocated a notion pertaining mostly to deliberation, reasonableness, design, heuristic procedure, what he, with A. Newell also called 'intelligent action' under the names of procedural or bounded rationality. It follows from the behaviouralist hypothesis that in a complex situation the actor and the object of action cannot be separated. The actor then is no longer a passive user of algorithms. The actor is given a participatory role in a two-level setting, with the need to identify the cognitive situation, which was illustrated in Tables 3.3 and 4.3.

Thus this behaviouralist, or behavioural, reflexivity entails a judgement of self-reference. The level of aspiration at the meta-level is to achieve a satisficing procedure for dealing with the object level problem. It entails an inquiry about D_m^* and $\overline{D}_m^p$, the meta-standard and the meta-procedural resources. An important consequence of recognizing the complexity of situation at the object level is thus to trigger an explicit inquiry into the foundations of the object-level standard. This is all the more noticeable as the object level standard is usually entrenched in habits and traditions and creates the intellectual climate under which actors operate. Therefore inquiring about it is doomed to create tensions of a deeper bearing than the tensions resulting from the debate and mutual criticism that are essential to scientific activity within the boundaries set by the standard reigning among a community. This kind of inquiry about the standard itself is by far less easily accepted. I recently attended a seminar about road traffic safety in which a doctoral student in economics was presenting a model based on assuming that car drivers are rational utility-maximising agents 'like agents in economics' according to him. I asked him a question about the evidence for this assumption and the protocol of validation against empirical evidence that was used. It triggered an answer from his adviser, a professor of economics who was also attending. The answer was that: 'scientific economics does not work this way but rather on formulating assumptions and testing them, like what is done in modern science in other fields'.

Implicit, but quite present behind this answer, is instrumentalism. There is nothing wrong with it if it is legitimate, that is, if it is checked by strict protocols of validation. It is known that they are extremely weak in this kind of economics. What tends to stand for a validating procedure is to proclaim that it imitates the methods used in other fields such as physics. What is not said is that in these fields the protocols of empirical validation do operate and render it possible for empirical evidence to be the justice of peace. It is then no surprise that the more remote and less visible the protocols of validation against empirical evidence are, the higher is the stickiness to first principles imitating in an inconsequential way what is done in the leading sciences.

A specific capacity of judgement is called for in this search for a satisficing solution. It includes the ability to question the often unnoticed dogmas defining the norms at work in an activity. This reflexive and inevitably critical capacity is in the very substance of the meta-judgement, and, therefore, of the process of complexity. In the end, behavioural reflexivity is a form of critical behaviouralism.

5.3.2 Composite Self-similarity

A. Intrinsic ambivalence

The notion of complexity with which we end, CX4, must be most unsettling to the reader since it combines the opposite ideas of irreducibility and reducibility, a feature which is, at least, paradoxical and seems to contradict the initial definition of complexity as irreducibility to a satisficing level of reduction.

This was the first meaning of complexity depicted as an obstacle, an irreducible resource gap. It was complemented by the process view: complexity is a process of search for a good enough pathway and outcome. These two constitutive properties are ever present either when we start with product at the object level and pursue with process (CX3), or when we start with process at the meta-level and pursue with product (CX4). Therefore the initial characterisation of complexity needs to be complemented. Complexity is not plain irreducibility. It combines reducibility at the meta-level, and actual (CX3), or potential (CX4), irreducibility at the object level.

Once the double logical-level pattern is taken into account this apparent paradox disappears. This ambivalence of deep complexity follows from its effective building block; the meta and object level structure of paired dualities is intrinsic to it. This intrinsic ambivalence may create some confusion. Thus it may be tempting to view deep complexity designed here as pertaining mainly or exclusively to method rather than to theory and statements on the substance of the disciplinary subject matter. This view might easily end in a criticism based on a supposedly limited, if not sterile, scope of complexity for the sake of substantive theory. These issues create the need for explicitly activating the distinction between the process of enquiry into the world *PEW* and the world *W* external to it. This distinction is generic. It operates at the meta- and the object logical levels. At the object level, we symbolise by *W1* the world external to the process of enquiry into it, and the process of enquiry itself by *W2*.

Reliance on this distinction becomes relevant at this stage of our argumentation because, on the one hand, we now dispose of the tools making it possible (effective building block of complexity *EBB*, CX3 and CX4) and, on the other hand, it is now necessary to sharpen the difference between classical complexity and CX3 and CX4. This difference is threefold. Its first aspect has been addressed since Chapter 2: it is a difference in the depth of complexity. The second difference resides in the content given to irreducibility and was developed in the last section: the irreducibility attached to CX3 and CX4 is a composite of reducibility and irreducibility; it is inherently ambivalent while the various types of irreducibility attached to the classical conceptions of complexity do not go beyond plain irreducibility. The third difference bears on the relationship between *W1* and *W2*. It is at the heart of our argumentation while complexity is classically dealt with in the literature as a property of the world *W1* external to the process of enquiry, with a noticeable exception. This exception will be evoked below after we go through the distinction between *W1* and *W2*. This distinction is not straightforward, since the process of enquiry into the world is itself part of the world at large which includes *W2* and *W1*. Yet the distinction is pragmatically useful: the operator, the process of enquiry, operates on a part only or a subset of the world *W*, and this part constitutes or contains the object of enquiry. This world is what is conceived of in the pair (*W2, W1)*.

W2 denotes the domains of method, investigation and learning. The world *W1* consists of the domain of the subject matter. Theory pertains to it and can thus be distinguished from method. Two cases can be envisaged for the relationship between *W2* and *W1*. Let us call them *A* and *B*. In the most common case, *A*, *W1* is considered to be external to *W2*. Case *B* occurs when this condition does not hold, that is, when the process of enquiry into a subject matter is taken as a subject matter itself. It is the exception evoked above. Then the subject matter is the process of enquiry at large, in which *PEW*, *W2* and *W1* overlap. This is what occurs when the subject-matter is epistemology, methodology or the method itself, and the aim is to theorise about. In this case method and theory belong to the unique domain of the process of enquiry. Complexity uniquely or predominantly connected with it illustrates this case and is most developed in work done by Edgar Morin and Jean-Louis Le Moigne.

While acknowledging the insights of case *B*, the notion on which we rely here includes *W1* conceived in the classical sense of case *A*. It follows that complexity represented by its effective building block contains necessarily both *PEW*, *W*, *W2* and *W1* parts, that is, a (*W2*, *W1)* duality at the object level. Unlike classical complexity, CX4 is not merely about *W1*, nor is it merely about *PEW* and *W2* like in case *B*, it is intrinsically about *both* *PEW*, *W2* and *W1*.

To recapitulate, the characterisation of complexity led to complement an initial formal building block (the *GP*∗*P* duality) with an effective building block (*GP*∗∗*P*). We identified these building blocks respectively as *FBB* (formal) and *EBB* (effective). CX3 and CX4 are best represented by *EBB* and the effective irreducibility it conveys. Effective irreducibility denotes the irreducible combination of reducibility and actual or potential irreducibility from which follows an intrinsic ambivalence.

This ambivalence ends in a necessary distinction about the domains of complexity based on the differentiation between *PEW*, *W*, *W2* and *W1*. Let us concentrate on the object level. CX4 can be defined over *W2* (case *B*) as well as over *W2* and *W1* (case *A*). In case *A* the subject matter belongs to *W1*, the purpose is to say something about the world external to *W2*, while the subject matter is *W2* itself in case *B*. The thinking presented here clearly comes under case *A*. This distinction adds to the ambivalence of complexity since it necessarily comprehends *W2* and *W1* in case *A*, while method and subject matter are both *W2* in case *B*. The '*A*' complexity of CX4 is therefore better adapted to our purpose than the '*B*' complexity. We rely upon it in this book without recalling its nature.

This can be expressed concisely by the use of set notation. *W2* and *W1* are non-overlapping subsets of *W* and the effective building block *EBB* stands for deep complexity:

$$W2 \cup W1 \subset W$$
$$W2 \cap W1 = \varnothing$$
$$EBB \subset W$$

Complexity represented by EBB can be conceived of as a multi-step sequence which can be reduced to the three steps of the operational pattern presented in Figures 5.2 and 5.3:

Case *A*

$$EBB \cap W2 \neq \varnothing$$
$$EBB \cap W1 \neq \varnothing$$

Case *B*

$$EBB \cap W2 \neq \varnothing$$
$$EBB \cap W1 = \varnothing$$

From this distinction, there follows a difference between an *A-EBB* or *A*-CX4, and a *B-EBB* or *B*-CX4. The *A*-complexity is inherently both *W2* and *W1* with the primacy of the *W2* level in CX4. The kind of complexity that we obtain finally in our research on the RISE is best represented by CX4 in case *A*. The paradoxical character of complexity is only apparent. From obstacle and pathway (CX3) to pathway and potential irreducibility (CX4) at once, *A*-complexity is not mere method nor mere theory or property of a subject matter, but both of them.

B. Logical level invariance

The formal and effective building blocks generate a multi-stage sequence in which they repeat themselves in a nested way as is pictured in Figures 5.2 and 5.3. This illustrates a self-similar process. Self-similarity needs to be explained. These words irresistibly evoke the notion found in fractal geometry. However the resemblance is mostly formal. The self-similarity which emerges in effective complexity is of a specific character. Let us explain this difference.

Benoit Mandelbrot introduced self-similarity in the following way: 'When each piece of a shape is geometrically similar to the whole, both the shape and the cascade that generate it are called self-similar' (Mandelbrot, 1983, 34). The image of the cascade comes from thinking of such a shape as is generated by a mechanism creating at each stage details smaller than those of the preceding stages. This self-similarity denotes a particular kind of fractality or *scale invariance*: a fractal structure or a fractal process cannot be characterised by a single scale of length or of time, which constitutes another form of irreducibility (West and Goldberger, 1987; Nottale, 1998). In our case a similar structure also repeats itself in a 'cascade' of steps but it has little to do with fractality or scaling. We are dealing with logical levels: (*GP***P*) and (*GP****P*) cannot be characterised by a single logical level. This is the central feature of the ambivalence of complexity CX4. This form of self-similarity is better depicted as a logical level invariance. However it is always a composite, not a plain, self-similarity since it links two elementary dualities of different qualities in a fluid, nested sequence in which the qualitative character (*W2* or *W1*; *GP* or *P*; meta-level or object level) depends on the relative position of the component dualities and includes a hierarchical ordering (primacy of *W2*, *GP* and meta-level). To conclude, the intrinsic ambivalence and the logical level invariance of complexity create a qualitatively differentiated self-similarity better depicted as composite self-similarity.

5.3.3 Conjunction

Non-separability reflects conjunction. The need for including this property was perceived pragmatically in Chapter 1 and found support in other attempts depicted in the literature. Our own enquiry on complexity relies heavily on it as is obvious from Chapters 3 to 5. The hindsight we now have provides an opportunity to reflect on the meaning of conjunction since it was shown that it does not eliminate the possibility of separation. Thus, a thorough appraisal of conjunction is needed.

Let us recall the initial rationale which arose from recognition of the excessively limiting character of the axioms of classical, two-valued Aristotelian logic, at least in the way they are usually used as bases for the logical conditions of scientific coherence. It led us to substitute an assumption of 'included middle' to the classical principle of excluded middle.

Let us also re-emphasise that what we do here is driven by practical considerations about doing science in a particular field about a specific issue, not by a general philosophical argumentation. And I have no claim to intervene in the domain of logics. I simply observe that there exist several logical systems, and that there is a priori no reason to prefer one logical system over others when they are equally consistent, apart from some specific and justified relevance in some specific context. Whether one is to be preferred to another in some activity is to be decided pragmatically. This is why I present the basic notions required here as principles and restrict the denomination of axioms to classical logic. Then, considering the developments of Chapters 4 and 5, the basic question is how to design a conjunctive setting which does not exclude the possibility of disjunction and separation. This follows from the need that was perceived in Chapter 1 to deal with non-decomposability and the ineliminable role of relationship. It was subsequently shown that, in addition to the pattern of non-separability, the very presence of process was essential to complexity. The axioms of Aristotelian logic, as they are commonly perceived, still play a fundamental role in Western thinking, notably the axioms of non-contradiction and of the excluded middle.

Yet they have been criticised for a long time. Hegel criticised what he called 'the law of the excluded middle' (Hegel, 1989, 438–439). Logical systems different from Aristotle's were formulated by several twentieth-century logicians, notably by Jan Lukasiewicz and Alfred Tarski. Alfred Korzybski emphasised that the 'law of identity' is never applicable to processes and that the 'law of excluded middle' represents only a limit case and therefore is unsatisfactory as a general principle (Korzybski, 1958 [1980], 405).

A. The Aristotelian axioms

It is important to notice that what can be found in Aristotle's writings about logic contained in his *Metaphysics* and *Organon (Analytics)* is less clear-cut than what has been crystallised in modern thinking as the non-contradiction and excluded middle axioms:

- *The axiom of identity* says that 'whatever is, is': A is A. It predicates the impossibility for the same thing to exist and not exist at once and under the same relationship. Under this axiom, the rationality of arguments requires that 'any notion or thing referred to in one constituent statement of the argument must be identical to that notion or thing when referred to in any other constituent statement of the argument' (Boland, 1998, 87).
- *The axiom of non-contradiction.* It is stated by Aristotle as the 'principle of contradiction' in the following terms: 'It is impossible that the same attribute both belongs and does not belong to the same subject at the same time, and under the same relationship, notwithstanding all other determinations which can be included in order to deal with logical difficulties' (*Métaphysique*, Γ,3,191–196).

  It is usually known under the form 'B cannot be at once and under the same relationship *A* and not-*A*' or 'No statement included in a rational argument can be both true and false', with a loss of attention to the conditions mentioned by Aristotle for this axiom to hold.
- *The axiom of excluded middle.* 'For any proposition, only its affirmation or its negation is true' (Aristotle, *Organon*, I, II, 61–62).Aristotle presents it as another form of the principle of (non-)contradiction (Aristotle, *Métaphysique*, Γ 7, 235–240).

  Any proposition *B* is either true or false. Given *A* and not-*A*, only *A* or not-*A* is true, there is no third which can be true; there is no middle ground such as 'partially true' or 'probably true'.

Comments

1. A striking gap appears in the way the axioms of classical logic have been popularised and de facto absolutised to ensure the rationality of argumentation in modern thinking, and the care with which Aristotle explicitly made them relative to conditions of simultaneity of time and sameness of relationship. These are quite limitating conditions. Whenever time is allowed to unfold and relationships to vary, these axioms cannot remain unchanged. Aristotle mentioned the axiom of non-contradiction as 'the strongest of all principles' in an explicit criticism of Heraclitus' denial of the principle of contradiction (*Métaphysique*, Γ 3, 195). This suggests indeed that the genuine forerunner of a vision including process and relationship was Heraclitus.
2. The notions of relationship and process are essential for complexity. There could not be irreducibility without a primary entity to be reduced. And reduction could not be envisaged without a distinction being performed.

   Irreducibility pertains to entities or notions that cannot be transformed into one single notion at a given logical level, that is, reduced to a kind of absolute meaning in which the only satisficing outcome is achieved when reduction to one entity is obtained. They are different, this difference cannot be eliminated, and yet these notions are not separable. Ineliminable or irreducible difference and non-separability characterise the irreducibility relationship. It is an internal relationship in the sense that its components are defined to a varying extent by the relationship. This gives it a primacy over its constituents. The character of a component or of an object thus depends on the contextual relationship. And the relationship is itself invariant to change of its components within its domain of validity. This can be summarised as the primacy of relationship over the substantive components. Yet separability is not ruled out, it governs non-complexity. But then the process of separation is informed by the possibility of reactivating the neutralised term whereas this is not possible when the reasoning starts from a given state of already reduced entities.

Because of internal relationship, the principle of identity operates for a given relationship. The apparently 'same' component becomes a different entity in a different relationship. Furthermore, the principle of contradiction requires us to keep in mind the general frame of meta- and object levels. This constituting property of complexity drives the reasoning away from disjunctive logic. It makes it possible and consistent to have irreducibility at the object level and reducibility at the meta-level for the same entity without a contradiction. This is however not possible within a given level and a given relationship defined at this level. If A is irreducible at the object level, it cannot be reducible at this same level, but it can be reducible at the meta-level.

B. Principles of conjunction

By 'principles of conjunction', I envisage a set of seven hypotheses (Table 5.1) that are foundational for subsequent theorising. The inclusion of relationship and process renders possible a larger degree of generality than the three classical axioms. They subsume them in the same way that complexity subsumes non-complexity, in the sense that the classical axioms hold whenever relationship and time can be neutralised. The excluded middle also becomes a limit case of a more general principle expressing the possibility for a third term not to reduce to one or the other of two mutually negating terms, and at the same time to be a compound of them, thus binding them. For this reason it may be called a *binding third* or *binding middle*. The term 'included middle' is also used but it introduces a sort of symmetry with the excluded middle which may be misleading since one is more general than the other.

In our pragmatic search for a set of consistent basic principles, it seems reasonable to render apparent two conditions of possibility for emphasising relationship and process. The act of relating and the property of being related necessitate that what is related is distinguished before being related. An act of distinction appears as antecedent to relating. And if there is an act of distinction then there is a prior action, symbolic or physical. Action appears prime.

Table 5.1 Principles of conjunction

1. Action
   Action is prime. It is symbolic or physical.
2. Distinction
   The primary cognitive act is to draw a distinction: *B* distinct from *A*.
3. Relationship
   What is distinguished is related through a relationship *R*: *A R B*
4. Process
   Entities unfold over time without any absolute beginning and predetermined end state.
5. Identity
   A is *A* at a given time and under a given *R*.
6. Non-contradiction (non-negation)
   There is no *C* such that *C* is *A* and not-*A* at once and under the same *R*.
7. Binding third (included middle)
   When process can operate and relationship vary, there exists *C* which can be *A* and not-*A*.

Comment

A difficulty lies in expressing the binding third since it takes its meaning only when relationship and process are activated, which entails that the fixity of notions and their negation are changed. *A* and not-*A* in the binding third mean distinct or 'different', and cover a range of an infinite number of possible differences including absolute negation in a two-valued pattern as a limit case. This change of meaning of the same apparent entities *A* and not-*A* is consistent with the principles presented here since it derives from the change of relationship: *A* and not-*A* strictly negating each other hold under the relationship of fixity (identity and non-contradiction) in a two-valued logic whereas *A* and not-*A* expresses a difference, among an infinity of possible differences, under a pattern allowing process and changing relationships. Principles 5 and 6 appear clearly as limit cases compared to the general principles 3, 4 and 7.

Another difficulty arises from the need to abandon binary oppositions. Including relationship and process does not mean excluding some fixity of entities. But it compels one to be aware of the need to characterise explicitly in every circumstance what is fixed and what is changing.

Complexity relies intrinsically on the conjunction which follows from both its essential non-separability (duality) and its processual character. The principle of the binding third (or included middle) synthesises these properties. It expresses a higher degree of generality than principles of identity and non-contradiction since these are valid only in the limit case of fixed relationship and disactivated process. This case is contained in the binding third in an otherwise more general setting, in which process operates and relationship varies, but can be neutralised temporarily for the sake of reasoning. Therefore, the binding third does not exclude the excluded middle as merely a limit case. There is an asymmetry between them: the binding third subsumes the excluded middle, whereas the excluded middle excludes the binding third.

Complexity derives from the relationship expressed in its formal building block *GP*P*. This relationship is fixed to the extent that it is definitional but it contains the possibility of being transformed into a non-complex relationship depending on what the situation is. It is therefore a fixed relationship which allows variations in the relative weights of its components. Furthermore, it is intrinsically connected to process both through containing process between *GP* and *P*, and through the effective building block *GP**P*. Only a pattern of conjunctive principles can take these characteristics into account.

5.3.4 Abduction

Abduction is a mode of inference which occupies a central place in the process of complexity described here, although it remains little known and used in comparison to the prevailing deductive and inductive modes. It was introduced by Charles Sanders Peirce.[2] Peirce argued that the logic of inquiry includes three types of inference: abductive, deductive and inductive, in which abduction is the necessary first stage. He wrote:

> [Induction] never can originate any idea whatever. No more can deduction. All the ideas of science come to it by the way of Abduction. Abduction consists in studying facts and devising a theory to explain them. Its only justification is that if we are ever to understand things at all, it must be in that way. Abductive and inductive reasoning are utterly irreducible, either to the other or to Deduction, or Deduction to either of them. (Peirce, 1931–35, vol.5, § 146)

Peirce described abduction as: 'a creative insight into how to resolve some surprising phenomenon' (Dyer, 1986, 23). Abduction is reasoning from consequent to antecedent. Deduction tests the conjecture provided by abduction: it defines the terms of a hypothesis generated by abduction and then formulates the hypothesis as a deductive argument, drawing out its consequences. Induction is the final stage: 'it takes the deduced consequences of a hypothesis, checks them with specific events in experience, and, on the basis of such sampling, makes a judgment as to whether the hypothesis is acceptable, needs modification or should be rejected' (ibid., 24).

These three modes of inference can be distinguished in the following way. Each mode includes a particular case, a general rule and the result of the operation of the rule and the case. It unfolds in a sequence of three steps but the order in which the case, the rule and the product are considered differs across the modes of inference. An example is: 'these balls are drawn from this bag' (case); 'all the balls drawn from this bag are white' (rule); 'these balls are white' (result).

Deduction is the move from the general claim that all the balls drawn from this bag are white (rule) and from the particular act of drawing balls from this bag (case) to the inference that these balls are white and the next balls drawn from the bag will be white (result).

Induction is the move from the particular observation that the balls drawn from this bag (case) are white (result) to the general claim that all the balls drawn from this bag are white (rule).

Abduction is the move from the particular observation of white balls (result) to a theory or mechanism intrinsic to white balls (rule) which disposes them to come from this bag (case).

These modes of inference are pictured in Figure 5.4 in which the successive steps are numbered from 1 to 3. Step 1 is the starting step, it symbolises what is taken as known from the start. Step 2 is intermediate. Step 3 is the ending point, it represents the goal, what one wants to know.

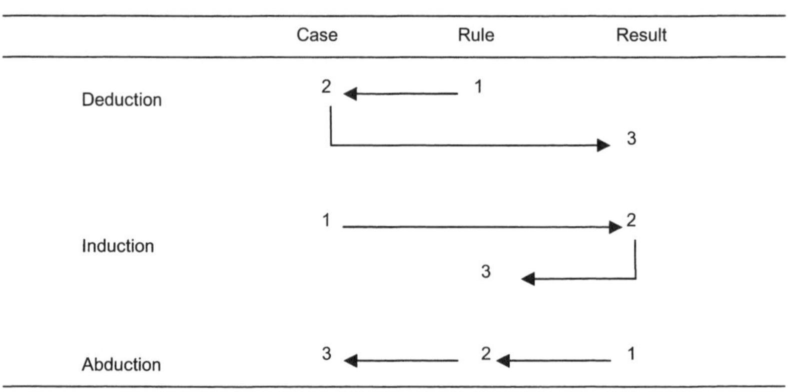

Figure 5.4 Three modes of inference

The connection with the complex duality $GP*P$ becomes apparent when it is realised that case, rule and result can be replaced respectively by the generative process GP, the relationship $*$, and the product P (Figure 5.5).

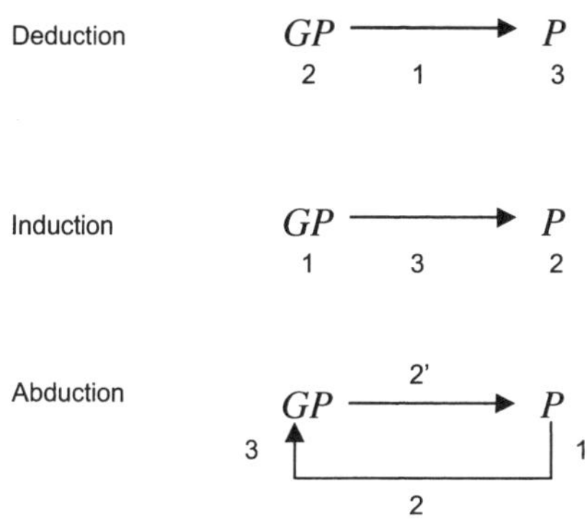

Figure 5.5 Deep complexity and modes of inference

Deduction and induction include the actualisation part only (⟶) of the recursive $*$ relationship, whereas it is fully included in abduction.

Only abduction takes *GP* as a goal, not as a given. Deduction and induction denote a unidirectional influence between *GP* and *P*. We showed in Chapter 4 that this is compatible with non-complexity. Only with abduction can the distinctive character of complexity be included. Abduction includes the recursive move from *P* to *GP* combined with the actualisation relationship, which makes the rule step composed of two parts, 2 and 2'. In abduction, starting with the product *P* (result, observation), it is aimed through 2 at characterising the process *GP* generating *P* through a relationship of actualisation 2'. Once *GP* is characterised, the test is: does this *GP* work, that is, does there exist 2' producing *P*? Then 2' is analogous to a rule of induction. And if 2' is found to work over a class of phenomena, it can be taken as a hypothesis in a deductive fashion.

Thus abduction does not substitute for deduction and induction. The three modes of inference are complementary but in an ordered way in which abduction tends to be prime. Abduction is a source of novelty in assumptions and ideas, deduction develops it and provides, with induction, checks and balances to abduction. No single method is self-sufficient without the other two as complements, in general. It follows that for abduction to be neutralised or ignored, one must assume that the situation on which the inquiry bears is simple enough, well structured, repeatable and confined to the identification of surface regularities between variables. An important aspect of abduction is that it enables one to inquire about singular, but robust, facts in scientific practice. The whole pattern of the inquiry about the state–economy relationship which led to the RISE is exactly abductive. It was summarised in Figure 1, Chapter 1. It can be reassessed now. I started with an empirical investigation whose result was the RISE pattern. Then I searched for a *GP* generating this representation, subject to the condition of abiding by the rules of scientific practice, that is, 2. Thus, to sum up: starting from a product, given a rule of scientific practice, how to design a *GP* generating *P* according to 2'? Anchored deep complexity (ADCX) was the name given to this *GP* in Chapter 1. After the characterisation of complexity in the subsequent chapters, ADCX became transformed into second-order complexity (CX3), and meta-complexity (CX4).

All in all, abduction is a way to give priority to what is important over what is general, although the concern with generality is never absent. Abduction together with induction and deduction in the application of the RISE to other countries is at the heart of the investigation which triggered this book.

5.3.5 Construction

Deep complexity CX4 does not bring a direct solution to a substantive problem. It proposes a pathway to a potentially satisficing situation. For this, it is necessary to mobilise the four organising principles established thus far. Behaviouralist self-reflexivity, the intrinsic ambivalence of composite self-similarity, the conjunctive pragmatic logic, and abduction entail an active participatory role for the operator or researcher. Intrinsic ambivalence pervades in the fact that CX4 combines an aspect which can be applied to an issue, and another aspect which does not lend itself to application but rather, to construction. The deep complexity that we established in section 5.2 provides a tool to be applied. It defines a framework and orientates the enquiry along the lines exposed in Tables 3.3 and 4.3, and in section 5.2. The part which pertains to the subject matter is informed by this tool but it does not bring necessarily a solution. There is no principle of sufficient reason which would make it possible to rely on a test-proofed set of technical and theoretical tools to be applied at the substantive or object level, and whose use would warrant a satisfactory solution to a problem. This statement may appear unpleasant. Yet it follows directly from the very definition of complexity. In the *GP***P* pattern, the conception of complexity presented here tells us that it is less difficult to address *GP* than *P*. Since the modus operandi of complexity tells us that it cannot be applied directly at the object level, it has to be constructed through relying firstly on the meta-level, and secondly on the object level without any general recipe operating at this level. Therefore CX4 requires a constant awareness of the interplay of the two levels and of the necessity of identifying the cognitive situation. Only the explicitly identified non-complexity of a situation entitles us to deal directly with the object level and therefore to dispense from activating the meta-level explicitly. This also entails the researcher's responsibility in the identification of the situation and the exposure to transparency and public criticism.

This pragmatic construction is the fifth organising principle. It complements abduction. This is exactly what we did in our research about the RISE (regime of interaction between the state and the economy). Let us remember that the initial question was 'What is the theory underpinning the RISE?' We are now in a position to answer that the RISE is a product *P* informed by a generative process *GP*. This *GP* is in turn informed by deep complexity CX4, itself relying on five organising principles. The initial anchored deep complexity ADCX was transformed into CX4. This *GP* is underpinning the RISE.

5.4 CONCLUSION: CX5

The full characterisation of deep complexity as process ends with an anchoring of the substantive open-ended alternative CX4. This anchoring consists in five organising principles (OPs): behaviouralist self-reflexivity (OP1), composite self-similarity (OP2), conjunction (OP3), abduction (OP4) and construction (OP5). It reflects the transformation that was operated from the initial heuristics about behaviouralist, conjunctive and abductive hypotheses in Chapter 1 to the present theoretical characterisation of deep complexity in its own right.

This characterisation consists in a fifth notion of deep complexity: CX5. It embodies the quantitative and the qualitative components, as CX4 augmented with the five organising principles:

$$\mathbf{CX5} = \text{CX4} + \text{OPs}\ (1, 2, 3, 4, 5)$$

Coming back to the agenda defined in Chapter 2 about ADCX, it seems that we have fulfilled three items at this point: intractability, open-endedness and its anchoring. There remains an unanswered issue about the kind of alternative CX5 is. Is it a theory? Isn't it merely contingent upon the specific situation which was described? Does it possess a more general bearing? Is it an alternative framework, and, therefore, does it bring an answer to the fourth component on the agenda? These questions point to the need to enquire into the scope for generality of CX5. This will be addressed in the next chapter.

NOTES

1. Original full sentence: 'If one must use metaphorical language, then let the metaphor be this: the mind and the world jointly make up the mind and the world', H. Putnam (1981), *Reason, Truth and History*, Cambridge: Cambridge University Press, xi.
2. Peirce (1931–35, 1984, 1986). Peirce's writings on logic and philosophy are typically fragmentary and reflect a temporal development in his thought (Fann, 1970, 5). Yet he stated in

1902 that abduction and the classification of arguments introduced by him in 1867 were still the key of his logic (Peirce, 1986, 588). Peirce believed that abductive reasoning which can be found in Aristotle's *Analytics* was 'imperfectly described under the name of apagoge' by Aristotle (Peirce, 1984, 22). He himself called it by different names at different times, notably hypothesis and retroduction, a term used later by N.R. Hanson (1965).

6. Generality

> What we call beginning is often the end
> And to make an end is to make a beginning.
> ...
> We shall not cease from exploration
> And the end of all our exploring
> Will be to arrive where we started
> And know the place for the first time.
>
> T.S. Eliot (1963)[1]

6.1 INTRODUCTION

We address in this chapter the issue of the generality of the notion of complexity that we obtained in Chapter 5. We symbolised it as CX5, the fifth notion of complexity resulting from the progressively developed theoretical specification of the irreducibility encountered in Chapter 1. From now on we will refer to it as CX5.

How and why the question of the generality of CX5 arises at this stage necessitates that we recall the progress made since Chapter 1 before we can define the issue at stake and a strategy for dealing with it.

6.1.1 The Progress Made

A. The birth of deep complexity

We started in Chapter 1 with enquiring about what theory could account for the empirically derived conjecture of a regime of interaction between the state and the economy or RISE. The RISE consists in a configuration of interdependent components. It was found irreducibly difficult to isolate and individualise the influences of specific components taken separately, independently from their relationships with other components and with the RISE itself. We also found that the notion of system or 'systems theory' did not help, although it was originally developed as a method for curing the limitations of thinking classically based on analytical decomposability into separate entities.

What we identified later as an ill-structured problem appeared initially as an irreducible obstacle. Several authors' contributions appeared as fundamental insights for our research: from Edgar Morin, the insight that radical uncertainty was not a cause for giving up with enquiry, but should be addressed in its own right; from John von Neumann, the intuition of complexity deriving from the relationship between a thing producing something and its product; from Heinz von Foerster, the legitimacy of self-reference; from Herbert Simon the distinction between substantive and procedural rationality; and from Jean-Louis Le Moigne, the idea that consistent reasoning is not compelled to rely exclusively on the axioms of classical logic, notably the excluded middle.

The combination of these ideas provided the resource for a heuristic construction of a general working hypothesis under the name of anchored deep complexity (ADCX). ADCX was a generative principle for the initial conjecture of the RISE viewed as its product. We established its acceptability through a comparison with the classical method of analysis. We suggested that this sort of complexity did not exclude classical analysis.

B. Anchored deep complexity (ADCX)

This finding triggered the question of where ADCX stands in the literature on complexity. It was addressed in Chapter 2. We found that in economics, it is Keynes's notion of uncertainty that comes nearest to ADCX. It fulfils three of the defining characteristics of ADCX but is clearly unsatisfactory on the fourth, anchoring. After a review of other frequently used forms of irreducibility that are present in the literature on complexity, we came to conclude that ADCX had no theoretically worked out equivalent although there is a growing literature covering two broad domains, the complex systems literature on the one hand, and complexity thinking on the other hand. The former bears on modelling complex systems, the latter is philosophical and methodological. They differ also about their relationship with classical science. The former relies heavily on computer simulations as a new tool besides classical analytical tools. But it develops within the classical science paradigm. The latter contains a reflection on the limitations of classical science but never delivers an alternative to it and resembles somewhat wishful thinking. This discussion nevertheless brought an insight about the need to draw a distinction between deep complexity (DCX), whose consistency cannot hold within the confines of the principles governing classical science and which calls for an alternative to it, and the kind of 'classical' complexity for which the issue of its foundations is practically never addressed to this author's knowledge, and which is therefore modelled within classical science. We denominated it as non-deep complexity (NDCX).

ADCX is a specific form of DCX. It triggers the question of how to accommodate it theoretically, that is, the question of specifying a generative principle for it. This brought us to the developments of Chapters 3 to 5.

C. From ADCX to CX5

It was obvious at the start of Chapter 3 that the kind of complexity entailed by ADCX required to be characterised in its own right before we could proceed to a theory of deep complexity. ADCX contains an essential feature of non-excludability of what is not DCX. It entails conceiving a threshold between ADCX and NDCX or, more broadly, between deep complexity and non-deep complexity. We examined current views on complexity in this respect and were forced to conclude that the question of how to endogenise this cutting point was left totally unanswered. This theoretical endogenisation is the task that was undertaken in Chapters 3 to 5 as a central aspect in the design of a generative principle for ADCX. At this stage it is important to recall that we shifted our main reference point from political economy and the RISE to safety science. Safety science bears on domains of experience in which irreducibility to total safety imposes itself in a much clearer and stronger way than irreducibility in economics or political economy or even, maybe, any other social science. These domains of experience concern notably industry and transport. Whereas there exists a body of knowledge on the basis of which current incidents and accidents can be statistically dealt with, there is no knowledge about reducing the potentiality of catastrophic events to nil. It is a radical irreducibility inherent to the very activity of safety. It is a potential of danger with actual – though rare – occurrences which cannot be eliminated. It is an accepted essential feature of these domains. Things go differently in economics. Economics contains no hard, ineliminable barrier in its subject matter into which the analysis which ignores it is bound to bang. When radical irreducibility is detected in economic theory, it is always possible to attribute it either to 'necessary' assumptions doing away with it which were not made, or to incompetent judgement. There is no general justice of peace for discriminating among different judgements, there is practically no hard protocol of validation in the actual world of economics. The contrast with safety science is striking. The irreducibility of the occurrence of catastrophic events is an intrinsic feature of its domain, not a product of uninformed analysis. The reference to this domain and other domains of experience synthesised in Tables 3.3 and 4.3 provided a firm basis for the characterisation of deep and non-deep complexity. CX5 is the outcome of this process.

6.1.2 The Issue at Stake

CX5 brings an answer to the question of designing a generative principle (*GP)* for ADCX and completes a second loop. It remains to clarify what kind of answer it is.

A. An answer to the initial question

The initial question was under what conditions deep complexity theorised in its own right might produce a generative principle for an ADCX subject to the two constraints of not excluding NDCX and abiding by scientific practice. The resulting CX5 relies on five mutually supporting pillars or organising principles (OP) numbered from OP1 to OP5. It confirms in a way the initial general hypothesis. But it denotes progress in it. Characterising complexity as a product and as a process led me to elaborate an articulate notion of complexity which no longer has the character of an hypothesis. The initial features of behavioural self-reflexivity, of an argumentation not tied to disjunctive reasoning, of abduction and of construction are characterised and organised in a more accurate fashion. Above all, CX5 contains an essential property which was produced inside the very abductive process of theorising. It is OP2 denoting an essential new feature denominated in different but equivalent ways as intrinsic ambivalence, composite self-similarity or logical level invariance. It could not be deduced from the first loop. OP2 combined with the other four OPs transforms deep complexity into a consistent composition, CX5, which was not 'discovered' but constructed all along, and whose central finding is the critical non-separability of the process of enquiry into the world (*PEW* or *W2*) and the world *W* itself containing *W2* and the world external to *W2*, or *W1*.

B. What kind of answer is it?

The non-separation of knowing and its object challenges deeply ingrained patterns of thought and action. There is little doubt that CX5 must appear weird and disquieting to the reader at this stage. It inevitably leads us to ask what kind of answer is this answer brought with CX5. What is its scientific status, since it seems to go against the basic tenet of the independence – or separation – of the world and the knowing process of the world?

Several additional questions arise about CX5. First, there is the view that CX5 may look so odd because it lacks something that would bring it closer to classical scientific practice. It raises an issue about the quality of its specification (is it well specified?) and an issue of its completeness (is it specified enough?). These two questions amount to asking for an assessment of the robustness of the specification of CX5. The former purely qualitative question orientates further enquiry toward contrasting CX5 with classical practice. The latter, completeness, cannot be dealt with in the absolute. It is conditioned by what is expected from CX5.

This raises a second set of questions about the effectiveness of CX5. The first goal of CX5 is straightforward. It is to improve the structure of an initially ill-structured problem-situation. It provides a clear criterion of what may be called an internal effectiveness. If it is achieved, it means that CX5 is sufficiently well specified and brings an answer to the issue of qualitative specification. The other notion of effectiveness follows from the way CX5 is distinguished from classical practice. It relies on a difference between principles that are axiomatic to both perspectives. Therefore a genuine issue of principle is present, however ambitious it may look: can CX5 be an alternative to the classical perspective?

This question triggers another question about what it means to be an alternative. A concise answer was made by Herbert Simon in his Nobel Prize paper:

> There is a saying in politics that 'you can't beat something with nothing'... The same principle applies to scientific theory. Once a theory is well entrenched, it will survive many assaults of empirical evidence that purport to refute it unless an alternative theory, consistent with the evidence, stands ready to replace it. (Simon, 1979, 509).

I propose to follow Simon and to extend his answer to a scientific perspective, and to call it 'Simon's test'. In the end, we will have to assess whether CX5 passes it or not.

A third question is about the generalisability of CX5. CX5 was built on the basis of specific situations in political economy and in safety science. Isn't it too specific in this respect?

However, one might ask as well whether generalisability could not be derived from the potential of generalisation contained in the characterisation of a 'situation' in Chapters 3 and 4. Once a the situation is informed by OP1 behavioural self-reflexivity, it delivers a general setting that seems relevant to any formally similar situation independently of its particular substance.

Yet though this reasoning may be relevant for practical purposes, it is not sufficient for scientific practice. The main reason is that its non-separationist basis runs against the ruling principle of classical science. This basis is the critical non-separation introduced in Chapter 4, which is intrinsic to CX5. It consists in the apparently paradoxical critical duality synthesised in (*GP**P*) in which the active role of the first term can be disactivated and reactivated in turn according to the character of the situation behaviouristically experienced, thus opening the way for the possibility of an oscillatory move between non-separation and separation, that is, between DCX and NDCX. An expression of this duality is the critical non-separation of *PEW* and *W*.

This apparently odd property calls for clarifying the scientific status of CX5, for defining its domain of validity and for characterising what kind of alternative it can be. How to make the criticality of the non-separation of *PEW* and *W* compatible with the effectiveness of CX5 as an alternative defines the issue of the generality of CX5. Indeed, once the issue of criticality is settled, it will appear that CX5 does not suffice to meet Simon's test of effectiveness. It will be necessary to complement it with three operational principles before we can define an ending step with a CX6 or Effective Deep Complexity (EDCX).

6.1.3 Strategy

The agenda defined above is immense. The clarification of where CX5 stands in scientific practice depends on fulfilling it. Two ways of tackling this problem can be envisaged. One might be to take the three groups of questions in a linear sequence, one after the other. The trouble is that they are interrelated: for instance, the quality of the specification cannot be settled without knowing the effectiveness of CX5, and the effectiveness depends on how robust the CX5 alternative can be.

Another way is to take this problem as a complex issue and to structure it with CX5 itself. It should provide a direct opportunity to test the relevance of CX5 and will be followed in this chapter.

It must be noted that it is in full continuity with CX5. Its OP5, the principle of construction, calls for constructing what construction means, apart from the very elaboration of CX5 itself and its five organising principles already carried out. Something more is needed now. The questions of the agenda cannot be answered by CX5 in its present state although its organising principles are the signposts on the path toward attempting to design answers. Constructing this path complementing CX5 is the task before us. It must also be noted that this task amounts to building a generalised *GP* for CX5, thus initiating a third recursive loop. Putting CX5 to work in order to build its own *GP* is in direct continuity with OP2, the principle of composite self-similarity, whose first test is to have CX5 work on itself. It will be undertaken through the use of the (*GP****P*) pattern combining the meta- and object levels. It will have to include the connection with the external world *W1*. It is therefore three consecutive levels that will need to be considered in this chapter. Moving bottom-up, there comes first the *W1*, substantive object-level proper. Then comes its meta-level $_m$, and finally the upper, meta-meta-level symbolised by $_{mm}$, both belonging to the process of enquiry into *W1*. The enquiry into the generality of CX5 requires that we progress in the reverse, top-down order. It sets the organisation of this chapter into five core steps.

The first step, on GP_{mm}, will be concerned with the search of a foundational perspective for CX5. It will be quite substantial and lead to a *critically transactional* perspective. This perspective will produce a P_{mm} which consists in a new principle, the principle of *autonomy* of CX5. It is an operational principle complementing the five organisational principles. Since it comes next to OP5, we symbolise it as OP6. It forms the immediate background of GP_m at the meta-level. It orientates it toward *situation recognition*, the second operational principle, or

OP7. The next, fourth step, P_m, will consist in harnessing OP7. It is *action in a deeply complex situation* which denotes the ending operational principle OP8.

The conclusion of this journey will be a new, enriched, and, it is claimed, complete notion of deep complexity as *Effective Deep Complexity* (EDCX) or CX6, to mark an ending point of the progression through a sequence of six successive notions of deep complexity. EDCX provides the tool that will be harnessed in the third part on operationality.

This chapter is unusually long. This is due to the unity of its theme and its important weight. Section 6.2 notably will extend over nearly 100 pages. I again ask for the reader's goodwill. Due to this specific organisation and in order to facilitate the readability of this chapter, I will recall graphically at the beginning of each section where it stands in the general argumentation (Figure 6.1).

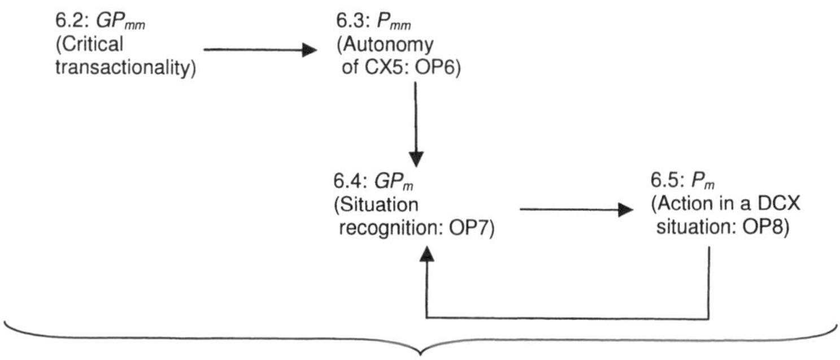

Figure 6.1 Chapter 6 in a nutshell

In the following, the particular subject matter of each section will be signalled by a grey shaded area. I start immediately with section 6.2 on GP_{mm}.

6.2 GP_{mm} IN SEARCH OF A FOUNDATION FOR CX5

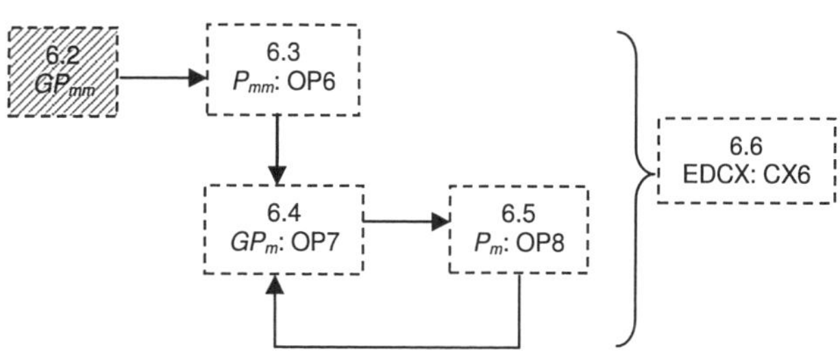

The task pursued in this section is to assess whether CX5 can be related to some definite foundational perspective. My hope is that it will also help clarify the argumentation. Paraphrasing Mark Blaug, I believe that it is hardly possible to understand something as unfamiliar as CX5 without subsuming it, or at least relating it, to something larger that is already familiar (Blaug, 1998). Couldn't we be satisfied with the foundations already evoked in Chapter 1? We took them as an assumption in the building of ADCX. They must be scrutinised again at this stage, and in a new way. We know now that CX5 is structured in a specific way and involves a specific relationship between the process of enquiry into the world, *PEW*, and the world *W* which includes both *PEW* as *W2* at the object level, and the world external to *W2*, that is, *W1*. The very process of construction (OP5) of CX5 emphasised *PEW* at the price of seemingly neglecting *W1*. Indeed it did not appear necessary to focus on *W1* in the very building process of CX5 since CX5 was designed from the origin on the basis of a specific problem in *W1*, namely the RISE, and later on in various other domains (Table 3.3). Once the robustness of the situation depicted in Table 3.3 was acknowledged, the remaining task was to design a *PEW*.

The task now is to reactivate *W1* and to make clear whether CX5 entails some definite perspective on it, and more broadly on *W*. The answer will be positive. It is a processual view of the world contemplated from the meta-meta-level. We symbolise it by W_{mm}. This result will be integrated in the reflection on the pair (PEW_{mm}, W_{mm}) which will take us rather far at the epistemological level. We will find indeed that if some of the available views on DCX do accommodate the non-separation of (PEW_{mm}, W_{mm}), none actually accounts satisfactorily for its criticality. We organise our argumentation in two steps, firstly on W_{mm}, secondly on (PEW_{mm}, W_{mm}).

I address this search of foundations for CX5 with the same caveat at the outset as for the conjunction principle (OP3) in Chapter 5: although it will by necessity bear on several issues of ontology and of the philosophy of knowledge, it is addressed pragmatically from a theoretician's standpoint, not a philosopher's one, in a domain of experience which is not philosophy. I will try to be clear on this unfamiliar subject-matter through contrasting systematically the main ideas and through following Ernest Nagel's advice that: 'scientific as well as philosophical ideas are best understood when the contexts in which they are employed are described, and their functions in those contexts are explained' (Nagel, 1986, xxvi).

6.2.1 W_{mm} The Processual World of CX5

What view of the world is consistent with the complex irreducibility that is intrinsic to CX5? In other words, does CX5 imply a particular conception of the world?

Let us recall that the world *W* in CX5 includes the world *W1* external to the process of enquiry, and the process of enquiry into the world (*PEW*), that is, ourselves, symbolised at the object level by *W2*. This definitional property challenges the common view of a world restricted to *W1*. It has important consequences whose discussion is the aim of this section.

Discussing the character of *W* at a foundational, meta-meta-level, cannot but trigger philosophical issues about ontology and about the substance of *W*. They are addressed below.

A. Reality and experience

The issue of reality at a foundational level cannot be disconnected from the philosophical question of realism. In our initial investigation on public expenditure it was a consideration of realisticness that drove us to retain robust features making up RISEs. Does this imply that the reality status of the world of CX5 pertains to an ontological realism? It is all the more relevant to address this question as a philosophical movement in social science has developed under the name of "critical realism" on the premises of a criticism of empirical realism and formal deductionism on the one hand, and of a notion of irreducibility broadly understood evoking an idea of complexity on the other hand (Lawson, 1997; Delorme, 1999).

Realism in its strong definition posits the existence of reality independently of the act of observation and leads to the normative view that science must depict this reality. It follows from a metaphysical, ontological view. Realism in its ontological or metaphysical meaning is about the notion of being, of what exists, as such. In philosophy, realism is the view that objects or some disputed kinds of entities exist independently of any perceiver. It was revived by Bhaskar as transcendental realism and adapted to social science by Lawson under the name of critical realism. It is developed mostly at a philosophical level and appears as a kind of general prescriptive programme for theorising. Scientific realism asserts 'the existence and operation of the objects of scientific enquiry absolutely (for the most part in natural science) or relatively (for the most part in social science) independently of the enquiry, or more generally of human activity', according to Bhaskar (1993). Transcendental realism conceived by him posits that it is a condition of the possibility of scientific activity (experimental and applied) that 'the objects of scientific enquiry (causal laws, generative mechanisms, structured things) not only exist but act independently of that activity-transfactually, in open and experimentally or otherwise closed systems alike' (ibid.). The adjective 'critical' denotes realism applied to social science. It is the term used by Lawson although he declares his preference for 'structural' or 'transfactual'. Transfactuality denotes the irreducibility of reality to events, and intransitivity denotes the irreducibility to our knowledge. This irreducibility originates from the layered and structured character of reality. It is layered in three hierarchised domains or levels (Figure 6.2) which are unsynchronised or out of phase, but overlapping.

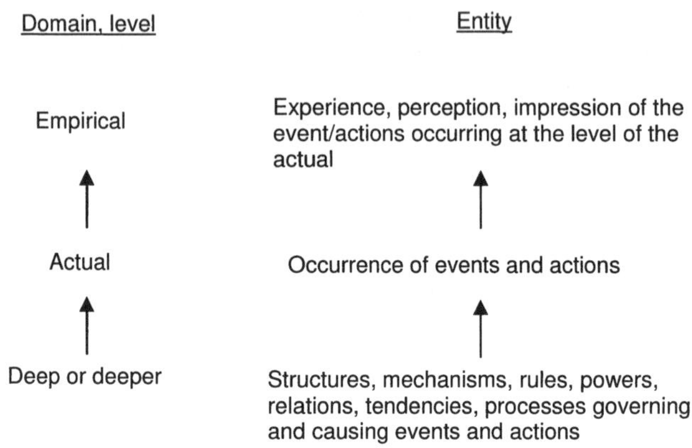

Figure 6.2 The layered reality of critical realism

Although critical realism emphasises the irreducibility of the deep reality to our knowing it, and therefore comes close to a notion of complexity, critical realism and the perspective of DCX developed here differ fundamentally in their implications for scientific practice. Critical realism is a philosophical view. DCX is a construction rooted in scientific practice with a commitment to integrate it with a foundational layer into a consistent set-up.

Yet critical realism is an involved construction whose reference to complexity renders it necessary to clarify its difference with DCX in more detail. We will come across critical realism several times in this chapter before we reach a final step of differentiation in section 6.3.

Bhaskar contrasts the realism he advocates – transcendental or critical – with empirical realism. The latter is said to prioritise epistemology and to presuppose an ontology grounded in sense experience. If sense experience produces atomistic events then reality must be atomistic. This epistemology, then, conceals a specific ontology (Fleetwood, 1996, 731).

Realism prioritises ontology. The nature of the world is believed to determine the way in which knowledge of it can be obtained. A hierarchy between ontology and epistemology is therefore established in which ontology is prime. Critical realism illustrates the tendency that from an ontological standpoint, it is tempting to shift from the metaphysical belief about what the world is to what should be known about it. The main drawback of critical realism is that, apart from its normative tone, it leaves in ambiguity how what should be known can be known scientifically. Bhaskar opposes 'his' realism to empiricism, pragmatism and idealism. Lawson opposes critical realism to idealism, nominalism and irrealism and abundantly criticises deductivism, empiricism and positivism (Delorme, 1999, 2). Although DCX differs from the above realism, it fits with none of the notions that are negated by realism, except pragmatism.

DCX can be said to convey a pragmatic view of the world in the way it arises from the cognitive and practical situations depicted in Chapter 3. Reality, 'realisticness' or pragmatic 'realism' rather than ontological realism are central features among the dimensions defining a cognitive and practical situation.

In this view there are phenomena which appear as real in the way they resist our attempts to modify or to ignore them. We do not know if they pertain to a deep reality which structures events that are actualised and can be empirically experienced. I know that I cannot fly in the air only with my arms used as wings. This impossibility reveals a pragmatic, phenomenal reality. We do not know what is the deep level of reality but we know that a generative process is deeper than its product and that any *GP* is itself the product of an even deeper *GP*. From the standpoint of experience, constraints and possibilities shape what appears as reality. Indeed the whole construction of CX5 reveals a pragmatist and phenomenological realist view in a sense that will be made explicit in section 6.2.2, C.2 below. We discuss below whether this perspective implies a specific view on the substance of the world.

B. Beyond atomism and reductionist holism

The particular view one adopts on the substance of the world can at the outset be expressed as a function of its distance to the two polar views of atomism and holism. It is hardly avoidable to refer to these views even when this dualism appears unsatisfactory.

However, these terms are often used with varying meanings. Before we reflect on an alternative, we need to make clear the notions for which an alternative is sought. An unease with this dualism appeared in works by R.W. Gerard (1958) who spoke of *orgs*; by F. Jacob (1971) who introduced the concept of the *integron*; and by A. Koestler with the concept of *holon* which is meant 'to supply the missing link between atomism and holism, and to supplant the dualistic way of thinking in terms of "parts" and "wholes"... by a multi-level, stratified approach' (Koestler, 1969, 197).

The path followed here is different. CX5 emerges from the perception of an irreducible difficulty to decompose a phenomenon in the way classical analysis commands to dissect it into elementary separate components. The triggering factor was that we could not rely on classical analytical techniques as a general framework to come to grips with the partial undecomposability of the RISE. It is therefore manifest that CX5 challenges what is commonly called atomism as a constant, general world-view.

B.1 Atomism and its Corollaries

Atomism is the view according to which the world is built up from simple and indivisible elements. The world is therefore an aggregate of separately existing elementary entities which are the 'basic building blocks' out of which everything is made. Atomism entails analytical reductionism, externality of relations and dualism. *Reductionism* is the claim than an object must be depicted or explained by relying solely on its basic elementary components. It does not relate exclusively to atomism. The kind of holism which relies on the notion of a whole as the sole source for explaining its components is also reductionist. *Externality of relations* is the belief that the role or the working of a component part is the same when separated out as it is when part of a whole. *Dualism* consists in 'organizing thought by means of all-encompassing mutually exclusive categories, with fixed meanings' (Dow, 1990, 143). It relies on an 'either – or', excluded middle type of reasoning and therefore differs from the duality that we introduced in Chapter 4.

Analytical reduction, when it is practiced as the general and undiscussed method of scientific enquiry, illustrates these meanings. It is one of the central features following from the axiomatic structure of Cartesian thought. This structure is exposed by Descartes at the beginning of his *Discours de la méthode* in his four rules for 'properly conducting one's reason'. The first rule is about the avoidance of 'precipitancy and prejudice' and the acceptance only of clear and distinct ideas for which there is 'no occasion to doubt' them (precept of evidence). The second rule is to 'divide each of the difficulties that I will examine into as many parts as might be possible and necessary in order best to solve them' (precept of reduction). The third rule requires 'to lead my thoughts in order, starting with the objects which are simplest and easiest to know to progress little by little, as if by degrees, to knowing of the more compound ones and even assuming order between the ones that did not naturally follow each other', (precept combining mechanism and a notion akin to sufficient reason.). The fourth precept (exhaustivity of enumeration), is 'to make everywhere such total enumeration and such general reviews that I could be ensured of omitting nothing' (Descartes, 1637 [2000]).

Here lies the core of Descartes's approach to science through the principles of analytical reduction in which analysis means identifying the simple entities in 'complex', compound or composite phenomena and showing how the latter can be reduced to the former. It is assumed that the components of the whole phenomenon are the same when examined separately as when they are playing their part in the whole, and that the principles for assembling the components into the whole are themselves *tractable*. This reasoning proved to be very successful in physical sciences, and greatly influenced Western-style thinking.

It has resulted in a kind of monopoly of this analytical thinking as the unique legitimate way of scientific thinking. It has even become a sort of natural state of serious science in mainstream economics. I have personally experienced for years how difficult it was, and still is, to explain to most of my fellow economic theorists that the analysis backed by the analytical thinking they practise is not the only way to be scientific. This overwhelming predominance of disjunctive analytical thinking in science, stemming from the hegemony of physics as *the* model of exact science, has been criticised for decades by many authors, notably, *inter alia*, Alfred North Whitehead (1929, 1979), Anatol Rapoport and William J. Horvath (1959), and David Bohm (1980).

B.2 Mechanism and Fragmentation

Among the widely unnoticed assumptions and consequences of this conceited scientism are *mechanism* (Lowe, 1951; Thoben, 1982), and *fragmentation*. In presenting the analytical view, Rapoport and Horvath note how it is natural to fall into the language appropriate for describing a mechanism, the 'working of the parts', and to hope to understand complexity by 'superimposing' the workings of the various parts. This approach proves effective in specific areas of investigation. The working of a complicated machine, the solar system and electro-magnetic theory provide paradigmatic examples in which superimposition and additivity 'work'. This classical picture, because of its success, 'has a terrible seductive power over the human mind. One is tempted to ask whether all complexities cannot be explained in this way' (Rapoport and Horvat, 1959, 72).

The general characteristic of classical physics is the analysability of everything into separate parts; these parts are considered to be working together in interaction as in a machine: 'The laws of physics, then, express the reason or ratio in the movement of all the parts, in the sense that the law relates the movement of each part to the configuration of all the other parts' (Bohm, 1980, 121). Moreover, in this mechanistic order, the elements are conceived as existing independently, and are assumed to be connected with each other through external relationships only. They interact through forces that do not bring any changes in their essential characters:

> The machine gives a typical illustration of such a system of order ... By contrast, in a living organism, for example, each part grows in the context of the whole, so that it does not exist independently, nor can it be said that it merely 'interacts' with the others, without itself being essentially affected in this relationship. (Bohm, 1980, 173)

It is even more present in human society. Bohm defines fragmentation as '*an attempt to extend the analysis of the model into separate parts beyond the domain in which to do this is appropriate, it is in effect an attempt to divide what is indivisible*'. The fragmentary approach:

> gives men a picture of the whole world as constituted of nothing but an aggregate of… 'atomic building blocks' and provides experimental evidence from which is drawn the conclusion that this view is necessary and inevitable. One might in fact go as far as to say that in the present state of society, and in the present general mode of teaching science, which is a manifestation of this state of society, a kind of prejudice in favour of a fragmentary self-world view is fostered and transmitted (to some extent explicitly and consciously but mainly in an implicit and unconscious manner). (Bohm, 1980, 15)

B.3 Holism and its Variants

The term 'holism' was coined by Jan Smuts, a South African statesman and philosopher, in his book *Holism and Evolution* (1926). In his words, '[Holism] regards natural objects as wholes… which are more than the sums of their parts, and the mechanical putting together of their parts will not produce them or account for their characters and behaviour' (Smuts, 1929, 640).

Opposing holism to atomism as polar notions is a matter of convenience. There are degrees in holism, from strong to weak, which combine, with various forms. In this way holism is not strictly symmetric with atomism. CX5 is compatible with a weak form of holism which will be defined below as a relational, organisation-based conception. Yet the plurality in the forms and the degrees of holism renders it problematic to use the epithet 'holist' without careful qualification in every instance.

This variety within holism can be illustrated in several ways. First, it can be defined as the view that an account of all the parts of a whole and their interrelations is inadequate as an account of the whole. Similarly, it is the view than an account of a part is inadequate without referring to the whole of which it is a part.

Second, holism can be ontological, methodological and epistemological, or relate to some property. In ontological holism, the world is a whole whose nature is not simply determined by the nature of its parts. Methodological and epistemological holism is the view that the best way to study and to know a subject matter is to treat it as a whole, and not merely to analyse the structure and the behaviour of its component parts. In 'property holism', the properties of the whole are not determined by, or not deducible from, the properties of its parts.

A third way is the close connection of holism with systems thinking. In social sciences, holism is the view that the proper object of these sciences is systems and structures which cannot be reduced to social agents. It opposes atomism and methodological individualism in various ways that are reflected in 'Holism puts the study of wholes before that of the parts' (Jackson, 2003, xv); in 'The systems paradigm … is holistic, but not in the usual (vulgar) sense of taking the whole; systems concepts are concerned with wholes and their hierarchical arrangement rather than with *the* whole' (Checkland, 1983 [1999], 13–14); and also in 'Being holistic in the management domain means using systems ideas and concepts'(Jackson, 2003, 301). A final important distinction needs to be made between a strong holism and weaker forms, these degrees depending upon the weight attributed to the whole in the explanation. When this weight is high it appears as if explanation might be reduced to the whole. This is a reductionist holism which does not fit with CX5. In a weaker interpretation, the parts of a whole understood as a complex system have mutual relations that do not exist for the parts in isolation (Simon, 1998, 170).

In all these distinctions we find a constant reference to wholes or systems which therefore seem to pre-exist enquiry. Is this reference needed? It does not seem necessary when we refer to organicness or organisation as characterised by a composition of entities between which the relations are internal rather than external, and in which the essential characteristics of any entity are outcomes of relations with other components. It is through this weaker relational notion of holism that the present argumentation on deep complexity is developed.

C. Process, relationality and openness

I have attempted to define in the previous section to what extent the polar notions of atomism and holism, and some of their variants, are views about the world that CX5 avoids. The worl-dview implied by CX5 is neither atomism nor reductionist holism. It relies from the start on the processual connection between *GP* and *P* and on the fact that the generative principle is indeed a generative process within the elementary *GP***P* loop. The fundamental duality (*GP****P*) itself denotes a processual paired connection between successive elementary loops. Process is therefore intrinsic to CX5. And it bears on *W1* and *W2* as well, through OP2. Process thus has a priority over product, both for *W1* and *W2*. Temporality and context, activity (what something *does* rather than *is*), and change are the cardinal factors for our understanding of the world. Process denotes an unfolding over time without absolute beginning and any predetermined end point.

Relationality can be external and internal. It is not limited to organicness or organicism. It does not follow from a predefined systems view. Relationality is more general than organicness since it includes both internal and external relations. However they are not treated on a par, the generative recursive relationship is given priority and it is in the specific situations in which it can be disactivated that the external relationship pattern holds. This is the reason why the view of the world of CX5 is better termed *relational* rather than organic.

CX5 does not exclude the possible relevance of addressing elementary separate components as well as addressing wholes or systems, provided it is relevant for the specific situation at stake. CX5 excludes only the -ism attached to these aspects and the way they tend to help transform local and provisional properties into extended and fixed properties deemed to have a general validity. This openness of CX5 follows from its processual and relational character.

Process and relationality allow us to address the particular substance of the subject matter that is relevant for investigation as a thing to be established, constructed or demonstrated rather than a preconceived substantive nature which would be valid in all circumstances. The position advocated here is coherent with a fallibilist stance which leaves open the options regarding the world and emphasises the knowing process.

Openness applies to any particular content of subject matter according to the pattern of Table 3.3. It is subject to the standard D^* in existence in a particular domain of experience, be it scientific practice in some discipline or whatever else. Openness thus combines an openness on the substance of the subject matter with a closure on D^*. Openness and relationality result in CX5 as being *integrative* rather than systemic to the extent that it does not prioritise any system view from the outset, but rather starts with experience and strives to identify and characterise the relations and their dynamics within their context. They may appear systemic, but as an outcome, a *P* of a process of enquiry, not a *GP*.

A final question bears on the apparent similarity with critical realism since Lawson also advocates process and relationality (Lawson, 1997, 2006). The basic difference is that CX5 does not make theory rely on its purported realism in correspondence with some deep reality whose nature is decided metaphysically. It does not compel theory to deal with this deep reality. It boils down to a fundamental difference about what can be argued in terms of theory of knowledge. The *W* of CX5 is known through an open, fallibilist process of construction. The *W* of critical realism is a metaphysical, ontological notion prior to enquiry, devoid of epistemic roots, which asks the knower to be a passive believer in something beyond his/her epistemic reach.

6.2.2 (PEW_{mm}, W_{mm}) An Epistemology for CX5

A. Introduction: a general warning to the reader

Commenting upon his own experience with the study of systems, Peter Checkland wrote: 'In fact, the dramatic – not to say traumatic – finding in our formative studies ... was that it simply was not possible to take any system as given' (Checkland, 1983 [1999], 278). We may paraphrase him in our case, replacing only the final words, by: 'it simply was not possible to take *PEW* as given and to consider *W* separately from *PEW*'.

Does there exist a theory of knowledge – an epistemology – accommodating what can be called the *critical non-separability* that is so essential to CX5? We will need first to define critical non-separability, in section B, and will suggest addressing non-separation and its criticality in two successive steps (sections C and D). The result of this review of the existing perspectives susceptible to accommodate these two aspects will appear rather mixed. Non-separation is accommodated by some pragmatist and constructivist approaches. But criticality appears to resist any satisfactory endogenisation, from the standpoint of research, in the perspectives which rely explicitly on a notion of deep complexity. Several major perspectives are close to DCX but differ unequivocally from CX5 with respect to criticality. These perspectives range from Piaget's genetic epistemology, Morin and Le Moigne's method of complexity, Checkland's soft systems methodology and Dewey's theory of inquiry, to Lawson's critical realism addressed in section 6.3. They are involved approaches for which it would be unsatisfactory to rely solely on our own synthesis without presenting to the reader how our argumentation proceeds. Our argumentation is itself rather involved and needs to be transparent. This necessity will force us to sharpen both the reasons why CX5 cannot be accommodated by these views, and therefore the notion of criticality itself. Hence the detailed enough developments that will follow.

It is at this point fair to say that the price to pay for this transparency will be in the length of the developments. A balanced presentation in terms of space would have it put in an appendix and summarise the argument in the core of this chapter. This is not our choice because these developments are intrinsic to the argumentation about GP_{mm}. We are involved in the construction of the generalisability of CX5 and need to make it as explicit as is needed. It is not a peripheral matter or an appendix issue to a core argument, it is the argument itself. It cannot be summarised because it relies on the critical analysis of important views on deep complexity which are still unevenly known or even ignored in the ongoing debates about the complexity movement in science.

The developments of this section, especially subsections D and E, will therefore be unusually lengthy. There will however be a gain in the identification of the central role played by criticality. With this hindsight, and with the conclusion that the available approaches on deep complexity cannot accommodate criticality enough, we will turn to another perspective, the one afforded by John Dewey's theory of inquiry. It is only at this ending stage about CX5 that Dewey's relevance to the process that we developed appears, although it remains partial. At least it provides a term to which CX5 can be referred, albeit critically. This almost 100 page section is organised as follows:

- B. The issue of the critical non-separability of CX5.
- C. Non-separability accommodated, but not critical.
- D. The problematic accommodation of criticality in complexity thinking.

- E. A post-Deweyan, critically transactional perspective.

B. The issue of the critical non-separability of CX5

The critical non-separability attached to CX5 was already evoked in the introduction to this chapter. We now engage in a discussion of it. We will address first the non-separability or non-separation of *PEW* and *W*, and we will envisage its criticality in a second step.

Remember that the world *W* comprises the world external to ourselves (*W1*) and ourselves (*W2*) to which we assimilate the process of enquiry into the world (*PEW*). The world *W* in *PEW* bears on *W1* and reflexively on the *PEW* itself, *W2*. Therefore process, relationality and openness are characteristic properties of both *W1* and *W2*. The relationship between *PEW* and *W* is part of the world at large. It is tangled since it comprises a process of enquiry into a world containing *W1* and the process of enquiry *W2*.

Relationality in *W1*, in the external world as a subject matter of enquiry, is a rather commonly accepted view which does not raise any issue of principle. Things go quite differently for the connection of *PEW* with *W*. It goes against the well-entrenched dogma of objectivity of science understood as the strict ontological and epistemological separation of *W* and *PEW*.

We designate by non-separation or non-separability this connection with the immediate necessary qualification of criticality meant to signal that it is not a plain, fixed, immutable non-separation. Non-separation will be best understood through first depicting the more familiar context of separation. We will find that it is accommodated by constructivist perspectives. However the most difficult problem is with criticality. We will make clear that this notion is only indirectly and loosely evoked in the perspectives on deep complexity whereas its endogenisation is required of any perspective susceptible to fully accommodate CX5.

The non-separation of *PEW* and *W* was encountered in Chapter 3. It is an essential property of CX5. It is especially expressed in OPs1, 2 and 3. The wording 'non-separation' may appear awkward to the extent that a positive denomination for this property of conjunction might have been preferred. The reason for retaining 'non-separation' is its explicit reference to the classical tenet of separation. Here, I recall Mark Blaug's advice that it is difficult to make sense of something unfamiliar without subsuming it, or at least relating it to something larger or different that is already familiar (Blaug, 1998, 24). Non-separation is unfamiliar. Its meaning derives from what is classically meant by separation and may be better explained through what non-separation is not. To separate means that any connection between the two terms is rejected either because of their mutual independence or because a constant priority is given to one term over the other, in which case one term is 'active', the other is passive or secondary, thus leading in practice to a quasi-separation. The postulate of objectivity illustrates the former in which *W* is considered independent from *PEW*. It is the defining aspect of objectivism. Both objectivism and its opposite, subjectivism, fit with the latter. In this case, separation is not absolute. It may support the idea that *W* is always dealt with by some knowing subject *PEW* and that it is a sort of non-separation. Yet it is clear that it is nothing but a trivial, passive non-separation. In CX5, non-separation prevails and can simultaneously be suspended in the specific, justified situation of non-deep complexity, and be reactivated if necessary. It is not trivial but active. Moreover it is not a plain non-separation. It derives operationally from a constant watchfulness and the exercise of critical judgement as to the character of the cognising situation from which the possibility of an oscillatory move between DCX and NDCX originates. Therefore, although it is active, it is not a radical or plain non-separation and is better denominated as a critical non-separation.

Criticality designates the existence of a threshold of deep complexity (DCX) and non-deep complexity (DNCX) or, here, a threshold of the non-separation of *PEW* and *W*, and its separation. Non-separation is the background, normal state. It can be suspended or disactivated locally and temporarily if there are justified reasons for considering that a situation is not deeply complex (NDCX). The critical character of CX5 signals the necessary and constant consciousness of the possibility of shifting from one state to the other. It follows directly from OP1 and is the outcome of experience in a given domain of experience. The criticality of non-separation means that it is not a plain non-separation or a plain deep complexity. It is quite demanding on the theory of knowledge susceptible to accommodate it, since it requires it to account for what negates it locally. This problematic endogenisation of criticality will appear to be a common weakness of existing perspectives on deep complexity.

C. Non-separability accommodated, but not critical

Since non-separation is unfamiliar, we pursue our strategy of clarifying concepts through relating, comparing and contrasting them with what is more familiar. The separation of subject and object, of *PEW* and *W*, is the commonly received view in science. It characterises what we may call separationist perspectives summarised in a first step, section C.1, before we address several non-separationist perspectives in section C.2.

C.1 What Non-separation is not: Separationist Perspectives

Separationist perspectives emphasise either *W* or *PEW* in such a way that the separated items exist independently of each other. The former are objectivist, the latter are subjectivist perspectives.

The objectivist view

Objectivism has been characterised in the following way by David Jonassen:

> The important metaphysical assumption of objectivism is that the world is real, it is structured, and that structure can be modelled for the learner. Objectivism holds that the purpose of the mind is to 'mirror' that reality and its structure through thought processes that are analyzable and decomposable. The meaning that is produced by these thought processes is external to the understander, and it is determined by the structure of the real world. (Jonassen, 1991, 28)

Two important objectivist traditions are positivism and realism.

- *Positivism*

Positivism, a term coined by Auguste Comte, designates a philosophical tradition based on a synthesis of Baconian, Galilaic and Newtonian empiricism on the one hand, and Cartesian rationalism on the other hand. It has become a term of polemical indictment with numerous meanings. In its generally accepted meaning, it denotes a basic emphasis on the empirical predictability of scientific statements.

Positivism is defined by Loïc J.-D. Wacquant as the theory of knowledge:

> which asserts the primacy of observation and the pursuit of causal explanation by way of inductive generalization. In the social sciences, it has become associated with three related principles: the ontological tenet of *phenomenalism* according to which knowledge can be founded on experience alone (verging on the fetishization of 'facts' as immediately available to sense-perception); the methodological tenet of the *unity of the scientific method* which proclaims that the procedures of natural science are directly applicable to the social world with the goal of establishing invariant laws or lawlike generalizations about social phenomena; and the axiological tenet of *neutrality* which refuses to grant normative statements the status of knowledge and maintains a rigid separation between facts and values. (Wacquant, 1993, 495)

The Cartesian method, with its central tenet that truth was established by deductive reasoning and not by observation and experiments, and its three other rules mentioned above in section1.1 of this chapter, inspired a tradition of deductive scientific thinking based on mechanistic analogies for the organisation of subject matter. The synthesis of the positivist vision of science comprises 'a *monistic* theory of scientific development and a *deductivist* theory of scientific structure' according to Bhaskar (1993, 468).

The logical primacy of data or *logical positivism* was proclaimed in the 1920s by the Vienna Circle: the goal of philosophical analysis was to be the logical analysis of the knowledge claims of positive, or empirical sciences. It was held that under the unity of science thesis all sciences shared the same method. Logical positivism was followed by *logical empiricism* in the 1940s and 1950s. Logical empiricism was less radically empiricist than logical positivism: it acknowledged the crucial importance of theory and emphasised notably the unity of science thesis, the hypothetico-deductive model, the deductive-nomological and inductive -probabilistic covering law models of scientific explanation, and the symmetry thesis between explanation and prediction. According to this thesis, the only difference between them is one of temporality: in explanation, the phenomenon described has already taken place, while prediction precedes it. Although classical positivism lost its influence in philosophy and among methodologists, positivism reorganised by the Popperian programme replacing verification by falsification, and mainstream scientific practice in social science, especially in economics, are evidence that positivism continues to reign as a scientific style and doctrine guiding method.

The methodological consequences of positivism on scientific research are overwhelming. Positivism manifests itself through its influence on theorising and the search for laws based on facts that are allegedly value-neutral or observer-neutral; on systematic data collection aimed at hypothesis-testing; and on the view that the world exhibits cause-effect relationships which can be discovered, at least partially, by structured observation. It proved immensely productive in physical science and contributed forcefully to the dogmas around which modern science is organised (Louçâ, 1997). They are the dogmas of *naturalism*, of *universalism* and of *objectivity*. Objectivity was evoked above. Naturalism is the claim that the rules for the knowledge of any element, be it human, social, living or artificial, are the same as those of nature or of physics in its variant of physicalism. Universalism entails the generalisation of the laws derived from observation and experiment. All in all, positivism is an approach to science which involves rules to govern theory appraisal or theory choice, rules which, if followed, lead scientists towards correct practice. It illustrates a sort of generalised principle of sufficient reason. It includes deduction, induction and quantification as necessary and sufficient forms of definition and description. Reductionism, atomism and mechanicism follow from these dogmas.

It is always difficult to discuss the methodological consequences of positivism critically because of several factors. The first is that it operates for a majority of scientists like ambient air operates for everybody. It is our natural environment and it goes largely unnoticed. Reliance on facts and the search for laws connecting facts, like what is done in 'modern science' is the alpha and omega of what appears to be a natural and unquestionable way of doing science. It follows that the positivist hypothesis goes almost unnoticed. It is the way our teachers were educated, the way they educated us, and the way pupils and students continue to be educated nowadays. Therefore questioning it and attempting to understand to what extent it constitutes a choice made by thinking subjects among other possible alternatives requires some maturity and detachment as to its potential adverse consequences in terms of an academic career.

Moreover positivism consists in a constellation of variants, which makes it difficult to reduce it to clear-cut methodological rules facilitating comparison and contrast. Notwithstanding these difficulties, the three general postulates of objectivity, of universality and of naturalism-physicalism entail rules to govern knowledge acquisition and theory appraisal. They are rules which, when followed, are deemed to lead scientists towards good practice, in a kind of extended principle of sufficient reason already mentioned. The positivist view asserts that the relationship between the world and the scientist consists in observation and prediction of a world composed of clearly discernable, divisible and measurable objects (facts, substantial things or events) which are not affected by the act of observation, and which are discovered or uncovered. Explanation becomes synonymous with prediction and causality.

In positivism causality consists in the action of impulses in a mechanical world ruled by laws derived from the certainty about the repetition of causal relations and allowing for prediction (Louçã, 1997, 20). Cause appears as the 'change in the independent variable' and cause – effect appears as a 'functional relation': this makes possible a general formalisation of causality as exogenous impulses in a mathematically treatable modelling. It is the main form of production of causal claims in positivism today. It is a concept of efficient cause instrumentally defined as exogeneity of the explanatory variable.

Repeatability of laws and determinism leave no place for other kinds of determination, such as circular or multiple determination, more suited to situations in which a cause may simultaneously be an effect. The belief in a causal and fully intelligible structure, the belief in the predictive capacity of theoretical statements, and the reliance on mechanistic reductionism, combined with the three postulates, give positivism its flavour of an unnoticed and hard-to-question intellectual environment.

All in all, positivism is a doctrine based on a particular style of scientific practice claiming the unity of science. Every time this particular founding choice is kept beyond question or remains unnoticed, positivism has won. Thanks to its successes in natural sciences, it became a kind of modern scholastic in social science. Although it is in disrepute among methodologists, it remains the prevailing style in mainstream economics. To summarise, the positivist methodology emphasises objectivity, the separation of object from subject, and the universality of the scientific method derived from it.

- *Realism*

The notion of realism was introduced above in the reflection on the kind of world that is implied by CX5. We address it here from the standpoint of the separation of *PEW* and *W*.

Realism is the philosophical position which asserts, following Bhaskar's definition: 'the existence and operation of the objects of scientific enquiry absolutely (for the most part in natural science) or relatively (for the most part in social science) independently of the enquiry, or more generally of human activity' (Bhaskar, 1993, 547). Realism is thus basically an ontological position postulating a reality existing prior to its observation or its representation. In its semantic formulation, scientific theories contain terms which refer to real entities. Scientific theories are true or false statements about the real world, which introduces one to a correspondence theory of truth. Given the postulate of objectivity in positivism already mentioned and the postulate that facts are the reality, semantic realism is the direct continuation of positivism. J.-L. Le Moigne recalls that in A. Comte's philosophy, 'what is positive is real' (Le Moigne, 1995, 7). Realism has also an epistemological formulation bearing on the knowability of reality. It has different forms depending on conceptions of knowledge and on what relevant reality is. At our level of scientific practice, several distinctions are needed, especially about realisticness, instrumentalism and again critical realism.

Realisticness is better viewed as a property of theories and assumptions, whereas realism is a theory of theories (Mäki, 1998) although we have used the term realism thus far in the common sense of a property of something being realistic. Developments in the twentieth century have modified the Comtian equation between positive and real. Today's positivism, especially in the empirical social sciences, is mainly instrumentalist. Instrumentalism asserts that theoretical terms are neither true nor false. It satisfies with correlation and prediction. It is agnostic about the ontological debate.

A recent development is the philosophy of transcendental or critical realism applied as critical realism to economic methodology in work pioneered by Lawson (1997). In Bhaskar's terms, critical realism arose from a general critique of the deductivist theory of scientific structure underpinning logical positivism. The cornerstone of deductivism was the theory of explanation according to which explanation proceeded by deductive subsumption under universal laws interpreted as empirical regularities (Bhaskar, 1994, 469). Bhaskar argued for an ontology identifying the domains of the real (or the deep), the actual and the empirical, and for a conception of science as proceeding 'by a continuing and reiterated process of movement from manifest phenomena, through creative modelling and experimentation, to the identification of their generative causes, which now became the new phenomena to be explained' (ibid., 469). In economics, realism emphasises the interdependencies of the economic system, their organic, complex (irreducible to simple phenomena) and evolutionary character preventing a formal representation. These interdependencies operate at the level of deep reality or structure of economic processes rather than at the surface level of appearance of events (empirical and actual) which are the normal focus of attention of positivist economists. Thus critical realism refers to the level of the nature of reality as understood by the theoretician. It is ontological and goes much further than the discussion of realism – or realisticness – of assumptions and theories.

Critical realism differs from positivism and from what may be termed classical realism with respect to the postulate of universality: for critical realists, 'ontological realism is consistent with epistemological relativism. We know the same world but under irreducibly historical (and better or worse) descriptions' (ibid.). The postulate of objectivity does continue to operate in critical realism, but without the monist view of positivism and classical realism. Pluralism follows from it: although the deep is understood to have an objective existence, there is no mechanism for establishing true knowledge of it in any absolute sense (Dow, 1996, 44).

There is however a fundamental presupposition which is common to the realist and the positivist stances: it is the givenness of the entities composing the world of interest for science. Givenness is one of the main themes on which R. Rorty bases his criticism of philosophy (Rorty, 1991). The only difference comes from the nature of the entities of interest. In the realist stance, they are real or actual objects to which theory must conform. It is an ontology of preconstituted objects postulating the givenness of this preconstituted reality. The positivist stance relies on the givenness of facts. Since facts are given, theory must model their regularities in a way enabling prediction. This view is an ontology of facts independent from observation. It postulates the givenness of preconstituted, already existing facts to be discovered and which remain simply ignored in the absence of sufficiently developed observing, measuring and experimental tools.

The subjectivist view

In contrast with objectivism, subjectivism refers to the theories of knowledge giving primacy to the subject. Most of these theories arise from a reaction against objectivism and its postulates. The consequence is the diversity of the theories since they are no longer unified by obeyance to universal postulates. In the limit, one might say that any theory not based on the primacy of object must in some way attribute a leading or, at least, a significatively active place to the subject. In this broad sense, the subjectivist view might tend to become the constellation of non-objectivist views. This might be permitted by the difficulty of drawing simple borderlines between most of the subjectivist epistemological traditions. However, distinctions must be made as is illustrated by the huge difference between the epistemological and methodological constructivism that will be discussed here on the one hand, and the anti-epistemology and anti-methodology versions of constructivism on the other hand. The latter are radical forms of subjectivism, while the former include an active role of subject but in a specific form which will be explained below and is better understood as standing beyond objectivism and subjectivism. This is very clear for CX5 although two of its organisational principles, behavioural reflexivity and construction, place high the subject's place, the other three organisational principles cannot be assimilated to a subjectivist view.

We will sketch out two classical forms of subjectivism, *apriorism* and *conventionalism*. Our aim is simply to organise elements of information about these views in order to contrast them later with the moderate, specific form of constructivism which can accommodate non-separation in CX5.

A first instance of apriorism is the Cartesian *cogito ergo sum*. To Descartes the only certain knowledge was his knowledge of his own thought. This position reinforced the dualism between conceptual knowledge and observation using the senses, between mind and matter (Dow, 1996, 26). It also reinforced the belief that 'the general nature of the world could be established by wholly non-empirical demonstrative reasoning' (Bullock and Stallybrass, 1981, quoted by Landry, 1995, 234). Bertrand Russell summarised it as: 'There is thus in all philosophy derived from Descartes, a tendency to subjectivism and to regarding matter as something knowable, if at all, by inference from what is known of mind' (quoted in Landry, 1995, 324). Kant's philosophy is also apriorist in the way it sees the knowing subject as being pre-equipped with fixed epistemic categories (innate or self-evident a priori knowledge and a posteriori knowledge) and actively engaged in structuring incoming perceptions within those categories (Landry, 1995, 324). It provides a justification for the deductive method as applied to axioms based on a priori knowledge but elicited by empirical observation. In physical sciences, it combines with induction from experimental information. However, as Dow mentions it, the difficulty of collecting data by experiment in the social sciences, notably economics, 'was one of the factors which led to a continued emphasis on deduction' (Dow, 1996, 26). In economics, it turned into a debate between those who favoured induction and those who favoured deduction from subjectively derived axioms. This debate does not seem to have disappeared. Instances of subjectism nowadays are, notably, Austrian subjectivism and the formal modelling based on an axiomatic approach to general equilibrium (Israel, 1996).

The conventionalist position represented by Henri Poincaré and Pierre Duhem holds that laws and theories are not summaries of passively received experience but are 'free creations of the mind for the simplest and most convenient interpretation of nature' (Bullock and Stallybrass quoted in Landry, 1995, 324). According to Keat and Urry (1975, in Landry, 1995, 324) one also finds in conventionalism 'the view that the truth or falsity of theories is "underdetermined" by empirical data. Observation cannot provide an objective control for science, the idea that agreed facts can enable us to choose between theories is denied'.

Conclusion on separationist perspectives

All in all, a common feature of the objectivist and subjectivist traditions is their reliance on the strong priority given to one term of the object and subject pair. In the objectivist view, the existence of a reality that is external and independent of the knowing subject is posited. The subject has a rather passive role in the process of knowledge production. To solve a problem is akin to a means–end exercise. The debate about the nature of the ends is often assumed to be of minor importance. Objectivism combined with a unitary view of science results in a self-assertive scientific practice in which knowledge is postulated to mirror reality. The subjectivist view emphasises the importance of the subject in the process of knowing. The existence of an independent reality is denied or considered of secondary importance. It does not constitute the ultimate test to validate the result of the knowing activity.

None of these traditions fits with CX5. CX5 necessitates a perspective in which both subject and object play a significant role in the activity of knowing. Several views offer such a perspective. We address them now.

C.2 Non-separationist Perspectives

In the last section we identified theories of knowledge which cannot be compatible with a non-separationist perspective. They are the objectivist (positivist, realist) and the subjectivist (apriorist, conventionalist) traditions. These polar traditions do not cover the entire spectrum of existing views although they seemingly attract the majority of discussions. Beyond these traditions are philosophical positions which, while rejecting objectivism and emphasising the role of subject, cannot be ranked simply in plain subjectivism. In marked opposition to objectivism is *constructivism*, a problematic term used as a common name for a broad and quite varied set of views. We alluded to it in Chapter 1, and OP5 signals the importance of construction in CX5. However there are other important non-separationist views which are not explicitly labelled constructivist but come close to it. They provide a kind of transition toward the explicitly constructivist views which appear potentially relevant to non-separation.

These traditions are *pragmatism*, *phenomenology* and *hermeneutics*. Constructivism would reject none of these views although it differs from them in its focus on the very process of constructing knowledge. In the face of a very ill-structured, deeply complex situation, action aimed at improving the situation is nothing but constructing knowledge. The kind of constructivism which seems relevant here was the background which helped formulate the method and the assumptions of Chapter 1. It is what I found in the writings of Le Moigne, Piaget, von Foerster, Varela, Morin, von Glasersfeld, and at an initially more distant, philosophical level, in Peirce's and Dewey's works.

I will sketch out the traditions which form a transition towards an unambiguous though moderate constructivist perspective accommodating non-separation both at the epistemological and methodological levels. These issues will be addressed in three steps about transition, a constructivist epistemology and a constructivist methodology.

Transition: three traditions

Among the traditions which accommodate non-separation in a more or less explicit way are pragmatism, phenomenology and hermeneutics. In the following, I have no pretence to summarise them in a representative way. I rather stick to what seems especially relevant for the present research. They all contain constructivist aspects that I will attempt to clarify when I address constructivism in its own right.

Pragmatism is characterised by William James as primarily a methodology which tries:

> to interpret each notion by tracing its respective consequences. What difference would it practically make to any one if this notion rather than that notion were true? If no practical difference whatever can be traced, then the alternatives mean practically the same thing, and all dispute is idle. Whenever a dispute is serious, we ought to be able to show some practical difference that must follow from one side or the other's being right. (James 1907, 1949, 45-46, cited in K. Hoover, 1994, 288)

This definition clarifies the original characterisation of pragmatism by its founder, Charles Sanders Peirce: 'Consider what effects, that might conceivably have practical bearings, we conceive the object of our conception to have. Then our conception of these effects is the whole of our conception of the object' (Peirce, 1931–35, vol. 5, 1).

John Dewey avoids the word 'pragmatism' in his *Logic: The Theory of Inquiry* because of the 'misunderstanding and relatively futile controversy [that] have gathered about the word' (Dewey, 1938 [1986], 4). He admits however that his book is

> thoroughly pragmatic in the proper interpretation of 'pragmatic', namely the function of consequences as necessary tests of the validity of propositions, provided these consequences are operationally instituted and are such as to resolve the specific problem evoking the operations. (ibid.)

From Peirce, James and Dewey to Rorty, one finds the common notion that truth involves beliefs being coherent, with knowledge being contextualised with regard to the presuppositions of a given community: truth tends to be in Peirce's thinking the ultimate limit to which the opinions of the relevant scientific community would converge, given their adherence to appropriate methods.

The advocacy of the importance of the situated subject and of human experience shared by all pragmatists may however have to be paid by the risks of subjectivism and practicalism: 'whatever works is true'. Hoover points out the difference between a 'modern pragmatism' exposed to these shortcomings, and Peirce's own concern with the ill-interpretations of pragmatism, which led him to propose to replace this term by the word 'pragmaticism, which is ugly enough to be safe from kidnappers' (Peirce, cited in Hoover, 1994, 288). Hoover argues that central to Peirce's work is a theory of inquiry in which criticism and criteria of validity of method (or 'truth') are central, unlike what may appear in Rorty's work evoked below. Hoover's claim is that a more Peircian pragmatism or 'pragmaticism' would help to avoid the risk of intellectual Balkanisation conveyed by modern pragmatism although many of the differences between Peirce and, say, Rorty 'reduce to matters of tone and emphasis. But tone and emphasis are part of what makes the difference between noise and music, prose and poetry' (Hoover, 1994, 288–289).

Phenomenology is used here for the philosophical method and movement that had its origins in the work of Edmund Husserl (1859-1938) in the twentieth century although the term had been used in a similar sense earlier, notably by Brentano, for describing phenomena. A phenomenon is a thing experienced, be it through the senses or otherwise (intellectually, psychologically, and so on). In Kant's philosophy phenomena contrast with noumena which are pure objects of reason, things in themselves, beyond any conceivable human experience. The term phenomenology implies a contrast with methods that seek to go beyond what is directly present in our experience. Phenomenology denotes the willingness to rely on phenomena of human experience as they present themselves in direct awareness (Kilminster, 1993, 460). It designates also the abstract philosophy deriving from this method.

Husserl aimed to develop a 'presuppositionless' philosophical method beginning with the 'total, unanalyzed cognitive situation' in which questions of the existence of objects were 'bracketed' in order not to take them as granted and to grasp their essences (Manicas, 1993, 466).

Phenomenology is not a doctrine but rather a movement made of various phenomenologies which have in common the notion of a mode of thinking based on experience and on a criticism of objectivism. As a methodological orientation in science, it opposes scientific realism and gives priority to describing lived experience in the everyday human life-world. Phenomenology may lean towards a subjectivist view in its readiness to concede primacy to the processes experienced by observers. This is indeed the way Checkland builds the methodology of his 'Soft Systems Methodology', combining phenomenology and hermeneutics, and contrasting it with a positivist stance (Checkland, 1999).

Intentionality, reflexivity, the rejection of the belief in the absolute externality of the world, the primacy of experience and the corollary of constant concern for the methods by means of which the knowledge of the everyday world of experience can be transformed into scientific knowledge, are features of phenomenology which are directly relevant to CX5 and have been present since the beginning of this research and in the OPs of CX5. Apart from its undoubtedly abstract character, phenomenology has also been criticised for its kind of first-person approach that is incompatible with the scientific third-person approach. Subjecting research to the standard D^* in its domain of experience is a way to answer it.

One of the main merits of the phenomenological standpoint lies in keeping active the question of how knowledge of everyday experience can be transformed into scientific knowledge. There is no ready-made answer to it. It needs to be argued. When scientific practice is taken itself as a particular everyday experience of scientists in a particular domain of experience, this practice of production of knowledge cannot escape the question about what theory of knowledge underpins it. 'What is the theory of knowledge supporting what you say?' is a question constantly kept alive in science by phenomenology.

Hermeneutics is the inquiry into, or the theory of, the nature or methods of interpretation. It can be seen as a study of the principles by which knowledge related to interpretation is obtained, which gives it an attribute of a theory of knowledge. From our standpoint two broad aspects stand out, namely a philosophical attack against objectivism and a methodological attempt with consequences for method in research.

At a philosophical level, hermeneutics is the term used by Richard Rorty in *Philosophy and the Mirror of Nature* (1979) to characterise the general orientation of his attack on what he regards as the central dogma of the Western philosophical tradition. This dogma is the mirror metaphor, the notion than the human mind and knowledge mirror the world, from which follows a correspondence theory of the knowledge of an objective world. Rorty's account is 'antirepresentationalist', by which he means a view of knowledge not 'as a matter of getting reality right, but rather as a matter of acquiring habits of action for coping with reality' (Rorty, 1991, 1).

In Rorty's view, knowledge tends to be more a matter of conversation and social practice than of accurate representation. Science is not a matter of discovering a true, objective reality independent of mind and language but rather a matter of constructing knowledge. Knowledge then appears as a broad network of mutually interpreting beliefs. The adequacy or validity of such a network cannot be judged from any independent standpoint. There is no such a standpoint.

Therefore it must be judged holistically, according to how the beliefs *cohere* and support each other (Hoover, 1994, 290). Inquiries are inevitably situated and contextual. The task therefore cannot be to specify invariant laws of human behaviour but to make that behaviour intelligible by interpreting it in relation to subjective intentions. In later works Rorty uses the term 'pragmatism' to designate his philosophy.

A less radical criticism, with methodological consequences for research, can also be found. The tradition of hermeneutics owes much to Wilhelm Dilthey (1833-1911) whose chief concern was to establish that the subject matter of social sciences was intrinsically different from that of the natural sciences, and was concerned not with an external world but with expressions of the human mind which become cultural artefacts by a process of 'objectification'. Gaining knowledge of this process required the method of understanding or *verstehen* which comprises a circular process of knowing called the 'hermeneutic circle', a means of perceiving social objects as both wholes and parts. An initial consideration of the whole leads to an understanding of the parts, which in turn enables a richer understanding of the whole, and reciprocally. Here I quote Checkland:

> A preliminary overview of subject matter is used to guide an examination of what the parts denote; this clarifies the concept of the whole, which at the end of the cycle must be perceived so that all the parts can be related to it. Thus there are no fixed or absolute starting points, only an iterative cycle which gradually leads to an increased understanding of social reality. The hermeneutic circle opposes a Cartesian faith in any self-evident starting point and there is no 'right' answer to the question of where to begin or end. (Checkland, 1999, 276)

This interpretive tradition of social science contrasts with the objectivist approach. Human beings in the social process are constantly creating the social world in interaction with others: 'They are negotiating their interpretations of reality, those multiple interpretations at the same time constituting the reality itself. There is no pre-given universe of objects but one which is produced by the active doing of subjects' (Giddens, quoted in Checkland, 1999, 277).

This embraces introspection, to which Dow seems to reduce the *verstehen* principle (Dow, 1996, 40). However this does not modify the importance of understanding in social science. Unlike a physical scientist, who cannot have an innate understanding of his/her subject-matter in any comparable way, a social scientist has the capacity to have knowledge of human behaviour from introspection.

The danger with hermeneutics is relativism and subjectivism, although most of its proponents deny this. Since it contains an attitude toward valid knowledge in which 'the consensus of a community rather than a relation to nonhuman reality is taken as central', similarly to pragmatism (Rorty, 1991, 23), this renders it necessary to clarify the criteria by which the 'consensus of the community' can be obtained.

Inter alia, each of the three perspectives brings into focus a particular property which can be found in CX5. Controlled openness in pragmatism, experience and clarification attached to phenomenology are properties which combine with the hermeneutic judgement found both at the start of CX5 with its OP1 (behaviouralist self-reflexivity) and in its further development. None of them would negate the other two. The ways in which CX5 connects with each of these views appear complementary. Yet, each of them taken individually remains partial. Can they be combined into a whole which would envelop them through its reliance on the leading thread of construction of knowledge common to them?

The epistemological constructivist view

- *Construction and constructivism: getting rid of confusions*

At this stage we are in a better position to appreciate what remains on the agenda. The three perspectives reviewed above are compatible with the non-separation of *PEW* and *W*, but in a rather general, programmatic way, without explicitly developing its meaning and its consequences. We are looking for an epistemological view that would embrace not only the non-separation of *PEW* and *W*, or of subject and object, but above all the criticality that is so essential to it and to CX5.

Let us recall that CX5 is the outcome of a reasoning based on an initial hypothesis of construction of an argument for addressing an ill-structured problem-situation, and abiding by scientific practice. One might therefore expect to find a connection between this assumption, the fifth organising principle 'construction', and the notion of a constructivist epistemological perspective. However this inference from construction to a constructivist view is not straightforward and necessitates to be argued. Not only is 'constructivism' a most confused term, but the insights gained in the construction of CX5 have transformed the initial heuristic conjecture into a theoretical notion in which the non-separability of *PEW* and *W* was not present initially.

Yet we cannot escape from the fact that the initial hypothesis of construction followed from a presentation of constructivism by J.-L. Le Moigne, itself inspired by J. Piaget's genetic epistemology. This background renders it necessary to make clear the conditions that an epistemology accommodating CX5 should fulfil and the extent to which it may fit with a constructivist epistemology.

The conditions set by CX5 pertain to three aspects of knowledge: its nature, its origin and its object. First, knowledge is introduced in CX5 under the concept of *PEW*, the process of enquiry into the world. *PEW* is itself part of the world at large. Therefore it cannot but conform to its general properties of process, relationality and openness. The fifth organising principle, construction, emphasises this processual feature of construction of knowledge, which may be better named as knowing. Second, knowing originates in CX5 from the interplay of *W2* and *W1*. It does not originate mainly and permanently from one or the other of these two terms. It is not the outcome of a mere subject-led thinking, nor a passive product mirroring an external object. It results from an active interplay structured by the critical possibility to neutralise *W2* provisionally and locally, when NDCX prevails, through relying on pre-given knowledge and algorithms which can be applied to a given problem-situation, and thus do not need to be constructed for this particular situation.

Third, the object of knowing is the world as *W* or *W1* which was characterised in the previous section. Although it was addressed before *PEW* and *W2*, it does not stand for an ontologically real world whose discovery would be the goal of knowing. It was characterised as process and relationality in such a way as to leave open the object of knowing and to avoid imposing on science the metaphysical task of discovering the true, deep structures of reality, and of judging scientific practice in terms of its distance to this deep reality.

It is at this stage that the fallibilist standpoint which has been present throughout this work connects most clearly with an epistemological constructivist view. This view is concerned with the nature, the origin, the construction, the structure and validity of knowledge, not with the ontological concern about the existence and ultimate nature of reality. The existence of a reality independent of the human mind is not necessarily denied. It is a different issue on which the epistemological constructivist view remains neutral (Klir, 1993, 30).

There are several varieties of constructivism, maybe as many as disciplines. Before we investigate deeper into the meaning of the constructivist epistemology that is envisaged here, it will be useful to point out what it is not, especially in the discipline of economics, given the confusion reigning in it about this term.

A major instance of confusion is in the use of the same word to denote quasi opposite notions. On the one hand, constructivism or constructivist rationality is the word used by Hayek (Diamond, 1980) to connote what V.L. Smith calls the standard socio-economic science model which stems particularly from Descartes, who advocated the use of reason to create deliberately rules of action and socio-economic institutions that yield socially optimal outcomes (Smith, 2003). Hayek denounced this belief as a 'fatal conceit'. On the other hand, constructivism is the term which underpins the 'postmodern' critique of rationality and of the belief in progress through science, and therefore contradicts the former meaning. In economics, the use seems to have settled to label constructivism what is also termed postmodernism and post-positivism (Backhouse, 1994, 5) including the 'rhetoric' approach of D. McCloskey (Dow, 1996, 42). With the 'scourge of constructivism' Blaug denounced a combination of 'the new anti-modernism, antifoundationalism, post-structuralism, hermeneutical deconstructivism, discourse analysis, radical relativism, end-of-philosophy critique' in 'endless variations' around the basic theme that 'science and literature are one and the same enterprise ... that scientific ideas are just as much social constructions as are poems and novels, and in short, that the world is nothing more than a representation of words' (Blaug, 1994, 130). According to Backhouse, Rorty's critique of epistemology, Latour and Woolgar's sociology of scientific knowledge and Fish's literary criticism were the bases for relating the definition of knowledge to the linguistic practices of particular communities with the result that theories can be appraised only from within specific communities without standards transcending them (Backhouse, 1994, 129). According to these methodologists, the result is to undercut the empirical aspirations of researchers, to downgrade prediction and causal explanation as central goals of economics, and to end in anti-epistemology and anti-methodology, that is, nihilism and generalised relativism under the name of interpretive understanding.

It is therefore little surprising that this constructivist view may be a scandal to the traditional realist and objectivist beliefs regarding knowledge and science in economic methodology (Knorr Cetina, 1998, 77).

It should be clear by now that the constructivist view underpinning CX5 is different from these instances. The kind of constructivism to which I will refer is an *epistemological* constructivism. It bears on the process of construction of knowledge. It says nothing about an ontological reality. Thus it is foreign to philosophical realism. However the kind of constructivism envisaged here does integrate *W* and its consequences for the process of knowing. Rather than developing these ideas at the outset and in the abstract, I will examine how they appear in selected, representative instances of constructivist contributions, in a sequence going from general constructivist perspectives to constructivist contributions to DCX or its equivalent, in the next paragraph.

The epistemological constructivist view connotes the perspectives in which knowledge does not originate mainly from *PEW*, or the subject, nor from *W*, or the object, but from their interplay, which a priori fits well with their non-separability. The criticality of this non-separation adds a central issue that will be addressed later. We concentrate here on non-separability.

Understood in this way, the constructivist view of knowing has a forerunner, Giambattista Vico, and two modern pioneers, John Dewey and Jean Piaget. None of them is easy reading. Vico is almost forgotten (Berlin, 2000). Dewey remained programmatic (Seltzer, 1977). Piaget was more developmental and ended with the formulation of a genetic epistemology. My own thinking was initially most influenced by the last. In the following, I will concentrate on Piaget and the contributions of two of his followers, Ernst von Glasersfeld and Jean-Louis Le Moigne.

The reason why I do not also rely on Dewey at this stage is quite pragmatic. Although Dewey's constructivism is close to Piaget's, Piaget offers an explicit epistemological view whereas this is more difficult to detect in Dewey's writings. Above all, as a French-speaking person, I found less difficult to grasp Piaget et al.'s writings than Dewey's *Logic*.

I am not alone here. E. Nagel, the author of the 'Introduction' to *Logic*, admits that Dewey's 'idiom of thought and expository style make his *Logic* difficult reading' (Nagel, 1986, xxvi). D. Schön reports that he found Dewey 'muddy and unintelligible' when he was a graduate student before he took *Logic: The Theory of Inquiry* as the basis for his doctoral thesis (Schön, 1992, 123). It was only when reaching the end of writing the manuscript of this book that, with hindsight, Dewey's *Logic* appeared in a new light to me. Dewey's relevance will be addressed below in subsection E.

Understanding Piaget also presents difficulties. Even a Piagetian expert like von Glasersfeld admits that Piaget is a difficult author: 'partly because statements about the basic concepts of his theory are scattered in many different volumes and he never produced a concise, comprehensive summary of his ideas; and partly because these ideas are incompatible with the general realist view' (von Glasersfeld, 2000).

These considerations may explain why there is so much confusion and suspicion nowadays about constructivist ideas.

- *Piaget: genetic epistemology or knowing as an adaptive activity*

Jean Piaget's genetic epistemology deals with the generation and meaning of knowing from child's cognitive psychology and learning to scientific knowing. It contains an Ariadne's thread about learning as adaptation, from early work on child learning (Piaget, 1937 [1954]) to his contributions on genetic epistemology and constructivism understood as an irreducible interaction between subject and object in the process of knowing in general, including scientific knowledge (Piaget, 1967, 1243):

> Intelligence (and thus the act of knowing) does not start with the knowledge of self, nor with the knowledge of things as such but with the knowledge of their interaction; it is through its simultaneous orientation towards both poles of this interaction that intelligence organises the world by organising itself. (Piaget, 1937 [1954], 311)

In the knowing activity, the subject has to *assimilate* the object to its cognitive structures otherwise the object could not be 'recognised'. And the cognitive structures are transformed by the information thus brought in by recognition of the object: they have to *accommodate* the 'newness' in the object. Knowing implies both an assimilation *to* cognitive structures and an accommodation *of* these structures. Knowledge production is then the result of an active interplay between a subject and an object.

In contrast with the objectivist view, knowledge is not a mirror copy of reality in Piaget's constructivism, although reality is reflected in it. And, in contrast with the subjectivist perspective, knowledge does not mainly reflect the subject's mind, although the subject's evolving knowing structures play an active role in knowledge production.

In Piaget's constructivist genetic epistemology, knowledge reflects the dialectical adaptation of an active subject with an object. Knowledge cannot be separated from action and adaptation. In scientific activity, problems arise from a recognised interest in adaptation by some subject bearing a judgement that something should be undertaken (Landry, 1995, 328). All in all, Piaget provides a theory of knowledge based on action. The interaction between the subject and its environment is a dynamic setting of adaptation comprising assimilation, accommodation and equilibration. Equilibration denotes the organisation of the subprocesses of accommodation and assimilation in an uninterrupted flow in which a mutual compatibility between diverging and disturbing tensions is involved. In this way "intelligence organises the world by organising itself" with the proviso that in order to avoid the plain subjectivism to which it might lead, one needs to add that intelligence organises the world subject to the condition that it is the world itself that sets the very conditions of appearance of intelligence (Miermont, 1995). We cannot escape from this reciprocal interplay.

The non-separation of *PEW* and *W* is therefore unambiguously grasped by Piaget as an irreducible interaction of subject and object in which knowing is an adaptive activity, a continuing construction of knowledge. What is the truth value of constructed knowledge? An answer is provided by Ernst von Glasersfeld, whose work is much influenced by Piaget's thinking and who brings the notion of *viability* in an *experiential world.*

- *Von Glasersfeld: viability in an experiential world*

Von Glasersfeld's emphasis on the world as an experiential world follows from his reaction against two requisites 'that have been considered fundamental in any *epistemological* discussion of knowledge' in the Western history of ideas. The first requisite is the independence of knowledge from the knowing subject; the second is that knowledge must represent 'a world of "things-in-themselves" in a more or less veridical fashion' and that 'it is tacitly taken for granted that a fully structured and knowable world "exists" and that it is the business of the cognizing human subject to discover what that structure is' (von Glasersfeld, 1991, 231).

These requisites pertain especially to realism. Challenges to them have a long history. It has been a major argument of the Sceptics, since Xenophanes in Greek antiquity, that even if someone succeeded in describing exactly what the world really was, there would be no way to know that it was the 'true' description:

> It is based on the assumption that whatever ideas or knowledge we have must have been derived in some way from our experience, which includes sensing, acting, and thinking. If this is the case we have no way of checking the truth of our knowledge with the world presumed to be lying beyond our experienced interface, because to do this, we would need an access to such a world that does *not* involve our experiencing it. (ibid., 230)

Furthermore, it is Kant who suggested that the concepts of space and time were necessary forms of human experience, rather than intrinsic characteristics of the world, which prevents us from knowing what the real world might be like 'because whatever we call structure is necessarily an arrangement in space, time, or both' (ibid., 231).

However, if no truth about a 'real' world can be derived from experience, experience supplies valuable and useful knowledge. It was one of the first critics of Descartes, Vico, who emphasised that all rational knowledge was the result of the knower's own construction: '*Verum est ipsum factum*' or 'to be true is one and the same as to be made' (von Glasersfeld, 1985, 94). As von Glasersfeld mentions, one finds a remarkable and apparently accidental echo of Vico in Piaget's statement that: 'To know is to construct or to reconstruct the object of knowledge in such a way as to capture the mechanism of that construction' (ibid., 1985, 94). And I should add that, after all, this is what the *GP*P* pattern of CX5 is all about.

Then, if on the one hand knowing cannot produce a true, mirror image of an objective world, and on the other hand, one does not want to end up with a solipsistic form of knowledge, 'one has to find a way of relating knowledge to reality that does not imply anything like *match or correspondence*' (von Glasersfeld, 1991, 232). Von Glasersfeld claims that such a conceptual alternative can be built thanks to the concept of adaptation supplied in Darwin's theory of evolution, as was first suggested by William James and Georg Simmel (von Glasersfeld, 1985, 95-97; 1991, 232). Knowing is an adaptive process with an evolutionary component, in which adaptation does not mean 'to become more like the "real" world of the environment', but to have found one possible way of surviving within the constraints set by the knower's environment. Von Glasersfeld's view prolounges Piaget's conception: knowledge is actively built by the cognising subject. Knowing is a process tending toward fit or viability. It serves the subject's organisation of the experiential world, not the discovery of an objective ontological reality (von Glasersfeld, 1991, 233).

An illustration was given here with the D^* constraint set by scientific environment. As von Glasersfeld states it:

> The fact that I am able to make the particular distinctions and coordinations *and establish their permanence in my experiential world* does not tell me anything other than the fact that it is one of the things *my experiential reality* allows me to do ... the viability of an action shows no more than that the 'real' world leaves us room to act in that way. (ibid., 234)

In this view reality becomes the experiential world in which we actually live. We cannot construct any reality we like. And we cannot adopt the constructivist principles as an absolute truth 'but only as a working hypothesis that may or may not turn out to be viable' (ibid., 233). This does not preclude objectivity. It arises when 'concepts, relations and operations that I have found to be viable in the management of my own experience, turn out to be viable also when I attribute them to the models of Others which I construct to manage my interactions with them' (von Glasersfeld, 1985, 99). Finally, it is worth recalling the epistemic status of the constructivist model of knowledge. It is no more than a model of the reasonable mind's organisation of experience, and not the description of some ontologically real entity. Von Glasersfeld's experiential constructivism 'deliberately and consequentially avoids saying anything about ontology'. In his own terms: 'It intends to be no more and no less than one viable model for thinking about the cognitive operation and results which, collectively, we call knowledge' (von Glasersfeld, 1985, 100).

The constructivist view advocated by von Glasersfeld 'does not require building blocks that are parts of ontological reality, but builds with elements that are accessible to the knower, i.e., elements found in, and belonging to, the knower's own eperiential world' (ibid., 1985, 97). The 'knower' extends to a knowing community. This focus on the world experienced by the knower community can protect research from relying on speculation or on features believed by self-proclaimed avant guarde minorities but not experienced by, or 'hidden' from, the majority.

To conclude, there seems to be nothing in these genetic and experiential epistemological views that would contradict the non-separationist pattern contained in CX5. If CX5 may be considered to be constructivist it is in the specific sense of contrasting not with objectivism alone, but with both objectivism and subjectivism. This opposition has to do with these -isms, that is, the constant and one-sided, excluding and systematic, not to say dogmatic, positions sometimes found in scientific debates.

- *Le Moigne: second-order systems*

Le Moigne is an author who has investigated most the epistemological foundations of systems thinking. His interest for this matter stemmed from his dissatisfaction with classical systems theory, that is, the so-called General

Systems Theory, and the gap which developed between the ambitious programme of this theory and its lack of a solid epistemological framework adapted to the ill-structured, analytically intractable issues which it was supposed to address. This gap has resulted in a lasting ambiguity in the systems movement, between those who behave as if the norm was technical and tied to 'hard' systems, and those who advocate a distinction between technical or first-order, object-based systems, and *systems of second generation* (Rittel, 1982), *second-order cybernetics* (von Foerster, 1960), *second-order systemics* (Le Moigne, 1995), *soft systems* (Checkland, 1999), and *critical systems* (Jackson, 2000).

The former attribute systemicity to objects belonging to the external world *W1* and deal with systems as objects in ways already evoked for the objectivist view. The latter claim that the ill-structured character of the problems at stake creates an issue of principle which cannot be grasped with the traditional view. They end up with a non-separationist perspective, although this term seems to be scarcely acknowledged by them.

Le Moigne places his thinking in a direct continuation of Vico, Piaget and von Glasersfeld, which explains why we evoke him here. But he is also a systems and complexity thinker whose explicitly mentioned references are Simon, von Foerster and Morin. The outcome is a combination of an epistemologically and methodologically oriented constructivist view. Following H.A. Simon in *The Sciences of the artificial* (1969 [1996]), Le Moigne emphasises the active representation of phenomena contained in scientific knowing, which involves conceiving and designing purposefully the representations that can be experienced and thus designing the actions that may be performed. It is a reminder that scientific reasoning deals not only with the regularities or laws which things should obey, but also with what things could be and could do, in the tradition of Vico's *ingenium.*

There follows what Le Moigne calls the methodological principle of intelligent action, which contrasts with what he terms the principle of sufficient reason of deductive logic, which he interprets as asserting that reality is ultimately explainable through deduction, thus providing a guideline for research based on classical logic, on the Cartesian precepts, and on a kind of alleged naturality of deductive logic which follows from its unbounded extension to a variety of domains. In contrast, the principle of intelligent action emphasises procedural rationality, heuristics, deliberation and argumentation in the reduction of the cognitive dissonance the subject experiences. It takes as its starting point not the question of solving a problem which is implicitly assumed to be well formulated, but the very question of formulating the problem before attempting to solve it. Feasibility, viability and plausibility replace the criterion of a general norm of truth.

- *Conclusion*

The constructivist views presented above provide a firm background for non-separability, once the adjective 'constructivist' is cleared of its surrounding confusion. Constructivism thus understood appears to synthesise the pragmatist, phenomenological and hermeneutic features which were pointed out above.

However these views still leave unresolved the theoretical issue of the accommodation of criticality. A next step will be to examine how this issue can be dealt with by constructivist contributions addressing DCX specifically, in the next subsection.

D. The problematic accommodation of criticality

We have discussed above how some constructivist epistemologies accommodate non-separation but do not take criticality explicitly into account. This can be tentatively explained by the fact that these perspectives do not address the subject matter of complexity proper. Our next task is therefore to examine whether and how criticality is dealt with in the constructivist perspectives which address deep complexity explicitly. Two broad perspectives stand out. One is developed from the standpoint of paradigmatic and epistemological thinking. Its initiators are Edgar Morin and Jean-Louis Le Moigne. The other derives from practice in management and has given rise to an abundant and diversified literature from which I select the Soft Systems Methodology initiated by Peter Checkland. This is the approach which seems closest to the questions asked here.

These perspectives are rather involved and both rely on a distinction between complexity and non-complexity tackled in their own ways. They are not foreign to the idea of a threshold but remain elusive and never endogenise it. Making this shortcoming clear is not straightforward. It needs to be argued, which will take all the more space as these perspectives are new and therefore need to be described, though schematically, before they can be discussed.

They appear to raise symmetric tensions. The former, that is, the standpoint of paradigmatic and epistemological thinking, is strong on foundations but weak on practice. The latter, that is, the standpoint of practice in management is strong on practice but weak on foundations. The discussion of these perspectives is organised below in three steps, by author: Morin on complexity and simplification (D.1), Le Moigne on systemic modelling (D.2), and Checkland on Soft Systems Methodology (D.3).

D.1 Edgar Morin on Complexity and Simplification

It seems impossible to discuss Morin's ideas without a prior clarification of their origins and context in a first stage. The next stage will be to present the substance of Morin's 'Method' of complexity. It will be discussed in a third stage.

Origins and context

Edgar Morin resembles John Dewey in at least two respects. His oeuvre is monumental. And he appears to many in the same way as Dewey appeared to Donald Schön. Let us recall how Schön reports that when he tried to read Dewey, he found him muddy and unintelligible, and later on he discovered that: 'Dewey's was generative muddiness: he was trying to say new things that were bound to seem muddy to anyone trained as I had been in the logical empiricism fashionable at the time. *Logic. The Theory of Inquiry* was the book that changed my mind about Dewey' (Schön, 1992, 123).

Morin tries to say new things. His idiom and his expository style make his Method difficult reading and even perplexing from the standpoint of scientific theory. But it is fair to say that Morin addresses what he calls a paradigmatic level rather than scientific theory. Yet Morin's thinking on the Method of complexity understood as a paradigm cannot leave in the dark the issue of its connection with scientific theorising. Morin's thinking develops on the basis of a critique of classical science, and of general systems theory and classical cybernetics. His response is in the 'alternative paradigm' of complexity. Complexity is an alternative to 'simplification' in Morin's wording. How to articulate complexity and simplification in scientific theory is therefore the way the issue of the criticality of DCX/NDCX in Morin's oeuvre can be discussed from the standpoint of the present book.

- *Morin's programme*

Morin's ambition is the search for a method to connect the human sciences, biology and physics. In this quest, Morin came to emphasise the central role of organisation and self-organisation understood as an irreducible composition of order, disorder and interactions. Complexity follows from this irreducibility.

Morin's crusade is directed against a ruling orthodoxy of separate 'continents' of physics, biology and the human sciences, anthropological and social. In his view, this present orthodoxy is the outcome of the European intellectual revolution of classical science. It generated a paradigm of simplification which has had great success but which also had mutilating consequences through excluding from scientific enquiry the features that could not be grasped by the paradigm and through setting rigid barriers between disciplines. Morin searches for a strategy of knowledge that would enable one to grasp or to create an articulation between sciences. Joining is the central theme.

Morin was already a leading French intellectual when he became involved in complexity thinking in what he depicts as his 'theoretical conversion' (Morin, 1973, 13) through the influence of a group of cyberneticians and biologists who started to meet in Paris in 1968 with Jacques Monod's support, and after a year spent in 1989 at the Salk Institute for Biological Studies in California. He became familiar with the revolution in genetics triggered by the discovery of DNA. He also got acquainted with the new cybernetics led by Heinz von Foerster.

Morin notices that the scientific revolutions of the past century, notably quantum physics, have set new challenges to separation contained in classical science. But no new paradigm has replaced it. This is what is ambitioned for organisation and complexity in Morin's view. Organisation, be it of matter, of the living, or of the anthroposocial domain, occupies a central place in volume 1 of *La Méthode* published in 1977. It is noticeable that almost three decades later, organisation is also central in the Nobel Prize of physics Robert Laughlin's *A Different Universe* (2005).

Morin covers an immense array of ideas. This may appear at first sight as a kind of huge subjective exercise in speculative thinking. Yet Morin has always been careful enough to admit his intellectual debts through both abundant references and acknowledging the direct help from scientists of various disciplines. Like all transdisciplinary writers, Morin has been attacked from all sides. He appears in his own terms as a 'poacher', not a sociologist, an anthropologist, a biologist, a physicist, a philosopher or an epistemologist, but a thinker addressing all these fields in turn (Bélanger in Morin, 1992a, Kofman, 1996, 5).

Morin's thinking about complexity is mainly contained in his oeuvre about Method. It is highly personal in style and possibly disconcerting for those who discover it without knowing Morin's overall project. In science, especially, it is expected to find tools for scientific activity in a work on method. This is not to be found in Morin's writing. He makes it clear that he deals with a meta-method rather than ready-to-use tools for research. His Method is about the principles of a strategy of knowledge consistent with the notion of complexity that he develops, which is indeed a deep complexity. Method cannot be summarised easily. It depicts a strategy for reasoning based on principles which, taken together, form a paradigm of complexity that will be explained below. Morin's publications comprise more than 40 books and numerous articles. *La Méthode* (Method) is Morin's magnum opus. It is composed of six volumes whose publication ranges from 1977 for the first volume, *La Nature de la Nature* (English translation published as *Method* in 1992), to 1980 (volume 2: *La Vie de la Vie*), 1986 (volume 3: *La Connaissance de la Connaissance*), 1991 (volume 4: *Les Idées*),

2001 (volume 5: *L'Humanité de l'Humanité. L'identité humaine*) and 2004 (*Ethique. La Méthode*, volume 6).

Morin differentiates his 'method' from what he terms 'methodology', the latter comprising tools and techniques, which seems to invert the meanings since methodology is commonly understood as a consistent set of principles guiding the use of methods. Yet, with this proviso in mind, one can hardly avoid asking what signposts for doing research are supplied by a contribution about 'method' like Morin's one. This has been the present author's attitude from the beginning.

- *My connection with Morin*

Morin's contribution to complexity thinking occupies a quite specific place in the argumentation developed in this book. It was a source of inspiration at the start, but since it is conceived at a paradigmatic level it has little to say about the intricacies of method and theory at the theoretical level. CX5 was developed almost independently of any explicit reference to Morin. Yet, in hindsight, a sentence from Morin that was quoted in a footnote of *L'Etat et l'économie* proved important in the subsequent research which led to the present book.

This sentence is: 'Uncertainty, indeterminacy, randomness and contradictions appear not as residues to be eliminated by explanation, but as ineliminable ingredients of our perception/conception of reality – thus spelling ruin for simplification as an explanatory principle' (Morin, 1992a, 381).

I discovered Morin's sentence quoted above at the beginning of the 1980s while Christine André, my co-author, and I were completing the manuscript of *L'Etat et l'économie*. We were facing a subject-matter that we had investigated statistically, theoretically, qualitatively and historically, and which appeared to resist any attempt we could make to reduce it to a satisfactory level of reduction such as a single general theory or thesis abiding by the standards of hypothesis testing ruling in the discipline of economics. I was especially concerned with the theoretical part and was unable to convert our findings into a single clear-cut theory, or into a master hypothesis which would have conveyed the belief that we were doing real theoretical work rather than mere statistics building, quantitative analysis and historical, institutional and qualitative description and analysis. 'What is the underlying theory?' was the recurring challenging question that arose. Our findings were not derived from hypothesis testing and deductive reasoning, they could not accommodate an 'all other things equal' assumption, and they relied on interdependencies between a plurality of factors calling for an interdisciplinary approach. It was not possible to do better than to identify an evolving configuration of heterogeneous and yet interrelated robust features of the state – economy relationship (what was to be termed a regime of interaction between the state and the economy after the comparison with Germany reinforced this finding). The RISE could not be reduced to a simpler and supposedly more theoretical and explanatory category with clear cause – effect relationships. The only path left for survival and for requesting resources to pursue the research of a more satisfactory theory was to invoke methodological pluralism. We understood it not as the idea that several methods could be combined in a kind of floating eclecticism, without some common leading thread, but as a way of survival in the field of economics and political economy based on a different method than the mainstream method.

This sentence of Morin's gave me the strength to stick to radical uncertainty or its equivalent of the perceived ill-structured character of my subject-matter as an ineliminable feature calling for further investigation. It had two consequences on me: a liberating effect with respect to the mainstream standard in my discipline, and a perplexing effect. At last I found a leading author stating forcefully exactly what I was facing. This had a tremendously encouraging effect and provided a legitimacy to my quest of a theory that would not mutilate or eliminate the irreducible features that we had identified. This book is the outgrowth of this theoretical investigation and therefore owes much to Morin's sentence.

However there is the other side of the coin. It is the last part of the sentence in which simplification as an explanatory principle is rejected. This is most ambiguous. It may convey the idea that simplification runs against scientific explanation and that complexity cannot be simplified (Morin, 1992b), which would run against the idea that a strategy of simplification necessarily accompanies any scientific endeavour. At least, it requires a further explanation of the meaning of a principle of simplification. Although it is envisaged as a principle which does not exclude simplification in specific cases, when it is relevant, it remains a problematic issue in Morin's view about complexity, as will be explained below.

Thus, perplexity came from Morin's rejection of simplification as an explanatory principle. In my view, a scientific claim cannot do without some degree of simplification. How to combine simplification and complexity in scientific practice summarises the effort pursued in this book. At issue here is the place of simplification or reducibility in complexity. Can simplification be admitted, but not as an explanatory principle? Morin's answer is yes. Then *how* can simplification be admitted? Getting an answer is not straightforward, it depends on the reasons why complexity is so much emphasised in Morin's works and on the way it is transformed into a principle of knowledge. A detour via Morin's oeuvre will be helpful at this point in order to understand the issue mentioned above.

Morin's Method: the paradigm of complexity

Morin's Method of complexity combines principles of knowledge which originate in his critique of classical science, of classical cybernetics and of the systems approach known as General Systems Theory. The complexity for which an adequate method is sought has its roots in Morin's interrogation on how to join or articulate the sciences addressing separately and in isolation the physical, the living and the anthropo-social universes. A fallibilist perspective follows from this broad interrogation. This perspective is in the nature of a paradigm – the paradigm of complexity. It is based on three main principles of knowledge. Its comparison with the 'paradigm of simplification' will necessitate a more complete characterisation. How this Method of complexity connects with method(s) in science will be asked in conclusion, thus bringing in the issue of criticality. The following development is therefore organised in four steps: Morin's three critiques; three principles of knowledge; the 'paradigm of complexity'; The 'Method of complexity' and scientific method.

- *Three critiques*

a. *The critique of classical science* Morin calls 'classical science' any scientific endeavour obeying the paradigm of simplification that we will define below. In Morin's view classical science has become more and more problematic – it even entered a state of crisis in the twentieth century – because it is based on an unbalanced mode of knowledge which gives a priority to our capacity to separate, and inhibits our capacity to relate and join (Morin and Le Moigne, 1999, 107). This mode of thinking relies on a master concept of determinism which entails a specific view of uncertainty as our 'temporary ignorance of a hidden order' (ibid.), rather than one of the permanent characters of our relationship with the universe. Hence a sort of hypertrophia of order at the cost of a profound quasi rejection of disorder.

Disorder is meant to cover ideas of chance, uncertainty, agitation, dispersion, disturbance, accident, noise and error (Morin, 1980b, 365) which are permanently present and operating with order, in encounters and interactions whose interplay creates, destroys and recreates organisation. Therefore a fundamental hypothesis is the ineliminable interplay of disorder, order, interactions and organisation in the physical, the living and the anthropo-social universes (ibid., 377–378).

Organisation as order *and* disorder rather than mere order is a master concept in Morin's view. It creates the need for attention to the classical view based on order. Order is rejected as a paradigm, not as a notion combined with disorder.

In Morin and Le Moigne's terms (1999), classical science is based on four pillars of certainty whose coherence relies on two rationalising postulates (Morin, 1991b, 225) and whose combination creates a simplifying mode of thinking. The pillars are order (deterministic and mechanistic conception of a world governed by laws to be discovered), separability, reduction and the 'logic of induction – deduction' combined with the Aristotelian axioms guaranteeing the formal validity of argumentation. The two underlying postulates are, first, the coincidence of logico-mathematical intelligibility with the underlying structures of objective reality and, second, Leibniz's principle of sufficient reason which states that 'no fact can obtain and no proposition can be true unless there is a sufficient reason why it should be thus and not otherwise' (Le Moigne, 1995, 29). These pillars and postulates are interdependent and reinforce each other in a very effective way leading to a paradigm of disjunction – reduction in which there is no room for irreducibility.

b. *The critique of classical cybernetics* Morin notes that 'Curiously, complexity only appeared in a marginal line between engineering and science, in the theory of systems, and in cybernetics' (Morin, 1985, 62). Indeed, although there are precursors to cybernetics and to systems theory as they developed after World War II, one must admit that the first full recognition of complexity as a scientific issue in its own right was by Warren Weaver (see Chapter 2) who in 1948 introduced in 1948 that the main challenge to science in the future would be organised complexity, thus linking complexity with organisation.

This connection is viewed by Morin as the central insight brought almost simultaneously by cybernetics and systems theory. Cybernetics was an inspiring source to Morin but with a fundamental proviso which necessitates differentiating a first and a second cybernetics. The first cybernetics was initiated by Norbert Wiener and W. Ross Ashby. It was a conceptual revolution with the notions of feedback and circular causation.

According to Morin, the main virtue of cybernetics is to have linked feedback and interaction, loop and process, regulation and stabilisation, finality and causality in an organisational way, and to have thus given birth to the first general science having organisation as its object. It is the first science applicable to physical, biological and anthropo-social phenomena that envisions a physical system, the machine, not as a function of its constitutive elements, but as a function of its organisational character (Morin, 1992a, 249).

Yet this first cybernetics had little room for disorder, and it subordinated communication to control and command. It is with the second-order cybernetics, introduced in the 1960s by H. von Foerster (von Foerster, 1960) that a communicational cybernetics could be envisaged (ibid., 251). It is on the problem of society that the deficiencies of the first cybernetics converge. After having noticed the promise offered by cybernetics, Morin denounces its bias toward control following from its bias toward relying solely on a notion of an artificial machine without a sufficient foundation.

Cybernetics was shaped in the framework of the dominant patterns of thought and action: 'After having gone, in the concept of machine, beyond reductionism which decomposed the whole into its elements, it developed reductionism which brings all living or natural machine-beings back to the model of the artificial machine' (ibid., 248). According to Morin, Wiener showed the necessity of a theory of the machine, but he did not work it out, so taken up was he with commanded machines. Cybernetics lacks fundamentally a theory of the organisation of feedback causality, finality, information and communication into an articulated setting, with its ambiguities and uncertainties. Cybernetics also lacks a principle of disorder. It gives a skeleton of organisation to living beings but takes away their life. The subordination of communication to command forces cybernetics to conceive biological organisation and social organisation as enslavement. Extending the vision of an engineer on machines onto the anthropo-social sphere, cybernetics tends to consider society as a vast machine to be functionalised.

Hence the call for a communicational organisation in which communication is not merely a tool of command. The second cybernetics initiated by Heinz von Foerster seems to fulfil this need (Andreewsky and Delorme, 2006).

c. *The critique of GST (General Systems Theory)* Although Morin mixes support and critique of systems theory (Morin, 1992a, 149), he is mainly critical of what was claimed to be a general systems theory but ended in substituting a new kind of reductionism to classical analytical reductionism.

Systems theory reacted to reductionism through its focus on the idea of the 'whole' or holism. Ludwig von Bertalanffy in particular, and the General Systems Theory movement in general, made valuable contributions with notions of the system as a whole not reducible to its parts, of hierarchy and of open system (Ashby, 1958b, von Bertalanffy, 1968). Yet, 'General System Theory has not explored theoretically the concept of system, beyond a few "holistic" truths schematically opposed to reductionism' (Morin, 1992a, 410). It has ignored the complexity at the heart of the global unity. Classical reductionism reduces the explanation of the whole to the properties of the parts considered in isolation. Holistic reductionism 'reduces the properties of the parts to the properties of the whole, likewise conceived in isolation' (ibid., 122). Although these two perspectives reject each other, they both stem from the same paradigm of simplification. The conception developed by Morin moves beyond reductionism and 'holism' and attempts to formulate a principle of knowledge which integrates the partial truths included in both views. It highlights the relations between parts and whole in a recursive process, in which none of the two terms is reducible to the other: the description or explanation of the parts depends on that of the whole which depends on that of the parts, and so on.

Therefore Morin opposes those systemist positions which, 'believing they have overcome the paradigm of simplification by refusing to reduce the system to its components, succumb to the paradigm by reducing all things and all being to the notion of system' (ibid., 150).

Against the pretence of a general theory of systems illustrated by GST, Morin advocates a system paradigm in which system is better understood as a generic rather than general concept rooted in a reductionist holism. A non-holistic principle of knowledge can be conceived in generic terms, that is, in terms of a paradigm. It entails breaking with the classical ontology of the object as something constituted of form and substance, decomposable into primary elements which can be isolated in a neutral, context-free space. GST relies on totality, on simplification through reducing the complex to a master concept of order, on dealing with complexity at the phenomenal level, and on system as a global unity, and therefore belongs to a paradigm of holistic simplification (Morin, 1992b). An alternative is to consider that system is a root-word for complexity rather than a master-word for totality. Genericity rather than generality, 'unitas multiplex' (Angyal, 1941 [1981]) rather than global unity, organisation rather than order, characterise what Morin terms the '*paradigm of complexity*'. *Unitas multiplex* connotes the complementary and antagonist terms simultaneously present in a system: it is a composition of unity out of diversity and of internal diversity out of unity. The central problem is not only about maintaining the relations between the whole and the parts, it derives also from the complex character of these relations. *Unitas multiplex* conveys this paradoxical character of organisation and of system.

Therefore complexity appears as a principle of knowledge defined at the level of a paradigm, that is, a set of fundamental notions that command or control thoughts, discourses and theories. Morin's Method is the 'method of complexity'.

- *Three principles of knowledge*

a. *The dialogic principle* Following Morin, 'dialogic' denotes a duality of logics, the 'complex unity of two logics or entities which are complementary, concurrent and antagonist, that is, which feed and complement each other but are also conflicting' (Morin, 2001, 281). In order to conceive their dialogical relationship, we must suspend the classical, Aristotelian logic in which order excludes disorder and disorder excludes order. A fundamentally complex relation between these two notions is needed (Morin, 1992a, 77–78). The principle of dialogics is to have a complementary – though antagonistic – interplay between notions which, in absolute terms, would reject each other (Morin, 1985, 66). It means that it is impossible to reach a sole principle or a master-word, be it uncertainty, chance, contradiction or organisation.

Therefore dialogic consists in the complex association – complementary, concurrent, antagonist – of logics which are both needed for the existence, functioning and development of an organised phenomenon (Morin, 1986, 98). It unites two antagonist principles or notions apparently excluding each other but that operate together and are indispensable to each other, like particles and waves in quantum theory (Morin and Le Moigne,1 999, 254).

It might be tempting to relate dialogics to Hegelian dialectics. In that case, it would be an inverted Hegelianism (Kofman, 1996) since in the dialogic between analysis and synthesis, the superior synthesis is absent. In Hegelian dialectics, contradictions are solved and cancel out into a superior unity. In dialogic, antagonisms do not vanish and are constitutive components of complex entities or phenomena.

The dialogic principle appears as a way to deal with the limitations of the axioms of simplification of classical, Aristotelian logic. But one cannot abandon classical logic. It is a tool for controlling thought on local, simple issues: 'Every fragmented operation of dialogical thinking obeys classical logic, but does not as a whole' (Morin, 1991a, 196). Morin insists on the need to go beyond Aristotelian logic, to envelop and relativise it through a weakened logic and a dialogical complex method (ibid.). The weakened logic that Morin mentions seems to envisage a mode of thinking including classical logic but not limited to it and not excluding aspects which would be ruled out by classical logic. The best instance of dialogic at work seems to be the association of order and disorder as ineliminable features of organisation. Our notions of irreducible duality, of the irreducible combination of reducibility and irreducibility, and of the principle of conjunction can also be taken as instances of dialogic though at a less abstract, more operationally specified level.

However there is a big difference between the generative pattern of duality in CX5 and dialogic. In (*GP*, *P*) the two terms and the logics they represent are not on the same footing. They are not symmetrical. *GP* can be provisionally disactivated. Their relationship is structured as an irreducible complementarity between a generative term and its product, in a recursive way, whereas no explicit structuring appears in dialogic. Indeed the (*GP*, *P*) couple expresses the very idea of criticality.

b. *Recursiveness* The recursion principle in Morin is similar to what we introduced in Chapter 3. It denotes a process in which the effects or products are in turn causing and producing the process itself. In such a process each element can be considered as cause or effect such that a product might also be an initial, producing stage.

Human beings produce society which produces human beings (language, culture, material means of existence). Recursiveness is at the centre of self-organising processes. Morin (1980b, 183) acknowledges the role of H. von Foerster in having emphasised it.

c. *The hologram principle* Morin uses the metaphor of the hologram to denote a principle of knowledge that is beyond analytical reductionism and holism. A hologram is a photography, a recorded interference pattern obtained by using lasers on photographic plates. A wave from an object and a reference wave are superposed. If this pattern is illuminated with a coherent source of light (a laser) similar to the reference wave, one of the orders of diffraction from the pattern will recreate the original object as a virtual image in a three-dimensional representation.

This metaphor is often applied to any system in which parts contain general information about the system as a whole. It was used by David Bohm in his 'implicate order' to consider the possibility that 'physical law should refer primarily to an order of undivided wholeness of the content of a description similar to that indicated by the hologram rather than to an order of analysis of such content into separate parts indicated by a lens', and therefore that each of its parts contains, in some sense, the whole, with the whole being enfolded in each of its parts (Bohm, 1980, 145–147).

In Morin's setting, the hologram principle combines whole and parts in a relationship which forbids the reduction of a whole to its parts or the absorption of parts by a whole. It is a kind of organisation of knowledge in which the 'whole is in the part which is itself in the whole' (Morin, 1986, 101): 'the world is inside our mind which is itself inside the world' (Morin, 1991b, 60).

This principle stands as an antidote to reductionism, be it analytical, holist or systemic reductionism. It is another way to state the Pascalian loop: 'I hold it impossible to know the parts without knowing the whole, or to know the whole without knowing each part in particular.' It complements recursiveness.

All in all these three principles provide alternatives to reductionism (hologram), to cause – effect causality (recursiveness) and to order, disjunction and the law of identity as general principles (dialogic). It is their interplay which produces the basis for a 'paradigm of complexity' presented next.

- *The 'paradigm of complexity'*

A paradigm is a pattern of thinking, a set of background assumptions taken for granted. It denotes in its Kuhnian meaning the general assumptions and laws, and the techniques for their application, that the members of a particular scientific community are taught to adopt and that set the standard for the way in which inquiry is to be conducted.

Morin points out that a paradigm is an underground, invisible and pervasive thought never explicitly formulated (Morin, 1991a, 215–216, 230–231, 236). It consists in 'the set of fundamental relations of association and/or opposition among a restricted number of master notions, these relations command or control every thought, discourse and theory' (Morin, 1992b, 372). The paradigm 'commands the epistemology which commands theory', and 'it controls the practice which follows from the theory' (Morin, 1991a, 213).

Complexity has a paradigmatic character because a full understanding and acceptance of its implications requires us to be conscious of the limitations of classical logic and science and of the methods which go with it. These limitations trigger a shift to the paradigmatic level. From the principles established at this level there arise three principles of dialogical, recursive and hologrammatic thinking as guidelines of reasoning which are the backbone of Morin's Method. It would be problematic to claim that these principles derive from an available paradigm of complexity, for such a paradigm does not yet exist. There are only increasing – though dispersed – signs of a rising consciousness of the consequences of the exclusion of complex organisation by the classical conception of intelligibility. There is a rationale for searching a mode of intelligibility that would account for complex organisation. It is the tentative set of principles which arise from contrasting them to the set of principles commanding or controlling classical science as they are detected by Morin.

Classical science is based on the idea that the complexity of the phenomenal world can be resolved through simple principles and general laws (Morin, 1990b, 304). It derives from several interdependent principles of intelligibility whose combination forms a 'paradigm of simplification'. Hence the assumption that a paradigm of complexity might be envisaged through the conjunction of principles of intelligibility contrasted to those of the paradigm of simplification (Table 6.1).

Morin explains how he slowly came to this conclusion with a list of principles whose precise number fluctuates between seven (Morin and Le Moigne, 1999, 261–265), ten (Morin, 1980, 357–8; 1991b, 138) and 12 or 13 (Morin, 1990b, 304–309). These variations give some freedom to clarify and systematise an otherwise multifaceted and hard-to-grasp thinking. I freely adapt Morin's view in Table 6.1 with a list of 11 principles. It is their conjunction which makes up the paradigmatic character of Morin's complexity. It includes the already evoked 'four pillars of classical science' (order, disjunction, reduction and binary logic) and their complex counterparts (principles 5, 7, 8, 10, 11), and the principles of recursiveness, dialogic and hologram (6, 11 and 3). These principles are interdependent and no a priori hierarchy is implied in their numbering from 1 to 11.

- *The 'Method of complexity' and scientific method*

The paradigm of complexity may look rather abstract and perplexing. From a scientific standpoint the main issue is how it can help in scientific research. This entails the mediation of a method. The Method conceived by Morin relies on the combination of the dialogic, recursive and hologram principles. However, these principles may still look abstract and rather remote from the requisites of everyday scientific practice that are usually envisaged when we evoke scientific method.

Table 6.1 A personal adaptation of Morin's view about the paradigms of simplification and complexity

Paradigm of simplification (principles of intelligibility of classical science)	**Paradigm of complexity**
1. Principle of universality De facto exclusion of singular phenomena Focus on universal laws	1. Inclusion of singular phenomena Focus on organisation
2. Exclusion of time irreversibility and of historical features	2. Inclusion of time irreversibility and of events and history
3. Reductionism	3. Hologram principle
4. Sovereign principle of order and determinism	4. Order, disorder, interactions and organisation
5. Organisation as order	5. Organisation as combination of order, disorder and interaction
6. Linear cause – effect principle as generalised causality principle	6. Circular and linear causal relationships Principle of recursiveness
7. Principle of isolation/disjunction of object with respect to its environment	7. Distinction rather than disjunction of object an its environment
8. Principle of absolute disjunction between perceived object and perceiving subject	8. Relationality of object with subject
9. Exclusion of any problematic of the subject from scientific knowledge	9. Possibility and necessity of a scientific theory of the subject
10. Principle of absolute reliability on classical binary logic of truth and falsity. Any contradiction appears necessarily as an error	10. Fallibilism and limitations of logic
11. Monopoly of 10: exclusion of dialogic	11. Dialogic principle

Is Morin's Method a scientific method? Morin's answer and the developments above clearly demonstrate that it is not a method which can find a direct application in science as a scientific method. It is a 'method for scientific method' or a meta-method. This difference is sometimes overlooked and causes repeated misunderstandings for those who reject the Morinian method in the name of its ineffectiveness in scientific activity.

Morin has himself emphasised the difference between the method entailed by the paradigm of complexity and scientific method. The former is a meta-method with respect to scientific methods. It includes them in the broader setting presented below.

First, Morin starts with method in the Cartesian sense of something which would permit 'rightly conducting reason and seeking truth in the sciences' (Morin, 1992a, 10). But he extends it to all knowledge, be it scientific or not. It is not limited to the set of rules which constitute scientific method. These rules are empirical (tests based on observation and experimentation), logical (coherence of theories, resistance to falsification), and ethical (the search of as much objectivity as possible) (Morin, 1990a, 256–257).

The meta-level character of Morin's Method compared with scientific method consists in *three* aspects. First is its *reflexive* character. Reflexivity is the thinking about oneself which can be interrogative, critical and controlling. This is made possible by the openness of the three principles of intelligibility. Reflexivity is thus intrinsic to them. A second source of this meta-level character is the search for an *articulation* between separate sciences and disciplines. This quest of a Method conceived as a reflexive articulation of the various domains of knowledge related to human condition constitutes Morin's self-avowed 'main obsession' (Morin, 2001, 11). The final reason for a meta-level is that it connotes *strategy* rather than a programme. Morin insists on differentiating 'methodology' understood by him as a programme and 'Method', a term which implies a mental and intellectual strategy illustrated by the three principles of knowledge (Morin, 1991a, 258).

Meta-method and method are associated in dialogic: the former includes the principles of intelligibility of complexity, the latter includes the techniques and tools called for in order to achieve a given kind of knowledge in a specific discipline. 'Every fragmented operation of dialogical thinking obeys classical logic, but does not do so as a whole process' (Morin, 1991a, 196): hence simplification and complexity co-dwell under the umbrella of the meta-method. It seems that method entails simplification and that Method is associated with complexity.

The dialogic principle advocated by Morin is not devoid of ambiguity. If every fragmented operation of dialogical thinking obeys classical logic for local, fragmented operations but does not as a whole (Morin, 1991a, 196) then dialogic combines classical logic for local, fragmented operations, and another rationale enabling to tackle other operations, what Morin calls a 'weakened logic' but does not explain. Is it a logic for the problems which are beyond the scope of classical logic, or is it the whole rationale of dialogic thus containing and relativising classical logic? Morin's developments seem to converge with the latter.

All in all a Morinian way to conclude this incursion into deep complexity is that a more adequate knowledge of organisation requires a different organisation of knowledge. It would have been impossible to make sense of this statement if we had not got immersed, though cursorily, into Morin's prose. This immersion also helps us understand what the present work owes to Morin, and how it differs from it. The issue is therefore how Morin's Method can help when scientific activity bumps into the obstacle of deep complexity. Although Morin does not refer to the term of criticality, he constantly acknowledges the local relevance of classical science, providing it is not taken as a paradigm of knowledge (1980b, 384, 391; 1991a, 195–196; 1992a, 15–16, 391; Morin and Le Moigne, 1999, 98, 141–150).

Discussion

Morin's Method of complexity is built upon the tension between the paradigms of simplification and of complexity. Morin identifies that classical science is underpinned by a paradigm, called by him a paradigm of simplification. This paradigm relies on principles which are effective in natural sciences, although the revolutions of the twentieth century (quantum physics, undecidability in logic) profoundly challenge it. And it is not adequate in anthropo-social sciences. These limitations call for an alternative paradigm which would not solve what are irreducible limitations, but host them as disorder, and combine it with order into a unified paradigm, the paradigm of complexity. The paradigm of complexity therefore contains simplification; in Morin's words, complexity is 'the union of simplification and complexity' (Morin, 1980a, 389) It echoes paradoxical irreducibility arrived at here, which states that irreducibility is the irreducibility of the pair (reducibility, irreducibility). Morin even mentions that 'the worst simplification' would be to repeat endlessly 'everything is complex, everything is hypercomplex' (Morin, 1990b, 312).

The main issue is therefore how complexity and simplification combine. At first sight, the former is at a paradigmatic level whereas the latter operates 'below', at a subparadigmatic level which ranges from epistemology and methodology to theory and the empirical level. However this view holds strictly only for natural sciences, those in which the principles of simplification operate adequately according to Morin. This apparently neat distribution of complexity and simplification across levels does not rule in anthropo-social sciences. If simplification is present in their practice, it cannot be on a principled basis. Therefore we are left with principles for a practice of complexity. At this level, they necessarily pertain to methodology and method, not to Method. How do they conform to the paradigm of complexity? Morin's construction faces here a heuristic issue: how to move, in his terms, from Method to methodology? How does simplification – or non-deep complexity in CX5 terms – articulate with deep complexity?

Once it is admitted that paradigmatic complexity does not eliminate simplification, several questions arise. First is the question of how complexity and simplification can coexist in everyday scientific practice. Is it a matter of choice? Of belief? Of something else? How does one move from one state to the other? It is the heuristic issue evoked above. Since complexity is given a priority, this question amounts to identifying when simplification becomes legitimate. But the reasoning can be inverted when it is addressed from the standpoint of the ruling existing scientific practice, that is, simplification. How can one move from simplification to complexity? Above all, complexity is now addressed at a subparadigmatic level, methodological and theoretical. What remains unnoticed and implicit with simplification must be explicited with complexity. How does paradigmatic complexity transform into methodological and theoretical complexity in scientific activity? Is it underpinned by a theory of complexity proper? Is there a threshold of complexity? This theoretical aspect is closely connected with the heuristic issue.

Finally there is an issue of strategy. Since the aim is no less than creating an alternative to the paradigm of simplification which currently dominates, what is the strategy envisaged for making this alternative effective? I admit that these issues pull Morin's paradigmatic thinking toward the sublevel of scientific theory. But it would seem odd to develop a thinking about a paradigm without inquiring about its consequences on method and theorising in scientific activity. Morin himself admits this need.

I will present Morin's answers in each case and compare them with CX5. This comparison will reveal shortcomings in these three accounts of heuristics, theory and effectiveness from the standpoint of scientific practice.

- *Heuristics: how to move from Method to method?*

How can Morin's Method inform scientific method? Morin's Method is indeed a meta-method. It consists in a meta-standpoint about specific sciences and disciplines. Therefore it would seem that it leaves entirely open the issue of the kind of scientific method that is adequate within sciences and disciplines. However, things are not so simple. The crux of the matter is whether simplification in a given scientific operation is acceptable or not, and why. At first sight, the Method of complexity will be called for whenever simplification is not acceptable. This compels us to investigate the way Morin presents acceptable and non-acceptable simplification and how it can be operationalised.

a. *When is simplification not acceptable?* We are driven back to the sentence evoked at the begining of this section in which Morin claims that uncertainty, indeterminacy, randomness and contradictions appear not as residues to be eliminated by explanation, but as ineliminable ingredients of our perception and conception of reality, 'thus spelling ruin for simplification as an explanatory principle'. With hindsight this last statement cannot but be restricted to a meta-level or to exact science. Although the duality between meta- and object levels is not investigated explicitly by Morin, it is clear from our own developments (Chapters 4 and 5) that to make sense, the phrase 'complexity is the union of simplification and complexity' requires that a meta-level complexity be differentiated from an object-level 'union of simplification with complexity'. Yet not all kinds of simplification are acceptable to Morin. From several of his writings, one may gather several circumstances of this type in which Morin rejects simplification. There appear at least five situations, that I list below.

A first reason given by Morin against the acceptance of simplification in a domain is when it is impossible to achieve the same degree of *objectivation* as in exact science. Morin explains that what he calls 'method', singled out here as 'Method', does not interfere and mix with the method operating in natural science because the degree of objectivation achieved in them permits reliance on the classical methods of simplification. Things go differently in human and social sciences because they cannot achieve the degree of objectivation of the exact sciences (Morin, 1990a, 259–260). The distinction between Method and methods is clear in the natural sciences but is more problematic in anthropo-social sciences. Therefore Method and methods blend in human sciences, including 'methodologies' with their own techniques and specific tools when they are adequate. One may infer that for Morin the method of social science combines aspects of method and meta-method principles of intelligibility contained in Method. Then the issue becomes to know how Method and methods combine and to what degree simplification is acceptable or relevant when one addresses the problem from the standpoint of scientific research.

A second reason against simplification is when *classical logic* is inadequate. Morin calls 'identitary-deductive logic' the logic based on the three axioms of identity, non-contradiction and excluded middle (Morin and Le Moigne, 1999, 148–150). It is acceptable when it addresses what can be 'isolated, fragmented, deterministic, mechanical'. Then it can be adequately applied to artificial machines, to the mechanical and deterministic aspects of the world, to stable entities. It leads to utilitarian intelligibility rather than understanding of what is complex. It satisfies our fundamental needs of sorting out the true from the false and of being able to affirm or to negate. This logic is practically and intellectually necessary. But it fails whenever removing ambiguity is misleading, whenever two opposite truths are related (dialogic), whenever complexity cannot be dissolved but at the price of a mutilation of knowledge and thought (ibid., 149; also Morin,

1980b, 389–390). The identitary-deductive logic is fitted only to our instrumental and manipulatory needs, be it manipulation of concepts or of objects. It is not fitted to all our needs of understanding. Therefore we cannot do without the identitary-deductive logic, but it cannot be the instrument of certainty and of absolute evidence. Complex thought does not call for the rejection of the identitary-deductive logic. Rather it calls for a dialogical combination of it 'segment after segment and for moving beyond it in the black holes in which it is no longer operational' (ibid., 150).

A third argument against simplification is when the interest for fragmentation is not appropriate, that is, when the circumstances which call for an 'interest for *useful simplifications*' are absent. These circumstances appear 'when we require clarity to isolate objects … In that sense, our universe appears to be extremely simple, decomposable, analysable … every time we need to remove all ambiguity from the environment … each time we need to cut it up into segments and manipulate it, our view of the universe becomes simple' (Morin, 1985, 67). But if our interest is the phenomenal world 'the world in which we live, existentially, politically, socially and anthropologically, there is no doubt that this world is one of complexity' which compels us to see it in a complex way if we do not want to 'seriously mutilate reality' (ibid.).

Fourthly, simplification collapses when the research interest is an exhaustive description or when it goes *beyond description*. The description of phenomena cannot be exhaustive. It must select some aspects, eliminate others and therefore simplify through the quest of 'order, unity, logical clarity … disjunction, reduction, selection, quantification' (Morin, 1990a, 264). Complex thought cannot but acknowledge this need for a minimum of simplicity. But simplification becomes problematic when more than description is intended and when the interest 'lies in reviewing fundamental problems of knowledge and understanding' in which case 'we find complexity' (ibid.).

A final, synthetic reason against simplification is *mutilation*. In Morin's words, complexity arises from the 'impossibility to simplify' in cases 'in which disorder and uncertainty impede knowing, in which the complex unit disintegrates whenever it is reduced to its elements, in which distinction and clarity disappear in causality and identity, in which contradictions challenge reasoning, in which the observing subject discovers his/her face through the observed object' (Morin and Le Moigne, 1999, 162). This impossibility to simplify means indeed an impossibility to simplify without mutilating. Mutilation, the removal of an essential part of something of interest, rather than simplification, appears as the enemy. One is tempted to infer that whenever simplification eliminates one of the properties mentioned above, it is a mutilating simplification. For Morin, simplifying in these cases must be akin to cutting a Gordian knot whose main characteristic is to combine two polar sides of complexity, an empirical side and a logical side. The former pertains to 'disorders, chance events, entanglements, inter-retroaction' contained in phenomena. The latter denotes causal circularity, unsolvable contradictions and logical paradoxes (ibid., 163). One may conclude that knowledge mutilates whenever it breaks this dialogic (1980b, 388–390) or when it cuts the Gordian knot of complexity. Simplification is not acceptable when it mutilates. Then how can we discriminate between mutilating and non-mutilating simplification?

b. *How not to mutilate?* From the above it is clear that most arguments against simplification boil down to a rejection of mutilation in Morin's mind. It leads one to ask how not to mutilate. Answering this question depends itself on the answers to two issues: How do we know when we mutilate? How should we proceed, with what heuristic, when there is a threat of mutilation?

Knowing when mutilation is occurring is in itself a problem. Can we rely on the circumstances of simplification listed above? The initial item, the degree of objectivation, refers more to minimising subjectivity than avoiding mutilation. Knowing when classical logic is inadequate is not straightforward at all for it seems to require a whole argumentation about the classical and the complex paradigms and its acceptance in a scientific community. The third and fourth circumstances refer to the scientists' research interests. The fourth case is about the interest in fundamental understanding, beyond description. It runs clearly against simplification, but is it still a scientific interest? Therefore, these items of the list help little. Only the third and the last, fifth, cases seem to remain relevant. The former is about 'useful simplification', the latter pertains to mutilation in general. Mutilation is a detrimental simplification. If we merge it with useless simplification we obtain a broad notion of mutilation.

The problem arises at this level. Theorising necessarily implies simplification. It is undertaken in all cases for the sake of useful simplification. Who would claim to work for useless simplification? Then how can it be decided either that a given simplification is useful or that there exists the need to go beyond it and abandon it? The examples afforded by Morin do not contain criteria on which an argumentation could be based in a discipline. The only way that is left seems either to rely, on the one hand, on the opinion of the majority or to follow the opinion of those who are most influential, or, on the other hand, to join Keynes's brave army of heretics. With Morin's instances, it can be sustained that every simplification is useful in a scientific discipline. If it is mutilating, it can be justified by the immediate need to remove ambiguity, with the proviso of correcting it in the future when new knowledge accrues. The only mutilation that would be excluded would be when it would exclude being corrected as new knowledge accrues. This is the way 'classical' science operates, and should feel comfortable with Morin's claims that understanding the phenomenal world can be addressed either scientifically when simplification is possible or in another, non-scientific, yet legitimate way, when it cannot be grasped with the available scientific tools and concepts. Then this complexity is deemed to develop outside of the scientific realm.

The usefulness or the non-mutilating character of simplification is not grounded in criteria enabling one to argue at the theoretical, infra-paradigmatic level in a discipline, in Morin. In this way these notions are insufficiently explained and endogenised. Complexity, or a method of complexity, therefore cannot be established on a firm scientific basis at the theoretical level.

If there are no general criteria for non-mutilation and useful simplification, then their legitimacy is left to those who decide. Who are they? A theory of operators is needed at this point. But it is absent. The 'terrific effectiveness' of classical science seems far from being effectively challenged by this complexity alternative. Something is lacking.

Our argumentation points to the shortcomings of relying on the relativity of mutilation to interests of knowledge without specifying the behavioural patterns informing them.

Another way to counter mutilation is through realisticness. This is done by Morin when he evokes an experiential realisticness: 'Its [classical science] good deeds have been and remain inestimable since the absolute primacy granted the concordance of observations and experience remains the decisive means of eliminating the arbitrary and the judgment of authority' (Morin, 1992a, 15–16). He also claims that: 'the antidote to irrelevant reasoning', what he calls the 'rationalising delirium' is 'empirical reality' (1990a, 282).

Yet again it helps little. The former sentence is in praise of classical science and of the way it works in natural sciences, following the distinction introduced by Morin between natural and anthropo-social sciences. The call for realisticness and reliance on empirical and experienced reality is welcomed. But this advice still tells us little on how to reckon mutilation.

A final way to deal with mutilation might be through the notion of a threshold in the same way as the need for a threshold of complexity was introduced in Chapter 3. Complexity as a remedy to mutilation would be called for beyond this threshold. This idea of a threshold or of a borderline between the simple and the complex is evoked by Morin with the immediate proviso that he finds it uncertain or impossible to establish (1980b, 387, 391; 1990a, 264).

These difficulties draw the very limits of Morin's view in scientific practice in social sciences. The criteria for identifying when the classical scientific method is no longer satisfactory are abstract and practically devoid of operationality to the extent that they rely on interests but do not explain how to discriminate in scientific practice between situations in which simplification is relevant, 'useful' or not mutilating, and those in which simplification is excessive, useless or mutilating. It is a problem to which CX5 provides an answer through behavioural reflexivity (OP1) rather than through a nomenclature and non-discriminating, underspecified notions.

Yet, even if the definitions of mutilation were taken for granted, there would remain the question of how to proceed in order to avoid mutilation. It is the issue of the heuristic. It badly needs to be solved since theorising is intrinsically a process of simplification. We need a heuristic frame that is consistent with the primacy of empirical reality, the dialogic of combined simplicity and complexity, the relativity of interests, and an indefinable threshold. We are told by Morin that method must combine simplicity with complexity in social science. Does it apply in every case? And how? If there is no operational threshold, does it mean that no heuristic can be defined? In that case, are there examples, operational reference points or case studies to which one could refer? Here we must reckon their absence and the essentially prescriptive tone of Morin.

It seems that in the absence of effective criteria or of a theory of the cognising subject operating in an environment, we are bound to endless debates over mutilation since there appears no reasoned way to convince each other. What is mutilation for one person may be a non-mutilating, necessary simplification in theorising for another person.

It is fair to recall that Morin's purpose was not to provide a theoretical framework. But when he does not stay at the level of paradigmatic thinking and engages into a connection of Method with method in anthropological and social sciences, it becomes necessary to investigate this connection: what are the clues, what is the heuristic for building a theoretical non mutilating frame? From a heuristic standpoint the basic requirement here is to help discriminate and establish an operational distinction between what is acceptable simplification and what is mutilation.

- *Theory*

For Morin, complexity denotes what cannot be simplified or grasped in a single, unified notion or master concept. He equates complexity metaphorically with an empirical and logical Gordian knot. It cannot be cut or disentangled without destroying its very defining characteristics (Morin, 1987; 1990a, 263–264; Morin and Le Moigne, 1999, 163).

a. *'Complexity is a Gordian knot'* This is the title of a paper by Morin (1987). This metaphor of the Gordian knot denotes an extreme difficulty to disentangle an intricate knot, the untying of which can be achieved only by the shortest and most drastic means, which amounts to mutilating it.

This metaphor runs throughout Morin's oeuvre but with varying components. In *La Méthode* Vol. I (1992a) one finds the Gordian knots of order and disorder (ibid., 48), of chance and necessity (ibid., 76) and of organisation founded on both communication and command which are knotted together in the concept of cybernetics (ibid., 236).

In Vol. II (1980b) Morin evokes the 'double game' played in complexity through the definitional struggle against simplification which itself necessitates to use simplification (ibid., 390). This double game is summarised in a way when complexity is said to be the union of simplification and complexity (ibid., 389).

However a most frequent reference by Morin is to the 'empirical and logical' Gordian knot of complexity (1980b, 358; 1987; 1991b, 105; 1985, 64–65; 1990a, 263–264; 1991a, 236, 238, 242; Morin and Le Moigne, 1999, 163). Morin introduces it in the following way: 'This is where the crucial problem lies: where does complexity fit in? On the empirical level with phenomena? On the theoretical level? With logic? With reality? With thought? ... Personally, I would put complexity at a level that is apparently logical but in fact paradigmatic' (1985, 64-65). This amounts to defining complexity in terms of an irreducible knot between two poles, an empirical and a logical one (1990a, 263–264; Morin and Le Moigne, 1999, 163). Does complexity belong to thought (logical pole)? Does it belong to the 'real world' (empirical pole)? Morin answers that he does not want to choose (1990a, 264).

Putting complexity at a paradigmatic level is consistent with the refusal to 'choose' at the logical (theoretical) and empirical (phenomenal) levels. It introduces a dividing line between a paradigmatic and sub-paradigmatic levels. The Gordian knot is left uncut at the latter, while complex thought develops at the former. Morin adopts a standpoint of thinking about complexity distinguished from a scientific standpoint concerned with theory and the phenomenal world, which is our standpoint. Two important consequences follow from this stance. They are the traps of simplifying simplification and of neutrality.

b. *The trap of simplifying simplification* The conception of complexity presented by Morin forbids simplifying it on a scientific ground. How then can it be envisaged to theorise complexity in its own right since theorising necessarily implies simplification? Morin seems to oppose this view: 'We must realise that the characteristic of theory is not to reduce the complex to the simple, but to express the complex into a theory' (1980b, 389). Yet this is not convincing. Why shouldn't the theory expressing the complex be a simplification of the complex? The Morinian idea that to 'simplify' the complex for a theorising purpose is inappropriate seems to be imprisoned in equating simplification with mutilation.

Let us pursue the metaphor and admit that cutting the Gordian knot would have drastic consequences. But why should it prevent cutting into the knot, partially, thus simplifying but not eliminating the intricacy, that is, retaining its irreducibility? For this we need to get rid of a static conception of the knot and model it dynamically. This is what the irreducibility of the (reducibility, irreducibility) couple of our OP2 of paradoxical irreducibility does. It means that we can simplify in our integrated dynamic way without abandoning irreducibility. This modelling is compatible with complexity in our setting.

To summarise:

1. Our standpoint is scientific practice. It differs from pure thinking about complexity.
2. It follows from the above that modelling complexity theoretically is necessary.
3. Modelling implies simplification. The Gordian knot metaphor strictly understood prevents us from modelling complexity in its own right. There exists a difference between thinking about complexity without subjecting it to the constraints of theoretical modelling, and modelling complexity subject to a constraint of irreducibility.
4. How to model, that is, to simplify, complexity while abiding by irreducibility is answered with CX5 and especially its OP2, composite self-similarity.

Once it is made clear that our standpoint is scientific practice, it follows immediately that we are not in a domain of thinking free from any constraint of action, but in the domain of action, informed by thinking. Modelling is action when it is compared to pure thinking. This entails a profound difference with thinking. Action, be it general or specific to some domain, cannot but be 'simplified' comparatively to thinking. While thinking has no limits apart from those of the thinker's mind, action takes place in space and time. The very actualisation of action, of doing or making, eliminates *ipso facto* other actions which were also possible before a particular action was taken and actualised at the 'same' place and time. Simplification is intrinsic to action even if it is symbolic action like modelling. Therefore there is no choice between simplifying or not. The choice is only about the kind of simplification one pursues in modelling. This is the basic reason why referring strictly to a Gordian knot in scientific practice is a trap.

c. *The trap of neutrality* A corollary of having a knot composed of elements left untouched is that it rules out any idea of conceiving a hierarchy between them since this would render thinkable to rely on a leading component and even to structure the knot possibly in terms of near decomposability in Simonian terms, which would negate the very concept of a non-simplifiable knot.

When the knot is taken as a non-separable duality we come closer to the notions evoked by Morin and in our research. In the empirical and logical Gordian knot, the two poles are treated on a par, complexity is both empirical and logical without any primacy of one of these terms over the other. This neutrality allows us to consider complexity from two standpoints. According to one, complexity consists in an attribute of human cognition, perception and action, and in joining what is spontaneously separated in our perception. According to the other, complexity is a property of the world considered independently from the epistemic subject although Morin states the principle that 'it is never in setting the knower aside that one goes towards complex knowledge' (Morin,1992a, 396).

Yet Morin speaks of 'the growth of complexity in organisation' (1980b, 118), of the 'complexification' of our cosmos (2001, 20), of the ubiquitous presence of complexity: 'Everything is complex, physical reality, logic, life, the human being, society, biosphere, the planetary era…' (Morin and Le Moigne, 1999, 163) thus echoing Simon for whom complexity is 'an ever-present phenomenon in the world' (Simon, 1999, 240).

This view blurs the unique, primary place of the subject, or of the *PEW*, the process of enquiry into the world. Refusing to cut into the Gordian knot means to be neutral between the theoretical and empirical poles while they cannot be on a par. When Morin states that 'complexity applies both to the phenomena and the principles which govern them, and to the principles (methodological, logical, epistemological) which govern our own thought about phenomena' (1980b, 358) is it without any hierarchy between these poles? Sentences like the ones cited above make sense only if a series of givens is taken into account. These givens are among the factors of Tables 3.3 and 4.3. They are givens emanating from cognising subjects in action in a situation. Complexity is epistemic before being objective and empirical.

This hierarchy in the non-separable duality characterises fundamentally deep complexity. It is a foundation of CX5. Deep complexity being primarily epistemic and 'meta' cannot be an untouched Gordian knot.

- *Strategy*

The issue of strategy follows from the paradigmatic character of complexity in Morin's thinking. It challenges head-on the classical framework. Can it be an alternative to it? What strategy may make the paradigm of complexity effective in science?

a. *Morin's claim for an alternative paradigm* Morin calls for a paradigmatic change in our way of thinking. The paradigm of simplification on which classical science is based remains broadly unnoticed. It is a non-explicit foundation combined with the 'terrible effectiveness' of classical science:

> through excluding complexity and retaining only what can be quantified and algorithmically dealt with, and thus isolating its objects and experimentation, it has paved the way for manipulation with its numerous technical achievements and its ignorance of the perverse effects that may ensue from these technical achievements. (Morin, 1991a, 226–227; Morin and Le Moigne, 1999, 120)

Since the paradigm of simplification remains not only unnoticed but also fully effective it comes as no surprise that Morin seeks to define an alternative to it. The following lines appear at the beginning of *Method* and summarise well the strategy proposed by Morin:

> I have discovered how useless it is to argue only against error. The latter is reborn ceaselessly from laws of thought which themselves are situated beyond polemic consciousness. I have understood how useless it was to prove things only at the level of the phenomenon: its message is soon reabsorbed by mechanisms of forgetfulness that stem from the self-defense of the threatened system of ideas. I have understood that it was hopeless to only refute: only a new foundation can ruin the old. This is why I think that the crucial problem is the one of the principle organiser of knowledge and what is vital today is not only to learn, not only to relearn, not only to unlearn, *but to reorganise our mental system to relearn to learn.* (1992a, 16)

Can the paradigmatic level of Morin's thinking provide an alternative to the ruling paradigm of simplification? What are the requisites of such an alternative? Are they met by the paradigm of complexity? And how can this strategy be extended to scientific theory?

b. *The requisites of an alternative to classical science* In pointing to the generally unnoticed presence of a paradigm which underpins classical science and in attempting to characterise an alternative paradigm of complexity, Morin apparently anticipated in 1977 Simon's Nobel lecture words of 1978 quoted above in this chapter: that an alternative to a paradigm must necessarily be another paradigm.

However, matters appear less simple here. It is certainly valuable to delineate the set of otherwise dispersed notions which appear to complement each other and to form a coherent cluster contrasting with the spontaneously accepted view. Yet the paradigm of simplification is itself supported by, and supporting, classical science. It is so to speak equipped with an epistemology, methodological principles, theoretical and empirical achievements that support each other and compose a consistent whole. This whole is indeed a genuine system of knowledge. Whatever the 'anomalies' that can be detected, this system is unlikely to be effectively challenged as long as an alternative system of knowledge does not emerge and address issues that the initial system cannot address. The strength of the paradigm of simplification is to be tied to an operational system of knowledge. The weakness of the paradigm of complexity is to be merely a paradigm without an operational system of knowledge.

In using the term 'system of knowledge' I envisage it in the full meaning of a system, that is, an organised composition of relations, internal and external, between component parts, making up a unified whole. Classical science finds its strength in its embededness in a systemic network of mutually supporting components ensuring its coherence and the cumulative character of its functioning, whatever its limitations are. The strength of classical science is reinforced by the lack of an alternative effective system of knowledge.

Focusing only on the paradigmatic aspect may not be problematic in thinking limited to the foundations. Things are likely to go differently when the focus is on scientific theory. The superiority of classical science is that it includes the various aspects required from scientific activity: theory about empirical phenomena, backed by methodology and epistemology consistent with the paradigm of simplification. The paradigm of complexity still lacks the case studies, the examplars, the theorising which could be contrasted with those of the classical frame. Furthermore these various components are interdependent and form a scientific system. The challenge for deep complexity is to achieve an alternative scientific system. It is not a matter of adding new aspects to the paradigm of complexity: their combination into a system will modify them. The problem is to integrate them into such a system.

The Method of complexity lacks an integration of generic aspects whose interplay founds the strength of classical science. To conclude, it can hardly be an alternative to classical science. It provides only a first step calling for further improvements.

c. *A problematic extension to scientific theory* What can a paradigm not derived from – and not supported by – practice, method, theory, case studies and examplars tell scientific theory? What help can it provide if it is not rooted in dissatisfactions and new insights experienced in the practice of science? The thinking about a paradigm of complexity brings a very useful reflection but it remains a one-bladed scissor to use Simon's metaphor. It is of little help when it is a pair of scissors that is needed. The blade of thinking cannot work without the blade of action. This duality is essential. It is at the heart of the heuristic and theoretical shortcomings detected above.

The task pursued here through the identification of shortcomings in the extension of the Method of complexity to science is not merely to criticise Method but to detect what features need to be included from the standpoint of scientific experience. Experience and thinking reinforce each other. Without Morin's paradigmatic thinking and its fifth principle it would have been difficult to pursue the research in the direction it took in this book. But it delivered no well-specified guidelines for scientific practice. They had to be constructed. On the other hand, without an initial anchoring in a robust experience, the heuristic and theoretical shortcomings of Method would hardly have been so manifest. CX5 differs basically from Morinian complexity in this respect: it is grounded in scientific experience and complements Morinian complexity by showing that in order to be relevant in science, complexity must remedy both the underspecification (threshold not worked out; system of knowledge not envisaged) and the misspecification (trap of the Gordian knot metaphor; simplification as a matter of nomenclature of simple instances) of Morinian complexity. It shows that what is relevant at the paradigmatic level cannot be extended directly at the sub-paradigmatic levels. From the interaction with experience there emerges a slightly different view of complexity which endogenises criticality in an essential way.

The difference between Morinian complexity and CX5 may be traced back to the initial questions. Morin looks for an alternative to the principles governing classical science and composing a paradigm. CX5 follows from a far less ambitious attempt to identify the conditions under which deep complexity can be effective in scientific practice liberated from its classical straitjacket.

Morin's refusal to cut into the logical and empirical Gordian knot creates a situation which does not compel facing the issue of articulating, integrating or making compatible what has been cut. In this case, it is the articulation of complexity with simplification, or of irreducibility with reducibility in the terms of CX5. Eschewing this issue leaves thinking on complexity comfortable at the sole paradigmatic level since it does not have to face the unpleasant constraints of theoretical and empirical action which force simplification. But this is a perverse consequence. Complexity thus limited to paradigmatic thinking lacks the primarily negative feedback from action, and has therefore neither to endogenise explicitly the notion of a threshold between complexity and simplification, nor to endogenise the conditions of the consistency and effectiveness of a genuine alternative system of knowledge. Dispensation from facing these constraints is a weakness from the standpoint of scientific experience.

A follower of Morin at the epistemological and methodological levels is Le Moigne. Whether the constraints mentioned above are addressed by him or not is examined next.

D.2 Jean-Louis Le Moigne on Systemic Modelling

In continuity with his constructivist epistemological perspective presented above, J.-L. Le Moigne has developed a modelling of complex systems that he contrasts with classical systems analysis.

Le Moigne's modelling comes close to methodology considered as a frame for putting epistemology into practice. It is a modelling of complex systems which is indeed a methodology and complements Morin's view of a paradigm. The connection of Le Moigne with Morin is very tight through their co-authoring of books and their common critique of classical science, of classical cybernetics and of classical systems theory (General Systems Theory or GST).

Le Moigne nevertheless pursues in a way von Bertalanffy's ambition of designing general systems as a model and a tool. The difference lies in his concern for an epistemological grounding of General Systems Theory, an aspect that von Bertalanffy and most other GST authors neglected far too much according to him. This is the basis for a new or second systemics distinguished from the first GST-style systemics.

The second systemics claimed by Le Moigne is in fact rooted in deep complexity because of the 'essential unpredictability' of the phenomena it addresses, following Paul Valéry, and because of the profound change it entails in scientific practice. It is therefore based on principles of systemic modelling that were presented above, and contrasted to the Aristotelian axioms, and to Cartesian principles of analytical modelling.

Its core concept is the General System (GS) or 'systemograph'. It is an abstract tool for modelling natural and artificial objects of study which has nothing to do with any general theory of systems. In the GS, 'system' denotes some entity conceived as a structure operating and evolving in an environment and having a finality, being goal-oriented. Unlike systems in general which denote primarily the phenomena that are represented, the GS is a model for conceiving models of objects of study, it is a meta-model.

The method following from the GS relies on two requirements which are deemed to ensure its validity. These two requirements consist in a double correspondence: the correspondence between a model of some object and the systemograph on the one hand, and the correspondence between a model and the object modelled on the other hand. Any model occupies a kind of intermediate position between the object of which it is a model and the systemograph. This systemic modelling requires that the correspondence between model and systemograph be isomorphic, that is, a one-to-one correspondence of elements; and that the correspondence between the model and the object of study be homomorphic, that is, a many-to-one mapping of some characteristics of the object onto its model. The search of isomorphism is an ideal and operates at a purely abstract level, while the modelling of objects cannot but aspire to be homomorphic and obey Korzybski's statement that 'the map is not the territory' (Korzybski, 1990, 56).

Systemic modelling thus conceived shifts the scientific method from analysis strictly understood to the design of models that are isomorphic to the General System and homomorphic to the objects of study. Analysis is not rejected but appears as an ancillary method having no absolute priority. The isomorphism with the systemograph provides a frame enabling one to address features that cannot be grasped by analysis. This frame is backed by an axiomatic. It was the basis for the initial stages of our investigation in this book. It appears especially well fitted with a deeply complex situation like the one of this book. With hindsight we discover that the characterisation of the situation achieved here with CX5 is consistent with the canonical form of a system proposed by Le Moigne with the General System.

All in all this methodology offers somewhat minimalist guidelines, but these are backed by an alternative epistemology. It is an apparently consistent framework composed of an epistemology and of a methodology. Is it enough? While it may prove to be sufficient from the standpoint of methodology, the particular experience exposed in this book shows that something more was required from the standpoint of empirical and theoretical research. Indeed the challenge I had to face was with theory, heuristics and strategy.

The theory of complexity that it proved necessary to build differs from the notion of complexity as plain irreducibility present in this methodology ('essential unpredictability' following P. Valéry, endorsed by Le Moigne). I had to integrate what was already missing in Morin, that is, action. Scientific practice does not reduce to thinking, epistemology and methodology, it necessarily integrates action through theory-making and empirical inquiry, and therefore cannot do without the reducibility intrinsic to action. This combination of reducibility and irreducibility cannot simply be alluded to, it requires to be given full status, it is intrinsic to the notion of complexity facing us. I characterised it as paradoxical irreducibility or OP2. Plain irreducibility dispenses from facing the issue of action and ends in antireductivism. Its antidote is not reductivism but paradoxical irreducibility. Le Moigne's claim that 'a complex phenomenon is modelled by a complex system' (Le Moigne, 1990) bypasses the unavoidable simplification entailed in the very action of modelling, a shortcoming that we detected in Morin's Gordian knot metaphor.

Another issue is heuristic. It bears, first, on how to identify the threshold between classical analysis and complex modelling and how to shift from one to other. It remains unanswered. Second, it pertains to valid modelling. From a scientific standpoint, it is not enough to rely on the principle of the two correspondences, especially between models and objects of study. How do we know that the correspondences are satisfactory or meet declared-in-advance criteria of validation? What are the heuristics? What are the appropriate examplars and the supporting case studies? How do we know or make sure enough that these correspondences are more adequate than classical modelling? Third, in the absence of answers to these questions, how can systemic modelling become an effective alternative to classical, analytical modelling in scientific activity? On the whole these shortcomings are similar to those detected in Morin's Method. However inspiring this epistemological and methodological thinking may be, it remains questionable when it is addressed from the theoretical and empirical scientific sides. Combining the various layers of scientific activity, from epistemology to empirical action and theory, into a coherent whole, in such a way that it appears as a possible alternative to the classical system of scientific knowledge, is not a trivial task.

Conclusion

The study of Morin's and Le Moigne's contributions to complexity thinking has revealed their fruitfulness, although they present limitations with respect to research. They paved the way for this research both positively and through the problems that they present and force us to address. Their clarification of some fundamental paradigmatic (Morin) and epistemological (Le Moigne) issues underpinning shortcomings of classical science, of General Systems Theory and of the first cybernetics, provided foundations that helped this author's own thinking on DCX. Their shortcomings in research demonstrate that the move from the epistemology and the methodology of complexity to actual research cannot reduce to a plain extension. Again, this is not a trivial matter. This shift requires to be constructed and to be more completely specified in terms of its heuristics, its theory, and its strategy of effectiveness. Simon's test operates fully at this point. In the present context it tells indeed that 'you can't beat' a cognitive scientific system – classical science – with a methodology of modelling, but that you may beat it only with another cognitive, scientific system bringing answers to problems which remain unanswered in the initial classical system, for example a structuring of problem-situations that are ill-structured in the initial system.

D.3 Soft Systems Methodology

Soft Systems Methodology (SSM) is a well-documented methodology among the approaches composing the soft systems thinking perspective. It addresses situations experienced in the management of organisations whose complexity is deemed to necessitate an alternative methodology to the classical one prevailing in hard systems. Therefore it deals with a form of deep complexity. SSM is an original and involved approach which touches in its own way upon some of the issues raised by CX5, notably the non-separation of *W2* and *W1*, a reflection on its connection with foundational perspectives, and the permanent question of the articulation between soft and hard systems.

In a nutshell, SSM raises a symmetric problem when compared with Morin and Le Moigne's views. The latter are strong on epistemological foundations and weak on empirical and theoretical aspects. SSM is strong on experienced deep complexity in the specific domain of management but is weak on its theoretical framework and on its scientific bearing. Both perspectives are not easy to capture in a way that does justice to their characteristics and nuances. With this in mind I proceed in the same way as for Morin and Le Moigne in concentrating on what I believe to be the main features that appear relevant for the connection with CX5, in terms of origins and context, and of substance, followed by a discussion.

Origins and context

SSM was founded by Peter Checkland at Lancaster University in the 1970s and has evolved until now. P. Checkland reports that when he came to start his work on systems he had completed a career of 15 years with ICI (Imperial Chemical Industries) in which he had been first a scientist, then a technologist and then a manager. These experiences had given him 'a taste for rubbing ideas against reality, so [he] was not inclined to be satisfied with the austere pleasures of General Systems Theory' (Checkland, 1999, 10). They also led him to criticise vigorously operations research (OR), systems engineering (SE) and systems analysis for management (SA), and to see them as instances of the divergence between textbook OR, SE and SA, and what practitioners actually do (Checkland, 1983).

There is an interesting parallel in Checkland and Le Moigne's respective stories. They respectively started their careers as a scientist (Checkland with ICI in the UK) and an engineer (Le Moigne with Shell in France) in the 1950s. After a decade or so in industry they both shifted to research and academic career (Checkland at Lancaster University, Le Moigne at the University of Aix-en-Provence-Marseille). They were looking for responses to the dissatisfactions they felt about the way systems theory and practice were unable to tackle the ill-structured problems they faced in their everyday management tasks. They both realised that these problems pertained to a kind of complexity which was challenging the classical methods and required building alternative methodologies. It was at this point that they came to follow different strategies, which is not surprising since they worked without knowing each other. It is noticeable that although Le Moigne mentions SSM, Checkland's writings are apparently innocent of any reference to Le Moigne's or Morin's works. Le Moigne attributed the flaws of General Systems Theory to its insufficient epistemological and methodological foundations and attempted to improve them through emphasising problem modelling rather than problem-solving.

Checkland also investigated the problem modelling side as it arose from experience in management and declared his intention to take systems thinking beyond the abstractions of GST on the one hand, and the constraints of specialised techniques on the other hand (Jackson, 2000, S8). After SSM had emerged in an action research programme, it was discovered that its process mapped well the notion of an appreciative system that Vickers had been developing in the 1960s and 1970s. Thus, although SSM was not an attempt to operationalise the concept of an appreciative system, in hindsight, Checkland came to present SSM as a process of an appreciative system in action. The appreciative system conceptualisation, SSM and soft system practice thus form a continuum characterised by the Vickers – Checkland couple. The similarity with Le Moigne arises again. Le Moigne discovered in the 1970s that his ideas matched to a very large extent those of Morin, and formed a continuum from Morin's paradigmatic thinking on complexity to Le Moigne's epistemological and methodological thinking.

Content

Six aspects appear as key components of Soft Systems Methodology. They are presented below.

- *Real-world problem-situations*

The Soft Systems Methodology is defined by its initiator as a system-based methodology for 'tackling *real-world problems* in which known-to-be-desirable ends cannot be taken as given' (Checkland, 1999, 318). A real-world problem is a problem which arises in the everyday world of events and ideas, and may be perceived differently by different persons. It contrasts with a laboratory problem, that is, a problem whose form, content and boundaries are defined by the investigator: it is the investigator who decides what to take into account and what to leave out. While the scientist may select the most difficult problem which in his/her judgement offers a reasonable chance of solution, 'real life pushes its problems upon us' (ibid., 72).

SSM was developed to investigate purposeful human activity characterising management and organisational studies. The main purpose of the methodology is to come to grips with the plurality of viewpoints and to generate debate and learning. The need to develop this approach arose because hard means – ends analysis was found to be inappropriate and ineffective for the often messy situations encountered in management.

Most management problems cannot be formulated as a search for an efficient means of achieving a defined end: ends, goals and purposes are themselves problematic. These are soft problems contrasted to hard problems, which can be formulated as the search for efficient means of achieving definite ends. This is analogous to the ill-structured, messy problems contrasted to the well-structured problems.

The frequent occurrence of ill-defined and ill-structured problems was at the origin of the distinction between hard and soft systems methodology. The hard methodology originated in natural science and was transferred into social science. Systems engineering illustrates it: 'an objective or end-to-be-achieved can be taken as given. A system is then engineered to achieve the stated objective' (ibid., 318).
Jackson formulates it in the following way:

1. There is a desired state, S1.

2. There is a present state, S0.
3. There are alternative ways of getting from S0 to S1.
4. Problem-solving consists of defining S1 and S0 and selecting the optimum means of reducing the difference between them. (Jackson, 2000, S4)

The methodology concentrating on goal-seeking, optimisation and 'how to do it' was found irrelevant to managers operating in contexts where goals and objectives, as well as the means of reaching them, are problematical. In ill-structured or messy problematical contexts there is no clear view on what constitutes the problem, or on what action should be taken in order to overcome the difficulties being experienced.

Since SSM addresses problems 'in which known-to-be-desirable ends cannot be taken as given', it is based upon a phenomenological stance defined by Checkland as a 'philosophical position characterized by a readiness to concede primacy to the mental processes of observers rather than to the external world' (Checkland, 315, 318). This position contrasts with the positive stance characterised by a readiness to concede primacy to the world as known through observation and experimental evidence, and considered as composed of facts and events which are given to the observer.

- *Problem modelling*

SSM shares – though unknowingly – with von Foerster, Morin and Le Moigne's thinking the notion that in complex situations the primary task of enquiry is problem modelling rather than problem-solving. This is also the backbone of DCX modelling. This convergence provides an opportunity to emphasise the central place of the distinction between problem modelling and problem-solving. Our inculcated habits of thinking and everyday behaviour spontaneously drive us toward the search for solutions to problems. This is coherent with hard systems thinking and every situation in which the problems addressed appear well defined and structured. Yet the techniques, methods and algorithms which apparently perform so well for these problems are themselves the outcomes of past problem modelling. But we do not need to know it and even to be reminded of it since these techniques, and so on, are readily available to be used. We simply assume implicitly, or have reasons to believe, that the problems to be solved are well formulated and modelled.

This emphasis on problem modelling does not mean that problem-solving is neglected. Only the belief that problem-solving is the normal stance in *every* circumstance is criticised. This distinction entails the question of how it is known that modelling or solving is the more appropriate. Is it attached to the social science domain as SSM might suggest? Does modelling subsume solving as SSM also suggests? Does SSM contain a theoretical framework about this issue? It will appear later on that SSM does not provide explicit answers to these questions.

- *Appreciative system and processual cycle*

In SSM, the actual practice of management is seen primarily as managing relationships, especially relationship maintaining rather than goal-seeking. This view finds an important support in Geoffrey Vickers's notion of an appreciative system (Vickers, 1995). It is a system of human activity composed of interactions between appreciations, actions and an environmental flux of events and ideas. Appreciation follows from our ability to perceive, to make judgements and to choose. It leads to action that becomes part of the flux of events and ideas unfolding through time. Events and ideas are inseparable and continually affect each other; their flux over time is imaged by Checkland and Casar as a two-stranded rope. Judgements are about facts (descriptive) and values (normative). They depend on standards about what is important or unimportant, relevant or irrelevant, and about what is good or bad, acceptable or not acceptable. The standards have no ultimate source. Their immediate source is the previous history of the system itself. Vickers's ideas originated in a reaction against the paradigm of goal-seeking and the cybernetic paradigm, and were expressed in the form of a model by Checkland and Casar (1986) and Checkland (1994).

Judgement-making is governed by relationship management rather than goal-seeking, the latter being a special case of the former. Judgements and actions are connected in a process organised like a system – an appreciative system – whose structure remains the same through time whereas its contents evolve and change. In Checkland's words, an appreciative system is 'a process whose products – cultural manifestations – condition the process itself' via the flux of events and ideas which 'ensures that it does not, through its actions, reproduce exactly itself' but a 'continually changed self', following Varela's notion of 'autopoietic systems' (Checkland, 1994, 82).

The initial opposition introduced between goal-seeking and relationship management is debatable. Why should relationship management be excluded from being a goal in its own right? This opposition stems in Vickers from his reaction against what he perceived as a main shortcoming of classical management reasoning personified, in his view, by H. Simon. The irony is that one may – as we do in this book – find an antidote in Simon's behaviouralist reasoning to what Vickers denounces in Simon's reasoning. But it is apparently overlooked or ignored by Vickers and by Checkland.

Notwithstanding this feature, the appreciative system provides a model broadly in phase with CX5. Apart from the analogy to autopoiesis and the reliance on systems models which were avoided in the construction of CX5, the emphasis on a recursive, cyclical open process echoes findings that were obtained with CX5.

- *Systemicity of PEW*

Beyond its emphasis on real-world problem-situations, on problem modelling, on the appreciative system and the processual cycle, a fourth insight of SSM is its emphasis on the attribution of systemicity or systems-like characteristics to the process of enquiry into the world (*PEW* or *W2*) rather than to the world *W* or *W1*. It is even the crucial distinction between hard and soft systems according to Checkland. This followed from realising that hard system methods were not adequate to the messy real-world problem-situations encountered in the management of organisations. The focus was therefore shifted to the *PEW* and to organising it as a learning system.

This is convergent with CX5 apart from two differences. First is the constant reference to the notion of system in SSM, whereas CX5 refers to process. Second, the world envisaged in SSM is the world outside ourselves. It is the *W1* of CX5. The *W* in SSM does not formally include *W2*, that is, ourselves as inquirers. The *W* in CX5 is about *W1* and *W2*. This is coherent with self-reflexivity introduced by the first organising principle of CX5. No such explicitly formulated inclusion of *W2* in *W* appears in SSM.

- *Learning*

Learning is a fifth key feature of SSM. It follows from acknowledging that models in SSM are not descriptions of the world or models of parts of the world as they are in Hard Systems Methodology (HSM). They are rather models 'relevant to' debate about the world. SSM is an 'epistemological device' serving coherent discussion about possible change. It is a dynamical cycle of learning and action. Modelling in SSM does not provide blueprints for design; it cannot tell 'what or how to do it'. It aims rather to tell what is required in a given situation.

SSM aims to structure a debate with people having a concern for the problem-situation. The structuring consists in 'comparing models and real world' and the purpose of debate is to find an *accommodation* (not necessarily a consensus) which enables action taken to improve the problem-situation. A cycle of action and debate develops, the whole cycle is 'itself a system which *learns* as the process of debate both illuminates the understanding of the situation and throws up new choices of relevant human activity systems' (Checkland, 1995, 50–51). The human activity system (HAS) denotes a structured set of activities connected together thus constituting a purposeful activity, a whole or system in which purposeful action represents an accommodation between a plurality of different and conflicting values and interests. Thus the HAS is a systems model of the activities people need to undertake in order to pursue a particular purpose (Jackson, 2000, S5).

- *Participation and validation*

SSM is participative to the extent that it 'aims to bring about improvements in areas of social concern by activating in the people involved in the situation a learning cycle which is ideally never ending'. It is flexible and iterative and entails that 'no objective and complete account of a problem-situation can be provided' (von Bülow, 1989).

The participation aspect of SSM brings with it a particular kind of *validation.* Since models in SSM are 'epistemological devices' their validity depends on their relevance and adequacy. Whether a model of an HAS is relevant in a particular study

> has to be answered by the learning process itself: In SSM you cannot know for sure whether or not a given root definition [the constitutive element of an HAS] and model are relevant: you *learn* your way to relevance by going round the [learning] cycle ... often many times in the course of a study. [This differs from the model validation in the hard approach where models] must be shown adequately to represent a part of the world. (Checkland, 1995, 53–54)

Validation in SSM relies on a 'declared in advance' intellectual framework of ideas in order to allow recovery of the process by which the results were obtained (Checkland and Holwell, 1998, 22–23). Recoverability expresses a type of validation that is intermediate between the too-strong repeatability criterion of classical science and the too-weak notion of plausibility. It means that the research ('action research') 'should be conducted in such a way that the whole process is subsequently recoverable by anyone interested in critically scrutinizing the research' (Checkland, 1999, A39-40).

Finally, Checkland's concern to clarify the foundations of SSM signals both support found in phenomenology, hermeneutics, action research and appreciative systems, and a rejection of positivism, the philosophical background of the hard systems approach. Yet specific formal hard modelling is not excluded, it is subsumed under the general stance of the soft approach.

Discussion

- *Insights and shortcomings of SSM*

A way to gain clarity in the contents of SSM is to compare it with its alternative, HSM. I summarise in Table 6.2 elements of comparison that can be found in the SSM literature. They are necessarily simplified but I believe that they are sufficiently representative. The items in the HSM column are denominated according to the way they are identified in the soft systems approach itself. This may be open to debate and will be discussed below.

Table 6.2 presents some major themes that recur in SSM and in its comparison with HSM. Overall, I found ten criteria of comparison. Entities in the cells are not absolute, exclusive notions. They are meant to point to the main feature on which the difference bears. Thus, to take an example, relationship maintainance is not exclusive in SSM: it is at least as important as goal-seeking, and answering questions about 'what' we should do is as significant as determining 'how to do it' (Jackson, 2003, 181–182).

Table 6.2 A comparison of Soft Systems Methodology (SSM) and Hard Systems Methodology (HSM) in management and organisational studies as it emerges from SSM literature

Criteria	HSM	SSM
1. Character of relevant problem-situations	Well structured	Ill-structured
2. Attribution of systemicity	The world is *W1*, outside ourselves *W1* is systemic	Ambiguity on the world *W* The process of enquiry into the world (*W2*) is systemic
3. Main task of enquiry	Problem-solving	Problem modelling
4. Actors' behaviour	Goal-seeking	Relationship management
5. Modelling style	Optimisation	Learning. Focus on process rather than on content
6. Status of models	Descriptions of the world	Devices to debate about the world
7. Expected use of models	Blueprints for design	Cycles of learning and action
8. Model validation	Representativeness of part of the world	Recoverability (relevance, adequacy, internal defensibility)
9. Foundations	Positivism	Phenomenology, Hermeneutics, Action research, Appreciative systems
10. Mutual interaction of HSM and SSM	Excludes SSM.	Subsumes HSM

SSM is based on practical experience. It has no claim to be a grand theory or an alternative to classical science. It is not prescriptive and does not tell us what to think or how to model. It simply stands as a way of thinking and modelling.

It brings an insightful view on modelling ill-structured problem-situations in management. On the whole none of the ten entries about SSM in Table 6.2 contradicts CX5. The emphasis on process rather than on content or product, on 'real-world' problem-situations rather than laboratory problems, on problem modelling rather than problem-solving, on the systemicity of *PEW* rather than *W*, on participation rather than mere representativeness, on learning to debate about the world, on the subsumption of hard modelling rather than its exclusion, are broadly in accord with CX5. Is this sufficient for making SSM a basic reference for CX5? To answer this question requires us to compare more closely each entry of SSM with CX5 (Table 6.3).

This comparison reveals noticeable differences with CX5 for each entry except entry 7 on learning and action. Table 6.3 is built on the same criteria as those of the comparison of soft with hard systems methodologies of Table 6.2, referred to by the figures in the first column of Table 6.3. Table 6.3 is therefore an extension of Table 6.2 to CX5. The most important differences between CX5 and SSM, which make the reference to SSM problematic, are reported in the fourth column of Table 6.3. Once totalised in this column, it is noticeable that the elementary differences concentrate in few recurrent problems about deficient criticality and integration, and about excessive looseness and specificity.

From the standpoint of CX5, these shortcomings can be organised under the three headings of deficient theorising, absence of mechanism articulating hard with soft problem-situations, and excessive specificity.

- *Deficient theorising of 'softness'*

Unstructured or complex problem-situations in management are equated with soft systems. SSM is a methodology of complex systems in management in which systemicity is primarily an attribute of *PEW*. In other terms, complexity or the source of 'softness' is perceived as an attribute of systems and is not worked out theoretically in its own right although the systemicity of *W2* is worked out. Since complexity is equated with human systems problems, does this mean that complexity is irrelevant for systems that are not human? Does it mean that human problems which are not systemic are excluded? In CX5, complexity is a property of situations which always involve human agency but that involve subject-matters which are neither limited to human systems nor compelling to an initial standpoint of systems or systems models taken for granted. CX5 relies on situated behavioural reflexivity rather than being an attribute of some given kind of system.

Table 6.3 SSM and CX5 compared

Criteria (similar to those of Table 6.2)	**SSM (cf. Table 6.2)**	**CX5**	**Difference with CX5 and problem with SSM**
1	Ill-structured problems as human systems problems	Focus on characterising and theorising irreducibility present in ill-structured problems *and* its articulation with reducibility of NDCX, well-structured problems, independently of systems. Characterisation of complex irreducibility prior to the use of systems models. Focus on problem-situations rather than on systems.	Too specific No notion of criticality No mechanism of articulation of DCX with NDCX
2	World (*W*) and process of enquiry into the world (*PEW*)	World *W* is *W1* (outside ourselves) *and W2* (ourselves) *PEW* as *W2* (self-reflexivity). *PEW* is the process of enquiry into *W1 and W2*.	Ambiguity on *W* (de facto equated with *W1*) due to absence of distinction between *W1* and *W2*
3	Problem modelling	Problem modelling *and* problem solving when NDCX	No mechanism of integration
4	Relationship management	Not limited to management of relationships	Too specific
5	Learning	Learning *and* optimisation when NDCX	No mechanism of integration
6	Models to debate about the world	Models help to debate about, *and* to describe, the world	No mechanism of integration
7	Learning and action	Intelligence of situations Learning *and* action	Convergence with CX5
8	Recoverability	Recoverability in domain of activity *i* subject to its standard D_i^*	Too loose
9	Phenomenology, etc.	OK with SSM but SSM silent on pragmatism and quasi silent on constructivism (Dewey, Bachelard, Piaget, von Foerster, deep complexity thinking)	Too loose and partial
10	Subsumption of hard systems alluded to	Subsumption made explicit and endogenised	Loose subsumption

SSM illustrates well a recurrent problem of the articulation of systems with complexity. In Checkland's words: 'We use systems models because our focus is on coping with the complexity in everyday life, and that complexity is always, at least in part, a complexity of interacting and overlapping relationships. Systems ideas are intrinsically concerned with relationships, and so systems models seem a sensible choice; and since they have been found, time after time, to lead to insights, they have not been abandoned' (Checkland, 1999, A24). Relying in this way on system as a tool taken for granted drives us naturally to address issues from the standpoint of an irreducible whole rather than mere irreducibility as a cognitive problem its in own right. The experience of the systems literature shows that the presence of 'whole' in 'irreducible whole' tends to obfuscate the component of irreducibility and to direct attention to the comparison with other systemic wholes. SSM originated in a reaction against goal-seeking systems and goal-seeking management theory connected with hard systems. The comparison made in Table 6.2 follows directly from this unquestioned standpoint and reveals a kind of path-dependency with respect to these premises. In this logic a soft system can be characterised independently of theorising on its softness. The practical experience of management displays at length instances which cannot be tackled in a hard way, and dispenses therefore with enquiring on the theoretical character of softness. A theory of softness or complexity may not be required in this context. But it is likely to convey severe limitations on the relevance of the reasoning for situations outside of management.

In hindsight, having a theory of complexity like CX5 renders it possible to use systems modelling in a more controlled way, which reverses the belief that the use of systems models might enable one to focus on complexity. It is claimed here that complexity adequately theorised comes before systems modelling.

- *Deficient articulation of 'soft' with 'hard' systems*

A consequence of the lack of a theory of 'softness' is the absence of a mechanism of articulation of 'soft' with 'hard' problems and systems. This shortcoming is abundantly documented in Table 6.3, in lines 1, 2, 3, 5, 6 and 10. It appears first with the lack of any notion of criticality between soft and hard or, in CX5 terms, between deep complexity DCX and non-deep complexity NDCX. It creates an incapacity to think about 'soft' and 'hard' notions otherwise than in terms of plain opposition. An instance of it is in line 3. Problem modelling in SSM is opposed to problem-solving of HSM, which leaves no room for problem modelling and problem-solving being endogenised into an integrative notion like CX5. This absence of an explicitly developed mechanism of integration appears whenever the difference between CX5 and SSM bears on an 'and' missing in SSM.

This shortcoming is complemented by the ambiguity or the excessive looseness of several central notions of SSM when they are compared with CX5 (lines 2, 8, 9 and 10). Let us take looseness. Thanks to it, it might be objected to the critique of the lack of a mechanism of integration made above that although such a mechanism is not explicitly worked out, there is nothing is SSM which would prevent appreciation and judgement from including hard features whenever needed. I agree, but this is precisely where the problem lies: SSM is too loose about its criterion of validation, about its foundational references, and most of all, about the way it subsumes hard systems modelling. It is one thing to say that subsumption exists through judgement and another thing to explain precisely how it operates, which is done in CX5 through the mechanisms contained in Tables 3.3 and 4.3, and OPs 1, 2 and 3.

- *Excessive specificity*

The problem of the excessive specificity of SSM is introduced in line 1 of Table 6.3 and indeed runs throughout SSM. It bears on the question whether SSM is limited to management or not. Even if it were limited to management, it could rely on a scientific framework whose relevance might be established for domains outside management. Let us consider these two questions.

In the introduction to the second edition of his book, Checkland makes clear that SSM addresses 'management, broadly defined … the kind of situations which we all have to deal with in both our professional and our private lives' (1999, A3). This notably extends the scope of SSM although most of the case studies seem to bear on management of organisations as usually understood. Beyond this extension is the issue of the scientific status of SSM. Since SSM rejects hard systems and the classical scientific tools underpinning them, in human activity systems, but subsumes hard systems, what kind of intellectual construction is it? Is it an alternative to a classical management methodology? The conditions required with Morin's paradigmatic complexity and CX5 apply as well here. The classical scientific framework backing hard systems is itself a system of scientific knowledge. It cannot be replaced or subsumed piecemeal with missing links in the candidate alternative to it. The big missing link in SSM is theory. The many practical and heuristic insights of SSM are loosely connected with epistemological foundations and lack the cement of a firm theoretical articulation of soft with hard features from a scientific standpoint. This characteristic thwarts any attempt to make SSM an overall reference point for CX5.

Checkland is almost silent on construction with one exception in which a parallel is drawn between a postmodernist view of an observer-community which constructs interpretations of the world, and the SSM accounts of deficient observer-communities, in different circumstances which 'construct interpretations of the world which are valid for them in their situation' and which provides 'an explicit constructivist process for the observer-community' (Checkland, 1994, 33–34).

If we may agree that 'GST (General Systems Theory) must pay for its generality with lack of content' (Checkland and Haynes, 1994, 190) we may also ask whether SSM is not bound to pay for its focus on practical human activity systems with excessive specificity and lack of generality.

E. A post-Deweyan, critically transactional perspective

E.1 Reclaiming John Dewey: Non-separation as Transaction

The results obtained thus far reveal a lasting gap between what is needed to accommodate CX5 fully and what is afforded by the perspectives based in some way or another on DCX or an equivalent of it. Although I do not contend to have been exhaustive, it seems at this point that none of the approaches reviewed above can be used as a reference perspective for CX5, for they lack a sufficiently specified treatment of the criticality of non-separation.

Why Dewey?

It was in the course of my research on this sixth chapter that I was driven to explore whether the kind of ill-structured, intractable situation conducive to DCX that I was already tackling in the domains of economics, of management science and of transport and industrial safety had also been studied in other domains. This is how I came across the issue of seemingly intractable policy controversies addressed by Donald Schön and Martin Rein in *Frame Reflection* (1994). My attention was stimulated by the importance they seemed to attach to Deweyan inquiry via Charles Lindblom (ibid., 52–53). Elsewhere, they referred to Deweyan transaction (Rein and Schön, 1991, 285), with an insistence by D. Schön on transaction and transactional inquiry, in which 'the inquirer does not stand outside the problematic situation like a spectator; he is *in* it and *in transaction with* it' (Schön, 1992, 122, 127). It prompted me to go back to Dewey's writings, especially *Knowing and the Known* written with A. Bentley (1949 [1973]) and *The Quest for Certainty* (1929 [1984]). It was a shock to me. I must say that I rediscovered Dewey and realised how my previous focus on *Logic: The Theory of Inquiry* had obfuscated my understanding of Dewey's thought. I mentioned above in D.1 how D. Schön initially found Dewey unintelligible. Schön adds that *Logic: The Theory of Inquiry* was the book that changed his mind about Dewey (Schön, 1992, 123). I should say that, unlike Schön, who was a philosopher, I got puzzled by *Logic* and it is *Knowing and the Known* that changed my mind about *Logic* and Dewey's thought.

I will be more explicit below about my own experience of making sense of Dewey because I suspect I am not alone in this case and my explanation of my experience may help others, and also because it is revealing of a deep challenge facing the communication of unconventional ideas, a challenge that this present book is also faced with.

My references to Dewey have appeared thus far in Chapter 1 and in the present chapter, with respect to pragmatism and some common traits of Dewey's and Morin's styles and the effort they require from their readers. These references are based on a unique source: *Logic: The Theory of Inquiry*. In it, I found that Dewey's discussion of the canons of Aristotelian logic confirmed the discussion of these axioms that I had initially found in Le Moigne. There is another lesson from *Logic* that I can better appreciate at this stage. It is the notion that inquiry means much more than mere investigation and develops as the transformation of an ill-structured situation into a better-structured one or, in Dewey's terms, the transformation of an 'indeterminate' situation into a 'determinate' one, a definition that will be discussed in a later paragraph. Indeed when we take the situation identified in Table 3.3 and the developments of Chapters 2 to 5, we find nothing noticeable in them that would go against the overall idea of Deweyan inquiry, although the argumentation about CX5 was constructed independently of any supposed Deweyan guideline, except for the decisive liberation from the excluded middle, shared by Dewey and some logicians. But that was all. I did not devote more time to what I had perceived as a difficult and unclear philosophical reading, at a really too large distance from what I needed for the purpose of theorising in my own field of experience. I felt that it was beyond my level of competence in philosophy and I was not willing to invest more time to come to grips with it, all the more as I doubted whether it might help in my own task.

I eventually discovered that Dewey was addressing in philosophy of knowledge issues that emerged in the development of CX5. Before I develop this point in the next section I believe it is necessary to explain why this proximity with Dewey did not appear earlier.

A late but timely rediscovery

Several reasons can explain this temporary sort of misunderstanding for Dewey. First is the difficulty with Dewey's language. I have already mentioned in C.2 that Ernest Nagel himself, the author of the introduction of the new edition of *Logic: The Theory of Inquiry* found that the 'idiom of Dewey's thought and his expository style make his *Logic* difficult reading' (Nagel, 1986, xxvi). It is reinforced by ambiguities, some of which were mentioned by Dewey himself, that are detrimental to a clear understanding and will be documented later on.

It was after I re-examined Dewey's possible connection with CX5 that I realised that inquiry alone was frustrating although it depicts a context which is not different from the context of Table 3.3. I was initially expecting to learn in *Logic* on what logical form I might base my research, when all that Dewey was saying was that logical forms arise within the operation of inquiry (Kaufmann, 1959, 831). My discomfort due to this kind of misunderstanding changed when I discovered that in a letter to Albert Balz annexed in an appendix in *Knowing and the Known*, Dewey acknowledged 'a certain cloudiness which obscures clear vision of what the book was trying to do' and was a 'source of misapprehension': 'The force of the word "Logic" in all probability, has overshadowed for the reader the import of what in my intention was the significant expression, *The Theory of Inquiry*' (Dewey, 1949 (1973], 204). I am among those who misapprehended Dewey's intention. And after reading these lines, I felt less uncomfortable about my own initial difficulties with *Logic*.

Another reason is the prominent place taken by *Logic* in Dewey's bibliography and the huge attraction it exerts on those, like this author, who were never taught Dewey's thought and who discovered it pragmatically through their readings, most of them mainly directing their attention toward *Logic* whereas it is in *Knowing and the Known*, a small book coauthored with Bentley, at the age of 90, that one finds the indispensable clarification of *Logic*.

Finally, how is it that I did not discern earlier that Dewey was talking of non-separation, in his own way, before working on the present chapter? A part of the answer is undoubtedly in Dewey's 'own way', another part comes from my following the common spontaneous focus on Dewey's 'theory of inquiry' which attracts attention to *Logic* at the price of the neglect of other works. However I believe that the main part of the answer comes from the very development of my argumentation.

It took me to be intellectually equipped with the CX5 I had developed to be able to make sense of Dewey. This illustrates how difficult it may be to shift from theory to philosophy and back again when this philosophy relies on a specific language and attitude of inquiry, differing from traditional ontological and epistemological contexts; just as the fact that CX5 requires to be envisaged in the unconventional context of the non-separability of *PEW* and *W* is likely to set up a barrier as long as we remain imbued with the separationist, conventional way of considering science.

The emphasis on non-separation as a foundational property is an outcome of the research which led to CX5. It could not arise before. It is not odd that it is thanks to this outcome, with the renewed questioning it involves, that Dewey's thought appeared in a new light. I simply was not ready to address Dewey from the standpoint of non-separation.

I must add that this new understanding arose from my new awareness of the crucial role of non-separation of *PEW* and *W* in CX5. It formed progressively along the path that was built through the successive chapters. It is an outcome of Chapter 5 and of the reflection conducted in the present chapter thus far. It could hardly have been raised in the initial steps of this research.

Non-separability is a result, not an initially assumed or imposed property. I took pains to find clues in a logic of inquiry when its appropriate subject-matter was a theory of inquiry as a *transactional* process. 'Transaction' is the term which denotes the way through which non-separation pervades Dewey's work over the last five decades of his life.

And yet a clarification of the notion of transaction contrasted with interaction did not occur before the publication in 1949 of *Knowing and the Known* by

Dewey and Bentley. It is through this collaboration that Dewey's thoughts were sharpened (Khalil, 2003, fn. 4).

E.2 The Transactional View

From transaction to inquiry: the main concepts

The experience related above illustrates how the usual focus on Dewey's *Logic: The Theory of Inquiry* may hinder a fuller understanding of his thought on non-separation. My claim is that the latter relies on Dewey's theory of *knowledge and action as inquiry*. These three notions hang together. Inquiry is tied to transaction, a specific type of action in Dewey's theory.

Logic is especially obscure on this aspect. Transaction was not clarified as a term denoting a specific concept before the publication of *Knowing and the Known* in 1949 with Arthur Bentley, although the substance of transaction as non-separation under a variety of specific forms pervaded Dewey's oeuvre for decades before.

From this vantage point the phrase 'transactional view' best synthesises Dewey's lifelong struggle against unwarranted dualisms in science. Transaction rather than inquiry appears therefore as the central notion. It is best understood when it is contrasted to interaction. Yet this clarification occurred only near the end of Dewey's life.

Transaction is the way non-separation appears under very diverse forms. It contrasts with interaction and self-action. It relies on distinguishing separation from distinction. And it is a procedure of inquiry and its outcome. All these terms need to be defined.

- *Transaction and related terms*

Dewey and Bentley present transaction as one of three levels of 'organization and presentation of inquiry ... those of Self-Action, Interaction and Transaction' which are 'all human behaviours in and with respect to the world, and ... all presentations of the world itself as men report it' (Dewey and Bentley, 1949 [1973], 132). They introduce these terms as:

> *Self-Action*: where things are viewed as acting under their own powers. *Inter-action*: where thing is balanced against thing in causal interconnection. *Trans-action*: where systems of description and naming are employed to deal with aspects and phases of action, without final attribution to 'elements' or other presumptively detachable or independent 'entities', 'essences' or 'realities' and without isolation of presumptively detachable 'relations' from such detachable 'elements'. (ibid., 132–133)

These three levels also denote three stages 'in the order of their historical appearance' (ibid., 132). The hyphenisation is irregular. It signals the prefix and the ever present component of action (ibid., 132). A transaction is the conversion of an ontological separation into a functional distinction envisaged within a more inclusive whole. It is characterised in different ways by Dewey and Bentley, but always with a common combination of internal relationality and process. It is internally relational since the very terms involved in a transaction derive their meaning and identity from the functional roles they play within the transaction. Transaction, seen as a dynamic, unfolding process becomes the primary unit of analysis rather than the constituent elements themselves. Transaction excludes the attribution of the aspects and phases of action to independently interacting elements or relations assumed to pre-exist in separation from one another. They are functional units defined by the role they play inside the transaction. The relations between terms are primarily dynamic, as unfolding, ongoing processes rather than as static ties among inert substances (Emirbayer, 1997).

Organism and environment are viewed in transaction as life-activity and form one of the most frequently used instances of transaction by Dewey: the hypothesis is to treat all human behavings, 'including knowings, as activities not of man alone, nor even primarily his, but as processes of the full situation of organism-environment; and to take this full situation as one which is before us within the knowings, as well as being the situation in which the knowings themselves arise' (Dewey and Bentley, 1949 [1973], 131) Therefore a transaction is 'neither something existing apart from observation nor as if it were a manner of observing existing in an observer's head independently of what is observed ... It is unfractured observation' (ibid., 131), the 'knowing known taken as one process' (ibid., 196), the 'seeing together, when research requires it, of what before had been seen in separations and held severally apart' (ibid., 134). Dewey and Bentley synthesise transaction as: 'Our own procedure is transactional, in which is asserted the right to see together extensionally and durationally, much of what is talked about conventionally as if it were composed of irreconcilable separates', and as if the subject matter were shattered 'into fragments in advance of inquiry' (ibid.,120–121).

Another instance is mind and body. Transaction converts them from separate things into a working distinction between mental and bodily activities within the wider system of action or behaviour: 'in just the degree in which action, behaviour, is made central, the traditional barriers between mind and body break down and dissolve' (Dewey quoted in Palmer, 2005, 5). The traditional barriers to agreed-upon solutions in epistemology 'stem from starting with body and mind as two separate things and trying to bring them together. Dewey's alternative is to start with human action and view the bodily and the mental as phases distinguished within this more inclusive whole' (ibid., 6).

This relational thinking contrasts with the substantialist viewpoint of self-action and inter-action. In 'self-action', 'things are viewed as acting under their own powers' (Dewey and Bentley, 1949 [1973], 132) independently of all other substances; organism alone is taken as the locus of behaviour.

In 'inter-action', 'thing is balanced against thing in causal interconnection' (ibid., 132), the relevant action takes place among the entities themselves rather than in their own, individual action. Entities remain fixed and unchanging throughout such interaction, each is independent of the existence of others. Newtonian mechanics provide a classical instance. Interaction relies on the view of separate, pre-existing parts, units or elements of action as operating upon one another. It emphasises the coming together, the reciprocal action or influence of separate persons or things on one another whereas transaction emphasises the coming together, the reciprocal influence of persons or things on one another that are distinguishable but inseparable aspects of occurrences.

Dewey and Bentley mention the use of the word 'transaction' by John R Commons in his *Legal Foundations of Capitalism* published in 1924 (ibid.,133). Indeed there is an even more striking coincidence in Commons' famous article on *Institutional Economics* (Commons, 1931). The contrast introduced by Commons between transaction as a unit of activity, and individual behaviour and the exchange of commodities, parallels transaction, self-action and interaction. It is worth quoting and meditating upon the whole passage where Commons defines an institution, and individual action as transaction:

> Thus an institution is collective action in control, liberation and expansion of individual action. These individual actions are really trans-actions instead of either individual behaviour or the 'exchange' of commodities. It is this shift from commodities and individuals to transactions and working rules of collective action that marks the transition from the classical and hedonic schools to the institutional schools of economic thinking. The shift is a change in the ultimate unit of economic investigation. The classic and hedonic economists, with their communistic and anarchistic offshoots, founded their theories on the relation of man to nature, but institutionalism is a relation of man to man. The smallest unit of the classic economists was a commodity produced by labor. The smallest unit of the hedonic economists was the same or similar commodity enjoyed by ultimate consumers. One was the objective side, the other the subjective side, of the same relation between the individual and the forces of nature. The outcome, in either case, was the materialistic metaphor of an automatic equilibrium, analogous to the waves of the ocean, but personified as 'seeking their level'. But the smallest unit of the institutional economists is a unit of activity – a transaction, with its participants. Transactions intervene between the labor of the classic economists and the pleasures of the hedonic economists, simply because it is society that controls access to the forces of nature, and transactions are, not the 'exchange of commodities', but the alienation and acquisition, between individuals, of the rights of property and liberty created by society, which must therefore be

> negotiated between the parties concerned before labor can produce, or consumers can consume, or commodities be physically exchanged.(ibid.)

These individual actions are not individual behaviours nor the exchanges of commodities. There is a striking coincidence between utility-oriented individual behaviour in Commons, and Dewey and Bentley's self-action. The exchange of commodities echoes interaction. Transaction in Commons takes the separate terms of the two substantialist views and converts them into distinctions within the more inclusive whole of a unit of activity.

- *Distinction and separation*

The word '*distinction*' designates the action of noting or making a difference between things, and the result of this action, a difference noted or made. The term '*separation*' denotes the act of dividing or splitting something into two or more things, and the result of this act. To be separate is to be 'withdrawn or divided from something else so as to have an independent existence by itself' (Palmer, 2005, 2).

Dewey was concerned with what he called *ontological separations*, that is, separations that are taken to have an ontological or real existence, to exist independently and externally to human observation and knowing. An ontological separation is a division assumed to have been there all along while a distinction is a difference noted (ibid., 3).

While a separation presupposes a distinction, a distinction does not imply a separation. In his letter to Balz, Dewey criticises the confusion which arises when 'distinctions which are indispensable to form and use in an efficient conduct of inquiry … are converted into something ontological, that is to say, into something taken to exist on its own account prior to inquiry and to which inquiry must conform' (Dewey and Bentley, 1949 [1973],203).

The traditional dualisms of subject and object, of organism and environment, of person and world, of observer and observed are examples of ontological separations among the 'hundreds of supposed ontological separations' to which Dewey applied his transactional strategy (Palmer, 2005, 11).

Dewey's transactional strategy (Palmer), view (Khalil) or approach relies on two phases (Palmer, 2005). The first phase reinterprets ontological separations as functional or methodological distinctions. The second phase envisages these distinguished items as interrelated aspects within more inclusive wholes. The separations are thus converted into phases of processes: organism and environment into life-activity, stimulus and response into coordination. Knowing and the known is reconsidered as 'the knowing known' which designates transaction as 'one process in cases in which in older discussions the knowings and knowns are separated and viewed as in interaction' (Dewey and Bentley, 1949 [1973], 196).

- *Inquiry*

Inquiry denotes 'the controlled or directed transformation of an indeterminate situation in one that is so determinate in its constituent distinctions and relations as to convert the elements of the original situation into a unified whole'(Dewey, 1938 [1986], 108). According to Dewey an indeterminate situation is 'uncertain, unsettled, disturbed, questionable … troubled, ambiguous, confused, full of conflicting tendencies, obscure' (ibid., 109). In his letter to Balz 11 years later Dewey specifies that occasions for inquiry cover 'features that are designated by such adjectives as confusing, perplexing, disturbed, unsettled, indecise; and by such nouns as jars, hitches, breaks, blocks – in short, all incidents occasioning an interruption of the smooth, straightforward course of behaviour and that deflect it into the kind of behaviour constituting inquiry' (Dewey and Bentley, 1949 [1973], 200).

A situation is indeterminate with respect to a given question if the established state of knowledge does not provide a warranted answer to this question. It is determinate in the opposite case. Inquiry is in short the determination of an indeterminate situation. The parallel with the sort of ill-structured problem-situations leading to CX5 is immediate, where the 'blocks' originate in features of irreducibility to satisficing levels of reduction that define deep complexity. That these notions are 'parallel' does not mean that they are similar, as will be shown in the next section.

Inquiry is transactional, 'autonomous', and it produces knowledge. The transactional character of inquiry is emphasised in *Knowing and the Known*: 'inquiry, a strictly transactional name … an equivalent of knowing (ibid., 193) although transaction is elsewhere only the third stage of inquiry, as we mentioned in the previous section. In hindsight, this transactional aspect can be detected in Dewey's definition of inquiry. However the word 'transaction' is used interchangeably with interaction in *Logic*. Interaction is most frequently used and is the only one of the two terms to appear in the analytical index. 'Transaction' appears in few instances. It is assimilated cursorily to 'entering into a contract' (Dewey, 1938 [1986], 24); in the next chapter, it is a process of activity, as organic life, that involves an environment and extends beyond the spatial limits of the organism (ibid., 32). Elsewhere, 'transaction' is used in a common sense meaning of 'the materials of legal regulations' (ibid., 105, 106).

'Autonomy of Inquiry' is the phrase mentioned by Dewey in his letter to Balz to recall that it was used in *Logic* with the purpose of serving 'as a key to understanding its contents' (Dewey and Bentley, 1949(1973], 201). This is not totally exact. It is the 'autonomy of logic', without capital letters, that figures in the first chapter of *Logic*:

> Logic is autonomous. The position taken implies the ultimacy of inquiry in determination of the formal conditions of inquiry. Logic as inquiry into inquiry is, if you please, a circular process; it does not depend upon anything extraneous to inquiry. ... It precludes the determination and selection of logical first principles by an a priori intentional act ... It precludes resting logic upon metaphysical and epistemological assumptions and presuppositions. The latter are to be determined, if at all, by means of what is disclosed as the outcome of inquiry; they are not to be shoved under inquiry as its 'foundation'. On the epistemological side, it precludes ... the assumption of a prior ready-made definition of knowledge which determines the character of inquiry. Knowledge is to be defined in terms of inquiry, not vice-verse, both in particular and universally. (Dewey, 1938 [1986], 28)

With this quotation, we are at the heart of the matter. It expresses the primacy of inquiry and illuminates Dewey's constant emphasis on the behaviour attributing a priority to the context of conduct of inquiry over what he calls the ontological context. In inquiry, 'all logical forms ... arise within the operation of inquiry and are concerned with control of inquiry so that it may yield warranted assertions. This conception implies ... that the forms *originate* in operations of inquiry. To employ a convenient expression, it means that while inquiry into inquiry is the *causa cognoscendi* of logical forms, primary inquiry is itself *causa essendi* of the forms which inquiry into inquiry discloses' (ibid., 11–12).

Inquiry is a continuing process. Knowledge is expressed in terms of outcome of this process. Knowledge is 'that which satisfactorily terminates inquiry ... it is knowledge because it is the appropriate close of inquiry' (ibid., 15). The 'convergent and cumulative' effect of continued inquiry 'defines knowledge in its general meaning. In scientific inquiry, the criterion of what is taken to be settled, or to be knowledge, is being *so* settled that it is available as a resource in further inquiry; not being settled in such a way as not to be subject to revision in further inquiry' (ibid., 16). Knowledge taken as a general term related to inquiry means 'warranted assertibility'. Warranted assertibility involves the references to inquiry as 'that which warrants assertion': if logical theory is the systematic formulation of controlled inquiry, logical forms 'accrue in and because of control that yields conclusions which are warrantably assertible' (ibid., 29, 105).

We find summarised here Dewey's core position: an operation-based logic (Burke, 1994, 13), logical forms which arise in a process exposed to revision in further inquiry with the background of a participatory theory of knowing, a transactional strategy, a pattern of inquiry and the reliance on the self-corrective process of science which compose a pragmatist overall pattern.

The rationale for transaction according to Dewey

It seems clear by now that non-separation is conceived by Dewey through transaction, and separation eventually through interaction. This leads to the issue of how and why one notion is retained rather than the other in research and whether and how they can possibly coexist. Does Dewey provide a theoretical frame? How does transactional non-separation arise in his writings? It is less problematic to answer the latter than the former. This is the reason why the former will be addressed in a following section. I will survey briefly below the sources for transaction which appear in the writings on which I am basing my analysis. I am not an expert of Deweyan doctrine and philosophy and I present the following ideas as an hopefully reasonable hypothesis which derives from my own, far from exhaustive reading of Dewey. My information is based on the references mentioned above which all deal, more or less directly, with non-separation and transaction.

At the outset, it is worth setting these issues in their Deweyan developmental perspective. The story of transaction is peculiar. It had been foreshadowed at least since Dewey's article on the reflex arc concept in psychology (Dewey, 1896 [1972]). It was given the name 'transaction' in 1930. It was hidden in the background of the definition of inquiry in 1938 and apparently not differentiated consistently from interaction until 1949 and Dewey's collaborative work with Bentley, at a time when Dewey was 90 years old, three years before his death. In hindsight, having the end of this story in mind, there is little doubt that the idea of non-separation as transaction pervades throughout Dewey's oeuvre. This lasting leading thread accompanied Dewey's long-lasting concern with *Logic*, the maturity of which took him some 40 years, as he himself mentions (Dewey, 1938 [1986], 5).

Let us start with, and to some extent recall, some firmly stated positions by Dewey, and Dewey and Bentley. They introduce transaction as the historically most recent level of organisation and presentation of inquiry with the understanding, however, that 'something of the old [self-action and interaction] and often much of it, survives within or alongside the new' (Dewey and Bentley, 1949 [1973], 132).

Inquiry is characterised as a 'strictly transactional name' (ibid., 193) which, by the way, seems to create an ambiguity with the above mention of three levels of inquiry, including the first two, non-transactional levels. Finally, transaction excludes epistemology: 'As far as this word [epistemology] directly or indirectly assumes separate knowers and knowns ... all epistemological words are ruled out under transactional procedure' (ibid.)

Yet, although Dewey did not develop a theory of knowledge in the usual sense of epistemology, he did elaborate a theory of inquiry synonymous with knowing.

Among the first influences on Dewey are those of C. S. Peirce and C. Darwin with Peirce's fallibilism and criticism of Cartesianism, notably of the Cartesian divide between thinking mind and extended matter, between *res cogitans* and *res extensa*.

The influence of Darwinian thinking on Dewey's philosophy permeates in the notion that a human being or community is like a natural organism that must function with respect to, and adapt to, an environment, from which follows the frequent reference to the organism and environment couple:

> Our position is simply that since man as an organism has evolved among other organisms in an evolution called 'natural', we are willing under hypothesis to treat all of his behavings including his most advanced knowings, as activities not of himself alone, nor even as primarily his, but as processes of the full situation of organism-environment; and to take this full situation as one which is before us within the knowings, as well as being the situation in which the knowings themselves arise. (ibid., 131)

Dewey and Bentley insist on the way environment is not external to organism, that they are not in interaction, but environment is a medium. The environment is:

> not something around and about human activities in an external sense; it is their *medium*, or *milieu*, in the sense in which a *medium* is *inter*mediate in the execution or carrying out of human activities, as well as being the channel *through* which they move and the vehicle by which they go on. (ibid., 185) An organism does not live *in* an environment; it leaves by means of an environment. (Dewey, 1938 [1986], 32)

Dewey was also influenced by William James who openly challenged in his *Principles of Psychology* (1890), notably in his chapter on The Stream of Thought, the 'common premise of both sensationalistic empiricism and [traditional] empiricism ... that the empirically given consists of disconnected elements' (ibid., 510).

Another source is Dewey's work in psychology with his famous article 'The Reflex Arc in Psychology' (1896), where he criticised the behaviourist conception of stimulus and response as tied to the mind – body dualism and argued for an alternative view, in which the organism interacts with the world through a self-guided activity that coordinates and integrates responses. Although the word 'transaction' was introduced by Dewey in 1930, the association of stimulus and response into a coordination constitutes a first instance of transactional non-separation. It had a clear implication for the theory of knowledge: the world is not passively perceived and known.

This view is thoroughly developed in *The Quest for Certainty. A Study of the Relation of Knowledge and Action* (Dewey, 1929 [1984]). Dewey explains the quest for certainty as a perennial disease of modern thought in its attempt to separate theory from practice, or knowledge from action. Knowledge is achieved not by trying to escape from conditions of doubt or uncertainty, but by active inquiry. What is known is not independent of the activity of knowing. Knowing becomes an act of participation. Dewey takes support in the advances of physics and formulates what he calls a 'Copernican revolution'. The change was brought by Einstein's theory of restricted relativity. It signified doing away with Newtonian absolutes in designating physical time as 'a *relation* of events, not an inherent property of objects' and marked the end, in natural science, of absolute space, time and motion as inherent properties and 'the substitution of the notion that they designate relations of events' (ibid., 116, 117). Next came Heisenberg's principle of indeterminacy, formulated in 1927, that Dewey was able to include in 1929: 'what is known is seen to be a product in which the act of observation plays a necessary role. Knowing is seen to be participant in what is finally known … The principle of indeterminacy thus presents itself as the final step in the dislodgment of the old spectator theory of knowledge' (ibid., 163).

Twenty years later, Dewey and Bentley stressed the 'increasing use of transaction … in physics' which started with James Clerk Maxwell in *Matter and Motion* and was pursued by Einstein and in quantum physics (Dewey and Bentley, 1949 [1973], 132, 133).

According to Dewey these scientific advances, and the extension of the scope of science in the twentieth century to psychology and other human sciences require a move away from the traditional view of objectivity: 'Mind is no longer a spectator beholding the world from without and finding its highest satisfaction in the joy of self-sufficing contemplation. The mind is within the world as a part of the latter's own ongoing process' (Dewey, 1929 [1984], 232). This constitutes a big reversal: 'In the Cartesian and Newtonian model, the observer was not just a spectator but an essentially unseen spectator whose task was to depict, reflect the external world, without affecting it in turn' (Toulmin, 1984, xvi). The world and man's knowledge of it from the standpoint of the knowing subject had already been addressed by Kant who claimed that he had effected a Copernican revolution in philosophy. However there is according to Dewey an 'opposition rather than agreement between the Kantian determination of objects by thought and the determination by thought that takes place in experimentation' with its overt and hypothetical content, and its differential content and testing by consequences: 'The old centre was mind knowing … The new centre is indefinite interactions … There is a moving whole of interacting parts, a centre emerges wherever there is effort to change them in a particular direction' (Dewey, 1929 [1984], 232).

Another source of non-separation comes from the difficulty in achieving a solution through agreement when the positions are set in an ontological context, for there is often little ground enabling discrimination between positions which each claim in their own way to be closer to reality than their rival. Our discussion about critical realism illustrated this. It implies a rejection of the separation attached to the ontological viewpoint. The traditional separationist epistemology is rejected as well. Dewey makes this point clear in his letter to Balz:

> Whatever relative novelty may be found in my position consists in regarding the *problem* as belonging in the context of the conduct of inquiry and not in either the traditional ontological or the traditional epistemological context … The failure of the controversy to arrive at solution through agreement is an important ground of the idea that it is worth while to take these constituents of controversy out of an ontological context, and note how they look when they are placed in the context of the use they perform and the service they render in the context of *inquiry*. (Dewey and Bentley, 1949 [1973], 201)

To conclude, the various sources for non-separation that we have detected in Dewey concur to the perspective, forcefully exposed in *The Quest for Certainty*, of a participant, non-separationist theory of knowing contrasted with the traditional spectator, separationist theory of knowledge. This participant conception of knowing is a basis for transaction, which transactional inquiry follows directly: 'The elimination of ontological reference that at first sight may seem portentous actually amounts to the simple matter of saying that whatever claims to be or to convey knowledge has to be found in the context of inquiry…' (ibid., 201). It is indeed the context of *transactional* inquiry. It constantly orientates the initial step of inquiry towards the position where the available, existing separations are not taken for granted, and instead orientates the initial step of inquiry towards the position where these are submitted to the transactional procedure.

E.3 A Critically Transactional Perspective

From the standpoint of research, something more specified than instances of the historical and contextual origins of a transactional view mentioned in the previous paragraph is needed. A theory of transaction is necessary in order to establish its consistency, to identify better its mechanisms and its limits, and to assess better its domain of relevance.

Transaction and the Theory of Inquiry

There seems to be no other candidate reference work to start the above task than *Logic: The Theory of Inquiry* since we have already mentioned that for Dewey, inquiry is 'strictly transactional'. However, this property is anything but clear in *Logic* and it is only thanks to the hindsight of the clarification brought 11 years later in *Knowing and the Known* that the specific status of transaction was to appear in an apparently consistent way. Reading *Logic* again with this clarification in mind invites us, then, to examine its theoretical bearing for transaction.

In doing so, it should not be forgotten that Dewey regarded *Logic* as a hypothesis, 'the detailed confirmation of which would have to be supplied by others in the future' (Nagel, 1986, x). The purpose here is less to criticise *Logic* than to bring material susceptible to help build a theoretical content of transaction that is compatible with the critical non-separability of CX5.

Let us recap what have learned about transaction and inquiry thus far:

- Inquiry is the transformation of an indeterminate situation into a determinate one.
- Transaction is the conversion of an ontological separation into a distinction within a more inclusive whole. The epithet 'ontological' indicates something taken to exist on its own account prior to inquiry and to which inquiry must conform.
- Transaction is a procedure of inquiry.
- Inquiry is a 'strictly transactional name'. Therefore inquiry is synonymous with transactional inquiry and renders it legitimate to view *Logic* as a theory of transactional inquiry.

Several questions arise immediately. Does a theory of transactional inquiry contain a theory of transaction? Can a theory of transaction be found in *Logic*? And how can transaction produce the determination of a 'doubtful, uncertain, blocked', and so on, that is, indeterminate situation? In other terms, what is the mechanism through which the use of transaction leads to successful inquiry?

Let us recall some basic features. The word 'transaction' appears very sparsely in *Logic* whereas the term 'interaction' is abundantly used. The two terms are never distinguished in *Logic*. This distinction is introduced late, in *Knowing and the Known*. Therefore it seems that one can safely contend that there is no theory of transaction in *Logic*. The theory of (transactional) inquiry is like the so-called theory of complex systems with respect to a theory of complexity: it does not contain a theory of transaction any more than a theory of yellow umbrellas, if it were to exist, would contain a theory of the yellow colour. We are left with the task of uncovering the mechanisms through which transaction contributes to inquiry. For the sake of clarification, let us go back to the roots of the transactional view.

The transactional view has been characterised by Daniel Palmer as the strategy applied by Dewey to problems preoccupying psychologists and philosophers. These problems result from treating conventional separations, divisions, dichotomies or dualisms as something ontological or real. Once something is accepted as real, the problem arises of how to fit the separate items together, how they interact (Palmer, 2005).

If one considers that this problem is a source of 'doubts, uncertainty', and so on, or in other terms, is a source of indetermination and of occasions for inquiry, then a way to determine things is to convert ontological separations into 'non-separations' or distinctions envisaged within a unified whole according to Dewey.

What seems especially problematic in separation for Dewey is the tendency to make it ontological, prior to inquiring about it. Such a separation appears unwarranted and undue.

Several questions arise at this point. Why does separation necessarily trigger an indeterminate situation? Can't there be cases or situations in which separation is compatible with determination in Dewey's terms? Dewey and Bentley themselves acknowledge the existence of 'thoroughly legitimate interactional procedures … like classical mechanics', but seem to rule out this possibility for 'psychologies, sociologies, and epistemologies' (Dewey and Bentley, 1949 [1973], 138). Is this difference a matter of domain or discipline of activity? Why is what is acceptable in classical mechanics rejected in the three domains mentioned? Separation and its ontological nature in these domains constitute the primary problem for Dewey. The thrust toward non-separation follows directly from it. It does not exclude the reference to interactional separation in some domains, but seemingly excludes it in others. This is the issue of the connection, coexistence or mutual exclusion of non-separation and separation, that is, of transaction and interaction. It will be discussed later on.

Beyond this connection of transaction with inquiry, there remains a lasting ambiguity in the association of the two terms in the phrase 'transactional inquiry' following from the 'strictly transactional' character of inquiry according to Dewey and Bentley. On the one hand, they designate inquiry as 'a strictly transactional name … an equivalent of knowing, but preferable as a name because of its freedom from "mentalistic" associations' (ibid., 193). On the other hand transaction is the third level of the 'organization and presentation of inquiry in the order of their historical appearance', coming after 'self-action' and 'inter-action', 'as a growing manner rapidly advancing to prominence in the growth of knowledge' (ibid., 132–133). Therefore it seems that inquiry can be also self-actional and interactional. How then can it be a 'strictly transactional name'? A way out of this apparent contradiction would be to introduce a distinction between a meta-level and an object-level transaction subsumed under the meta- transaction. But this is seemingly never envisaged by Dewey and Bentley. This brings us to the articulation between the levels of inquiry, especially transaction and interaction.

At this point, whatever one might detect in *Logic* about a transactional content, but without the name, and in *Knowing and the Known*, one has to admit that some basic features of a genuine theory of transaction are wanting, notably with respect to its consistency, and its mechanisms and limits.

How inquiry can be both strictly transactional and include the other two modes of action is an issue of consistency. It will be suggested below that CX5 provides a pattern solving this problem.

If inquiry does not exclude interaction, how, then, is interaction connected with transaction? How can separation and non-separation coexist? This is the issue of the criticality of non-separation that will be addressed in the last section. Criticality is missing in transaction. It will be argued below that the frame fully relevant for CX5 is *critical* transaction.

The transactional view in a CX5 pattern

CX5 seems to be echoed by the transactional view to a degree that no other perspective offers. In our quest for a view which was adequate for CX5 we had to move step by step until we hit the issue of non-separability as the basic divide: it is non-separability, not only within the world *W1* external to the observer *PEW*, but primarily of *PEW* and *W*, in which *W* comprises *W1* and *W2*. This non-separability of subject and object was shown to be present in various perspectives. It is with Dewey that we find maybe the first – with the exception of Vico – and firmest argumentation for a reversal of the separationist, spectator theory of knowledge, and in favour of a non-separationist theory of participatory knowing. The primacy of experience illustrated in Table 3.3 is echoed by Dewey's autonomy of inquiry. The qualitative irreducibility of DCX is echoed by the irreducibility of transaction to separation. And the notions of process, relationality and openness are emphasised both in CX5 and in transaction.

At this stage, the transactional view might therefore seem to be a good candidate for accommodating CX5. However a closer look at inquiry and transactional inquiry will reveal that there exist important differences with CX5 beyond obvious resemblances. And there remains the central question left unanswered of the connection of transaction with research. We address these issues now.

First, is CX5 'inquiry'? There are several reasons to answer positively. The whole process of CX5 can be seen as an inquiry whose initiation occurs when we feel a disruption in activity and do not know how to go on.

In the Deweyan sense, inquiry is the directed transformation of an indeterminate situation into a determinate situation. CX5 is less ambitious in its terms but is conducted in a similar spirit: from the situation depicted in Table 3.3 to OPs 1 to 5, it consists in the controlled transformation of an ill-structured situation into a better-structured situation – though not necessarily fully determinate and liberated from uncertainty, doubt and so on. The only claim of CX5 is that the process brings an improvement in the structure of the problem-situation as assessed through explicit, declared-in-advance criteria.

However, a fundamental difference lies in the sources of the initiating disruption in activity. In Dewey, the source of inquiry is in an ontological separation which brings a difficulty in connecting previously separated items that is important enough to trigger a shift toward abandoning the initial ontological context and toward designing a non-separation. In CX5, the source of the deeply complex irreducibility lies in the incapacity to reduce or to separate up to a satisficing level of reduction. This incapacity is serious enough to trigger the search for another satisficing way of reduction or simplification. This difference is likely to orientate the ensuing developments into specific, divergent directions. This issue will be addressed in the concluding paragraph.

The bulk of the remaining interrogation is on transaction. Is CX5 'transactional' inquiry? Les us recall as a starting point that:

- The theory of inquiry as exposed in *Logic* is not an explicit theory of transaction or non-separation, although the statement that inquiry is 'strictly a transactional name' in *Knowing and the Known* renders legitimate to see *Logic* as a theory of transactional inquiry.
- Transaction is a specific kind of action, alongside interaction and self-action: they are three successive stages of inquiry, in which transaction is the last one. Therefore inquiry can hardly be strictly transactional unless transaction subsumes the other stages. This aspect is seemingly not addressed explicitly in *Knowing and the Known*. We retain the transactional character of inquiry and therefore the subsuming status of transaction.

Transaction is the conversion of ontological separations into working distinctions envisaged within more inclusive wholes. In CX5 terms it is a process of transformation and its outcome. It comprehends a procedure of inquiry and its outcome. And transaction is itself the product of a procedure, at the meta-level. Its main generative principle is a theory of participatory knowing. It can be characterised in a CX5 pattern as shown on Figure 6.3.

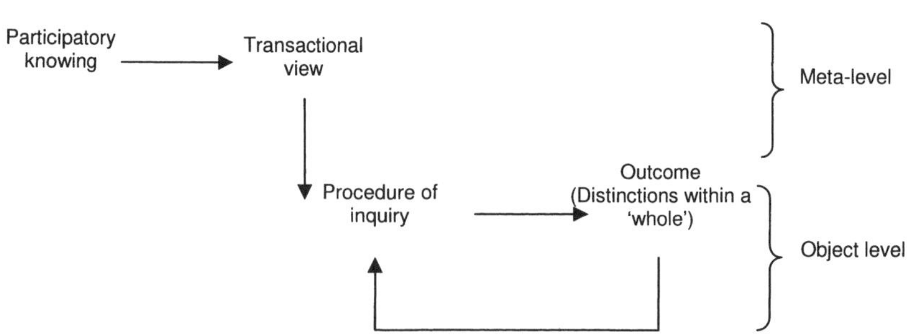

Figure 6.3 The transactional view in a CX5 pattern

The outcome of inquiry is new knowledge which arises from envisaging what was severed apart as functional distinctions within a whole or a 'system' in Dewey's language. It is provisional. Inquiry is a continuing process. Hence the recursive loop. The pattern of Figure 6.3 is dynamical. It has no claim to represent Dewey's thought fully. It is merely intended to picture how it connects with CX5 and how the CX5 generic pattern provides a structuring of transaction in which its basic aspects, that are dispersed in Dewey's writings and waiting for completion, are organised into a unified setting. Recall that we discovered firstly that inquiry did not make sense without transaction, and secondly that transaction could not itself make sense without a participant theory of knowing. The CX5 pattern makes it possible to introduce explicitly this subsuming status of transaction. It also renders it possible to model the Deweyan transactional view as the circular composition of the connections between the three cornerstones of participatory knowing, transaction and inquiry. These notions are strictly interdependent in what appears as a Deweyan thinking on non-separation. The picture of a circular transactional view follows from this interdependence. Figure 6.4 sketches how they hang together, as announced at the beginning of this section.

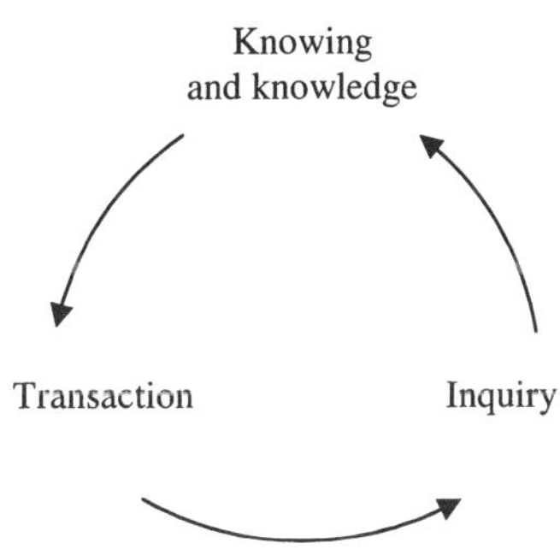

Figure 6.4 The Deweyan transactional circle

Figures 6.3 and 6.4 synthesise how the overall transactional view can be structured by using the CX5 generic pattern. Transaction appears as a generative principle and its product, as *GP* and *P*. It subsumes transaction, interaction and self-action taken at the object level. Knowing is taken as a short-cut for the process of knowing itself and its outcome, knowledge.

Each one of the three notions is specifically Deweyan and structured by CX5 when necessary. Hence, knowing is underpinned by a participatory rather than a spectator theory of knowledge. Transaction is both a meta-level subsuming notion and the subsumed object-level procedure of inquiry covering transaction, interaction and self-action, rather than an unstructured, underspecified coexistence of these notions. Inquiry is autonomous, as an alternative to the spontaneous, general obeyance to an ontological context or a separationist perspective in CX5 terms.

Transaction reshaped with CX5

The remaining issue is about the connection of non-separation, as transaction, with separation which covers interaction and self-action, and that we reduce to interaction for the sake of simplicity. What is the theoretical rationale for following one or the other of these kinds of conduct of inquiry?

In this section, we are no longer dealing with a CX5 presentation of the connection of transaction with inquiry and the theory of knowledge as symbolised in Figures 6.3 and 6.4. This time, we intend to explore the internal working of the connection of transaction with interaction. We will not satisfy with the general definition of transaction as conversion of separation into distinction.

When transaction is envisaged from the standpoint of theory and research, the habitual question about its intriguing character becomes even more insistent: how can it be held that scientific investigation should shift, when there are occasions for inquiry, from the study of things spontaneously observed, existing in their own right, 'already there' before investigation, to the relations of things appearing as terms of distinctions within more inclusive wholes? The norms of good practice in conventional science impose uniformly that objects be taken as imposing their existence to observers. Otherwise, the researcher cannot but justify his/her willingness to make use of the transactional procedure only through arguing the interest for it compared to the common, interactional or separationist procedure. Such an argumentation cannot but be based on a mechanism for the choice of one or the other. This mechanism is the connection between them. In CX5, it consists in the critical character of (*PEW, W*) symbolised by OP2, and through which a meta-level irreducibility subsumes the pair (irreducibility, reducibility) at the object level. Irreducibility and reducibility have their direct equivalents in non-separation and separation, or transaction and interaction, respectively. Can a connecting mechanism be found in Dewey and Bentley's transactional view? We will start with their treatment of this question. It will prove to be wanting, which will invite us to assess how CX5 may bring a more satisfactory answer.

Dewey and Bentley's problematic connection of transaction with interaction

With CX5 in mind, attention is immediately drawn to what the object of non-separation or transaction is. It is much dispersed in the transactional view, though it was initially about organism and environment, and subject and object. According to Palmer, already quoted, there are hundreds of separations to which Dewey applied his transactional strategy. A specific feature is the absence of any hierarchy or organisation among them. The transactions set out by Dewey were never structured into a pattern of transactions.

In CX5 the structure is immediate. There are two kinds of non-separations, about (*PEW, W*) and within the subject matter *W*. There is a hierarchy: (*PEW, W*) is prior. It forces us to make clear why this priority exists and how it shapes other distinctions.

One might nevertheless assert that there is a notion of priority of transaction in Dewey through his insistence on the primacy of the context of inquiry over the ontological context (Dewey and Bentley, 1949 [1973], 202). It implies the primacy of transaction over interaction, but at a general level, without any specification of its mechanism in research. However, Dewey and Bentley admit the existence of 'thoroughly legitimate interactional procedures' (ibid., 138) and, according to Palmer, mention that they themselves 'employ both interactional and transactional observation', and stress the utility of 'specialized interactional treatments within the wider transactional presentation' (Palmer, 2005, 9–10).

Yet it seems that whatever effort is made, ambiguity and elusiveness are the words that are appropriate to describe Dewey and Bentley's thought on transaction, from the standpoint of theoretical research. These aspects are documented below, across transactions first (undifferentiated transactions) and inside the very notion of transaction (unstructured transaction).

- *Undifferentiated transactions*

Dewey and Bentley's treatment of transaction suggests first an interrogation about the substance of transaction. The transactions applied to the numerous separations evoked above by Palmer seem to compose a broad set of transactions without any distinction among them as to their theoretical status. They seem to belong to an undifferentiated population of transactions in which one finds Dewey's initial examples of transactions between organism and environment as life activity, and subject and object as participatory knowing, and cases of transactions envisaged strictly inside the subject-matter external to the inquiring subject. In CX5 terms, the former pertains to (*PEW, W*), the latter to *W1*, external to *W2*. This distinction is essential. It entails the priority of (*PEW, W*). There is no such distinction between the two kinds of transactions in Dewey and Bentley.

An example of transaction inside *W1* is their reference to the advances introduced in physics by Maxwell and Einstein, in which they claim they find support for introducing transaction in their own fields of study. They acknowledge that in contrast with his transactional treatment of physical phenomena, Einstein 'remained strongly self-actional … in his attitude towards man's activity in scientific enterprise' (Dewey and Bentley, 1949 [1973], 135). Indeed Einstein fought constantly against any idea of a connection between *PEW* and *W* and opposed Bohr in this respect. The trouble with Dewey and Bentley is that they provide no further comment. It is as if they endorsed a kind of objectivist belief for transaction, following Einstein, at the price of a neglect of participatory knowledge, a cornerstone of the transactional view. In Dewey and Bentley's terms, Einstein's view of knowledge is on the ontological side. Then there seems to exist a serious ambiguity in their applause of a transactional Einstein in *W* and their actual neglect of Einstein's anti-transactional position on (*PEW, W*).

Although Dewey emphasised participatory knowledge in *The Quest for Certainty*, the notion that transaction bears primarily on it and necessitates one to distinguish this domain of relevance from the external world domain is never systematised either by Dewey or by Dewey and Bentley. One of the insights of CX5 appears clearly here: it is the structuration and the hierarchy it introduces in the connection of *PEW* with *W*, which avoids the above ambiguity.

- *Unstructured transaction*

Setting aside this ambiguity of transactions, how is the connection of transaction and interaction organised by Dewey and Bentley? One of their answers is that transaction is called for '*when research requires it*'. Transaction is 'the seeing together, when research requires it, of what before had been seen in separations' (Dewey and Bentley, 1949 [1973], 134); it is 'the right to see in union what it becomes important to see in union' (ibid, 135). In addition, interaction is 'the right to see in separation what it is important to see in separation – each in its own time and place' (ibid., 135). Likewise they claim to 'employ both interactional and transactional observation … in the same spirit in which physicists perforce use both particle and wave presentations' (ibid., 121).

Elsewhere the idea of requirement of research is complemented with the reference to the *field of activity*. Transaction appears as a matter of historical stage of development in a field when they present it as the procedure 'now needed in the field where we work' (ibid.).

In a third answer, transaction appears activated and deactivated in turn, depending on the *stage of inquiry*: transaction is the 'functional observation of (the) full system, actively necessary to inquiry at some stages, held in reserve at other stages' (ibid., 122).

There seem to be no other clues from Dewey and Bentley as to the use of transaction or interaction. The articulation of transaction and interaction seems to be a matter of requirement of research, in certain fields – those where the authors work, that is, psychology, sociology and epistemology; it also seeks support in the latest advances in physics (ibid., 132, 135), and it depends on the stage of inquiry without further explanation.

They say that transaction can be 'held in reserve'. If it is thus deactivated it must be balanced by an active interaction. Beyond the reasons given about the 'why', the 'how' remains unexplained. Dewey provides us with a pattern of (transactional) inquiry. The pattern of interaction is known: it is classical, separation-based science. But there is a void in the pattern of the connection of transaction with interaction. Our concern is with connection from the standpoint of research. Beyond saying that transaction and interaction coexist, we need to know how. How can one be held in reserve and the other be active or deactivated if the former ceases to be held in reserve and is reactivated? When it is taken into account that classical practice is interactional, then the *why* and the *how* one can shift to transaction is not a trivial issue. There is also little doubt that we cannot expect to find precise guidelines for theory-making at a philosophical and abstract level like Dewey's. Yet the position which emerges from CX5 is that the philosophical level should not be disconnected from the methodological and other levels. The linkage whereby the shift from interaction to transaction and vice versa occurs needs to be explicitly specified.

From the standpoint of research, and of CX5, it helps little to say that transaction or interaction should be used when "research requires it", without any indication on the substance of what makes it required. The same goes for the reference to stages of inquiry. And the connection of transaction with the historical development of certain fields is totally foreign to the rationale for non-separation in CX5. The possibility of oscillation between transaction and interaction suggested through the 'active' necessity of transaction at some stages and holding it in reserve at other stages is welcome. But the mechanism which commands it remains unknown.

However, in defence of Dewey and Bentley, one can maintain that their discussion is at a philosophical level and is by construction bound to deal with philosophical notions. The 'requirements of research' emerge in the very process of inquiry. A decision on their specific nature cannot be taken prior to inquiry. This is premised on the very priority of setting the problem addressed in what Dewey calls 'a context of inquiry', thus contrasted to the 'ontological context' of interaction and self-action. But then, inquiry in this context is transactional by nature. We are driven back to an essential ambiguity: how can there be room for oscillation between transaction and interaction in a transactional context? Is this oscillation an oscillation of contexts rather than of procedure within contexts? Then the recurrent question would come: what is the mechanism for deciding for one context rather than the other? 'Judgement' might be the answer. We may also come to this conclusion in the present work. However, the structuring on which a judgement is based is likely to make a big difference. This structuring could hardly be left to be forever the outcome of 'successful inquiry' through the ongoing 'self-corrective process of scientific inquiry' (Kaufmann, 1959, 827, 830). The present research leading to CX5 is an outcome of an inquiry. If it is to possess some generalisability, it may be useful for other research, thus avoiding the exhausting task of starting every new piece of research as if nothing had been done before. This is the main reason why this structuring should be made explicit in the design of the transactional view susceptible to accommodate CX5. My claim is that the phrase 'critically transactional perspective' conveys best what is required by CX5.

The very ambiguities detected here, in Dewey and Bentley's treatment of transaction and interaction in relation to the requirement of having explicit criteria for using one or the other, create a genuine ill-structured problem-situation.

Criticality through CX5

At stake with the articulation of transaction with interaction, there is the continuity with interaction, that is, with classical scientific practice and research. From the standpoint of research, the disconnection of transaction from interaction is most damaging. It makes transaction appear as a product of a kind of wishful thinking, possibly relevant in philosophical discussion, but ineffective in scientific practice.

The CX5 pattern provides a critically transactional way to design a connection between the irreducibility to separation, that is, transaction, on the one hand, and its reducibility, that is, interaction, on the other hand. These are converted into an object-level distinction envisaged from a meta-level, subsuming transaction or irreducibility. This pattern is the one exposed in OPs 1 to 5 of CX5. From their initial status of ambiguously coexisting notions activated and disactivated in turn, transaction and interaction become structured as phases within a more inclusive process in which transaction subsumes interaction.

At this stage it is necessary to find an adequate structuration. It is the meta-level transaction, which, like CX5, makes it possible to disactivate and activate transaction and interaction in turn at the object level (Figure 6.5).

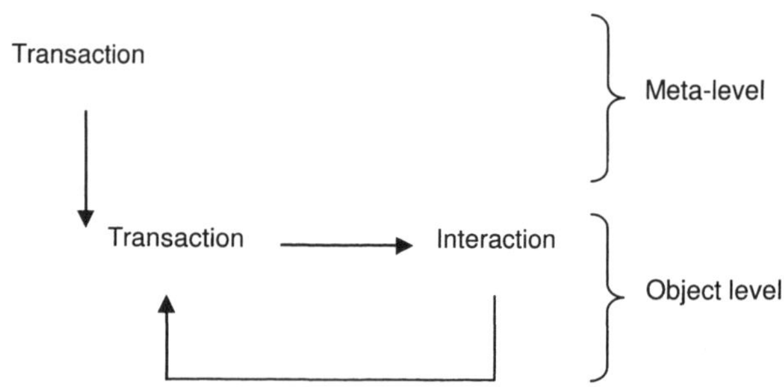

Figure 6.5 Transaction and interaction in a CX5 pattern

This is the foundation on which the criticality of transaction arises. It relies on a hierarchy in which transaction subsumes interaction. Interaction is the product

(P_o) of transaction as a generative principle (GP_o) at the object level. Whenever the problem-situation is or becomes determinate or well structured, transaction (GP_o) is held in reserve or deactivated and interaction (P_o) operates without any explicit consideration of its GP_o, as if it were independent of it. It loses its apparent independence in such cases where the situation is or becomes indeterminate.

The character of a situation depends in CX5 on a behaviouralist pattern that is socialised through the D^* constraint. Indeterminateness and determinateness have equivalents in non-satisficing and satisficing. However, the latter are structured by a behaviouralist pattern whereas the former have no such structuring specific pattern. Thanks to this pattern the criticality of non-separation is endogenised in CX5 thus maintaining a continuity in the conduct of inquiry between the separationist and non-separationist procedures. These features are summarised in Table 6.4.

Though it is much simplified, this first comparison of CX5 with the three components of the Deweyan circular transactional view shows similarities and differences. They are similar in their reliance on a participatory theory of knowing. Inquiry is initiated by a disruption in activity and ignorance about how to go on. This feature is common to both views. However, the substance of the problem is different: in one case it is to move toward non-separation; in the other case it is to design a better-structured situation. Transaction and its reliance on distinction may superficially look common to both approaches. However, distinction derives from an initial separation in Dewey whereas it is the structured basic unit of analysis in CX5. The criticality of non-separability appears once more as the key differentiating factor.

Table 6.4 A sketchy comparison of the Deweyan circle with CX5

Components	Deweyan transactional view	Counterparts in CX5
1. Theory of knowing	Participatory	Participatory
2. Transaction	From ontological separation to distinction within a whole	Theorising irreducibility. Basic unit of analysis is a structured, hierarchised distinction (GP_*P)
3. Inquiry	Transformation of an indeterminate situation into a determinate one	Transformation of a deeply ill-structured problem-situation into a better- structured one
4. Combination of 1, 2 and 3	• Non-separation as transaction • Transactional strategy • Primacy of context of transactional inquiry: Autonomy of inquiry	• Critical non-separability • Critically transactional view • Context of critically transactional inquiry

This is possibly the main insight of CX5 for the transactional perspective. Once the latter is reshaped as being critically transactional through the CX5 pattern, the ambiguities that we detected disappear and the connection with research is endogenised. The next step is to pursue the inquiry and conceive how the connection with research can develop substantially through operational principles at the levels of methodology, method and theorising.

With the CX5 pattern, the connection of transaction with interaction becomes the *transaction of* transaction with interaction. CX5 provides a transactional pattern for transaction. In Deweyan terms, CX5 is the 'more inclusive whole' into which the initially de facto separated transaction and interaction are converted into distinguished inseparable moments of a unified process, that is, CX5. CX5 is a transaction, a critical one rather than a plain Deweyan transaction. Yet, although CX5 appears on the whole to belong to a transactional perspective, should we satisfy with this labeling or should we retain the *critically* transactional character of CX5, thus signalling the connection with separability and the necessary continuity that it implies in research? This is the issue addressed below.

Two pathways to non-separation

It was shown in the previous section how CX5 brings an answer to the issue of the connection of non-separation with separation, that is, of transaction with non-transaction as interaction. Criticality provides this connection. The way criticality emerges was documented in Chapters 3 to 5. Although it retains the word 'transaction', the notion of critical transaction is not the plain Deweyan transaction. Its specific character needs to be established. This will be done in a first step through a systematic comparison with the Deweyan transactional view. It will appear in a second step as an alternative perspective, the one sought for GP_{mm}.

Since non-separation is a common essential feature of the transactional view and of CX5 they might easily be equated to one another. That would be misleading. The reasons for this are not straightforward and require explanation. This is done in Table 6.5. A systematic comparison is pursued through nine headings provided by the various steps and components of inquiry, ranging from the initiating problem to the still pending issues, through the built-in thrust, the central concepts, the substance of the argumentation developed, its outcome, the underlying theory of knowledge, the resulting perspective and its scope. The only complete similarity is the participatory theory of knowing under the sixth heading.

The 'vertical' composition of the nine items in each one of the two columns shows their specific coherence. Three big differences must be pointed out.

The *first* difference is about the origins of non-separation. It is immediately present in Dewey's thought as the negative of dualisms, as a way to react to them, even though it was not named 'transaction' before 1930 and not clarified before

1949. Non-separation appears as a 'necessity', present from the beginning in Dewey, under the different forms of coordination in psychology, of participation in a theory of knowledge, and of the latest advances in physics (Maxwell, Einstein) taken as exemplary instances of transaction. In this respect CX5 is a symmetric of Dewey's transaction. Non-separation is an outcome of inquiry in CX5. This difference explains why the operational thrusts are dissimilar although these initial problems trigger quasi-similar indeterminate situations of inquiry.

Table 6.5 Two pathways to transactional and critically transactional views

Steps and components of inquiry	Dewey Transactional view	CX5 Critically transactional view
1. Initiating problem	Ontological 'excess' of dualism or separation, in psychology and epistemology	Irreducibility to a satisficing level of reduction, in economics and safety management
2. Built-in thrust	Reduce separation, convert separation into non-separation	Transform non-satisficing reduction into satisficing reduction
3. Central concepts	Non-separation as transaction from the start Inquiry	Behaviouralist reflexivity and structured, hierarchical distinction (GP,P) in a double recursive loop ($GP^{**}P$)
4. Argumentation developed	Transactional inquiry	Theorising of irreducibility Critical irreducibility ensuring the connection of irreducibility (non-separation) with reducibility (separation)
5. Outcome	Theory of inquiry Autonomy of inquiry	A theory of complex non-separation Non-separability as outcome of research Critical non-separability
6. Underlying theory of knowledge	Participatory knowing	Participatory knowing
7. Resulting perspective	Transactional view Context of inquiry first	Critically transactional view
8. Scope	Psychology and epistemology	Any deeply ill-structured problem-situation
9. Pending and unsettled issues from the standpoint of research	Elusive underspecified connection of transaction with interaction	CX5 treatment of CX5 still incomplete: 1) Begun with GP_{mm} foundation above: CX5 is critically transactional 2) Awaiting to be complemented with P_{mm} (methodology), GP_m (method) and P_m (theory)

The initial thrust is toward non-separation in Dewey because of an initial hitch or block due to separation, that is, to an 'excessive' prior reduction. Dualism is excessive when it takes an ontological character, which follows from the historically constructed and ingrained habit of viewing as notions existing independently of, and prior to inquiry, what needs instead to be addressed in a context of inquiry first.

In CX5 the triggering factor was the irreducibility to a satisficing level of reduction. CX5 originates in an experience of research. Because of an initial incapacity to achieve a sufficient level of reduction or separation, the ensuing non-separation appears as an ineliminable constraint requiring one to work with it and to theorise about it. It compels one with a built-in necessity to design a bridge, a connecting mechanism to shift from irreducibility to reducibility, or from transaction to interaction in Deweyan terms.

There is no such compelling need to articulate transaction with interaction in Dewey. If one could imagine that the starting point might have been against excessive reduction to 'one-sided selection' in epistemological theory (Dewey, 1938 [1986], 507) then there would have been no thrust toward how to reduce in a more satisfactory way, as is developed in CX5. When you come from an excess of reduction, your concern is to reduce it. When you come from a lack of satisfactory reduction, as in CX5, your concern is to move from an ill-structured to a better-structured situation, that is, a situation more satisfactorily – here, satisficingly – reduced in the end.

It seems that Dewey never derives the transactional character of inquiry from the very limitations of knowledge. He seems to rely on the potential gains of envisaging in a transactional context what was blocked, because it was seen in an ontological context. Non-separation has a philosophical origin in the Deweyan transactional view, either as an initial hypothesis or as an outcome of philosophical reasoning. In CX5, non-separation is an outcome of theoretical research.

A *second* difference follows from the undifferentiation and the absence of structuring of transaction which were analysed above. They have implications for the way the subject-matter of non-separation is organised.

We have already mentioned the high variety of couples of notions considered as transactional by Dewey. They range from mind and matter, subject and object to organism and environment. We even evoked instances of relationality in physics taken by Dewey as inspiring sources for transactional thinking. These cases bear both on the world external to the observer and on the couple (*PEW, W*) or subject and object. There is no structuring, no hierarchy in the instances of transactions in Deweyan thought. This aspect contrasts neatly with CX5 where the non-separation of (*PEW, W*) is prime.

Yet the above non-separation is not only prime in CX5, it is so in a critical way. The very notion of criticality and its endogenised mechanism constitute the *third* major difference from Dewey. Although a coexistence of transaction and non-transaction is present in Dewey's thinking, an explicitly specified and endogenised mechanism of criticality is absent.

In CX5, critical irreducibility is the mechanism of conversion of non-separation into separation and vice versa. This mechanism provides the link which was missing between philosophical thinking and action as theoretical research outside of philosophy. It does not consist in a mere addition to the views evoked above in this chapter, be they Piagetian or Morinian. It is in the nature of an internal relationship and involves a linkage and its consistency between several stages of a chain, ranging from a theory of knowledge to action and vice versa.

CX5 is transactional but critically so, not plainly: it is transactional at the meta-level, and possibly transactional or interactional at the object level. This is in the same way that CX5 means irreducibility at the meta-level and irreducibility or not at the object level. It depends upon the character of the problem-situation at the object level. It obeys an explicitly built-in procedure which ensures continuity of interaction with transaction. It enables a shift from interaction to transaction when the situation proves ill-structured and interactionally intractable, and from transaction to interaction when the situation becomes non-deeply complex. It relies entirely on the procedure and the criteria by means of which a problem-situation can be identified as DCX or not.

In stressing the primacy of inquiry, Dewey:

- evokes the possibility of deactivating it – 'holding it in reserve';
- evokes 'occasions for inquiry';
- but does not explain the mechanism whereby the shift from interaction to transaction and vice versa can occur;
- and seems to be satisfied with assuming de facto that the 'relationality' or transaction observed in physics (in the shift from Newton to Einstein, and to Bohr and Heisenberg) should pervade in psychology, in other human sciences and in epistemology.

A final aspect of these differences is in scope. CX5 extends the relevance of a critically transactional strategy well beyond the domains envisaged above by Dewey, to any deeply complex situation, whatever the domain or discipline.

The critically transactional alternative in its epistemological context

The perspective offered by CX5 is critically transactional. How this feature differentiates it from the Deweyan transaction was explained in the previous paragraph. It remains to establish where this approach stands in the context of other critical views in an epistemological context.

Beyond the Deweyan transaction, we are now in a position to synthesise what is meant by criticality and where it stands with respect to other perspectives which contain also an explicit reference to being 'critical'. From this standpoint, CX5 is critical in several ways:

- CX5 is critical because 'it starts from the problem', following K. Popper (Backhouse, 1994, 9). Like the Popperian critical rationalism, the critically transactional perspective combines a deliberate openness to criticism with the idea that knowledge is fallible and that 'rationality is critical debate' (Boland, 1998, 88). Unlike the Popperian construct, CX5 is not a philosophy of science. It addresses only scientific practice, ranging from its founding principles to its actual and empirical functioning.
- CX5 is also critical in virtue of OP1, its behavioural self-reflexivity, since reflexivity is the ability to be critical or suspicious of one's own intellectual assumptions (Calori, 1998, 301). It pertains to the active character of the relationship between *PEW* and *W*. It is active because behavioural self-reflexivity is called for in order to identify the problem-situation. A judgement of satisficing is present. No fixed rule or algorithm can substitute for it. Behaviour does not reduce to the sole application of some rule, but it implies the construction of a pathway. This sense of criticality pervades the Deweyan notion of 'intelligent action' (Dewey, 1929 [1984], 160, 170–171, 194) and its connection with judgement, that is, the 'selection and arrangement of means to effect consequences and with choice of what we take as our ends' (ibid, 170).
- CX5 is also critical in the sense of 'critical systems' designed in order to assess the question 'Which methodology should be used and when?' (Flood and Carson, 1993, 10). It comes close to the 'critical systems practice' advocated by Jackson and its three commitments to critical awareness 'of different systems, methodologies and methods' and to human emancipation and pluralism (Jackson, 2003, 303).
- But above all, CX5 is critical for a reason which does not exist in these 'critical' perspectives and which is embedded in OP1 and OP2. The mechanism of criticality originates in OP1, the post-Simonian self-reflexivity. It calls for a judgement structured by the capacity to detect whether satisficing, subject to a norm D^*, is achieved or not with respect to a specific issue. OP2 is the principle of paradoxical irreducibility or composite self-similarity. OP2 means that the pair (*PEW, W*) is irreducible, active and open. However it cannot be maintained active and open in a consistent way without a closure. The mechanism of closure is necessarily at an 'upper', meta-level. It informs and constrains the object-level openness. The paradox of simultaneously having a closure and an openness is only apparent once the nested duality of levels is kept in mind. It is the

> mechanism through which several habitually maintained oppositions get dissolved and reorganised into OP2. Criticality designates a situation or point in time when a critical decision must be made. A decision is critical when it entails a radical change in an important aspect of what is the object of the decision. In this way, disactivating and reactivating *PEW* in (*PEW*, *W*) is a critical decision. Criticality also denotes the situation in which this potentiality of shifting to one or the other of seemingly opposite notions is constantly maintained active and open. OP1 and OP2 in combination make it possible to endogenise this potentiality of a change of state through the articulation of a meta-level with an object level: transaction at the meta-level allows transaction and non-transaction at the object level. The same goes for meta-level non-separation and object-level non-separation-and-separation, for irreducibility (meta-level) and irreducibility-and-reducibility (object level). It follows that most characteristics of CX5 are a matter of degree rather than absolutes and their negations. In this way 'critical' opposes to 'plain' and to several 'isms'. It denotes the endogenisation of the turning point between DCX and NDCX.

Criticality is thus an antidote to the poisonous use of equating transaction with the 'isms' of holism, systemism, organicism and even transactionalism. Although it relies on the active and open character of (*PEW, W*), CX5 is not a plain eclecticism: it is controlled and informed by OP1 to OP5. The form of scientific practice that it implies is one leaving (*PEW, W*) open, subject to the rules of scientific practice. This is a necessary closure. It means that in the end there is a primacy of *PEW*, but at an upper logical level.

To summarise:

- CX5 is not plain irreducibility but irreducibility-and-reducibility;
- CX5 is not plain DCX but DCX and non-DCX (NDCX);
- CX5 is not plain transaction but transaction and non-transaction (interaction);
- CX5 is not plain non-separation but non-separation and separation;
- CX5 is not plain openness but openness and closure.
- CX5 is not against reduction but against reductionism as a general stance;
- CX5 is not against objectification but against objectivism as a general stance;
- CX5 is not against subjectivity but against subjectivism as a general stance;
- CX5 is not against positivity but against positivism as a general stance;
- CX5 is not against separation but against separationism as a general stance.

The critically transactional perspective of CX5 is presented in its general scientific context in Table 6.6. The goal is to make clear where the divide with other perspectives takes place.

Table 6.6 The context of the critically transactional perspective of CX5

Nature of scientific activity	Scientific perspective	Preconception on how to develop scientific knowledge	Epistemology	Context of scientific practice
Shared view: scientific activity as process of knowing and production of knowledge about some object of interest, exposed to criticism and systematically put to the public test	Classical	Separationist	Spectator theory of knowledge	Ontological
	Transactional	Non-separationist	Theory of participatory knowing	Context of inquiry: • transactional (Dewey) • critically transactional (CX5)

It is a divide, not a separation, because the critically transactional view subsumes the classical perspective, in the sense of a non-transactional view. The divide occurs on the basis of what may be considered as a common, shared conception of the nature of scientific activity as a process of knowing and of production of knowledge about some object of interest, this process being exposed to criticism and systematically put to the public test.

It is on the basis of this shared view that the division occurs between scientific perspectives ('classical' and transactional), preconceptions on the development of scientific knowledge (separationist and non-separationist), epistemology (spectator theory of knowledge and participatory theory of knowing), and the context of scientific practice (ontological or of inquiry). CX5 pertains to a context of inquiry in a critically transactional way.

It seems preferable to retain the phrase '*critically transactional*' rather than 'non-separationist' because of its positive connotation and its explicit reference to criticality. It points to the origin of the epistemological divide in an exact manner, after Dewey. This critically transactional, post-Deweyan alternative is also critical to the extent that it subsumes the separationist practices. It offers in this sense another instance of openness, with a closure on the nature of scientific activity. Finally, it is the answer to the initial question of this section: it is the foundational meta-generative principle GP_{mm}.

6.3 P_{mm} METHODOLOGY: OP6

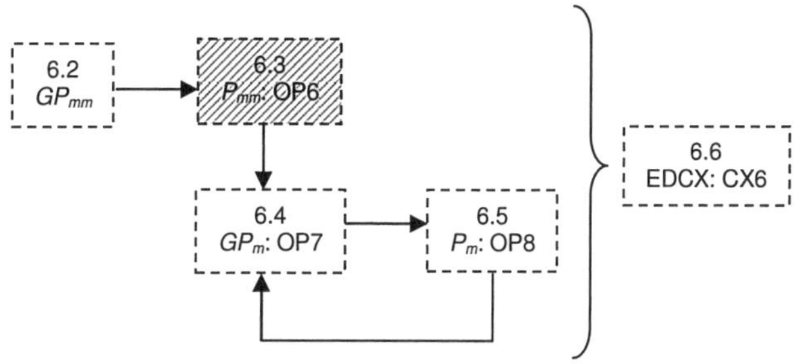

The previous section has provided a firm epistemological grounding for the critical non-separability or critical transactionality of CX5. It entails a subsuming oscillation between DCX and NDCX or non-separability and separation of *PEW* and *W*. It pertains to deeply complex situations. In virtue of the principle of construction OP5 this critical transactionality necessitates to be harnessed and put into play at the P_{mm}, GP_m and P_m levels. At this stage the issue of methodology arises at the P_{mm} level. Does critical transactionality imply a specific methodology? We will contrast the methodological requirements of CX5 with two other significant methodologies in order to determine whether they accommodate what is required by CX5. These methodologies are *methodological constructivism* in management science, and the methodology of *critical realism* in social science. They are compatible at first sight with the notions of being 'critical' and of dealing with complex phenomena in social science. And they provided the substance of a debate a few years ago that we will use as a basis for our discussion. It will help sharpen the requirements of a critical methodology and our understanding of the reasons why none of them, and seemingly no other available methodology, satisfactorily accommodates CX5. The object of the second part of this section will therefore be to work out a methodology for CX5. It will be established that CX5 has essential properties of asymmetry and inequivalence which led to a principle of autonomy of CX5. It will be the sixth principle, symbolised as OP6.

6.3.1 The Issue of Methodological Criticality

The purpose of this subsection is to clarify the difference between the methodological criticality of CX5 and seemingly related constructivist and critical realist methodologies. This comparison will be facilitated by drawing support from an exchange about the relevance of a constructivist methodology for research in strategic management which took place a few years ago in the *Strategic Management Journal.* It originated in the advocacy of a constructivist methodology, contrasted to realism, by Raza Mir and Andrew Watson (2000). Their criticism of realism triggered a reaction in defense of a methodology of the critical variety of realism or critical realism by Kai-Man Kwan and Eric W.K. Tsang (2001) and a response by Mir and Watson (2001). This debate provides an opportunity for discussing the pros and cons of these methodologies. It raises issues going far beyond research in strategic management and will allow us to ask whether these methodologies might accommodate CX5. The answer will be negative in both cases, but for different reasons, thus indicating some aspects that should be integrated in order to accommodate CX5.

A. Two 'critical' methodologies in debate

A.1 Mir and Watson's Constructivist Methodology

Mir and Watson introduce constructivism as a school of thought denoting that research is basically theory-dependent insofar as the theoretical positions held by researchers guide 'what gets construed as a research problem, what theoretical procedures are used, and what constitutes observations and evidences' (Mir and Watson, 2000, 941). It is theory or preconceived notions (a default theory) that drives what counts as observation, what research design and experiments will be acceptable, what techniques are legitimate, and what problems are worthy of attention. Researchers appear as actors 'rather than mere information processors or reactors' who are part of a network that creates knowledge and ultimately guides practice rather than impartial, detached, value-neutral subjects who seek to uncover clearly discernable objects or phenomena. Researchers are part of communities of practice with shared assumptions. Mir and Watson list six important assumptions which, they claim, are shared by all constructivists:

> Knowledge is theory-driven; … the separation of subject and object is not feasible; … the separation between theory and practice is equally unfeasible; … researchers are never 'objective' or value-neutral; … research occurs within a 'community' of scholarship where mutually held assumptions are deployed to create 'conversations'; … constructivism constitutes a methodology. (ibid., 942–944)

The last assumption has a direct bearing on what a researcher may expect from constructivism thus understood. A methodology contains assumptions on how to acquire knowledge. It is distinct from the method or the techniques that are used in the process of enquiry. A methodology defines a frame which informs research. Within this frame, a variety of methods can be used. Being about acquisition of valid knowledge, methodology depends on what valid knowledge is, which pertains to epistemology. Therefore one cannot eschew the issue of defining what valid knowledge consists of, even when the focus is on methodology.

Mir and Watson's answer endorses epistemological relativism. In this view, theory is contingent and contextualised. Clues to what 'good research' is appear in what is advocated and what is excluded. They primarily argue for 'transparency at the level of assumptions and premises. Such transparency renders research *contestable*, and separates good research from bad, the counterintuitive from the tautological, and the contingent from the over generalized' (Mir and Watson, 2001, 1170). Other components of valid research in their account are sensitivity to context, history and perspective, rigour about methodology and circumspection about generalisability, added to transparency, contestability and intellectual humility.

What they exclude can be derived from the way they contrast constructivism with the methodological tradition of realism. They detect three major problems of realism in strategy research: theories are treated as a measure of a 'reality out there'; theories overlook the existence of multiple realities in organisations; and 'researchers write their presence completely out of the research, in an attempt to give an objective character to their accounts' (Mir and Watson, 2000, 946).

Mir and Watson mention an abundant literature relying on a constructivist methodology in a variety of fields ranging from mathematics, physics, chemistry and biology to economics, anthropology, sociology, political science, psychology and education (ibid., 944). They identify methods or techniques which may, as they see them, lay the foundation for a constructivist agenda for strategic management research. They claim that several 'research techniques' are suitable for constructivist inquiry. These techniques include 'ethnography … institutional analysis … textual analysis … appreciative inquiry … and historical analysis' and can be accompanied with quantitative methods such as statistical analysis (ibid., 947). They finally argue for a 'healthy mix of realist and constructivist perspectives' (ibid., 950), which may look surprising given their criticism of realism, and leave unexplained the question of how to mix them.

A.2 Enter Critical Realism: Kwan and Tsang's Criticism

Kwan and Tsang's reaction criticises a lack of clarification in constructivism and an inadequate understanding of realism by Mir and Watson (Kwan and Tsang,

2001). They claim that constructivism is not an improvement over critical realism, and is subsumed by it.

Their first point looks well taken. Mir and Watson fail to distinguish between different types of constructivism and to clarify that they stand in a moderate position. They also fail to distinguish different kinds of realism, notably 'dogmatic' realism from critical realism (Kwan and Tsang, 2001, 1165), although Kwan and Tsang seem to endorse the following list of underlying principles of realism given by Mir and Watson (2000, 944–945):

- the best theories are those that are close to the truth;
- the truth of a theory explains (and is the only explanation of) its predictive validity;
- science is moving progressively towards a true account of phenomena;
- the claims made by any theory are either true or false; and
- only through the deployment of 'reason' can a theory be proven or refuted.

While both kinds of realism believe in the third and fourth principles, dogmatic realists 'further believe that current theories correspond (almost) exactly to reality', an attitude inspired by 'a primitive version of positivism which believes in indubitable observations as raw data and that an infallible scientific method can safely lead us from these data to universal laws' (Kwan and Tsang, 2001, 1165).

In contrast, critical realists, though believing in the first and fourth principles, would not take progress towards a true account of phenomena for granted. And they would not accept the second and fifth principles. Precisely because they believe that reality exists independently of our minds and that it is structured (deep, actual and empirical levels), they believe that our knowledge of it is fallible. Therefore current theories are not mirrors of reality, verification and falsification are never conclusive, and prediction is unwarranted especially in social science. Critical realism is anti-positivist. It emphasises that the actual events that we observe in the empirical domain are produced by generative mechanisms which reside in the deep domain. Events depend on contingent conditions. And critical realism can accommodate the context-driven nature of theory creation since theories are products of the mind's activities at the epistemological level, which is compatible with maintaining that there is a mind-independent reality at the ontological level.

A.3 Response and Discussion

Mir and Watson argue in their response that constructivism and critical realism in strategy research are compatible but not equivalent. The compatibility can be seen from the features that are common to both views as mentioned by Kwan and Tsang. However, Mir and Watson reject the claim that constructivism might be subsumed under critical realism. They argue that critical realists still subscribe to the realist notion that there exists an 'inherent mind-independent' order of things while constructivists 'attribute structures not to a mind-independent reality, but rather to the generative (and therefore constructive) act of researchers' (Mir and Watson, 2001, 1169)

In order to gain clarity, in Table 6.7 I contrast the implications of constructivism and critical realism as viewed by Mir and Watson. It remains to assess whether these perceptions are representative and helpful for CX5.

Although Mir and Watson seem at times to restrict their discussion to strategic management research, they extend it to other fields when they list in support of constructivism a variety of constructivist contributions in a number of fields, be they natural or social, thus implying that they address the constructivist methodology independently of a reference to a specific field.

Table 6.7 A synthesis of Mir and Watson on a constructivist perspective and critical realism

Methodological constructivist perspective	**Methodological consequences of critical realism**
Focus on the manner in which researchers constitute theories in the act of describing things	Predicated upon an inherent order of things graspable by research
Theory is an act of generation.	Theory is the formalisation of an underlying reality.
Reality as a construction of the researcher	Our grasp of reality is partial but we can hope to achieve a better knowledge of reality.
Realities as essentially products of different contexts, perspectives, sense-making mechanisms	Reluctance of critical realism to distance itself from the contention that a true explanation of reality is possible.
Overdetermination of phenomena. Replication is not the central issue	Replication of empirical tests is a key to matching the reality they address.

The debate above is indeed a case in point of some of the problems presented by the use of the constructivist and critical realist terms. It explains why I avoid the use of the term 'constructivism' for CX5 although, as was mentioned in this chapter, the CX5 perspective might be termed 'constructivist' but *critically* so. The kernel of the problem is in the epithet 'critical'. The perspective of CX5 is in disagreement with this constructivist view under four headings. It will also appear in a fundamental disagreement with the critical realist methodology

The first problem concerns the 'healthy mix of realist and constructivist perspectives'. It is an instance of unspecified eclecticism in the absence of any clue about how to combine the two views. Constructivist perspectives are replete with recognitions of the relevance of mixing contrasted notions but no one, to this author's knowledge, provides a mechanism thanks to which it would turn into an effective methodology. Secondly, Mir and Watson fail to differentiate ontological and epistemological views of constructivism. Their presentation of a reality as a construction of the researcher (ibid., 1171) without qualification is especially contentious. They add confusion when they want to illustrate it by taking a decline in the U.S. stock market as an example of a phenomenon that is socially constructed by actors (in this case, investors). It is difficult to understand how it is also a construction of the researcher. It is also difficult to see how the above sentence fits with their concluding statement that: 'reality is as much a manifestation of our own social construction as it is of natural forces beyond our control and understanding' (ibid., 1173). Then, either Mir and Watson's scope is limited to strategic management or social science and the former sentence makes sense but it is not clear what 'natural forces' evoked in the latter are manifest in social reality; or Mir and Watson aim to cover the social and natural domains, like in the second sentence, but then it is difficult to see how nature is an unqualified construction of the researcher. This confusion might be avoided if the ontological aspect of reality and its epistemological and methodological aspect relevant to methodological constructivism were clearly distinguished, something which Mir and Watson fail to do.

The constructivism that was presented above with Piaget and von Glasersfeld does not address ontology in any specific way. It does not reject having a view on the world but this view originates from a cognitive standpoint. It is fallibilist, therefore it preserves an openness and introduces one single broad hypothesis on the world perceived and experienced as processual and relational. This is the view exposed above and which fits with CX5. It is one thing to say that reality is a construction of the researcher, and another to say that from an epistemological standpoint the researcher participates in the construction of reality and that the reality experienced itself has an influence on the researcher and on the process of knowledge production. CX5 fits with the latter but obviously not with the former.

Thirdly, their argumentation about overdetermination is oversimplified. Overdetermination means that phenomena have multiple potential causalities, 'an overdetermined process … is determined by each other process' (ibid., 1172). According to Mir and Watson, if all events are determined by 'potentially infinite causalities, an empiricist search for linearity in causality or a realist search for a replicable reality is futile' (ibid., 1172). If it is taken at face value, such a statement is hardly acceptable in research. Not all events are overdetermined. Research on a particular topic in a discipline is always conducted locally and whether local causalities can be detected or not, and replicated or not, depends on the particular situation. When it is simple enough, stable or transparent, and well circumscribed, to use the terms we introduced in situation recognition (Chapter 3) one would find difficult to understand why looking for causalities would be futile.

While everything may be overdetermined at a (very) general level, its linear projection on the local levels of research is hardly acceptable. This is a clear instance of a failure to distinguish a general and a local level in research. Its consequence is not only an oversimplification, but it is also irrelevant to a variety of situations.

B. An unresolved problem

B.1 The Critical Realist View Reassessed

Finally, the presentation of critical realism by Mir and Watson may ironically render obvious a weakness of constructivism due to the absence in it of a clear criterion of truth or validity of theories, while true explanations of reality would be possible in critical realism. It is notably with respect to the notion of truth that a more elaborate view of critical realism can be found in Tony Lawson's discussion of truth in economics (Lawson, 1997).

Lawson claims that truth as correspondence between discourse and extra-discursive reality is misleading:

> [The] thesis of the (existential) intransitivity of objects or ontological realism (that things in general exist and act independently of our knowledge of them) must be tied to the thesis of the historical transitivity of knowledge or epistemological relativism (that there is no way to know what exists except under particular, historically transient, descriptions) … creative subjects do not constitute the world (as in idealism including its post-modernist or pragmatist variants) but also … thought cannot be regarded as a mechanical function of the world (as in empiricism). Rather, knowledge must be seen as consisting of stuff that is socially produced, typically symbolically mediated and formed, historically specific, and materially irreducible to its (intransitive) objects'. (ibid., 239)

In order to capture the fallible, historically transient, and transformable characteristics of knowledge, the notion of knowledge as *expression* is preferable to correspondence or mapping according to Lawson. This 'fallibility and transformability' of knowledge does not preclude the possibility of objective truth 'as something which holds or exists independently of any individual's beliefs'. Indeed, 'propositions are true, or contain truth, by virtue of the way that the world is' (ibid., 239, 240).

In its objective aspect under consideration in critical realism, the term truth functions both as an attribute of propositions and as a property of the reality expressed. This inherent duality exists also for terms such as 'scientific law', 'explanation' and 'history'. To know their meaning we usually need to know their context. Following Bhaskar, this duality can be seen as epistemic–ontic or expressive–referential: it turns on the condition that: 'while the *referents* of discourse, i.e. the conditions and states of affairs which form the intransitive objects or knowledge, exist (relatively) independently of us, they can only be *expressed* by us via human mediation in cognitive discourse'. Truth appears as an expressive–referential dual. In its expressive or epistemic aspect, truth designates 'the truth-values, truth-judgments and truth-claims' of scientific activity and discourse; in its referential or ontic aspect, truth designates the referents, the states of affairs expressed 'which exist relatively independently of us and by virtue of which our claims are (or are not) true' (ibid., 241).

There is no external point for determining the truth of a proposition: 'There is no way of comparing the world and a sentence to see whether they match. The fallibility of knowledge must be accepted' (ibid., 242). A judgement is called for. Truth judgements will incorporate 'ontological/evidential'components as well as pragmatist (persuasiveness, simplicity, standard of rhetoric, vested interests) and coherentist (consistency) considerations. An epistemic relativity of knowledge is thus accepted, that is: 'there is no way of knowing what exists except under particular, historically transient, interest-guided descriptions' (ibid., 243) but it does not necessarily imply a judgemental relativism, that all theories are equally valid. A necessary condition for a judgemental rationality is the conjunction of epistemic relativism with ontological realism: the commitment to realism entails that a priority be given to 'the power of some theoretical claim to illuminate a (relatively) mind independent reality' (ibid., 243).

Explanation, both pure and applied, relies in part on retroduction or abduction. Competing theories are to be assessed empirically on the basis of their explanatory power 'which may reduce to predictive power in those conditions, such as experimental control, where one (set of) mechanism(s) can be materially insulated' (ibid., 244).

Lawson's argument is therefore less simple than what appears in Table 6.7. I relied heavily on his book for the sake of transparency and in order to reproduce its particular tone and its normative orientation.

B.2 The Criticality of CX5 Not Accommodated

After having come across constructivism and critical realism several times on our way toward constructing an answer to the issue raised by our initial cognitive dissonance in this book, we reach for the first time a stage where the divide with CX5 can be finally identified and given a name, something which was previously impossible because of the very progressiveness of the process of construction and of the incompletion of CX5. *Criticality*, understood as endogenised oscillation, denotes this divide. It is closely tied to the *non-separation* both of *PEW* and *W*, and in *W1*, understood as a *critical non-separation*. Let us take the two methodologies one after the other, before we propose a synthesis.

Mir and Watson emphasise that constructivism focuses on the manner in which researchers constitute theories. The constructivist theorising is an act of generation, whereas its realist equivalent is a formalisation of an underlying reality consisting in an inherent, mind-independent order of things. They maintain the quite contentious claim that constructivists see reality itself as a construction of the researcher (Mir and Watson, 2001, 1171). Critical realism seems to come close to CX5 in its basic ontological assumptions of internal relationality, process and uncertainty (Lawson, 2006) and its methodological traits emphasising the search of generative mechanisms, retroduction or abduction, appreciative theorising, history-friendly models, and interdisciplinarity (Castellacci, 2006).

Both perspectives profess an opposition to positivism and empirism although they diametrically oppose each other about the sense of influence between subject, or the process of enquiry into the world *PEW*, and object, or the world *W*. This influence goes clearly from *PEW* to *W* in constructivism, and in the opposite way, from the external world *W1* to *PEW*, in critical realism. This opposition brings us back to an age anteceding Dewey, Piaget and von Glaserfeld.

Notwithstanding his ceaseless criticism of mainstream economics, Lawson overlooks that its cornerstone is much deeper than positivism, empirism and deductivism. It is separationism, especially the separation of *PEW* and *W*, which is the basis of objectivism. Critical realism cannot accept a situation in which complexity is not intrinsic to objects lying in *W1*, and in which it is deep enough to create a cognitive dissonance in a *PEW* which is necessarily active if it is to perceive a deep cognitive gap and to support behavioural reflexivity OP1. The problem is deeper than positivism or empirism, it is with separationism. It may appear as an irony that a perspective so obsessed with deep reality as critical realism overlooks that separationism is a real problem at a deeper level than its habitual criticism of the way social science, notably economics, works.

Uncertainty is said to be pervasive in the ontologically complex world of critical realism but it never pervades *W2* or *PEW*. It remains inside *W1*. This uncertainty never attains the researcher *PEW*, which would compel looking into the black box and admittitng its active role. It still looks like an unsurpassable taboo for the separationist view to which both the economics mainstream and critical realism belong. Only knowledge as 'stuff … socially produced' and its 'epistemic relativism' is acknowledged to play a significant but not preponderant role in judgemental rationality, in combination with ontological realism.

On the whole the epithet 'critical' in critical realism has a different meaning than in the critical non-separation of CX5. In critical realism, it means 'critical of plain realism', whereas it denotes the oscillation between *PEW* and *W* in CX5. There is no oscillation in critical realism. Separation can never be suspended in it. What is critical in it is realism itself which cannot do without separation complemented with epistemic relativism. Epistemic relativism results from the lack of true access to reality, it cannot be avoided.

In critical realism, knowledge originates mainly from a world limited to the external world *W1*; the task of science is to express it; *PEW* remains constantly passive; this one-way influence can be symbolised as:

$$W1 \longrightarrow PEW$$

It contains no sense of an oscillatory interplay of *W* and *PEW*.

Methodological constructivism emphasises the epistemic side through an essentially one-way influence. Although it alludes to a 'mix' or a 'middle path' with critical realism, in Mir and Watson's version, it proposes no mechanism for it. Knowledge originates in it mainly from *PEW*. It can be symbolised as:

$$PEW \longrightarrow W$$

In CX5, this relation is fully oscillatory and endogenised: at times it can be with a priority on *W1*, with a given *PEW*, at times the priority is on *PEW*. The mechanism consists in the combination of the five OPs using the tools designed for recursive thinking. It can be symbolised basically as:

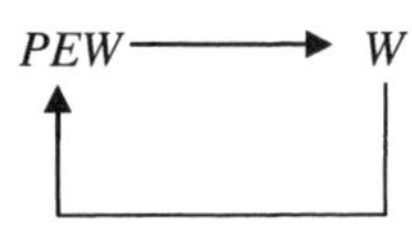

and

$$(PEW{**}W)$$

in which: *PEW* is the generic process of enquiry into the world *W*; *W* includes *W1* and *W2*; *W1* is the world external to *W2; W2* is the process of enquiry into *W1*.

As we already stated in 6.2 above, *PEW*, or knowing, experiences and organises the world *W* which itself sets the conditions for the *PEW* which experiences and organises the world *W* which and so on.

We synthesise in Table 6.8 the results that we have obtained at this stage about criticality. We rely on contrasting four perspectives, including Dewey's, with respect to oscillation and its endogenisation, the two components of criticality. Oscillation bears on non-separation–separation or its equivalent transaction–interaction in Deweyan terms. It operates at two levels in CX5, at the level of the relationship of *PEW* with *W*, and at the level of the external world *W1*.

Table 6.8 Four perspectives contrasted from the standpoint of methodological criticality

Main sources	Non-separation, transaction: Of *PEW* and *W* — Oscillatory	Of *PEW* and *W* — Not oscillatory	In *W1* — Oscillatory	In *W1* — Not oscillatory	Criticality as endogenised oscillation
Dewey	Quasi; not endogenised	/	Quasi; not endogenised	/	No
Mir and Watson on constructivist methodology	Unspecified 'healthy mix' or 'middle way'	*PEW* → *W*	?	?	No
Lawson on methodology of critical realism	/	*W1* → *PEW*	Partially, at surface level, as epistemic relativism	Ontological realism: from deep structures to surface phenomena	No
CX5	Oscillatory; endogenised	/	Oscillatory; endogenised	/	Yes

The former has already been abundantly documented above. The latter bears on the relationality of *W1*, especially internal relationality. It can be suspended provisionally and leave room to external relationality, that is, mechanistic and atomistic features provided it is explicitly justified.

We refer to terms like separation, non-separation, transaction and relation to designate notions which in all rigour differ from non-separability, transactionality and relationality: the former usually designate a specific actualisation of the general potential denoted by the latter, respectively.

Criticality means an endogenised oscillation. Oscillation denotes the two-way possible shift from any term of a duality to the other. It is endogenised rather than exogenous, spontaneous or casual when it obeys, or is explained by, a specific mechanism produced within the modelling.

We find in Dewey an ambiguous, quasi-oscillatory move between notions taken as if they coexisted in a kind of repertoire since each of them becomes relevant 'when research requires it'. It remains unclear whether research may require it within a given domain as research proceeds, or whether it is a matter of coexisting domains, some in which transaction is relevant, others in which interaction is called for. Hence the adverb 'quasi'. Endogenisation is at any rate absent.

The comparison contained in Table 6.8 is straightforward for constructivism and critical realism since it directly transposes our comments above. None of these perspectives appears methodologically critical. Only CX5 displays an endogenised oscillation.

The next step will be to assess what kind of oscillation is contained in CX5. Are there other views on oscillation? Is CX5 different from them? This issue will be addressed next and will help identify an additional property, that is, asymmetry.

6.3.2 A Methodology for Criticality: The Autonomy of CX5

We learned in the last section that more than non-separability is required: it is an *oscillatory* non-separability and its mechanism which define criticality sharpened in the course of the discussion of constructivist and critical realist methodologies. We now know that the methodological challenge is to accommodate criticality, that is, the endogenised oscillation of *PEW* and *W*, and in *W1*. This double oscillation amounts to the oscillation between non-separation and separation in both the pair (*PEW, W*) and the external world *W1*: non-separation prevails when the situation is DCX, the same goes for separation when the situation is NDCX. In the end, it is an oscillation between DCX and NDCX. Several questions arise at this point.

First, we need to know if the notion of oscillation is new or if it is already present in methodological thought, in which case its possible relevance to the present problem should be assessed. It should be assessed mainly, and this is the second question, with respect to the guidance it might provide for the orientation of action in one or the other direction. It is a way to address the general methodological question: What are the principles for the conduct of action? CX5 already tells to identify the problem-situation as was done in Table 3.3. But this is not enough. It is even putting the cart before the horse since a prior requirement is to have the resources enabling us to identify a situation in an informed way. This will bring to the fore the issue of *asymmetry* and of its corollary of *inequivalence*, the combination of which will lead to the principle of the *autonomy* of CX5.

A. From oscillation to asymmetric oscillation

The theme of oscillation was already encountered in Piaget's argumentation about the priority to be given to the subject or to the object in the act of cognition. Other noticeable forms of oscillation are between the whole and parts, and between the complex and the simple. They have a prestigious pedigree in the literature.

The oscillation between the whole and parts was evoked by Blaise Pascal and mentioned in Chapter 2. Let us recall it:

> Since everything, then, is both caused and causing, dependent and supporting, mediate and immediate, and all hold together by a natural and unnoticed bond which ties things most distant and most different, I hold it equally impossible to know the parts without knowing the whole and to know the whole without knowing the parts in detail. (Pascal, 1662 [1963], 527)

One may find an echo of this in Wilhelm Dilthey's interpretive method of understanding comprising a circular process of discovery called the 'hermeneutic circle'. It consists of an iterative cycle in which an initial consideration of the whole leads to an understanding of the parts, which in turn enables a richer understanding of the whole (Checkland, 1999, 276). This cycle can similarly be triggered by an initial consideration of the parts leading to address the whole which in turn, and so on.

The oscillation between the complex and the simple was expressed by Henri Poincaré in 1902:

> No doubt, if our means of investigation became more and more penetrating, we should discover the simple beneath the complex, and then the complex from the simple, and then again the simple beneath the complex, and so on, without ever being able to predict what the last term will be. (Poincaré, 1902(1968], 164)

Other instances could also be found in the literature on the implications of paradoxical reasoning (Barel, 1979; Bernard-Weil, 1988; Wunenburger, 1990).

Oscillation means that instead of taking for granted one or the other of the above alternatives, an imperative is to leave these alternatives as open options, indeed as open potential moments or stages envisaged in a more inclusive process.

But then the problem of the mechanism for performing the oscillation arises immediately. The instances of oscillation mentioned above are devoid of such a mechanism. A danger of an otherwise unspecified and undetermined oscillation is the infinite move from one alternative to the other. We encountered it when self-reflexivity was introduced in Chapter 1, with its potential infinite regress. The solution was to decide about a *cutting point*. This entailed the risk of being arbitrary. Solving this problem was the goal of the parts following the initial chapter of the present book. In a similar vein, a frequent criticism to generalised interdependence and systems theory is that everything holds together 'and reciprocally'. We mentioned in Chapter 2, about internal relations, Whitehead's view that: 'In so far as there are internal relations, everything must depend on everything else. But if this be the case, we cannot know about anything till we equally well know everything else'. Whitehead's solution was to propose a nested hierarchy of sets of internal relations. Simon introduced the near decomposability of what he called 'complex systems' (Simon, 1969 [1996]). In both instances, the solution rests on a notion of *hierarchy*.

Other ways of coping with oscillation can be found. They range from *methodological pluralism* to *floating eclecticism* and even *anarchism*. As was already mentioned, *methodological pluralism* is a weak standpoint in the absence of a leading thread structuring it. 'Openness' to different methods in the face of quasi ignorance or fallible knowledge remains a necessary, but defensive standpoint as far as it is most often used in social science, especially in economics, as a means to justify the practice of non-reductionist and non-positivist methods in contrast to a scientistic mainstream. Methodological pluralism has value, but more as a basis. It points to the need of a unified methodological specification enabling methodological openness or pluralism.

Eclecticism in social science tends inevitably to turn into an unanchored, floating eclecticism. It is due to the essential difficulty in designing an empirical justice of peace like the one existing in natural science through separation and the strict and clear-cut protocols of validation which characterise it. This essential feature of social science renders it all the more important to pay a restless attention to how theories are obtained. A firm methodological specification is what is left to rely upon when there is endless disagreement on the theoretical results. One may even contend that a central difference between natural and social sciences lies in their ways to ascertain that a theory works or not: the protocols of empirical validation are incomparably safer in natural science than in social science. This reinforces the need to compensate this weakness of social science by a carefully specified and explicitly transparent exposition to the public of the generating mechanisms through which their theoretical statements are produced. Finally, *anarchism* says that anything goes or, similarly, that no particular method goes, except the method which consists in rejecting any method. It is a way to exacerbate a kind of generalised oscillation in which the reliance on reasonable criteria has been replaced by almost anything susceptible to prevail in the face of counter-arguments, or to enforce belief by, or upon, others.

There seems to be no other noticeable solution to underspecified oscillation. We are therefore driven back to a discussion of hierarchy. Hierarchy designates in Whitehead and Simon a unique ordering, either descending or ascending in a chain of successive degrees of influence or determination, and which applies to the external world *W1*. CX5 is agnostic about it. It does not licence any specific view of *W* except the generic perspective of process, relationality and openness. It does not imply the existence of an a priori hierarchy, and does not exclude the possibility of some hierarchy as well. If there is a form of hierarchy in CX5 it is in the basic pair (*GP*, *P*) or (*PEW, W*): action by a human actor is prime and manifests itself as *PEW* or knowing in the organisation of (*PEW, W*). But it is embedded in a circular relationship, which, after Piaget and von Glasersfeld, consists in a *PEW* which experiences and organises a world *W* which sets itself the conditions under which *PEW* experiences and organises a world *W*, and so on. It appears as a circular or oscillating hierarchy which may also be depicted as an asymmetric oscillation.

The phrase *asymmetric oscillation* may better depict the functioning of CX5 for it covers another essential aspect, the asymmetry of DCX and NDCX. Asymmetry in CX5 originates in the possibility to disactivate and reactivate *GP* in (*GP*, *P*) and in its (*PEW, W*) form. *PEW* is neutralised when it is believed that separation holds and the situation is NDCX: then a taken for granted *PEW* may be applied to a varying *W*. It is activated when the situation is identified as DCX.

Asymmetry can also be shown to arise in the following way. The basic argument results from the very defining properties of irreducibility and of a complex situation introduced here: non-deep complexity holds whenever deep complexity can be neutralised. Deep complexity is the general case. A deeply complex or non-separationist approach makes it possible to integrate non-complexity whenever it is appropriate according to Table 3.3 and OP1. Conversely a non-deeply complex or separationist approach does not make it possible to integrate deep complexity.

By definition, a classical, NDCX approach cannot accommodate DCX, whereas a DCX approach subsumes NDCX. Similarly, it is not possible to accommodate the criticality of the non-separation of *PEW* and *W* with a non-critical pattern, whereas it is possible to accommodate separation, that is, non-criticality, with a critical approach.

In sum, oscillation designates on the one hand the possibility of a move from DCX, under its form of CX5, to NDCX, and on the other hand the possible move from NDCX to CX5. The whole question is: Once in NDCX, how can the move to CX5 occur? It could occur through a similar development as the one which led to CX5 in this book. It would be very lengthy and inconsistent with the availability of CX5. Therefore it would seem more sensible to experience Table 3.3 first with the awareness of the already available CX5 pattern. It means that CX5 is needed to shift back to it. The whole procedure is subsumed by CX5, a property which defines the asymmetric character of oscillation.

The whole question can also be stated in terms of the identification stage evoked at the beginning of this section: What are the resources needed to start and conduct the identification? If the resources available are NDCX, then there is no way to identify the situation as DCX because of the absence of a DCX structuring, by definition. If the resources are deeply complex, in the sense of including the

CX5 pattern, then the capacity to differentiate NDCX and DCX exists. This is the essence of the asymmetry of CX5.

B. Inequivalence and the autonomy of CX5: OP6

Asymmetry characterises the subsumption of NDCX by DCX. It is a solution to the need of an explicitly designed mechanism of oscillation that was detected in the previous section. This asymmetric oscillation and its subsuming property suggest strongly that a prior role should be given to CX5. Yet this suggested inference brings us on to new ground, that is, the value of asymmetry from the standpoint of the methodological process. How should research be conducted? Should it start from DCX and develop accordingly? Or why couldn't it start classically, from NDCX, and progress according to the successes and difficulties it would meet, and lead to complexity in case this necessity would impose itself? The claim held here is that these two alternatives are not equivalent and that the former has a higher methodological value. We develop this argument now.

Instances of these alternatives can be found in the literature. An early claim for the priority of a form of non-separation or conjunction was made at the beginning of the twentieth century by Alexander Bogdanov, a Russian author who developed a reflection on organisation under the name of tektology, and who appears as a forerunner to post-World War II systems developments. According to Bogdanov the acts of joining and separation, or conjunction and disjunction, are basic organisational mechanisms in which conjunction is the primary moment. Any event, any change of phenomena, any development of organisational forms can be conceived 'as a chain of two acts: the act of joining what was separated, and the act of separating what was bound together' (Bogdanov, 1921 [1980], 64–65).

A similar view was expressed by biologist Paul Weiss in his criticism of the step-by-step hypothesis in the analysis of systems in biology which could be extended to complex systems in general (Weiss, 1969). According to Weiss, the living system is 'a system to begin with', life is process, not substance, at the beginning there is coexistence, cooperation rather than isolated things. This led him to be reluctant to accept Simonian near-decomposability, to accept the mechanical interpretation of systems, and to any synthesis following from a separationist starting point (ibid., 6–19).

The priority of non-separation over separationist reduction has also been forcefully advocated by Karl Popper in *Objective Knowledge: An Evolutionary Approach* (Popper, 1972). Popper addressed reduction as contrasted to emergence in the fields of physics and chemistry, both being 'sciences which make assertions about all physical things and physical states, including living organisms' (ibid., 290). He discussed the reductionist claim 'that all the findings of chemistry can be fully explained by (that is to say, deduced from) the principles of physics … and that we may also reduce one day all the biological sciences to physics', with the reduction of chemistry to physics meaning '*theoretical* understanding: the *theoretical* penetration of the new field by the old field'. If the reduction of life to physical terms proves impossible then 'we might speak of life as an emergent property of physical bodies, or of matter' (ibid., 290–292). Although Popper finds 'conceivable, although not yet certain, that the reduction of chemistry to physics will be completely successful', and 'though less likely, that we may one day have good reductions of biology, including physiology, to physics, and of psychology to physiology, and thus to physics', he concludes in a defence of the primacy of emergence: 'So I would say: let us work out in every case the arguments for emergence in detail *at any rate before attempting reduction*' (ibid., 294).

Emergence appears as an outcome of irreducibility. It is therefore a form of complexity, even of deep complexity. It is present in social science as well, where its consequences for analysis are certainly no less difficult to tackle than in biology.

An alternative to 'complexity first' is the step-by-step process of moving from simplified conceptions to others of greater complication and so, it is supposed, being more satisfactory. This process of gradually complicating the picture with the aim of making it more satisfactory (realistic, encompassing) is often referred to as the *method of successive approximation* (Lawson, 1997, 127) and sometimes, with a rather negative connotation in social science, as disjointed or stepwise incrementalism.

One of the necessary conditions for the relevance of this method is that the effects of the causal factors considered in 'isolation' interact mechanically or at least in some predictable fashion. As Lawson states, this condition

> becomes apparent once we take note of the fact of emergent properties, novel kinds, internally related structures and other forms of complex objects which possess properties at their own level, irreducible to their component parts. For in these cases it makes little sense to attempt to understand their natures by looking at component bits or parts *as if existing separately in isolation*. Only if the individual factors operate the same way in isolation as they do in combination, and there are no powers of the more complex entity irreducible to those of its parts, i.e. if the various factors are atomistic in their interrelations, does it seem that the method can be expected to be of use. (ibid., 129)

Lawson's proposed alternative comes close to Weiss and Popper's views. It is to treat entities of the world 'at their own level of being' (ibid., 130), that is, like atoms if they behave in isolation, and organically if they behave non-atomistically and are characterised by internal relation and emergence, which is the case for the social domain.

This kind of argument relies on internal relationality, organisation and emergence in *W1*, the external world. It suggests a sort of qualitative jump. This qualitative jump is fully acknowledged in CX5, not only because of these potential properties of *W1*, but essentially because of the active relation of *PEW* and *W*, prior to what occurs in *W1*. This active non-separation is the cornerstone of CX5. Not only does CX5 subsume NDCX through asymmetry, but it structures a situation bound to remain ill-structured with NDCX. CX5 does not mean 'enlarging the scope' within a separationist approach. It means shifting from a separationist to a non-separationist strategy in which there is room for a *locally* separationist argumentation.

A final argument would be to maintain that ultimately the developments of this book illustrate a methodology of step-by-step construction. Why not leave it to research starting conventionally with NDCX to decide whether it should go beyond the borderline of separation and shift to a functional equivalent of CX5? Although there is in the absolute no a priori impossibility for such a procedure, one may be highly sceptical about its consistency and its relevance. How could it be believed that the process which led to CX5, that some might find excruciatingly intricate, could be replicated or rebuilt at will and in ignorance of the availability of CX5? Beyond that, the search cost of ignoring CX5 would be very high. It is easier to get to DCX when starting with a DCX pattern than when starting with an NDCX pattern, the reliance on CX5 is more efficient than reconstructing without it.

At this point, it seems that we can safely claim that starting an inquiry with DCX as CX5, or with NDCX, are not equivalent. To summarise, several factors explain the gain of starting with CX5. Firstly, it subsumes NDCX and therefore makes room to NDCX wherever it is appropriate. It illustrates the French saying 'Qui peut le plus peut le moins' which can be translated as 'He/she who can do the most can do the least', those who can do the hard things can readily do the easy ones, but it does not work the other way round. What is simplified 'from the non-deeply complex' cannot include aspects simplified 'from the deeply complex' whereas the converse is not true and creates an inequivalence. Is it required to include aspects simplified from the DCX? Yes, if there exist reasons for believing in a deeply ill-structured problem-situation. If there are no such reasons, then simplifying from the NDCX is appropriate. At any rate an informed decision requires the prior awareness of DCX as CX5. The second factor of inequivalence is that CX5 helps structure an ill-structured situation. Thirdly, DCX saves time and effort in this task, compared with NDCX, and is more cost efficient. The inequivalence of DCX and NDCX is symbolised in Figure 6.6.

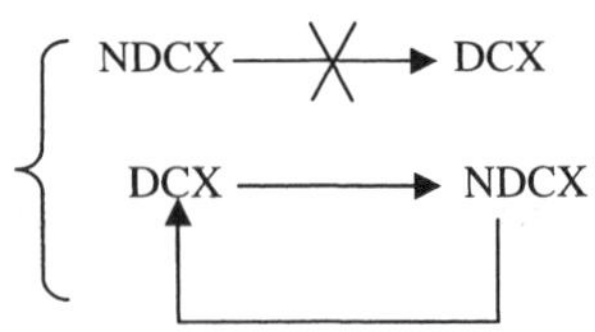

Figure 6.6 Inequivalence in CX5

Figure 6.6 summarises our argumentation. It represents inequivalence as the combination of two relationships. First is the de facto impossibility of moving from NDCX to DCX. Second is the recursive construction of DCX in which the asymmetric oscillation between DCX and NDCX makes them mutually dependent but with a priority to DCX due to its superiority in terms of subsumption, of structuration and of search cost.

Inequivalence relies in sum on fallibility, on a consciousness of the limits of knowledge and on the awareness of the enlargement of the scope of investigation permitted by the DCX pattern: not only does it include what NDCX includes, but it also includes features that are excluded by NDCX.

Inequivalence establishes the autonomy of CX5. It tells us that in order to recognise whether a problem-situation is NDCX or DCX, it is necessary always to act initially as if it were deeply complex. It is a new principle which complements the five organising principles. In effect, it puts into operation OP5, the principle of construction. It can therefore be denominated as an operational principle, with the same OP acronym as the five OPs but with number 6. We state it as the principle of autonomy of CX5, OP6: *Always behave initially as if the problem-situation were deeply complex.*

6.4 GP_m HARNESSING OP6: FROM AUTONOMY TO SITUATION RECOGNITION OP7

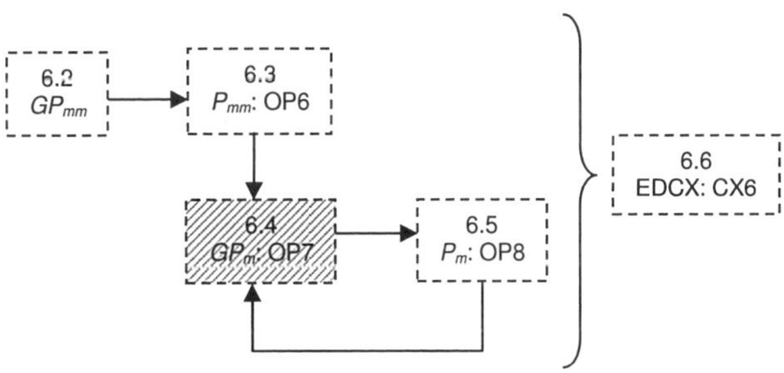

We have established in sections 6.2 and 6.3 the generality of deep complexity CX5 as the autonomy (P_{mm}) of critical non-separability or critical transactionality (GP_{mm}). It provides the pattern in which our whole pragmatic construction has its roots. We now know better where we started from and why our argumentation developed in a specific way. These epistemological and methodological stages cannot however stand on their own in isolation from what they permit to deliver at the meta-level. The meta-level is concerned with the consequences of asymmetry, inequivalence and autonomy for the cognitive situations which constitute the object of the reasoning on deep complexity. A direct consequence of the operational principle of the autonomy of CX5, OP6, is the need to identify deeply complex and non-deeply complex situations.

At the meta-level, the generative principle GP_m calls for harnessing OP6. It will produce a seventh principle, of situation recognition: OP7. Harnessing it in turn through the move from GP_m to P_m, will lead to the eighth and last principle, the principle of action in a deeply complex situation: OP8.

Sections 6.2 and 6.3 paved the way for a more direct and less intricate continuation of our argumentation in the present and the next sections, hence the sort of acceleration which will be permitted by the shorter developments to come.

How is the autonomy of CX5 put into operation? This time the answer is straightforward: there seems to be no other way than following what was done for constructing CX5, in virtue of autonomy itself. This implies that the five organisational principles be put into play. But then, couldn't it be feared that everything might be complex or connected with everything else in a complex way? This is the place where criticality is so important in its role as an antidote to this potential misleading tendency. Through its constitutive asymmetry and inequivalence, OP6 ensures a constant awareness of the potentially oscillatory character of a situation. The very existence of OP6 warrants that 'everything' is not complex. It remains therefore to identify the character of a problem-situation with OP6 as the immediate, initial resource to have in mind.

How to recognise a situation in terms of deep complexity or non-deep complexity starts with being conscious of OP1, behaviouralist self-reflexivity. It goes on through the kind of check list contained in Table 3.3 in which seven dimensions operate in order to detect the character of the situation, which arises as an eighth dimension. This detection is scarcely straightforward. It necessitates a judgement which itself emerges from a social process or debate. There is a growing literature on social judgemental procedures in situations which are similar to complex situations although they lack the pattern of complexity developed here. An instance is 'Post-Normal Science'. It will be evoked in Chapter 8.

It is not our task to engage in these procedural details. And we do not limit ourselves to the situations which appear de facto as complex. We do not take complexity for granted or as attached intrinsically to some particular type of phenomenon. Although the principle of asymmetry OP6 tells us to behave as if deep complexity were always present, it is complemented by the principle of situation recognition (OP7). OP6 is the necessary prior step in order to characterise the situation that is experienced. This recognition of situation is itself a necessary consequence of OP6. If there are good reasons to believe that the situation is satisficing to the participants or the stakeholders, then it is not deeply complex and the classical procedures apply.

6.5 P_m PUTTING DEEP COMPLEXITY TO WORK: OP8

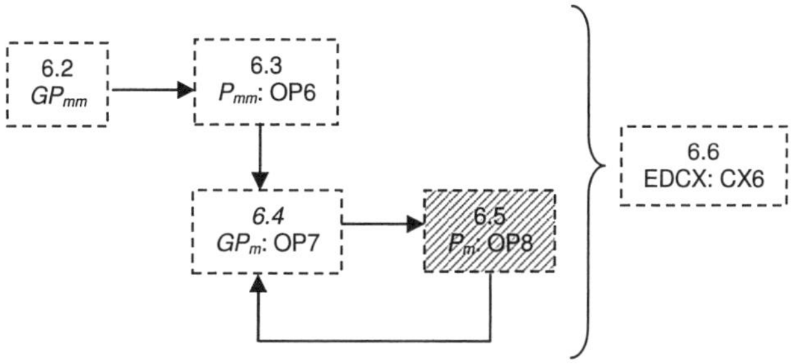

OP8 designates the outcome of putting deep complexity to work. It is the operational principle of 'action in a deeply complex situation'. It is the eighth and last principle of deep complexity (DCX). Action is pervasive in DCX, from self-reflexive behaviour (OP1) to the identification of a given situation (OP7). In that way, it comprises choice. But it goes beyond it. It also includes putting something to work and implementing it.

Putting OP7 to work leads immediately to two possibilities about the character of the problem-situation. If it is NDCX, the usual, classical procedures apply. If it is DCX, it leaves wide open the question of what can be done or of what to do. This is the subject-matter of this section on the product P_m of GP_m. There are indeed two sides to P_m. On the one hand P_m follows from GP_m and the upper steps in a sort of top-down way. It is in this way informed by CX5, and it cannot but be compatible with it and critical transactionality. On the other hand P_m is at the articulation with the object level. The object level GP_o*P_o is informed byP_m and it can in turn influence P_m, in a kind of bottom-up way. Given the unfolding of time the characterisation of the experiential situation at the object level is not fixed once and for all. The situation can become NDCX in cases in which it was initially found deeply complex, and conversely. Hence the two-way flux of information between the object level and the meta-level via P_m. The overall pattern was described in Chapter 5. We therefore need at this stage to include explicitly the object level GP_o*P_o in order to investigate what reference points can be established for articulating the meta-level with the object level. P_m is an interface. At this stage only a pattern of general conditions of action can be envisaged. How they fit with specific issues will be addressed in Chapter 8.

It will be argued below that OP8 needs to include five sub-principles structured as five steps. They are the priority to the experiential problem-situation P_o, complexification, complex reduction, action and validation, and learning and oscillation.

The first three steps are concerned with the issue of how to move from an initial P_o to its generative principle GP_o. GP_o will arise as the outcome of a complex simplification or reduction. How to put GP_o to work is the next issue, addressed in the fourth and fifth steps.

6.5.1 Priority to the Experiential Situation P_o

OP8 is the convergence point of two moves. It is both the meta-product of the process of construction of the generality of DCX, and the product of action following from the character of the problem-situation at the object level. The rationale of the former is to complete the design of DCX and lead to action at the object level. The rationale of the latter is to take action at the object level. Its explicit consideration and articulation with the meta-level process developed thus far is the ending stage of this construction of deep complexity.

The first step in OP8 is also the first instance in which the principles of CX5, which are established at a meta-level, are faced with the object level. This is the reason why OP8 pertains both to the meta- and object levels.

In virtue of OP2, we need an OP8 which works at the meta-level as well as at the object level. In Chapter 5, Figure 5.2, P_m informs directly the generative process GP_o at the object-level. Here lies a big difference with the procedure starting from the object-level problem-situation. It is the situation experienced. What is experienced is normally not transparent enough and well structured so as to make the connection between what is experienced and its generative process sufficiently clear. The whole logic of CX5, and especially its OP4 of abduction, indicate the direction for modelling what appears ill-structured and irreducible as the product of events, tendencies and actions that engendered it. It is a P_o. P_o is the problem-situation as it is experienced at the object level. If it appears deeply complex, it means at least that its connection with a generative process GP_o is not satisficing. This may include a lack of knowledge about GP_o itself. Then, the task is to design it. This is the difference with Figure 5.2. In it, P_m connects directly with GP_o. This is consistent when GP_o is already known or is assumed to be satisficing. Before knowing GP_o and obtaining the situation of Figure 5.2, there is the inquiry or action stemming from P_o. This action begins when P_o is reckoned as being so ill-structured that it triggers a deeply complex situation.

It is this GP_o, once it has been established, which appears in Figure 5.2. Here the issue is the move from the initial, experiential situation P_o, to a GP_o such that it generates P_o. This GP_o has to be designed. In the course of action the direct connection is between P_o and P_m. We can therefore assume that the initial deeply ill-structured problem-situation is a P_o, the product of a GP_o. There follows from it that the orientation of action is to structure better the initial situation P_o. This action requires to be itself structured and modelled. This modelling is our concern here. Whether the action following from it, or likely to follow from it, improves the problem-situation or not, will provide a criterion for its validation.

P_o is the product of events, tendencies and actions. Events and tendencies are themselves the products of actions, past and present, in human and social science. All this can be simplified and P_o viewed as the outcome of action. Although we do not include the natural domain, that is, the domain of things not directly and entirely caused by human action, it is not foreign to human action since any problem-situation implies a *W2*, whatever its *W1* is, natural or anthropo-social.

6.5.2 Complexification

Starting from the experiential situation meant to avoid getting rid of the strongest difficulties and evacuating them through ad hoc assumptions. Complexifying it first, before any attempt at simplification, is the second and most counterintuitive step. It goes against the spontaneous, intuitive move toward the attempt to simplify the problem-situation through dividing it into components that are supposed to become easier to grasp. Why complexify a situation that is already perceived as deeply ill-structured?

A first element of the answer originates from the author's own experience with deeply complex situations. Experience tells us that at any rate simplification and modelling is a necessary step. It tells us also that there is a difference between the simplification or modelling obtained after an initial complexification, and the simplification obtained from what is initially taken for granted. Illustrations will be given in the final chapter. Complexifying renders it possible to become aware of aspects which might be excluded by the spontaneous tendency to divide an intricate phenomenon into separate pieces that are supposedly easier to understand, control or instrumentalise. This is the argument of *inequivalence* already present in OP6.

A next argument follows from *pragmatic consistency*. The way the problem-situation presents itself may be loaded with conventions which worked in the past but not in this case. Then the reduction based on an initial situation possibly containing conventions, and which blocks, is bound to be a dead end. When a situation is initially perceived as deeply complex because no further satisficing reduction works, it would be absurd to insist reducing it further. The status quo, no change, would also be absurd. The only way left open is to complexify it.

Another argument is *enlargement* and its closely connected aspects of *transaction* and *contextualisation*. Enlarging the scope is the way to inquire about whether the initial irreducibility might be due to the fact that some features of the problem are not taken into account. Once it is enlarged, one cannot exclude beforehand that some new features may modify the outcome of reduction and make unforeseen aspects become relevant. It is a way of putting transaction to work, that is, to convert initially blocking separations into distinctions envisaged in a more inclusive setting. Enlarging creates the opportunity for bringing new distinctions. Although there is no assurance that it will deliver a solution, the hope is that it will prepare the way to structure the ill-structured problem-situation. The first element of structuration here is that there must be some limit to enlargement. CX5 provides this through (*GP**P*). According to it, P_o depends in some way on a GP_o itself connected to a P_m, itself to a GP_m, and so on. Complexification makes it possible to envisage these successive levels as contexts rather than as determining factors. It is the analysis subsequent to this complexifying phase that can sort out the determining and non-determining aspects. The enlargement advocated here means more than simply adding new aspects or putting more details on the map in order to come closer to the terrain. It is a complex enlargement in the sense that it is not confined to a given map but it includes the possibility of changing the boundaries of the map.

To illustrate it, I will use an increasingly known brain-teaser. Consider the following. Draw a square on a sheet of paper with its four vertices, the four middles of its sides, and its centre. Connect all of them with no more than four straight lines without lifting your pen and without retracing any line.

I have experimented for years with this exercise as a pedagogical tool for initiating my student classes to deep complexity thinking. Usually, after some time, one or a few students would come with a solution, but the majority of them would remain blocked. When those who get a solution are asked to solve the problem with fewer than four lines, the usual reaction is amazement, at least for those who are not already familiar with this puzzle. It is not by any means new and it has variants in the way its terms are stated, which may lead to slightly different views about its meaning. An instance of it in the context of business management is what the *Harvard Business Review* presented in two issues as the 'nine-dot dilemma' (HBR, 1990, 1991). Letters from readers helped improve the terms of the problem as initially stated by HBR's editor. They proposed new solutions, though they all remained within the overall notion that nine dots were to be connected, as stated by HBR.

The standard solution is to go outside or to think across the 'boundaries' (Figure 6.7a). It can be improved by thinking 'imaginatively about matters of substance … and reaching beyond conventional categories' (HBR, 1990, 10) through enlarging the dots and using three straight lines (Figure 6.7b). This was not the final word. A reader suggested that the dots could be further expanded and become spots connected without using straight lines (Figure 6.7c). One may debate whether enlarging the dots is compatible with the terms of the puzzle although the same reader stated that 'spots are dots far away, but dots are spots up close' (HBR, 1991) which makes it depend on the distance from which the dots are contemplated. No doubt, other solutions might be conceived. There is no one best solution. A simpler version of this puzzle has also been taken as emblematic of the systems approach (Le Moigne, 1994, 289–290).

Now let us come back to our terms. The way the puzzle is stated here does not mention dots for drawing the nine entities of the square. However ill-structured the problem may appear at first sight, solving it does not rely primarily on enlarging dots. Rather it depends on our ability to enlarge the ingrained belief that makes us think spontaneously that vertices, and so on must be represented by dots whatever the circumstances and the context are. There is no constraint here, no explicitly mentioned compulsory scale for representing the nine entities.

Complexification operates through assessing what the constraints are in a given context and what is left open subject to these constraints. In a deeply ill-structured problem-situation, assuming that the problem is correctly stated from the start is the first thing to avoid.

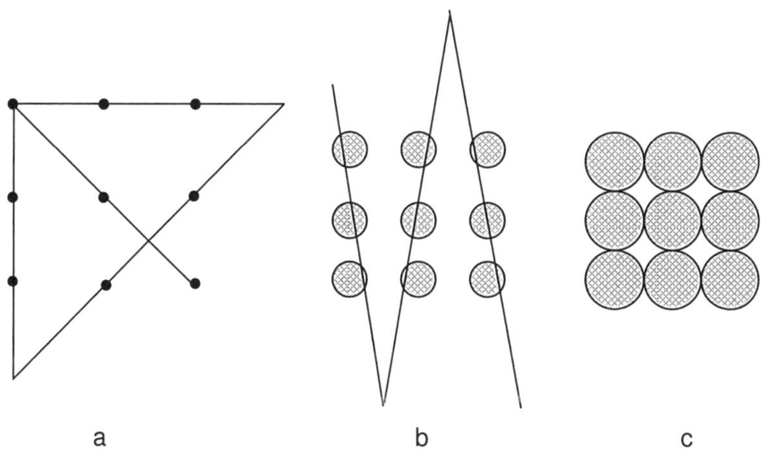

Figure 6.7 The nine-dot or square dilemma

For the HBR, the solution of this dilemma illustrates 'thinking across boundaries, or integrative thinking', the 'ultimate entrepreneurial act' of 'business creativity' (HBR, 1990, 9). This is well taken. However, one may wonder whether enlarging the dots into spots is not going too far outside the boundaries. In the alternative formulation it is the initial spontaneous observer's or 'problem-solver's' behaviour that is in need of enlargement in order to reflect on the way the problem is stated and possibly needs to be reformulated and freed from having to start with dots when nothing in the terms compels this.

Complexification as enlargement of the scope enables us to probe whether a hidden, tacit assumption or routine is operating. Enlarging the scope is commonly suspected and often rejected in conventional science on the ground that in addressing features that are too remote and too numerous, it makes analytical theorising practically impossible. Yet when a situation P_o is experienced as being ill-structured, it might be dangerous to exclude that it might be due to the exclusion, consciously or unconsciously, of aspects that have an influence on P_o but cannot be integrated in the modelling because of the particular assumptions and constraints of this modelling. Behavioural self-reflexivity (OP1) operates fully at this point. The aim is not to reject reduction, it is to envisage a different, potentially more satisficing reduction. Complexification is a transitory and iterative process. It contains no a priori boundary to the development of enlargement apart from constraints of remaining subject to D^*, the standard of good practice in science. It includes consistency and validation. In the puzzle above, nothing in the solution proposed is inconsistent with the terms of the problem. And the value of the solution that is proposed depends on whether the problem-situation gets better structured and whether its outcome is an improvement. The enlargement stops at the point beyond which validation cannot be performed in application of the wisdom according to which the more you enlarge, the more difficult it is to validate. A complementary wisdom is that, in social science, the more you reduce, the more it may become meaningless.

There seems to be no way to fix a point of equilibrium. It all depends upon the purpose at hand and satisficing as exposed in Table 3.3, and synthesised in OP1, behavioural self-reflexivity. The limit to complexifying arises from validation. It is another moment of OP8, which comes after the simplification of what has been complexified, and its putting to work. Although OP8 starts with P_m and P_o sequentially, it is a circular process of interdependent moments. The adjusted degree of complexification depends on its validation. Validation is tied to the action that follows from putting to work the outcome of modelling the complexified phenomenon creating the situation. Modelling consists in a complex reduction coming next to the complexification stage. It is addressed below.

6.5.3 Complex Reduction

Complexification calls for simplification as the next step. This simplification will take the form of a complex reduction to the extent that it is structured by the goal of designing a GP_o for P_o. It is an organised simplification or modelling. How it is organised, what are its substance and its method, what is its expected outcome, are the main questions that arise.

A. Organisation of reduction

The organisation of reduction obeys CX5. Its modelling is unsurprisingly structured according to the five organisational principles of CX5 and the $GP^{**}P$ pattern. It has been abundantly explained above.

B. The substance of reduction

The substance of reduction bears on *W1*, the world external to the actor or the observer. Although we cannot but address it at a necessarily high level of generality, we will claim that this substance derives from P_o in a specific way and calls for a method which will specify and complement the abduction of OP4. In the social domain, *W1* consists in actions, structures, events and ideas. In any problem-situation, one finds a combination of these component aspects with a *PEW* or *W2*. When P_o is deeply ill-structured, it includes both *W1* and an active *W2*. It can be claimed at least that action is ever present in P_o in the sense that P_o cannot be separated from the action through which it is perceived as being deeply ill-structured beyond its presence in *W1*.

The problem-situation P_o may therefore be viewed as the product of actions and tendencies following from a generative principle GP_o. Finding or designing a connection between P_o and a GP_o such that P_o can appear as produced by GP_o is the task before us. Since the situation is deeply complex, we know that looking for substantive determinants of actions making up P_o will not be satisficing. We have to make do with a procedural setting allowing both that determinants be identified and dealt with through causal relationships, thus leaving space for NDCX, and that the rest be DCX. We need to take into account both the potential reducibility of actions, and their irreducibility to NDCX causality.

We therefore need an open-ended notion about the generation of actions. The concept of '*context of action*' seems to meet this requirement. Actions depend on attitudes and behaviours which are themselves shaped in varying fashions by their environment and context. A context of action designates the conditions, material and immaterial, under which people act. It consists in the structures, the relationships and the qualities which compose the conditions in which action takes place. Ideally the more proximate and immediate these conditions are with respect to action, the better knowing them should enable us to understand action. Yet these immediate conditions are themselves the outcomes of, or permitted by, their own immediate conditions which are therefore more distant, or mediate, with respect to action. And it is possible to go further with still more distant conditions.

One may imagine trivial contexts of action in which there is a determinate, transparent and stable or law-like connection with action which would justify reasoning in deterministic or probabilistic terms for the prediction of action, that is, in NDCX terms. However, safety management and accident prevention tell us that even in the most constrained organisations deviances may build up, are even inevitable as 'efficiency-thoroughness trade offs' (Hollnagel, 2004), and leave room for actions creating unwanted outcomes and major accidents, as was abundantly evoked in Chapter 3. In a deeply complex situation, one cannot rely on the belief that an accurate sequence of the process of generation of a P_o can be traced back to a GP_o. Room must be left for the unpredictable and genuinely surprising, that is, the irreducible, in our representation of the generating process.

Instances of contexts of action and their nested patterns are abundantly documented in the literature on safety and accident analysis. Most of the contributions on safety reviewed in Chapter 3, notably by Reason, Rasmussen and Vaughan, rely heavily on contexts of action. A recent addition to this perspective is Hollnagel's conceptualisation of 'sharp end – blunt end' relations in organisational and systemic accident models, with unsafe acts and local workplace factors at the sharp end and, moving toward the blunt end, successive levels ranging from management, to company, to regulator, to government and, still more 'distant' or enveloping, to moral and social norms (Hollnagel, 2004, 62–63). Another instance is in the RISE with its hierarchy going from social and constitutional norms to institutional and organisational forms, and to local conditions.

Another aspect of this nested character of contexts of action is the distinction between structural and functional. The former refers to an architecture, a framework. It connotes the framework into which the institutions, the habits, the routines and the conventions shape the dynamics of everyday activity. Even in highly constraining activities such as manufacturing, chemicals, and so on, operators build efficiency-thoroughness trade-offs (ibid.) which create functional conditions of action that are at some distance from the nominal way to operate. This suggests a more general issue about how the articulation of structural with functional conditions operates. This leads to the question of how these different levels and qualities are interrelated and themselves structured into a whole setting which may appear itself as being a global context for the component contexts of action.

The notion of context of action presents two difficulties, one about the limits when the contexts are remote, and the other about its identification. There cannot be a fixed rule or limit for the former. It is a matter of balance between the need to be selective enough in order to design an organised composition of relations and contexts whose validity can be tested. Identifying contexts of action and their components is the second issue, especially when action takes place within regularities that remain unnoticed because they have been there all along.

Experience tells us that dealing with contexts of action related to complex situations necessitates complementing the method of abduction with an explicit awareness of several methodological orientations.

C. The method of reduction

A central element of method is abduction, the fourth organisational principle of CX5. It follows from the *GP*P* overall pattern and was abundantly documented. However, when we come to concrete issues there arises the question of how to put it to work. A general answer is to develop *GP*P* and search for generating influences on P_o structured into a pattern of contexts of action, which was exposed above. Then the question becomes how to facilitate this search. From our experience, several mutually interdependent tools and practices appear especially helpful and are worth being singled out. They are comparison, integration, interplay and cross-disciplinarity.

C.1 Comparison

When something is so problematic as to create a DCX situation it may be tempting to compare it with other supposedly similar situations, but apparently working better and to try to emulate these experiences. It is a kind of benchmarking. The literature on the management of organisations, be they private or governmental, and the literature on economic policy are overloaded with expositions of success stories and the ways the less successful might take advantage of them. It all boils down to a generalised method of *comparison*. And it is trivial that to be relevant, the things compared must be comparable. Comparison becomes especially problematic when the things compared belong to contexts which differ from one another. Then, unless internal relations do not exist or are so weak that they can be ignored, it is impossible not to take explicitly into account the contexts of the things that are compared.

How to take the contexts into account is a most difficult issue. A context is not quantifiable, not measurable. And the danger of the call for contextualisation is the lack of limits it may convey, and the drift toward the reductionist holism that we evoked at the beginning of this chapter. Notwithstanding this difficulty, the comparison of problem-situations cannot be developed without referring to their context, here, their context of action. The task is then to design a structured setting in which contexts are included, and to compare these contexts within this setting defined broadly enough so as to be a common framework. Before we address this expected outcome of complex reduction, we need to complete the method of comparison.

The interest of comparison can be suggested in the following way. Let us start with a P_o to be compared to another, P_o'. They can be indicators of levels of performance of a given activity, say road safety governance in two countries, leading to different outcomes P_o and P_o' measured in terms of casualties. If the countries are not too dissimilar, they may have quasi-similar structural contexts of action, but different functional contexts. Then attention will be focused on understanding the differences between the components of these contexts. Comparing them may help detect connections between these functional components and P_o, and sort out what appears determinist, causalist, that is, NDCX, and what is only a potentiality. This will be illustrated in Chapter 8 with a comparison of the British and French road risk regulation regimes.

To sum up:

- Comparison is a lever to trigger change and hopefully improve a situation.
- No comparison is valid without due reference to the contexts of the things which are compared.
- Comparison is a tool for identifying contexts, notably contexts of action, provided the comparison bears on structured settings which contain the specific contexts to be detected.

C.2 Integration

In its common sense, integration means the inclusion of aspects which would otherwise not be included. In this sense, it was already present in complexification and it is an important feature of it. The reason integration is singled out here follows from several specific traits of integration which are well beyond inclusion. First, integration has to do with the organisation of relations and contexts of action into a structured setting. Second, integration connotes the combination of holistic and atomistic aspects into a unified whole. Both traits converge on the notion of an organised and processual composition of relationships designed with respect to the generation of P_o and envisaged in their relation to an external environment.

These properties define an open system. Then why not refer plainly to a system rather than using terms like 'setting', 'whole' or 'composition'? The answer pertains precisely to a third specific trait of integration which helps clarify the difference it brings when it is compared to system. This question also provides an opportunity to contrast deep complexity with the systems and the classical, analytical perspectives, in Table 6.9.

Table 6.9 Deep complexity CX5 contrasted to separationist scientific perspectives from the standpoint of integration

	Separationist perspectives		**Deep complexity**: CX5
	Classical analytical	Systems	
Thinking	Thinking locally	Thinking globally	Thinking integratively
Theoretical modelling	Model locally Analytical frame	No unified, structuring frame	Frame of integrative modelling
Action	Act locally	Act locally	Act locally

The comparison is made in terms of their typical styles of thinking, theoretical modelling and action. The choice of these three notions stems from the way the systems approach is said to differ from the analytical perspective: 'think globally, act locally' is the systems motto which supposedly would be contrasted with the analytical 'think locally, act locally'. However, this formulation is shaped by its dependence on the systems motto. It bypasses the modelling stage for which the systems approach is weak, whereas the analytical perspective relies on a strong, unified modelling framework. CX5 also provides a unified modelling framework bridging the upper and lower levels.

Then, why again single out integration since it is already contained in CX5? It is a way to signal the difference between CX5 and systems. In our developments, we could not rely on a supposed 'systems theory' or on a systems typology because they are not established solidly enough. They lack a unified, complete modelling framework. The 'systems approach' could not be a method for designing deep complexity. This is not to deny the importance of the notion of system. But it is only an outcome of deep complexity.

Integration serves to point to what the CX5 process is, that is, the generation, in the end, of a system-like setting independently of the use of a systems theory.

C.3 *Interplay and Cross-disciplinarity*

We take interplay as synonymous with interaction but retain the former here in order to avoid the ambiguity that the use of interaction without qualification might create after its introduction in a specific way by Dewey.

There are three aspects to interaction. The first one pertains to the fact that action takes place *in* a complex situation, not *on* it. The actor is not contemplating the situation from the outside but intrinsically takes part in the emergence of the situation. And the latter's very complexity means that it cannot be controlled satisficingly. There is no initial criterion or tool for controlling or stopping the process from which the complexity of situation arises. Therefore action is in some way bound to *interact with the phenomenon of interest* and accompany its processual character. Experience, co-evolution, watchfulness and assessment of experience appear as forms of 'action for knowing', as means of learning about the phenomenon. A second aspect is *interaction across disciplines*. Most of the time action in a complex situation is *cross-disciplinary*. There is an obvious reason for this due to the fact that complexity usually arises from intractable obstacles in a discipline and calls for searching for new ways outside of the initial discipline. This move does not guarantee that a solution will be achieved but it necessitates to communicate and include a cross-disciplinary participation in the overall action since no one can alone, in isolation, have the same level of competence on a variety of cross-disciplinary issues as the actors who are already familiar with these respective disciplines.

A final kind of interaction is the *interaction with the stakeholders*. They are obviously part of the overall assessment on whether the situation is satisficing or not. Citizens' juries illustrate this participatory process. No assessment of a problem-situation and no judgement of validity on a purely individual basis, in isolation of peers and stakeholders, can be accepted. This suggests two comments:

- These procedures may look resource-consuming and difficult to organise. These three forms of interaction vary in importance according to the problems at stake. The role of citizens' juries in nuclear waste management is a priori different from what occurs in road safety.
- Interplay or interaction illustrates best the notion of openness and closure that is present in all aspects of action in a complex situation.

D. The outcome of reduction

The primary outcome that we expect from reduction is a generative process GP_o. Deep complexity means by definition that a satisficing outcome on P_o cannot be achieved directly. Only generative action is left. This fundamental aspect is downplayed in the current discourse that assesses the merits of theories and explanations in terms of their final outcomes P_o, which is consistent with its separationist nature. The theory of deep complexity developed here establishes the legitimacy of not aiming at P_o in an initial step and of focusing on GP_o.

GP_o emerges as the outcome of a construction in which CX5 is enriched with substance connected by hypothesis with the objec-level initial situation P_o. GP_o combines CX5 with a composition of contexts of action and relationships that appear relevant to the generation of P_o as it is experienced, and that are ascertained through comparison, integration, interplay and cross-disciplinarity. However this primary outcome would remain partial if it were not envisaged explicitly in its connection with P_o, in the inclusive way of the $GP*P$ structuring.

The model which arises will therefore include what pertains to GP_o (relations and contexts of action – nested character of contexts of action between immediate, mediate and distant – and structural or functional), to P_o, and their recursive connection, and is symbolised by GP_o*P_o. GP_o will especially express how what is structural and static gets articulated with what is functional and connects with the dynamics of action. Satisficing insights may hopefully emerge, and non-satisficing aspects may subsist. It seems safe to assume that a final solution to the deep complexity of the situation will not be achieved in one blow. Iteration, experiencing and learning will be necessary. This will take time. The situation itself will evolve. Interacting and co-evolving with the phenomenon at the source of deep complexity is of utmost importance. It is the sense in which the modelling of a deeply complex phenomenon and situation cannot but be processual, relational and open-ended.

An important notion is regularity. It denotes the presence of a durable feature over some period of time. It is this type of feature that renders possible to identify some unity and structure in an otherwise dynamic and evolving process. It is precisely because some features remain roughly unchanged over some period of time, or change more slowly than others, that the other features can be contrasted to them as being evolving. Unchanging features in a process denote a coherence within their own context when they retain some durability. In an overall process composed of activities, actions, contexts of actions and their relationships, the term *regime of action* seems to convey both the notion of regularities and of openness to process and change. This is the way a characterisation of a regime of action emerges from CX5 and complex reduction.

The $GP_o{*}P_o$ pattern can therefore be designated as a regime of action. It comprises two subregimes, structural and functional (Figure 6.8). Their intersection (A) symbolises how structural features are converted into functional ones. P_o emanates from the functional subregime and is not separated from it. It is not the output of an input–output system. It is best understood as an outcome and a recursive source within an overall functional, dynamic setting, symbolised by the functional subregime.

A deeply complex regime of action is defined and evolving over time though retaining its basic features over some period. It is also defined with respect to an external environment, a notion which marks the point where the reference to contexts stops and beyond which is the external environment.

This notion of regime of action will be put to work on the governance of road safety in Chapter 8.

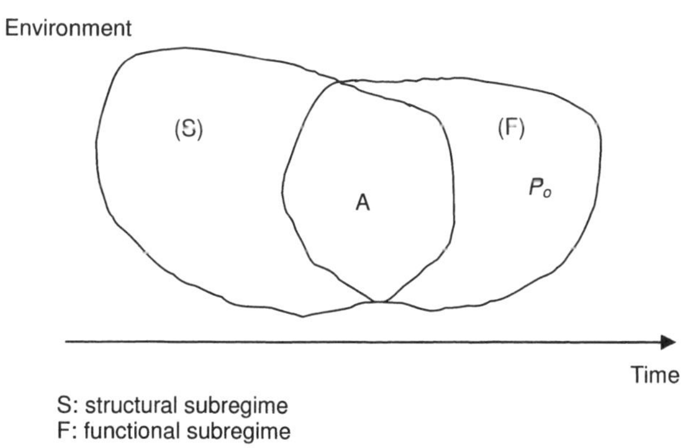

Figure 6.8 A snapshot of the deeply complex regime of action

6.5.4 Action and Validation

Action and assessment or validation are tightly connected. To validate is to assess the P_o outcome which will result from putting $GP_o{*}P_o$ to work.

There is no available toolkit whose established general validity would dispensate from having to justify it and would therefore enable us to move directly to the search for a solution to P_o. Modelling starts with the problem of formulating the problem, of discussing it with respect to a regime of action to be constructed before attempting to solve it. It is symbolised by the move from P_m to the object level.

This is understandably disquieting although two classical criteria apply, namely internal coherence and realism. Internal coherence imposes a consistency of knowing and action with the framework of the eight principles of DCX, under the constraint D^* of good practice in the field. Realism means that no core assumption or statement blatantly negating the experiential world is admissible. However this differs from realism to the extent that validation cannot be reduced to a test of truth correspondence against some external true reality.

Beyond these criteria, the validity of the process depends upon the answers to the two questions mentioned in introduction to OP8. First is the structuring of an ill-structured problem-situation. This is the task performed by CX5, in the move from P_m to $GP_o{*}P_o$ at the object level. Second is the issue of whether the DCX modelling $GP_o{*}P_o$ is susceptible to improve the empirical, object-level experienced situation. This is external validation. To assess it, it is by definition of DCX not possible to rely solely on causality relations or computer simulation. In order to gain knowledge about how P_o is susceptible to be affected by a change of GP_o, there seems to be no better way than taking action on GP_o and judging whether the new experiential situation P'_o is an improvement in terms of the problem which created the initial situation.

This may look very difficult to implement. Yet it points to the direction in which an effort is called for. It helps us to remain aware of the simplification that the direct focus on P_o entails. What needs to be assessed is primarily a process before its outcome. And it should be stated in a way making sense for those who are concerned and informed, both with *PEW* (scientists, and so on) and with the object level (external world agents).

In this sense validation is processual, through creating variation either by way of implementation or by comparison. It relies on assessing change and judgement by the stakeholders. Instances of reliance on judgement are not rare in science, though not informed by an explicitly deep complex setting. They range from Keynes's advocacy of judgement (Chapter 2), Checkland's focus on recoverability rather than plausibility in this chapter, R. Nelson on whether an explanation 'rings right to those who know the details of the field' (Nelson, 1995, 85), to N. Oreskes, K. Shrader-Frechette and K. Belitz about how a model may 'ring true' if it is consistent with our experience of the world (Oreskes et al., 1994, 644).

Finally there is the case when stakeholders cannot agree on what is a satisficing solution. The DCX modelling cannot substitute to it, but it brings an open-ended framework susceptible to structure the disagreement and to host the diverging points of view. It simply assumes a minimum basic agreement on a framework for making clear the material on which the stakeholders disagree. In this case, the inquiry should be complemented by a counter-inquiry in a vein that recalls that a prime feature of scientific knowing is not only to be exposed to criticism, but to cultivate transparency and make every possible effort to render criticism possible.

6.5.5 Learning and Oscillation

Action in a complex situation is a process. It has no final end point although it needs to come to a halt at some point, when it is 'satisficing enough'. However, its implementation may make new aspects appear, other disappear, new information and different knowledge arise and, overall, create a new appreciation. It is not a one-shot or 'ballistic' decision procedure. It unfolds over time. Experiencing and learning are demanding: most often, it takes time to be prepared to accept spending time.

The logical-level duality is fundamental. It structures the articulation between the closure of the representation at the meta-level and its openness at the object level. In this way it accepts what may appear as eclecticism at the object level, provided it abides by the meta-level principles exposed here.

Both the outcome of action through time and the possibility of combining different views subject to meta-level closure render it possible to make difficulties and certitudes evolve. One cannot rule out that features which made the situation appear deeply complex initially will evolve and make the situation become non-deeply complex. Conversely new sources of complexity may appear in the course of action implementation. One needs to beware of taking for granted what appeared in a specific fashion at a point in time. Constant watchfulness is needed.

Even when validation is obtained, one needs to be on guard against treating the situation as constant, and to be prepared to learn from change and evolution. Process and its openness impose to be ready to accept an oscillatory fluidity of knowing and action, and of deep complexity and non-deep complexity. It implies the possibility of reverting iteratively to the product P_m of the identification stage. Therefore action in a deeply complex situation does not bear on the object-level regime of action only. It includes the identification of the problem-situation OP7 and leads to an overall regime of action comprising the product of OP7 and OP8.

To conclude, the internal functioning of OP8 is formalised in Figure 6.9. It is schematised as an overall instantaneous loop of a spiralled process in the flux of events and ideas unfolding over time.

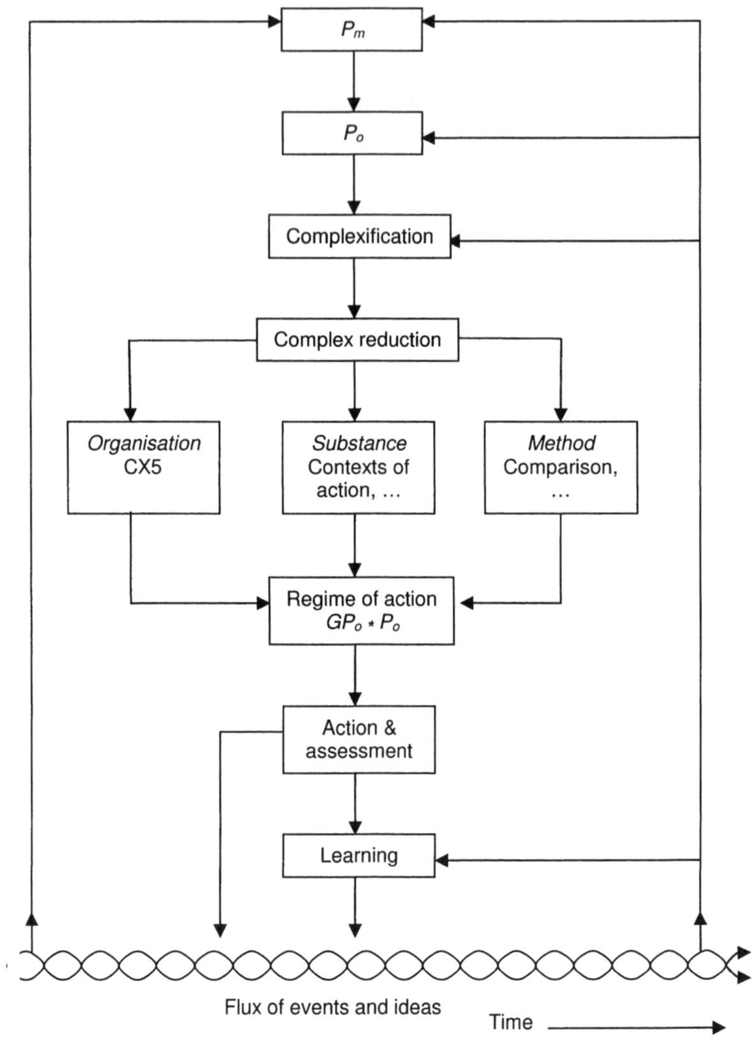

Figure 6.9 The internal functioning of OP8

OP 8 takes its full meaning in its own context of deep complexity (Figure 6.10). The organisation of deep complexity is hopefully made clear in this figure, with the distinction between an overall deeply complex regime of interaction including

PEW, or the observer, and the object-level regime of action bearing on the subject matter of the world external to *PEW*.

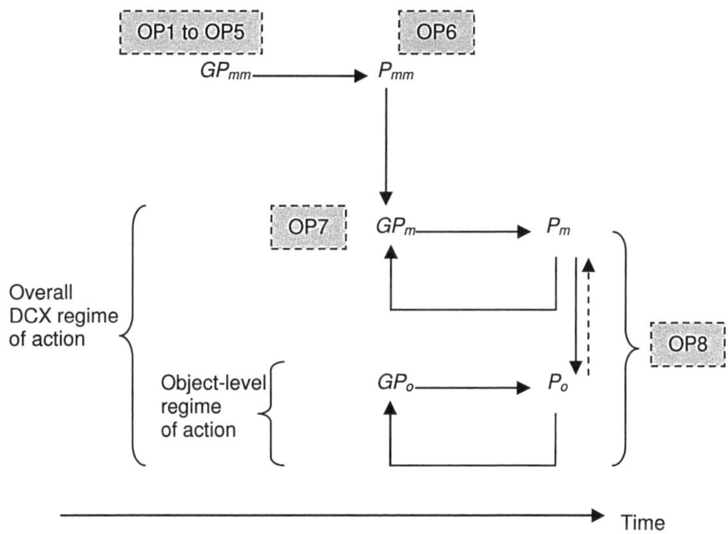

Figure 6.10 OP8 in the context of deep complexity

6.6 EFFECTIVE DEEP COMPLEXITY (EDCX OR CX6)

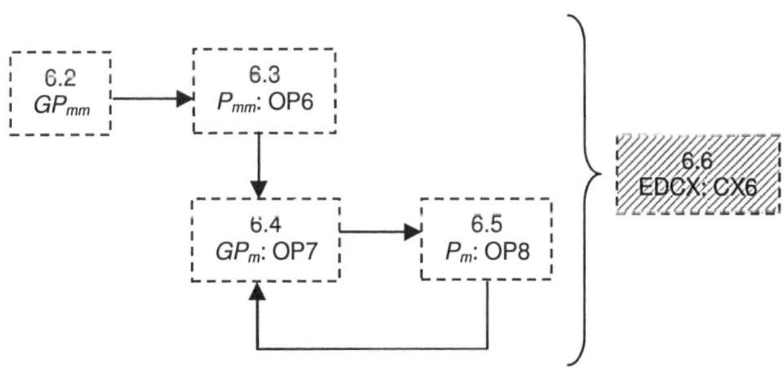

We are reaching a final stage in the characterisation of deep complexity DCX. The substance of DCX achieved with OP7 and OP8 in the previous section adds to the notion of CX5 which was obtained with the five organisational principles and OP6, the principle of autonomy of CX5. This enriched notion of deep complexity includes principles which render it possible to put CX5 into action in a structured pattern. The notion of deep complexity arrived at here is effective; it explicitly combines theoretical principles and principles for action. It constitutes therefore an ending step in our progressive modelling of a structured, satisficing behaviour in response to the kind of obstacle found in Table 3.3. In the same way as we used symbols to identify the intermediate steps from CX1 to CX5, we designate this final notion of deep complexity as CX6 and will refer to it as Effective Deep Complexity (EDCX) or CX6.

Deep complexity as CX6 is therefore no longer mere thinking about knowledge and action. It is specified as a theory of deeply complex situations and becomes an effective modelling. This modelling is also a general formal framework. How CX6 is effective in these two ways, as a theory of deep complexity proper, and as a formal framework, is addressed in the next two sections.

6.6.1 A Theory of Deeply Complex Situations

A constant theme of the present research has been that complexity badly needed a theory of complexity. We claim at this stage that CX6 or EDCX brings a theory of deep complexity proper. Let us discuss first how CX6 is a theory, second what kind of theory it is.

A. How Effective Deep Complexity is a theory

A theory is a self-consistent set of propositions, a model which provides principles of analysis, of explanation or of understanding of a subject matter. It relies on some basic assumption, a methodology and methods, specific concepts, and tools.

Analysis classically denotes the process of separating the constituents of a whole and discerning the manner in which they are interrelated. But the separation and interrelations can be understood and practised in quite diverse ways, which illustrates the ambivalence of the word 'analysis'. On the one hand it denotes the approach to which the systems approach is opposed, that is, the constant separationist attitude in *W1*. We envisaged it in this way in Chapter 1 and came to substitute separationism to it, to denote its exclusive reliance on separation and its corollary of reductionism. It was discussed above with inequivalence. It is the exact negation of the OP8 initial step of complexification which says 'No separation previously to complexification'. On the other hand analysis connotes the process of drawing distinctions, of distinguishing parts and of arguing about their behaviour and their possible connections with the issue of their provisional and local separation being considered as open. It relies on distinction and integration in an inclusive way as is proposed throughout CX6.

It is in the above general sense of theory that we denounced the lack of theoretical specification of complexity in the literature on complexity. This lack appears as a missing link in the chain through which the foundations and methodology inform theory which itself informs – and is informed by – the empirical world. Empirically based complexity illustrated by Soft Systems Methodology, and computer-based complexity appear underspecified as to their theoretical foundations. And deep complexity thinking derived from epistemological, ontological and methodological thinking remains underspecified as to its theoretical mechanisms and empirical practical implications.

The *subject-matter* of EDCX is deep complexity defined as the irreducibility to a satisficing solution within a separationist setting. This property is constitutive of the deeply ill-structured character of a problem-situation. EDCX does not guarantee a final solution but it does bring a structuring to deeply ill-structured problem-situations. The basic essential *assumption* is the principle of behaviouralist reflexivity OP1. Given the singularity of any deeply complex situation the *method* is primarily abduction (OP4) combined with all the other principles from OP2 to OP8. The *fundamental concepts* are duality and paradoxical irreducibility transformed ultimately into the master notions of critical non-separability and process. Four root dualities are at work in EDCX: procedural and substantive rationality; meta- and object levels; generative process *GP* and its product *P*; and the process of enquiry into the world and the 'world' itself, both as (*PEW*, *W*) and (*W2*, *W1*). The permanent combination of these dualities is the defining characteristic of EDCX. From them there follows the qualitative, the quantitative and the processual characterisation of deep complexity which achieves a final step with CX6. The *basic tools* are the generic recursive loop *GP*∗*P* and its nested pattern *GP*∗∗*P*.

The combination of these constituents composes the set of the eight principles OP1 to OP8. This combination is the theory of Effective Deep Complexity or CX6.

B. The kind of theory Effective Deep Complexity is

The domain of EDCX is any deeply ill-structured problem-situation irrespective of the specific field, activity or scientific discipline in which the situation arises. The immediate consequence is that it brings a structuration to the ill-structured. It helps sort out the deeply complex and what is not deeply complex through the recourse to the check list supplied by Table 3.3 which applies to a variety of situations. Then EDCX appears as a theory of what a DCX or a NDCX situation is, how it arises, and what its consequences are for action.

The typical outcome of EDCX is best symbolised by the (*GP*, *P*) process. By construction, the primary outcome of CX6 theorising is on the generative principle *GP*. This will undoubtedly be disconcerting at first sight for the usual view expecting results to bear on the level of *P*, the product in (*GP*, *P*). Yet it is totally consistent with having a deeply ill-structured problem-situation to begin with. The primary focus of EDCX is on *GP* and the recursive consequences which follow from harnessing it. EDCX is by essence a *generative*, *dynamic* and *processual theory* oriented toward *action*.

It is summarised in Figure 6.11. It illustrates the basic fact that EDCX is not to be applied to a problem in the way a tool or an algorithm can be selected into a repertoire and applied to a NDCX situation. Harnessing EDCX always requires a construction (OP5): the initial issue is not to solve a well-defined problem, it is to set the problem first. This is the task of the situation recognition (OP7) informed by the availability of the complex 'toolkit' CX5 and OP6. If the situation is found to be NDCX then the separationist setting is relevant. If the situation is found to be DCX, then OP8 operates. This process is likely to evolve through time, symbolised by the arrow at the bottom, as learning occurs and changes in the items of Table 3.3 defining a situation may occur. Hence the oscillatory potential setting, pictured by the dotted loops linking DCX and NDCX backwards to OP7.

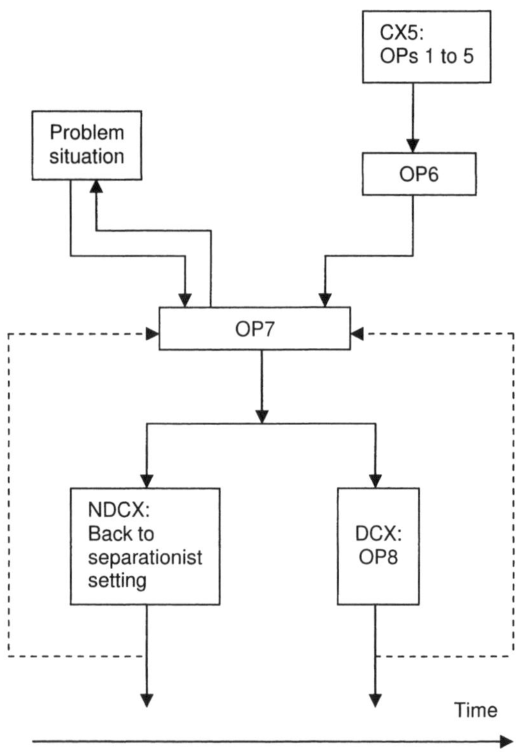

Figure 6.11 Effective Deep Complexity CX6 in a nutshell

The potential oscillatory unfolding through time completes the generative, dynamic and processual character of Effective Deep Complexity. It is schematised in Figure 6.12.

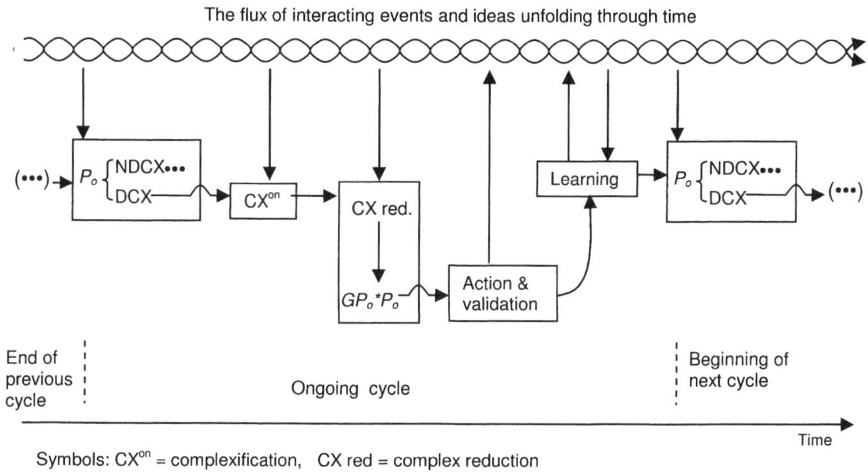

Figure 6.12 The dynamics of Effective Deep Complexity

6.6.2 A Theoretical and Practical Formal Framework

Beyond being a theory proper, CX6 operates as a formal framework for theorising action in any problem-situation because of OP6, the principle of autonomy. This formal frame is based on a master notion of critical non-separability. It constitutes an alternative to the conventional separationist perspective. And it differs from the systems perspective, although it can be viewed as a system itself.

A. Critical non-separability and process

Beyond the non-separability of *PEW* and *W*, and in *W1*, a new domain of non-separability is included in CX6. It is the non-separability of knowledge and action. This kind of non-separability is emphasised by Dewey, as a participatory theory of knowing, in *The Quest for Certainty*. It is intrinsic to the pragmatist view of validation on which CX6 relies (6.5.5) and which renders action an inherent component of the overall process of knowing. It is no longer possible to rely on a kind of principle of sufficient reason through which the recourse to the right tool in a given situation – as if the operator were only a spectator – would be sufficient to establish the validity of the operation. The interplay of OP1, OP2, OP3, OP5,

OP7 and OP8 is the way this non-separation of knowledge and action is intrinsic to CX6.

The addition of this third variety of non-separation brings a complete, final characterisation of non-separability. It is contrasted with the separationist perspectives which have been evoked thus far in Table 6.10.

Table 6.10 Effective Deep Complexity contrasted with three separationist perspectives

	Contrasted perspectives	
Domains of separation / non-separation	CX6	Alternatives to CX6: positivist, objectivist, critical realist
1. (*PEW, W*)	Critical non-separation	Separation in all cases
2. *W1* (World external to *PEW* as *W2*)	Agnostic, with priority to process, relationality and openness	Analytical separation before any possible combination into a more inclusive whole (positivist and objectivist)
	Internal relationality in the social domain	Internal relationality only in critical realism and systems perspective
3. Knowledge and action	Non-separation in most cases Processual validation Critical judgement	Separation Truth value of knowledge mostly assessed independently from action
Overall common characteristic	Critical non-separability and process	Separation

The outcome is twofold. First and foremost, it indicates where the divide between CX6 and the classical perspectives occurs and it points to *critical non-separability* or *transactionality, and process* as being the master notion defining EDCX.

A by-product of this outcome is semantic. Until this present stage, we have used interchangeably the terms 'non-separation' and 'non-separability', and have made them equivalent to transaction and transactionality. Although one might argue that using one term would be preferable, and that sticking to transaction would avoid the awkward use of a negative term, the gain in using both terms is to point explicitly to what each of them negates. Non-separation contrasts in a clear-cut way with separation and maintains a continuity with separationism. Transaction points to the conversion of ontological separates into distinctions within an encompassing whole.

Non-separability, or transaction, appears as a general term covering the three types of non-separation, for the first time in this book. It is always critical. Its criticality results from the criticalities of its three components. Even knowledge and action is critical since addressing knowledge as subject-matter separately from putting it into play, as pure theorising, cannot be ruled out at the outset as it is likely to create a non-deeply complex situation. Non-separation of knowledge and action holds whenever the situation is deeply complex.

Finally, process is ever present in CX6 and endogenised through the organising principles and the eighth, operating principle. It is intrinsic to CX6.

B. An effective alternative to the separationist perspective

Theorising deep complexity entailed the need to characterise how it differs from non-deep complexity and non-complexity in its general sense, and how the knowledge produced is valid over a class of situations. To perform this task, it appeared necessary to go through a sequence of successive steps ranging from the initial empirical experience of a deep obstacle to looking for an underlying theory, itself to be informed by a method itself shaped by a methodology being itself compatible with a theory of knowledge. These successive moves were triggered by the quest for knowing the level at which the divide between the competing perspectives occurs. This quest led in the first part of this chapter to identifying separability and its negation as the fundamental dividing source. The perspective of deep complexity arrived at relies on critical non-separability and process. The other perspectives are separationist. This divide occurs at the level of preconceptions. Fallibilism forms the basic context of deep complexity and of critical non-separability.

It is often claimed however that the value of the positivist and of most objectivist perspectives in science is their reliance on a chain of links, from epistemology to theory and practice, which both warrants their internal consistency and makes them deliver theoretical and empirical outcomes. They are effective in this sense, whereas their critics most often remain either mainly on a methodological ground, with no theoretical outcome or strictly empirical, historical, descriptive and monographic, with little theoretical substance. This classical, separationist chain is detailed in Table 6.11. It includes critical realism although critical realists claim their rejection of positivism, but share much with it, as appears along the chain. A rather spectacular insight emerges from structuring the positivist, objectivist and realist perspectives around the notion of separation: they all share similar orientations on each of the links of the chain. They can therefore be considered as constituting a unique, separationist framework when they are contrasted to CX6.

Table 6.11 EDCX as an alternative to the separationist framework

	1 Preconception about the world	2 Epistemology	3 Methodology	4 Method	5 Theory	6 Practice
Separationist perspective in science	A world *W1* external to the observer	Spectator theory of knowledge: • positivist • objectivist • realist (including critical realist)	Truth as: • correspond-ence • prediction	Use of separationist tools	Product theory	On product *P* first
Effective Deep Complexity	A world *W* including *W1* and the observer	Participatory processual theory of knowing	Experience of a problem situation and behavioural reflexivity first; OPs 1 to 6 and judgement	OPs 7 and 8	Generative theory first	On generative principle *GP* first

The outcome of the present research is that CX6 offers a complete alternative to the separationist view and makes up what can be called an Effective Deep Complexity (EDCX). Each cell is filled in. Recall that in CX6, for (*PEW, W*), non-separation is constitutive of the meta-level, whereas the possibility of separation or non-separation is at the object level. The external world *W1* appears at the object level. These links hang together, they form a consistent chain which can be contrasted term by term with the separationist chain. It seems therefore that we can claim that CX6 meets Simon's requirement and is an effective alternative theoretical frame to the separationist view. For the first time we may consider that the RISE, in Chapter 1, is more than a mere heuristic conjecture: it is an abstract entity informed by, and part of, a full-fledged theoretical frame. It is a theoretical notion operating as a generative hypothesis calling both for further theorising on specific instances and for being harnessed in economic policy debate and action. Instances of other outcomes of CX6 will be presented in Chapter 8.

Beyond being an alternative framework, a fundamental aspect is that CX6 subsumes the separationist frame. We are no longer in the excluding logic of the classical debates. CX6 is inclusive. It subsumes the classical, separationist frame in an open, potentially oscillatory way. It does not claim a monopoly over inquiry provided the conditions for this openness at the object level are warranted by a meta-level closure on CX6. Without it, openness would again boil down to fundamentally unstructured and senseless floating eclecticism. CX6 welcomes by construction a diversity of views on some phenomenon of interest that is irreducible to a single view, under the condition that these views are explicitly compatible with CX6. It provides a structured, unified and yet open way of inquiry. CX6 helps structure deeply ill-structured problem-situations.

6.7 CONCLUSION

Paraphrasing T.S. Eliot, the end of our exploring deep complexity is to know the place for the first time. The name describing CX5 is *critical transactionality*. And the name describing CX6, the augmentation of CX5 with operational principles, is *critically transactional effective deep complexity*, thereafter simplified as EDCX or CX6.

Deep complexity itself takes on a modified meaning compared to its initial definition in Part I. It denotes a critical irreducibility to a satisficing level of reduction. Satisficing makes deep complexity depend on a judgement of satisficing which relies on behaviouralist self-reflexivity OP1, and on situation recognition OP7. Its criticality denotes its oscillatory character. Because of criticality, this definition could not be completed before the completion of the present chapter and of Part II. Operationalising EDCX is addressed in Part III.

NOTE

1. T.S. Eliot (1963), *Little Gidding*, in *Collected Poems 1909–1962*, London: Faber & Faber Ltd.

Part III

Operationality

'To make an end is to make a beginning' said T.S. Eliot. Effective Deep Complexity CX6 is an end and a beginning in the overall process of self-reflexive recursion which generated it. It brings an answer and an end point to the question raised in Table 4.3 and its three-level recursive reasoning. The purpose of this final part is to take CX6 as a beginning and put it to work.

An intrinsic characteristic of CX6 is that knowledge and action are tied to each other. The identification of depth, or of its absence, cannot be the outcome of speculative thinking and cannot conceivably arise without the prior cognitive and practical experience of a problem-situation. The domain of operation of CX6 is a priori any deeply ill-structured problem-situation irrespective of the field, of the discipline, or of any particular kind of activity.

It has been a constant feature of the argumentation developed in the preceding chapters to emphasise the *construction* of EDCX and to maintain a distance with the spontaneous tendency to *apply* some available, taken-for-granted, tools. Now that we have completed the construction phase, we can envisage applying what has been constructed. Entering this application stage requires however that what is to be applied be unambiguous and made as clear as possible. The very construction of CX6 was recursive and consisted, in hindsight, of making what was a still-to-be-defined reflexive complexity work on itself. The first instance of operationalisation of CX6 was on its own construction, in Chapter 6. This is where a clarification is needed. Pulling the threads together will be pursued in the synthesis proposed in Chapter 7. It will open the way for applying CX6 in two specific domains in Chapter 8.

7. Synthesis

> We often think that when we have completed our study of *one* we know all about *two*, because 'two' is 'one and one'. We forget that we have still to make a study of 'and' … that is to say, of organization.
>
> Arthur Eddington (1928)[1]

7.1 INTRODUCTION

The purpose of this chapter is to establish how the CX6 that results from Chapter 6 can be made fully operational. Pulling the threads together will hopefully make clear how CX6 is the outcome of six successive steps and of four successive recursive loops, in section 7.2.

We will also need to organise the implication of one insight of EDCX: the world addressed by EDCX is not merely the world *W1* external to *W2*, the process of enquiry into it, but *W1 and W2*. Yet the aim is to put EDCX to work on *W1*. Hence the need to characterise EDCX first from the standpoint of the world of ideas to which *W2* belongs (section 7.3) and from the standpoint of the experiential situation, that is *W1* and *W2*, in section 7.4.

7.2 PULLING THE THREADS TOGETHER

7.2.1 Six Steps to Deep Complexity as CX6

CX6 is the end point of a seemingly rather intricate construction. We are now in a position to contemplate it from a distance and with the benefit of hindsight to summarise its leading thread in a nutshell (Table 7.1). CX6 has been modelled in six steps, from CX1 to CX6, as a box-within-boxes arrangement of levels of complexity from the elementary to the most encompassing.

Table 7.1 The road from CX1 to CX6

Symbols	$\hat{D}^i$: level of difficulty or of resources required to match a given level of aspiration in dealing with a task *i*			
	$\overline{D}$: maximum level of difficulty that can be dealt with satisficingly with the resources			
	D^* : level of resources required to match the standard of good practice in a given activity			
	$DD^i \equiv \hat{D}^i - \overline{D}$			
CX1 :	$DD^i > 0$	subject to	$\hat{D}^i \geq D^*$	
CX2 :	$DD^{ip} > 0$	subject to	$\hat{D}^i \geq D^*$	*p*: procedural resources
				Table 3.3
CX3 :	$DD_o^{ip} > 0$	subject to	$\hat{D}_o^i \geq D_o^*$	*o*: object level
	$DD_m^{ip} \geq 0$	subject to	$\hat{D}_m^i \geq D_m^*$	*m*: meta-level
				Table 4.3
CX4 :	$DD_{mm}^{ip} = 0$	subject to	$\hat{D}_{mm}^i \geq D_{mm}^*$	*mm*: meta-meta-level
	$DD_m^{ip} = 0$	subject to	$\hat{D}_m^i \geq D_m^*$	
	DD_o^{ir} indeterminate	subject to	$\hat{D}_o^i \geq D_o^*$	*r* = *p*, *s* (*p*: procedural resources, *s*: substantive resources)
CX5	= CX4 + OPs 1 to 5 = critical transactionality			
CX6	= CX5 + OPs 6 to 8 = Effective Deep Complexity			

CX1 is the expression of irreducibility as a cognitive resource gap in performing a task *i*, and that cannot be reduced to zero. It is the positive difference between the difficulty of achieving a level of aspiration $\hat{D}^i$, measured by an 'amount' of cognitive resources, and the amount of available resources $\overline{D}$. The term 'cognitive' is taken in the broad sense of covering purely cognitive and practical resources. No measurement of the resources is done and is needed in our argumentation. It is an intermediary notion which allows us to formulate the lack of cognitive resources conveyed by irreducibility in relative and comparative terms. This gap is always subject to the constraint that the level of aspiration is not lower than the standard of good practice in the field to which *i* belongs.

A full Simonian setting appears in CX2 with the differentiation of the cognitive resources between substantive and procedural resources. Its development was described in Table 3.3.

CX3 is the first expression of deep complexity. It appeared with the introduction of a second-order deep complexity (SODCX) denoting the move from a first-order or object level of reasoning to a second-order, meta-level of reasoning. It entails stepping outside the mental habit of taking as given what is available at the meta-level in order to deal with object-level problems even when there is an irreducible obstacle at this object level. It implies therefore devising new resources at the meta-level and solving the problem expressed in procedural terms as $DD_o^{ip} > 0$ at the object level, and $DD_m^{ip} \geq 0$ at the meta-level to denote that either reducibility can be obtained ($DD_m^{ip} = 0$) or that irreducibility holds ($DD_m^{ip} > 0$) and necessitates to shift to the meta-meta-level. To achieve this implies in turn that this meta-level obstacle be treated as the de facto object level of a still 'upper', meta-level, which, in this case, is the meta-meta-level. This bottom-up process was described in Table 4.3. It calls for producing a $DD_m^{ip} = 0$, that is, a solution at the meta-level. This outcome cannot but be the product of a meta-meta-level process whose substance is to be satisficing at this *mm* level. It is expressed as:

$$DD_{mm}^{ip} = 0 \quad \text{s.t. } \hat{D}_{mm}^{i} \geq D_{mm}^{*}$$

The turn towards CX4 appears at this point. This end point of the bottom-up process becomes the beginning of a top-down process from CX4 to CX6.

CX4 is the formal expression of a framework designed at the meta-meta-level and made available at the meta-level ($DD_m^{ip} = 0$) to address the object-level problem-situations. However it can be any situation at this level, either deeply complex or not. The object-level cognitive gap is therefore indeterminate, it can be nil, or even negative in case of simplicity or mere complication, and whether it bears on the substantive or the procedural sides is also indeterminate.

At this point, the task is to transform this formal setting CX4 into a substantial framework, that is, to give a substance to the foundational $DD_{mm}^{ip} = 0$, and to make it operational for substantive matters. It entails first clarifying out the principles coming into play in the construction of a way out at the meta-level. They are the five organising principles (OP) ranging from OP1 (behaviouralist self-reflexivity), to OP2 (composite self-similarity), to OP3 (conjunction), to OP4 (abduction) and to OP5 (construction). The union of CX4 with these principles makes up CX5. It provides an anchoring to the initial, heuristically built hypothesis about 'anchored deep complexity' (ADCX) of Chapter 2, and converts it into a theoretical conjecture. Then it entails assessing the degree of generalisability of this conjecture. This was addressed through putting to work the generic pattern of double recursive duality $GP^{**}P$, thus going successively through GP_{mm}, P_{mm}, GP_m and P_m in Chapter 6.

The foundational status ($DD_{mm}^{ip} = 0$) of CX5 emerged at the meta-meta generative principle level (GP_{mm}) as critical transactionality. It was complemented by three operational principles at the respective successive levels: OP6 (autonomy of CX5) at the P_{mm} level; OP7 (situation recognition) at the GP_m level, and OP8 (action in a deeply complex situation) at the P_m level. The combination of CX5 with these three operational principles makes up CX6 or effective deep complexity (EDCX).

It should be noticed that the identification of CX5 as critical transactionality and of the eight organisational and operational principles emerged as a response to the issues that appeared with the formal expression of CX4 and the possible generalisability of CX5. The formal expression of CX4 called for constructing the ingredients conferring it a value as a theoretical conjecture and leading to CX5. These ingredients were the five organisational principles. The construction of EDCX was undertaken by putting CX5 to work on the very problem of its generalisability. It was taken as a deeply complex problem-situation requiring to be addressed with the CX5 pattern, that is, the $GP^{**}P$ setting. It is the very complexity of the problem that pulled to investigate it through the former successive meta-meta and meta levels. In hindsight, with the benefit of knowing the outcome of this reasoning, it may look obvious to have followed a strategy which indeed consisted in filling the cognitive gap $\hat{D}^i - \overline{D} > 0$ by creating cognitive resources susceptible to raise $\overline{D}$ up to the level $\hat{D}^i$ at the meta-meta level.

It is at last a simple way which made it possible to explain that there is no miracle in the transformation of complexity as an obstacle into a support for judgement but at the meta-levels. At the meta-meta level the five organising principles and critical transactionality are the $\overline{D}_{mm}$ resources warranting the consistency of the new knowing framework and ensuring that $DD_{mm}^{ip} = 0$ through raising $\overline{D}_{mm}$.

Similarly, at the meta-level, the three operational principles are the $\overline{D}_m$ resources bringing an effective substance to $DD_m^{ip} = 0$ through raising $\overline{D}_m$.

As the formulation of CX4 tells, these new resources do not bring a solution to the object-level problem-situation. The top-down procedure depicted by CX4 is compatible with any type of situation at the object level. The gain lies in the better-informed judgement that this structuring renders possible. It may notably enable us to address the initial problem-situation in a new way and possibly improve it. An illustration in safety management will be given in Chapter 8.

Finally it is to be noticed that another way to reduce the cognitive gap might be to reduce the level of aspiration $\hat{D}^{i}$. But it is strictly limited by the standard D^{*}, to which $\hat{D}^{i}$ cannot be inferior, and which is not modifiable at will. The substance of D^{*} depends on the logical level: at the object level, D_{o}^{*} is the norm of scientific practice; at the meta-level, D_{m}^{*} represents the norm of consistency and relevance of methodology; and at the meta-meta level, D_{mm}^{*} stands for the norm of consistency and relevance of the epistemological and ontological foundations.

All in all the construction of EDCX consisted in a combination of a quantitative conceptualisation ($DD^{i} > 0$) with the qualitative setting *GP*∗∗*P*. The procedure described here from CX1 to CX6 is shaped mainly by the former in the move from a formal step CX4 to a substantial theoretical conjecture CX5, and in the end to a complete theory CX6. A different reading of the same process can be developed from the standpoint of the latter. It is synthesised in Table 7.2.

7.2.2 The 'Three Plus One' Recursive Loops of CX6

Our argumentation can also be synthesised as a logical sequence of three recursive loops (*GP*∗*P*) represented by the columns of Table 7.2, and a fourth loop (Figure 7.1). These loops do not necessarily coincide with the parts, the chapters and the steps described in the last section. As with the six steps to CX6, this simple characterisation in loops appears in hindsight, after the result was obtained. They could not be planned beforehand. Each loop is characterised by its generative process, its development and its product which will itself appear as the starting point of the next loop. Every *GP* can be schematised as consisting of a purpose and an object of enquiry. Its development comprises a method, the main hypotheses and their development proper. Its product consists in its direct outcome, its value and practical implication, and the pending issue driving to the next loop.

Table 7.2 Synthesis of the process which led to CX6

	Experience	Modelling	
	Loop 1 **Chapters 1 and 2**	**Loop 2** **Chapters 3, 4, 5**	**Loop 3** **Chapter 6**
Purpose and object	Improve knowledge about an empirical 'complex' conjecture (RISE)	What theory for ADCX?	What anchoring for CX5? Generality as combination of depth and effectiveness
Method	Reliance on empirical construction Abduction	Focus on irreducibility proper. Resort to safety management	Put CX5 to work. Three logical levels
Main hypotheses	Belief in importance of careful construction and reading of empirical evidence ADCX hypothesis	Behaviouralist self-reflexivity Cognitive gap (*GP,P*) recursive pattern	Generality as a complex problem Addressing it through the CX5 framework
Development	Search of a theoretical corpus accommodating ADCX	Theorising behavioural irreducibility in its own right (from CX1 to CX4) Organisational principles of CX4	Participatory knowing Critical transactionality Operational principles of CX5
Outcome	Originality of ADCX	CX5	CX6 or Effective Deep Complexity (EDCX)
Value	Heuristic conjecture	Theoretical conjecture	A complete theoretical framework
Practical implication	Necessity to pursue the search of a theoretical anchoring for ADCX	Consistent basis to complete the theorising of deep complexity	Threefold character of CX6: • A theory of deeply ill-structured situations • A cognitive framework • A decision-and-action support process
Pending issue	What theoretical value?	What degree of generality of CX5?	What operationality of CX6?

The first loop runs from the desire of not doing away with the RISE and knowing it better to establishing the originality of the heuristic conjecture that it produced and the issue of its theoretical value. The second loop starts with this question of theorising ADCX and produces CX5 with the pending problem of its degree of representativeness or generality. It is addressed in the third loop and leads to Effective Deep Complexity. It is a complete theoretical framework which has the threefold character of being a theory of ill-structured problem-situations; an alternative and encompassing cognitive framework; and of being a decision support framework. The pending issue is to put CX6 to work.

This can be readily done since CX6 is the end point that was called for in Table 4.3 and is deemed to be a theoretical setting which underpins the RISE. Then we enter a fourth loop, from the meta-level to the object level. We dispose of a meta-product P_m which can be put to work on a new object-level problem-situation (Figure 7.1).

The fourth loop is represented partially in Figure 7.1. It includes the information of the problem-situation, which can be symbolised as GP_o*P_o at the object level, and by CX6 or EDCX at the meta-level GP_m*P_m. In turn, in function of the difficulties encountered in dealing with GP_o*P_o, a shift back from the problem-situation to the meta-level is possible. This move back does not bear on CX6 as such, but on the particular content given to GP_m*P_m in case the initial content it was given does not lead to a satisficing object-level situation. There is no guarantee that this reshaping of the substance of GP_m*P_m will be satisficing. What EDCX tells is that not obtaining a final solution is not the end point of the process and that it calls for readdressing the issue, and that it can be done in a consistent way through the EDCX pattern.

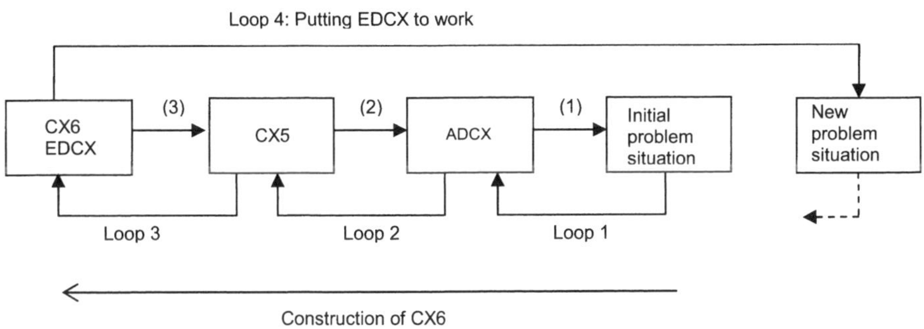

Figure 7.1 The four recursive loops of CX6

The arrows numbered (1) to (3) connect each *GP* to its *P* in the first three loops. They denote the value conferred to the *P* by the *GP* that has been constructed:

- (1) stands for the heuristic conjecture that ADCX is for the problem situation;
- (2) denotes the theoretical conjecture that CX5 is for ADCX;
- (3) stands for the generality conferred to CX5 by CX6/EDCX.

7.3 THE THREEFOLD CHARACTER OF EFFECTIVE DEEP COMPLEXITY

EDCX is a threefold intellectual construct comprising a theory of deeply ill-structured problem-situations, a cognitive framework, and a decision support framework. It belongs to the world of ideas, theories and doctrines. Therefore its operationality can be assessed first by comparing these aspects to the way they appear in the already available formulations and doctrines.

7.3.1 A Theory of Deeply Ill-structured Problem Situations

Before an end result was reached, it was difficult to explain both how '*deeply* ill-structured' differed from the common terminology of ill-structured problems, and how the reference to *situations* differed from the common habit of referring complexity to systems. With EDCX in mind, it seems no longer possible to claim that insisting on radical uncertainty in economics is unduly destructive and nihilist, as Coddington claimed about Keynes (Coddington, 1982). There is now a theoretical appraisal of those problem-situations which prove to be so deeply ill-structured to those who deal with them that they cannot be dealt with satisficingly in the current cognitive scientific framework and require either abandoning the task or stepping outside the framework. EDCX provides a substantial theoretical content to the latter. Its two basic requirements and resources are behavioural self-reflexivity (OP1) and an awareness of the possibility of depth with the judgement of depth that it implies (OP7, situation recognition). In other words it simply calls for being aware of, and keeping in mind, Tables 3.3 and 4.3. This is the minimum practical requirement for exerting a judgement on a situation.

EDCX brings two central distinctions. First is the distinction between deep complexity (DCX) and non-deep complexity (NDCX) which includes all the notions commonly denoted under the term 'complexity'. In an extended way, NDCX may designate anything that is not DCX, ranging from 'ordinary' complexity to complication and simplicity. However equating NDCX with 'complexity' and other notions would create an ambiguity.

It is more appropriate to consider that DCX and NDCX are two forms of an encompassing notion of complexity. When the complexity of complex systems is evoked in the theoretical literature it is indeed non-deep complexity that is at play since the recognition of the need to shift to a different cognitive framework is never addressed head on. It is evoked only in general, more speculative and philosophical discussions but without noticeable repercussions on theorising. Therefore EDCX renders it apparent that the literature on theoretical complex systems or 'complexity theory' leaves unexplored a whole domain of complexity.

A second distinction follows from the central place of the notion of cognitive situation. EDCX is a theory of deeply complex situations, not a theory of complex systems. It pertains to situations. It calls into question the usual, spontaneously made connection of complexity with complex systems. Indeed it disconnects in part complexity from systems. A situation is deeply complex not because it is a complex system, but it can be decided to represent it by a system. Beyond this central distinction, the autonomy of EDCX (OP6) illustrates its encompassing, subsuming status: it contains NDCX. If a notion can be equated with complexity generally understood, it is EDCX, of which NDCX is a subset. EDCX can be viewed as a system, not a property of a system except in the quite specific case in which one considers a deeply complex issue about the system formed by the union of the observing system and the observed system, in which case this issue would be a property of this global system.

When a complex system is evoked, it pulls invariably toward characterising the system and making complexity a property of it, with the result that it is the system and its behaviour that are at the centre of interest, and that distracts one from being compelled to address complexity directly in its own right.

To summarise, EDCX substantiates how problematic it would be to continue to think of complexity in terms of complex systems without a theoretically founded knowledge of complexity in its own right.

7.3.2 An Alternative Cognitive Framework

A. The transdisciplinary level

Effective Deep Complexity brings structuration to ill-structured problem situations, where there was none, irrespective of the particular field or discipline. In bringing this structuration it encompasses de facto any problem situation through its autonomy (OP6) established in Chapter 6. It does not exclude the standard framework but subsumes it. It emerges as an organised totality of internally related, mutually dependent components and their relations. It ranges from the foundational stage to the practical level. It therefore has all the attributes defining a system. It forms a consistent, complete, effective alternative to the standard system of knowledge. Rather than having complexity as a property of complex systems, it is 'system' that appears as a consequence of Effective Deep Complexity. It is based on fallibility as critical tansactionality, the oscillatory conversion of ontological separates into working distinctions, and its operational principles.

Another way in which EDCX is an alternative framework arises through comparing it with the classical disjunction-based framework and with the systems approach.

Advocates of systems theory commonly present it in terms of a 'think globally, act locally' phrase which differentiates it from a 'think locally, act locally' kind of motto of the classical, analytical approach. Yet in its reliance on thinking and action it omits the intermediate stage of theoretical modelling on which the classical framework is especially strong with its analytical framework. One must admit the weakness of the systems approach in this domain: it lacks a unified, structuring modelling framework, a feature which explains the permanent confusion reigning about the so-called systems theory. This modelling and thinking domain is where the difference brought by EDCX operates most: it is an integrative modelling grounded in critical transactionality and its conjunctive foundation. 'Think integratively' reflects this. These characteristics of the three cognitive frameworks were sketched out in Table 6.10, in the wording of CX5. They are rephrased in Table 7.3 with the benefit of CX6/EDCX.

Table 7.3 Three scientific perspectives

	Systems approach	**Classical approach**	**Effective Deep Complexity**
Thinking	Think globally	Think locally	Think integratively
Theoretical modelling	No unifying and structuring body	Disjunctive, analytical framework	Conjunctive, critically transactional framework
Action	Act locally	Act locally	Act locally

B. Economic theory

EDCX has two main consequences in economics: it displaces the dividing line between a mainstream and non-mainstream, and it fills a gap between a formally based, unified economics, and floating eclecticism. On the first account it sets a heavy doubt on the relevance of the opposition to neoclassical economics which has become the obsessional rallying cry of most heterodox schools of economic thought. Neoclassical economics is a particular way of relying on a scientific framework based on disjunction and separation. It shares this constitutive characteristic with many sectors of so-called heterodox views, although it remains a tacit premise which does not seem to be clearly perceived and nurtures the confusion reigning in heterodoxy. Evolutionary and institutionalist economics, the post-Keynesian perspective and *régulation* theory, among others, illustrate schools of thought which are struggling endlessly against the neoclassical mainstream and often against each other, to define what they are.

They remain blind to the fact that most of the issues on which they insist are deeply ill-structured problems which call for a non-separationist, conjunctive pattern of knowing. The major part of theoretical work done in these schools obeys the disjunctive, separationist tacit premise. Keynes's comment about the brave army of heretics doomed to fail in their attacks on the classsical citadel is entirely relevant to today's situation: a major part of the dissenting economists rejects neoclassical conclusions while accepting their tacit scientistic premise. EDCX redefines the dividing line: it is between perspectives based on a conjunctive, non-separationist system of knowing, and those which espouse the conventional scientistic wisdom of disjunction and separation.

Effective Deep Complexity also fills a gap between the disjunctive scientific block and the floating eclecticism that we identified in Part I. One may indeed distinguish two broad methodological sensibilities in the way economics and political economy are addressed nowadays. The first is the mainstream which has already been defined here. The second is the constellation of floating, unanchored eclectic approaches. They share a criticism of 'neoclassical economics', notably of what they denounce as its lack of realisticness. A part of them also reflects a disdain for ordinary-language economics and its absence of mathematical formalisation which is deemed to deprive it from a scientific content. Parts of *régulation* theory and of evolutionary economic theory illustrate this. It leads them to ad hoc formalisations and empirical modelling, and open-ended discourse, without a complete alternative architecture that could be contrasted to the neoclassical one. Some insist on empirical inquiry as a way out of the endless debates on methodology, as if empirical substance could be a substitute to the lack of a firm cognitive framework informing it. Others seem to be content with discourse based mainly on ordinary language or, in Keynes's terms, on ordinary logic. In Keynes's thinking, it relied on the belief that there is no intermediate logic between the classical, formal logic and ordinary language. We claimed in Chapter 2 that this assimilation of formalised logic with disjunctive logic is a flaw in Keynes's thought. The issue is with disjunctive logic, not with its formalised character. It was possible to introduce a specified set of hypotheses which make up a conjunctive pattern, the third organisational principle (OP3) of EDCX.

It seems therefore that we are left with three perspectives: the disjunctive predominating view in science, with its exclusion of deep complexity; the floating eclecticism and ordinary language discourse, with their open-ended substance but their absence of explicit closure; and the open-ended substance with a closure brought by Effective Deep Complexity.

However seemingly ambitious it may appear to qualify EDCX as being an alternative cognitive system, we have to admit that it fulfils Simon's test for any candidate perspective to be an effective alternative to the prevailing disjunctive framework, as has been documented in Chapter 6. This alternative is a call for scientific humility in science, especially social science with its particular exposure to deeply ill-structured problem-situations. The challenge is to overtake the ingrained prejudice that to do science about social matters means the same exactness of outcomes and the same demonstrative and conclusive character of conclusions as in natural science.

7.3.3 A Decision-and-action Support Process

Effective deep complexity relies on a connection between knowing and action. Its three operational principles of autonomy (OP6), situation recognition (OP7) and action in a deeply complex situation (OP8) make of it a genuine decision support framework irrespective of the discipline and of the type of activity, be it scientific research or any activity likely to engender a deeply ill-structured problem-situation.

Given the reflexive and recursive character of EDCX, decision is essential to it since it calls for an initial judgement about the situation (OP7) and to decide whether to deal with it in an NDCX or a DCX way. This decision calls for assessment. This can only be done through taking action and experiencing (OP8). EDCX is a decision-and-action support process.

The three operational principles therefore appear as landmarks for action, but in a specific sense. They are the product of a meta-process and do not imply a priori any determinate outcome at the object level: the object-level outcome results from putting to work OP8 and is a priori open ended. Moreover EDCX is not normative. It says simply that if the situation is deeply complex, then EDCX as a theory of this kind of situation provides a specific pattern of decision and action that is appropriate to the situation and likely to help the decision-maker structure his/her information and gain in knowledge of the situation. By the very definition of an ill-structured situation, EDCX brings a structuring where there was initially no satisfactory structure.

Given an awareness of CX5 and its critical transactionality, OPs 6 to 8 have important practical implications. First, since there is now an encompassing alternative to the common spontaneously shared disjunctive manner of doing science, it is no longer possible to behave as before, as if there were no alternative. There is a *judgement of depth*, and a choice to be made (OP7) in the context of a general a priori deeply complex situation (OP6). The usual spontaneous ranking, in which non-deep complexity comes before a possible deep complexity, is reversed. With OP6, any NDCX development about a problem needs to be justified especially in a domain like social science in which the routinised protocols of empirical validation of natural science most often cannot operate. How the problem can be dealt with in an NDCX way becomes the prime question.

A logical, necessary consequence of the autonomy OP6 of Effective Deep Complexity is that the NDCX appraisal of problems is acceptable only if it is duly justified, or in obviously NDCX problem-situations. Both cases will inevitably trigger a reflection on the status, scientific or not, of the knowledge at stake. EDCX implies no a priori ranking. The norm D^* denotes good practice in a given activity, be it scientific or whatever else. In the context of this book, the reference is with scientific knowledge and practice.

Finally, if a deeply complex situation is detected after OP7, OP8 follows immediately from it. Let us recall its five stages:

1. Start with the experiential problem-situation.
2. Complexify: activate the CX5 pattern, enlarge, compare, map the situation in the setting of Table 3.3, think in terms of *GP* first.
3. Simplify on the basis of what is obtained in stage 2. Justify explicitly how the frontier of what is taken as granted is set, and to what extent the reduction is performed.
4. Put to work the outcome of stage 3, check, assess and validate.
5. Learn and possibly engage in a process of revision following from stage 4, leading to a shift back to an earlier stage if necessary and if resources and time available permit it.

Being prepared for this process is important in order to alleviate the stress that an ill-structured unwanted event may create. The literature on management does not ignore this need to be prepared for acutely adverse situations (Crozier, 1995).

7.4 EFFECTIVE DEEP COMPLEXITY AND THE EXTERNAL WORLD *W1*

7.4.1 The Experiential Problem-situation

W1, the world external to the process of enquiry *W2*, manifests itself through the experiential situation. The first experiential, deeply complex situation on which EDCX bears is the one encountered in this book. EDCX appears as an answer to the situation which was provoked by the RISE. The extent to which EDCX connects with the RISE itself requires to be further specified.

The RISE denotes a situation observed in an overall process. EDCX sees it as the product P_o of a generative process GP_o , both being defined at the object level of W1. It takes it as a unique phenomenon that is tackled abductively.

Figure 7.2 depicts the *GP**P* process through which *W1* and *W2* are connected in the problem-situation. The problem-situation is made up of the object level and the meta-level situations. EDCX proper covers GP_m, P_m and GP_o: GP_m is the situation recognition (OP7), P_m is the principle of action in the situation (OP8) put to work at the object level (GP_o). The whole situation is part of a process denoted by the arrow of time.

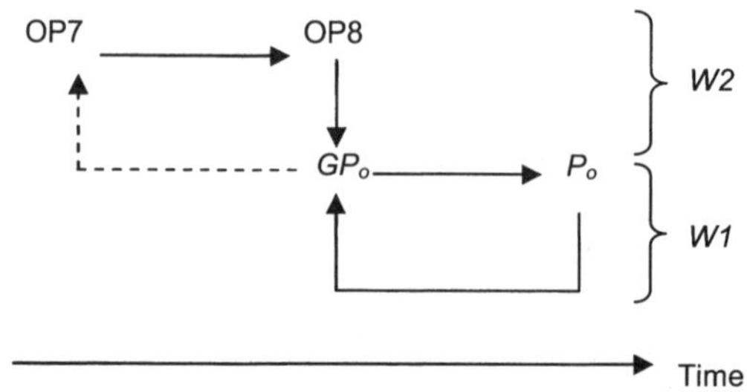

Figure 7.2 The experiential problem-situation

In the conventional disjunctive framework, P_o is analysed with a GP_o. The origin of GP_o is given. There is no need to shift to a meta-level of inquiry. Depth, the property of the situation which would push to convert GP_o into the open-ended product of a meta-deliberation, has no place in a disjunctive setting whereas the conjunctive setting of EDCX makes it relevant. The consequence is that while it is a theory of P_o that is sought in the conventional, not deep procedure, in EDCX the theory bears on the overall process *GP* that generates P_o, and which includes the meta-level and GP_o.

Deeply complex situations invariably involve an object and a meta-level taken in a processual perspective. EDCX is a theory of this duality generalised as *GP**P*. In this pair, *P* is the irreducible complex product of a generative principle which includes both the object and the meta-levels.

P cannot be reduced to an object-level product given a disactivated *GP*, by the very definition of the deeply complex situation it triggers in combination with the variables of Table 3.3. In this sense EDCX brings a distinction between a *process* theory, which it is, and a *product* theory, which it is not. It converts the problem of devising a solution for *P* into a problem of designing a *GP*. It creates a situation in which *P* becomes intelligible as a part of a generative process including the object-level world and the process of enquiry into the world. Again, the situation created by the RISE and its accompanying conditions is one in which it cannot be separated from its generative principle. To repeat, EDCX cannot substitute to an intractable notion at its own level of intractability, that is, the object level. It renders possible to reappraise the RISE in a broader setting of which the initial notion is a part, and with an unchanged obedience to scientific practice in the present case.

In the case of the RISE, its generative GP_o can be identified as containing a variety of factors, some economical, others not, some analytically tractable, others not, without pushing aside what is not tractable into the 'all other things equal', and taking for granted what can be grasped analytically and/or quantitatively.

The passing of time and learning are likely to make some of the variables that contribute to define the situation as in Table 3.3 change and the whole situation evolve, and convert it in a not deeply complex situation, and so on. OP8 operates fully here. As a decision support framework, EDCX applies as well to the economist or the scientist as to any actor facing a deeply ill-structured problem situation irrespective of the activity.

In the end, whether *W2*, as EDCX, implies a determinate *W1* or not is given an answer by the very intrinsic setting of EDCX: *W1*, as a product, is open-ended. Nevertheless EDCX orientates the broad kind of substance of *W1* as process and relation.

EDCX cannot prescribe a direct solution in *W1*. It creates a new situation in which action, what is done or can be made, is prime. In this situation a solution in *W1* may be possible whereas it would be meaningless or unintelligible without EDCX. EDCX views events and objects in *W1* as processual and relational, which can be symbolised by a $GP \rightarrow P$ relationship at least, as a local part of $GP{**}P$.

In sum, the *W1* implied by *W2* (that is, by EDCX) is:

- $GP_o{*}P_o$ if the problem-situation created in *W1* is DCX (deeply complex);
- $GP_o \rightarrow P_o$ if the situation in *W1* is NDCX (not deeply complex).

Instances of uses of EDCX in *WI* will be presented in Chapter 8 with road safety governance, and economic theory and policy.

7.4.2 Complex Duality: A Critically Transactional Systemic Process

To conclude, the complex duality of *GP* and *P* forms the building block of the critically transactional systemic process (CTSP) of which EDCX consists. This duality differs from a trade-off in the sense of an either–or exchange of mutually exclusive terms. It denotes an essential tie between terms that are necessary to each other but in a dynamic tension in process, with varying weights and in a hierarchy. They are therefore not separable and taken in transaction. The *GP*, *P* pattern introduces a recursive and hierarchical process and facilitates an abductive reasoning. This duality comprises the logica-level duality of the elementary $GP{*}P$: it relies intrinsically on the meta-level and object-level pattern, that is, on $GP{**}P$.

It is this 'double' duality that unfolds through the meta- and the object levels. Its extension depends on the deep, or not deep, complex character of the situation. This concatenation of dualities composes a cognitive system which can be viewed as a 'complex system'.

However it needs to be stressed that our argumentation and EDCX do not follow from a systems perspective theory but rather from a processual perspective which ends with systemic considerations. Therefore one should avoid conflating 'complex system theory' conventionally understood, and the kind of complexity discussed here, although EDCX possesses systemic properties. It is best depicted as a systemic process, that is, a process with systemic properties (Figure 7.3).

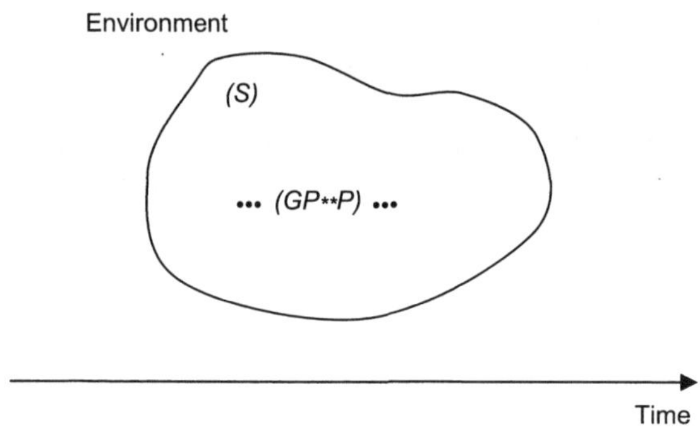

Figure 7.3 Effective Deep Complexity as a systemic process

EDCX has the characteristics of an open dynamic system which can be defined by the representation of something (*S*) as a composition and organisation of interactions between components, with respect to an environment, and that is evolving and transforming over time. 'Interactions' are understood not in the Deweyan sense, but in the more general sense of mutual relationships between active components, these relationships being in process and mostly internal.

The transactionality of EDCX resides in the conversion of the salient elements of the initial problem-situation into distinctions structured by the *GP****P* duality and its concatenation. It is critical, which means that it can always be simplified into a non-deeply complex setting and again complexified, depending upon the judgement of satisficing about the situation (Table 3.3). Criticality is an essential difference with the complex systems literature. A constant theme of 'complex systems' is emergence, either strictly tied to systems or related to process as in Arthur's 'process and emergence' perspective. With criticality, emergence is not systematic, it may not be present when the problem situation turns out to be not complex. This CTSP (critically transactional systemic process) reflects what appears indeed as a fundamental, generic complex duality.

The next issue is about the implication of this complex duality for action. An answer is already provided by OP8. It contains broad guidelines that we would like to see more specified. The limit is in the variety of concrete situations and in the fact that every situation calls for the construction of an argumentation that is informed by guidelines but whose substance is particular and cannot be disposed of by a general framework. The guidelines have to be declined in accordance with every particular situation. It is a matter of judgement. The examples presented in Chapter 8 will illustrate it.

The initial binding constraint is in the resources that are needed for exerting a judgement of complex satisficing. Behavioural self-reflexivity OP1, be it individual or social, is this primary resource. It is at the basis of the chain of the organising and operating principles which make up EDCX. It is not normative or prescriptive. It follows simply from the exploration of the implications of a fallibilist initial attitude.

NOTE

1. A. Eddington (1928 [1958]), *The Nature of the Physical World*, Ann Arbor, MI: University of Michigan Press, 103.

8. Applications

> If you desire to see, learn how to act.
> Act always so as to increase the number of choices.
> Heinz von Foerster (2003)[1]

8.1 INTRODUCTION

Putting EDCX to work or 'applying' it *in* – rather than *to* – problem-situations requires several resources. The first resource is twofold: it is the willingness to 'try and test' EDCX, and the capacity to think dually. Thinking dually is not a new religion. It is the first step in putting complex duality to work. There is no doubt that it still must appear rather weird on first inspection, and leave sceptical those in social science who feel comfortable with the disjunctive scientific framework. To those who feel uncomfortable with it, the good news is that an alternative exists and that it is possible to step outside the disjunctive framework, although it cannot alleviate the risks for careers that are under the control of mainstream peer committees, at least as long as EDCX is in its infancy and there is no credible alternative to the mainstream. Effective Deep Complexity implies a judgement about a problem situation. It starts with the action taken to deal with it. EDCX informs and structures this action notably with its seventh and eighth principles, OP7 and OP8. It implies that one actualises a second kind of resources, those needed for judgement. They depend on being informed of EDCX.

A third aspect is new for the scientific debate in social science. It follows from the availability of an effective alternative to what was considered thus far as being without any credible alternative. It goes beyond issues of realism or realisticness. At stake is the judgement of situation, deeply complex or not, implying respectively a conjunctive or a disjunctive setting. Since the former is encompassing, it implies that any recourse to the latter needs to be justified.

Fourth, the focus of complex duality is on *GP*, the generative process, whenever the situation identified is deeply complex. It entails that the course of action is a search and discovery process. This seems especially relevant for the highly complex situations that can be found in the areas of economic policy, of nuclear waste management or of climate change, among others. They are domains in which values are in dispute and seem incommensurable. In these cases, policy decision and action cannot be conceived as resulting from one centre of rationality.

Some agreed framework for disagreeing and debating is needed. It cannot but be participatory although every aspect cannot be suspended to a vote. Leadership is required but within a duality with participation. It even suggests a complex recursive duality in which leadership is the generative process and participation its active dual which feeds back on it, processually.

Finally a corollary of the focus on *GP* is a watchfulness on the *P* that will be produced, and a readiness to reinterpret and revise the process. It reflects a learning process. It requires that the means for watchfulness and revision be implemented. The latter requires a capacity for flexibility. Both necessitate a capacity for experiencing.

All in all, decision and action in complex duality means taking action and creating variation without being certain or even being capable of probabilising *P*, but with a certainty on what is to be avoided in *GP*. Then in a deeply complex situation the first thing to avoid is the lack of duality and the spontaneous tendency to one-sidedness. It is in the experience of specific problem-situations that the declension of these guidelines will take place by necessity and illustrate applications of EDCX. I have selected two situations, in road safety management and in economic theory and policy. They are presented below.

8.2 ROAD SAFETY GOVERNANCE

This section presents how EDCX was harnessed to road safety governance in research led by Sylvain Lassarre and this author on a comparison of France with Great Britain (Delorme and Lassarre, 2005, 2009). The main focus was to gain an understanding of the reasons why the long-run statistics of fatalities in road accidents display an almost constant difference between the two countries and make each one appear as a sort of mirror of the other (Figure 8.1). The ultimate goal was to gain insight about the French situation and to construct knowledge likely to contribute to improving action about road safety in France. The general working hypothesis was that beyond the wealth of available sophisticated quantitative, statistical studies in this domain, it would be necessary to inquire into the often evoked but left unexplored domain of qualitative factors at the country level, notably the institutions and organisation of road safety. The goal was not only to improve knowledge about these factors, but also to construct an integrated view through their articulation with quantitative factors into a unified setting.

Thanks to funding from the French Ministry of Transport and the 'Programme de recherche et d'innovation dans les transports terrestres' (PREDIT), it was possible to enable British and French researchers and experts to work together. It has been a truly cross-disciplinary team who accepted engagement in research based on an empirical, experienced situation but with an unknown expected outcome and, at any rate, with the perspective that everyone be more or less pulled outside his/her own discipline. This is an opportunity to acknowledge their cooperation.

On the whole 14 British and French experts worked in cooperation on the two projects. Beyond the team leaders, Robert Delorme and Sylvain Lassarre (INRETS: Institut National de Recherche sur les Transports et leur Sécurité, Marne-la-Vallée, France), the contributors to the two publications included: Richard E. Allsop (University College, London), Jeremy Broughton (Transport Research Laboratory, Crowthorne, UK), Laurent Carnis, Didier Chabanet, Pierre-Alain Hoyau (all with INRETS), Amy Aeron-Thomas, Brigitte Chaudhry, Agnès Saudrais-Hough (all with RoadPeace, London), Hervé Chomienne (University of Versailles), Ken Spence (Transport Initiatives Ltd, Leeds), Jean Orselli (Conseil Général des Ponts et Chaussées, Paris) and Stephen G. Stradling (Transport Research Institute, Napier University, Edinburgh). An extension of the EDCX model to six European countries was developed by Vojtech Eksler (2009).

8.2.1 The Problem-situation

In France, 4620 persons were killed in road accidents in 2007. The corresponding figure was 2946 in Great Britain. The first year in the past for which a reliable comparison of fatalities is possible is 1953, when the number was 7668 in France. It increased annually to a maximum of 16 545 in 1972 and then declined regularly. In Britain, it was 5090 in 1953, then it increased to a maximum of 7985 in 1966, remained on a plateau until 1972, and declined afterwards.

The long-run trend of road unsafety is its spectacular decline in industrial countries. A common indicator is the ratio of the number of fatalities per year to a measure of the volume of traffic, usually the number of vehicle-kilometres (in billions of veh-km). It has fallen from 167 in 1953 to 8.5 in 2006 in France while the traffic increased from 46 to 555 billion veh-km between the same years. The corresponding figures are 78 (1953) and 6.3 (2006) persons killed by billion veh-km in Great Britain with a rise in road traffic from 65 to 511 billion veh-km.

These figures suggest that France has been lagging constantly behind Britain. This is confirmed by annual time series covering the years 1953 to 2007. However a spectacular change occurred in France between 2002 and 2003, with the vigorous measures decided in summer 2002 by the head of state and that were rapidly implemented. The ratio was 13.1 in 2002. It fell to 10.3 in 2003. These same years the figures were 7.1 and 7.2 for Britain.

The figures for persons killed provide partial information on the damage due to road accident casualties. More complete information would include injuries (serious and slight) but their international comparison is rendered quite problematic by the differences in definitions across countries. Figures for deaths refer to persons killed immediately or who died within 30 days of the accident. This definition is international and provides reliable information for comparisons.

The comparison of the annual fatality rates between Great Britain and France between 1953 and 2007 reflects a striking parallelism when it is expressed in logarithms and mapped as in Figure 8.1. An almost constant gap seems to have been present until 2002. It was spectacularly reduced in 2003. It has again remained almost constant since 2003, but at a lower level than before.

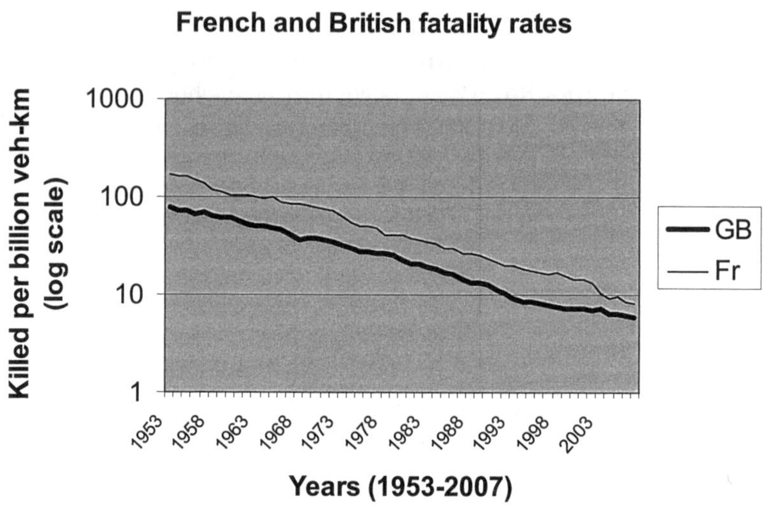

Figure 8.1 Fatality rates (per 10^9 veh_km)

The ratio of the French to the British fatality rates remained quasi constant, at a level of two over the 50 years extending from 1953 to 2002. It declined neatly in 2003 and has remained since then at a level of 1.4 (Table 8.1).

Table 8.1 Ratio of French to British fatality rates (1953–2007)

Annual arithmetic mean								
1953–62	1963–72	1973–82	1983–92	1993–2002	1953–2002			
2.0	2.1	1.8	1.9	2.1	2.0			
Recent years								
2000	2001	2002	2003	2004	2005	2006	2007	2003–07
2.0	2.0	1.9	1.4	1.5	1.5	1.4	1.4	1.4

On average the ratios of decline of road unsafety have been the same in France and Great Britain, except for the singular year 2003. That year, the beginning of the implementation in France of automatised radars for controlling and enforcing speed limits had an immediate effect, which suggests that speeding was a significant source of the gap with Britain. The gap has remained almost constant again after 2003, but at a lower level of 1.4. This gap, although it was larger, was already there more than 50 years before. Its constancy suggests that both countries are like mirrors to each other. Are there features that are present in Britain that would explain why it appears so difficult for France to catch up? Do these features point to their lack of equivalence in France?

8.2.2 Concepts and Modelling of Road Risk

Road risk analysis is normally based on consideration of the three main components of road transport: the road users, the vehicles and the roads. The goal of road safety is to prevent traffic accidents. Accidents result from failures in the interactions between and within the components of a traffic situation, notably in the interactions between road users (drivers, motorcyclists, cyclists, pedestrians and so on). Each of the three components needs to be decomposed into homogeneous subcategories by transportation mode, age, gender, and so on for users; by types of vehicles, vehicle speed, and so on for vehicles; by motorways, main roads, rural roads, streets, road width, number of lanes, speed limit, and so on for roads. 'Road' is shorthand for infrastructure and physical environment (including weather and light conditions). In cross-country comparisons the differences in the distributions of these components are significant and need to be taken into account.

Accidents as such provide only partial information on the traffic safety situation. It depends also on the conditions which prevail before the accident, and on the degree of seriousness of the injuries once the accident has occurred. The former denote the exposure, the latter the consequence. There are therefore three dimensions: traffic exposure, accident risk and accident consequence.

The exposure designates the units or the magnitude of the activity in which the accidents occur (quantitative indicator of involved units, distance travelled, time spent in traffic, and so on). A common aggregate indicator is the number of vehicle-kilometres of traffic over a given period of time.

For the consequences, we concentrate over accidents generating person casualties. They range from slight to severe injuries and fatalities. We limit the international comparison to fatalities.

A usual definition of risk in road safety is the ratio between the number of accidents or casualties (casualties are injuries, or only fatalities) and exposure. In this sense, the overall risk of being killed in road traffic in France in 2007 was still 1.4 times higher than in Great Britain.

The change in the road safety situation depends on the interdependent changes in the three dimensions. The expected number of casualties (E) can be expressed by a multiplicative dimensional relationship between exposure, risk and consequence:

$$\text{E (casualties)} = \text{Exposure} \cdot \frac{\text{Accidents}}{\text{Exposure}} \cdot \frac{\text{Casualties}}{\text{Accidents}}$$

$$= \text{Exposure} \cdot \text{Risk} \cdot \text{Consequence}$$

A classical representation of traffic safety follows from combining the three safety dimensions and the three road traffic components in a 3 x 3 matrix. It is usually called the Haddon matrix, after the contribution made by William Haddon through his research and leadership of the US National Highway Traffic Safety Administration and later the Insurance Institute of Traffic Safety, in the 1960s and 1970s (Haddon, 1972; Runyan, 2003). From previous work by J.E. Gordon in 1949 on the epidemiology of accidents placing injury control 'within the public health framework in which health problems are conceptualised to result from interactions among the host, agent, and environment', and J.J. Gibson, in 1961, who elaborated on this notion by classifying agents of injury in terms of various forms of energy, Haddon expanded upon this conceptualisation of injury epidemiology and prevention by depicting the phases of the accident process as pre-crash, crash and post-crash. These phases correspond to three rows that are crossed with three columns consisting of host (road user), agent (vehicle and energy related to speed and mass), and the environment, either physical (road, street) or physical and social. The Haddon matrix provides a sort of checklist of the factors that enter into the definition of a road safety situation.

However, the focus on fatalities requires one to understand how one passes from road traffic to accidents with fatalities. Here road safety appears as a challenging domain when it is compared with accident prevention analysis in industry, and with other modes of transport.

First, road accidentology does not fit with the systemic perspective that is emphasised for hazards and accidents in tightly coupled industrial activities like those evoked in Chapter 3 with Perrow's thesis about normal accidents. Erik Hollnagel (2004) contrasts three main types of accident models: sequential, epidemiological and systemic, which differ mainly with respect to their assumptions about causality.

In the sequential approach, the goal is to describe specific cause–effect mechanisms such as unsafe acts, mechanical failures and accident blackspots. The accident is the result of a sequence of factors that occur in a specific order. It is basically assumed that it is possible to reason from accident occurrence to underlying specific causes and well-defined links in a sequence of causal series.

The epidemiological approach relies on an analogy with the spreading of a disease in which the outcome is a combination of factors, some of which are manifest, others latent. Latent conditions, performance deviations rather than unsafe acts, resident pathogens (Reason, see Chapter 3), and carriers are the main features of what appears as a causal network between host, agent and environmental factors. Rather than focusing on eliminating or containing specific causes, as is done in the sequential approach, the goal here is to create or strengthen the defences and barriers.

In the case of tight couplings and non-linear interactions, no specific direction of causality can be identified. The potential for accident arises from the inevitable performance variability and functional non-linear resonance. In this systemic perpective, Hollnagel advocates understanding how the system functions rather than seeking to identify well-specified failure pathways. He even subtitled his book about accident prevention '*How to improve safety by understanding the nature of accidents rather than finding their causes*' (Hollnagel, 2004).

At this point it seems that the sequential approach can help in simple, local, and well-specified situations. At a regional or country level, the factors which are at play are so numerous and heterogeneous that it is more appropriate to recourse to the epidemiological perspective.

This is reinforced by a second aspect of road accidentology, that is, its original position among other modes of transport. One might ask why the tools which render safety high in commercial aviation or in railways in industrialised countries could not be applied to road traffic. Let us briefly compare safety in road traffic and in commercial aviation from the standpoint of their operating conditions and their accidentology (Table 8.2).

On the whole, except for some particularities, safety characteristics more or less similar to those in aviation operate in railways. Their main difference to road safety is that in the latter, users are the operators in an activity distributed simultaneously over entire populations and territories.

Road safety could therefore hardly be dealt with without an analysis of the distributions of characteristics over heterogeneous populations of millions of road users, of vehicles, and environmental factors. This epidemiological perspective seems fully appropriate to the comparison of fatalities at a country level between France and Great Britain.

In the analysis conducted by S. Lassarre (Delorme and Lassarre, 2009), six main factors supposed to account for the difference were isolated. They all pertain to differences in risk exposure but for different reasons. First there are differences that are due to structural factors. They affect the three components of road traffic. These are the users (differences in their distribution by gender and age, and in their mobility); the vehicles (differences in distribution by categories between cars, light and heavy goods vehicles, motorcycles, and so on); and the physical environment (urbanisation, and the distribution of roads: built up, rural, motorways, 2 x 2 lane roads).

Table 8.2 Road safety and commercial aviation safety systems compared

	Commercial aviation safety system	**Road safety**
Operating conditions	• Highly qualified operators • Users are not the operators • Integrated international organisation • Little individual autonomy, priority to procedures • Commitment to maintaining a high safety level	• Activity structuring almost everyone's everyday life • Users are operators • Mass phenomenon • Combining a minority of occupational operators with a majority of amateurs • High individual autonomy • Uneven safety culture
Accidentology	• Small number of accidents but sizable casualties • High visibility • Immediate international concern • Asymptotic level of safety (10^{-6}) achieved since the end of the 1970s • Difficult and limited gains of safety in present system, on average	• Many "small-size" fatalities • Diffused accidents • No immediate statistical summation of casualties • No front-page coverage by the media • Room for large safety gains within present system
Overall control characteristics	• Internationally integrated control • Tight coupling	• Uneven control across countries • Loosely coupled activity • Loose systemic characteristics

Once these factors are taken into account, there remain the factors which depend on the users' behaviour and that can be measured by average indicators of speed, drink driving and seat belt fastening, notably as regards rear seats. These are the main factors.

Speed appeared as a key factor of differentiation between the two countries: it was higher in France on motorways and rural roads, but similar in urban areas. It was estimated, on the basis of year 2000 data, before the French turn of 2002–03, that a reduction of average speed would notably reduce the lag with Britain. The method followed the principles presented in Kleinbaum et al. (1982), and the World Health Organization procedure (WHO, 2002) for the estimation of the parts attributable to the various risk factors that would result from changes in exposure, relatively to the British situation taken as the reference level. For speed it was combined with the model based on kinetic energy in transport: the risk of crash is assumed to be proportional to speed; in the crash, the risk of being injured is also proportional to speed, and the risk of fatal injury is proportional to the energy released in the crash (Nilsson, 2004). These dimensions are multiplicative and result in the fact that the fatality rate is proportional to the power four of the average speed.

It was predicted that if speeds and the distribution of traffic volumes were similar in France to those of Britain, the number of fatalities would be reduced by one-third. The differences in exposure to the three risks (speed, alcohol, deficient seat belt fastening) were estimated to account for 80 to 90 per cent of the difference in the French and British fatality rates.

Let us start from the 2002–03 turn. It is attributable to a change in French road safety policy which triggered an overall decline of average speed on motorways and highways through the implementation of automatised control sanctions via radars. It was complemented by a reinforcement of drink driving control. A new plateau seems to have been reached, at least temporarily, with a stabilised lag at a 1.4 level.

Then once the attributable parts of the difference have been measured, there remains an as yet unanswered question about the reasons for the past long-run stability of this difference, and for the possible new stabilisation after 2003, but at a lower level. Are there more fundamental factors at play? Are there factors underlying the long-run difference that remain unaffected? Are the recent change and its effects rooted in underlying factors which would ensure their duration? Beyond the narrow reading of the curves, there arises the whole issue of the qualitative aspects of road safety. Here we hit at a most perplexing problem of statistical comparisons of road safety. There exists a profound discrepancy between the widely accepted idea that the historical paths and their legacies, the institutions and the organisations of road safety management, differ across countries, notably between France and Great Britain, and the quasi total absence of any attempt at integrating these aspects in the information bases upon which analysis is done, which are purely quantitative. When qualitative aspects are evoked, it is in a merely anecdotal way, as a casual addition to the core statistical framework, or as a part of concluding comments on the interest of taking them into account in further studies, which boils down to wishful thinking.

This is a clear instance of an ill-structured problem situation. There seems to be no way in which the qualitative and quantitative dimensions of road safety could be grasped into an integrated framework through the use of the methods and tools of information and analysis that are available in this domain. It can therefore be viewed as a deeply ill-structured problem situation in which it may become appropriate to harness Effective Deep Complexity. This task is pursued next.

8.2.3 An Activity Model of Road Safety

With EDCX, we are driven to consider road safety as a more or less integrated activity with its structural and organisational aspects on the one hand, and its functional, operational features on the other hand. Road unsafety can be viewed as a process running from activities implying road traffic, the unwanted consequences of which are road accidents, injuries and persons killed.

Road accidents are the unwanted products of an activity. It calls for building a modelled representation of this activity rather than taking accidents only as either undesired events grasped through their specific causes or through focusing on the attribution to components. EDCX suggests to look for a way to take into account both the non-deeply complex part of road unsafety (statistical analysis) and the deeply complex part triggered by the issue of the articulation of qualitative and quantitative factors whose necessity results from the cross-country comparison.

A. Actors and activities

A prior requirement was to dispose of an integrated view of the actors and the activities on which road safety depends in practice. The first actors of road safety are the road and street users. Safety depends on their behaviours while driving, riding and walking. Road safety is also the outcome of the activity of actors whose specific task is to enhance road safety as their specialised occupation, in government or local authorities, and in other institutions (non-governmental organisations, insurance business and business organisations, notably). Important road safety actors are also those responsible for health and safety in business organisations whose activity includes road traffic, and the members of the health care sector for the public of road users at large.

The list of the fields of activity connected to road safety is longer. They can be structured according to the components of the Haddon matrix. They will therefore include the activities connected with users and their attitudes and behaviours (education, training, information and communication – notably communication campaigns), with vehicles, with infrastructures (roads and streets), and with the traffic environment (traffic engineering, management of mobility). They will also include the pre-accident, accident and post-accident features. There are two groups of pre-accident activities: the group of prevention and the insurance business, and the group of control and enforcement, law, regulation, justice and courts. Activities related to the accident occurrence proper are those connected to dampening down the effects of the energy liberated in the crash, either through embarked technical devices (airbag, and so on) or through safety equipment on roads and streets. They are part of the activities specifically concerned with vehicles and infrastructures that were evoked above.

The immediate post-accident activities include the emergency rescue services and hospital services. The post-accident activities also comprise the less visible aspects of information-building and research on road safety. The quality of the latter depends heavily on the quality of information. And they both aim at contributing to improve road safety.

This list comprises 11 headings. All actors, except public actors (government and local authorities) do not operate on all of them, as is clear from Table 8.3. Indeed Table 8.3 shows that the public actors occupy the central place among the actors of road safety. Since the international comparison cannot be exhaustive about the actors of road safety, the observation above points to the rationale for focusing on public actors at least.

Table 8.3 Fields and actors of road safety

Fields	Actors		
	Road users	Road safety actors	
		Government Local authorities	Other: NGOs, etc.
1. Education	*	*	*
2. Training	*	*	*
3. Information-Communication	*	*	*
4. Vehicles	*	*	*
5. Infrastructures (roads, streets)		*	
6. Road traffic engineering Management of mobility		*	
7. Prevention, insurance business		*	*
8. Control and enforcement Regulation. Justice and courts		*	
9. Emergency rescue		*	
10. Hospital		*	
11. Information – research		*	*

B. Contexts of action

Among the popular reasons that are often evoked to explain the safety lag between Great Britain and France is the difference in road users' cultures. By their very culture, British users would be more respectful of regulations than the French. This is a widespread belief that our study did not confirm. Shortly after the implementation of automatic speed cameras in the north of France, notably in Pas-de-Calais, the British media reported the complaints of British drivers who declared their surprise at having been fined for speeding although they were used to behaving in this way in the past on French roads, without being fined. This example is telling. British drivers on French roads were used to behaving more or less like other drivers, mostly French, on French roads. The same goes for French drivers on British roads. The particular immediate context of action, more than culture, explains behaviour.

Road users' behaviours depend to a large extent on the contexts in which they operate. This conforms to Gigerenzer and Selten's ecological rationality or reasonability, and to Rasmussen's behaviour-shaping mechanisms (Chapters 1 and 3 above). The immediate context of action is also evoked in the same vein by Erhard Friedberg (Friedberg, 1997). To paraphrase Reason, you cannot change the human condition, but you can change the conditions under which people operate (Reason, 1998).

Contexts of action are more or less distant or immediate. The former include education, training, information, communication, control and enforcement, and courts. The latter comprise the immediate surrounding traffic conditions, that is, what other road users do around you while you are operating. They also include the vehicle characteristics, infrastructure and weather conditions. Another category is central, it is the characteristics of action by road safety actors. It is a powerful defining factor of the context of road users' actions, and it is likely to differ across countries. Given the important place of road safety actors, notably public actors, in road safety activity, a second level of context of action therefore needs to be taken into account. It is the context of action of road safety actors themselves, in addition to the context of action of road users, of which road safety actors are a part.

The context of action appears at the articulation of the actions it shapes, that is, the functional dynamics, on the one hand, and of the structural and organisational conditions that shape itself, on the other hand. It is both shaping and shaped. It is at the intersection of the structural and functional characteristics of road safety. EDCX suggests to model these aspects as a road risk regulation regime (R4).

C. The road risk regulation regime (R4)

The notion of a road risk regulation regime, or R4, follows directly from the regime of action implied by EDCX and evoked in Chapter 6, figure 6.7. The term regulation is taken in the broad sense of the set of actions aimed at reducing the gap between an experienced level of unsafety and a more satisficing, lower level. This level is ideally zero fatality. It is the proclaimed Swedish strategy. In other countries, it is simply to reduce the fatality rate as much as possible, year after year, sometimes with quantitative targets being defined.

R4 is a systemic process made up of the activity relationships and components of which fatalities are the unwanted products (Figure 8.2).

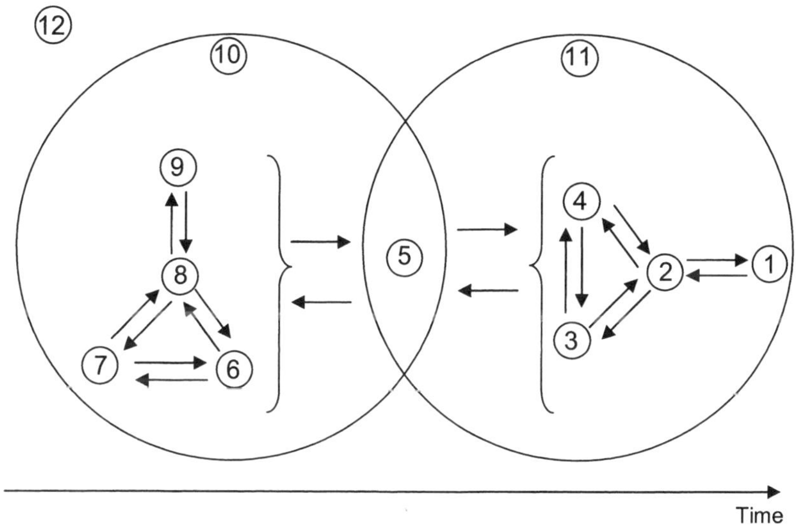

Symbols:

1 Number killed
2 Risk (speed, etc.)
3 Road traffic
4 Road safety action
5 Context of action (immediate, more distant)
6 Structuring of actors
7 Structuring of road safety activities by fields
8 Organisation of road traffic and road safety
9 Institutions, legislation
10 Structural subregime
11 Functional subregime
12 Environment

Figure 8.2 The road risk regulation regime

In Figure 8.2, fatalities are connected to risk via the chain of risks (speed, and so on), accidents, injuries and fatalities evoked in last section. Road risk depends itself on road traffic and road safety action, which are both shaped by their contexts of action that are schematised by the intersection of the functional subregime with the structural subregime. On the structural side, the context of action depends on both the structuring of actors and of activities, themselves shaped by the organisation of road traffic and road safety, itself shaped by law and the institutions of road safety.

D. The French and British R4s in the concrete

Our general hypothesis is that an improved understanding of the fatality rate gap between France and Great Britain can be obtained from characterising fatalities within their respective processual, systemic activity contexts. R4 provides the common framework thanks to which lasting differences can be identified and interpreted. This task cannot be performed otherwise than via an empirical investigation of the experiential British and French R4s.

The results are summarised in Table 8.4. They follow from a systematic comparison of the items included in Figure 8.2, except for the structuring of the fields of road safety activity whose distribution undoubtedly differs between the two countries, but the amount of research resources that an accurate inquiry would have required was well beyond this research's funding limits.

The shorthand term 'organigram' for the item about organisation designates simply the organisational charts or structures. They differ neatly and reflect the differences of the institutional set-ups and historical legacies. They are documented in the research but cannot be detailed here. An instance relates to police forces with road safety responsibilities. There are three police forces in France (police nationale, gendarmerie, and compagnies républicaines de sécurité or CRS). In Great Britain, there is one police organisation which is divided into forces with responsibilities for different geographical regions. Since our focus is on activity, it is especially worthwhile to scrutinise the context of action. An important difference was found in the contexts of action of public actors of road safety.

Table 8.4 Stylised French and British speed R4s

	Great Britain	**France**
Environment	High population density Quasi similar volume of traffic	Lower population density Quasi similar volume of traffic
Institutions	Historical legacy of decentralisation Centralising reforms since the 1978s	Historical legacy of centralisation Decentralising reforms since 1982
Organisation	'Organigram'	'Organigram'
Fields of road safety activity (structuration)	Not documented here	Not documented here
Actors: • **road safety** • **road traffic**	Local Authorities and Department for Transport Local strategy of road safety and governmental strategy	Governmental bodies, prefects, general councils (départements) 'Local road safety policy' mainly defined at the government level
Immediate context of action of public road safetv actors	Relative intensity on professionalisation, integration and evaluation	Relative weakness
Road safety action (fields 1 to 11 of Table 8.3: case of field 8)	Distributed automatised control and enforcement	Centralised automatised control and enforcement
Traffic safety: speed	No noticeable recent decline	Noticeable recent decline
Number of fatalities	Declining long-run trend, recent slowdown	Declining long-run trend, acceleration at end of period
Overall character of R4 speed	Distributed	Under prevailing influence of higher politico-administrative levels

Three factors appear especially discriminating: they are professionalisation, integration or coordination, and evaluation (Table 8.5). An indicator of professionalisation is the number of road safety officers operating with local authorities: more than 600 in Great Britain, less than 20 in France at the *département* level. These figures do not include the persons having a full-time responsibility in road safety at the other politico-administrative levels. Yet there are grounds for believing that the overall relative inferiority of France would not be dramatically changed by their inclusion. Integration refers to coordination. A clear instance is with the police forces: integration is a priori greater with one police force than with three distinct forces and the mechanically created issue of the coordination of their actions. Evaluation refers to public action evaluation.

These three factors are interdependent and form a configuration which was identified as the PIE factor (professionalisation, integration, evaluation). The level of PIE is self-sustained in a circular mutual dependence. Thus, low evaluation and integration imply an absence of pressure toward a higher professionalisation, and are compatible with low professionalisation. In the same vein, low integration and professionalisation are compatible with the quasi absence of public policy evaluation since the resources required for evaluation include a high degree of professionalisation, and evaluation would be likely to put the lack of integration into question. Finally, low professionalisation and no evaluation can go along with low integration since there is no pressure to change it. A low intensity and density of PIE can therefore be coherent and self-sustainable. It still depicts the French case at the beginning of the twenty-first century although reforms have been undertaken recently. It is compensated for by a discretionary capacity of action at the top politico-administrative levels. The situation is the inverse in Great Britain. The relatively high level of PIE and its dense extension across local authorities render governmental big turns in this domain more unlikely than in France.

Table 8.5 The PIE factor

	Great Britain	France
Professionalisation	Dense presence of road safety officers	Few road safety officers
Integration	Effective (local transport plans) though uneven	Calls for more coordination and partnerships
Evaluation	Effective and widespread	Very limited

Road safety action in Table 8.4 refers to the fields listed in Table 8.3. Field 8, control and enforcement, is selected in the table. It was subjected to an important change with the implementation of automatised cameras for speed control which began in 1993 in Great Britain, in 2002 in France. It reflected two different overall procedures, distributed in Great Britain, centralised in France. The bottom line of Table 8.4 contains a characterisation of R4s with respect to speed. Each R4 synthesises the entries in each column, read vertically, from top to bottom. It is manifest that a coherence arises in each column. Its prevailing feature is its distributed character in Great Britain whereas the French R4 denotes a prevailing influence of the higher politico-administrative levels. This does not mean that the British road safety action is necessarily more coherent than the French one. The French R4 denotes a coherence in its greater reliance on impulsions originating from the higher governmental level. The 2002–2003 turn was triggered and managed successfully in this way. Its weakness is to be exposed to changes in political priorities in the future. On this ground, the British R4 is more organic and based on a broader distribution of responsibilities between local authorities and the government.

Concluding remarks

To assess the difference brought by EDCX, we can refer to Figure 8.2. The quantitative epidemiological approach covers items 1, 2 and 3. EDCX includes also the quality of road safety action 4 as another component of risk exposure, and items 5 to 12. It draws attention to the need to integrate the very characteristics of road safety action itself into road safety management. Road safety action differs qualitatively across countries. It is one aspect of enlarging the scope when road safety is studied as an activity reflected in a regime of action, and here, a regime of regulation. EDCX indicates orientations for action that can be put to work, assessed and revised if necessary. In this way it creates a new situation in which elements that were deemed relevant but remained outside the scope of quantitative, statistical analysis can now be included. EDCX does not bring a solution. It simply creates a situation in which improvements are possible. These improvements do not consist in the direct transfer of what seems to work better elsewhere. Here, as in any organised and involved phenomenon, benchmarking requires articulating local action aimed at improving the situation with the enduring regularities on which the overall coherence depends.

8.3 ECONOMIC ISSUES

The purpose of this section is to assess how the threefold character of Effective Deep Complexity, or EDCX, applies to the economy, in terms of a theory of deeply complex situations, of an alternative framework, and of a decision-and-action support process. If we compare the task with what was done with road safety, there is one central difference. It originates in the higher order of complexity depth that most complex economic issues reflect. It renders impossible to dig inside the (G_o, P_o) object-level mechanisms of issues, at a general level. It is only in particular, specific problem situations that it can be envisaged to actualise these mechanisms. Yet it is not an absolute loss of substance, for the main challenge in economic theory is to escape from taking for granted in every case a hypothetico-deductive setting available as a P_m, a meta-level product. It is at this meta-level that the way the object-level problems are informed takes place.

Economic policy, and the economic theory that inevitably informs it, either immediately or from a distance, are faced with a big challenge nowadays. EDCX is not a miraculous solution to this but it can help structure it in a different way. The main shortcoming to which EDCX points is the recurrent reluctance or incapacity of economic policy to take more seriously the essential complex duality that arises in every modern economy. This shortcoming reflects the situation in economic theory. Although the fact that every sustainable market economy is a mixed economy is admitted by some (Guesnerie, 2006), it is still described as if it were a mere adjunct or addition to a core market, and coming after the market. The very intrinsic combination of market and non-market logics from the start, as in the RISE, remains foreign to conventional economic theory. To paraphrase biologist Paul Weiss about systems (see Chapter 6), the way to grasp this complex duality is to consider that a mixed economy is not a market to which some non-market additions would have been made 'afterwards', it is a mixed entity to begin with. Although many heterodox perspectives may be viewed as instances of approaches to the mixed economy, the problem is that they do not appear as effective complete alternatives able to grasp the deeply complex duality of many mixed situations. Their insights about the mix are therefore doomed to be no more effective than the disjunction-based theoretical bodies to which they belong.

8.3.1 A Theory of Deeply Complex Economic Situations

A. In praise of a new mixed economy

The mixed economy has been said to stand as 'the crowning economic achievement of the twentieth century' (Rodrik, 2007, 195). After capitalism was 'unleashed in its full force' in the nineteenth century, it became 'tamed' and its productivity was boosted in the twentieth century 'by supplying the institutional underpinnings of market-based economies'. These institutional innovations which 'enhanced the efficiency and legitimacy of markets' notably in the second half of the twentieth century range from central banks to fiscal policies, to antitrust and regulatory authorities, to social insurance and political democracy to make the above institutions 'accountable to the citizenry' (ibid.). It seems that only market fundamentalists could reject this view. The irony is that although there is likely a wide agreement on this functioning of market capitalism, most of the time its theory has been heavily disputed and despised. The 'brave army of heretics' evoked by Keynes would not only include the institutionalists but also the ordo-liberal, post-Keynesian and *régulation* theory schools. True, they do not focus on the 'mixed economy' proper, though they emphasise the institutional basis of the market economy that is constitutive of a mixed economy. As a matter of fact, the very phrase 'mixed economy' has become a kind of dirty word in standard economic theory and has remained synonymous with intoxicating government and interventionist state, at least until the 2008 financial crisis. These beliefs are even reinforced by the widespread, ingrained dualism of 'market-and-state' as if everything that is not 'market' in the economy were necessarily 'state'.

It is one of the insights of the research on the RISE to have established that in order to characterise the interactions between the state and the economy it is necessary to envisage them in the broader setting of the quite involved and evolving arrangement of institutional and organisational forms beyond mere market and public hierarchy.

The damaging consequence of the dichotomous divide between market and state is to enhance one-sided doctrines and to make theory oscillate in a to-and-fro way between one dominating term or the other. After Keynes highlighted the limitations of the classical school and seemed to have legitimated the post-World War II mixed economic management in Western countries, the growing inflation and monetary and financial instability of the 1970s supplied the ground for denouncing the inefficiency of this economic management and for propagating the promises of its polar opposite, that is, a strategy enhancing the market and downsizing the role of government.

It succeeded in giving rise to an extended neoliberal ideology and in nourishing the market bias of contemporary economic theory that Herbert Simon constantly denounced (Simon, 1991, 27–28; 2000, 11). Rather than opposing notions taken as quasi ontological separates, EDCX converts them into distinctions within a unified setting in process, in which they are structured as a *GP* and a *P* in turn. It is the essence of its principled duality as opposed to the dichotomous dualism of separates.

A duality between what and what? The RISE appears as a mixture of market and other behavioural logics and forms of interaction between economic agents. The former include competition as the core logic underpinning market behaviour. It also includes cooperation and coercion. These comprise notably hierarchies, alliances and networks. These non-market logics and forms of interaction constitute institutions and organisational forms. Their common trait is to consist in organisation understood in its generic bearing of a logic and property of interaction governed by rules and regularities, implicit or explicit, in contrast with competition as the characteristic logic and property of the market governed,in principle, by the exploitation of opportunities and search for advantage in as free and as non-distorted a way as possible.

The RISE is a subspace of any economy. In a market economy, competition is the driving logic but it is not self-regulating and is organically embedded in an institutional and organisational fabric. Organisation covers a wide spectrum. It may range from a minimal meaning of property rights and rule of law to an extreme degree of totalitarian society.

In this way the elementary building block of a market economy can be defined as the duality of competition and organisation (Figure 8.3). EDCX structures it in taking competition as its generative principle and organisation as its product. Why are these terms ordered in this way rather than the converse? History explains it. None of these two terms is prior to the other on a logical basis. History teaches however that all forms of economies and societies that put organisation first, as their generative principle, became dictatorial and totalitarian and ended in catastrophic collapses. The examples of such trauma abound in the past century. Taking the logic of competition as the generative principle of market-led economies aims simply at recognising its role as an engine of dynamism calling for its organisation in a pattern evolving according to the periodic crises that are intrinsic to market economies. Historical experience tells us that the ingredients of this duality are in continual tension and influence each other. Unleashed competition creates imbalances and excesses which call for reactions and responses through organisation. But its very success is likely to reinforce it and make it appear sooner or later as an impediment to the promises of freer economic activity. Organisation as a product thus feeds back on the need for more competition which in turn will be perceived positively during a time and negatively through its excesses, thus calling for a renewed organisation and so on. There is nothing mechanical in the succession of these tensions. It depicts simply the historical experience of market capitalism and its oscillating move from unleashed capitalism to a mixed economy as evoked by Rodrik, but with the opposite tendency of a new unleashing of market, notably financial markets, at the end of the twentieth century and the beginning of the twenty-first century.

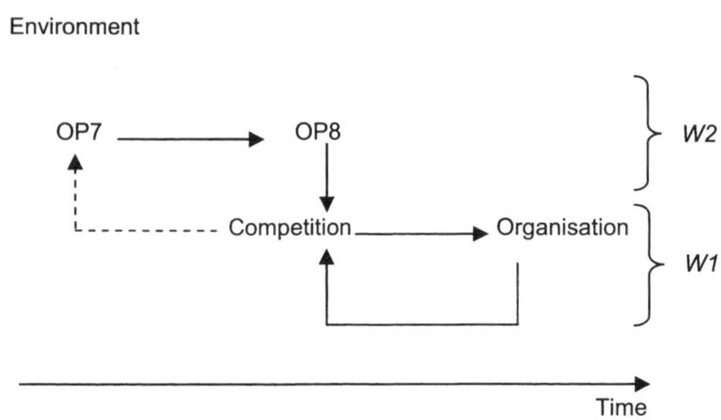

Figure 8.3 EDCX and the market economy

All in all, EDCX provides a theoretical depiction of a market economy understood as a CTSP, a critically transactional systemic process whose dynamics reside in the complex duality of a logic of competition and a logic of organisation in which the former is the generative principle and the latter is the product. Why this particular distribution of the two terms rather than the inverse? The reason is supplied by history. None of these terms is superior to the other on a logical basis. History teaches however that there is no form of economy and society having put economic organisation first, as their generative principle, that did not end in totalitarian dictatorship and catastrophe. The examples of such trauma abound in the twentieth century. Taking the logic of competition as the generative principle of market led economies underscores its role as an engine of dynamism calling for its organisation in a pattern evolving according to the periodic phases of instability that are intrinsic to any market economy. This mixture encompasses the traditional (market, state) mixed economy. In this sense the terms which depict it are those of *new mixed economy.* It is also new because its relevant framework is less and less national but tends to become national and international or global in the present-day historical development of capitalism. It is addressed below.

Emphasising this duality may look like Veblen's comment that: 'All this is simple enough. It is so simple and is so obvious that it is difficult to see it until it has been pointed out, and after it has been pointed out it seems to have been unnecessary to speak of it' (Dorfman, 1972, 51). Yet it is not trivial to theorise in a unified setting, as a duality proper, notions which are usually grasped in a dichotomous way.

B. The politico-economical trilemma of our time

Dani Rodrik suggests, by analogy with the standard 'impossible trinity' (fixed exchange rates, capital mobility and monetary autonomy) of open-economy macroeconomics, a different kind of trilemma that he calls the *political trilemma* of the world economy (Rodrik, 2007, 199). I would like to suggest in turn, by analogy with Rodrik's political trilemma, a different kind of trilemma, one that we might call the *politico-economical* trilemma, which includes the new mixed economy.

The first trilemma is a familiar result of open-economy macroeconomics. It tells that countries cannot simultaneously maintain independent monetary policies, fixed exchange rates and international capital mobility. If a government chooses to have two of these features, it has to give up the third.

In Rodrik's extended trilemma, the three nodes are international economic integration – or globalisation as 'enhanced trade and financial integration', the nation-state and mass politics. Although the implied claim is that it is possible to have at most two of these three things, as in the standard trilemma, it is less familiar and needs to be explained. By the term *nation-state* Rodrik denotes the 'territorial-jurisdictional entities with independent powers of making and administering the law'. He uses the term *mass politics* 'to refer to political systems where (a) the franchise is unrestricted; (b) there is a high degree of political mobilisation; and (c) political institutions are responsive to mobilized groups' (ibid., 200).

Rodrik explains that:

> If we want true international economic integration, we have to go either with the nation-state, in which case the domain of national politics will have to be significantly restricted, or else with mass politics, in which case we will have to give up the nation-state in favour of global federalism. If we want highly participatory political regimes, we have to choose between the nation-state and international economic integration. If we want to keep the nation-state, we have to choose between mass politics and international economic integration. (ibid., 200)

The outcome of this reasoning is thus to characterise three limit pairs, each with its own logic. The nation state–globalisation pair implies what Rodrik, after Thomas Friedman (1999), calls the Golden Straitjacket. The nation state–mass politics pair implies what he calls a 'Bretton Woods compromise'. And the globalisation–mass politics pair calls for global federalism.

The Golden Straitjacket designates a world where national markets are fully integrated but politics remains organised nationally. Friedman notes:

> To fit into the Golden Straitjacket a country must either adopt, or be seen as moving toward, the following golden rules: making the private sector the primary engine of its economic growth, maintaining a low rate of inflation and price stability, shrinking the size of its state bureaucracy, maintaining as close to a balanced budget as possible, if not a surplus, eliminating and lowering tariffs on imported goods, removing restrictions on foreign investment, getting rid of quotas and domestic monopolies, increasing exports, privatizing state-owned industries and utilities, deregulating capital markets and making its currency convertible, opening its industries, stock, and bond markets to direct foreign ownership and investment, deregulating its economy to promote as much domestic competition as possible … When you stitch all of these pieces together you have the Golden Straitjacket. (Friedman, 1999, 86–7)

Once the rules of the game are set by the requirements of the global economy, there is a pressure to shrink politics through, as Rodrik notices: (1) insulating economic policy-making bodies (central banks, fiscal authorities, and so on) from political participation and debates; (2) curbing down and privatising social welfare insurance; (3) replacing developmental goals with the imperative to maintain market confidence.

The 'Bretton Woods compromise' is the option implied by the renunciation of complete international economic integration. Until the end of the 1970s, the Bretton Woods–GATT (General Agreement on Tariffs and Trade) regime consisted in a loose set of rules leaving enough space for countries to follow their own development orientations and maintain restrictions on capital flows provided they removed a number of restrictions on trade and did not discriminate among their trade partners. This compromise vanished in the 1980s under several pressures coming from a lasting high inflation and financial instability, the growing criticism of the so-called Keynesian spirit of economic policy orientations with which it was linked, and its replacement by a neoliberal ideology encouraged by the curbing of inflation, the coming to power of Margaret Thatcher in 1979 in the United Kingdom and of Ronald Reagan in 1980 in the USA, and the economic growth that was observed. It was encouraged by the collapse of the USSR in 1989.

Global federalism does not yet exist. It would relocate politics and government at the global level and actualise the need of balancing economic globalisation with global governance.

The upshot of this argumentation is that if we represent these limit situations by the vertices and the sides of a triangle, the actual situation lies somewhere between these limits, as a composition of these dimensions.

In what follows, I suggest that the essential duality mechanism of EDCX helps envisage a different, not purely political framework, though finding support in parts of Rodrik's trilemma (Figure 8.4). The three vertices of this deeply complex, politico-economical dilemma are globalisation, the nation-state with national mass politics, and the competition-organisation duality. The nation-state level includes national governance, national economy and mass politics, as defined by Rodrik, which are essentially developed at the national level.

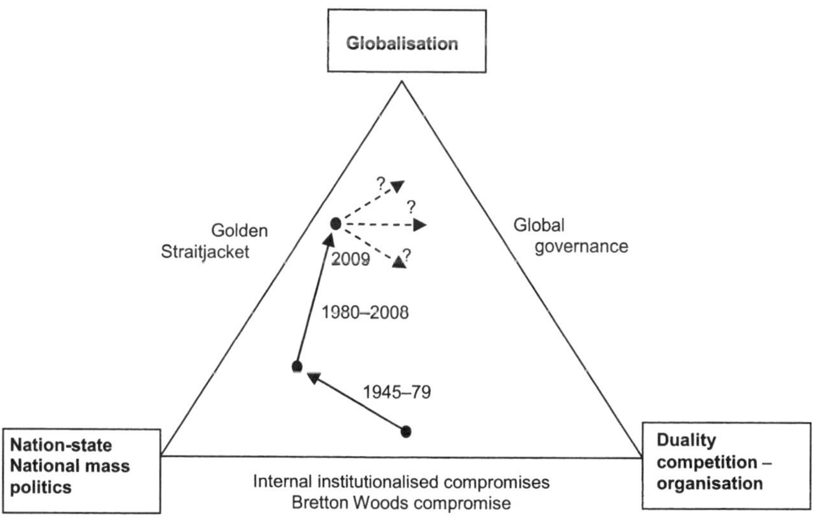

Figure 8.4 The politico-economical trilemma of market economies

The duality of the logics of competition and organisation as a node is meant to point out that it is the core problem of the working of any economy and that its internal mixture is open to a variety of possible combinations, all of which result from constructions in history. It modifies the very sense of the trilemma since this duality proper cannot be eliminated by the choice to abide by globalisation and retain a nation-state governance (the Golden Straitjacket). Yet, the trilemma works fully through the neutralisation it implies of one term of the duality, here, organisation. The working of the Golden Straitjacket implies that competition works fully and that its dual of organisation or reorganisation through modified regulation intended to monitor the non-self-regulating character of unleashed competition is, so to speak, disactivated to a broad extent.

The Bretton Woods compromise implied a particular duality with a specific organisation which went under heavy pressure in the 1970s and was followed by the thrust toward globalisation and a competition logic which developed at a much faster rate than organisation. The financial crisis of 2008 is one of its upshots. It has accelerated the recognition that more international coordination is needed. Whether it is treated as a short-run concern to remedy events viewed as temporary difficulties, without affecting the belief in the basically self-regulating character of competitive markets, including financial markets, or whether it is aimed at reorganising the fundamental mechanisms of the duality, is the choice that is at stake nowadays.

The combinations of competition and organisation vary across countries. They depend on internal and international conditions. They are shaped inside countries by institutionalised, history-dependent compromises. Internationally, the Bretton Woods compromise managed a way of articulating an active role of nation-states with international rules. Globalisation makes it now necessary to envisage a new, more involved articulation, between the need of a global governance, the existence of nation-states, and the management of the (competition $*$ organisation) duality.

8.3.2 An Alternative Analytical Framework

Contemporary economic theory is plagued by two things: the scientism of its mainstream, and the lack of an effective alternative to it.

A. The scourge of scientism

The *Oxford English Dictionary* defines scientism in two ways: as a belief in the omnipotence of scientific knowledge and technique; and as the view that the methods of physical science are applicable in all inquiry, especially in the human and social sciences. The latter is especially relevant for contemporary mainstream economic theory and its claim to use the methods of 'modern science' as mentioned in Chapter 6, and is addressed here. Its exact meaning needs to be specified for it is likely to vary among authors. Scientism was denounced notably by Friedrich Hayek and Karl Popper. Although they both attacked historicism in social science in the name of its alleged scientistic character, their views of scientism are different and may help understand the notion of scientism envisaged here.

For Hayek, the methods of natural and social sciences are irreducible to each other. Scientism, the slavish imitation of the methods of the physical sciences, overlooks crucial aspects of social reality such as perception, intent and anticipation. Scientism pervades objectivism (the view that true sciences make reference to observable, objective reality), collectivism (the tendency to treat aggregate concepts, like 'society' or 'the economy' as actual objects of study) and historicism (the search of historical laws that govern the evolution of the collective entities). The actual subject-matter of the social sciences is premised for Hayek on a common structure of human minds consisting in the perceptions and beliefs on the basis of which we act. They are the starting point for the study of the actions and facts of social science. From these subjective opinions of individual agents, the social scientist 'builds up' to the level of complex social phenomena using a compositive method (Caldwell, 1998, 223), whereas in the natural sciences, we start with complex phenomena and attempt to go back to their most elementary components in an analytical way (Lacroix, 1992, 92).

The task of the social scientist is to understand how individual human action leads to aggregate phenomena which, although they are the result of human action, are not the result of human design, and relate to what Hayek calls a spontaneous order. The social scientist is very seldom in a position to predict the precise outcome of a particular situation and to rely on controlled experiment, because of the complexity of the subject-matter of social sciences. Often the best that one can do is to disprove a theory by the observations of events which according to the theory are impossible, or to 'explain the principle on which certain phenomena are produced' (Caldwell, 1998) or, still, to envisage 'pattern prediction' (Hayek, 1975, [1989]).

Popper also denounced historicism as an instance of scientism and of a wrong understanding of the scientific method. But unlike Hayek, Popper does not contrast the methods of social and natural sciences. For him, they differ only in degree within a unity of the scientific method whose paradigmatic illustration is physical science with its deductive-nomological methodology (that is, oriented towards stating scientific laws), its recourse to experimentation, trial solutions subject to criticism, refutations and error elimination. Popper even claims that economics approximates this method and that other social sciences should follow what is done in economics. Therefore scientism consists in a wrong imitation of the method of physical science, for Popper, whereas the very methodological imitation of natural science is unwarranted for Hayek. Popper's advocacy of the unity of scientific method contrasts clearly with Hayek's dualism of methods.

EDCX is still different though it contains Popperian and Hayekian aspects. In emphasising the reference to scientific practice from the beginning, I was especially concerned with what is common to science in the daily work of scientists, that is, a process of production of a kind of knowledge whose unique, differentiating characteristic is to be continually exposed in a transparent way to public criticism and testing through declared-in-advance criteria. It is not tied to some specific essence of phenomena of whatever particular scientific domain, but to cognitive situations and judgement. Its general methodological perspective is abductive and encompasses other methods. The methods of physical science are acceptable as far as they lead to satisficing results, which amounts to non-deep complexity. But things are different for deeply complex problem-situations.

In the dominant part of economic theory that is overtly scientistic, scientism consists in importing the methods of physical science as a generally valid methodology. It occurs in an economics world in which the tools which allow one to achieve clear-cut results in physical science, and thus a form of satisficing, do not work generally. Economics and social science are more likely to reveal deeply complex problem-situations than natural sciences because the tools which allow the latter to achieve demonstrative and conclusive results (controlled experimentation, repeatability, stabilised and accepted protocols of validation) simply do not exist on a general basis in the former. This non-demonstrative and non-conclusive character of economics was already emphasised by J.M. Keynes in the 1930s, as we mentioned in Chapter 2.

EDCX favours economics and social science as a critical process of knowing whose testing rests on an open-ended intersubjective consensus of what is the case, in the way Popper defined an open society. To continue to act in the economy – and elsewhere – as if we possessed the scientific knowledge enabling us to transcend the obstacles set forth by deeply complex situations may become a serious obstacle to the advance of human knowledge, to paraphrase Hayek. Or, more plainly stated, it may become a serious obstacle to dealing with the mounting human, politico-strategic, developmental, environmental and climatic challenges on Planet Earth in the years to come.

To sum up, physical and social sciences differ through the techniques on which they can rely to put to work their common generative process of scientific practice. EDCX advocates a scientific practice based on criticism and experiencing, aiming at error elimination when it can be unambiguously performed and, above all, at critical valuation.

B. Another game in town[2]

In economics, there is a plurality of theoretical perspectives that differ from the mainstream view. A partial list of them includes, notably, Keynesian theory, institutionalist thought, *régulation* theory, evolutionary political economy and some less well-known views such as the Ordo-liberal original perspective, George Soros's thinking, the Post Normal Science movement in ecological economics and even an important part of the complex systems perspective. Several of them, and the reasons why they come close to deep complexity, were evoked in Chapter 2.

Among others, Soros's theses on 'reflexive theory' and the instability of financial markets also consist in a recognition of the irreducibility of observed phenomena to the equilibrium analytical framework, and in the defence of an alternative to it (Soros, 2002; Bryant, 2002).

'Post-Normal Science' (Funtowicz and Ravetz, 1993; Ravetz, 1999, 2004) is a label denoting the conduct of research when 'facts are uncertain, values in dispute, stakes high and decisions urgent' (Ravetz, 1999). It contrasts with T.S. Kuhn's 'normal science', that is, the sort of research that is devoted to 'puzzle-solving' within a paradigm that is accepted uncritically (Ravetz, 2004). As Ravetz states it, when the assumption that the policy environment is 'normal' holds, routine puzzle-solving by experts provides an adequate knowledge base for policy decisions. In 'normality', either science or policy, the process (routine work on small-scale problems) is managed largely implicitly, and is accepted unwittingly by all those who wish to join it. In a post-normal problem situation:

> even the professionals' skills and commitment are insufficient ... deep uncertainty or even ignorance swamps our knowledge, and ... the value-commitments of participants set incompatible frameworks for the policy issue in dispute. Although decisions need not be urgent, the features about radical uncertainty, incommensurable values and high decision stakes suggest strongly that when 'science' is applied to them, the conditions are anything but normal. (Ravetz, 1999, 649)

In such a context hard policy decisions must be made 'where our only scientific inputs are irremediably soft' (ibid.). Resolving such issues requires new skills and attitudes. Assertive scientific demonstration gives way to open-ended dialogue. Post-Normal Science has been applied to several fields beyond ecological economics such as food safety, medicine and climate change (Hulme and Turnpenny, 2004). The essential feature of this perspective is its methodology. It has given rise to a variety of attempts to build appropriate tools (Van der Sluijs et al., 2006).

All these views share a common distrust and contempt from the scientific establishment in economics. Things occur as if any sort of thinking not resembling the canons of committees' consensus about emulating 'modern science' (essentially mathematical and hypothetico-deductive formalisms whatever the absence of strict protocols of empirical validation) were a priori condemned to be considered as non-serious science by this scholastic.

It is fair to say that the lack of a unified framework creates a confusion and an incapacity to devise firm criteria for assessing the value of most dissident views. In the absence of an alternative framework, the unique, standard framework is bound to rule effectively.

The thesis defended here is therefore that a noticeable source of this rather frustrating debate lies within these non-standard perspectives themselves. To become a possible effective alternative to the scientific mainstream theory, a challenging perspective needs to pass the Simon's test and to bring insights to problems that mainstream theory cannot tackle. Although it may look totally out of reach, one may detect common features among these perspectives. DCX is one such salient feature for the theoretical perspectives discussed in Chapter 2. In this way EDCX brings with its conjunctive framework the anchoring that was sought and may be viewed as an effective alternative to the disjunctive framework.

An objection to the interest of having an alternative framework may be that it is too abstract. It calls for showing what difference it makes empirically. I offer what follows in Table 8.6 as an answer. It contains a schematised comparison between a standard and an evolutionary perspective of the overall strategy of economic transition that was followed in the 1990s in Central and Eastern European countries after the collapse of the Soviet bloc. I had the privilege to coordinate an international team from 1993 to 1995 researching the economic transformations in Central and Eastern European countries, including Russia. It resulted in a special issue of Emergo in 1995, and the publication of a book in 1996 (Delorme, 1996). This research mixed Western, Central and Eastern European experts, a majority of whom discovered each other, and who accepted working in the unusual way of building robust observations first, before attempting to theorise them, without any predefined end-state. These authors were Christine André, Amit Badhuri, Robert Boyer, Laslo Bruszt, Bernard Chavance, Jerzy Hausner, Branko Horvat, Rouslan Koumakhov, Tadeusz Kudlacz, Victor Kuznetsov, Eric Magnin, Jacques Sapir, Guy Standing, David Stark, Jacek Szlachta and this author.

The research developed in a context in which the debate was between a 'shock therapy' and a gradual strategy of structural transformation. The former was favoured by the influential economic circles advising international organisations and the governments that were concerned, and it prevailed. There rapidly appeared a feeling of discrepancy between, on the one hand, the errors that were made although they were based on a rather unified body of standard economic theory (Portes, 1994), and on the other hand, several views advocating more pragmatism and less overconfidence in market fundamentalism. Our research was among the latter. Its result was to highlight the diversity of the national situations due to the diversity of historical paths and of institutional and organisational arrangements, thus nourishing a view that the actual situations were less 'black or white' than a strictly narrow application of market-led microeconomics would have it. Market and institutions, or competition and organisation, emerged as recurring dualities throughout the research. It underpinned the perception of an irreducibility to the standard analysis. This irreducibility was however not yet conceptualised as a deep complexity.

Table 8.6 The divide between the standard perspective and an alternative, evolutionary perspective about economic transition in Central and Eastern European countries in the 1990s

	Standard perspective	Alternative perspective
Normative principle guiding economic policy orientations	• Pareto criterion of allocative efficiency. General equilibrium of competitive markets as paradigmatic example of a well-functioning economy	• Economic performance dependent on capacity to cope with change and on capacity to satisfy human needs defined through democratically agreed procedures and respecting basic universal values
Prevailing view of change and evolution	• End-state-driven • Pre-established model as norm of reference • Transition: viewed as a move from one coherent order to another	• Open-ended • History-bound process. Paths of extrication with differences in kind • Transformation: plurality of logics of action
Prevailing mode of reasoning	• The economy as a self-contained system • Universality • Typological reasoning Homogeneity • Priority to determinateness. One best way, single exit. Priority to analytical tractability • More 'either–or' than 'more or less' view of economic problems • De facto exclusivism	• Economy embedded in the socio-historical fabric • History and context dependency • Population thinking. Diversity • Indeterminateness permitted Pragmatism. Priority to the empirically robust and meaningful (hard facts) • More 'more or less' than 'either–or' view of economic problems • Inclusivism: subsumes standard approach, accepting its local relevance, for suitably identified situations
Typical outcome	• Equilibrium-driven • Macroeconomic convergence	• No asymptotic state • Plurality of capitalist trajectories
Expected result and its likelihood	• High, if decision makers, notably governments, follow economists' advice	• Varying across countries. Evolution does not necessarily entail progress. Decline, political setbacks are possible

Adapted from Delorme (1995b)

As a matter of fact it was rapidly recognised that these results suffered from the major shortcoming of not being underpinned by a unified theoretical framework. I undertook a systematic comparison of the standard perspective, contrasting it with what arose from our research and that I called an 'evolutionary perspective' in order to convey its complex processual character, and for lack of a better term.

Table 8.6 is a simplified version of the initial comparison. It retains selected items of it, without any modification in the terms used in the study. The terms in each column are reduced to those that are given a priority in each perspective. The first column contains the characteristic properties and features that emerged from the debates and decisions that were taken in order to monitor rapid transitions toward market economies. Though it is impossible to go into the details contained in the original sources, it is manifest that the vertical totalisation of the first column displays a unified, equilibrium-driven, underpinning framework. The second column was filled differently. It had no *a priori* unity. Each of its entries resulted from asking whether there was a counterpart to each corresponding entry of the first column. The outcome is the column entitled 'alternative perspective'. Although the vertical totalisation of this column reflects a consistency based on an open-ended process and an overall encompassing character with respect to the standard perspective, its weakness was the lack of a unified theoretical framework of which it would have been the product. I was far from Effective Deep Complexity at that time. The developments of the present book allow me now to put the name of Effective Deep Complexity on this alternative perspective.

This case study suggests at least that there was an alternative strategy that might have been envisaged at the beginning of the 1990s although it could not be grounded on a unified theoretical framework. It might have entailed a slower transition. Would it have been worse than what was put into action and experienced until now? It is naturally impossible to answer. Yet it remains to be demonstrated that it would have had worse consequences than the kind of 'quick and chaos' process, and the authoritarian return to order with an apparent economic prosperity based on oil and gas experienced since 2000 in Russia.

8.3.3 An Economic Decision-and-action Support Process

How can Effective Deep Complexity support economic decision and action? It seems that two answers can be given. One is general and says that EDCX works in relation to the economy in the same way as it does in relation to any deeply complex situation, whatever the subject matter, the domain or the discipline are. In this way, there is nothing to add to Chapter 7. Another answer is more specific to economic policy. It is that EDCX brings a difference in economic policy, both in theory and in actual policy. This is a challenging claim which will be explained in what follows. In order to avoid any ambiguity, let it be made clear what it is not or it cannot be. It is not the claim to prescribe a solution to major economic policy problems but to create a situation in which a solution may be possible, thus paraphrasing Keynes about the revision of the Treaty of Versailles and the settlement of Europe after World War I (Keynes, CW, III, 117).

And it cannot be the direct transposition of the modelling of road safety management to economic policy decision and action. The main reason is that although these issues both follow from deeply complex problem situations, most important issues of economic policy are by far much more complex than those of road safety policy.

A. Complex, organised duality

The main difference brought by EDCX lies in the overall *GP**P* structuring of the problem-situations. *P* in road safety consists in casualties to people, killed and injured. Its generating process can be traced back through risk analysis and a variety of factors whose diversity can nevertheless be modelled in a setting based on structural and functional aspects of what appears as a road safety system. A connection between the level of product and its generating factors could be envisaged. Levers of decision and of action could be identified as an outcome of the enquiry.

In comparison, in many economic problems, every term of the *GP**P* pattern is complexified by a multiplicating factor up to a level of diversity and heterogeneity that creates an irreducibility to a model in which a clear-cut connection between product and generative factors could be established. This is the essence of emergence, the appearance at the global level of properties that cannot be deduced from the properties of the component parts, an instance of which is Brian Arthur's process and emergence perspective of economic analysis contrasted to equilibrium economics. It is precisely at this point that EDCX tackles the issue as deeply complex, calling for: (1) a decision as to whether to continue in a disjunctive way, or to step outside the received view and shift to a conjunctive framework in which deciding on how to deal with the problem is an inclusive part of the problem; and (2) putting decision-making to work through action aimed at assessing its value in an experiencing process of trial solutions, failures and exercise of judgement. There is much more of an emergence problem in economics than in road safety.

The task in road safety is to improve safety subject to law and the highway code. The task of economic policy is to contribute to improve the welfare of the population. There is little debate on the means to affect sources of safety in road safety. They rely on shaping users' behaviour, on vehicles, on infrastructure and on the enforcement of rules. There is no enforcement in economics that could be equivalent to the highway code. The existence of a rather well-identifiable connection between *P* and *GP* in road safety allows one to define illegal deviations from the highway code and to sanction them. There is no such general connection in economics. It is, comparatively, a multifarious subject-matter involving simultaneously diverse levels of activity (individual, managerial, global), a heterogeneity of activities (production, distribution of income, consumption investment), a plurality of forms (material goods, services, money, finance) and multiple tangled interdependencies, all these features being crowned by disputed causation connections, values also in dispute, and uncertainties about outcomes.

The consequence is that whereas it proved possible to go inside the $GP_o{*}P_o$ relation in road safety in an effective way, the same is not possible on a general basis for economic policy decision-making and action. It does not allow us to model economic activity and policy as a systemic process based on a distinction between structural and functional features unless we stay at a very abstract and ineffective level of description. The very intricacy and variety of economic matter forces us to leave open the specific contents of the $GP_o{*}P_o$ innumerable elementary processes through which economic activity unfolds. The lesson of EDCX is to focus on what is common to these processes. It operates as the framework and context setting the boundaries inside which these $GP_o{*}P_o$ processes unfold. This framework is a meta-level $GP_m{*}P_m$: it is the (competition * organisation) duality.

It is the answer to the question: 'On what to act?' Many combinations between the two terms are possible and may range from one-sided to balanced situations. One-sided situations are unstable and inconsistent with truly open societies. The duality needs to be maintained as duality, however evolving it may be. The issue about acting on it is to manage a dynamic compromise between the engine of the functioning of markets and competition, on the one hand, and the necessary rules and organisation making the whole sustainable and consistent with economic and social aspirations, on the other hand.

Maintaining the (competition * organisation) duality active and effective is the key intellectual challenge that has to be faced nowadays. Several empirical illustrations will be given below. Before we move to them, we need to address the 'how' of acting on the duality.

Maintaining a concern for duality as an essential imperative of economic action and policy goes against the spontaneous attractor of one-sidedness in knowledge and in behaviour. Each of the examples below taken from the issues of globalisation, of the failed European Union constitution, and of the present financial and economic crisis, illustrates spectacularly what is meant by one-sidedness and its consequences. They show how what seems obvious common sense is the object of an extraordinarily strong resistance in the belief systems of the majority which has shaped economic theory and influenced economic policy since the beginning of the 1980s, in Western counties first and elsewhere later on.

There is therefore a clear stake in informing duality by a theoretical alternative framework, as was done above, and in making it operational. Duality as a principle for decision has important implications on economic policy making in non-trivial, non-non-deeply complex situations. Duality reflects deep complexity and cannot be encapsulated into the classical view of the point-like decision maker of first cybernetics whose economic counterpart evokes the authoritarian-like steermanship underpinning economic policy that pervades in most economics textbooks.

The very duality setting pushes away the notion of substantially well-settled one-sided truths and compels us to remain watchful about how to strike a balance between two terms in continual tension, none of them having the capacity to supersede its dual durably. The only truth is that the duality is ineliminable and is hierarchised in a recursive way from *GP* to *P* to *GP* and so on.

Managing to maintain a balance is never-ending. Its outcome can be at most temporarily stabilised. It continually questions our certainties and evidence that we have taken for granted and makes them evolve *de facto*. It goes against many economists' hubris and arrogance, and keeps active a positive anxiety following from the humility that is called for, while impulsing the need to keep some control. Not being cast a priori in a one-sided substantive truth implies relying on a procedure rendered acceptable to a majority although its outcome is certain to none. It therefore calls for a participatory decision making process. This does not mean that every decision must be decided by a vote, but simply that one individual, one decision entity, is less knowledgeable and reasonable alone than through a participatory or collegial decisio-making process. This does not dispense with the necessary leadership, but a leadership that is itself necessarily combined with participation. It creates another specific duality in which the *GP*-leadership secretes a *P*-participation to be reasonable and effective which itself, in turn, as time and its accompanying flux of events and ideas goes by, causes a changed *GP*, and so on.

In sum, keep duality active to keep options open. How GP_o*P_o is substantiated depends on the situation at stake. It varies according to the flux of events and ideas. What must be avoided is to deal with it with the NDCX toolkit even when the situation is DCX. EDCX tells us that if decision and action are to be consistent with the DCX character of the situation, then it is necessary to maintain options open at the object level. It makes it all the more necessary, then, to dispose of a meta-level pattern setting the bounded space inside which openness operates at the object level. The complex duality of competition*organisation in a market economy is schematised in Figure 8.5.

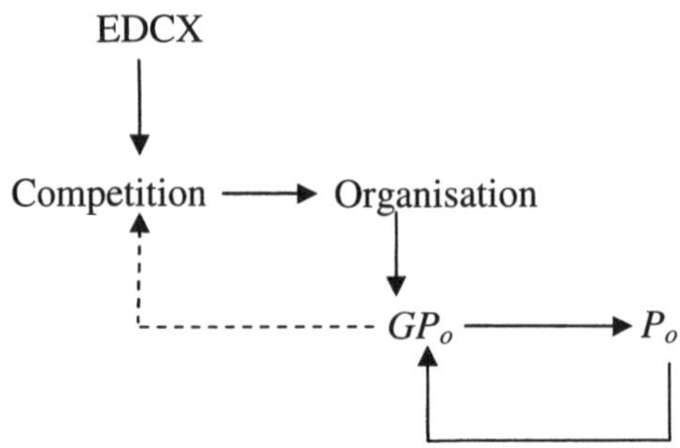

Figure 8.5 The duality of competition and organisation

B. Globalisation without complex duality

Globalisation is both economic and financial. It denotes enhanced trade and economic and financial integration. The second half of the twentieth century was characterised by the succession of two clearly different phases of globalisation.

The first was the Bretton Woods system which lasted for about three decades after the end of World War II. It achieved a sort of compromise between removing the most important restrictions on trade flows, and allowing national governments the freedom to run their own macroeconomic policies and to erect their own visions of the welfare state. The second phase, under which we are, is marked by a continual push toward market opening and deregulation. It is a one-sided process whose consequence is a continual shrinking of national policy space that is depicted by Friedman's 'Golden Straitjacket'. China, India and a few other Asian counties were able to play the globalisation game without liberalising their import regimes until well after their economies had taken off, and used industrial polices strategically to take greater advantage of world markets (Rodrik, 2007).

On the whole globalisation may well have achieved a level from which the further pressure to market opening may become counterproductive. The Achilles heel of globalisation is the imbalance between the global nature of markets and the national scope of governments. Following Rodrik, no country's growth prospects seem to be significantly constrained today by an insufficient openness of the international economy. The threat is that national policy space will shrink to such levels that governments will be unable to deliver the policies that their electorates want, and that instability and mass rejection will arise.

In EDCX terms, the (competition $*$ organisation) duality takes here the form of a (market opening $*$ national policy space) duality. Continual market opening as global market access is the driving force. Too much of it is at the risk of instability and little social and political support from those it is supposed to help sooner or later. Supporters of continual market opening evoke the risk of going back to protectionism and even autarchy if more room were left to national policy space. As a matter of fact we are far from it today; a one-sided market opening process is prevailing.

Rodrik has aptly diagnosed the limits of this continual opening of markets and the threat it presents for the global economy (ibid.). Rich and poor countries alike need some breathing space in the global economy: the rich to revive the social compacts, the poor to have the room to engage in exchange rate and industrial policies that may conflict with the World Trade Organisation and International Monetary Fund rules of good behaviour. Rodrik claims that the time has come to consider a new bargain in the negotiation on the rules of the game between rich and poor countries. They should stop thinking in terms of exchanging market access and instead consider exchanging policy space. The challenge then is to design procedures that will ensure that the policy space is used for socially desirable purposes, while limiting its beggar-thy-neighbour protectionist potential. This thinking converges with the consequences of EDCX. The challenge is to manage a dynamic and delicate compromise of the processual duality between the extreme of excess market opening and its potential of instability, and its opposite of policy space in autarky, which would be unsustainable. The challenge is also for economic theory to free itself from the pendulum shifts from one extreme to the other. Thinking in terms of complex duality would be significant progress.

C. The story of the failed European Union constitution

A rather fascinating illustration of the one-sidedness to which EDCX points is contained in the defunct project of treaty which intended to create a constitution for the European Union. It was signed in 2004 by the heads of states or governments of the 25 member states of the union and needed to be ratified by all member states. Its main aims were to replace the overlapping set of existing treaties that followed the Treaty of Rome signed in 1957 which created a 'common market' between six founding countries (Belgium, France, Germany, Holland, Italy and Luxemburg). It also aimed to codify human rights throughout the EU, and to streamline decision-making.

It was in process of ratification in 2005. In France a big majority of politicians, of intellectuals and of the media – all the TV and radio networks – campaigned in support of the treaty. The French voters rejected it in a referendum (29 May). They were followed by the Dutch (1 June).

Eighteen other member states ratified the text while seven postponed the ratification process. It marked the end of the project for a constitution. Following a period of reflection, it was decided in 2007 to replace it by a Reform Treaty known as the Treaty of Lisbon, also subject to ratification by all member states. Irish voters rejected it (12 June 2008), while it was due to enter in application by 1

January 2009. This highlights the difficulty of streamlining decision-making in what is now a 27-member state organisation.[3]

The constitution project (European Union, 2004) mentioned the enhancing of a 'social market economy' and of an 'internal market where competition is free and undistorted' (article I.3). It contained a chapter on economic and monetary policy which defined a model of economic policy by stating that the 'activities of the Member States and the Union shall include ... the adoption of an economic policy ... conducted in accordance with the principles of an open market economy with free competition' (art. III.177) or 'shall act ... in accordance with the principle of an open market economy with free competition' (art. III.178).

Nowhere in this project can one find an explicit statement about competition combined with its organisation as a basis for economic policy. The only instance is the prohibition of the 'prevention, restriction or distortion of competition within the internal market' that is detailed in articles III.161 to III.169. It is a set of rules ensuring the enforcement of free competition, including a limited list of aids granted by the member states that 'shall be compatible' with the internal market (aids of a social character to individuals, after natural disasters) or that 'may be considered to be compatible' with the internal market (promotion of less developed areas, projects of common European interest, promotion of culture and heritage conservation).

To the market bias of contemporary economic theory denounced by H. Simon (Simon, 1991, 2000), the constitution project added a market bias of European economic policy. The question is whether it was so important as to make an issue of it. There are three arguments that can be used in defence of the project but that do not appear convincing when they are assessed with EDCX.

First is the reference to a 'highly competitive social market economy' mentioned right at the beginning (article I.3). It is indeed used as a slogan which deviates from the original notion of 'as much market as possible, as much state as necessary', which seems to describe best the experience of a social market economy followed notably in Germany. The genuine social market economy does not separate the two branches. It forms a duality that we evoked in Chapter 2.

According to a second argument, the 'social clause' introduced by the Charter of Fundamental Rights of the Union (dignity, freedom, equality, solidarity, citizen's rights and justice) should be sufficient to balance the market bias. Article III-117 mentions that: 'the Union shall take into account requirements linked to the promotion of a high level of employment, the guarantee of adequate social protection, and a high level of education, training and protection of human health'.

It makes clear a profound asymmetry with the 'economic clause'. The latter is a clearly defined set of rules whose violation is illegal and enforced through explicit procedures which may involve the European Court of Justice. The former is no more than a set of intentions. Not taking into account 'the requirements ... of a high level of employment' cannot be enforced by law and court. There is no consensus on the means to be used for achieving this central goal of economic policy. The only consensus is on taking it as an objective. What may be incompatible with high employment cannot be coined in a law. This reflects the dispute in economic theory. Therefore the authors of the project of treaty cannot be blamed for it. But it is wrong to believe that the market bias is balanced by the social clause when the former is a binding legal constraint while the latter is a set of objectives of which the most important cannot be expressed as a legal constraint. A way to avoid this essential imbalance would have been to include explicitly the duality and the reference to organisation in the economic policy clause, thus reducing its brutal one-sidedness by exposing it to politico-economical deliberation by appropriate institutions. A suggestion is that articles III-177 and 178 might have been complemented by the addition of the reference to 'free competition *within a framework ensuring that it is sustainable'* or viable. It would have compelled one to reflect on, and to create, the means appropriate for a genuine legislative and governmental framework of decision-making at the EU level that would be needed to envisage a politico-economical compromise, rather than abandoning the functioning of the economy to a sheer market bias.

The final argument in favour of the project was that its economic part simply reproduced what was already in the Treaty of Rome and its successors. It is true that the economic aspect of the European integration has been governed since its inception by the elimination of barriers to the mobility of goods and services, and of labour and capital. In this way it has been market-oriented since its beginning. But the 2004 project was a constitutional treaty. It had a status of fundamental law due to last for a long time and whose modification procedure would have been in practice very difficult if not impossible to implement. This was a new context although it was naturally also a treaty like the other European treaties, as its supporters used to claim. But then why call it a 'constitution'? Its constitutional character precisely made the difference. Whereas the market orientation of the existing treaties was a strategy for enhancing economic integration in otherwise modifiable treaties, the emphasis put on free competition in a constitution made of it a normative enforced model of economic policy. It illustrates internal relationality: similar words in different contexts take on different meanings.

The conception of economic policy contained in the project of a European constitutional treaty was flawed not because of its market orientation but because of its one-sidedness and its essential inconsistency in the deeply complex situation European integration creates. EDCX is neutral on the substance and the kind of balance between competition and organisation but it is not neutral on the necessity to recognise fully this duality in its own right.

D. The global financial crisis of September and October 2008

The financial crisis which burst in September and October 2008 offers an extraordinary instance of what is meant by a lack of EDCX duality in thinking, deciding and acting about a subject-matter which creates a deeply complex situation. Although there was little hindsight at the time these lines were written, in November 2008, the crisis was well documented by the debates that had been going on for months between commentators and experts about the global economic and financial issues, on which I will rely here.

The global financial crisis began with the bankruptcy of Lehman Brothers, on 15 September, 2008. It entered an acute phase marked by failures of other important American and European banks, and efforts by the American and European governments to rescue distressed financial institutions.

This global crisis had been preceded by a liquidity crisis which first hit in July and August 2007. It is widely agreed that this liquidity crisis resulted from a nascent subprime mortgage crisis and housing bubble in the United States. The first victims were, apart from the people who lost their homes, the banks and institutions directly involved in home construction and the securitisation of mortgage lending, notably Northern Rock, a major British bank, and Bear Stearns in the US. The former was taken over by the British government in February 2008, the latter was acquired in March by JP Morgan Chase through the assistance from the US government.

In July 2008, Indy Mac Bank, a big mortgage lender, collapsed. Two other prominent mortgage lenders, Fannie Mae and Freddie Mac, were taken over by the US government on 7 September. 16 September, the US government seized control of AIG (American International Group), one of the world's biggest insurance groups. By mid-September, of the five Wall Street's top investment banks, three had disappeared as independent entities (Bear Stearns, Lehman Brothers and Merril Lynch) leaving Morgan Stanley and Goldman Sachs on the market. David Leonhardt commented in the NewYork Times, 27 September, 2008 that 'The last few weeks, by any standard have been extraordinary for America's economy and its financial system'.

What went wrong? The subprime mortgage crisis is often cited as the triggering factor of the global financial crisis which burst in September 2008. The connections in the sequence of events are beyond doubt. However, they explain only partially why local contractions of liquidity in housing in the US suddenly became transformed into the most important financial crisis of capitalism since 1929. Other factors must have entered into play.

The American housing bubble peaked in early 2006 and was followed by a rapid decrease which began in summer 2006. For a number of years prior to that, starting in the early 1990s, borrowers had been encouraged in the belief that they would be able to refinance at more favourable terms in the future by declining lending standards, an increase in loan incentives such as easy initial terms, and a long-term trend of rising housing prices. However refinancing became more difficult when interest rates began to rise and housing prices started to drop in 2006–07 in many local areas in the US. Home prices ceased to go up as anticipated, easy initial terms expired and adjustable-rate mortgages started to go up. Defaults and foreclosures accelerated in 2007 and triggered financial difficulties for lenders which exploded in the financial crisis of September 2008.

Yet the housing bubble was not unique to the US. According to the IMF *World Economic Outlook*, the biggest apparent housing overvaluations occurred between 1997 and 2007 in Ireland, the Netherlands and the UK. Four causes might explain them: very low long-term real interest rates, low nominal interest rates, economic stability and, above all, the liberalisation of mortgage finance.[4] Still there seems to have developed in the US more than in other countries a combination of factors that led to the present situation. Among them are the developments of a shadow banking system, of financialisation and systemic risk, of a specific economic climate, and regulatory failures. The shadow banking system denotes the new institutions that developed since the 1990s and that, like banks, borrow short and in liquid forms and lend or invest long in more illiquid assets via the use of credit derivative instruments such as mortgage-backed securities. They include investment banks, hedge funds and other non-bank financial institutions which are often affiliated to major banks but may be off the banks' regular balance sheets. As they are non-depository institutions, they do not have access to the central bank's lender-of-last-resort support. In conditions of market illiquidity they can go bankrupt if they are unable to refinance their short-term liabilities. The present crisis was triggered by a run on non-banks by investors, not by banks' depositors. This run started when the deleveraging after the asset bubble explosion led to uncertainty about which institutions were solvent.[5] The run propagated to highly leveraged or indebted institutions.

Financialisation denotes the trend in which profit-making increasingly occurs through financial channels rather than through commodity production and trade. It refers to the greatly expanded role of financial motives, of capital market financial systems over bank-based financial systems, and of financial actors and institutions in the operation of domestic and international economies.

There are undoubtedly several combined reasons which triggered the crisis. The aim here is not to engage in an analysis of them. Simply, one aspect seems to have played an important role and is totally relevant here: it is the lack of regulation of the shadow banking system. It is a lack of action in a complex situation. One person, the Chairman of the Fed, was especially exposed in this domain.

The bubble burst would have had smaller consequences if the market for derivatives (the financial instruments intended to hedge against risks whose values are derived from underlying assets) had not increased fivefold since 2002 and reached an overall huge size[6] (from $106 trillion to $531 trillion in the first semester of 2008). It would also have had smaller consequences if the interconnections between instruments likely to trigger chain reactions in the case of a shock had been less tightly coupled. Tight coupling of the fabrication processes in industry is a major theme of industrial safety management. Its equivalent in banking is systemic risk.

It looks all the more threatening with the unregulated shadow banking system. The bubble might also have developed less if it had not been encouraged by a supportive economic context in the US marked by a long period of rapid growth, low inflation, low interest rates and unregulated financial innovation (securitisation, off-balance-sheet financing) [7] with net equity extraction from residential property viewed increasingly as a permanent source of income generation[8] in an overall consumption- and debt-based economy.

On top of that, risk management (Institute of International Finance, 2008), credit rating agencies and regulatory authorities failed. Of special interest to us is the domain in which deliberate action might have been taken to deal with this situation, that is, regulation.

The Chairman of the Federal Reserve from 1987 to 2006, Alan Greenspan, advocated a limited role for government. He maintained that risks could be handled by the markets themselves and appeared as a champion of deregulation. Three stages can be detected in the way he expressed himself publicly, from 2004 to October 2008. At the top of his fame, Greenspan, who was once lauded as the 'Oracle' or the 'Maestro', wrote: 'Not only have individual financial institutions become less vulnerable to shocks from underlying risk factors, but also the financial system as a whole has become more resilient.' [9]

He wrote in March 2008 that although

> The current financial crisis in the US is likely to be judged in retrospect as the most wrenching since the end of the second world war … it is … crucial that any reforms in … the structure of markets and regulation do not inhibit our most reliable and effective safeguards against cumulative economic failure: market flexibility and open competition. [10]

This article attracted a number of critical comments. In his reply to them Greenspan pointed out his 'judgment that free competitive markets are by far the unrivalled way to organize economies', and concluded that: 'We have tried regulation ranging from heavy to central planning. None meaningfully worked. Do we wish to retest the evidence?'[11]

Greenspan appeared on October 23, 2008 with the Chairman of the SEC (Securities and Exchange Commission), Chris Cox, and former Treasury Secretary John Snow, at a Congress hearing in Washington examining the role of federal regulators in the current crisis. Representative Henry Waxman, the committee Chairman, blamed the Fed for failing to curb aggressive lending practices, the SEC for allowing credit rating agencies to operate under lax standards, and the Treasury for opposing 'responsible oversight' of financial derivatives. Greenspan admitted that the crisis had 'found a flaw' in his thinking but said that the kind of heavy regulation that could have prevented the crisis would have damaged US economic growth.[12] He also declared that the housing bubble became clear to him in early 2006 and that he did not 'forecast a significant decline because we had never had a significant decline in prices'. He added that forecasting in the early years what was ultimately going to happen to subprimes was beyond anybody's capability in 'this extraordinary complex global economy', in which there are always people raising issues about problems emerging 'but who are wrong half the time'. Then, 'What to do?' His answer was that: 'we are not smart enough as people. We just cannot see events that far in advance'.

From the standpoint of complex duality these statements illustrate two things. First is the negation of the very idea that organisation, mainly under the form of regulation here, is the necessary dual of the operation of competitive markets. Free competitive markets are even deemed to be the best way to organise the economy: free market generation becomes conflated with organisation. We should be grateful to Greenspan for having involuntarily expressed in such a transparent way what is meant by a one-sided view and for helping explain *a contrario* the empirical bearing of complex duality in actual economic life.

Greenspan stood in the way of modernising the US monetary and financial regulatory system. The regulatory failure is clear. He argued that there is no middle way between almost completely free financial markets on the one hand, and repressed ones on the other. This is typically a one-sided view which goes against the notion of continually managing an evolving balance between competition and its supervision and regulation.

Second, how can it be that the commonsense idea that sooner or later any bubble has to face the question of what will happen when prices go down, and the lessons from Keynes and Minsky about the instability of the fully free operation of financial markets, have not been considered more seriously? (Guttmann and Plihon, 2008).

A part of the answer is undoubtedly in Greenspan's self-acknowledged ideology. This widespread ideology could feel comfortably at home within the intellectual climate of unleashed free markets and globalisation that has been shaped in Washington, London, the elite universities of North America and Europe, the European Commission, and the leading media, and that has prevailed since the 1970s. Another part follows from the scientist content that appears as a corollary of this context. It pervades the way risk management was considered. While in office, Greenspan emphasised that the Fed had a responsibility both for money and for the whole economy. He convincingly argued that his task was akin to global risk management.

Yet, however sophisticated the models of risk developed at the Fed might have been, Greenspan had to admit at the Congress hearing that although 'the Federal Reserve had as good an economic organization as exists, and I would say, in the world … all these extraordinary capable people were unable to foresee the development of this critical problem which undoubtedly was the cause of the world problem with respect to mortgage-backed securities'. The models manifestly did not integrate the systemic risk caused by unregulation.

According to Rama Cont, the whole approach of risk should be revised in order to take better into account 'economic fundamentals'.[13] Here EDCX would suggest considering the duality (competition∗organisation) as one such economic fundamental.

More organisation and regulation of financial intermediation may be costly in terms of dynamism and innovation, but it should be assessed against the risk and the cost of overall instability. This extends to one-sided globalisation. Here one would find it hard not to agree that everything possible must be done to prevent the foreseeable recession from turning into something worse, such as widespread social unrest, nationalism and xenophobia.[14]

E. 2009: economic crisis and global challenges

At the time when these lines are written, in June 2009, the financial slump has evolved into a major financial and economic crisis. Though it is too soon to tell how the second half of 2008 and the first half of 2009 will feature in history books, there should be no doubt that this situation presents several huge challenges and is deeply complex. I will rely, in an inevitably sketchy way, on the main recent economic policy events and on a selection of economists' contributions that appear especially relevant in order to identify these challenges. In so doing, I wish to avoid supplying a too personal view. I will naturally have to ask how EDCX fares in this context.

The leaders of the G20 major advanced and emerging economies met in November 2008 in Washington for the first summit on financial markets and the world economy. They agreed a new approach to economic cooperation and a strengthening of the financial regulatory system and of international financial institutions. In December 2008, the UK government issued a statement entitled '*Managing the global economy through turbulent times*' which pointed out that the 'unexpected scale of the turbulence in international financial markets and its impact on real economies has become a global crisis' (HM Treasury, 2008, 3). The next six months did not invalidate it. The UK government's statement underlined the need to prevent the current downturn from being 'unnecessarily deep and prolonged', and to manage the risks of contagion to emerging and developing markets, which will 'require a new and decisive systemic approach from economic and financial policy makers around the world' (ibid., 5).

The G20 met again in April 2009 in London and decided on a '*Global Plan for Recovery and Reform*'. It is a combination of well-meaning declarations – restore confidence, growth and jobs, repair the financial system, rebuild trust, reform international financial institutions, promote global trade and investment, reject protectionism, build an inclusive, green, and sustainable recovery – and a few specific decisions which consist in a $1000 billion global deal through trebling the resources available to the International Monetary Fund, and a new allocation of special drawing rights. These decisions are a welcome first step toward more international cooperation and governance, but they fall short of what would be necessary to meet the needs of the moment. It has become clear that the outburst of the financial crisis in 2008 was only the most visible symptom of an overall situation which has structural roots and needs to be addressed with a long-run view.

Although this is not the place here to engage a thorough analysis of the crisis, it reveals an overall situation which combines five main challenges, some of which are well documented in the ongoing debates, the fifth one remaining evoked only by a minority of economists although it is of utmost importance. They pertain to finance, to global macroeconomic imbalances, to economic growth and climate change, to globalisation and development, and to an intellectual gap.

First is the financial challenge. It has two aspects. One relates to the lack of regulation and was evoked above. The other follows from the finance-led capitalism that has prevailed since the end of the 1970s. It relies on the dominance of financial motives and on an emphasis on the strategic position of the financial investors. The macroeconomic implications of this trend and its restraining effects on growth have been abundantly commented (Stockhammer, 2004). The challenge is to reorient the financial sector to serve first and foremost the business sector and innovative projects (Phelps, 2009).

Global macroeconomic imbalances denote the gap that has settled for years between countries with current account surpluses and countries with current account deficits. This issue has been abundantly analyzed, notably by Barry Eichengreen (2007). Guttmann and Plihon characterise it as a situation in which surplus countries – a notion which includes commodity producers, emerging market economies (notably China), and some industrial nations (notably Germany and Japan) – have been able to pursue export-led growth strategies and sustain them by lending their surpluses to the one country willing and able to act as the world's 'consumer of the last resort', that is, the United States. The US is by far the main deficit country, it absorbs about three-quarters of the world's aggregate trade imbalances, and has thus been able 'to live consistently beyond its means with the help of the surplus nations' savings'. They observe that this 'symbiotic relationship ... has been supported by a crucial asymmetry in the world economy stemming from the use of the leading power's national currency as international money in cross-border transactions' (Guttmann and Plihon, 2008, 20). They add that since the US 'has not had to face an external constraint like anyone else' and surplus economies 'have no interest in letting their currencies appreciate much or slow down the torrid pace of their expansion otherwise, global imbalances have been allowed to persist and grow to the point of triggering acute conditions of global crisis' (ibid., 24). As the discretionary stimulus measures taken by governments in response to the crisis will boost fiscal deficits, and as their private sectors are over-indebted, the imbalances are likely to continue. However, will the US capacity for excess consumption come to a limit as the need for an adjustment is likely to be imposed by the crisis? This issue was not evoked in the G20 summit declaration. Yet a first sign in this direction is the proposal of a reform of the international monetary system made by Zhou Xiaochuan, the Governor of the People's Bank of China (Zhou, 2009).

The third challenge is about the link between growth and climate change. How to orientate economic growth toward economising on non-reproducible natural resources and combating global warming is a central issue. It is a domain in which the political economy of growth centred on innovation, reallocation, and education (Acemoglu, 2009) appears especially relevant. The G20 summit mentioned its commitment to this issue and to reach agreement at the United Nations Climate Change Conference to be held in Copenhagen in December 2009.[15]

Globalisation and development is the fourth issue. Globalisation should contribute to economic development understood essentially as poverty alleviation and human development in an environmentally sustainable manner. In the way globalisation is envisaged in the World Trade Organization agenda, one cannot deny that it is positively connected with growing international trade. Yet one would hardly disagree with Dani Rodrik that the manner in which globalisation has developed has until now favoured macroeconomic imbalances and financial instability, has had an 'adverse impact on equality and social peace in many countries', and will continue to generate tensions and periodic crises because of its weak political legitimacy (Rodrik, 2009). Two main weaknesses stand out. They are the lack of global leadership, and the market bias of globalisation at work. On the first account, history tells us that a global economic order is difficult to establish in the absence of a dominant economic power. The US economy has lost its past, post-World War II dominant position. It has no successor. Maybe the world is gradually moving in the long run toward a multipolar global economic pattern with deepening regional integration (Guttmann and Plihon, 2008, 29). On the second account, the market bias of globalisation equating development with maximum trade and market access has been denounced forcefully by Rodrik. Rodrik advocates a developmental perspective in which trade is a means to an end, not an end in itself. This perspective includes several conditions: trade rules have to allow for diversity in national institutions and standards; non-democratic countries cannot count on the same trade privileges as the democratic ones;

countries have the right to protect their own institutions and development priorities but they do not have the right to impose their institutional preferences on others (Rodrik, 2007, 225–233). In Rodrik's terms, it is a view of an international trade regime that puts development first. It has several implications. It implies first that nations, developing as well as rich, articulate their needs 'not in terms of market access, but in terms of the policy autonomy that will allow them to exercise institutional innovations that depart from prevailing orthodoxies' (ibid., 235–236). Second, it implies that rather than tending to impose uniformity, global governance manages the interface between different national systems. This view echoes closely the institutional diversity that we underlined in Chapter 1 and in this chapter. Third and foremost, this perspective implies a shift from a market-exchange mindset to a development mindset (ibid., 233–236). This is the most fundamental challenge because it conditions the other changes that are called for.

These considerations lead to the fifth, intellectual challenge. The issues evoked above are immense. Though one cannot ignore the role of the ideological, economic and geopolitical interests at stake, and the limits to stressing the intellectual dimension of the situation, the latter is an aspect as essential as the former. This is well perceived by Rodrik when he writes that it is only through a change in the overall mindset of trade negotiations that significant change can be accomplished (ibid., 215). Guttmann and Plihon call for a 'meta-theory revolution, akin to Keynes' macro-theory revolution seventy years ago' (Guttmann and Plihon, 2008, 32).

From the Effective Deep Complexity standpoint, this situation is deeply complex. Yet, however huge and intricate the issues may be, I submit that it is possible to detect two leading threads which run through the first four challenges briefly evoked above. One is the emphasis on the excesses that resulted, and still result, from the one-sided view of the gains of the quasi unlimited extension of the market competition logic. The other is the repeated call for new institutions and reorganisation: the financial excesses calling for a reorganisation of the financial sector; the global macroeconomic imbalances calling for an international monetary reform; institutional innovation for managing growth and global warming; reorganisation of global governance and of the trade negotiation principles. These convergent, though independently conceived views bring flesh to the complex duality of the competition and organisation logics of EDCX which might otherwise have remained a formal and abstract idea to many people.

EDCX operates at two levels, the object level and the meta-level. The first four challenges operate at the object level only. The mindset shift implied by EDCX operates at the meta-level and envelops the object level. It pertains to the organisation of ideas and of knowledge accommodating the deeply complex character of the situation. The challenge implied by EDCX is a shift from a non-deep complexity (NDCX) mindset to a deep complexity (DCX) mindset. It contains the specific shift from a market-exchange mindset to a development mindset which stands at the object level. I described in Chapter 2 how a similar shift at the meta-level was exercised by Keynes. In this way, the whole argumentation of this book has been to construct the firm anchoring that was missing in Keynes's reflection.

The task implied by this intellectual challenge is immense. EDCX forces us to debate about the character of the situation. Far from leading to paralysis, given the size of the stakes, it provides a structured framework that is fully cognisant of its limits. It underscores the limits to the possibilities of changes implied by the first four challenges. In the absence of a traumatic giant shock such as World War II, and in the absence of a global leadership, there remains to help a shift of mindsets toward taking our knowing limits more seriously, and acting accordingly.

8.4 CONCLUSION

The instances of applications of Effective Deep Complexity in deeply complex situations that have been presented in this chapter illustrate the consequences of the non-deeply complex governance of deeply complex situations.

In road safety governance, the focus on the causes of accidents, either in a sequential way or in the epidemiological fashion of attributable quantitative factors at a national level, is useful but it reflects a fragmented view of a many-sided activity. It can be enriched by a more integrated perspective such as that brought by Effective Deep Complexity. In political economy, the precocious failure of the European Union project for a constitution was the welcome failure of the willingness to implement a non-deeply complex straitjacket in a deeply complex situation. And the intensity of the financial crisis can be viewed, at least in part, as the outcome of polarised ideology, doctrine and practice imposed upon deeply complex material. The current global economic crisis creates a deeply complex problem-situation. Effective Deep Complexity highlights the need to address it with intellectual and behavioural resources that accommodate its deeply complex character.

NOTES

1. Heinz von Foerster (2003), *Understanding Understanding*, New York: Springer, 227.
2. I borrow the phrase 'game in town' from Robert Solow who, in presenting estimates of social rates of return to fixed investment said about them: 'what the inveterate gambler said about the dishonest roulette wheel: "I know the wheel is crooked, but it's the only game in town" ' (Solow, 1965, 68).
3. The Irish electorate reversed its decision in a second referendum in 2009. The Treaty of Lisbon entered into force on 1 December 2009.

4. M. Wolf (2008), 'Why Greenspan does not bear most of the blame', *Financial Times*, 9 April.
5. N. Roubini (2008), 'The shadow banking system is unraveling', *Financial Times*, 9 September.
6. P.S Goodman (2008), 'In crisis, a critical look at champion of deregulation', *New York Times*, 18 October.
7. M. Wolf (2008), 'The end of lightly regulated finance has come far closer', *Financial Times*, 17 September.
8. S. Roach (2008), The Economists' Forum, *Financial Times*, 10 April.
9. A. Greenspan (2004), 'Risk and uncertainty in monetary policy', *American Economic Review*, 94 (2): 33–40.
10. A. Greenspan (2008), 'We will never have a perfect model of risk', *Financial Times*, 17 March.
11. A. Greenspan (2008), 'A response to my critics', *Financial Times*, 7 April.
12. *Financial Times*, 24 October, 2008.
13. Interview with R. Cont, *Le Monde*, 18 September, 2008.
14. M. Wolf (2008), 'Preventing a global slump must be the priority', *Financial Times*, 28 October.
15. The Copenhagen Summit was attended by 192 countries. It ended on 18 December 2009 with a weak agreement judged meaningful by some (it recognised that climate change is a major challenge), disappointing by others (it did not contain any legally binding commitment for reducing CO_2 emissions).

General conclusion

Complexity and deep complexity are two different things. Deeply complex situations differ from the complexity commonly envisaged in complex systems and in the scientific discourse on complexity in general. Complexity has become a catchword that conflates different meanings. Deep complexity encompasses complexity or, more broadly, non-deep complexity. Non-deep complexity cannot host deep complexity because its very consistency relies on the consistency of the analytical framework to which it belongs, which is disjunctive or separationist, whereas deep complexity calls for a conjunctive, non-separationist analytical framework.

Deeply complex problem-situations require to be addressed in a deeply complex way, with appropriate methods and tools. Excluding deeply complex problems from the scope of scientific inquiry impoverishes scientific research. And the polarisation of perspectives that is generated by one-sided views is damaging, for it leads to treating in a non-deeply complex way issues that may be deeply complex and therefore require to be dealt with in a deeply complex manner. The result is that deeply complex problems cannot be grasped with a non-deeply complex framework. They require a deeply complex analytical framework. Effective Deep Complexity is such a framework. It brings a new kind of analysis which relies first on a behaviouralist awareness of the distinction between non-deep complexity and deep complexity. The concept through which this distinction can be drawn is central to Effective Deep Complexity. This concept is behaviouralist self-reflexivity (OP1). Let it be stressed that not all situations in social sciences are deeply complex, and that deep complexity is not tied to social sciences proper but to cognitive situations whatever the domain is, scientific or not, as well as social or otherwise. Scientism is misleading and damaging not because of some intrinsic character of social science but because it consists in the transposition to situations that may be deeply complex of concepts, methods and tools that were built for, and are effective in, non-deeply complex situations, but are not appropriate to deeply complex situations. This distinction between deeply complex and non-deeply complex situations is central to Effective Deep Complexity. It demarcates it fundamentally from the perspectives based on the distinction between natural and social sciences (Hayek), or on the divide between science and non-science (Popper).

Another lesson is that deep complexity requires that the knowledge or knowing situations be explicitly activated as objects of inquiry and judgement rather than being neutralised or left aside by the most common, spontaneous focus of attention on how to apply the classical analytical concepts and tools to substantive problems.

The third lesson is that deeply complex situations can be dealt with in a structured way. Any deeply ill-structured problem-situation can be analysed as a complex duality. This requires an analytical shift away from the classical analytical framework. Effective Deep Complexity consists in a critically analytical framework.

As an analytical framework, it contains analysis, that is, 'the resolution or breaking up of anything complex into its various simple elements' according to the *Oxford English Dictionary*. After Effective Deep Complexity, there appears a divide on the nature of the 'simple elements' and the way in which they combine. In classical analysis, the basic elements are like indivisible entities or atoms externally and mechanistically related: the role of a part is the same when separated out as it is when part of the whole; parts interact through forces that do not bring any change in their essential characteristics, like in a machine; and superimposing the workings of the parts is deemed to explain the working of the whole. In Effective Deep Complexity analysis, the basic element is a recursive relationship between a generative process *GP* and its product *P*. But it is critically so. It is not fixed once and for all. It is active and can be deactivated and reactivated in turn, depending on the cognitive situation.

The criticality of Effective Deep Complexity stems intrinsically from the active duality of its elementary unit of analysis or building block. It reflects the essential inclusion of a turning point between deeply complex and non-deeply complex situations. Classical analysis applies *a priori* when the situation is non-deeply complex. In Effective Deep Complexity, the formal building block symbolised by *GP*P* always operates as a part of an effective building block symbolised by the pair *GP**P*. Effective Deep Complexity consists in the concatenation of these building blocks inside and between successive logical levels. Internal relations, contextualisation and reflexivity are ever present and reflect the non-atomist and non-mechanist character of Effective Deep Complexity. This new kind of analysis does not exclude classical analysis when the situation is identified as being non-deeply complex. Whenever the situation is, or becomes, non-deeply complex, these characteristics are neutralised, and conversely. This is the essence of the criticality of Effective Deep Complexity.

Criticality renders effective a kind of analysis not restricted to the separationist straitjacket, but which encompasses it and relies on its own tools, thus organising a continuity between the analysis of deeply complex problem-situations and classical analysis. Fallibility, behaviouralist self-reflexivity and processual duality are among its key properties.

Effective Deep Complexity produces a kind of analysis in which the primary task is to identify the cognitive situation (OP7), after which the divide toward deep complexity or non-deep complexity may occur. For this divide to be possible, it is necessary to start with the Effective Deep Complexity apparatus in mind. This is the first operational resource. It is the autonomy of Effective Deep Complexity, or OP6. It allows one to be watchful about the conditions under which non-deep complexity is appropriate. In turn, having OP6 in mind necessitates being aware of the organisational principles of Effective Deep Complexity. The first organisational resource is the one enabling one to have a judgement about the situation. It is behaviouralist self-reflexivity OP1. It is subject to the norm ruling in a given activity. It is therefore a socialised self-reflexivity.

If the key words pertaining to Effective Deep Complexity were to be selected, they would include fallibility, criticality, behaviouralist self-reflexivity, recursive duality and process.

The main obstacle to decision and action in deeply complex situations like those that economic theory and policy contain, together with other areas in social sciences, is intellectual and behavioural. It blocks stepping outside the prevailing disjunctive analytical framework. Effective Deep Complexity offers a way to unblock this obstacle in the economy and elsewhere. Yet there is little doubt that resisting EDCX will still prevail. For how long? Remember Jean-Jacques Rousseau's epigraph of Chapter 4. Almost three centuries later on, may we hope that if scientists, as 'men' – and women – 'of learning', still 'have sometimes fewer prejudices than others', that the second part of Rousseau's reflection has become outdated, and that they no longer 'more tenaciously retain those they have'?

Effective Deep Complexity does not solve deeply ill-structured problem-situations directly, but it provides a structured framework within which a strategy for dealing with these problems can be designed and implemented.

If Effective Deep Complexity has any value, it is to improve our judgement and to help us do something constructive about the deeply ill-structured problem-situations life forces us to face, in economics, in safety management and elsewhere.

References

Acemoglu, D. (2009), *The Crisis of 2008: Structural Lessons for and from Economics*, www.cepr.org

Ackoff, R.L. (1979), 'The future of operational research is past', *Journal of the Operational Research Society*, **30**, 2, 93–104.

Adam, C. and P. Tanney (eds) (1969), *Oeuvres de Descartes. Correspondance I*, Paris: J. Vrin

Albin, P.S. (1998), *Barriers and Bounds to Rationality. Essays on Economic Complexity and Dynamics in Interactive Systems*, with an introduction by D.C. Foley, Princeton, NJ: Princeton University Press.

Allen, C.S. (2005), *Ideas, Institutions and Organized Capitalism: Germany, Europe and 21st Century Economic Policy Models*, retrieved from http://www.arches.ugal~csallen

Amable, B. (2000), 'Institutional complementarity and diversity of social systems of innovation and production', *Review of International Political Economy*, **7**, 4, winter, 645–687.

Amable, B. (2005), *Les cinq capitalismes. Diversité des systèmes économiques et sociaux dans la mondialisation*, Paris: Seuil.

Amable, B., R. Boyer and F. Lordon (1997), 'The *ad hoc* in economics: the pot calling the kettle black', in A. d'Autume and J. Cartelier (eds), *Is Economics Becoming a Hard Science?* Cheltenham, UK and Lyme, NH, USA: Edward Elgar Publishing, 252–275.

Amalberti, R. (1996), *La conduite de systèmes à risques*, Paris: Presses Universitaires de France.

Amalberti, R. (1997), *Notions de sécurité écologique : le contrôle du risque par l'individu et l'analyse des menaces qui pèsent sur ce contrôle. Approche psycho-ergonomique.* Monographie du Séminaire du Programme Risques Collectifs et Situations de Crise, Paris: CNRS, November.

Amalberti, R. (1999), 'Les effets pervers de l'ultra-sécurité', *La Recherche*, 319, 66–70.

Amalberti, R. (2001), 'The paradoxes of almost totally safe transportation systems', *Safety Science*, **37**, 2-3, 109–126.

Andreewsky, E. and R. Delorme (eds) (2006), *Seconde cybernétique et complexité. Rencontres avec Heinz von Foerster*, Paris: L'Harmattan.

Angyal, A. (1941, [1981]), 'A Logic of Systems', in F.E. Emery (ed.), *Systems Thinking:* vol.1, Harmondsworth: Penguin, 27–40.
Aoki, M. (2001), *Toward a Comparative Institutional Analysis*, Cambridge, MA: MIT Press.
Aoki, M. (2007), 'Endogenizing institutions and institutional changes', *Journal of Institutional Economics*' **3**, 1, 1–31.
Argyris, C. (1993), *Knowledge for Action, A Guide to Overcoming Barriers to Organizational Change*, San Francisco, CA: Jossey-Bass.
Aristotle (1970a), *La métaphysique I*, transl. J. Tricot, Paris: J. Vrin.
Aristotle (1970b), *Organon IV. Les seconds analytiques,* transl. J. Tricot, Paris: J. Vrin.
Arrow, K. (1974), *The Limits of Organization*, New York: Norton & Co.
Arthur, W.B. (1999), 'Complexity and the economy', *Science*, **284**, 107-109.
Arthur, W.B., S.N. Durlauf and D.A. Lane (eds) (1997), *The Economy as an Evolving Complex System II*, Reading: Perseus Books.
Ashby, W.R. (1956), *An Introduction to Cybernetics*, London: Chapman & Hall.
Ashby, W.R. (1958a), 'Requisite variety and its implications for the control of complex systems', *Cybernetica*, **1**, 2, 83–99.
Ashby, W.R. (1958b), 'General Systems Theory as a New Discipline', in Klir (1991), op. cit., 249–257.
Ashby, W.R. (1973), 'Some Peculiarities of Complex Systems', *Cybernetic Medicine*, **9**, 1–8.
Augier, M. and J.G. March (eds) (2004), *Models of a Man. Essays in Memory of Herbert A. Simon,* Cambridge, MA: MIT Press.
Avenier, M.-J. (ed.) (1997), *La stratégie 'chemin faisant',* Paris: Economica.
Bachelard, G. (1937), *Le nouvel esprit scientifique*, Paris: Presses Universitaires de France.
Backhouse, R. (ed.) (1994), *New Directions in Economic Methodology*, London: Routledge.
Bainbridge, L. (1987), 'Ironies of Automation', in J. Rasmussen, K. Duncan and J. Leplat (eds), *New Technology and Human Error*, Chichester: Wiley, 271–283.
Barel, Y. (1979), *Le paradoxe et le système. Essai sur le fantastique social*, Grenoble: Presses universitaires de Grenoble.
Bartley, W.W. III (ed.) (1977), *Lewis Carroll's Symbolic Logic*, New York: CN Potter Books.
Bateson, G. (1972), *Steps to an Ecology of Mind*, New York: Chandler Publ. Co.
Beck, S., F. Klobes and C. Scherrer (eds) (2005), *Surviving Globalization? Perspectives for the German Economic Model*, Dordrecht: Springer.
Bennett, C.H. (1988), 'Logical Depth and Physical Complexity', in R. Herken (ed.), *The Universal Turing Machine A Half-Century Survey*, Oxford: Oxford University Press, 227–257.

Bennett, C.H. (1989), 'Computational Measures of Physical Complexity', in D. Stein (ed), *Lectures in the Sciences of Complexity*, Santa Fe Institute Studies in the Sciences of Complexity, Reading, MA: Addison-Wesley, 787–798.

Bennett, C.H. (1990), 'How to Define Complexity in Physics, and Why', in W.H. Zurek (ed.), *Complexity, Entropy, and the Physics of Information*, Santa Fe Institute Studies in the Sciences of Complexity, vol. VIII, Reading, MA: Addison-Wesley, 137–148.

Berlin, I. (2000), *Three Critics of the Enlightenment*, edited by H. Hardy, London: Pimlico.

Bernard-Weil, E. (1988), *Précis de systémique ago-antagoniste*, Limonest, France: L'Interdisciplinaire.

Bhaskar, R. (1993), 'Philosophy of science' and 'Realism', in W. Outhwaite and T. Bottomore, op. cit., 467–469, 542–549.

Billings, C. (1997), *Human Centred Aviation Automation*, Hillsdale, NJ: Lawrence Erlbaum Associates.

Bird, R.M. (1970), *The Growth of Government Spending in Canada*, Toronto: Canadian Tax Foundation.

Blaug, M. (1994), 'Why I am not a constructivist. Confessions of an unrepentant Popperian', in R. Backhouse, op. cit., 109–136.

Blaug, M. (1998), *Lectiones Jenenses,* Heft 16, Iena: Max Planck Institut

Bogdanov, A. (1921 [1980]), *Essays in Tektology*, Seaside California: Intersystems Publications.

Bohm, D. (1980), *Wholeness and the Implicate Order*, London: Routledge & Kegan Paul.

Boland, L.A. (1998), 'Critical rationalism', in J.B. Davis et al., op. cit., 86–88.

Boyer, R. (2002), 'Introduction', in R. Boyer and Y. Saillard, op. cit., 1–10.

Boyer, R. and Y. Saillard (eds) (2002), *Régulation Theory. The State of the Art*, London: Routledge.

Braithwaite, R.B. (1973), Editorial foreword, J.M. Keynes (1921 [1973]), *A Treatise on Probability*, op. cit.

Brown, G.S. (1969), *Laws of Form*, London: George Allen & Unwin.

Brown-Collier, E.K. (1985), 'Keynes' view of an organic universe: the implications', *Review of Social Economy*, 43, 14–23.

Bryant, C.G.A. (2002), 'George Soros's theory of reflexivity: a comparison with the theories of Giddens and Beck and a consideration of its practical value', *Economy and Society*, **31**, 1, 112–131.

Burke, T. (1994), *Dewey's New Logic. A Reply to Russell*, Chicago, Il: The University of Chicago Press.

Caldwell, B. (1991), 'Clarifying Popper', *Journal of Economic Literature*, March, 1–33.

Caldwell, B. (1998), 'Hayek, Friedrich A.', in J.B. Davis et al.; op. cit., 220–226.

Calori, R. (1998), 'Philosophizing on Strategic Management Models', *Organisation Studies*, **19**, 2, 281–306.

Cannon, W.F. (1968), 'Darwin's vision in *On the Origin of Species'*, in G. Levine and W. Madden (eds), *The Art of Victorian Prose*, New York: Oxford University Press, 154–176.

Carabelli, A.M. (1988), *On Keynes's Method*, Basingstoke: Macmillan.

Carabelli, A. M. (1995), 'Uncertainty and measurement in Keynes: probability and organicness', in S. Dow and J. Hillard (eds), *Keynes, Knowledge and Uncertainty*, Aldershot, UK and Brookfield, VT, USA: Edward Elgar Publishing, 137–160.

Castellacci, F. (2006), 'A critical realist interpretation of evolutionary growth theorising', *Cambridge Journal of Economics*, **30**, 861–880.

Casti, J.L. (1979), *Connectivity, Complexity and Catastrophe in Large-Scale Systems*, New York: John Wiley.

Casti, J.L. (1994*), Complexification. Explaining a Paradoxical World Through the Science of Surprise*, London: Abacus.

Casti, J.L. (1997), *Reality Rules: I. Picturing the World in Mathematics–The Fundamentals*, New York: John Wiley.

Chaitin, G. (1996), 'Les suites aléatoires', *Pour la Science*, Hors-série, April, 68–73.

Checkland, P.B. (1983), 'OR and the Systems Movement, Mappings and Conflicts', *Journal of the Operational Research Society,* **34,** 8, 661–675.

Checkland, P.B. (1991), 'From Framework through Experience to Learning: The Essential Nature of Action Research', in H.E. Nissen, H.K. Klein and R. Hirscheim (eds), *Information Systems Research*, Amsterdam: Elsevier, 397–403.

Checkland, P.B. (1994), 'Conventional Wisdom and Conventional Ignorance: The Revolution Organization Theory Missed', *Organization*, **1**, 1, 29–34.

Checkland, P.B. (1995), 'Model Validation in Soft Systems Practice', *Systems Research*, **12** ,1, 47–54.

Checkland, P.B. (1999), *Systems Thinking, Systems Practice*, Chichester: Wiley.

Checkland, P.B. and A. Casar (1986), 'Vickers' Concept of an Appreciative System: A Systemic Account', *Journal of Applied Systems Analysis*, **13**, 3–17

Checkland, P.B. and M.G. Haynes (1994), 'Varieties of systems thinking: the case of soft systems methodology', *Systems Dynamics Review,* **10**, 2-3, 189–197.

Checkland, P.B. and S. Holwell (1994), 'Action Research: Its Nature and Validity', *Systemic Practice and Action Research* , **11**, 1, 9–21.

Checkland, P.B. and S. Holwell (1998), *Information, Systems and Information Systems*, Chichester: Wiley.

Checkland, P.B. and J. Scholes (1990), *Soft Systems Methodology in Action*, Chichester: Wiley

Chick, V. (1992), *On Money, Method and Keynes, V. Chick's Selected Essays*, P. Arestis and S. Dow (eds), Basingstoke: The Macmillan Press.

Churchman, C.W. and W. Ulrich (1980), 'The Status of the Systems Approach: Reply to Bryer', *Omega*, **8**, 3, 277-–280.

Clower, R.W. (1994), 'Economics as an Inductive Science', *Southern Economic Journal*, **60**, 4, 805-–814.

Clower, R.W. and P. Howitt (1997), 'Foundations of Economics', in A. d'Autume and J. Cartelier (eds), *Is Economics Becoming a Hard Science?*, Cheltenham, UK and Lyme, NH, USA: Edward Elgar Publishing, 17–34.

Coddington, A. (1982), 'Deficient Foresight: A Troublesome Theme in Keynesian Economics', *American Economic Review*, **72**, 480–7.

Colander, D. (1994), 'The art of economics by the numbers', in R. Backhouse (ed.), op. cit.

Colander, D. (2003), 'Are Institutionalists an Endangered Species?' *Journal of Economic Issues*, **37**, 1, 111–122.

Comim, F. (2000), 'The Santa Fe approach to complexity: a Marshallian evaluation', *Structural Change and Economic Dynamics*, **11**, 25-–43.

Commission of the European Communities (CEC) (2000), *Communication on the Precautionary Principle*, Brussels: COM 1, February.

Commons, J.R. (1931), 'Institutional Economics', *American Economic Review*, **21**, 648-–657.

Crozier, M. (1995), *La crise de l'intelligence. Essai sur l'impuissance des élites à se réformer*, Paris: InterEditions.

Csanyi, V. (1989), *Evolutionary Systems and Society: A General Theory*, Durham, NC: Duke University Press.

Davis, J.B., D.W. Hands and U. Mäki (eds) (1998), *The Handbook of Economic Methodology*, Cheltenham, UK and Lyme, NH, USA: Edward Elgar Publishing.

Davidson, P. (1991), 'Is Probability Theory Relevant for Uncertainty? A Post Keynesian Perspective', *Journal of Economic Perspectives*, **5**, 1, 129–144.

Delahaye, J.-P. (1994), *Information, complexité et hasard*, Paris: Hermès.

Delahaye, J.-P. (1995), *Logique, information et paradoxes*, Paris: Pour la Science, Belin.

Delahaye, J.-P. (1997), *Le fascinant nombre π*, Paris: Pour la Science, Belin.

Delorme, R. (1984), 'A New View on the Economic Theory of the State. A Case Study of France', *Journal of Economic Issues*, XVIII, 3, 715–744.

Delorme, R. (1992), 'Economic Intervention in the History of the French and other European States: A Comparative Study', in A.A. Zini Jr (ed.), *The*

Market and the State in Economic Development in the 1990s, Contributions to Economic Analysis, Amsterdam: North-Holland, 23–50.
Delorme, R. (1994), 'Economic Diversity as Cement and as a Challenge to Evolutionary Perspectives' in R. Delorme and K. Dopfer, op. cit., 1–17.
Delorme, R. (1995a), 'The Case for Controlled Pluralism: A Bottom-up Approach', in A. Salanti and E. Screpanti (eds), *Pluralism in Economics: Philosophical Implications and Methodological Consequences*, Aldershot, UK and Brookfield, VT, USA: Edward. Elgar Publishing, 105–123.
Delorme, R. (1995b), 'An Alternative Theoretical Framework for State-Economy Interactions in Transforming Economies', *Emergo*, Autumn, 5–24.
Delorme, R. (ed.) (1996), *A l'Est, du nouveau. Changement institutionnel et transformations économiques*, Paris: L'Harmattan.
Delorme, R. (1997), 'Evolution et complexité: L'apport de la complexité de second ordre à l'économie évolutionnaire', *Economie Appliquée*, **50**, 3, 95–120.
Delorme, R. (1999), 'A propos du réalisme critique en économie', *Economie Appliquée*, **52**, 1, 63–92.
Delorme, R. (2001), 'Ordnungstheorie and the Theory of Régulation Compared from the Standpoint of Complexity', in A. Labrousse and J.-D. Weisz , op. cit., 247–271.
Delorme, R. (2002), 'The state as relational, integrated and complex' in R. Boyer and Y. Saillard (eds), op. cit., 115–121.
Delorme, R. and C. André (1983), *L'Etat et l'économie*, Paris: Seuil.
Delorme, R. and K. Dopfer (1994) (eds), *The Political Economy of Diversity*, Aldershot, UK and Brookfield, VT, USA: Edward Elgar Publishing.
Delorme R. and S. Lassarre (eds) (2005), *L'insécurité routière en France dans le miroir de la comparaison internationale. Comparaison entre la France et la Grande-Bretagne*, Arceuil: INRETS.
Delorme, R. and S. Lassarre (eds) (2009), *Les régimes français et britannique de régulation du risque routier: la vitesse d'abord,* Paris: INRETS.
Descartes, R. (1637 [2000]), *Discours de la méthode*, Paris: CF Flammarion.
Dewey, J. (1896 [1972]), 'The Reflex Arc Concept in Psychology', *Psychological Review*, **3**, 357–370, in J.A. Boydston (ed.) *John Dewey, The Early Works*, **5**, Carbondale and Edwardsville, IL: Southern Illinois University Press, 96–109.
Dewey, J. (1929 [1984]), *The Quest for Certainty: A Study of the Relation of Knowledge and Action*, The Later Works 1925–1953, **4**, Carbondale and Edwardsville, IL: Southern Illinois University Press.
Dewey, J. (1930 [1984]), 'Conduct and Experience', *Psychologies of 1930*, in J.A Boydston (ed.) *John Dewey, The Later Works*, **5**, Carbondale and Edwardsville, IL: Southern Illinois University Press, 218–235.

Dewey, J. (1938 [1986]), *Logic: The Theory of Inquiry*, The Later Works 1925–1953, **12**, Carbondale and Edwardsville, IL: Southern Illinois University Press.

Dewey, J. and A.F. Bentley, (1949 [1973]), *Knowing and the Known*, in R. Handy and E.C. Harwood (eds), *Useful Procedures of Inquiry* (94–209). Great Barrington, MA: Behavioral Research Council, http://transactionalview.org.

Diamond, A.M. Jr (1980), 'F.A. Hayek on Constructivism and Ethics', *Journal of Libertarian Studies*, **IV**, 4, 353–365.

Dobzhansky, T. (1962), *Mankind Evolving. The Evolution of the Human Species*, Newhaven, CT: Yale University Press.

Dorfman, J. (1972), *Thorstein Veblen and his America*, Clifton, NJ: Augustus M. Kelley.

Dosi, G. and M. Egidi (1991), 'Substantive and procedural uncertainty', *Journal of Evolutionary Economics*, **1**, 145–168.

Dow, S. (1990), 'Beyond dualism', *Cambridge Journal of Economics*, **14**, 143–157.

Dow, S. (1991), 'Keynes's epistemology and economic methodology', in R.M. O'Donnell, op. cit., 144–174.

Dow, S. (1995), 'Uncertainty about uncertainty', in S. Dow and J. Hillard (eds), *Keynes, Knowledge and Uncertainty*, Aldershot, UK and Brookfield, VT, USA: Edward. Elgar Publishing, 117–127.

Dow, S. (1996), *The Methodology of Macroeconomic Thought*, Cheltenham, UK and Brookfield, VT, USA: Edward Elgar Publishing.

Dupuy, J.P. (1982), *Ordres et désordres. Enquête sur un nouveau paradigme*, Paris: Seuil.

Durand, N. and J.-M. Alliot (1999), 'Peut-on supprimer le contrôle au sol?', *La Recherche*, 319, April, 57–61.

Dyer, A.W. (1986), 'Veblen on Scientific Creativity: The Influence of Charles S. Peirce', *Journal of Economic Issues*, XX, 1, 21–41.

Eatwell, J., M. Milgate and P. Newman (eds) (1987), *The New Palgrave: A Dictionary of Economics*, London and New York: Macmillan and Stockton.

Eichengreen, B. (2007), *Global Imbalances and the Lessons of Bretton Woods*, Cambridge, MA: MIT Press.

Eksler, V. (2009), 'Road mortality in Europe: a regional approach', Doctoral dissertation, Université de Versailles.

Elster, J. (1989), *Solomonic Judgments*, Cambridge, UK and Paris, France: Cambridge University Press and Editions de la Maison des Sciences de l'Homme.

Emirbayer, M. (1997), 'Manifesto for a Relational Sociology', *American Journal of Sociology*, **103**, 2, 281–317.

Eucken, W. (1939 [1950]), *The Foundations of Economics*, London, Edinburgh and Glasgow: William Hodge.
European Union (2004), Treaty establishing a Constitution for Europe, *Official Journal of the European Union*, **47,** 16.12.2004, HTML/PDF.
Falletta, N. (1985), *Le livre des paradoxes*, Paris: Belfond.
Fann, K.T. (1970), *Peirce's Theory of Abduction*, The Hague: Martinus Nijhoff.
Fichter, M. (2005), 'The German Way', in S. Beck et al., op. cit.
Finch, J. and M. Orillard (eds) (2005), *Complexity and the Economy*, Cheltenham, UK and Northampton, MA, USA: Edward Elgar Publishing.
Fischhoff, B. (1975), 'Hindsight ≠ Foresight: The Effect of Outcome Knowledge on Judgment Under Uncertainty', *Journal of Experimental Psychology: Human Cognition and Performance*, **1**, 3, 288–299.
Fischhoff, B., S. Lichtenstein, P. Slovic, S. Derby, and R. Keeney (1981 [1999]), *Acceptable Risk*, 2nd edition, Cambridge: Cambridge University Press.
Fleetwood, S. (1996), 'Order without equilibrium: a critical realist interpretation of Hayek's notion of spontaneous order', *Cambridge Journal of Economics*, **20**, 729–747.
Flood, R.L. and E.R. Carson (1993), *Dealing with Complexity*, New York: Plenum Press.
Foster, J. (2005), 'From Simplistic to Complex Systems in Economics', *Cambridge Journal of Economics*, **29**, 6, 873–892.
Foster, J. (2006), 'Why is Economics Not a Complex Systems Science?', *Journal of Economic Issues*, **XL**, 4, 1069–1091.
Friedberg, E. (1997), *Local Orders. Dynamics of Organized Action*, Greenwich, CT: JAI Press.
Friedman, M. (1953), *Essays in Positive Economics*, Chicago, IL: Chicago University Press.
Friedman, T.L. (1999), *The Lexus and the Olive Tree: Understanding Globalization*, New York: Farrar, Straus & Giroux.
Funtowicz, S.O. and J.R. Ravetz (1993), 'Science for the post-normal age', *Futures*, 25, 739–755.
Garnsey, E. and J. McGlade (eds) (2006), *Complexity and Co-evolution: Continuity and Change in Socio-economic Systems*, Cheltenham, UK and Northampton, MA, USA: Edward Elgar Publishing.
Garrison, R.W. (1995), 'Review of K.I. Vaughn's Austrian Economics in America: The Migration of a Tradition, *Southern Economic Journal*, **62**, 1, 279–281.
Gell-Mann, M. (1995), *The Quark and the Jaguar. Adventures in the Simple and the Complex*, New York: W.H. Freeman & Company.
Génelot, D. (1998), *Manager dans la complexité*, Paris: INSEP Editions.
Georgescu-Roegen, N. (1979), 'Methods in Economic Science', *Journal of Economic Issues*, **13**, 2, 317–328.

Georgescu-Roegen, N. (1988), 'The Interplay Between Institutional and Material Factors: The Problem and its Status', in J.A Kregel, E. Matzner and A. Roncaglio (eds), *Barriers to Full Employment*, London: Macmillan, 297–326.

Gerard, R.W. (1958), *Concepts of Biology,* National Academy of Sciences, National Research Council Publication 560, Washington D.C.

Gerrard, B. (1992), 'From *A Treatise on Probability* to the *General Theory*: continuity or change in Keynes's thought?' in B. Gerrard and J. Hillard, *The Philosophy and Economics of J.M. Keynes*, Aldershot, UK and Northampton, MA, USA: Edward Elgar Publishing, 80–95.

Gigerenzer, G. (2004), 'Striking a Blow for Sanity in Theories of Rationality', in M. Augier and J.G.March (eds) op. cit., 389–409.

Gigerenzer, G. and R. Selten (eds) (2001), *Bounded Rationality. The Adaptive Toolbox*, Cambridge, MA, MIT Press.

Granger, G.G. (1990), 'Epistémologie', Paris: Encyclopaedia Universalis.

Guesnerie, R. (2006), *L'économie de marché*, Paris: Le Pommier.

Gupta, S.P. (1967), 'Public Expenditure and Economic Growth: a Time Series Analysis', *Public Finance*, XXII, 423–466.

Guttmann, R. and D. Plihon (2008), *'Consumer Debt at the Center of Finance-Led Capitalism'*, paper presented at the colloquium on Globalisation and Inequality, University of Paris-Nord, 17–18 January, http://www.univ-paris13.fr/CEPN/Texte_colloque_170108.pdf

Haddon, W.A. (1972), 'A logical framework for categorizing highway safety phenomena and activity', *Journal of Trauma*, 12, 193–207.

Hall, P.A. and D. Soskice (eds) (2001), *Varieties of Capitalism. The Institutional Foundations of Comparative Advantage*, Oxford: Oxford University Press.

Hamouda, O.F. and J.N. Smithin (1988), 'Some remarks on "Uncertainty and Economic Analysis" ', *Economic Journal*, **98**, March, 159–164.

Hanson, N.R. (1965), *Patterns of Discovery. An Inquiry into the Conceptual Foundations of Science*, Cambridge, MA: MIT Press.

Harvard Business Review (1990), 'Thinking Across Boundaries', From the Editor, November-December, 9—10.

Harvard Business Review (1991), 'Crossing Boundaries: The Nine-Dot Dilemma', March-April.

Hayek, F.A. (1945), 'The Use of Knowledge in Society', *American Economic Review*, XXXV, 4, 519–530.

Hayek, F.A. (1967), 'The Theory of Complex Phenomena', in F.A. Hayek, *Studies in Philosophy, Politics and Economics*, Chicago, IL: University of Chicago Press, 22–42.

Hayek, F.A. (1975 [1989]), 'The Pretence of Knowledge', Nobel Memorial Lecture, 11 December, 1974, *American Economic Review,* **79**, 6, 3–7.

Hayek, F.A. (1978), *New Studies in Philosophy, Politics, Economics and the History of Ideas*, Chicago, IL: University of Chicago Press.
Hayles, N.K. (1991), *Chaos and Order*, Chicago, IL: University of Chicago Press.
Hegel, F. (1989), *Hegel's Science of Logic*, Translated by A.V. Miller, Atlantic Highlands, NJ: Humanities Press International.
Heiner, R.A. (1983), 'The origins of predictable behavior'. *American Economic Review*, **73**, 4, 560–591.
HM Treasury, Cabinet Office (2008), *Managing the global economy through turbulent times,* www.hm-treasury.gov.uk
Hofstadter, D. (1985), *Gödel, Escher, Bach. Les brins d'une guirlande éternelle*, Paris: InterEditions.
Hollnagel, E. (2004), *Barriers and Accident Prevention*, Aldershot: Ashgate.
Hoover, K.D. (1994), 'Pragmatism, Pragmaticism and Economic Method', in R.E. Backhouse, op. cit, 286–315.
Hulme, M., and J. Turnpenny (2004), 'Understanding and managing climate change: the UK experience', *Geographical Journal*, **170**, 2, 105–115.
Hutchison, T.W. (1984), 'Institutionalist Economics Old and New', *Journal of Institutional and Theoretical Economics*, **140**, 1, 20–29.
Israel, G. (1996), *La mathématisation du réel*, Paris: Seuil.
Jackson, M.C. (2000), 'Checkland, Peter Bernard (1930 -)', *Systems Research and Behavioral Science*, **17**, Special Issue, s3–s10
Jackson, M.C. (2003), *Systems Thinking: Creative Holism for Managers*, Chichester: John Wiley & Sons.
Jacob, F. (1971), *La logique du vivant*, Paris: Gallimard.
James, W., (1890 [1983]), *The Principles of Psychology*, Cambridge,MA: Harvard University Press.
Jonassen, D.H. (1991), 'Objectivism versus constructivism: Do we need a new philosophical paradigm?', *Educational Technology Research and Development*, **39**, 3, 5–14.
Kahneman, D., P. Slovic and A. Tversky (eds) (1982), *Judgment under Uncertainty: Heuristics and Biases*, Cambridge: Cambridge University Press.
Kaufmann, F. (1959), 'John Dewey's Theory of Inquiry', *Journal of Philosophy,* **56**, 21, 826–836.
Keynes, J.M. (1936 [1965]), *The General Theory of Employment, Interest, and Money,* New York: Harcourt, Brace & World.
Keynes, J.M. (1971–1979), *The Collected Writings of John Maynard Keynes*, vol. III (A Revision of the Treaty, 1922 [1971]), V (*A Treatise on Money*, 1930 [1971]), VIII (*A Treatise on Probability*, 1921 [1973]), IX (*Essays in Persuasion*, 1931 [1972]), X (*Essays in Biography*, 1933 [1972]), XIII (*The General Theory and After, Part I, Preparation*, 1973 [1979]), XIV (*The*

General Theory and After, Part II, Defence and Development, 1973 [1979]), XXIX (*The General Theory and After. A Supplement*, 1979), D. Moggridge (ed.), London: Macmillan.
Khalil, E.L. (2003), 'The context problematic, behavioural economics and the transactional view: An introduction to "Symposium: John Dewey and economic theory"', *Journal of Economic Methodology*, **10**, 2, 1–24.
Kilminster, R. (1993), 'Phenomenology', in W. Outhwaite, and T. Bottomore, op. cit, 461–463.
Kirzner, I.M. (1987), 'Austrian School of Economics', in J. Eatwell, et al., op. cit., vol. 1, 145–151.
Kleinbaum D., L. Kupper and H. Morgenstern (1982), *Epidemiological Research: Principles and Quantitative Methods*, New-York: Van Nostrand Reinhold.
Klir, G. (1991), *Facets of Systems Science*, New York: Plenum Press.
Klir, G. (1993), 'Systems science: a guided tour', *Journal of Biological Systems*, **1**, 1, 27–58.
Knight, F.H. (1921 [1964]), *Risk, Uncertainty and Profit*, New York: Sentry Press, Augustus M. Kelly.
Knorr Cetina, K. (1998), 'Constructivism' in I. Davis et al., op. cit, 75–78.
Koestler, A. (1969), 'Beyond atomism and holism – the concept of the holon', in A. Koestler & J.R. Smythies, op. cit., 192-232.
Koestler, A. and J.R. Smyhies (eds) (1969), *The Alpbach Symposium. Beyond Reductionism. New Perspectives in the Life Sciences*, London: Hutchinson & Co.
Kofman, M. (1996), *Edgar Morin. From Big Brother to Fraternity*, London: Pluto Press.
Korzybski, A. (1958 [1980]), *Science and Sanity. An Introduction to Non-Aristotelian Systems and General Semantics*, Scranton, PA: Haddon Crafstmen.
Kwan, K.-M. and E.W.K. Tsang (2001), 'Realism and Constructivism in Strategy Research: A Critical Realist Response to Mir and Watson', *Strategic Management Journal*, **22**, 1163–1168.
Labrousse, A. and J.-D. Weisz (eds) (2001), *Institutional Economics in France and Germany. German Ordoliberalism versus the French Regulation School*, Berlin: Springer.
Lacroix, A. (1992), 'Popper, Hayek: différence et indifférence', *Philosopher*, **12**, 83–102.
Landry, M. (1995), 'A Note on the Concept of "Problem"', *Organisation Studies*, **16**, 2, 315–343.
Langlois, R.N. (1986), 'Coherence and Flexibility: Social Institutions in a World of Radical Uncertainty', in I. Kirzner (ed.), *Subjectivism, Intelligibility and*

Economic Understanding: Essays in Honor of the Eightieth Birthday of Ludwig Lachmann, New York: New York University Press, 171–191.

Langlois, R.N. (1994), Risk and uncertainty', in P.J. Boettke (ed.), *The Elgar Companion to Austrian Economics*, Aldershot: E. Elgar, 118–122.

La Porte, T. and P. Consolini (1991) 'Working in Practice but not in Theory: Theoretical Challenges of "High-Reliability Organizations"', *Journal of Public Administration Research and Theory*, **1,** 1, 19–47.

Laughlin, R. (2005), *A Different Universe: Reinventing Physics from the Bottom Down*, New York: Basic Books.

Laviolette, M. (1995), 'Fuzzy Logic: Great Hope or Grating Hype?', *Chance*, **8**, 4, 15–20.

Lawson, T. (1985), 'Uncertainty and economic analysis', *Economic Journal*, **95**, December, 909–927.

Lawson, T. (1988), 'Probability and uncertainty in economic analysis', *Journal of Post Keynesian Economics*, **11**, 1, 38–65.

Lawson, T. (1994), 'Uncertainty', in G.M. Hodgson, W.J. Samuels and M.R. Tool (eds) *The Elgar Companion to Institutional and Evolutionary Economics*, Aldershot, UK and Brookfield, VT, USA: Edward Elgar Publishing, 350–357.

Lawson, T. (1997), *Economics and Reality*, London: Routledge.

Lawson, T. (2006), 'The nature of heterodox economics', *Cambridge Journal of Economics*, **30**, 483–505.

Lehmbruch, G. (2001), 'The Institutional Embedding of Market Economies: The German Model and its Impact on Japan', in W. Streeck and K. Yamamura, *The Origins of Nonliberal Capitalism: Germany and Japan in Comparison,* Ithaca, NY: Cornell University Press, 39–93.

Le Moigne, J.-L. (1990), *La modélisation des systèmes complexes*, Paris: Dunod.

Le Moigne, J.-L. (1994), *La théorie du système général. Théorie de la modélisation*, Paris: Presses Universitaires de France.

Le Moigne, J.-L. (1995), *Les épistémologies constructivistes*, Paris: Presses Universitaires de France.

Lévy-Leblond, J.-M. (1991), 'La physique, une science sans complexe?', in F. Fogelman-Soulie (ed.*), Les théories de la complexité. Autour de l'oeuvre d'H. Atlan*, Paris: Seuil.

Loasby, B.J. (1976), *Choice, Complexity and Ignorance*, Cambridge: Cambridge University Press.

Loasby, B.J. (1988), *The Mind and Method of the Economist, A Critical Appraisal of Major Economists in the 20th Century*, Aldershot , UK and Brookfield, VT, USA: Edward Elgar Publishing.

Louçã, F. (1997), *Turbulence in Economics, An Evolutionary Appraisal of Cycles*

and Complexity in Historical Processes, Cheltenham, UK and Lyme, NH, USA: Edward Elgar Publishing.
Lowe, A. (1951), 'On the Mechanistic Approach in Economics', *Social Research*, **18**, 4, 403–434.
Lupasco, S. (1951 [1987]), *Le principe d'antagonisme et la logique de l'énergie*, Monaco: Le Rocher.
Mäki, U. (1998), 'Realism. Realisticness', in J.B. Davis et al., op. cit., 404–409.
Mandelbrot, B. (1983), *The Fractal Geometry of Nature*, NewYork: W.H. Freeman & Company.
Manicas, P.T. (1993), 'Philosophy', in W. Outhwaite and T. Bottomore, op. cit, 461–462.
Marchionatti, R. (2002a), 'Dealing with Complexity. Marshall and Keynes on the Nature of Economic Thinking', University of Torino Economics-CESMEP, Working Paper Series No. 1/2002.
Marchionatti, R. (2002b), 'What Don't Economists Know Now that Marshall Knew a Century Ago?' University of Torino Economics-CESMEP, Working Paper Series No. 2/2002.
Marshall, A. (1961), *Principles of Economics*, London: Macmillan.
McCloskey, D. (1989), 'The Very Idea of Epistemology. A Comment on Standards', *Economics and Philosophy*, **5**, 16.
McGlade, J. (2003), 'The map is not the territory: complexity, complication and representation', in R.A. Bentley and H.D.G. Maschner (eds), *Complex Systems and Archeology: Empirical and Theoretical Applications*, Salt Lake City: University of Utah Press, 111–119.
Miermont, J. (ed.) (1995), *Dictionnaire des thérapies familiales*, Paris: Payot.
Milgrom, P., Y. Qian and J. Roberts (1991), 'Complementarities, Momentum, and the Evolution of Modern Manufacturing', *American Economic Review*, **81**, Papers and Proceedings, 84–88.
Mir, R. and A. Watson (2000), 'Strategic Management and the Philosophy of Science: The Case for a Constructivist Methodology', *Strategic Management Journal*, **21**, 941–953.
Mir, R. and A. Watson (2001), 'Critical Realism and Constructivism in Strategic Research: Toward a Synthesis', *Strategic Management Journal*, **22**, 1169–1173.
Mirowski, P. (1989), *More heat than light: economics as social physics, physics as nature's economics*, Cambridge: Cambridge University Press.
Morin, E. (1973), *Le paradigme perdu: la nature humaine*, Paris: Seuil.
Morin, E. (1980a), 'Au-delà du déterminisme: le dialogue de l'ordre et du désordre', *Le Débat*, November, 105–122.
Morin, E. (1980b), *La Méthode. 2. La Vie de la Vie*, Paris: Seuil.

Morin, E. (1981), 'Peut-on concevoir une science de l'autonomie?' *Cahiers internationaux de Sociologie*, **72**, 257–267.
Morin, E. (1985), 'On the Definition of Complexity', in *The Science and Praxis of Complexity*, Tokyo: United Nations University, 62–68.
Morin, E. (1986), *La Méthode. 3. La Connaissance de la Connaissance*, Paris: Seuil.
Morin, E. (1987), 'La complexité est un nœud gordien', *Management France*, 59, 4–8.
Morin, E. (1990a), 'Messie, mais non', in D. Bougnoux, J.-L. Le Moigne, S. Proulx (eds), *Arguments pour une méthode (Autour d'Edgar Morin)*, Paris: Seuil, 254–268.
Morin, E. (1990b), *Science avec conscience*, Paris: Seuil.
Morin, E. (1991a), *La Méthode. 4. Les Idées. Leur habitat, leur vie, leurs mœurs, leur organisation*, Paris: Seuil.
Morin, E. (1991b), *Introduction à la pensée complexe*, Paris: ESF éditeur.
Morin, E. (1992a), *Towards a Study of Humankind*, volume 1: *The Nature of Nature*, with an introduction by J.L.R. Bélanger, New York: Peter Lang. American edition of *La Méthode. 1. La Nature de la Nature*, Paris: Seuil, 1977.
Morin, E. (1992b), 'From the Concept of System to the Paradigm of Complexity', *Journal of Social and Evolutionary Systems*, **15**, 4, 1992, 371–385. Translation of 'Le système, paradigme ou/et théorie', in AFCET: *Modélisation et maîtrise des systèmes techniques, économiques et sociaux,* Suresnes: Editions Hommes et Techniques, 1977, T. 1, 44–53, and in E. Morin, 1990b, 238–255.
Morin, E. (1994), *La complexité humaine*, with an introduction by H. Weinmann, Paris: Flammarion. .
Morin, E. (2001), *La Méthode. 5. L'Humanité de l'Humanité. L'identité humaine*, Paris: Seuil.
Morin, E. (2004), *La Méthode. 6. Ethique*, Paris: Seuil.
Morin, E. and J.-L. Le Moigne (1999), *L'intelligence de la complexité*, Paris: L'Harmattan.
Morris, C. (1971), *Writings on the General Theory of Signs*, The Hague: Mouton.
Mugur-Schächter, M. (1997), 'Les leçons de la mécanique quantique', *Le Débat*, 94, 169–192.
Nagel, E. (1986), 'Introduction' to Dewey (1938 [1986]), *Logic: The Theory of Inquiry*, op. cit.
Nelson, R. (1995), 'Recent Evolutionary Theorizing About Economic Change', *Journal of Economic Literature*, **33**, 48–90.

Nilsson, G. (2004), 'Traffic Safety Dimensions and the Power Model to Describe the Effect of Speed on Safety', Lund Institute of Technology and Society, Traffic Engineering.

North, D.C. (1994), 'Economic Performance Through Time', *American Economic Review*, **84**, 3, 359–368.

North, D.C (1998), 'The Institutional Foundations of East Asian Development: A Summary Evaluation', in Y. Hayami and M. Aoki (eds), *The Institutional Foundations of East Asian Economic Development*, Basingstoke, UK: Macmillan/IEA, 552–560.

Nottale, L. (1998), *La relativité dans tous ses états. Au-delà de l'espace-temps*, Paris: Hachette.

O'Donnell, R.M. (1989), *Keynes: Philosophy, Economics and Politics*, London: Macmillan.

O'Donnell, R.M. (ed.) (1991), *Keynes as philosopher-economist*, London: Macmillan.

O'Driscoll, G.P. and M. Rizzo with a contribution by R.W. Garrison (1985), *The Economics of Time and Ignorance*, Oxford: Basil Blackwell.

Oreskes, N., K. Shrader-Frechette and K. Belitz (1994), 'Verification, Validation, and Confirmation of Numerical Models in the Earth Sciences', *Science*, **263**, 4 February, 641–646.

Outhwaite, W. and T. Bottomore (eds) (1993), *The Blackwell Dictionary of Twentieth-Century Social Thought*, Oxford: Blackwell.

Palmer, D.K. (2005),'John Dewey's Transactional strategy', Transactional View.org Online Article, www.transactionalview.org

Pascal, B. (1662 [1963]), *Pensées*, in *Oeuvres complètes*, Paris: Seuil.

Paté-Cornell, M.E. (1993), 'Learning from the Piper Alpha Accident: A Postmortem Analysis of Technical and Organizational Factors', *Risk Analysis*, **13**, 2, 215–232.

Pavard, B. and J. Dugdale (2000), *An Introduction to Complexity in Social Science*, GRIC-IRIT, Toulouse: http://www.irit.fr/COSI/training

Peacock, A.T. and J. Wiseman (1967), *The Growth of Public Expenditure in the United Kingdom*, London: George Allen & Unwin.

Peirce, C.S. (1931–35), *Collected Papers of Charles Sanders Peirce*, C. Hartshorne and P. Weiss (eds), vol. 5, Cambridge, MA: Harvard University Press.

Peirce, C.S. (1984), 'Some Consequences of Four Incapacities', in *Writings of Charles S. Peirce*, **2**, 1867–1871, E. Moore et al. (eds), Bloomington: Indiana University Press, 211–242.

Peirce, C.S. (1986), *Writings of Charles S. Peirce: A Chronological Edition*, vol. 4, E. Moore and C.J.W. Kloesel (eds), Bloomington: Indiana University Press.

Peirce, C.S. (1878 [1992]), 'How to Make our Ideas Clear', in N. Houser and C. Kloesel (eds), *The Essential Peirce. Selected Philosophical Writings*, vol. 1, Bloomington and Indianapolis: Indiana University Press, 124–141.

Perlman, M. and C.R. McCann (1996), 'Varieties of uncertainty', in C. Schmidt (ed.), *Uncertainty in Economic Thought*, Cheltenham, UK and Brookfield, VT, USA: Edward Elgar Publishing, 9–20.

Perrow, C. (1999a), *Normal Accidents. Living with High-Risk Technologies*, Princeton, NJ: Princeton University Press.

Perrow, C. (1999b), Organisations à hauts risques et 'normal accidents', Monographie du Séminaire du Programme Risques Collectifs et Situations de Crise, Paris: CNRS, June.

Phelps, E. (2009), *Letter to the Honorable Gordon Brown*, 17 March, www.capitalism.columbia.edu/

Piaget, J. (1937 [1954]), *The Construction of Reality in the Child*, New York: Basic Books.

Piaget, J. (1967), 'Les courants de l'épistémologie scientifique contemporaine' in J. Piaget (ed), *Logique et connaissance scientifique*, Paris: Gallimard, 1125–1271.

Poincaré, H. (1902, [1968]), *La Science et l'hypothèse*, Paris: Flammarion.

Popper, K.R. (1972), *Objective Knowledge An Evolutionary Approach*, Oxford: Clarendon Press.

Popper, K.R. (1982), *The Open Universe, An Argument for Indeterminism*, London: Hutchinson.

Portes, R. (1994), 'Transformation Traps', *Economic Journal*, **104**, 1178–1189.

Potts, J.D. (2000), *The New Evolutionary Microeconomics: Complexity Competence, and Adaptive Behavior*, Cheltenham, UK and Northampton, MA, USA: Edward Elgar Publishing.

Prigogine, I. and I. Stengers (1984), *Order out of Chaos. Man's New Dialogue with Nature*, New York: Bantam Books.

Pryor, F.L. (1968), *Public Expenditures in Communist and Capitalist Nations*, London: George Allen & Unwin.

Rapoport, A. and W.J. Horvath (1959 [1968]), 'Thoughts on Organization Theory', *General Systems*, **4**, 87-91; reprinted in W. Buckley (ed.), *Modern Systems Research for the Behavioral Scientist. A Sourcebook*, Chicago, IL: Aldine Publishing Company, 71–75.

Rasmussen, J. (1997), 'Risk management in a dynamic society: A modelling problem', *Safety Science*, **27**, 2/3, 183–213.

Rasmussen, J. and A. Jensen (1974), Mental Procedures in Real Life Tasks. A Case Study of Electronic Troubleshooting, *Ergonomics*, 17, 293–307.

Rasmussen, J. and I. Svedung (2000), *Proactive Risk Management in a Dynamic Society*, Karlstad, Sweden: Swedish Rescue Services Agency.

Ravetz, J.R. (1999), 'What is Post-Normal Science', *Futures*, **31**, 7, 647–653.
Ravetz, J.R. (2004), 'The Post-Normal Science of Precaution', *Futures*, **36**, 3, 347–357.
Reason, J. (1993), *L'erreur humaine*, Paris: Presses Universitaires de France.
Reason, J. (1998), *Managing the Risks of Organizational Accidents*, Aldershot: Ashgate.
Rein, M. and D.A. Schön (1991), 'Frame-reflective policy discourse', in P. Wagner, C. Hirschon Weiss, B. Wittrock and H. Wollmann (eds), *Social Sciences and Modern States. National Experiences and Theoretical Crossroads*, Cambrige: Cambrige University Press, 262–289.
Rittel, H. (1982), 'Systems Analysis of the "First and Second Generations"' in P. Laconte, J. Gibson and A. Rapoport (eds), *Human and Energy Factors in Urban Planning*, NATO Advanced Intitute Series, The Hague: Martinus Nijhoff, 35–63.
Rittel, H.W.J and M.M. Webber (1981), 'Dilemmas in a General Theory of Planning' in F. E. Emery (ed.), *Systems Thinking*, vol. 2, Harmondsworth: Penguin, 81–102.
Rodrik, D. (2007), *One Economics. Many Recipes. Globalization, Institutions, and Economic Growth*, Princeton, NJ: Princeton, University Press.
Rodrik, D. (2009), *The Bumpy Road Ahead*, www.koreatimes.co.kr, 14 June.
Rorty, R. (1979), *Philosophy and the Mirror of Nature*, Oxford: Basil Blackwell.
Rorty, R. (1991), *Objectivity, Relativism, and Truth*, vol. 1, Cambridge: Cambridge University Press.
Rosen, R. (1977), 'Complexity as a System Property', *International Journal of General Systems*, **3**, 227–232.
Rosen, R. (1985), *Anticipatory Systems*, Oxford: Pergamon Press.
Rosen, R. (1991), 'Complexity and System Descriptions', in G. Klir, op. cit., 477–482.
Rosenhead, J. and J. Mingers (eds) (2004), *Rational Analysis for a Problematic World Revisited, Problem Structuring Methods for Complexity, Uncertainty and Conflict*, Chichester: John Wiley & Sons.
Rosser, J.J.B. Jr (1991), *From Catastrophe to Chaos: A General Theory of Economic Discontinuities*, Boston, MA: Kluwer.
Rosser, J.J.B. Jr (2000), 'Aspects of dialectics and non-linear dynamics', *Cambridge Journal of Economics*, **24**, 311–324.
Rosser, J.J.B. Jr (ed.) (2004), *Complexity in Economics*, Cheltenham, UK and Northampton, MA, USA: Edward Elgar Publishing.
Rotheim, R. (1989-90), 'Organicism and the role of the individual in Keynes's thought', *Journal of Post Keynesian Economics*, **12**, 2, 316–326.
Rubinstein, A. (1998), *Modeling Bounded Rationality*, Cambridge, MA: MIT Press.

Runyan, C.W. (2003), 'Introduction: Back to the Future. Revisiting Haddon's Conceptualization of Injury, Epidemiology, and Prevention', *Epidemiologic Reviews*, **25**, 1, 60–64.

Salthe, S.N. (1993), *Development and Evolution. Complexity and Change in Biology*, Cambridge, MA: MIT Press.

Sargent, T.J. (1993), *Bounded Rationality in Macroeconomics*, Oxford: Oxford University Press.

Schön, D.A. (1987), *Educating the Reflective Practitioner: Toward a New Design for Teaching and Learning in the Professions*, San Francisco, CA: Jossey-Bass.

Schön, D.A. (1992), 'The Theory of Inquiry: Dewey's Legacy to Education', *Curriculum Inquiry*, **22**, 2, 119–139.

Schön, D.A. and M. Rein (1994), *Frame Reflection. Toward the Resolution of Intractable Policy Controversies*, New York: Basic Books.

Science et Vie (2000), 'Tokaimura: accident impossible en France?', *Science et Vie*, January, 102–109.

Selten, R. (2001), 'What is Bounded Rationality?', in G. Gigerenzer and R. Selten, op. cit., 14–36.

Selten, R. (2004), 'Herbert A. Simon opened my eyes', in M. Augier and J.G. March, op. cit., 163–167.

Seltzer, E. (1977), 'A comparison between John Dewey's Theory of Inquiry and Jean Piaget's Genetic Analysis of Intelligence', *Journal of Genetic Psychology*, **130**, Second Half, June, 323–335.

Shackle, G.L.S. (1972 [1992]), *Epistemics and Economics, A Critique of Economic Doctrines*, New Brunswick: Transaction Publishers.

Shannon, C.E. and W. Weaver (1949), *The Mathematical Theory of Communication*, Urbana, IL: University of Illinois Press.

Simon, H.A. (1947 [1976]), *Administrative Behavior*, New York: Macmillan.

Simon, H.A. (1976), 'From Substantive to Procedural Rationality', in S. Latsis (ed.), *Method and Appraisal in Economics*, Cambridge: Cambridge University Press, 129–148.

Simon, H.A. (1978), 'Rationality as Process and as Product of Thought', *American Economic Review*, **68**, 2, 1–16.

Simon, H.A. (1979), 'Rational Decision Making in Business Organizations', *American Economic Review*, **69**, 4, 493–513.

Simon, H.A. (1985), 'Human Nature in Politics: the Dialogue of Psychology with Political Science', *American Political Science Review*, **79**, 2, 293–304.

Simon, H.A. (1987a), 'Rationality in Psychology and Economics', in R.M. Hogarth and M.W. Reder (eds), *Rational Choice. The Contrast Between Economics and Psychology*, Chicago, IL: University of Chicago Press, 25–40.

Simon, H.A. (1987b), 'Behavioural economics' and 'Satisficing', in J. Eatwell et al., op. cit., vol. 1, 221–225 and vol. 2, 243–245.
Simon, H.A. (1991), 'Organizations and Markets', *Journal of Economic Perspectives*, **5**, 2, 25–44.
Simon, H.A. (1992), 'Letter to J.-L. Le Moigne. February 3, 1992', *Revue Internationale de Systémique,* 606.
Simon, H.A (1969 [1996])), *The Sciences of the Artificial*, Cambridge, MA: MIT Press.
Simon, H.A (1999), 'Coping with Complexity'; in GRASCE, *Entre systémique et complexité, chemin faisant... Mélanges en l'honneur du Professeur Jean-Louis Le Moigne*, Paris: PUF, 233–240.
Simon, H.A. (2000), 'Can there be a science of complex systems', in Y. Bar-Yam (ed.), *Unifying Themes in Complex Systems*, Cambridge, MA: Perseus Books, 3–14.
Smith V.L. (2003), 'Constructivist and Ecological Rationality in Economics', *American Economic Review*, **93**, 2003, 465–508.
Smithson, M. (1989), *Ignorance and Uncertainty. Emerging Paradigms*, New York: Springer.
Smuts, J.C. (1926), *Holism and Evolution*, London: Macmillan
Solari, S. (2000), 'Le rôle de l'Etat dans l'économie italienne. Un essai d'analyse institutionnelle comparée,' Doctoral dissertation, St Quentin-en-Yvelines: Université de Versailles.
Solari, S. (2005), *Istituzioni ed Organizzazione dei Processi Economici*, Milan: Giuffré Editore.
Solow, R.M. (1965), *Capital Theory and the Rate of Return*, Chicago, IL: Rand McNally & Company.
Soros, G. (2002), *On Globalization*, New York: Public Affairs.
Stacey, R.D, D. Griffin and P. Shaw (2000), *Complexity and Management. Fad or Radical Challenge to Systems Thinking?*, London: Routledge.
Stigler, G.J. (1961), 'The economics of information', *Journal of Political Economy*, **69**, 213–225.
Stockhammer, E. (2004), 'Financialisation and the Slowdown of Accumulation', *Cambridge Journal of Economics*, **28**, 5, 719–741.
Streeck, W. (2005), 'Requirements for a useful concept of complementarity', *Socio-Economic Review*, **3**, 2, 363–366.
Tanzi, V. and L. Schuknecht (2000), *Public Spending in the 20th Century: A Global Perspective,* Cambridge: Cambridge University Press.
Thoben, H. (1982), 'Mechanistic and Organistic Analogies in Economics Reconsidered', *Kyklos*, **35**, 2, 292–306.
Toulmin, S. (1984), 'Introduction' to Dewey (1929 [1984]), *The Quest for Certainty*, op. cit.

Triendl, R. (1999), 'Les déboires du plutonium japonais', *La Recherche*, 319, 30–32.

Tsoukas, H. and M.-J. Hatch (2001), 'Complex thinking, complex practice: the case for a narrative approach to organizational complexity', *Human Relations*, **54**, 8, 979–1013.

Uterwedde, H. (2003), 'Le capitalisme rhénan n'est pas mort', *Sociétal*, 40, 35–38.

Vallée, R. (1990), 'Sur la complexité d'un système relativement à un observateur', *Revue Internationale de Systémique*, **4**, 2, 239–243.

Van der Sluijs, J.P., J.-M. Douguet, P.H.M. Janssen, M. O'Connor and A.C. Petersen (2006), *Tools to Assess Uncertainty in a Deliberative Perspective. A Catalogue*, Université de Versailles: Cahiers du C3ED, 06-02.

Varela, F.J. (1979), *Principles of Biological Autonomy*, New York: Elsevier/North- Holland.

Vaughan, D. (1996), *The Challenger Launch Decision, Risky Technology, Culture and Deviance at NASA*, Chicago, IL: University of Chicago Press.

Vaughn, K.I. (1992), 'The problem of order in Austrian economics: Kirzner vs Lachmann', *Review of Political Economy*, **4**, 3, 251–274.

Vaughn, K.I. (1994), *Austrian Economics in America. The Migration of a Tradition*, Cambridge: Cambridge University Press.

Veblen, T. (1898), 'Why is economics not an evolutionary science?', *Quarterly Journal of Economics*, **12**, July.

Vickers, G. (1995), *The Art of Judgment, A Study of Policy Making*, London: Sage.

Villiers, J. (1998), 'Le mur de l'automatisation', in Académie Nationale de l'Air et de l'Espace (ed.), *La Relation Homme-Machine dans l'Aéronautique*, Toulouse : Teknea, 205–237.

Von Bertalanffy, L. (1968), *General Systems Theory*, New York: George Braziller.

Von Bülow, I. (1989), 'The bonding of a problem situation and the concept of a system's boundary in soft systems methodology', *Journal of Applied Systems Analysis*, **16**, 35–41.

Von Foerster, H. (1960), 'On self-organizing systems and their environments,' in M.C. Yovits and S. Cameron (eds), *Self-Organizing Systems*, Oxford: Pergamon Press, 31–50.

Von Foerster, H. (1977), 'Les objets: gages de comportements propres' (Objects: Tokens for Engenbehavior), in B. Inhelder, R. Garcia, J. Vonèche (eds) , *Epistémologie génétique et équilibration. Hommage à Jean Piaget*, Actualités pédagogiques et psychologiques, Neuchatel: Delachaux et Niestlé, 76–92.

Von Foerster, H. (1988), 'La construction d'une réalité', in P. Watzlawick, (ed.), *L'invention de la réalité*, Paris : Seuil, 45-69.

Von Foerster, H. (2003), *Understanding Understanding, Essays on Cybernetics and Cognition*, New York: Springer.

Von Glasersfeld, E. (1985), 'Reconstructing the Concept of Knowledge', *Archives de Psychologie*, **53**, 91–101.
Von Glasersfeld, E. (1991), 'An Exposition of Constructivism: Why Some Like it Radical', in G. Klir, op. cit., 229–238.
Von Glasersfeld, E. (2000), 'Ernst von Glasersfeld answers', April, http//www.oikos.org/vonansapr00.htm
Von Neumann, J. (1961), 'The General and Logical Theory of Automata', in *John Von Neumann Collected Works*, vol. V, A.H. Taub (ed.), Oxford: Pergamon Press, 288–318.
Von Neumann, J. (1966), *Theory of Self-reproducing Automata*, Edited and completed by A.W. Burks, Urbana, IL: University of Illinois Press.
Wacquant, L.J.D. (1993), 'Positivism', in W. Outhwaite and T. Bottomore, op. cit., 495–498.
Weaver, W. (1948), 'Science and Complexity', *American Scientist*, **36**, 4, 536–544.
Weiss, P.A. (1969), 'The living system: determinism stratified', in A. Koestler & J.R. Smythies, op.cit., 3–42.
Weisz, J.-D. (2005), 'Les Etats et l'économie en Allemagne. Les territoires de l'Etat inséré et la réorganisation des systèmes publics allemands.', Doctoral dissertation, Paris: Université Paris Nord, 4 volumes.
West, B.J. and A.L. Goldberger (1987), 'Physiology in Fractal Dimensions', *American Scientist*, **75**, July–August, 354–365.
Whitehead, A.N. (1929, [1979]), *Process and Reality*, Corrected Edition, New York: Free Press.
Winslow, E.G. (1986), 'Human logic and Keynes's economics', *Eastern Economic Journal*, XII, 4, 413–430..
Winslow, E.G. (1989), 'Organic Interdependence, Uncertainty and Economic Analysis', *Economic Journal*, **99**, December, 1173–1182.
Wolfram, S. (2002), *A New Kind of Science*, Wolfram Media Inc.
World Health Organization (WHO) (2002), *The World Health Report 2002*, www.who.int/whr/2002
Wunenburger, J.-J. (1990), *La raison contradictoire. Sciences et philosophie modernes: la pensée du complexe*, Paris: Albin Michel.
Zhou, X. (2009), *Reform the International Monetary System*, www.pbc.gov.cn

Index